ANALYSIS OF ECONOMIC TIME SERIES

A Synthesis

This is a Volume in
ECONOMIC THEORY, ECONOMETRICS, AND MATHEMATICAL
ECONOMICS

A Series of Monographs and Textbooks

Consulting Editor: KARL SHELL

A complete list of titles in this series appears at the end of this volume.

ANALYSIS OF ECONOMIC TIME SERIES
A Synthesis

Marc Nerlove
Department of Economics
Northwestern University
Evanston, Illinois

David M. Grether
Division of the Humanities and Social Sciences
California Institute of Technology
Pasadena, California

José L. Carvalho
Fundação Getúlio Vargas-EPGE
Rio de Janeiro-R.J., Brazil

ACADEMIC PRESS New York San Francisco London 1979
A Subsidiary of Harcourt Brace Jovanovich, Publishers

ACADEMIC PRESS, INC.
111 Fifth Avenue, New York, New York 10003

United Kingdom Edition published by
ACADEMIC PRESS, INC. (LONDON) LTD.
24/28 Oval Road, London NW1   7DX

Library of Congress Cataloging in Publication Data

Nerlove, Marc, Date
  Analysis of economic time series.

  (Economic theory and mathematical economics)
  Bibliography: p.
  1. Economics––Statistical methods. 2. Time–
series analysis. I. Grether, David M., joint author.
II. Carvalho, José L. , joint author. III. Title.
HB137.N47   330'.01'51   78–26059
ISBN 0–12–515750–9

PRINTED IN THE UNITED STATES OF AMERICA

80 81 82 83 84 9 8 7 6 5 4 3 2

For
Mary Ellen, Susan, and Gelda

CONTENTS

vii

PREFACE

In this book my coauthors and I attempt to integrate several topics in time-series analysis: (1) the formulation and estimation of distributed-lag models of dynamic economic behavior; (2) the application of the techniques of spectral analysis in the study of the behavior of economic time series; and (3) unobserved-components models for economic time series and the closely related problem of seasonal adjustment. The research underlying the book began a long time ago, and I would like to take the opportunity afforded by this preface to set down some of the intellectual antecedents of the book, as well as to acknowledge many debts and much assistance.

My interest in the formulation and estimation of distributed-lag models began with my work on agricultural supply analysis in 1954–1956; in 1970, however, I began to realize the possibilities inherent in combining time-series models with models of dynamic optimization. Many ideas in this connection were developed in the course of a Workshop on Lags in Economic Behavior held under the auspices of the Mathematical Social Science Board at the University of Chicago in the summer of 1970. I am grateful to the workshop members and to the coleaders of the workshop, G. S. Maddala and David Grether, for their important contributions in this connection. I must also acknowledge with gratitude the many discussions I had with Dale W. Jorgenson in the course of preparing some of this material for presentation as the Henry Schultz Memorial Lecture at the Second World Congress of the Econometric Society.

Spectral analysis of economic time series is now a fashionable topic, but in the early 1960s spectral analysis was little known among economists. In the late 1950s Milton Friedman was a fellow of the Center for Advanced Study in the Behavioral Sciences at Stanford in the same year as John Tukey, a key figure in the development of modern time-series techniques. Tukey introduced Friedman to spectral-analytic techniques, with which the latter experimented in his studies of the demand for money. In discussions in 1959, Friedman told me of this work and convincingly argued that spectral analysis was a sensitive tool for uncovering data anomalies, such as cycles due to the number of trading days in a month. Some time later, Robert Aaron Gordon became chairman of the President's Commission to Appraise Employment and Unemployment Statistics and asked whether I would consult with the staff with respect to the problem of seasonal adjustment. Particularly troublesome were the issues of defining seasonality and of assessing the effects of seasonal adjustment procedures in terms of that definition. Recalling my discussions with Friedman, it occurred to me that spectral techniques might be a way of resolving both the issue of definition and the issue of effect. Thus, much of the concern of this book with both seasonality and spectral analysis may be traced to the influence of Friedman and Gordon. I should also like to acknowledge many helpful discussions with, and much assistance in data acquisition from, Margaret E. Martin, who was at that time the Staff Director of the Commission. I must, as well, express my great debt to Emanuel Parzen, who taught me the elements of spectral analysis and patiently explained its somewhat arcane terminology, and to the spectral-analysis study group that I organized at Stanford, which included David Grether, Joseph B. Kadane, and G. S. Maddala.

Seasonal adjustment rests in part on the idea that a time series can be decomposed into two or more separate but not directly observable components. Moving-average or autoregressive time-series models originated in the work of Slutsky and Yule in the early part of this century. The current popularity of the work of G. E. P. Box and Gwilym M. Jenkins on time series rests principally on their discovery of practical methods of formulating and estimating mixed moving-average autoregressive models for time series and the use of such results in forecasting. The idea of combining two or more such mixed moving-average autoregressive models to obtain a new kind of "unobserved-components" model I owe to interchanges in 1962–1963 with Henri Theil, who was then Director of the Econometric Institute at the Netherlands School of Economics. Working with his assistant S. Wage, I extended a simple forecasting model that Theil had developed and derived an explicit form for the forecasts as a weighted average of past errors. Theil's influence has been profound, and the ideas formed during the year at the Institute recur again and again throughout this book.

Many of my students and colleagues have greatly assisted in the research which underlies this volume, but none more so than my coauthors, David M. Grether and José Luiz Carvalho. Grether's Stanford University Ph.D. dissertation (1968) forms the basis for Chapters I, VI, parts of XIII, and Appendices A, D, and G. His paper on distributed lags and signal extraction (1977) reports on related research also discussed in Chapter XIII. Carvalho's University of Chicago Ph.D. dissertation (1972) forms the basis for Chapter XIV and parts of Chapter XIII. His work also led us into the research on multiple time-series analysis, described in Chapters VII (Section 7) and XI, in which he actively participated during two visits to Evanston in 1974 and 1975.

I have benefited greatly from the aid of, and interchange with, a number of extraordinarily able research assistants. At Stanford University, George Fishman, Bridger Mitchell, Karl Shell, David Couts, and Kenneth F. Wallis contributed to early work on this book, and at Yale University, I had the assistance of Elizabeth Boekelman. At the University of Chicago, Uri Ben-Zion and Michael P. Ward assisted and helped to shape many of my ideas about the analysis of economic time series. In the final stages of the book, my coauthors and I were fortunate to have the able assistance of Seiichi Kawasaki, George Sweeney, and Bruce Vavrichek at Northwestern University.

Our greatest debt has been the continuing support of the National Science Foundation through a series of grants to Stanford University (G-16114 and GS-142), to Yale University (GS-1721), to the University of Chicago (GS-2670 and GS-39872), and to Northwestern University (SOC 74-21194). In addition, a senior postdoctoral fellowship from the Foundation in 1971–1972 enabled me to begin work on the book itself. I also wish to acknowledge gratefully the John Simon Guggenheim Memorial Foundation and the Program for the International Exchange of Persons of the U.S. Department of State, whose fellowships enabled me to spend the academic year 1962–1963 at the Netherlands School of Economics, and the Federal Reserve Board, which supported some of the work underlying Chapters VI and IX. Needless to say, neither the National Science Foundation, the U.S. Department of State, the Guggenheim Foundation, nor the Federal Reserve Board are responsible for the ideas expressed in this book.

Andrew Melczer and Quang Vuong have proofread the entire manuscript and the galley and page proofs and have ably assisted in the preparation of the index. Gloria Feigenbaum and Stina L. Hirsch have typed our manuscript. Mrs. Hirsch has also assisted in the several revisions that have been undertaken since 1975.

Many friends and colleagues have been good enough to read our work, or parts of it, and to give us the benefits of their comments and criticism.

An inevitable dimness of memory prevents me from thanking all those who deserve our thanks, but I gratefully acknowledge the more recent comments of C. W. J. Granger and Christopher Sims. Three patient colleagues, T. Amemiya, E. J. Hannan, and K. F. Wallis, have commented extensively on the entire manuscript. Time constraints and the desire to have a published, if not perfect, book have prevented us from taking account of their strenuous efforts to save us from error as fully or as completely as they—and we—would have liked. We, not they, bear the responsibility for the final text.

Marc Nerlove

ANALYSIS OF ECONOMIC TIME SERIES

A Synthesis

Chapter I
A HISTORY OF THE IDEA
OF UNOBSERVED COMPONENTS
IN THE ANALYSIS
OF ECONOMIC TIME SERIES

1. Introduction

In the statistical literature dealing with the analysis of economic time series it is common practice to classify the types of movements that characterize a time series as trend, cyclical, seasonal, and irregular. The idea that a time series may best be viewed as being composed of several unobserved components is by no means universal, but it plays a fundamental role in certain areas of application, e.g., the choice of methods for seasonal adjustment. In contemporary discussions of the unobserved-components model, the components typically are taken as given, and relatively little attention is paid to their exact interpretation. Indeed, it is sometimes said that such components cannot be precisely defined.

In this chapter we review the literature on the trend, cyclical, seasonal, irregular model to gain some understanding of the current uses of the model; in particular, we explore the origins of the model and how it came into use in economics. The survey that follows is not intended to be a complete historical review of the uses of the unobserved-components model; much of the literature on the subject consists of discussions of operational techniques for estimating the various components, and no attempt is made to cover that part of the literature. The literature dealing with the existence of long cycles is also not treated in any detail.[1] The survey that follows is somewhat episodic, emphasizing the earliest literature and that of the past thirty years.

---

[1] For a summary of the writings on long cycles, see Fellner (1956). See also Kondratieff (1935) and Schumpeter (1939).

2. Background

The idea of unobserved components is basically a way of looking at data. Throughout history man has observed various phenomena, noted regularities, and formulated "laws" based upon observed regularities; hence, the exact beginning of any particular attitude toward empirical observation is difficult to date. A society subject to changes of seasons or in which a calendar is in general use must recognize more or less formally the approximately periodic occurrence of certain events. Deviations from regular periodic occurrence must somehow be explained, although the explanation may be different in different cultures; for example, when a solar eclipse predicted by a Babylonian astronomer failed to occur, the failure might be explained as the result of the intervention of some supernatural power. Later, small unexpected deviations in the orbits of planets might be attributed to random shocks. Here, we concentrate on only those developments that appear to have influenced economics and the analysis of economic data.

The notion of unobserved components appears to have become common in economics during the period 1825–1875. In tracing the history of this idea, it is important to keep in mind the nature of scientific inquiry during this period, in particular the role of statistics. In this connection, the remarks of Stanley (1856) are relevant.

> The axiom on which . . . [statistics] is based may be stated thus: that the laws by which nature is governed, and more especially those laws which operate on the moral and physical condition of the human race, are constant, and are, in all cases best discoverable—in some cases only discoverable—by the investigation and comparison of phenomena extending over a very large number of individual instances. In dealing with the individual human being everything is uncertainty; in dealing with MAN in the aggregate, results may be calculated with the precision and accuracy of a mathematical problem . . . .
>
> This, then, is the first characteristic of statistics as a science: that it proceeds wholly by the accumulation and comparison of registered facts;—that from these facts alone, properly classified, it seeks to deduce general principles, and that it rejects all *a priori* reasoning, employing hypothesis, if at all, only in a tentative manner, and subject to future verification.[2]

3. Origins

The notion that a series of observations is composed of separate unobserved components was important in the calculation of planetary orbits by seventeenth century astronomers. In the course of the eighteenth century more accurate instruments for observing the movements of the planets became available; it

---

[2] The quotation is from Lord Stanley's presidential address to Section F of the British Association for the Advancement of Science. The speech was given the day after a resolution was passed "which has enlarged the scope of our duties so as to include, in addition to statistics, properly so called, Economic Science, in general" (1856, p. 305); the remarks quoted in the text were prepared before the resolution was passed.

was discovered that Kepler's laws did not hold exactly. The discrepancies between observations and predictions based on Kepler's laws were minor so that the laws were approximately correct. Thus the notion that Kepler's laws gave the mean position of a planet and not its exact position, i.e., that the position actually observed was the mean plus some irregular fluctuations, became common.[3]

Comparison of the contemporary observations with previous records later revealed that slow persistent changes in planetary orbits were taking place. Thus, a distinction was made between secular and periodic movements. Slow changes were especially apparent in the orbits of the moon, Jupiter, and Saturn. Explanation of these changes occupied some of the great mathematicians of the eighteenth and early nineteenth centuries, including Laplace, Euler, and Lagrange. In discussions of these problems "secular change" was frequently mentioned. In 1787 Laplace showed that the secular change in the behavior of Jupiter and Saturn was in fact periodic with a period in excess of 900 years. Similarly, the secular movement in the behavior of the moon was also shown to be of a very long-term periodicity.[4] Explanations of the orbits of Jupiter and Saturn and of the moon were major triumphs of celestial mechanics and gave further strength to Newton's theory of gravitation.[5]

The use of distinctions among different types of changes was not confined to discussion of planetary orbits. For example, Cannon and Jensen (1975) state that "The secular decrease of the earth's rotation rate due to tidal interaction with the sun and moon was known to nineteenth century physicists, who theorized about the existence of short-term fluctuations in the rotation rate of the solid earth due to daily, seasonal, decadal, and irregular changes in its moment of inertia as well as exchanges of angular momentum between the solid earth and the oceans, atmosphere, and liquid core."

Early writers on economic subjects, when dealing with periodicities, occasionally made explicit references to astronomy as the source of their ideas. For example, in 1838 Cournot said, "as in astronomy, it is necessary to recognize the *secular* variations which are independent of the *periodic* variations."[6] Jevons (1884, p. 4) remarks that his studies of short-term fluctuations use the methods of astronomy and meteorology.

One of the earliest writers in economics to mention cycles and to suggest a statistical correction for them was Sir William Petty (1899).

---

[3] See Pannekoek (1961, p. 280).

[4] See Whewell (1847, Vol. II, pp. 232–235).

[5] Newton's laws are relatively easy to solve for orbits if only two bodies are involved. If three bodies are involved, one obtains a set of second order differential equations that cannot be integrated. The solution can only be obtained as an approximation, and the calculations are enormous. To obtain the accuracy needed often required years of computation. See Pannekoek (1961, pp. 299–307) and Whewell (1847, pp. 101–107, 213–252).

[6] Cournot (1927, p. 25); also cited by Mitchell (1928).

Suppose a man could with his own hands plant a certain scope of Land with Corn, that is, could Digg, or Plough, Harrow, Weed, Reap, Carry home, Thresh, and Winnow so much as the Husbandry of this Land requires; and had withal Seed wherewith to sowe the same. I say, that when this man hath subducted his seed out of the earth and given to others in exchange for Clothes, and other Natural necessaries; that the remainder of Corn is the natural and true Rent of the Land for that year; and the medium of seven years, or rather of so many years as make up the Cycle, within which Dearths and Plenties make their revolution, doth give the ordinary Rent of the Land in Corn.[7]

For Petty, the cycle of seven years, in contrast to later writers, is of little interest per se. Its importance is that one must allow for it in order to determine the ordinary rent of the land. Petty's calculation was intended to determine the value of the land and thus makes sense on economic grounds, i.e., as the determination of the value of an asset from the stream of payments it yields.[8]

That Petty was not searching for periodicities or very concerned with short-term regularities can be seen in his *A Treatise on Ireland* published in 1687. Here Petty passed up an opportunity to make what probably would have been the earliest seasonal adjustment (1899, Vol. 2, pp. 584–588). Petty had quarterly data from the first quarter of 1685 through the first quarter of 1687. To assess the direction of change over the period he compared the first three quarters of 1685 with the three quarters ending with the first quarter of 1687. From the data it appears that the second quarter figures are larger than the fourth quarter figures, but Petty made no correction for this. Admittedly, two years are not much to base a seasonal adjustment on; but Petty displayed the necessary courage on other occasions.

Probably the first attempt to find and to explain periodicities in economic data was that of the famous astronomer Sir William Herschel, who reported in 1801 on his attempt to find a relation between sunspots and the price of wheat. Among other early students of economic fluctuation were Robert Everest and Hyde Clarke.[9] Everest (1843) speculated that the famines in India might be periodic and examined data on wheat prices to test his speculation. One series led him to suspect a period of 18 years, suggesting a lunar influence to him; from other data he found evidence for a cycle of approximately 10 years. Hyde Clarke also searched for a physical explanation for cycles.[10]

---

[7] Cited by Mitchell (1928, p. 333).

[8] Although Petty later showed an understanding of capitalization (1899, Vol. 1, pp. 107–108, p. lxxii), at the time he wrote the *Treatise of Taxes and Contributions* (1662), in which the quoted statement appears, the idea of discounting an infinite stream of payments was not clear to him. In calculating the value of land he took a certain number of years' rent, and he explicitly ruled out an infinite horizon. "If we say an infinite number, then [the value of] an Acre of Land would be equal to [the value of] a thousand Acres of the same Land; which is absurd . . ." (1899, Vol. 1, p. 45).

[9] Both cited by Jevons (1884).

[10] Cited by Jevons (1884, pp. 222–223). In his discussion of Hyde Clarke's paper "Physical Economy—A Preliminary Inquiry into the Physical Laws Governing the Periods of Famines and Panics," published in the *Railway Register* in 1847, Jevons remarks, "In the third page of his paper he (Hyde Clarke) tells us that he had previously written a paper on the laws of cyclical action

Interest in periodicities was not confined to economics. For example, Guy (1843) examined data on disease and mortality to see if the seasons and temperature had any obvious effects. The meteorological literature abounds with examples which appear to be clearly influenced by the success of the idea of unobserved components in astronomy. For example, Forbes (1832) examined barometric oscillations and gave the average fluctuations for the four seasons of the year. He also gave a formula that he claimed gave the mean barometric fluctuation for any point on earth. Along with the idea of unobserved components, one finds in this literature the idea that the laws governing atmospheric events can be discovered by careful observation.[11] Forbes states that

> One of the most important features of recent improvements in the mode of studying the group of facts which meteorology presents to us, is the analytical method of discussing observations, extracting as it were, from the data which nature presents to us, laws which shall best represent them, instead of framing clumsy hypotheses, to which it became a secondary object to apply the facts. (1832, p. 261)

Forbes was clearly optimistic that, with the new methodology, the laws of nature would be quickly discovered and quoted approvingly John Herschel who saw "the speedy disclosure of relations and laws, of which, at present, we can form but a very imperfect notion" (1832, p. 261).

The adoption of the model of unobserved components and separate periodicities in meteorology was important for the development of the model in economics. Of the three men who first used the model to study short-term fluctuations in economic data, two were sometime meteorologists. Also the Dutch meteorologist, Buys Ballot, is occasionally cited as being one of the first to analyze time-series data using a components model (Guilbaud, 1951). We discuss his work in detail in Appendix A; however, it appears that he had little influence on the English language literature of the nineteenth century.

---

printed in *Herapath's Railway Magazine* for 1838. 'At this time,' he says, 'it was my impression that the period of speculation was a period of ten years, but I was led also to look for a period of thirteen or fourteen years . . .'" (1884, pp. 222–223). This is a rather obscure reference for a bibliographer, but a search of the magazine referred to makes it understandable; apparently no such paper exists. Possibly Jevons erred because Hyde Clarke wrote a number of things on a variety of topics in the publication at that time (including a rather disturbing piece about a recent widespread outbreak of volcanic activity). At one point (Clarke, 1838, p. 291) he asks, "Why are there golden ages in literature and the arts? Why are there revolutions in politics? Why sudden periods of progress in science?" This seems to be about as close as he gets to the subject. The only other possibility seems to be an anonymous piece titled "On the Mathematical Law of the Cycle," which appeared in the November 1838 issue of *Herapath's Railway Magazine*. For a complete discussion of early investigations of cycles in economics the reader is referred to Jevons (1884).

[11] The paper by Forbes appeared in the *Edinburgh Journal of Science*, in which Charles Babbage published many of his early papers. Meteorological data were frequently published there, the accumulation of it being a project of the editor D. Brewster, and it was not uncommon for the average value for a season or a month to be determined from several years' data.

4.   Nineteenth Century Contributors

J. W. Gilbart

The earliest study of seasonal patterns in economic phenomena known to us is the work of J. W. Gilbart.[12] Gilbart was a banker who managed a joint stock bank in Ireland for several years and later one in London. He wrote extensively on banking and also published *Logic for the Million*, a book intended to explain the art of quantitative reasoning to the masses. In 1841, he testified before a committee of the House of Commons which was investigating reforms of the banking system. Gilbart appeared as a witness at the request of the Joint-Stock Bank Committee of London; his testimony was designed to show that the private banks had little active control over their issuance of notes, merely responding passively to local trade conditions. Also, he argued that conditions varied in different locales so that it would be unreasonable for the private banks to attempt to have their issuance of notes parallel that of the Bank of England. Specifically, he claimed that the conditions governing the circulation of the country banks, the Bank of England, banks in Scotland, and banks in Ireland were all different. He based his argument on data giving the circulation of notes of banks in the various regions. With regard to the country banks he said:

> I find that the highest point of fluctuation in each year of the circulation of country banks is the end of April, and that the lowest point in each year is the end of August; those two periods divide the year into equal parts; I have constructed a table, which shows the amount of the country circulation on the last Saturday of April, August, and December from the year 1834 to 1839 inclusive, from which it appears that the highest amount of circulation is in April and the lowest in August; proving that the country circulation is governed by local causes, and cannot be regulated by the foreign exchange .... The general law is, that the circulation always makes one circuit in the year, being at its lowest point in August, and advancing to December, and continuing to advance to its highest point in the month of April, and then descending to its lowest point in August.   (Bell, 1842, pp. 41–42)

In the table he presents, two of the six years deviated from the pattern described, but in both cases Gilbart offered explanations of special circumstances that he felt could account for the discrepancy.

Regarding the circulation of the Bank of England, Gilbart testified that

> The first circumstance that affects the circulation of the Bank of England, as apart from those laws which affect the country circulation, is the payment of the periodical dividends; those dividends are payable in January, in April, in July, and in October; and from the accounts published by the committee I find that the monthly average circulation of those months is generally higher than of the two months which follow.   (Bell, 1842, p. 43)

To support his claim, Gilbart presented a table giving the circulation for each month for the years 1834 through 1839. His testimony about the banks of Ireland and Scotland was similar.

---

[12] Gilbart's early work on seasonal patterns is described by him in several places including the articles cited by Jevons (Gilbart, 1854, 1856); the discussion of his statements in 1841 on the subject is based on Bell (1842).

The argument that the conditions affecting the demand for notes of the several types of banks were peculiar to each type was a fairly common one at these hearings, and several witnesses mentioned the seasonal pattern of circulation to support their arguments. Gilbart's testimony was by far the most detailed on the subject, and he may well have influenced the testimony of the others. Indeed, one of the other witnesses, Vincent Stuckey, appeared at the request of the same committee that had authorized Gilbart to testify. Further, the data on which Gilbart's testimony was based were publicly available, and the argument is a rather natural one, especially for a banker who is likely to be aware of seasonal demand for currency in his area. So one would be on weak ground in arguing that there was *general* interest in seasonal patterns or unobserved components of time series.

Gilbart seems to have been extremely proud of his testimony and quoted it from time to time in his other publications. It is noteworthy that his later interest in this work emphasized that he had discovered laws (sometimes LAWS) of the circulation of currency. Whatever his original purpose in making the study, the finding of laws governing the circulation of currency was the major accomplishment. In his original testimony he did refer to the "law," but the emphasis is greater in his later writings. In *Logic for the Million* he wrote:

> When our figures are chronological facts, new and highly important truths are sometimes ascertained by merely observing if any specific facts recur at certain periods. When we have ascertained any uniformity in the occurrence of events, we call the uniformity a LAW.[13]

In two later papers, he followed up his earlier work, giving some further details and comparing the seasonal patterns for 10 years before and 10 years after the Bank Reform Act of 1844. He found little change. In assessing the impact of the act he argued that the restrictions imposed on the note issuance of the private banks had been binding. He stated that there was a heavy penalty for a bank's exceeding its legal maximum in note circulation.

> The average is taken every four weeks. If a banker finds that in the first three weeks he has exceeded his limit, he stops his own issues and sends to London for a supply of five-pound and ten-pound Bank of England notes. Even this may not be sufficient, and then he sends his clerks round to all the neighboring banks asking. "Have you got any of our notes? If you have, we wish to pay them immediately, in order to keep down our average." Thus in some instances the country circulation has become in one sense a *regulated* currency. It is so regulated that in every fourth week the amount is less than in either of the preceeding weeks. (Gilbart, 1856, pp. 295–296)

Gilbart analyzed several short cycles—monthly, quarterly, and annual—and clearly supposed that it was legitimate to treat the different periodicities separately. Though his work was all in a single area, money and banking, he believed his approach to be of general applicability. It should be pointed out that he did not explicitly view his work in terms of unobserved components and made no

[13] Gilbart (1865, p. 232); also quoted in his paper (1854, p. 297).

reference to the trend or irregular, though some of his work was in fact explanation of irregular fluctuations. For example, when arguing for a "law" that was
violated in two of the six years for which he had data, he claimed unusual
transitory factors had obscured the true pattern.

Charles Babbage

Of the men who made early studies of periodicities in economic phenomena,
possibly the most interesting is Charles Babbage. Babbage was a man of
considerable genius and delightful eccentricity. He was acquainted with most
of the leading scientists of his day and made contributions in several fields. His
main interest was in calculating machines, and he spent years and large sums
of money attempting to construct mechanical calculating engines. These labors
were, by and large, fruitless due to lack of financial support and the fact that his
designs called for precision in tooling largely beyond the capabilities of the day.
While some models were constructed, his dream of an "analytical engine" was
not fulfilled until the coming of modern computers. Babbage wished to use his
machines for the construction and printing of mathematical tables and delighted
in finding and pointing out errors in published tables. He advocated gathering
data from many sources and pooling all "constants" of nature where they would
be accessible to all. His interests led him at various times into mathematics,
physics, meteorology, astronomy, shipbuilding (in 1818 he made drawings of a
four-man submarine), economics, and operations research.[14]

One of Babbage's last published papers, "Analysis of the Statistics of the
Clearing House During the Year 1839" (1856), is of major interest in this survey
of the history of unobserved-components models. In an analysis based on
daily observations for 1839, Babbage carefully examined the data to discover
patterns in the average daily clearings; he studied fluctuations within the week
and the month, giving tables of the average for the first, second, etc., day of the
month as well as the average for Monday, Tuesday, and so on.

Examining the average daily clearings, he noted that the largest clearings
were usually on Saturday and the least on Thursday. He discovered that, in all
but two weeks, either the largest amount of clearings was on Saturday or there
was some special factor (such as Inland Bills coming due) that increased the
clearings for some other day. By omitting all days when some disturbing
cause was at work and averaging all the remaining Mondays, Tuesdays, etc.,
he obtained the typical pattern for a normal week. He also explained how to
calculate the magnitude of the disturbance due to some special event.

> Taking as before any week in which only one disturbing force occurs, proceed thus: omit the
> clearings of the day on which the disturbing cause acts; take the sum of the clearings of the
> other five week days; take from the *average* week the sum of the clearings of *its* same five days;
> then, as the sum of the five *average* weekdays is to its remaining day, so is the sum of the

---

[14] A summary of his life and work is given by Morrison and Morrison (1961); this book also
contains excerpts from his writings. A recent biography is Mosely (1964).

five days of the week taken, to the *natural* value of its remaining day; if there was no other cause acting, subtract this last result from the amount of the clearing due to the exceptional day, and the remainder is the amount due to the exceptional cause alone. (Babbage, 1856, p.34)

This was surely one of the earliest attempts to calculate explicitly the irregular component in an economic time series.

Babbage considered the study of short-term fluctuations an important field and felt that one of the benefits of such studies would be improved forecasting. "If we could arrive at some means of obtaining the proportions in which this amount [exchange] has varied in past times, it would be a very useful guide to the future" (1856, p. 28). He advocated that more studies of the type he made be undertaken and explicitly likened the study of economics to meteorology.

> The complicated phenomena of the atmosphere can only be explained by long continued and daily observations of the barometer, thermometer, hygrometer, and various other instruments. In the equally complicated phenomena of currency and exchange, we have little hope of fully unravelling their laws, except through patient observations continually made and published, of those monetary transactions which are constantly fluctuating. The weekly returns of the Bank of England may perhaps be considered as our economical barometer, and other commercial publications be likened to other instruments; but, I believe, few will be found of greater importance than the publications of returns from the Clearing House. (1856, p. 37)

Later another former meteorologist, William Stanley Jevons, was to suggest that the methods of meteorology and astronomy be used to study economic phenomena, but the parallel was never again so strongly stated as by Babbage.

William Stanley Jevons

While Babbage, Gilbart, Clarke, and Everest had some interest in economic fluctuations, William Stanley Jevons was the first to study the problem seriously in a variety of contexts. Although Jevons' statistical work is primarily remembered in connection with his sunspot theory, his interest in periodicities was really much broader. As did his predecessors, Jevons hoped to discover the laws governing economic fluctuations and looked to some physical explanation for them. Such motivation was not the only reason for his studies, and his views are in many ways similar to those of modern students of the subject.[15]

Jevons' attempt to explain economic cycles by sunspots was one of his last major undertakings, and he wrote a number of papers on the subject toward the end of his life. His *The Periodicity of Commercial Crises and its Physical Explanation* (1884, pp. 206–220) contains a postscript written in April of 1882 only five months before his death. Jevons had painstakingly examined long series of prices and records of panics and wherever he looked he found a 10–11 year cycle. This corresponded to the cyclical period of sunspots as he knew it, and it is hard

---

[15] This point is brought out very well in Keynes' essay (1951, pp. 267–280) on Jevons. Keynes stresses Jevons' early interest in seasonality and his concern with the analysis of empirical data in economics that "is shifting and complicated, and will only yield up its answer if it is arranged, compared and analysed for the discovery of uniformities" (1951, p. 268).

not to sympathize with Jevons' enthusiasm for this "beautiful coincidence." His interest in sunspots led him to study early writings on cyclical phenomena, and even if his writings on this topic are otherwise useless, they do contain a good summary of previous investigations of economic cycles.

Sir William Petty's idea of averaging over a cycle to obtain a mean or normal price was employed by Jevons in his *A Serious Fall in the Value of Gold Ascertained and its Social Effects Set Forth* (1863). In this tract, Jevons attempted to determine whether the value of gold had diminished following the gold discoveries of the mid-nineteenth century. To see whether the price level had in fact risen, Jevons found it necessary to correct for temporary fluctuations in prices. His procedure was to compare prices in the years 1851–1862 to the average price over the cycle of 1845–1850. He concluded that the value of gold had declined.[16]

It is clear that Jevons viewed economic series as being composed of separate periodicities, and he advocated a study of the periodicities one at a time.

> Every kind of periodic fluctuation, whether daily, weekly, monthly, quarterly, or yearly, must be detected and exhibited not only as a subject of study in itself, but because we must ascertain and eliminate such periodic variations before we can correctly exhibit those which are irregular or non-periodic and probably of more interest and importance.   (1884, p. 4)

The elimination of seasonal and other regularities was an essential first step in any empirical study of economic changes. In *On the Study of Periodic Commercial Fluctuations* (1862), in which the preceding statement occurs, Jevons presented several seasonal estimates and explained their importance as follows:

> The chief use of the table of quarterly variations, however, is that we may by its use eliminate these variations from the whole variation of the year, by simple subtraction. We then ascertain the nature of the yearly variation which is due to natural causes, as distinguished from the artificial distinctions of months and quarters.   (1884, p. 6)

Thus, for Jevons, the knowledge of periodicities could have application in determining policy, and the study of such periodicities was worthwhile even if one lacked an explanation for or a precise definition of them. The idea of basing policy on recognized regularities is clearly stated in *On the Frequent Autumnal Pressure in the Money Market, and the Action of the Bank of England* (1866).

> If it be clearly known that in the early part of October there is a normal demand for currency far greater than at any time of the year, then I take it to be an expedient and necessary policy of the Bank to prepare themselves for it somewhat beforehand, and when it does occur, to let their reserves run down to a lower point than they would do at any other time of the year, knowing that the excess of currency will in the natural course of events return.   (1884, p. 180)

In this paper, Jevons commented that much attention in the press was given to the panic in October of 1865. He went on to note that tightness in the money

---

[16] In the course of this investigation, Jevons gave one of the first treatments of the problem of index numbers. It is interesting to note that Cournot's reference to secular and periodic variations was made in a similar context: the determination of a standard of value.

market during the fall was an annual event, and explained its cause. He constructed a seasonal pattern and calculated what the figures in October, 1865 should have been on the basis of the usual fluctuation. He concluded that, "The drain of 1865 is ... considerably beyond, and in fact about double of what is shown as the normal change in my average tables" (1884, p. 174). Later he discussed the usefulness of this type of calculation and provided a rationale for eliminating regularities from economic data.

> We should learn to discriminate what is usual and normal ... from what is irregular and abnormal. It is a matter of skill and discretion to allow *for the normal changes.* It is the abnormal changes which are alone threatening or worthy of ... attention.   (1884, p. 181)

Jevons' attitude toward the proper study of economic time series is not very different from some of the views currently expressed. The idea of eliminating the variations due to "the artificial distinctions of months and quarters" to determine the "variation which is due to natural causes" is not essentially different from the modern notion of adjusting series to obtain estimates of the trend and cyclical components. Moreover, Jevons fully developed the notion that policy decisions should be based on observed regularities.

5.   Recent Developments

The modern literature on unobserved components is more difficult to survey than the earlier, partly because of the greater volume of material published in the twentieth century, but also because more elaborate procedures for dealing with unobserved components have become possible with the development of more sophisticated statistical techniques and computational capabilities. These developments have led to greater interest in technique so that relatively more attention has been given to methods themselves and relatively less to the reasons for using them.

One of the first writers to state explicitly the assumption of unobserved components was Persons (1919, 1925). As Persons saw it, time series were composed of four types of fluctuations.

> 1. A long-time tendency or secular trend; in many series such as bank clearings or production of commodities, this may be termed the growth element;
> 2. A wavelike or cyclical movement superimposed upon the secular trend; these curves appear to reach their crests during the periods of industrial prosperity and their troughs during periods of industrial depression, their rise and fall constituting the business cycle;
> 3. A seasonal movement within the year with a characteristic shape for each series;
> 4. Residual variation due to developments which affect individual series, or to momentous occurrences such as wars or national catastrophes, which affect a number of series simultaneously.   (1919, p. 8)

Persons' articles are frequently cited in works dealing with unobserved components. During the 1920s there was considerable interest in this type of model, and a number of technical articles appeared dealing with problems of seasonal adjustment and trend removal.[17] In these articles, Persons is usually cited as a pioneer in the field. While Persons' definitions are a convenient starting point for discussing twentieth century developments, his work did not appear to have had any significant effect on the way in which people thought about the separate components.

In the first edition of his text, *Elements of Statistics* (1901), Bowley discusses the meaning of a time series smoothed by taking a five-year-centered moving average (in this case exports).

> The smoothed line . . . represents the general tendency of the value of exports, when accidental and temporary variations are removed. If it were possible to separate entirely variations of short period from secular changes . . . we may suppose that we should obtain a result represented by this line. In it there are no sudden changes even in rates of growth, while the addition and subtraction year by year of relatively small quantities would produce precisely that irregular fluctuating line from which the smooth line was obtained. (1901, p. 154)

In the fifth edition (1926), the quoted statement is repeated exactly, and Bowley adds, "The direction of the smooth line at any date may be called the *trend* of the series at that date" (1926, p. 137). He then discusses some methods of trend removal including Persons' own ideas. Thus the major difference between what a student learned about the trend in 1901 and what he learned in 1926 was its name. We do not intend to minimize Persons' own contribution or the contributions of others, but merely to point out that the basic ideas about the meaning of the components were fixed at a relatively early date. Later work refined and systematized these notions, but much of the conceptual content of this literature predates the modern period.

Several of the major elements can be found in Persons' statement. *One element is the essentially empirical nature of the definitions of the components.* That the definitions are not precise is recognized by many writers. Burns and Mitchell, for example, say that "It is difficult to give a satisfactory theoretical interpretation of seasonal adjustment . . ." (1947, p. 44). Burns, in his book devoted to measuring and analyzing trends, admits that there "is probably no concept in the whole field of contemporary 'quantitative' economics that is vaguer than that of secular trend" (1934, p. 30). Even if one could provide a rigorous definition of secular change, in practice the definition used for estimation must be empirical since the length of the series of observations determines what can be recognized as being cyclical and what cannot. Moreover, the meaning for estimation of the definition of one component depends upon the definitions of the others. As Kuznets says, "The precision of our knowledge of these [secular] movements depends to a large extent upon the definiteness of our conception of cyclical variations" (1930, p. 60).

It should be emphasized that the business cycle referred to by Persons is not an exact cycle in the sense of being strictly periodic or of having a fixed ampli-

---

[17] See, for example, the *Journal of the American Statistical Association* during the period in question. By comparison with earlier volumes of this journal, there is a clear increase in interest in components models following Persons' paper.

tude. As Mitchell stated it:

> To the [students of business cycles] "the cycle idea" does "have more content than mere variability"; but it does not have the content of periodicity. (1928, p. 467)

> In no case are the fluctuations highly regular; but in many cases they are far from haphazard.... Further, the cyclical-irregular fluctuations of series which individually show semblance of regularity are found to have tolerably regular relations with one another—relations many of which have been suggested by economic theory. (1928, p. 466)

The lack of precision in the definitions of such concepts clearly does not lead those who use them to view them as empty. There is even some feeling that questions of precise definition are not especially important. As Burns puts it,

> What the most appropriate denotation of secular trend should be is perhaps less important than that the term have real economic content, a fairly unequivocal meaning, and a uniform use in any given investigation. (1934, p. 30)

Burns' statement seems to imply, however, that he thought the term well defined.

The nature of the definitions has influenced the literature on method. Procedures for estimating components must be judged on empirical grounds, and it is often difficult to see on what basis certain technical decisions are made. Furthermore, ambiguity in the definitions necessarily leaves room for a range of opinions as to what the best methods are. For example, Shiskin, in discussing the handling of extreme seasonal–irregular ratios, says:

> Our standard technique for identifying extremes is to calculate for each month the average of the squared deviations (sigma squared) from a preliminary curve ... fitted to the ratios, and to define all ratios falling outside some multiple of sigma as extreme .... The standard program uses limits of twice sigma for this purpose. Some users of this program have suggested increasing the number of items defined as extreme by reducing control limits to $1\frac{1}{2}$ or 1 sigma .... The following control limits have also been proposed: 1.8, 2.5, 2.7, and 3.0 .... on the other hand, others have suggested discontinuing the distinction between extreme and other ratios. (OECD, 1961, p. 103)

Another element implicit in Persons' statement is the idea that *the separate components are to some extent dependent on different causal forces*. The strength with which this assumption is held varies considerably. Frickey writes:

> One view is that we can best give rationality to the statistical process of separating the various elements in a time series ... by thinking of this process as one of analyzing the effects of particular groups of causes .... If the conventional classification of time-series fluctuations is accepted, the statement may be made more precise by saying that in computing lines of secular trend and curves of cyclical variation, we are trying to separate by statistical devices, the effects of two sets of causal influences—one set operating in general gradually and over comparatively long periods of time, and the other set operating in a more oscillatory manner and producing fluctuations of shorter length. (1942, p. 37)

Frickey goes on to say that this does not characterize his own views, and Burns takes a stronger position in rejecting what he calls the "question-begging notion that secular trends are measures of the effects of causes independent of those generating the cyclical, seasonal, and random variations ..." (1934, p. 32).

Nevertheless, the idea that the different components reflect different causal sources of movement persists, though it is currently only apparent in discussion of seasonal and irregular variations.

That statistical decomposition is not intended to effect strict causal separation affects the interpretation of the results. Burns and Mitchell are especially explicit on this point.

> Seasonally adjusted figures no more show what the behavior of time series would have been in the absence of seasonal forces than indexes of physical production show what production would have been in the absence of changes in relative prices; or than figures on per capita income show what income would have been in the absence of income inequalities. (1947, p. 47)

Unfortunately, they do not say precisely what it is that seasonally adjusted figures do show.

While a major source of seasonal variation is, no doubt, the weather, the weather may influence other components as well. For example, it is occasionally pointed out that a seasonally adjusted series may be affected by the weather, provided only that the weather is "unseasonal." Shiskin notes that "it is possible that the irregular factors vary more in certain months than in others (possibly because of the weather)" (OECD, 1961, p. 104). Shiskin's statement illustrates well the rejection in contemporary literature of the causal separation by components. A component may depend primarily on a certain set of identifiable forces, but it is not necessarily true that these forces affect only that one component. For example, the irregular component shows the results of major shocks to the economy, but this does not mean that these shocks could not start or aggravate a cyclical movement.

Persons mentions that the rise and fall of the cyclical components of time series constitute the business cycle, while the seasonals have a "characteristic shape for each series." This suggestion that the cyclical components tend to move together *more* than do the seasonal components brings out the third major theme in Persons' statement: *The interrelationships that hold among components of one kind may be different from those that hold among other components.* Frickey is especially explicit on this point.

> Quite possibly, for example, the system of equations inherent in long-time secular relationships may be altogether different from the system inherent in short-time cyclical relationships, and by mixing the two types of variation (i.e., by using non-analyzed or improperly analyzed data) we may get in our results not truth, but confusion. (1942, p. 5)

Differing relationships are not restricted to cyclical and trend components alone. Seasonal patterns may vary greatly from one series to another, but the seasonal fluctuations are not assumed to be independent of each other. For example, Mitchell writes, "From the activities directly affected by climatic or conventional seasons, acting separately or in union, seasonal influences radiate to all other activities, probably without exception" (1928, p. 237). In his book on seasonal patterns, Kuznets (1933) investigates the seasonal patterns in related series, e.g., the harvesting and marketing of agricultural commodities.

Abramovitz's (1964) study of long swings in construction provides another example of the importance of interrelationships among corresponding components of different series. He finds evidence for long swings in construction not simply from movements in construction statistics but in the behavior of other economic factors as well.

> The long swings in the growth of output appear to have involved related swings occurring at about the same time in many other areas of American development. They were matched by waves of immigration and population growth, of additions to the labor force, of land sales by the federal government, and of business incorporations. They were also accompanied by swings in the volume of internal migration, in the rate of growth in our cities, in the value and volume of imports, in the balance of payments and capital imports, in the flow of specie across our borders, in the rate of growth of our money supply, and in the rates of change of interest rates, of prices, and of money and real wages. Whatever their ultimate nature, therefore, it appears that the long swings in economic growth have been phenomena ramifying widely through our economic life and involving a complex set of interconnections and responses. (1964, p. 2)

Although interrelationships among components are stressed in theoretical discussions, surprisingly these relationships are usually not considered in statistical adjustment of economic time series. In estimating the components of a number of series, it is common practice to treat each series individually. Any relations within the group of series are considered only informally and then usually as a way of appraising the results.

Shiskin, for instance, says that one of the criteria for judging seasonal adjustment is the "reasonableness" of the results and gives the following example.

> The unreasonableness of the results of the electronic computer adjustment of the U.S. unemployment series for 1958 led to widespread objections to it. The pattern of the 1958 recession and revival in the U.S. was V-shaped in most broad measures of business activity . . . . The decline from mid-1957 to April, 1958 was sharp, as was the upturn that followed. On the other hand, the official unemployment series, adjusted by the standard Census method, showed a rise to April, 1958, a decline to June, 1958, another rise to August, 1958, and then a more prolonged decline. In comparison with other general business indicators, the movements in unemployment were unreasonable, and required either a good economic explanation or a technical explanation of why the seasonal adjustment method did not give good results in this instance. (OECD, 1961, p. 85)

The practice of dealing with series individually has not gone unquestioned. Frickey was one to express dissatisfaction on this count.

> When we attack time series singly, we are . . . confronted with an embarrassment of riches; a host of possibilities appears. Further, in time series decomposition, we should look forward to obtaining a unified and consistent interpretation of our array of analyzed series . . . such unity we can hardly hope to attain by dealing with series one at a time. (1942, pp. 52–53)

The literature on seasonal adjustment deals almost exclusively with the calculation of "endogenous" seasonal factors, although some interest in the possibility of using other variables is expressed occasionally.

So far, apart from some work done on fuel and power statistics little use seems to have been made of exogenous variables in the seasonal relationship. There is a clear limit to the extent to which further refinements of internal relationships will lead to the improvement of seasonal adjustment; thus it may therefore be desirable to pay rather more attention to this type of relationship. (OECD, 1961, p. 65)

6.   Application to Seasonal Adjustment and "Current Analysis"

Two distinct purposes lie behind the division of a time series into two or more unobserved components. The most prominent involves the search for regularities or "laws" governing economic fluctuations. In some cases a definite physical force, e.g., sunspots, is assumed responsible for cycles; in others no single force is identified—the regularities are simply noted or explained in general terms. Another purpose can be seen in Jevons' early work. The study of unobserved components is a way of extracting the information in a time series; any periodicity, being relatively predictable, can serve as a guide to policy makers. For Jevons, however, deviations from regularity were more important and more interesting. The crisis of October 1865 was noteworthy because it exceeded in seriousness what would have been expected on the basis of past October experiences. Noting the discrepancy between what was expected, based on a seasonal pattern, and what actually occurred constitutes a way of appraising the current economic situation.

One of the major uses of the unobserved-components model is in what is called "current analysis." In 1919, Persons stated that one of his goals was to "contrive a method of handling business statistics which will make it easy to determine the significance or levels of significance of each item in dictating current conditions and possibly those of the immediate future" (1919, p. 7). More recently, Shiskin wrote,

A principal purpose of studying business statistics is to determine the stage of the business cycle at which the economy stands. Such knowledge helps in forecasting subsequent cyclical movements and provides a factual basis for taking steps to moderate the amplitude and scope of the business cycle. (1958, p. 1539)

One aspect of the use of unobserved components in assessing business conditions is the reliance on seasonally adjusted data. In fact, much of our understanding of the purposes of seasonal adjustment derives from reading this particular literature. Seasonal adjustment is considered in detail in Chapter VIII, and our discussion of that use of unobserved-components models is deferred until then.

It was mentioned earlier that the imprecise definitions of the components make interpretation of the estimates of such components difficult. Shiskin's paper provides some insight into the meaning of seasonally adjusted series and of estimates of cyclical components. For "current analysis," at least, the study of separate components seems to be a form of prediction. The Economics Branch and Shiskin are not interested in the *value* of the cyclical component, but rather in determining which "stage of the business cycle" the economy is in. Similarly, seasonal adjustment makes forecasting easier because it allows one to determine changes in cyclical movements earlier than does mere inspection of raw data. The difficulty of exact interpretation comes in part from an ambiguity in what is being forecast. Since cycles are assumed to last two or three years, knowledge of the current position on a cycle provides information about the future but not direct information about the future of any real economic time series.[18] Further, since cycles are not strictly periodic and since the relations among series are only "tolerably regular," it is hard to assess the information contained in any single adjusted series. Without the assumption of strict periodicity or a precise frame-work to analyze the interrelationships among different series, it is necessary to examine the behavior of a large number of series.

The selection and analysis of indicators of business conditions has been studied at the National Bureau of Economic Research. This work, primarily associated with Geoffrey Moore, is an extension and revision of work originally undertaken by Burns and Mitchell.[19] All series showing seasonal variation are adjusted prior to study. Series are classified as leading, lagging, and coincident dependent on their past behavior when compared with peaks and troughs of the National Bureau's reference cycle. A large number of economic time series have been studied in determining the actual list of indicators used, and other measures such as diffusion indices have been constructed. The list of indicators has been revised occasionally and current observations and various summary statistics are published in *Business Conditions Digest* (1961-present).[20]

The basic assumption underlying business indicators is that relationships in the timing of movements of economic time series are "tolerably regular." Thus the past can only be an imprecise guide to future developments. For example:

> If the current expansion were to continue through all of 1957, it will have lasted forty months. In the National Bureau's business cycle chronology covering the past 100 years, there are only five expansions (out of twenty-four) that lasted as long as forty months . . . four of these expansions encompassed major wars, and one was the recovery from the Great Depression. Clearly, if the present expansion extends through 1957 without a setback, it will establish a new precedent. (Moore, 1961, p. 123)

There is considerable emphasis in the literature on business cycle indicators on the principle that a list of indicators alone cannot be a perfect vehicle for forecasting; economic reasoning and analysis are essential. For example, Burns states that "subtle understanding of economic change comes from a knowledge of history and large affairs, not from statistics or their processing alone—to

---

[18] The problem of time-series decomposition is sometimes explicitly treated as an estimation problem. Shiskin (OECD, 1961) states that the Census Methods are tested against artificial series whose components are known. Godfrey and Karreman (1967) also treat seasonal adjustment as an estimation problem and compare several methods using a variety of seasonal models.

[19] A brief account of the history of business indicators is given by Fabricant (1961, pp. 3–12).

[20] Previously titled *Business Cycle Developments*.

which our disturbed age has turned so eagerly in its quest for certainty" (1934, p. 34). This remark illustrates a major difference between the trend-cycle–seasonal–irregular model as currently interpreted and the unobserved-components model employed by earlier astronomers and meteorologists. A model with strictly periodic components, components each of which depends upon a distinct set of causes, definitely does suggest that the future can be determined by mechanical data handling alone.

7.   Application to the Historical Analysis of Business Cycles

Another important application of the unobserved-components model is in the historical analysis of business cycles and involves searching for "hidden" regularities, much as earlier time series analysts used periodogram analysis to search for "hidden periodicities." Such studies have gone quite out of fashion in recent years due in part to the development of large-scale econometric models, but interest in methods of analysis based on unobserved components viewed as a descriptive device may re-emerge in connection with extensive simulation studies based on such large-scale models. The early literature on business cycles, however, is definitely illuminated by viewing it in terms of the unobserved-components model.

One of the main threads running through the theory of business cycles prior to the 1930s is the distinction between forced oscillation and free oscillation theories of business cycles. As described by Hotelling (1927, p. 289), a forced oscillation theory requires some particular "regularly recurring cosmic cause which influences the economic system but is not influenced by it." Jevons' sunspot theory is an early example of this; Henry Moore's work provides a later one. Forced oscillation theories are no longer very common due, no doubt, to the "tenuousness . . . of the long chain of causation which they are forced to postulate" (1927, p. 289). Such theories do, however, illustrate still another use of unobserved components.

Henry Moore's analysis of business cycles was based on a theory of forced oscillation. For Moore, a cycle was "mathematically defined with definite period, amplitude and phase . . ." (1923, p. 5), and he was openly critical of theories in which the cycle was not completely regular and that did not associate distinct causal forces with the various components. In his study of time series, Moore calculated the periodogram, a method well suited for analyzing series with a few exact periodicities. Moore's primary observation was that there was a prominent eight-year cycle in rainfall data for the Ohio Valley. Moore studied other meteorological data and concluded that the eight-year cycle was a general phenomenon. Moore saw an eight-year cycle in crop yields and also in the production of industrial products (pig iron). In 1914, Moore believed that he had traced the source of economic cycles to fluctuations in rainfall. His complete explanation was presented in his 1923 book; the eight-period cycle coincides with the period between the conjunction of Venus and Earth. Moore argued that Venus interfered with solar radiation and that this caused the fluctuation in rainfall.[21]

The work of Arthur F. Burns and Wesley C. Mitchell, *Measuring Business Cycles*, is especially significant in the study of business cycles by means of the components model. This model plays a key role in the determination of the scope of their study and in all preliminary processing of the data. All series showing seasonal variation are smoothed to eliminate these fluctuations as a first step in the analysis. Burns and Mitchell state the logic of this procedure clearly: The interrelationships among the seasonal components are not at all the same as those holding among the secular and cyclical components so it is reasonable to ignore the seasonal variations.

> Seasonal fluctuations vary endlessly from one business activity to another, but they are a comparatively regular factor within each activity. Since the seasonal pattern, by and large, is much the same in years of "good" business and years of "bad" business, our analysis of cyclical movements can be facilitated by putting the seasonal fluctuations provisionally out of sight. The effects on business enterprise of an increase in activity that is expected to last at most a few months are very different from an increase that is expected to continue for years. For one thing, seasonal increases do not lead men to expand their investments as does rapid secular growth. (1947, p. 40)

This view is quite similar to Jevons' notion that to study one type of fluctuation, one should eliminate all other sources of variation. There is, however, an additional element in Burns and Mitchell's statement. Economic agents recognize and react differently to the separate components in the time series that concern them. In addition to being largely irrelevant to the object of study of Burns and Mitchell, seasonal variations are something of a nuisance, playing a role analogous to measurement errors in the more usual type of econometric analysis.

> That the removal of seasonal variation can facilitate the analysis of the interrelations of the cyclical movements in different activities will be plain to any reader who takes the trouble to study Chart 3 which depicts the movement in recent years of industrial production, railroad freight traffic, and department store sales in the United States, before and after adjustment for seasonality. The seasonal variations follow an individual course in each series, and obscure the protracted fluctuations in freight traffic and department store sales. When the variations associated with the seasons of the year are removed, the underlying fluctuations in economic fortune come clearly to the surface and can be readily traced in the several series. (1947, pp. 44–46)

[21] For a description of Moore's work see Stigler (1962). Moore's work shows he had some interest in astronomy and used periodogram analysis. Schuster (1898) was, of course, the principal investigator to apply this form of analysis to astronomical phenomena in his development of methods for searching for hidden periodicities. Beveridge (1921, 1922) early exploited periodogram analysis in the study of meteorological and economic phenomena. W. L. Crum, who applied the method to economic time series at about the same time (1923), was clearly influenced by astronomical research; indeed, it is interesting to note that Crum's doctoral dissertation (published 1918) was not in economics at all but concerned the perturbations caused by the near approach of an asteroid. Later, Bradley and Crum (1939) were to write critically on the use of periodogram analysis and related methods on the ground that the notion of a cycle is vague and the available length of economic time series is too short.

Furthermore, business cycles themselves are viewed as an unobserved component in the time series being analyzed.

> Business cycles are a type of fluctuation found in the aggregate economic activity of nations that organize their work mainly in business enterprises: a cycle consists of expansions occurring at about the same time in many economic activities, followed by similarly general recessions, contractions, and revivals which merge into the expansion phase of the next cycle; this sequence of changes is recurrent but not periodic; in duration business cycles vary from more than one year to ten or twelve years; they are not divisible into sub-cycles of similar character with amplitudes approximating their own.   (1947, p. 3)

Burns and Mitchell's study is, in effect, a search for hypotheses. The search involves the examination of a great number of economic time series. From these series dates of peaks and troughs in business cycles are determined. These in turn define what Burns and Mitchell call "reference cycles." The specific cyclic patterns for the individual series are also studied. To allow for variation in duration of different cycles, cycles are divided into nine phases and the series are averaged over each of these phases to obtain specific cycle patterns. Timing relations among the series are investigated, and Burns and Mitchell consider the possibility of secular change in the cyclical patterns. Although certain of the calculations contain corrections for intercycle trend, Burns and Mitchell do not attempt to separate the cyclical and secular components in the series they analyze.

Measuring Business Cycles was the subject of Tjalling Koopmans' critical review "Measurement without Theory" and of a lively exchange between Koopmans and Rutledge Vining.[22] Koopmans distinguishes between what he calls the "Kepler stage" and the "Newton stage" in science and suggests that Burns and Mitchell's work corresponds to the "Kepler stage" in economics. Koopmans is clearly doubtful that the separation of the Newton and Kepler stages will yield fruitful results in economics and stresses the complementarity between theory and measurement.

> My *first argument*, then is that even for the purpose of systematic and large scale observation of such a many-sided phenomenon, theoretical preconceptions about its nature cannot be dispensed with, and the authors do so only to the detriment of the analysis.   (1965a, p. 190)
> This then, is my *second argument* against the empiricist position: Without resort to theory, . . . conclusions relevant to the guidance of economic policies cannot be drawn . . . .   (1965a, p. 196)
> However, the extraction of more information from the data requires that, in addition to the hypotheses subject to test, certain basic economic hypotheses are formulated as distributional assumptions, which often are not themselves subject to testing from the same data . . . . The greater wealth, definiteness, rigor, and relevance to specific questions of such conditional information extractable without hypotheses of the kind indicated, provides the *third argument* against the purely empirical approach.   (1965a, p. 200)

---

[22] See Koopmans (1965a,b) and Vining (1965a,b). For a comparison of Burns and Mitchell's work with Frickey's see Ames (1948). See also Gordon (1949).

Koopmans also criticizes Burns and Mitchell for focusing their attention on the behavior of certain aggregates rather than on the behavior of economic agents.

> This shift of attention from underlying human response to their combined effects is a decisive step. It eliminates all benefits ... that might be received from economic theory—by which I mean in this context the theoretical analysis of the aggregate effects of assumed patterns of economic behavior of groups of individuals. (1965a, p.191)

Koopmans' forceful criticism of Burns and Mitchell's empiricism could well be applied to most of the work discussed so far. Hypotheses such as the trend-cycle–seasonal–irregular hypotheses are directly concerned with the behavior of series of numbers, not with the behavior of economic agents, and such hypotheses have nothing explicit to say about the choice or meaning of observed series.

The distinction between the kinds of movements which characterize separate components has important implications. Burns and Mitchell, for example, mention the difference between the impact on investment of changes that are expected to last for a substantial period of time and the impact of changes that are viewed as representing transitory phenomena. Adjustment may be quite different if it is in response to a change that is a regular seasonal fluctuation than if it is in response to a one-time change. A department store, for example, may increase its volume substantially during the Christmas season. The fact that the Christmas buying rush comes regularly each year makes it relatively easy to adjust to the temporary increase in demand. Extra workers at this time of year can readily be obtained; indeed many people enter the labor force at this time since they know that many stores will increase their staffs and they themselves need extra cash. High school and college students who are on vacation provide additional sources of short-term workers. Suppliers also can anticipate such changes and can be expected to prepare for increased orders. If consumer demand were to increase suddenly but at a different time of the year, the adjustment of the stores would certainly be different from the response to the increase in early December. Ultimately one would hope to explain the differences in response in terms of expectations, conditions in the labor market, and suppliers' inventories rather than by simply classifying movements as seasonal or nonseasonal. As a first approximation or in partial equilibrium analysis such a classification may be satisfactory.

The present form of the trend-cycle–seasonal–irregular model is quite different from its original form. Fluctuations of the components are no longer assumed to be strictly periodic, and it is now generally acknowledged that the same causal forces may affect more than one component. Recent work has provided a number of refinements in the model, more systematic applications of it, and substantial technical advances in the handling of the many statistical problems inherent in the model. Yet the essence of the model itself seems little altered since the time of Jevons.

Chapter II
INTRODUCTION TO THE THEORY
OF STATIONARY TIME SERIES

1. Introduction

Time-series analysis is based on two fundamental notions: the idea of unobserved components, which we have explored in detail in the preceding chapter, and a more probabilistic theory based on parametric models. As we have seen, the former is largely a nineteenth century development, whereas the probabilistic theory originated early in the twentieth century, partly in response to criticism of the methods then in use. The two ways of treating time series are, however, highly complementary; indeed, much of this book is devoted to our attempt to integrate the two approaches.

The idea of unobserved components not only lies behind the traditional decomposition of an economic time series into three or four components but is also the central idea in harmonic analysis of time series. In this type of analysis, the time series, or some simple transformation of it, is assumed to be the result of superposition of sine and cosine waves of different frequencies. However, since summing a finite number of such strictly periodic functions always results in a perfectly periodic series, which is seldom observed in practice, it is usual to add an additional stochastic component, sometimes called "noise." Thus one is led to search for "hidden periodicities," i.e., the unknown frequencies and amplitudes of sinusoidal fluctuations hidden amidst noise. The method for doing so is *periodogram analysis*, suggested by Stokes (1879) and used by Schuster (1898) to analyze sunspot data and later by others, principally William Beveridge (1921, 1922), to analyze economic time series.

Spectral analysis is a modernized version of periodogram analysis modified to take account of the stochastic nature of the components themselves. If it is assumed that economic time series are fully stochastic, it follows that the older technique is inappropriate to their analysis and that considerable difficulties in the interpretation of the periodograms of economic series may be encountered.

The disrepute into which periodogram analysis fell in the twenties was due largely to these problems of interpretation: Not only was the estimated periodogram very jagged in appearance, suggesting the presence of a very large number of cyclic components for which no economic explanation could be found, but additional observations actually seemed to make things worse. It is now known that these difficulties are due to the awkward statistical properties of the periodogram estimated for series that do not have exact periodicities but rather are generated by a stochastic mechanism. In the next chapter we discuss, among other things, how modern techniques of spectral analysis modify the periodogram in order to make of it a tool suitable for the study of stochastic time series that are not the result of superimposing harmonic components and noise.

At the time when harmonic analysis proved to be inadequate for the analysis of economic and social time series, another way of characterizing such series was suggested, more or less simultaneously, by the Russian statistician and economist, Eugen Slutzky (1927), and the British statistician, G. U. Yule (1921, 1926, 1927). Slutzky and Yule showed that if we begin with a series of purely random numbers and then take sums or differences, weighted or unweighted, of such numbers, the new series so produced has many of the apparent cyclic properties that were thought at the time to characterize economic and other time series. Such sums or differences of purely random numbers and sums or differences of the resulting series are the basis for moving-average or autoregressive schemes or mixed processes, which are the basic mechanisms for generating time series considered in this book. There is, however, nothing incompatible with looking at time series as generated by processes of this sort and the way in which spectral analysis looks at them; indeed, spectral analytic and parametric characterizations of time series can be quite complementary.

2. What Is a Stationary Time Series? Ergodicity

Consider a random variable x_t subscripted by an index t that, let us say, belongs to a set of such indices T.[1] If T is a finite collection of integers, we are in a familiar class of problems: The set of $\{x_t; t \in T\}$ defines a finite dimensional vector $x = (x_1, \ldots, x_N)'$ where the elements of T have been put into correspondence with the first N integers. x has some multivariate distribution $F(v_1, \ldots, v_N)$. Now let T be the set of *all* integers $T = \{\ldots, -1, 0, 1, 2, \ldots\}$. The set $\{x_t; t \in T\}$, or $\{x_t\}$ for simplicity, defines an *infinite* vector. We call such

---

[1] Uppercase letters are frequently used to denote random variables, a practice we shall not follow in this book.

a vector a *discrete time series*. While we shall analyze discrete time series almost exclusively in this book, it is useful to note here that if T were a set consisting of a continuum of real numbers, we would call $\{x(t)\}$ a *continuous time series*. Now for any subset T_k of k elements of T, $\{x_t; t \in T_k\}$ is equivalent to a finite dimensional vector and therefore to a multivariate random variable. The way to discuss properties of a finite set of random variables is, of course, to characterize their joint distribution; indeed, we may characterize time series by the joint distribution functions of the random variables corresponding to the subsets T_k, where T_k is *any* finite subset of T.[2]

Let the probability that a collection $x_{t_1}, \ldots, x_{t_k}$ is such that $x_{t_1} \leq v_{t_1}, \ldots, x_{t_k} \leq v_{t_k}$ be given by $F_{T_k}(v_{t_1}, \ldots, v_{t_k})$ for any finite subset $T_k = \{t_1, \ldots, t_k\}$ of T. Define a new subset of T, $T_k + \tau$ as

$$T_k + \tau = \{t_1 + \tau, \ldots, t_k + \tau\}.$$

Then $\{x_t\}$ is called a *stationary time series* (sometimes, *strictly* stationary) if and only if

$$F_{T_k}(\cdot) \equiv F_{T_k} + \tau(\cdot) \tag{1}$$

for all finite subsets T_k of the index set T such that $T_k + \tau$ belongs to T; that is, $F_{T_k}(\cdot)$ depends only on differences between the t's. To modify this definition for continuous time series, i.e., when T consists of a continuum of real numbers, it suffices to take T_k to be a finite set of k points in T and τ to be any real number such that $t_i + \tau$ is in T for $i = 1, \ldots, k$.

The above definition may be restated in terms of the characteristic functions associated with the distributions F_{T_k} since these functions completely characterize those distributions even when some or all of the moments of the latter fail to exist (Lukacs, 1970, p. 11). The characteristic function of a random vector z is defined as

$$\varphi_z(u) = E\{e^{iu'z}\}, \tag{2}$$

where u is a vector of real numbers of the same dimension as z. (Appendix B surveys certain prerequisite theory of functions of a complex variable used throughout this chapter and succeeding chapters.) The expectation on the right-hand side of (2) always exists no matter what the distribution of z. Let

$$z(k) = (x_{t_1}, \ldots, x_{t_k}) \quad \text{and} \quad z_\tau(k) = (x_{t_1 + \tau}, \ldots, x_{t_k + \tau});$$

then our previous definition for a stationary time series reduces to

$$\varphi_{z(k)}(u) \equiv \varphi_{z_\tau(k)}(u) \tag{3}$$

for any finite subset T_k of T. As before, (3) implies that the characteristic function, and hence the distribution, depends only on the differences between the t's.

For a discrete time series, we may define the *mean* (generally a function of t) as Ex_t if Ex_t exists. If $\{x_t\}$ is stationary, the mean cannot depend on t. Let

[2] See Hannan (1970, p. 4) and Billingsley (1968, p. 228) for further discussion.

$Ex_t = \mu$ for all $t \in T$; then we can define the autocovariance of x_t for lag τ as

$$\gamma(t, \tau) = E[x_t - Ex_t][x_{t+\tau} - Ex_{t+\tau}]. \tag{4}$$

If $\{x_t\}$ is stationary,

$$Ex_t = Ex_{t+\tau} = \mu$$

and $\gamma(t, \tau)$ depends only on the lag τ, so we write $\gamma(\tau)$ or γ_τ. Clearly the variance of x_t is γ_0 independently of t for a stationary time series.

These definitions carry through for a continuous *stationary* time series as well; $\gamma(\tau)$, however, is now a function of the continuous variable τ.

Processes or time series for which properties $Ex_t = \mu$ and $E(x_t - \mu)(x_{t+\tau} - \mu) = \gamma_\tau$ are called *covariance stationary* or *stationary to the second order.*[3]

While stationarity is in general a stronger condition than covariance stationarity, they are the same for an important class of processes: A process $\{x_t\}$ for which the distribution function $F(v_{t_1}, \ldots, v_{t_k})$ is multivariate normal for any finite subset T_k of T is called a *Gaussian process* or time series. For such time series, stationarity and covariance stationarity are equivalent.

The characteristic function for a stationary Gaussian process is

$$\varphi_x(u; t \in T_k) = \exp(iu'\mu_k - \tfrac{1}{2}u'\Gamma_k u), \tag{5}$$

where

$$\mu_k = \begin{bmatrix} Ex_{t_1} \\ \vdots \\ Ex_{t_k} \end{bmatrix}$$

and

$$\Gamma_k = \|E(x_{t_j} - Ex_{t_j})(x_{t_{j'}} - Ex_{t_{j'}})\|, \qquad j, j' = 1, \ldots, k.$$

The notation $\| \quad \|$ signifies the elements of a matrix are contained between the two sets of double lines. The elements of Γ_k depend only on the differences $|t_j - t_{j'}|$. Clearly, since the distribution depends only on first and second moments, covariance stationarity and stationarity are the same. Moreover, for many applications one relies only on the properties of first and second moments so covariance stationarity is usually sufficient.

A process $\{x_t\}$ may be thought of as an infinite dimensional random variable. Suppose that we observe *one* member of this population. Such an observation is called a *realization* of the process $\{x_t\}$. Let us denote the value of such a single observation by $\{\xi_t\}$. The *infinite sample mean* is

$$m = \lim_{N \to \infty} \frac{1}{2N+1} \sum_{t=-N}^{N} \xi_t, \tag{6}$$

---

[3] A process is said to be stationary to the order p if moments up to the pth order are independent of t.

if the limit on the right exists. Similarly the *infinite sample autocovariance* is

$$c(\tau) = \lim_{N \to \infty} \frac{1}{2N+1} \left\{ \sum_{t=-N}^{N} \xi_t \xi_{t-\tau} - (2N+1)m^2 \right\}$$

$$= \left\{ \lim_{N \to \infty} \frac{1}{2N+1} \sum_{t=-N}^{N} \xi_t \xi_{t-\tau} \right\} - m^2, \tag{7}$$

for $\tau = 0, \pm 1, \ldots$ when the limit on the right exists. The *infinite sample auto-correlation* is defined as

$$r(\tau) = c(\tau)/c(0), \qquad \text{for} \quad \tau = \pm 1, \ldots$$

when $c(\tau)$ exists for $\tau = 0, \pm 1, \ldots$ and $c(0) \neq 0$.

The question of when the limits involved in the definitions of the sample moments above exist is connected with the question of stationarity. In fact the following "law of large numbers" can be established (Doob, 1953, p. 465):

Theorem.   If $\{x_t\}$ is stationary and if g is any function of the k random variables $x_1, \ldots, x_k$ such that $g(x_1, \ldots, x_k)$ is a well-defined random variable and such that, for any τ,

$$E|g(x_{t_1}, \ldots, x_{t_k})| = E|g(x_{t_1+\tau}, \ldots, x_{t_k+\tau})| < \infty \tag{8}$$

exists, then the *finite* sample means

$$\frac{1}{2N+1} \sum_{\tau=-N}^{N} g(\xi_{t_1+\tau}, \ldots, \xi_{t_k+\tau}) \tag{9}$$

converge with probability 1 to the random variable

$$\bar{g} = \lim_{N \to \infty} \frac{1}{2N+1} \sum_{\tau=-N}^{N} g(\xi_{t_1+\tau}, \ldots, \xi_{t_k+\tau}). \tag{10}$$

If the process $\{x_t\}$ is also what is called *ergodic* (or in this case *strongly ergodic*), the random variable $\bar{g}$ is a constant with probability 1 such that

$$\bar{g} = E\{g(x_{t_1}, \ldots, x_{t_k})\} = E\{g(x_{t_1+\tau}, \ldots, x_{t_k+\tau})\}. \tag{11}$$

The notion of ergodicity is a rather deep one. We shall try here to make it intuitively clear by connecting it with the problem of inference, to which it is related but not fundamentally so. What the above results say is that *when a process is both stationary and ergodic, a single realization allows us to infer everything about the probability law generating that process.* In particular, the sample moments for finite stretches of a realization approach with probability 1 the population moments as the stretch of the realization becomes infinite if the process is both stationary and ergodic; i.e., the finite sample moments converge to the infinite sample moments, which are equal to the population moments with probability 1.

If one has a stationary process and can only observe (a part of) one realization, one might as well assume the process to be ergodic since there is no operational way to tell the difference. To assert that the process is ergodic simply amounts to assuming that those elements of the stochastic structure are fixed that are in fact fixed for the one realization that will be observed. Of course, it is possible to construct a model of a process that is not ergodic without attributing any operational significance to the model. For example, let r be a random variable with finite mean and let φ be uniformly distributed on the interval $[-\pi, \pi]$. One can show that $r\sin(\lambda t + \varphi)$ for fixed λ is stationary; however, it is deterministic in a sense to be made more precise below, for a single realization contains in effect *only one* observation on r and only one on φ (really none, if the origin from which we measure t is arbitrary).[4]

The notion of ergodicity is quite distinct from the notion of stationarity but is nonetheless usually not defined for nonstationary processes since these do not possess stable probability laws.

Thus far we have considered only single processes, although in applications we often must deal with several processes. The notions introduced above can be generalized by considering the formulation of new processes through the combination of others having a joint distribution. Moreover, we can show that all of the manipulations that can be performed on ordinary random variables can be performed on processes; such operations give rise to new processes. Let $\{x_t^{(1)}\}, \ldots, \{x_t^{(n)}\}$ be n processes, $t \in T$. Suppose that these variables have a joint distribution function $F(v_{t_1}^{(1)}, \ldots, v_{t_k}^{(1)}, \ldots, v_{t_k}^{(n)})$ for any finite index set T_k. If $f(x^{(1)}, \ldots, x^{(n)})$ is a well-behaved function, then $\{y_t\}$, where

$$y_t = f(x_t^{(1)}, \ldots, x_t^{(n)}), \tag{12}$$

is a well-defined process since y_t is a well-defined random variable for given t. In particular sums and differences and, indeed, any finite linear combinations with constant coefficients are well-defined processes.

The processes $\{x_t^{(1)}\}, \ldots, \{x_t^{(n)}\}$ are said to be *jointly stationary* if

$$F(v_{t_1}^{(1)}, \ldots, v_{t_k}^{(n)}) \equiv F(v_{t_1+\tau}^{(1)}, \ldots, v_{t_k+\tau}^{(n)}) \tag{13}$$

for any finite index set T_k and for any τ such that $T_k + \tau$ belongs to T. It is apparent that the process $\{y_t\}$, defined by (12), is stationary if the processes $\{x_t^{(1)}\}, \ldots, \{x_t^{(n)}\}$ are jointly stationary. If processes are jointly stationary they are individually so; the converse, however, is not true.[5] This is evident since

---

[4] Let $\{x_t\}, t \in T$, be a process defined as follows: $x_t = re^{i(\lambda t + \varphi)}$, where $r \sim n(\mu, 1)$, λ is a fixed frequency, and φ is uniformly distributed on the interval $[-\pi, \pi]$; the definition of stationarity may be seen to apply by deriving the joint distribution of the pair $(x_t, x_{t+\tau})$, the triplet $(x_t, x_{t+\tau_1}, x_{t+\tau_2})$, etc.

[5] For example, let the processes $\{x_t^{(1)}\}$ and $\{x_t^{(2)}\}, t \in T$, be defined as follows:

$$x_t^{(1)} = a_1 \cos t + b_1 \sin t + a_2 \cos 2t + b_2 \sin 2t,$$

$$x_t^{(2)} = a_2 \cos t + b_2 \sin t + a_1 \cos 2t + b_1 \sin 2t,$$

where

$$Ea_1 = Ea_2 = Eb_1 = Eb_2 = 0, \qquad Ea_1^2 = Eb_1^2 = \sigma_1^2 < \infty, \qquad Ea_2^2 = Eb_2^2 = \sigma_2^2 < \infty,$$

$$Ea_1a_2 = Eb_1b_2 = Ea_1b_2 = Ea_2b_2 = Ea_1b_1 = Eb_1a_2 = 0.$$

Each of these two series is weakly (covariance) stationary, but they are not jointly stationary.

joint stationarity is a property of the joint distribution, while stationarity of the individual processes depends only on the marginal distributions.

Let $v_1^{(1)}, \ldots, v_k^{(n)}$ be n sets of k fixed numbers. The processes $\{x_t^{(1)}\}, \ldots, \{x_t^{(m)}\}$, for $t \in T$, are said to be *independent* if, for any finite index set T_k, the joint distribution function can be factored into the product of the marginal distribution functions:

$$F(v_{t_1}^{(1)}, \ldots, v_{t_k}^{(n)}) \equiv \prod_{j=1}^{n} F_j(v_{t_1}^{(j)}, \ldots, v_{t_k}^{(j)}), \qquad (14)$$

for any T_k and any set $v_{t_1}^{(1)}, \ldots, v_{t_k}^{(n)}$. A corresponding definition can be given in terms of characteristic functions (Cramér, 1946, p. 188). The *infinite sequence* of processes $\{x_t^{(1)}\}, \ldots$ is independent if every finite subsequence consists of independent processes. A sequence of independent processes that are individually stationary are also jointly stationary.

Consider the process $\{x_t\}$. Choose an integer τ and form the process $\{y_t = x_{t+\tau}\}$. If $\{x_t\}$ is a stationary process, then so will $\{y_t\}$ be. Furthermore, the processes will be jointly stationary.[6] In the same way one can show that the processes $\{x_t\}, \{x_{t-1}\}, \ldots, \{x_{t-h}\}$ are all jointly stationary. We can form the process $\{y_t\}$ where

$$y_t = a_0 x_t + a_1 x_{t-1} + \cdots + a_h x_{t-h}. \qquad (15)$$

$\{y_t\}$ will clearly be stationary for h finite. We now need to consider such sums when the number of terms tends to infinity, and therefore we also need to define a suitable notion of convergence.

Let $\{\zeta_t^{(1)}\}, \ldots, \{\zeta_t^{(m)}\}, \ldots$ be a sequence of processes. For an arbitrary t this defines a sequence of random variables:

$$\zeta_t^{(1)}, \ldots, \zeta_t^{(m)}, \ldots.$$

These random variables converge in probability to a random variable ζ_t if for every δ and $\epsilon > 0$ there exists an n such that for all $m > n$

$$\text{Prob}\{|\zeta_t^{(m)} - \zeta_t| > \epsilon\} < \delta. \qquad (16)$$

We say the sequence of processes $\{\zeta_t^{(1)}\}, \ldots$ converges to the process $\{\zeta_t\}$ if (16) holds for any $t \in T$. If the sequence $\zeta_t^{(1)}, \ldots$ for arbitrary t is convergent and if the processes $\{\zeta_t^{(1)}\}, \ldots$ are all stationary, the limit process $\{\zeta_t\}$ will be stationary as well.

Let $\{x_t\}$ be a stationary process; then a necessary and sufficient condition for the infinite sum process $\{y_t\}$, defined by

$$y_t = \sum_{j=0}^{\infty} a_j x_{t-j}, \qquad (17)$$

---

[6] To prove this, write out the joint distribution for $x_{t_1}, \ldots, x_{t_k}$ and $x_{t_1+\tau}, \ldots, x_{t_k+\tau}$ and note that this joint distribution is unaffected by adding θ to τ since the joint behavior of $\{x_t\}$ and $\{x_{t+\tau}\}$ is uniquely determined by the distribution function of $\{x_t\}$ alone if it is stationary.

to be stationary is that the sequence $\{y_t^{(1)}\}, \{y_t^{(2)}\}, \ldots,$ where

$$y_t^{(m)} = \sum_{j=0}^{m} a_j x_{t-j}, \tag{18}$$

be convergent in the sense defined in the previous paragraph. We should also like the right-hand side of (17) to converge in the sense of convergence in the mean. It may be shown that sufficient conditions for convergence in this sense are that, uniformly in p,

$$\lim_{n \to \infty} \sum_{j=0}^{n} a_j E x_{t-j} = E y_t \tag{19}$$

$$\lim_{n \to \infty} \frac{1}{n} E\left\{ \sum_{j=n}^{n+p} a_j x_{t-j} \right\}^2 = 0, \tag{20}$$

although convergence may occur under weaker conditions (Anderson, 1971, pp. 398–399, 414–415). It follows from (20) that

$$\lim_{n \to \infty} \text{var}(y_t^{(n)}) = \text{var}(y_t) < \infty. \tag{21}$$

Let $\{\epsilon_t\}$ be a process formed of identically distributed random variables with zero mean and unit variance such that $E\epsilon_t \epsilon_{t'} = 0, t \neq t'$. Such a process is sometimes called *white noise* for reasons that are discussed in the next chapter. The process $\{x_t\}$, where

$$x_t = \sum_{j=0}^{n} b_j \epsilon_{t-j}, \tag{22}$$

is called a *finite (one-sided) moving average*. Let $b_0, b_1, \ldots$ be an infinite sequence such that $\sum_{j=0}^{\infty} b_j^2 < \infty$. Then the *infinite one-sided moving average* $\{x_t\}$, where

$$x_t = \sum_{j=0}^{\infty} b_t \epsilon_{t-j}, \tag{23}$$

is a well-defined stationary process with mean 0 and variance $\sum_{j=0}^{\infty} b_j^2$.[7]

---

[7] Using the definition of $\{x_t\}$ and the condition on $\sum_{j=0}^{\infty} b_j^2$, one can obtain an explicit expression for

$$\gamma(\tau) = E x_t x_{t-\tau} = E\left\{ \sum_{j, j'=0}^{\infty} b_j b_{j'} \epsilon_{t-j} \epsilon_{t-j'-\tau} \right\} = \sum_{j=0}^{\infty} b_j b_{j+\tau},$$

since it is assumed that $E\epsilon_t = 0$ and

$$E\epsilon_t \epsilon_{t'} = \begin{cases} 1, & \text{if } t = t' \text{ for all } t \text{ and } t' \\ 0, & \text{otherwise.} \end{cases}$$

This expression for γ_τ may be used to show that the condition given in (20) is satisfied since

$$\frac{1}{n} E\left\{ \sum_{j=n}^{n+p} b_j \epsilon_{t-j} \right\}^2 = \frac{1}{n} E\{x_{t-n} - x_{t-(n+p+1)}\}^2 = \frac{1}{n} E\{x_t - x_{t-p-1}\}^2$$

$$= \frac{2}{n} \left\{ \sum_{j=0}^{\infty} b_j^2 - \sum_{j=0}^{\infty} b_j b_{j+p+1} \right\},$$

which clearly tends to zero with n uniformly in p.

Processes of a slightly more general form than (23),

$$x_t = \sum_{j=-\infty}^{\infty} b_j \epsilon_{t-j}, \qquad \sum_{j=-\infty}^{\infty} b_j^2 < \infty \qquad (24)$$

are called *linear processes*. Such processes are always ergodic (Hannan, 1970, p. 204).

3. The Wold Decomposition Theorem

Further insight into the meaning of a stationary time series may be obtained by an important theorem proved by Herman Wold in 1938. The object of Wold's theorem is to show how an arbitrary stationary time series can be decomposed into two parts, one of which is of the form (2.24), and one of which can be predicted exactly from at most an infinite past of a realization of the process and is deterministic in a sense to be made more precise below. Our discussion is far from rigorous.

Let $\{x_t\}$ be a zero-mean stationary process with finite variance, σ_x^2. Let n be an integer and consider the variables $x_t, x_{t-1}, \ldots, x_{t-n}$ for fixed t. Consider a linear combination of $x_{t-1}, \ldots, x_{t-n}$ for *predicting* x_t,

$$\hat{x}_t = a_1 x_{t-1} + a_2 x_{t-2} + \cdots + a_n x_{t-n}, \qquad (1)$$

and choose $a_1, \ldots, a_n$ so as to minimize $E(\hat{x}_t - x_t)^2$. Since

$$E(\hat{x}_t - x_t)^2 = E \left\{ \sum_{i,j=1}^{n} a_i a_j x_{t-i} x_{t-j} - 2 \sum_{j=1}^{n} a_j x_t x_{t-j} + x_t^2 \right\},$$

differentiating with respect to a_i gives us the *normal* equations for the determination of the a's

$$\sum_{j=1}^{n} a_j E x_{t-i} x_{t-j} = E x_t x_{t-i}, \quad i = 1, \ldots, n, \qquad \text{or} \qquad \Gamma a = \gamma, \qquad (2)$$

where

$$\Gamma = \begin{bmatrix} \gamma_0 & \gamma_1 & \cdots & \gamma_{n-1} \\ \gamma_1 & \gamma_0 & \cdots & \gamma_{n-2} \\ \vdots & \vdots & & \vdots \\ \gamma_{n-1} & \gamma_{n-2} & \cdots & \gamma_0 \end{bmatrix}, \qquad \gamma = \begin{bmatrix} \gamma_1 \\ \vdots \\ \gamma_n \end{bmatrix}, \qquad \text{and} \qquad a = \begin{pmatrix} a_1 \\ \vdots \\ a_n \end{pmatrix}.$$

So $a = \Gamma^{-1} \gamma$. Note that the assumption that $\{x_t\}$ is stationary implies that Γ is symmetric about both diagonals. If we write

$$x_t = \hat{x}_t + u_t^n, \qquad (3)$$

where u_t^n is the "residual," we can easily show that

$$Eu_t^n = 0,$$
$$Ex_{t-k} u_t^n = 0, \qquad k = 1, \ldots, n. \qquad (4)$$

First,

$$Eu_t^n = -E(\hat{x}_t - x_t) = -E\hat{x}_t + 0 = -\sum a_j E x_{t-j} = 0.$$

Second,

$$Ex_{t-k}u_t^n = E\{x_{t-k}x_t - x_{t-k}\hat{x}_t\} = \gamma_k - \sum_{j=1}^n a_j \gamma_{|k-j|}, \qquad k = 1, \ldots, n,$$

where γ_k is the autocovariance of $\{x_t\}$ for lag k. But the a's were chosen according to (2) so the expression on the right is zero for $k = 1, \ldots, n$. Of course, this is intuitive since if the residuals were correlated with the past x's, the latter could be used to "explain" the part of x_t that is "unexplained," and the a's could not then minimize $E(\hat{x}_t - x_t)^2$.

In a similar fashion we can obtain

$$x_{t-1} = \hat{x}_{t-1} + u_{t-1}^n, \tag{5}$$

where $\hat{x}_{t-1}$ is a linear combination of $x_{t-2}, \ldots, x_{t-n}$ with coefficients chosen so that $E[(x_{t-1} - \hat{x}_{t-1})^2]$ is minimized. It should be clear from the above that $E(u_{t-1}^n) = 0$, and $E(x_{t-k} \cdot u_{t-1}^n) = 0$, $k = 2, 3, \ldots, n$. Notice that from (4) we obtain

$$E(u_t^n \cdot u_{t-1}^n) = E(u_t^n(x_{t-1} - \hat{x}_{t-1})) = 0.$$

Substituting (5) and (1) into (3) yields

$$x_t = u_t^n + a_1 u_{t-1}^n + a_2' x_{t-2} + \cdots + a_n' x_{t-n} = u_t^n + a_1 u_{t-1}^n + \xi_t^n(1), \tag{6}$$

where $\xi_t^n(1)$ depends only on x's prior to x_{t-1},

$$E(u_{t-k}^n \xi_t^n(1)) = 0, \qquad k = 0, 1, \qquad \text{and} \qquad a_1 = E(x_t u_{t-1}^n)/E(u_{t-1}^n)^2.\text{[8]}$$

Continuing in this fashion we obtain

$$x_t = u_t^n + b_1 u_{t-1}^n + b_2 u_{t-2}^n + \cdots + b_j u_{t-j}^n + \xi_t^n(j), \qquad j \le n-1$$
$$= \eta_t^n(j) + \xi_t^n(j),$$

where

$$E(u_{t-s}^n \xi_t^n(j)) = 0 \qquad \text{for all} \quad s \le j,$$
$$b_j = E(x_t u_{t-j}^n)/E[(u_{t-j}^n)^2], \tag{7}$$

and

$$E((u_{t-i}^n)^2) \ge E((u_{t-k}^n)^2) \qquad \text{for} \qquad i > k = 0, 1, \ldots.$$

Applying this same construction to each of the x's yields

$$x_{t-i} = \eta_{t-i}^n(j) + \xi_{t-i}^n(j), \qquad 0 \le j \le n-1. \tag{8}$$

---

[8] Essentially this is a result standard in least-squares theory: The expression on the right-hand side of (6) is the projection of x_t on $x_{t-2}, x_{t-3}, \ldots, x_{t-n}$ and u_t^n. u_t^n is orthogonal to $x_{t-2}, x_{t-3}, \ldots, x_{t-n}$.

In every case ξ^n_{t-i} depends only upon the x's in the remote past, and by construction,

$$E(\eta^n_{t-i}(j)\xi^n_{t-i}(j)) = 0, \qquad j = 0, 1, \ldots, n-1.$$

An alternative way of obtaining the same decomposition is as follows: Take

$$\hat{\hat{x}}_t = \sum_{j=0}^{k} b_j u^n_{t-j}, \qquad k \le n-1,$$

with the $\{b_j\}$ being chosen to minimize $E((x_t - \hat{\hat{x}}_t)^2)$. Since the u^n's are uncorrelated, the solution for $b_1, \ldots, b_j$ is given by (7) so that again we obtain the decomposition (8) with ξ^n being the residual. If the u^n's vanish so that η^n is zero, then the x's are deterministic in that they can be predicted perfectly (zero-mean-square error) using information from only the distant past.

Wold's decomposition theorem states that

$$x_t = \eta_t + \xi_t, \qquad \eta_t = \sum_{j=0}^{\infty} b_j u_{t-j}, \qquad \sum b_j^2 < \infty, \tag{9}$$

where

$$
\begin{aligned}
E(u_t u_s) &= \sigma^2, && t = s, \\
&= 0, && t \ne s, \\
E(\eta_t \xi_s) &= 0 && \text{for all } t, s,
\end{aligned}
$$

and ξ_t is deterministic.[9]

We do not provide a rigorous proof of this theorem, though the previous discussion (which, strictly speaking, holds only for n finite) is intended to be suggestive. (See Wold, 1938, pp. 75–89; Anderson, 1971, pp. 420–421.) Consider the problem of choosing $\hat{x}_t = \sum_{j=1}^{\infty} a_j x_{t-j}$ so that $E(x_t - \hat{x}_t)^2$ is minimized. If this problem has a solution, it will be characterized by equations (2). We still have x_t decomposed as in (3) with $E x_{t-k} u_t = 0$, $k = 1, 2, \ldots$, and $E u_t = 0$. The residuals u_t are called the *innovations* of the process $\{x_t\}$ since they are that part of the current value that cannot be "explained" on the basis of past values. It can be shown that $\hat{x}_t$ and u_t are uniquely defined although the a's may in certain cases not be uniquely defined (Cramér, 1946, p. 304). Now

$$u_{t-1} = x_{t-1} - a_1 x_{t-2} - \cdots, \qquad u_{t-2} = x_{t-2} - a_1 x_{t-3} - \cdots, \qquad \text{etc.,}$$

so that

$$E u_t u_{t-k} = E u_t \{x_{t-k} - a_1 x_{t-k-1} - \cdots\} = 0, \qquad k \ne 0. \tag{10}$$

---

[9] Strictly speaking, ξ_t is *linearly* deterministic. An example is the time series generated by $\xi_t = e^{i(vt+u)}$, where u is uniformly distributed over the interval $(-\pi, \pi)$ and v is independently distributed with arbitrary distribution function. Indeed, under the assumptions made, x_t is itself white noise, in the sense that the best linear predictor of the current value is 0 (see Cox and Miller, 1965, p. 336, exercise 8.1).

Hence, the innovations of the process $\{x_t\}$ are uncorrelated. Moreover, $Eu_t^2 = \sigma_u^2$ for all t by stationarity. We cannot, of course, say they are independent unless $\{x_t\}$ was assumed to be a Gaussian or normal process to start with.

One way to think of this decomposition is to consider the subspace spanned by the time series $\{x_t\}$ in a Hilbert space (complete, infinite dimensional vector space in which inner product and distance are defined). Here x_t is resolved into two components: One lies in the subspace spanned by $x_{t-1}, x_{t-2}, \ldots$ and the other part u_t is orthogonal to that subspace (see Parzen, 1967, pp. 253–319; Hannan, 1970, pp. 136–137).

Corresponding to (1) and (3) we now have

$$x_t = u_t + \sum_{j=1}^{\infty} a_j x_{t-j}. \tag{11}$$

Substituting for x_{t-1} gives

$$x_t = u_t + a_1 u_{t-1} + a_1 \left(\sum_{j=1}^{\infty} a_j x_{t-1-j} \right) + \sum_{k=2}^{\infty} a_k x_{t-k} = \eta_t^1 + \xi_t^1.$$

Substituting again this time for x_{t-2} yields

$$x_t = u_t + a_1 u_{t-1} + (a_2 + a_1^2) u_{t-2} + \text{(terms involving earlier } x\text{'s)}$$
$$= \eta_t^2 + \xi_t^2.$$

Continuing in this fashion gives

$$x_t = \eta_t^k + \xi_t^k, \qquad \eta_t^k = \sum_{j=0}^{k} b_j^k u_{t-j}, \qquad \xi_t^k = \sum_{j=k}^{\infty} \delta_j x_{t-j-1}. \tag{12}$$

At each step $E(\eta_t^k \cdot \xi_t^k) = 0$; in fact

$$
\begin{aligned}
E(u_{t+j} \xi_t^k) &= 0, & j \geq 0 \\
E(u_{t-j} \xi_t^k) &= 0, & j \leq k.
\end{aligned}
\tag{13}
$$

Assuming that $\{\eta_t^k\}$ and $\{\xi_t^k\}$ converge in mean square to $\{\eta_t\}$ and $\{\xi_t\}$ (in a rigorous discussion convergence should be proved), we eventually get $x_t = \eta_t + \xi_t$, and in view of (13)

$$E(\eta_t \xi_s) = 0, \qquad s, t = 0, \pm 1, \ldots.$$

Thus we have expressed $\{x_t\}$ as the sum of two mutually uncorrelated processes, one of which $\{\eta_t\}$ is a linear combination of the innovations, while the other $\{\xi_t\}$ depends linearly upon the remote past of the process.

To gain further insight into the meaning of the decomposition, consider the following series of projections:

$$x_t \text{ on } x_{t-1}, x_{t-2}, \ldots, \qquad x_t \text{ on } x_{t-2}, x_{t-3}, \ldots, \qquad \ldots, \qquad x_t \text{ on } x_{t-k}, x_{t-k-1}, \ldots.$$

For each we have the representation

$$x_t = \hat{x}_t^{(k)} + u_t^{(k)}, \qquad k = 1, 2, \ldots. \tag{14}$$

The $u_t^{(k)}$'s have similar properties to the u_t'''s discussed above. Let $\sigma_u^2(k)$ be the variance of these "kth order" innovations. Clearly $\sigma_x^2 \geq \sigma_u^2(k) \geq 0$ and is non-decreasing as k increases. Hence the sequence $\sigma_u^2(1), \sigma_u^2(2), \ldots$ must tend to a limit $\sigma_u^2(\infty)$. If this limit is σ_x^2, we call the process $\{x_t\}$ purely nondeterministic. The meaning of this is that a *linear* combination of x's in the remote past has little predictive ability. This, as one can see, is very much like the "independence" of remote segments that is a condition for ergodicity.[10]

If the limit $\sigma_u^2(\infty) = 0$, then we say the process is *linearly* deterministic. Since the sequence $\sigma_u^2(k)$ is nondecreasing, we must then have $\sigma_u^2(1) = \sigma_u^2(2) = \cdots = 0$. This means that we can predict x_t without error if we know its entire past (possibly only part of its past). Furthermore, any segment, however remote, is just as good as a more recent segment in this respect. It is important to note that a process can be completely deterministic but not linearly so. For example, the process $\{y_t\}$ with $y_t = e^{i(\lambda t + \varphi)}$, where φ and λ are independent random variables both distributed uniformly on the interval $[-\pi, \pi]$, is clearly deterministic in the sense that once λ and φ are chosen, y_t is determined forever.[11] But the process is not *linearly* deterministic because no *linear* combination of past values can predict the current value with zero variance. The proof, however, requires some further considerations.

Returning to the original line of argument assume $0 < \sigma_u^2(\infty) < \sigma_x^2$. Let $k \to \infty$ and let the processes $\hat{x}_t^{(k)}$ and $u_t^{(k)}$ tend to the limiting processes ξ_t and η_t, respectively, in the sense discussed in the previous section of this chapter. Since

$$E(\hat{x}_t^{(k)} u_t^{(k)}) = 0 \qquad \text{for all } k,$$

it must be true that $E\xi_t \eta_t = 0$ as well. Since

$$E(\hat{x}_t^{(k)} u_{t-\tau}^{(k)}) = 0 = E(\hat{x}_{t-\tau}^{(k)} u_t^{(k)}) \qquad \text{for all } k, \text{ any } \tau \geq 0,$$

it must be true as well that

$$E\xi_t \eta_{t-\tau} = 0 = E\xi_{t-\tau} \eta_t.$$

Thus the whole process $\{\xi_t\}$ is orthogonal to $\{\eta_t\}$. Both have mean zero and are stationary. Indeed, it can be shown they are jointly stationary. Now $\{\xi_t\}$ is determined only by the remote past of $\{x_t\}$. Therefore if it does not tend to zero in probability, it is natural to call this the *deterministic component*. The process $\{\eta_t\}$, on the other hand, must be purely nondeterministic. Were there no deter-

---

[10] While stationary time series that are purely linearly nondeterministic in the sense used here must be ergodic, there are cases of stationary, purely *deterministic* time series that are nonetheless ergodic. An example is a time series defined by

$$x_1 = \begin{cases} 1 & \text{with probability } 0.5 \\ -1 & \text{with probability } 0.5 \end{cases}$$

and $x_t = -x_{t+1}$ for all t.

[11] See footnote 9.

ministic component, it would be $\{x_t\}$ itself; and if it were zero in the limit, $\{x_t\}$ would obviously be purely deterministic.

It follows from Wold's theorem that any purely nondeterministic process can be written as a one-sided moving average with a white noise input. This representation is extremely important in spectral theory and in the theory of optimal prediction and extraction.

The component $\{\xi_t\}$, which is determined, as indicated, only by the remote past of $\{x_t\}$, can be shown to be linearly deterministic (Anderson, 1971, p. 421). It can be shown that the deterministic component ξ_t in the Wold decomposition

$$x_t = \xi_t + \eta_t \tag{15}$$

is essentially of the form[12]

$$\xi_t = \sum_{j=1}^{m} z_j^t \tag{16}$$

where $z_j^t = c_j e^{i\lambda_j t}$, λ_j is fixed, and $c_j = (a_j + ib_j)/2$, where[13]

$$Ea_j = 0 = Eb_j, \qquad Ea_j^2 = 1, Eb_j^2 = 1, \qquad Ea_j b_j = 0,$$
$$Ea_j a_{j'} = 0 = Eb_j b_{j'} = Ea_j b_{j'}, \qquad \text{for all } j \neq j'.$$

(We could replace the variances of a_j and b_j by σ_j^2 above.) The autocovariance function of the component is

$$E\xi_t \bar{\xi}_{t-\tau} = \gamma_\tau = E \sum_{j,\, j'=1}^{m} z_j^t \bar{z}_{j'}^{t-\tau}$$

$$= E \sum_{j,\, j'=1}^{m} c_j \bar{c}_{j'} e^{i\lambda_j t} e^{-i\lambda_{j'} t} e^{i\lambda_j \tau}$$

$$= \sum_{j,\, j'=1}^{m} (E c_j \bar{c}_{j'}) e^{i(\lambda_j - \lambda_{j'})t} e^{i\lambda_j \tau} = \sum_{j=1}^{m} e^{i\lambda_j \tau}, \tag{17}$$

[12] See Doob (1953, p. 576). What Doob says is that such a time series has a "line" spectrum. Compare our discussion in Chapter III, Section 3.

[13] Here z_j is a *complex random variable*. We may define such a variable $z = x + iy$ in terms of its random real and imaginary parts, x and y respectively. From the definition we have

$$Ez = (Ex) + i(Ey), \qquad Ez\bar{z} = E(x^2 + y^2), \qquad Ez_1 \bar{z}_2 = E\{x_1 x_2 + y_1 y_2\} - iE\{x_1 y_2 - x_2 y_1\},$$

where $\bar{z}$ is the complex conjugate of z.

We define

$$\text{cov}(z_1, z_2) = Ez_1 \bar{z}_2 - (Ez_1)(E\bar{z}_2)$$

and say z_1 and z_2 are *orthogonal* if $\text{cov}(z_1, z_2) = 0$. Note if z_1 and z_2 are orthogonal, x_1, x_2, y_1, and y_2 are not necessarily mutually uncorrelated. This definition makes the variance of z

$$\text{var}(z) = Ez\bar{z} - EzE\bar{z} = E\{(x - Ex)^2 + (y - Ey)^2\}$$

always a real positive number.

where the bar above a variable indicates its complex conjugate (Doob, 1953, pp. 486–488). Note that $\{\xi_t\}$ is stationary to the second order but is linearly deterministic. If a_j and b_j are assumed $n(0, \sigma_j^2)$ and independent for all j, then $\{\xi_t\}$ is strictly stationary. It is obvious intuitively that $\{\xi_t\}$ cannot be ergodic since each of its components clearly is not. A rigorous proof, however, requires a proper rigorous definition of ergodicity, which we have not given here.

Essentially the Wold decomposition divides the process $\{x_t\}$ into an ergodic and a linearly deterministic part.[14] One might also term this representation *canonical:* Every process stationary at least to second order can be represented as the sum of two mutually uncorrelated processes, one linearly deterministic component (the sum of a denumerable number of sine and cosine terms with fixed frequencies and random amplitudes) and one nondeterministic component representable as a one-sided moving average with white noise input. A linearly deterministic component, as shown, is essentially a stochastic trigonometrical series. In the next chapter we shall see that by enriching the spectrum of frequencies we can represent such processes in another canonical form, namely a stochastic trigonometric integral.

[14] This is not to be confused with nonergodic. See footnote 10.

Chapter III
THE SPECTRAL REPRESENTATION AND ITS ESTIMATION

1. Introduction

In this chapter we present two rather different ways of introducing the spectral density function for stationary stochastic processes. First we give a development based upon the Wold decomposition theorem and the auto-correlations of a time series. Next we show how the spectral distribution function of a stationary time series can be derived from the representation of such a process in terms of random variables defined in the frequency domain rather than in the time domain. Although either development alone would be sufficient, our experience has been that some prefer the first approach since it is somewhat more direct and mathematically simpler, while others prefer the second since it leads to a better intuitive understanding of spectral ideas.

Much of the material presented requires a knowledge of the elements of the theory of complex variables. A brief overview of the requisites is given in Appendix B. Some results from the theory of Fourier series and transforms are needed, especially for our discussion of spectral estimation, which we have included at the end of this chapter. A discussion of the elements of Fourier analysis is included in Appendix C.

2. Covariance Generating Functions

Consider a purely nondeterministic process $\{x_t\}$:

$$x_t = \sum_{j=0}^{\infty} b_j \epsilon_{t-j} = B(U)\epsilon_t, \tag{1}$$

where

$$E(\epsilon_t) = 0, \qquad E(\epsilon_t \epsilon_s) = \begin{cases} \sigma^2, & t = s, \\ 0, & t \neq s, \end{cases}$$

$$B(U) = \sum_{j=0}^{\infty} b_j U^j,$$

and U is the backward shift operator such that $U^j x_t \equiv x_{t-j}$. For reasons that were discussed in the previous chapter in connection with one-sided infinite moving-average processes, it is clear that, in order for the variance of $\{x_t\}$ to be finite, we must have $\sum_{j=0}^{\infty} b_j^2 < \infty$. In what follows, we make the somewhat stronger assumption that $\sum_{j=0}^{\infty} |b_j| < \infty$. The autocovariance function for $\{x_t\}$, derived for the general one-sided moving-average process in the previous chapter, is

$$\gamma(\tau) = \gamma(-\tau) = \sigma^2 \sum_{j=0}^{\infty} b_j b_{j+\tau}. \tag{2}$$

Note that we have changed notation slightly so as to make the autocovariance functions of the lag τ rather than a subscripted variable. For example, if $b_j = \lambda^j$ so that

$$x_t = \sum_{j=0}^{\infty} \lambda^j \epsilon_{t-j}, \qquad |\lambda| < 1, \tag{3}$$

the autocovariance function is

$$\gamma(\tau) = \sigma^2 \sum_{j=0}^{\infty} \lambda^{2j+\tau} = \begin{cases} \dfrac{\sigma^2 \lambda^{\tau}}{1 - \lambda^2}, & \text{for} \quad \tau \geq 0 \\ \dfrac{\sigma^2 \lambda^{-\tau}}{1 - \lambda^2}, & \text{for} \quad \tau < 0 \end{cases} = \frac{\sigma^2 \lambda^{|\tau|}}{1 - \lambda^2}.$$

The *autocovariance generating transform* for a time series $\{x_t\}$ is defined as

$$g(z) = \sum_{j=-\infty}^{\infty} \gamma(j) z^j, \tag{4}$$

where z is a complex variable, provided the series on the right-hand side of (4) converges for z contained in an annulus about the unit circle.[1] In the example above, for $b_j = \lambda^j$ the generating transform is

$$g(z) = \sum_{j=-\infty}^{\infty} \frac{\sigma^2}{1 - \lambda^2} \cdot \lambda^{|j|} z^j = \frac{\sigma^2}{1 - \lambda^2} \left[\frac{1}{1 - \lambda z} + \sum_{j=1}^{\infty} \lambda^j z^{-j} \right]$$

$$= \frac{\sigma^2}{1 - \lambda^2} \left[\frac{1}{1 - \lambda z} + \frac{\lambda z^{-1}}{1 - \lambda z^{-1}} \right] = \sigma^2 \frac{1}{(1 - \lambda z)(1 - \lambda z^{-1})}. \tag{5}$$

---

[1] See the discussion in Appendix B of the Laurent expansion of a function of a complex variable.

Notice that this series converges on the unit circle and in an annulus around it. Indeed, in this example the series converges for all z such that $|\lambda| < |z| < 1/|\lambda|$ and nowhere else.

Substituting (2) into (4) yields

$$g(z) = \sum_{j=-\infty}^{\infty} \gamma(j)z^j = \sigma^2 \sum_{j=0}^{\infty} \sum_{k=0}^{\infty} b_k b_{k+j} z^j + \sigma^2 \sum_{j=1}^{\infty} \sum_{k=0}^{\infty} b_k b_{k+j} z^{-j}$$

$$= \sigma^2 \sum_{k=0}^{\infty} b_k^2 + \sum_{j=1}^{\infty} \sum_{k=0}^{\infty} b_k b_{k+j}(z^j + z^{-j}) = \sigma^2 B(z)B(z^{-1}). \tag{6}$$

The last equality in (6) gives what is called the *canonical factorization* of the covariance generating function. Thus, in general, the autocovariance generating function converges on the unit circle and in an annulus surrounding it. The example may be rewritten compactly as

$$x_t = \sum_{j=0}^{\infty} \lambda^j \epsilon_{t-j} = \sum_{j=0}^{\infty} \lambda^j U^j \epsilon_t = \frac{1}{1 - \lambda U} \epsilon_t. \tag{3'}$$

Lagging x_t one period, multiplying by λ, and subtracting gives

$$x_t - \lambda x_{t-1} = (1 - \lambda U)x_t = \epsilon_t. \tag{7}$$

In general, a process satisfying

$$A(U)x_t = \epsilon_t \tag{8}$$

where $A(U)$ is a polynomial and $\{\epsilon_t\}$ is a white noise input is called an autoregressive process and may or may not be stationary. In stationary cases it is not necessary to restrict the degree of $A(U)$ to be finite. When $g(z)$ is the autocovariance generating transform of a stationary process that *has no zeros* and is analytic both on the unit circle and in an annulus about the unit circle, then the process $\{x_t\}$ has both a moving-average and an autoregressive representation. For under these circumstances, $\log g(z)$ is analytic in an annulus about the unit circle and therefore has a Laurent expansion there:

$$\log g(z) = \sum_{j=-\infty}^{\infty} c_j z^j = c_0 + \sum_{j=1}^{\infty} c_j z^j + \sum_{j=1}^{\infty} c_{-j} z^{-j}. \tag{9}$$

Clearly we can take

$$B(z) = \exp\left(\sum_{j=1}^{\infty} c_j z^j\right), \qquad \sigma^2 = e^{c_0}. \tag{10}$$

$B(z)$ is analytic inside a circle with radius greater than one and therefore has a Taylor's series expansion there of the form

$$B(z) = \sum_{j=0}^{\infty} b_j z^j, \tag{11}$$

which yields immediately the moving-average representation of the process by equating powers of z with length of lag in (II.2.22).[2] On the assumption that $\log g(z)$ is analytic, we have also that

$$[B(z)]^{-1} = \exp\left(-\sum_{j=1}^{\infty} c_j z^j\right) = A(z), \tag{12}$$

where $A(z)$ is analytic inside the same circle and thus has a Taylor's series expansion

$$A(z) = \sum_{j=0}^{\infty} a_j z^j. \tag{13}$$

$A(z)$ is the generating transform of the autoregressive representation. Clearly, a necessary condition that $A(z)$ exist for a stationary process whose covariance generating function in canonical form is $\sigma^2 B(z)B(z^{-1})$ is that $B(z)$ shall have no zeros on the unit circle. Indeed, to make the factorization unique we observe that $g(z)$, being symmetric, has a zero outside the unit circle corresponding to every one inside the unit circle so that we can separate these zeros by appropriate choice of the factors $B(z)$ and $B(z^{-1})$. If this is done so that $B(z)$ has zeros only outside the unit circle, the factorization will be unique and $A(z)$ will be given as in (12).[3]

Although perfectly acceptable stationary processes such as $y_t = \epsilon_t - \epsilon_{t-1}$ do not possess autoregressive representations, we shall generally suppose throughout this book that the processes with which we deal have both moving-average and autoregressive representations. Stationary processes that have both a moving-average and an autoregressive representation are called *invertible*. One way to view the requirement of invertibility is as a condition for identifiability in the usual econometric sense. Consider, for example, the process

$$x_t = \epsilon_t - \rho\epsilon_{t+1}, \qquad |\rho| > 1,$$

where $\{\epsilon_t\}$ is white noise with variance σ_+^2, which is stationary and has exactly the same covariance generating transform as the process

$$x_t = \epsilon_t - \rho\epsilon_{t-1}, \qquad |\rho| < 1,$$

where $\{\epsilon_t\}$ is white noise with variance σ_-^2. But the first process is not invertible, whereas the second is. Moreover, since the covariance generating transforms

---

[2] In equation cross references, the numbers preceeding the decimal points give the chapter and section numbers. These numbers will be omitted when the equation referred to is in the same chapter or section.

[3] As an example of this result, it is instructive to obtain the autoregressive representation of $\{x_t\}$ where $x_t = \epsilon_t - \rho\epsilon_{t-1}$, $|\rho| < 1$, and $\{\epsilon_t\}$ is white noise with variance σ^2. The covariance generating transform is thus $g(z) = \sigma^2(1 - \rho z)(1 - \rho z^{-1})$ so that $\log g(z) = \log \sigma^2 + \log(1 - \rho z) + \log(1 - \rho z^{-1})$. But $\log(1 - \rho z) = -\sum_{j=1}^{\infty} (\rho z)^j/j$ is that part of the Laurent expansion containing positive powers of z; thus $A(z) = \exp[\sum(\rho z)^j/j] = \exp[-\log(1 - \rho z)] = \sum_{k=0}^{\infty}(\rho z)^k$. That is, the corresponding autoregressive representation is $x_t + \rho x_{t-1} + \rho^2 x_{t-2} + \cdots = \epsilon_t$.

for the two processes are identical, they have the same autocovariances and there is no way to distinguish empirically between them. The requirement of invertibility thus serves to identify a priori which process we are talking about when both describe the data equally well.

When $|\rho| = 1$, as in the earlier example, the two processes discussed in the preceding paragraph are still stationary, although neither is invertible. The requirement of invertibility serves to rule out this case altogether.

Of substantial practical importance is the case of a time series with a *rational covariance generating function*. In this case, by definition, the autocovariance generating function may be written as the ratio of two polynomials:

$$g(z) = P(z)/Q(z). \tag{14}$$

If $Q(z)$ has roots on the unit circle, then $\{x_t\}$ cannot be regarded as stationary for it has no moving-average representation. On the other hand, if $Q(z)$ has no such roots, we know that because $g(z)$ is symmetric in z and z^{-1}, both $P(z)$ and $Q(z)$ must be as well and hence can be factored as

$$g(z) = \frac{\sigma^2 \prod_{k=1}^{m} (1 - \beta_k z)(1 - \beta_k z^{-1})}{\prod_{k=1}^{n} (1 - \alpha_k z)(1 - \alpha_k z^{-1})}. \tag{15}$$

Note that σ^2 has been chosen so that the leading coefficients of $P(z)$ and $Q(z)$ are both one. (These coefficients cannot be zero because of the nature of $g(z)$.) In line with the convention mentioned earlier to ensure a unique factorization, we suppose $|\beta_k| \leq 1$ and $|\alpha_k| < 1$. If the strict inequality holds in the first instance, the process has an autoregressive as well as a moving-average representation; the latter has the generating transform

$$B(z) = \prod_{k=1}^{m} (1 - \beta_k z) \Big/ \prod_{k=1}^{n} (1 - \alpha_k z) \tag{16}$$

and the former $A(z) = [B(z)]^{-1}$. Requiring a one-sided moving-average representation with $\sum |b_j| < \infty$ ensures a unique factorization of the denominator; the requirement that the process also be invertible ensures a unique factorization of the numerator. Without both such requirements the process will not be "identifiable" in the usual econometric sense.

Processes with a rational covariance generating transform are typically represented as an autoregression equal to a noise input that is not white; i.e.,

$$\prod_{k=1}^{n} (1 - \alpha_k U)x_t = \prod_{k=1}^{m} (1 - \beta_k U)\epsilon_t. \tag{17}$$

If a process $\{x_t\}$ is defined by (17), it follows that we may write

$$x_t = \frac{\prod_{k=1}^{m} (1 - \beta_k U)}{\prod_{k=1}^{n} (1 - \alpha_k U)} \epsilon_t + \zeta_t \tag{17'}$$

where $\prod_{k=1}^{n} (1 - \alpha_k U)\zeta_t = 0$.

Thus, for example, for a first-order autoregressive process the specification

$$x_t - \lambda x_{t-1} = (1 - \lambda U)x_t = \epsilon_t \qquad \text{implies} \qquad x_t = \sum_{j=0}^{\infty} \lambda^j \epsilon_{t-j} + A\lambda^t.$$

The point is that unless we restrict attention to purely nondeterministic processes, the specifications

$$x_t = \frac{1}{1 - \lambda U} \epsilon_t \tag{18a}$$

and

$$(1 - \lambda U)x_t = \epsilon_t \tag{18b}$$

are not equivalent. Of course, since λ is in absolute value less than one in this case, the distinction is not important if the process is observed after it has been in operation a long time. In addition, much of the theory presented, e.g., prediction and signal extraction, is identical for both specifications. Thus, in order to keep the exposition uncluttered, we shall generally treat the two specifications as being equivalent and transfer freely between them.

Consider a purely linearly nondeterministic process $\{x_t\}$ with covariance generating function $g(z)$; the *spectral density function* for this process is defined by

$$f(\lambda) = \frac{1}{2\pi} g(e^{i\lambda}) = \frac{1}{2\pi} \sigma^2 B(e^{-i\lambda})B(e^{i\lambda}) = \frac{1}{2\pi} \sum_{j=-\infty}^{\infty} \gamma(|j|)e^{-ij\lambda}. \tag{19}$$

Thus the spectral density function is the Fourier transform of the autocovariance function, i.e., proportional to the autocovariance generating function evaluated on the unit circle.[4] Since the complex conjugate of $e^{i\lambda}$ is $e^{-i\lambda}$ and since $\gamma(j)$ is equal to $\gamma(-j)$, the spectral density is a real valued function. Further, since

$$\frac{1}{2\pi i} \oint_{|z|=1} g(z) \frac{dz}{z^{j+1}} = \gamma(j), \tag{20}$$

it follows that

$$\int_{-\pi}^{\pi} f(\lambda)\,d\lambda = \frac{1}{2\pi i} \oint_{|z|=1} g(z) \frac{dz}{z} = \gamma(0) = \text{var}(x).$$

So the integral of the spectral density function over $(-\pi, \pi)$ is the variance of the process. The spectral density, in effect, gives the decomposition of the variance of $\{x_t\}$ by frequency bands, and $\int_{\alpha}^{\beta} f(\lambda)\,d\lambda$ can be thought of as the part of the variance "due to" or associated with frequencies in the interval (α, β). This interpretation will become clearer following the discussion of the theory of the spectral representation.

Suppose that the process $\{x_t\}$ is white noise so that

$$\gamma(j) = \begin{cases} \sigma^2, & j = 0, \\ 0, & j \neq 0. \end{cases}$$

[4] See Appendix C, Section 5, "Fourier Transforms and 'Windows.'"

In this case the spectral density function is a simple constant[5]

$$f(\lambda) = \sigma^2/2\pi, \qquad -\pi < \lambda < \pi. \tag{21}$$

Generally, one might think of a pure noise process as being one without any cyclical or periodic components or properties at all. From this example we see that in fact a white noise process has contributions from all frequencies but all contribute equally, producing completely unsystematic behavior. This example also brings out another factor in interpretation of spectra, namely, it is not the presence of power in a frequency band that is associated with regularities in the behavior of the process but rather the amount relative to that in other bands of similar size.

3. The Spectral Representation of a Stationary Time Series

It is not necessary to assume stationarity for the development of the spectral representation but only covariance, or weak stationarity. It is, however, convenient to work with complex-valued time series until the last moment and then to make the necessary specialization.

Let $\{x_t\}$ be a stationary complex random process defined on the basis of previous definitions of a real stationary process. Let $\{x_t\}$ have zero mean. We define the autocovariance function of $\{x_t\}$ as

$$\gamma(\tau) = Ex_t \bar{x}_{t-\tau} = \overline{\gamma(-\tau)}. \tag{1}$$

Note that the variance–covariance matrix of a set of k values of the process $\{x_t\}$, say $t, t+1, \ldots, t+k-1$, is no longer symmetric but what is called Hermitian:

$$\Omega = \begin{Vmatrix} \gamma(0) & \gamma(-1) & \cdots & \gamma(-k+1) \\ \gamma(1) & \gamma(0) & \cdots & \gamma(-k+2) \\ \vdots & & & \vdots \\ \gamma(k-1) & & \cdots & \gamma(0) \end{Vmatrix}$$

$$= \begin{Vmatrix} \overline{\gamma(0)} & \overline{\gamma(1)} & \cdots & \overline{\gamma(k-1)} \\ \vdots & & & \vdots \\ \overline{\gamma(-k+1)} & & \cdots & \overline{\gamma(0)} \end{Vmatrix} = \bar{\Omega}'.$$

[5] Conversely, suppose that the spectral density is uniform on the interval $(-\pi, \pi)$: $f(\lambda) = k$, $-\pi < \lambda < \pi$; then

$$\gamma(\tau) = k \int_{-\pi}^{\pi} e^{i\lambda\tau}\, d\lambda = \begin{cases} 0, & \text{if } \tau \neq 0, \\ 2\pi k, & \text{if } \tau = 0, \end{cases}$$

or

$$\gamma(0) = \sigma^2 \qquad \text{if we take } k = \sigma^2/2\pi.$$

In our discussion of linearly deterministic processes we considered processes $\{x_t\}$ of the form

$$x_t = \rho e^{i\lambda t}, \qquad (2)$$

where ρ is random and λ is a fixed frequency in $[-\pi, \pi]$. Now let us examine the conditions for stationarity of such a process. Note that x_t can be real only if ρ is complex. Now

$$Ex_t = e^{i\lambda t}E\rho$$

does not depend on t if and only if $E\rho = 0$. So $E\rho = 0$ is a necessary condition for stationarity. If $E\rho = 0$ then

$$Ex_t\overline{x_{t-\tau}} = \text{cov}(x_t, x_{t-\tau}) = \gamma(\tau) = (E\rho\bar\rho)e^{i\lambda\tau}, \qquad (3)$$

which does not depend on t in any case. Thus $E\rho = 0$ is also sufficient for second-order stationarity of the process $\{x_t\}$. If $\{x_t\}$ is Gaussian, second-order stationarity implies strict stationarity, but if not, more complicated conditions, which we do not examine here, must be imposed.

Now let

$$x_t^{(N)} = \sum_{j=-N}^{N} \rho_j e^{i\lambda_j t}, \qquad (4)$$

where the ρ_j are complex random variables and where the λ_j are $2N + 1$ distinct fixed frequencies equally spaced in the interval $[-\pi, \pi]$. Clearly for stationarity we must have

$$E\rho_j = 0, \qquad j = 0, \pm 1, \pm 2, \ldots, \pm N. \qquad (5)$$

Now consider

$$\text{cov}(x_t, x_{t-\tau}) = E \sum_{j=-N}^{N} \sum_{j'=-N}^{N} \rho_j\bar\rho_{j'}e^{i\lambda_j t}e^{-i\lambda_{j'}(t-\tau)}$$

$$= \sum_{j,j'=-N}^{N} (E\rho_j\bar\rho_{j'})e^{i(\lambda_j - \lambda_{j'})t}e^{i\lambda_{j'}\tau} \qquad (6)$$

This will depend on t unless for every j, j' such that $\lambda_j \neq \lambda_{j'}$, $E\rho_j\bar\rho_{j'} = 0$, i.e., unless the complex random variables $\rho_j, j = 0, \pm 1, \ldots, \pm N$ are all mutually orthogonal. If they are, $\{x_t\}$ is stationary to the second order provided (5) also holds, and the autocovariance function for $\{x_t\}$ is

$$\gamma(\tau) = \sum_{j=-N}^{N} (E\rho_j\bar\rho_j)e^{i\lambda_j\tau}. \qquad (7)$$

Provided only that the series converges with probability 1 there is no reason why we cannot let $N \to \infty$. When $E\rho_j = 0$, a necessary condition for stationarity, it is sufficient for

$$x_t^{(N)} = \sum_{j=-N}^{N} \rho_j e^{i\lambda_j t}$$

to converge to a well-defined random variable x_t for all t, as $N \to \infty$, that

$$\sum_{j=-N}^{N} E\rho_j \bar{\rho}_j = \sum_{j=-N}^{N} \text{var}(\rho_j) \to \sigma^2$$

as $N \to \infty$. This obviously implies that

$$\lim_{j \to \infty} E|\rho_j|^2 = 0,$$

but such a condition is not sufficient (Wold, 1938, p. 41). Since the λ_j are equally spaced in the interval $[-\pi, \pi]$, letting $N \to \infty$ means taking these frequencies ever more densely in this interval.

To proceed further we must reconsider the concept of a continuous random variable on an interval. As indicated above, a continuous stationary stochastic process is defined on an interval in a manner exactly analogous to the definition of a discrete series on an index set. Let $\{\zeta(t)\}$ be such a process; $\{\zeta(t)\}$ is said to have *orthogonal increments* if, for any $t_1 < t_2 < t_3 < t_4$ in the interval on which $\{\zeta(t)\}$ is defined,

$$E[\zeta(t_4) - \zeta(t_3)][\overline{\zeta(t_2)} - \overline{\zeta(t_1)}] = 0. \tag{8}$$

Note that the discrete analog of a continuous process with orthogonal increments is one with uncorrelated differences, i.e., a simple random walk.

Let $\{\zeta(\lambda); \lambda \in [-\pi, \pi]\}$ be a continuous process with zero mean and orthogonal increments on the interval $[-\pi, \pi]$ such that $E\zeta(\lambda_1)\overline{\zeta(\lambda_2)} = 0$ for λ_1 and λ_2 in nonoverlapping intervals. It can be shown that, in the limit as we fill in the frequencies λ_j ever more densely in the interval $[-\pi, \pi]$, the sum $x_t^{(N)}$ defined in (4) converges, in mean square for fixed t, to the stochastic integral

$$
\begin{aligned}
x_t &= \int_{-\pi}^{\pi} e^{i\lambda t} \, d\zeta(\lambda) \\
&= \lim_{\substack{\max|\lambda_k - \lambda_{k-1}| \to 0 \\ N \to \infty}} \left\{ \sum_{k=-N+1}^{N} e^{i\lambda_k' t} [\zeta(\lambda_k) - \zeta(\lambda_{k-1})] \right\}, \tag{9}
\end{aligned}
$$

where λ_k' is an arbitrary frequency in the interval $[\lambda_{k-1}, \lambda_k]$ and

$$-\pi = \lambda_{-N} < \lambda_{-N+1} < \cdots < \lambda_{N-1} < \lambda_N = \pi.$$

At points of discontinuity it is conventional to take $\zeta(\lambda)$ to be continuous on the right. Because only differences of $\zeta(\lambda)$ enter (9), $\zeta(\lambda)$ is in fact uniquely defined only up to an additive random variable. Convergence of the sum $x_t^{(N)}$ defined in (4) to the stochastic integral occurs in the sense that

$$E|x_t^{(N)} - x_t|^2 < \delta \tag{10}$$

for any $t \in T$ and any $\delta > 0$ and for some N sufficiently large. Since $x_t^{(N)}$ is stationary and has finite variance, this in turn implies that

$$\lim_{N \to \infty} \text{Prob}\{|x_t^{(N)} - x_t| > \epsilon\} = 0, \qquad \text{for} \quad t \in T \quad \text{and} \quad \epsilon > 0.$$

See Yaglom (1962, pp. 36–43).

It is a remarkable fact, first proved independently by Kolmogorov (1940) and Cramér (1942), that every discrete process stationary to the second order can be represented in the form of the stochastic integral appearing in (9). An analogous representation for continuous processes also exists, the main difference being that the limits of integration in (9) must be taken to be $(-\infty, \infty)$ rather than $(-\pi, \pi)$. Note how remarkable this result really is. After all, the $x_t^{(N)}$ as defined by (4) are linearly deterministic. Nonetheless, any stationary process, including those that are purely linearly nondeterministic, can be represented as the "limit" of such processes.

Let $\lambda_1 < \lambda_2$ be distinct fixed frequencies and consider

$$\text{var } \zeta(\lambda_2) = E \left\{ \left[\int_{-\pi}^{\lambda_1} d\zeta(\lambda) + \int_{\lambda_1}^{\lambda_2} d\zeta(\lambda) \right] \overline{\left[\int_{-\pi}^{\lambda_1} d\zeta(\lambda) + \int_{\lambda_1}^{\lambda_2} d\zeta(\lambda) \right]} \right\}$$

$$= \text{var } \zeta(\lambda_1) + \text{var} \left\{ \int_{\lambda_1}^{\lambda_2} d\zeta(\lambda) \right\}. \tag{11}$$

Thus, var $\zeta(\lambda)$ is a nondecreasing, nonnegative, real-valued function of λ. Because of the convention that $\zeta(\lambda)$ is taken to be continuous from the right at any points of discontinuity, the function

$$F(\lambda) \equiv \text{var } \zeta(\lambda) \tag{12}$$

will also be continuous from the right. Take the limit of $F(\lambda)$ to be zero as $\lambda \to -\pi$ *from below*, since any positive value can be attributed to $F(\lambda)$ as $\lambda \to -\pi$ *from above*. From (9)

$$\sigma_x^2 = \text{var } x_t = E \left\{ \left[\int_{-\pi}^{\pi} e^{i\lambda t} d\zeta(\lambda) \right] \overline{\left[\int_{-\pi}^{\pi} e^{-i\lambda t} d\overline{\zeta(\lambda)} \right]} \right\}$$

$$= E \left[\lim_{\substack{\max|\lambda_k - \lambda_{k-1}| \to 0 \\ \max|\lambda_j - \lambda_{j-1}| \to 0 \\ N \to \infty}} \left\{ \sum_{k=-N+1}^{N} e^{i\lambda_k t} [\zeta(\lambda_k) - \zeta(\lambda_{k-1})] \right\} \right.$$

$$\left. \left\{ \sum_{j=-N+1}^{N} e^{-i\lambda_j t} [\overline{\zeta(\lambda_j)} - \overline{\zeta(\lambda_{j-1})}] \right\} \right], \tag{13}$$

where λ'_k and λ'_j are arbitrary points in the intervals $[\lambda_{k-1}, \lambda_k]$ and $[\lambda_{j-1}, \lambda_j]$, respectively. Because $\zeta(\lambda)$ has orthogonal increments

$$\sigma_x^2 = \lim_{\substack{\max|\lambda_k - \lambda_{k-1}| \to 0 \\ N \to \infty}} \left[\sum_{k=-N+1}^{N} E|\zeta(\lambda_k) - \zeta(\lambda_{k-1})|^2 \right]$$

$$= E \int_{-\pi}^{\pi} d\zeta(\lambda) \int_{-\pi}^{\pi} d\overline{\zeta(\lambda)} = F(\pi), \tag{14}$$

which could also be written as $\int_{-\pi}^{\pi} dF(\lambda)$, where

$$E\, d\zeta(\lambda)\, d\overline{\zeta(\lambda)} = dF(\lambda). \tag{15}$$

Thus, if $\{x_t\}$ is normalized so that $\sigma_x^2 = 1$, the function $F(\lambda)$ has all the properties required of a distribution function: it is nonnegative, nondecreasing, continuous from the right, and takes on the values 0 at $-\infty$ and 1 at $+\infty$. For this reason $F(\lambda)$ is called the *spectral distribution function* of the process $\{x_t\}$. $F(\lambda_1), \lambda_1 \leq \pi$, shows the fraction of the variance of $\{x_t\}$ contributed by increments of the process $\{\zeta(\lambda)\}$ up to λ_1. $\{\zeta(\lambda)\}$ is called the spectral process associated with $\{x_t\}$ and (9) is called the *spectral representation* of $\{x_t\}$.

Even before the spectral representation theorem was proved, Khinchin (1934) showed that the correlation function of any discrete stationary random process can be represented as an integral of the form

$$\gamma(\tau) = \int_{-\pi}^{\pi} e^{i\lambda\tau}\, dF(\lambda), \tag{16}$$

where F has the properties of a distribution function. Note that we are assuming $\gamma(0) = 1$. Conversely, corresponding to any distribution function F, Khinchin showed that the integral on the right-hand side of (16) is the correlation function of a stationary random process. [Again, to generalize to the continuous case, it is only necessary to replace the limits of integration by $(-\infty, +\infty)$.] The result (16) follows readily from the spectral representation of $\{x_t\}$, although the latter was proved after Khinchin obtained his result, and indeed with its aid, by replacing x_t and $x_{t-\tau}$ in

$$\gamma(\tau) = E x_t \overline{x_{t-\tau}}$$

by the corresponding spectral forms. Thus, $\gamma(\tau)$ is the characteristic function of the spectral distribution function; there is thus a one-to-one correspondence between the two. All the information about the process contained in its moments is contained in its spectral distribution function, and vice versa.[6]

---

[6] Alternatively, we could say (although this involves some complexities not yet discussed) that $\gamma(\tau)$ is the Fourier transform (up to a scalar multiple) of the spectral density function $dF(\lambda)$. [The complexities involve the meaning of $dF(\lambda)$ at a point of discontinuity of $F(\lambda)$.] Note that setting $\tau = 0$ gives exactly (14) back again. We are assuming $\gamma(0) = 1$.

If $\{x_t\}$ is a real-valued process,

$$x_t = \bar{x}_t \qquad \text{for all} \quad t \in T.$$

It follows from (9) that

$$x_t = \int_{-\pi}^{\pi} e^{i\lambda t} \, d\zeta(\lambda) = \int_{-\pi}^{\pi} e^{-i\lambda t} \, d\overline{\zeta(\lambda)} = \int_{-\pi}^{\pi} e^{i\lambda t} \, d\overline{\zeta(-\lambda)}, \qquad (17)$$

so that $\zeta(\lambda) = \overline{\zeta(-\lambda)}$ if $\zeta(\lambda)$ is the spectral process associated with a real time series. Write

$$\zeta(\lambda) = \tfrac{1}{2}[U(\lambda) - iV(\lambda)], \qquad (18)$$

where $U(\lambda)$ and $V(\lambda)$ are real functions. Then (17) implies that $U(\lambda)$ is an even function and $V(\lambda)$ is an odd function; i.e.,

$$U(-\lambda) = U(\lambda), \qquad V(-\lambda) = -V(\lambda). \qquad (19)$$

Since the product of two even functions or two odd functions is even and the product of an even and an odd function is odd, since $\cos \lambda t$ is even and $\sin \lambda t$ is odd, and since the integral of an odd function over an interval symmetrical about the origin is zero, (9) may be rewritten

$$x_t = \int_{0}^{\pi} \cos \lambda t \, dU(\lambda) + \int_{0}^{\pi} \sin \lambda t \, dV(\lambda), \qquad (20)$$

where $U(\lambda)$ and $V(\lambda)$ are mutually orthogonal *real* processes on the interval $[-\pi, \pi]$ with orthogonal increments, such that

$$dF(\lambda) = \tfrac{1}{4}\{E[dU(\lambda)]^2 + E[dV(\lambda)]^2\}. \qquad (21)$$

Clearly, $dF(\lambda) = dF(-\lambda)$, except at $\lambda = -\pi$ where a discontinuous jump may occur by convention, so $dF(\lambda)$ is symmetric about $\lambda = 0$ and certainly real; hence,

$$\gamma(\tau) = 2 \int_{0}^{\pi} \cos \lambda \tau \, dF(\lambda), \qquad (22)$$

which also follows directly from (16) when $\{x_t\}$ is a real-valued process.

The purely real spectral representation of $\{x_t\}$ yields further insight into the nature and significance of the representation itself. Essentially what the spectral representation amounts to is the substitution of "many" random variables $\{\zeta\}$, or $\{U\}$ and $\{V\}$, with simple properties or interrelations, for a "single" random process $\{x_t\}$ characterized by a complex structure of interdependencies. In many mathematical problems this is standard operating procedure: We transform our problem by replacing it with an equivalent problem involving orthogonal variables. Thus, in matrix algebra it is often convenient to transform the co-ordinate axes so that certain matrices become diagonal. This is exactly analogous to the replacement of $\{x\}$ by $\{\zeta\}$, or $\{U\}$ and $\{V\}$, in the study of time-series problems. We may think, in terms of the random variables U and V, of replacing x by components that are not only orthogonal at different frequencies but are exactly $90°$ out of phase at the same frequency, or *in quadrature*. This interpretation plays an important role in understanding the meaning of the cross-spectral distribution function of two time series to which we turn below.

When the process under consideration is a purely linearly deterministic process of the form (4), the spectral distribution function $F(\lambda)$ is a *step function* with steps at the frequencies λ_j equal to $E\rho_j\bar{\rho}_j$. This result follows directly by comparing (7) and (16)

$$\gamma(\tau) = \sum_{j=-N}^{N} (E\rho_j\bar{\rho}_j)e^{i\lambda_j\tau} = \int_{-\pi}^{\pi} e^{i\lambda\tau} \, dF(\lambda).$$

The Stieljes integral on the right reduces to the sum when $F(\lambda)$ is a step function with steps at the frequencies λ_j by virtue of the definition

$$\int_{-\pi}^{\pi} e^{i\lambda\tau} \, dF(\lambda) = \lim_{\substack{|\lambda_k - \lambda_{k-1}| \to 0 \\ N \to \infty}} \sum_{k=-N}^{N} e^{i\lambda_k\tau}[F(\lambda_k) - F(\lambda_{k-1})]$$

for $-\pi = \lambda_{-N} < \cdots < \lambda_0 < \cdots < \lambda_N = \pi$. Thus $F(\lambda)$ will, in general, contain a step-function component that corresponds to the purely linearly deterministic portion of the Wold decomposition.

It is a classical result (Doob, 1953, p. 488) that every distribution function such as $F(\lambda)$ may be decomposed into the sum of three components:

$$F(\lambda) = F_1(\lambda) + F_2(\lambda) + F_3(\lambda). \tag{23}$$

$F_1(\lambda)$ is an absolutely continuous nondecreasing function with derivative $f(\lambda)$ almost everywhere.[7] $F_2(\lambda)$ is a nondecreasing step function of the type just described, i.e., corresponding to the spectral distribution function of a linearly deterministic process. $F_3(\lambda)$ is the so-called singular component, which is zero almost everywhere in the mathematical sense. It does not have a practical meaning in the present context and is usually combined with $F_2(\lambda)$ or disregarded in discussions of the subject.

In the Wold decomposition, every covariance stationary process is expressed as the sum of two uncorrelated covariance stationary processes, one linearly deterministic, the other purely nondeterministic. The spectral distribution function $F(\lambda)$ is also decomposed into two corresponding parts, disregarding $F_3(\lambda)$, namely, a step function $F_2(\lambda)$ and an absolutely continuous function $F_1(\lambda)$. One suspects that $F_1(\lambda)$ is the spectral distribution function of the purely nondeterministic part in the Wold decomposition. Indeed, this is the case, and the stronger result also holds that an absolutely continuous spectral distribution function is a necessary and sufficient condition for a covariance stationary

---

[7] Absolute continuity is a strong form of continuity that implies the existence of a derivative almost everywhere (i.e., except on a set of measure zero) over any interval in which it characterizes a function (Kingman and Taylor, 1966, pp. 231–232).

process to have a moving-average representation (Doob, 1953, pp. 499–500). In what follows we explore in a nonrigorous way the relation between the derivative of an absolutely continuous spectral distribution function, i.e., the *spectral density function* of a stationary process, and its moving-average representation. For the remainder of this discussion we consider only purely linearly nondeterministic processes.

It follows from (2.6) that, for processes that contain no purely linearly deterministic component, the autocovariance generating transform exists and is given by

$$g(z) = \sum_{\tau = -\infty}^{\infty} \gamma(\tau) z^{\tau} = \sigma^2 B(z) B(z^{-1}). \tag{24}$$

On the unit circle, i.e., for $z = e^{-i\lambda}$, $-\pi \leq \lambda \leq \pi$, we have

$$g(e^{-i\lambda}) = 2\pi f(\lambda) = \sum_{\tau = -\infty}^{\infty} \gamma(\tau) e^{-i\tau\lambda}$$

$$= \gamma(0) + 2 \sum_{\tau = 1}^{\infty} \gamma(\tau) \cos \tau\lambda, \tag{25}$$

so we see that on the unit circle the autocovariance generating function is proportional to the spectral density function.[8] Furthermore,

$$f(\lambda) = (\sigma^2/2\pi) |B(e^{i\lambda})|^2. \tag{26}$$

Because $B(z)B(z^{-1})$ is analytic in an annulus containing the unit circle, we see that spectral density functions for processes of the type considered are absolutely continuous functions of λ.

The two definitions of the spectral density given in this chapter are equivalent. Equation (26) follows from the fact that if $F(\lambda)$ is absolutely continuous, its derivative $f(\lambda)$ is of bounded variation and never negative since $F(\lambda)$ is nondecreasing. Thus $f(\lambda)$ must have a Fourier series expansion. Moreover, since $g(z)$ converges in an annulus containing the unit circle, the coefficients $\gamma(\tau)$ of the powers of z in (24) must be proportional to the coefficients in the Fourier series expansion. Since $F(\lambda)$ is assumed to be absolutely continuous in this discussion, (16) implies that $f(\lambda)$ is the inverse Fourier transform of

---

[8] Since $g(z)$ converges in an annulus containing the unit circle and since $\gamma(\tau) = \gamma(-\tau)$, on the unit circle we have

$$g(e^{-i\lambda}) = \gamma(0) + 2 \sum_{\tau = 1}^{\infty} \gamma(\tau) \cos \lambda\tau.$$

Now, it is a necessary (but not sufficient) condition that the terms of a convergent series tend to zero. Thus $\lim_{\tau \to \infty} \gamma(\tau) \cos \lambda\tau = 0$, but since $\lim \cos \lambda\tau \neq 0$, we must have $\lim_{\tau \to \infty} \gamma(\tau) = 0$. This is another way of saying that dependence at a distance must be slight for a stationary time series that has no linearly deterministic component.

$\gamma(\tau)$; thus

$$f(\lambda) = \frac{1}{2\pi} \sum_{\tau=-\infty}^{\infty} \gamma(\tau)e^{-i\lambda\tau}, \tag{27}$$

which is equivalent to (26).

Given an absolutely continuous spectral distribution function, conversely one can always find a moving-average process with that spectral distribution function. However, this representation will not be unique unless the conditions required for invertibility are imposed upon $B(z)$ (Whittle, 1963, pp. 25–26; Hannan, 1960, pp. 13–16).

Equation (26) shows why the representation of $g(z)$ as $\sigma^2 B(z)B(z^{-1})$ is often called the *canonical factorization of the spectral density function*. This factorization must evidently exist for all processes of the type considered.

Graphs of the spectral densities of four simple processes are presented in Figs. 1–4: Fig. 1 shows the spectral density of white noise; Fig. 2 exhibits the spectral density of a simple first-order autoregression $x_t - 0.5x_{t-1} = \epsilon_t$; Fig. 3 shows that for a first-order moving average $x_t = \epsilon_t + 0.5\epsilon_{t-1}$; and Fig. 4 shows that the second-order autoregression with complex roots has a "humped" shape rather different in appearance from either the first-order autoregression or the first-order moving average.

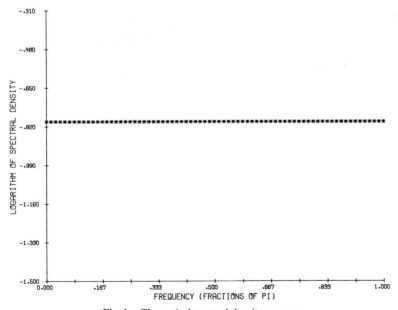

Fig. 1. Theoretical spectral density: $x_t = \epsilon_t$.

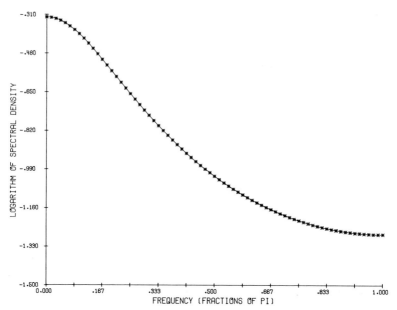

Fig. 2.   Theoretical spectral density: $x_t = [1/(1 - 0.5U)]\epsilon_t$.

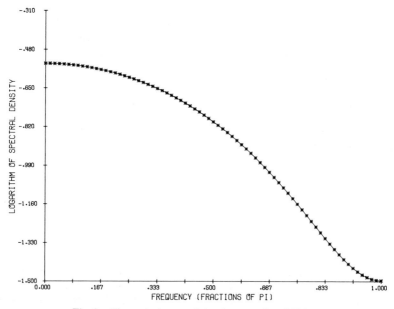

Fig. 3.   Theoretical spectral density: $x_t = (1 + 0.5U)\epsilon_t$.

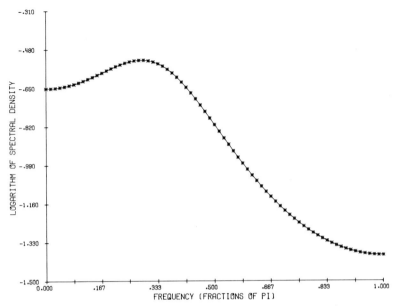

Fig. 4.   Theoretical spectral density: $x_t = [1/(1 - 2U + 4U^2)]\epsilon_t$.

4.   The Cross-Spectral Distribution Function of Two Jointly Stationary Time Series and Filtering

In this section we introduce the cross spectrum for two zero-mean stationary time series. Consider two jointly covariance stationary time series $\{x_t\}$ and $\{y_t\}$; the cross-covariance generating function is defined as

$$g_{yx}(z) = \sum_{-\infty}^{\infty} E(y_t x_{t-\tau})z^\tau = \sum_{-\infty}^{\infty} \gamma_{yx}(\tau)z^\tau, \tag{1}$$

when the summation on the right converges (although not necessarily uniformly).[9] The cross-spectral density function is defined as

$$f_{yx}(\lambda) = (1/2\pi)g_{yx}(e^{i\lambda}). \tag{2}$$

Since in general $\gamma_{yx}(\tau)$ and $\gamma_{yx}(-\tau)$ are not equal, the cross-spectral density is complex valued and

$$f_{xy}(\lambda) = f_{yx}(-\lambda) = \overline{f_{yx}(\lambda)}. \tag{3}$$

---

[9] Since we are now dealing with two time series, both autocovariances and their generating transforms and cross covariances and their generating transforms, as well as both spectral densities and cross-spectral densities, will henceforth bear two subscripts signifying the series to which they refer.

Suppose that y_t is equal to the sum of two nondeterministic covariance stationary processes $\{x_t\}$ and $\{u_t\}$, and assume that these latter processes are uncorrelated for all lags; i.e.,

$$E(x_t u_{-\tau}) = 0, \qquad \text{for all } \tau. \tag{4}$$

In this case it is clear that

$$f_{yy}(\lambda) = f_{xx}(\lambda) + f_{uu}(\lambda), \qquad f_{xu}(\lambda) = f_{ux}(\lambda) = 0, \qquad f_{yx}(\lambda) = f_{xx}(\lambda). \tag{5}$$

If

$$y_t = A(U)x_t + u_t, \tag{6}$$

where $E(x_t u_{t-\tau}) = 0$ for all τ and $A(z) = \sum_{j=0}^{\infty} a_j z^j$, then

$$\begin{aligned}
f_{yy}(\lambda) &= A(e^{i\lambda})A(e^{-i\lambda})f_{xx}(\lambda) + f_{uu}(\lambda), \\
f_{xu}(\lambda) &= f_{ux}(\lambda) = 0, \\
f_{yx}(\lambda) &= A(e^{i\lambda})f_{xx}(\lambda).
\end{aligned} \tag{5'}$$

To verify the last equality in (5'), note that

$$E(y_t x_{t-\tau}) = E\{A(U)x_t x_{t-\tau}\} + E\{u_t x_{t-\tau}\} = \sum_{j=0}^{\infty} a_j \gamma_{xx}(\tau - j). \tag{7}$$

Thus it follows that

$$\begin{aligned}
g_{yx}(z) &= \sum_{\tau=-\infty}^{\infty} \sum_{j=0}^{\infty} a_j \gamma_{xx}(\tau - j)z^\tau = \sum_{j=0}^{\infty} a_j z^j \sum_{\tau=-\infty}^{\infty} \gamma_{xx}(\tau - j)z^{\tau-j} \\
&= A(z)g_{xx}(z).
\end{aligned} \tag{8}$$

Thus, whenever two series are related by a model such as (6), called a distributed lag model, the ratio of the cross-spectral density to the spectral density of the exogenous variable is proportional to the Fourier transform of the lag coefficients.[10] The operator $\sum_{\tau=0}^{\infty} a_\tau U^\tau$ is called a one-sided linear filter. We say that $\{y_t\}$ is obtained by such a filter with input $\{x_t\}$ plus "noise" $\{u_t\}$. $|A(e^{i\lambda})|^2$ is sometimes called the transfer function of the filter, while $A(e^{i\lambda})$ is called the frequency response function.

The quantity

$$R^2(\lambda) = |f_{yx}(\lambda)|^2/f_{yy}(\lambda)f_{xx}(\lambda) \tag{9}$$

is called the *coherence* between x and y at frequency λ. Note the similarity between the coherence and the usual squared correlation coefficient.

In this example

$$f_{yy}(\lambda) = [|f_{yx}(\lambda)|^2/f_{xx}(\lambda)] + f_{uu}(\lambda), \tag{10}$$

---

[10] See Chapter XIII, Sections 1 and 2 for a detailed discussion.

so that

$$f_{uu}(\lambda)/f_{yy}(\lambda) = 1 - R^2(\lambda). \tag{11}$$

Thus the coherence gives the percentage of the variance at each frequency "due to" or accounted for by the distributed lag model (6). Note that if the two series are related *exactly* by a linear filter, the coherence is equal to one at every frequency. Even when the two series are not related by a distributed lag model, the interpretations of the cross-spectral density and coherence are similar to those just given.

Given a pair of jointly stationary processes $\{y_t\}$ and $\{x_t\}$, consider the problem of predicting y_t by a linear combination of the x's with the weights chosen to minimize the expected squared error. The problem is to minimize

$$V = E\left\{\left(y_t - \sum_{\tau=-\infty}^{\infty} \delta_\tau x_{t-\tau}\right)^2\right\} \tag{12}$$

by choice of δ's. Differentiating (12) with respect to δ_k and setting equal to zero gives

$$E(y_t x_{t-k}) = \sum_{\tau=-\infty}^{\infty} \delta_\tau E(x_{t-\tau} x_{t-k})$$

or $$\tag{13}$$

$$\gamma_{yx}(k) = \sum_{-\infty}^{\infty} \delta_\tau \gamma_{xx}(k-\tau), \qquad k = 0, \pm 1, \pm 2, \ldots.$$

Multiplying both sides of (13) by z^k and summing over all k gives

$$\sum_{-\infty}^{\infty} \gamma_{yx}(k)z^k = \sum_{k=-\infty}^{\infty} \sum_{\tau=-\infty}^{\infty} \delta_\tau \gamma_{xx}(k-\tau)z^k$$

$$= \sum_k \sum_\tau \delta_\tau z^\tau \gamma_{xx}(k-\tau)z^{k-\tau}$$

or

$$g_{yx}(z) = \delta(z)g_{xx}(z). \tag{14}$$

If we take $u_t = y_t - \delta(U)x_t$, then equation (6) holds with $A(z)$ equal to $\delta(z)$. Thus $f_{yx}(\lambda)/f_{xx}(\lambda)$ is proportional to the Fourier transform of the coefficients of the linear operator giving the least-squares estimate of y_t based upon the entire history of the sequence $\{x_t\}$. Notice that the interpretation of $R^2(\lambda)$ is the same as before, though the lag distribution is not in general the result of any necessary causal relation between the series. In fact, from (14) it is apparent that $\delta(\ )$ is in general a two-sided operator.

Consider now two jointly stationary zero-mean time series $\{y_t\}$ and $\{x_t\}$. Our discussion extends without difficulty to the case in which there are more than two such series. Each of the series has the spectral representation

$$x_t = \int_{-\pi}^{\pi} e^{i\lambda t} \, d\zeta_x(\lambda), \qquad y_t = \int_{-\pi}^{\pi} e^{i\lambda t} \, d\zeta_y(\lambda), \tag{15}$$

where $\{\zeta_x(\lambda)\}$ and $\{\zeta_y(\lambda)\}$ are continuous processes with zero mean and orthogonal increments on the interval $[-\pi, \pi]$. One can also show that if $\{x_t\}$ and $\{y_t\}$ are jointly as well as individually stationary, then

$$E\zeta_j(\lambda)\overline{\zeta_k(\lambda')} = \begin{cases} 0, & \text{for } \lambda \text{ and } \lambda' \text{ in nonoverlapping intervals,} \\ F_{jj}(\lambda), & \text{for } \lambda = \lambda' \text{ and } k = j, \\ F_{jk}(\lambda), & \text{for } \lambda = \lambda' \text{ and } j \neq k. \end{cases} \tag{16}$$

(j and k represent either the subscript x or y.) F_{xy} is called the *cross-spectral distribution function*.

If $\{x_t\}$ and $\{y_t\}$ are each linearly nondeterministic, $F_{xy}(\lambda)$ has a derivative $f_{xy}(\lambda)$ called the *cross-spectral density function*. If $B_x(z)$ and $B_y(z)$ are the generating transforms of the two sets of coefficients in the moving-average representations of these time series, we can write

$$f_{xy}(\lambda) = \frac{1}{2\pi} g_{xy}(e^{i\lambda}) = \frac{\sigma_{12}}{2\pi} B_x(e^{i\lambda})B_y(e^{-i\lambda}), \qquad -\pi \leq \lambda \leq \pi. \tag{17}$$

As before, the cross-spectral density function and the cross-lag covariance function

$$\gamma_{xy}(\tau) = Ex_t y_{t-\tau} \tag{18}$$

are Fourier transform pairs:

$$\gamma_{xy}(\tau) = \int_{-\pi}^{\pi} e^{-i\lambda\tau} dF_{xy}(\lambda) = \int_{-\pi}^{\pi} e^{-i\lambda\tau} f_{xy}(\lambda) d\lambda, \qquad \tau = 0, \pm 1, \ldots. \tag{19}$$

Recall that we have assumed $Ex_t = 0 = Ey_t$; Eq. (18) may be modified in the usual way if this is not the case. Note that $\gamma_{xy}(\tau)$ is, in general, different from $\gamma_{yx}(\tau)$ and that $f_{yx}(\lambda)$ is generally complex. Setting $\tau = 0$ in (19), and comparing the result with (15), shows that $f_{xy}(\lambda)$ decomposes the contemporaneous covariance between the two time series into that due to in-phase sinusoidal components at various frequencies, and that due to components 90° out of phase or in quadrature. Moreover,

$$g_{xy}(e^{i\lambda}) = 2\pi f_{xy}(\lambda), \qquad -\pi \leq \lambda \leq \pi,$$

establishes a relation between the cross-spectral density function and the cross-lag covariance generating function.

The coherence is like a squared correlation coefficient in the frequency domain, i.e., between the random variables into which the time series $\{x_t\}$ and $\{y_t\}$ have been decomposed by their spectral representation.

If we think of the relation between the series $\{y_t\}$ and $\{x_t\}$ as being expressed in terms of their sinusoidal components at each frequency, we can imagine this relationship in terms of a difference in *phase* and a difference in *amplitude*. Let $\{y_t\}$ and $\{x_t\}$ be expressed in spectral form as in (15) and write the spectral process of each in polar form

$$d\zeta_y(\lambda) = \rho_y(\lambda)\exp i\varphi_y(\lambda), \qquad d\zeta_x(\lambda) = \rho_x(\lambda)\exp i\varphi_x(\lambda). \tag{20}$$

Then we may write

$$E \, d\zeta_y(\lambda) \, \overline{d\zeta_x(\lambda)} = f_{yx}(\lambda) = E\{\rho_y(\lambda)\rho_x(\lambda) \exp i[\varphi_y(\lambda) - \varphi_x(\lambda)]\},$$
$$E|d\zeta_y(\lambda)|^2 = f_{yy}(\lambda) = E\rho_y^2(\lambda), \tag{21}$$
$$E|d\zeta_x(\lambda)|^2 = f_{xx}(\lambda) = E\rho_x^2(\lambda).$$

An interpretation of the cross-spectral density function and related quantities may be given in terms of regression "in the frequency domain" (Nerlove, 1964, pp. 271–274). The ratio $f_{yx}(\lambda)/f_{xx}(\lambda)$ may be interpreted as a complex regression coefficient in the frequency domain; that is, as an estimate of

$$d\zeta_y(\lambda) \, \overline{d\zeta_x(\lambda)}/|d\zeta_x(\lambda)|^2 = [\rho_y(\lambda)/\rho_x(\lambda)] \exp i[\varphi_y(\lambda) - \varphi_x(\lambda)].$$

The quantity $\rho_y(\lambda)/\rho_x(\lambda)$ is called the *gain* of y over x at λ; the quantity $\varphi_y(\lambda) - \varphi_x(\lambda)$ is the *phase shift*. If we write $f_{yx}(\lambda)$ in terms of its real and complex parts, called respectively the *cospectral density* and the *quadrature spectral density*,

$$f_{yx}(\lambda) = c_{yx}(\lambda) + iq_{yx}(\lambda), \tag{22}$$

we see that the estimate of gain is $(c_{yx}^2(\lambda) + q_{yx}^2(\lambda))^{1/2}/f_{xx}(\lambda)$, and the estimate of phase shift is $\arctan\{q_{yx}(\lambda)/c_{yx}(\lambda)\}$.

It can be shown that if the filter in (6) is a two-sided symmetrical filter so that

$$y_t = \sum_{j=-\infty}^{\infty} a_j x_{t-j} + u_t,$$

where $a_j = a_{-j}$, then the phase shift of y with respect to x will be absent. This is because

$$A(e^{i\lambda}) = \sum_{j=-\infty}^{\infty} a_j e^{i\lambda j}$$

is real if $a_j = a_{-j}$ for all j so that $f_{yx}(\lambda)$ is real from (5'); hence, $q_{yx}(\lambda)$ vanishes. Note that for asymmetrical filters, of which one-sided filters such as that in (6) are the most important case, phase shift must, in general, occur.

5. Estimation of the Autocovariance Function and the Spectral Density Function

In this section we consider briefly the problem of estimating the spectral density function and the autocovariance function for normal processes with zero mean and having an absolutely continuous spectral distribution function (i.e., a one-sided moving-average representation in the Wold decomposition). We do not consider cross-spectral estimation in this book; the reader is referred to Jenkins and Watts (1968) or Fishman (1969) for a detailed discussion.

Returning now to the subscript notation for the autocovariances, for processes with a one-sided moving-average representation (1.1) and assuming

$\sigma^2 = 1$, the autocovariance function is given by

$$\gamma_\tau = \sum_{j=0}^{\infty} b_j b_{j+\tau}. \tag{1}$$

Moreover, if we further specify that $\epsilon_t \sim n(0, \sigma^2)$ for all t so that $\{x_t\}$ is Gaussian, the fourth-order moment of $\{x_t\}$ is given by

$$E[x_t x_{t+\tau} x_s x_{s+v}] = \sum_{j,k,m,n} b_j b_k b_m b_n E[\epsilon_{t-j} \epsilon_{t-k+\tau} \epsilon_{s-m} \epsilon_{s-n+v}]$$

$$= \gamma_\tau \gamma_v + \gamma_{t-s} \gamma_{t-s+\tau-v} + \gamma_{t-s-v} \gamma_{t-s+\tau} \tag{2}$$

(Anderson, 1971, p. 467; Hannan, 1960, p. 33).

The condition that the sample autocovariance function defined below converges in probability to the population value, i.e., is a consistent estimate of that value, is that

$$\lim_{n \to \infty} \frac{1}{n} \sum_{s=0}^{n-1} E[x_{s+t} x_s x_t x_0] = \gamma_t^2 \tag{3}$$

(Doob, 1953, p. 494; Hannan, 1960, p. 32). Thus, replacing τ by s and v by $-s$ in (2) and comparing the result with (3), we see that it is necessary and sufficient for (3) that

$$\lim_{n \to \infty} \frac{1}{n} \sum_{s=0}^{n-1} \gamma_s^2 = 0. \tag{4}$$

The condition for the sample autocovariance function to be a consistent estimate of the population value may be interpreted as a condition in the *rate* at which the dependence between values, which are s periods apart, of the process falls off with increasing s.[11]

Now suppose we have a finite number T of observations on the values of $\{x_t\}$, $x_1, \ldots, x_T$. There are basically two ways to estimate γ_τ: The first is a *biased* estimate

$$c_\tau = (1/T) \sum_{t=1}^{T-|\tau|} x_t x_{t+|\tau|}, \qquad \tau = 0, \pm 1, \ldots, \pm M, \quad M \leq T - 1. \tag{5}$$

The second is an unbiased estimate

$$c_\tau' = \frac{1}{T - |\tau|} \sum_{t=1}^{T-|\tau|} x_t x_{t+|\tau|}, \qquad \tau = 0, \pm 1, \ldots, \pm M, \quad M \leq T - 1. \tag{6}$$

---

[11] The analogous condition that the sample mean converges to the population mean for a stationary Gaussian time series is that $\lim_{n \to \infty} (1/n) \sum_{s=0}^{n-1} \gamma_s = 0$ (Doob, 1953, p. 489; Hannan, 1960, p. 31). This is weaker, of course, than (4).

It can be seen that

$$Ec'_\tau = \frac{1}{T - |\tau|} \sum_{t=1}^{T-|\tau|} \gamma_\tau = \gamma_\tau$$

and

$$Ec_\tau = \frac{1}{T} \sum_{t=1}^{T-|\tau|} \gamma_\tau = \gamma_\tau \left(1 - \frac{|\tau|}{T}\right) \tag{7}$$

so that c_τ is asymptotically unbiased.[12]

The difference between c_τ and c'_τ that is important for estimation is that c_τ is a positive definite function of τ, whereas c'_τ is not (Parzen, 1961, p. 981). This means that, if c'_τ is used in the computation of the estimates of the spectral density, the latter could turn out to be negative (Feller, 1966, Vol. 2, pp. 585–586, theorem due to Bochner). Since the spectral densities are to be interpreted as variances, it is apparent that the possibility of a negative estimate is a disturbing one; indeed, in practice it does occasionally happen that a negative estimate is obtained when c'_τ rather than c_τ is used in the computation.[13] Tukey has argued (private communication about 1962) that the possibility of such negative estimates provides a useful diagnostic tool; on the other hand, the problem occurs with such regularity in the analysis of raw economic time series that some method seems desirable for dealing with the underlying difficulty other than the suppression of the possibility of negative estimates by using c_τ rather than c'_τ.

To obtain the covariance between estimates of the autocovariance function at two different lags and the variance of a single estimate we proceed as follows. Let

$$a_\tau = 1 - |\tau|/T.$$

From (7) $Ec_\tau = a_\tau \gamma_\tau$ so that, from (2), assuming τ and v are positive,

$$E\{c_\tau - Ec_\tau\}\{c_v - Ec_v\}$$

$$= \frac{1}{T^2} \sum_{t=1}^{T-\tau} \sum_{s=1}^{T-v} E\{x_t x_{t+\tau} x_s x_{s+v}\} - a_\tau a_v \gamma_\tau \gamma_v$$

$$= \frac{1}{T^2} \sum_{t=1}^{T-\tau} \sum_{s=1}^{T-v} \{\gamma_\tau \gamma_v + \gamma_{t-s}\gamma_{t-s+\tau-v} + \gamma_{t-s-v}\gamma_{t-s+\tau}\} - a_\tau a_v \gamma_\tau \gamma_v. \tag{8}$$

---

[12] Note that since all our observations are taken to be deviations from the sample mean and we are assuming no linear or polynomial trends, we implicitly assume that the mean of the series is known to be zero. This is important to the proof that c'_τ is unbiased (Anderson, 1971, p. 448). When the mean is unknown, both estimates are biased although the bias tends to zero as the number of observations increases (Anderson, 1971, pp. 449, 463–464).

[13] The proof that c_τ is a positive definite function is a straightforward application of the definition (Feller, 1966, Vol. 2, p. 585). A similar argument establishes that c'_τ is not. Moreover, it can be shown that, although c_τ is biased, it is the minimum mean-square error estimate (bias squared plus variance) of γ_τ (Schaerf, 1964).

Thus,

$$E\{c_\tau - Ec_\tau\}\{c_v - Ec_v\} = \frac{1}{T^2} \sum_{t=1}^{T-\tau} \sum_{s=1}^{T-v} \{\gamma_{t-s}\gamma_{t-s+\tau-v} + \gamma_{t-s-v}\gamma_{t-s+\tau}\}. \quad (9)$$

Because of a condition such as (4), which requires the autocovariance function to fall off at a rapid rate in order that the process be ergodic for second moments, it can be shown that the right-hand side of (9) tends to zero as $T \to \infty$ (Hannan, 1960, p. 40; Anderson, 1971, p. 464).

Similarly, setting $\tau = v$ in (9) yields an expression for the variance of c_τ

$$E\{c_\tau - Ec_\tau\}^2 = \frac{1}{T^2} \sum_{t,s=1}^{T-\tau} \{\gamma_{t-s}^2 + \gamma_{t-s-\tau}\gamma_{t-s+\tau}\}. \quad (10)$$

Although the right-hand side of (10) also tends to zero as $T \to \infty$, the variance *relative* to the mean does not if τ increases too; indeed, it can be shown that

$$E\{c_\tau - Ec_\tau\}^2/Ec_\tau \to \infty \qquad \text{as} \quad \tau/T \to 1. \quad (11)$$

It is this result that, in part, accounts for the failure of the sample autocorrelation function to damp down as it should for a stationary, linearly nondeterministic process (Hannan, 1960, p. 43). To illustrate (10), consider the first-order autoregressive process

$$x_t - \rho x_{t-1} = \epsilon_t, \qquad E\epsilon_t = 0, \qquad E\epsilon_t\epsilon_{t'} = \begin{cases} 0, & t \neq t', \\ \sigma^2, & t = t', \end{cases}$$

with autocovariance function

$$\gamma_\tau = \sigma^2 \rho^{|\tau|}/(1 - \rho^2). \quad (12)$$

Substituting in (7) and (10)

$$\frac{E\{c_\tau - Ec_\tau\}^2}{Ec_\tau} = \frac{\sum_{t,s=1}^{T-|\tau|} \{\rho^{|t-s|}\rho^{|t-s|} + \rho^{|t-s-|\tau||}\rho^{|t-s+|\tau||}\}}{T(T - |\tau|)\rho^{|\tau|}(1 - \rho^2)}. \quad (13)$$

For fixed T this expression increases without bound as $\tau \to T$; even when T increases as long as $(\tau/T) \to 1$, it will also increase without bound. Even without such a limiting result, however, it can be seen that the autocovariance function will fail to damp down properly for long lags both because of the sizable variance of the estimate at those lags and because of the correlation of estimates for adjacent lags. As we shall see, the opposite side of this coin is the exceedingly erratic behavior of the so-called periodogram ordinates.

Earlier we saw that the spectral density of a process with absolutely continuous spectral distribution function was proportional to the covariance generating function evaluated along the unit circle:

$$f(\lambda) = \frac{1}{2\pi} \sum_{\tau=-\infty}^{\infty} \gamma_\tau e^{-i\lambda\tau}. \quad (14)$$

Given a finite stretch of a time series, say $x_1, \ldots, x_T$, one could estimate at most T values c_τ, $\tau = 0, 1, \ldots, T - 1$. Thus one might consider the estimate

$$\hat{f}(\lambda) = \frac{1}{2\pi} \sum_{\tau=-(T-1)}^{T-1} c_\tau e^{-i\lambda\tau} = \frac{1}{2\pi} \sum_{\tau=-(T-1)}^{T-1} \frac{1}{T} \sum_{t=1}^{T-|\tau|} x_t x_{t+|\tau|} e^{-i\lambda\tau}. \tag{15}$$

Now consider the expression

$$\left(\frac{T}{2}\right) I_T(\lambda) = \left| \sum_{t=1}^{T} e^{i\lambda t} x_t \right|^2 = \sum_{t=1}^{T} e^{i\lambda t} x_t \sum_{t'=1}^{T} e^{-i\lambda t'} x_{t'} = \sum_{t,t'=1}^{T} x_t x_{t'} e^{i\lambda(t-t')}$$

$$= x_1 x_1 e^{i\lambda(0)} + x_1 x_2 e^{i\lambda(-1)} + \cdots + x_1 x_T e^{i\lambda(1-T)}$$
$$+ x_2 x_1 e^{i\lambda(1)} + x_2 x_2 e^{i\lambda(0)} + \cdots + x_2 x_T e^{i\lambda(2-T)}$$
$$+ \cdots + x_T x_1 e^{i\lambda(T-1)} + x_T x_2 e^{i\lambda(T-2)} + \cdots + x_T x_T e^{i\lambda(0)}$$

$$= e^{i\lambda(0)}\{x_1 x_1 + x_2 x_2 + \cdots + x_T x_T\} + e^{i\lambda(1)}\{x_2 x_1 + x_3 x_2$$
$$+ \cdots + x_T x_{T-1}\} + e^{-i\lambda(1)}\{x_1 x_2 + \cdots + x_{T-1} x_T\}$$
$$+ \cdots + e^{i\lambda(T-1)}\{x_T x_1\} + e^{-i\lambda(T-1)}\{x_1 x_T\}$$

$$= \sum_{\tau=-(T-1)}^{T-1} e^{-i\lambda\tau} \sum_{t=1}^{T-|\tau|} x_t x_{t+|\tau|}$$

$$= \sum_{\tau=-(T-1)}^{T-1} e^{-i\lambda\tau} T c_\tau = 2\pi T \hat{f}(\lambda) \tag{16}$$

(as defined in (15)).[14] The expression

$$I_T(\lambda) = \frac{2}{T} \left| \sum_{t=1}^{T} e^{i\lambda t} x_t \right|^2 = 4\pi \hat{f}(\lambda) = 2 \sum_{\tau=-(T-1)}^{T-1} c_\tau e^{-i\lambda\tau} \tag{17}$$

is called the periodogram of the partial realization of $\{x_t\}$. It is usually evaluated at the equispaced frequencies

$$\lambda = 2k\pi/(T), \qquad k = 0, 1, \ldots, \left[\tfrac{1}{2}T\right] \tag{18}$$

in the interval $[0, \pi]$, where $\left[\tfrac{1}{2}T\right]$ is the greatest integer less then or equal to $\tfrac{1}{2}T$. (Note that $I_T(\lambda)$ is a function of λ symmetrical about the origin in the interval $[-\pi, \pi]$.)

[14] Note that the expression $\sum_{t=1}^{T} e^{i\lambda t} x_t$ in the first line of (16) is the finite Fourier transform of the sequence $x_1, \ldots, x_T$. In an economic context, T is generally relatively small; computing the Fourier transform of a sequence of observations or of the autocorrelations (weighted or unweighted) of such a sequence presents no special computational problems. In other contexts, however, such as ocean-ography or seismology, many tens of thousands of observations are often available. Since a number of operations proportional to T^2 are necessary for the computation of the sum above [two multiplications and an addition for each value of λ and each value of t, where $[T/2]$ values of λ are chosen as in (18)] it is clear that the computational burden may be severe when T is large. Fortunately, when T is an exact power of two or can be made so by the addition of fictitious observations or the deletion of some of the available data, a method known as the fast Fourier transform is available, which greatly reduces the number of computations required. Credit for resurrecting this method is generally given to Cooley and Tukey (1965). See also Hannan (1970, pp. 263–273).

Since $Ec_\tau = [1 - |\tau|/T]\,\gamma_\tau$,

$$\lim_{T \to \infty} E\hat{f}(\lambda) = \frac{1}{2\pi} \lim_{T \to \infty} \sum_{\tau = -(T-1)}^{T-1} Ec_\tau e^{-i\lambda\tau}$$

$$= \frac{1}{2\pi} \lim_{T \to \infty} \sum_{\tau = -(T-1)}^{T-1} \left(1 - \frac{|\tau|}{T}\right)\gamma_\tau e^{-i\lambda\tau} = f(\lambda), \qquad (19)$$

where $f(\lambda)$ is the spectral density of the process $\{x_t\}$ at λ. Thus

$$EI_T(\lambda) \to 4\pi f(\lambda) \qquad \text{as} \quad T \to \infty. \qquad (20)$$

That is, $(1/4\pi)I_T(\lambda)$ is an asymptotically unbiased estimate of the spectral density. However, it can be shown that it is not a consistent estimate.

It is useful to illustrate the proof for the special case of a Gaussian white noise process: $\{\epsilon_t\}$, $\epsilon_t \sim n(0, 1)$, independently of t. In this case we have

$$E\{I_T(\lambda_1)I_T(\lambda_2)\} = \frac{4}{T^2} E \left| \sum_{t=1}^{T} \exp(i\lambda_1 t)\epsilon_t \right|^2 \left| \sum_{t=1}^{T} \exp(i\lambda_2 t)\epsilon_t \right|^2$$

$$= \frac{4}{T^2} E\left\{ \sum_{s,t,u,v=1}^{T} \epsilon_s\epsilon_t\epsilon_u\epsilon_v \exp i\{(s-t)\lambda_1 + (u-v)\lambda_2\} \right\}. \qquad (21)$$

Now

$$
\begin{aligned}
E\epsilon_s\epsilon_t\epsilon_u\epsilon_v &= 3, & s &= t = u = v, \\
&= 1, & s &= t, & u &= v, & t &\neq u, \\
&= 1, & s &= u, & t &= v, & s &\neq t, \\
&= 1, & t &= u, & s &= v, & s &\neq t, \\
&= 0, & \text{otherwise.}
\end{aligned}
$$

It follows that

$$E\{I_T(\lambda_1)I_T(\lambda_2)\} = \frac{4}{T^2} \left\{ 3T + T(T-1) + \sum_{s \neq t} \exp\{i[s(\lambda_1 + \lambda_2) - t(\lambda_1 + \lambda_2)]\} \right.$$

$$+ \left. \sum_{s \neq t} \exp\{i[s(\lambda_1 - \lambda_2) - t(\lambda_1 - \lambda_2)]\} + 0 \right\}$$

$$= \frac{4}{T^2} \left\{ T^2 + \sum_{s,t=1}^{T} \{\exp[i(s-t)(\lambda_1 + \lambda_2)] \right.$$

$$+ \left. \exp[i(s-t)(\lambda_1 - \lambda_2)]\} \right\}$$

$$= \frac{4}{T^2} \left\{ T^2 + \left| \sum_{s=1}^{T} \exp[is(\lambda_1 + \lambda_2)] \right|^2 + \left| \sum_{s=1}^{T} \exp[is(\lambda_1 - \lambda_2)] \right|^2 \right\}$$

$$= \frac{4}{T^2} \left\{ T^2 + \left| \frac{1 - \exp[i(\lambda_1 + \lambda_2)(T+1)]}{1 - \exp[i(\lambda_1 + \lambda_2)]} - 1 \right|^2 \right.$$

$$+ \left. \left| \frac{1 - \exp[i(\lambda_1 - \lambda_2)(T+1)]}{1 - \exp[i(\lambda_1 - \lambda_2)]} - 1 \right|^2 \right\}, \qquad \text{for} \quad \lambda_1 \neq \lambda_2,$$

$$(22)$$

and

$$E\{I_T(\lambda_1)I_T(\lambda_2)\} = \frac{4}{T^2}\left\{T^2 + \left|\frac{1 - e^{2i\lambda(T+1)}}{1 - e^{2i\lambda}} - 1\right|^2 + T^2\right\}, \quad \text{for} \quad \lambda_1 = \lambda_2 = \lambda \neq 0.$$

The expression $|[(1 - e^{i\mu(T+1)})/(1 - e^{i\mu})] - 1|^2$ may be reduced as follows:

$$\left|\frac{1 - e^{i\mu(T+1)} - 1 + e^{i\mu}}{1 - e^{i\mu}}\right|^2 = \left|e^{i\mu}\frac{(1 - e^{i\mu T})}{1 - e^{i\mu}}\right|^2 = \frac{(1 - e^{i\mu T})(1 - e^{-i\mu T})}{(1 - e^{i\mu})(1 - e^{-i\mu})}$$

$$= \frac{2(1 - \cos \mu T)}{2(1 - \cos \mu)} = \frac{2\sin^2(\mu T/2)}{2\sin^2(\mu/2)}.$$

Consequently,

$$E\{I_T(\lambda_1)I_T(\lambda_2)\} = \frac{4}{T^2}\left\{T^2 + \left[\frac{\sin\{(\lambda_1 + \lambda_2)T/2\}}{\sin\{(\lambda_1 + \lambda_2)/2\}}\right]^2\right.$$

$$\left. + \left[\frac{\sin\{(\lambda_1 - \lambda_2)T/2\}}{\sin\{(\lambda_1 - \lambda_2)/2\}}\right]^2\right\} \quad \text{for} \quad \lambda_1 \neq \lambda_2,$$

and

$$E\{I_T(\lambda_1)I_T(\lambda_2)\} = \frac{4}{T^2}\left\{2T^2 + \left[\frac{\sin \lambda T}{\sin \lambda}\right]^2\right\}, \quad \text{for} \quad \lambda_1 = \lambda_2 = \lambda \neq 0,$$

and

$$E\{I_T(\lambda_1)I_T(\lambda_2)\} = \frac{4}{T^2}\{3T^2\}, \quad \text{for} \quad \lambda_1 = \lambda_2 = 0. \tag{23}$$

From (23),

$$\lim_{T \to \infty} E\{I_T(\lambda_1)I_T(\lambda_2)\} = \begin{cases} 4, & \lambda_1 \neq \lambda_2, \\ 8, & \lambda_1 = \lambda_2 = \lambda \neq 0, \\ 12, & \lambda_1 = \lambda_2 = \lambda = 0. \end{cases} \tag{24}$$

Since $f_{\epsilon\epsilon}(\lambda) = 1/2\pi$ (see footnote 5), (20) implies that $EI_T(\lambda) \to 2$; it follows that

$$\text{var}\{I_T(\lambda)\} \to \begin{cases} 8 - 4 = 4, & \lambda \neq 0, \\ 12 - 4 = 8, & \lambda = 0, \end{cases} \tag{25}$$

$$\text{cov}\{I_T(\lambda_1), I_T(\lambda_2)\} \to 4 - 4 = 0, \quad \lambda_1 \neq \lambda_2.$$

Thus $I_T(\lambda)$ is not a consistent estimate of $f(\lambda)$, for although it is asymptotically unbiased, its variance does not tend to zero. Furthermore, the correlation, even between adjacent periodogram ordinates, does tend to zero. This means that the periodogram will have a very jagged and erratic appearance for large T despite the fact that in this case the true spectrum is uniform. (See the periodogram graphed by Hannan (1960, p. 56).)

When the process considered is not Gaussian white noise, similar results can be derived, although the proof is considerably more difficult. It can be shown that for a purely linearly nondeterministic process $\{x_t\}$ with spectral density $f_{xx}(\lambda)$,

$$\text{cov}\{I_T(\lambda_1), I_T(\lambda_2)\} \rightarrow \begin{cases} 0 & \text{for} \quad \lambda_1 \neq \lambda_2, \\ [4\pi f_{xx}(\lambda)]^2 & \text{for} \quad \lambda_1 = \lambda_2 \neq 0, \\ 2[4\pi f_{xx}(0)]^2 & \text{for} \quad \lambda_1 = \lambda_2 = 0 \end{cases} \tag{26}$$

(Hannan, 1960, pp. 54–55; Olshen, 1967; Anderson, 1971, pp. 484–488). When the process is not purely linearly nondeterministic, the results are more complicated at those frequencies at which jumps occur in the spectral distribution function. At these frequencies $EI_T(\lambda) \rightarrow \infty$ (Bartlett, 1955, pp. 275–276; Grenander and Rosenblatt, 1957, pp. 91–94). It is this fact that forms the basis for the use of the periodogram to test for hidden periodicities. Unfortunately, it is implausible to assume that any but a negligible number of economic time series contain an exact periodicity so that methods for estimating the spectral density function or related quantities for processes with absolutely continuous spectral distribution functions assume considerable importance. It is to this subject that we now turn.

Since the periodogram ordinates are uncorrelated in the limit, one might naturally think of averaging these asymptotically uncorrelated random variables in order to achieve an estimate with variance that does tend to zero as the number of observations increases. Indeed, it is possible to do just this and obtain estimates of the corresponding averages of the spectral density function that are consistent.[15] Note, however, that only *averages* of spectral densities for purely linearly nondeterministic stationary time series can be consistently estimated, *not* the value of the density function itself *at* a specific point.[16] Much of the literature on spectral analysis deals with the appropriate and optimal form of such averages and the problems involved in interpreting estimates of averages of functional values rather than function ordinates.

Until recently, the chief difficulty in implementing the above suggestions has been the lengthy computations involved in calculating the periodogram ordinates, especially for fairly long time series. Recently, however, the so-called fast Fourier transform has made it possible to compute periodogram ordinates extremely efficiently (Cooley and Tukey, 1965; Cooley *et al.*, 1967).[17] Most

---

[15] Indeed, this was exactly the basis of Bartlett's famous 1946 suggestion for estimating spectral averages. See also Bartlett (1950).

[16] Because the spectral density function for a real time series is symmetric about the origin, it is customary to estimate and plot such averages only for bands centered on equispaced frequencies in the interval $[0, \pi]$.

[17] See also Bloomfield (1976, especially Chapter 4, "The Fast Fourier Transform," pp. 61–76). Bloomfield's book is an extensive discourse on harmonic analysis of time series, based almost entirely on Fourier transforms of the series themselves made possible by the development of this computationally feasible method.

Pukkila (1977, pp. 32–39) uses an alternative method to speed up the computation of the periodogram ordinates based on a recursive calculation of the necessary sines and cosines. He reports

people today would probably prefer to use weighted averages of the periodogram ordinates, but formerly, when this was not computationally feasible, procedures were based on averaging the estimated autocovariances and then taking the Fourier transform of the much smaller number of averaged autocovariance estimates (Blackman and Tukey, 1958; Fuller, 1976, pp. 275–326).

Both weighted and unweighted averages of the periodogram ordinates and/or the estimated autocovariances correspond to weighted averages of the true spectral density function over the entire range of frequencies, although typically, of course, the weight is concentrated in a more-or-less narrow band of interest. Much of the time-series literature up to 1965 deals with the problem of choosing weights for the autocovariances in an appropriate manner. In this literature the weighted average of the true spectral density function that one estimates is called a *window*, and we speak of viewing the spectral density function through a window. Nonzero weights outside the frequency band of interest are referred to as *side lobes*. The fact that certain windows, corresponding to particular weighting schemes for the autocovariances, have negative side lobes is of great concern since very large values of the spectral density function even at distant frequencies can cause seriously distorted estimates in the band with which one is mainly concerned. Since frequencies near zero account for much of the variance in economic time series (values of the spectral density function are often 10,000 times as great as the values at higher frequencies), the problem is an especially serious one in the analysis of economic time series. The phenomenon that results in this type of bias is called *leakage*.

The two most widely used windows formerly discussed in the time-series literature are the Tukey–Hanning window and the Parzen window. The first does have negative side lobes but substantially better properties than crude averages of the periodogram ordinates. The second has no negative side lobes, but is less sharply focused than the Tukey–Hanning window in the following sense: In order to achieve an estimate with a given approximate variance (approximate because the small-sample properties of spectral estimates are effectively unknown), averages of the true spectral density function over certain frequency bands must be estimated; apart from the sidelobe issue, these bands are broader the smaller the desired variance of the estimate and may be made narrower (so that the estimates have greater "resolution") only at the cost of a higher variance of the estimate. The greater part of the total weight, for a

---

that this method saves nearly 90% of the time required, as compared with methods using the standard sine and cosine function routines. A similar suggestion for recursive calculation of the necessary sines and cosines is made by Otnes and Enochson (1972, pp. 140–143). Pukkila also suggests the importance of "tapering" the series prior to the calculation of the periodogram ordinates since these estimates are otherwise biased towards values corresponding to a periodogram of white noise. "Tapering," which will not be discussed here, is analogous to weighting the autocovariances themselves when computing their Fourier transforms.

given approximate variance, is concentrated in a narrower band for the Tukey–Hanning window than for the Parzen window. Our estimates presented in subsequent chapters are all based on weighted averages of the autocovariances using the Parzen window.

Weighted averages of the periodogram ordinates are usually expressed in the form of weighted averages of the autocovariances of the time series, which are used in place of the "raw" autocovariance estimates in (15).[18] To each such *lag window*, as such a system of weights is called, there corresponds a particular weighted average of the spectral density function. The weights attached to the values of the true spectral density are called a *spectral window*. Dhrymes (1970, p. 442) gives a convenient summary of various types of lag windows and the corresponding spectral windows. If $\hat{c}_\tau = a_\tau c_\tau$ are the weighted autocovariances used to compute the spectral density and if M is the maximum lag at which the raw autocovariances are estimated, then the lag window for equally weighted periodogram ordinates is

$$a_\tau = \frac{\sin(\tau\pi(M/N))}{M\sin(\tau\pi/N)}, \qquad |\tau| < N - 1, \tag{27}$$

and the corresponding spectral window is

$$A(\lambda) = (1/\pi)(\sin\lambda)/\lambda, \tag{28}$$

where λ is the frequency on which the average or band is centered (Hannan, 1970, pp. 275–276). The Tukey–Hanning estimate corresponds to the lag window

$$a_\tau = \begin{cases} \frac{1}{2}[1 + \cos(\pi\tau/M)] & \text{if } \tau = 0, \pm 1, \ldots, \pm M, \\ 0 & \text{otherwise}; \end{cases} \tag{29}$$

and the corresponding spectral window is

$$A(\lambda) = \frac{\pi^2}{\pi^2 - (M\lambda)^2} \frac{\sin M\lambda}{\lambda}. \tag{30}$$

The Parzen lag window is

$$a_\tau = \begin{cases} 1 - 6(\tau/M)^2 + 6|\tau/M|^3 & \text{for } \tau = 0, \pm 1, \ldots, \pm[M/2], \\ 2(1 - |\tau/M|)^3 & \text{for } \tau = \pm([M/2] + 1), \ldots, \pm M, \\ 0 & \text{otherwise}; \end{cases} \tag{31}$$

---

[18] If, however, a fast Fourier transform is used on the data, it will then be more convenient to compute the new periodogram estimates and average these across frequency bands. When very large amounts of data are available, as will usually be the case when a fast Fourier transform technique is warranted, equally weighted averages are typically used. Although such averages do not estimate equally weighted averages of the true spectral density function, the large amount of available data will usually permit sufficiently narrow bands so that leakage presents little problem. "Tapering" the series prior to the calculation of the periodogram ordinates also mitigates the problem and is especially advisable in the case of short series. See Pukkila (1977, pp. 61–76).

and the corresponding spectral window is

$$A(\lambda) = \frac{3}{4M^3} \left[\frac{\sin(M\lambda/4)}{\lambda/4} \right]^4. \tag{32}$$

The notation $[M/2]$ means the largest integer less than or equal to $M/2$. It can be shown that the Tukey–Hanning spectral window is more narrowly focused about the central frequency λ but that it has negative side lobes. The Parzen window, on the other hand, is clearly always nonnegative, but it can be shown that it is not as sharply focused as the Tukey–Hanning window (Fishman, 1969, pp. 90–97).

Provided one is willing to treat the data appropriately, the precise nature of the window really matters very little. If the true spectral density is rather flat, bias due to leakage is bound to be small; the difficulty in the analysis of economic time series arises primarily because there is such substantial variation in the level of the spectral density over the frequency range. If the data could be transformed so that the spectral density were nearly flat, the problem would not arise. Since white noise (serially independent random values with common variance) has a perfectly flat true spectral density, Tukey called such transformation of the data *prewhitening*. Of course, the nature of the transformation required to reduce a given time series to white noise is unknown; if it were known, there would be no need to estimate the spectral density of the series since its structure could be completely described by the nature of the transformation required. In Nerlove (1964), a modification of a prewhitening device originally suggested by Tukey is adopted. Repeated differences of the form $x(t) - 0.75x(t - 1)$ were taken until the resulting estimated spectral densities were, apart from seasonal peaks, approximately flat (variation of the normalized spectral density was confined to within one power of ten). Such transformations were called quasi-differences. A less labor-intensive method has been suggested by Parzen: An autoregression is fitted by a stepwise least-squares procedure that will admit few coefficients in the final result; the estimates are then used to transform the data to residuals from the final regression equation. This procedure occasionally results in strange estimates of the spectral density from a finite series, especially when the series is trending but with a sharp drop or break (as might, for example, be due to a strike), but inspection of the series itself and the estimated autoregression generally serves to guard against this possibility. The Parzen procedure is used in all of the analyses presented in this book.

Although prewhitening greatly reduces problems of the interpretation of estimates that arise because of leakage, it often leads to difficulties of interpretation itself. For example, quasi-differencing or removal of an autoregression often reduces the level of the spectral density very near the origin quite substantially—considerably more than at neighboring, but not quite so low, frequencies. One consequence is an apparent peak at a low frequency (corresponding to a sinusoidal component with a relatively long period). One might be inclined to accept this as evidence of a cyclical component of fairly long period, whereas in fact it is nothing more than an artifact of the estimation procedure. For this reason, Nerlove (1964) introduced an additional device, called *recoloring* by contrast to the initial transformation of the data which Tukey had termed *prewhitening*. This is nothing more than the division of each estimated value of the average spectral density function by the known transfer function of the filter used to prewhiten the data; this yields a better estimate of the spectral density function of the original data.[19] Indeed, Durbin has shown, in an unpublished note written in 1963, that prewhitening-estimation recoloring reduces the bias in estimates of spectral averages due to leakage by a factor that depends on the nature of the window and on the rate of change in the spectral density of the original series, compared with the rate of change of the spectral density of the prewhitened series in the vicinity of the frequency upon which the estimate is centered. All spectral densities presented in this book are recolored estimates based on the estimated spectral densities of autoregressively prewhitened data.

Nerlove (1965) presents methods for recoloring the cross spectra of two series that have been prewhitened by different filters. It is apparent that none of the important quantities, such as gain or phase, are affected if the series are prewhitened by the *same* filter. Indeed, coherence is unaffected even if the two series are prewhitened by two different time-invariant linear filters.

Jenkins and Watts (1968, pp. 363–421) discuss practical problems of cross-spectral estimation and interpretation, including the need for what they call "alignment" prior to estimation when the cross-lag covariance function has a large peak. Since the cross-spectral density function is little used in the studies reported here, we do not survey the problems of cross-spectral estimation here. These are discussed extensively by Bloomfield (1976, pp. 209–233).[20]

---

[19] Note that $f_{uu}(\lambda)$ may be set to zero in (4.5), since the transformation of the data is exactly known.

[20] We do estimate distributed-lag and multiple-time-series models in the so-called frequency domain, but our procedures involve use of the cross-periodogram ordinates rather than the cross-spectral density functions.

Chapter IV
FORMULATION AND ANALYSIS OF
UNOBSERVED-COMPONENTS MODELS

1. Introduction

In Chapters II and III we developed the theory of stationary time series and their spectral representations, with special emphasis on time series containing no linearly deterministic component. Such a time series may be represented as a one-sided, possibly infinite, moving average of a white noise input. Moreover, the spectral distribution function of such a time series $F(\lambda)$ is absolutely continuous in the interval $(-\pi, \pi]$, with derivative $f(\lambda)$ of bounded variation and never negative; this derivative is the spectral density function and proportional to the squared modulus of the generating transform of weights in the moving-average representation $B(z)$ evaluated on the unit circle. For this reason, as noted, the factorization of the autocovariance generating transform defined in equation (III.3.24) is called the canonical factorization of the spectral density function:

$$g_{xx}(z) = \sigma^2 B(z)B(z^{-1}).$$

When $B(z)$ has no zeros on the unit circle [conventionally, to identify the process its zeros are then taken to lie outside the unit circle and those of $B(z^{-1})$ to lie inside], the time series $\{x_t\}$ has a purely autoregressive representation; the weights of past x's in this representation have generating transform $A(z) = 1/B(z)$. In this case the representation is said to be invertible, as indicated in Chapter III.

Of special importance in the theory we develop in this chapter are stationary time series, which may be represented in terms of a finite autoregression with input given by a finite moving average of white noise; such processes are said to have rational spectral densities since their autocovariance generating transforms may be represented as the ratios of two polynomials

$$g_{xx}(z) = \sigma^2[Q(z)Q(z^{-1})/P(z)P(z^{-1})],$$

where σ^2 is the variance of the white noise input to the moving-average part of the process generating the time series.

In the previous chapter, we also introduced the notion of jointly stationary time series and defined the cross-lag covariance generating transform and its associated cross-spectral density function. The canonical factorization of the cross-spectral density function, analogous to the canonical factorization of the spectral density function, plays a major role in the theory of prediction and extraction for unobserved-components models, which is developed in the next chapter.

In the present chapter, we show how unobserved-components models, which capture much of the flavor of those used by economic statisticians of the nineteenth and early twentieth centuries, may be formulated by superimposing simple mixed moving-average autoregressive models with independent white noise inputs. The estimation of such unobserved-components models and their application to the formulation of distributed-lag models are topics left to Chapters VII and XIII, respectively.

2.   Unobserved-Components Models and Their Canonical Forms

Using the backward shift operator U, introduced previously, we may write an ordinary mixed moving-average autoregressive process with zero mean $\{x_t\}$ as

$$H(U)x_t = G(U)\epsilon_t, \tag{1}$$

where

$$E\epsilon_t = 0, \qquad E\epsilon_t\epsilon_{t'} = \begin{cases} \sigma^2, & t = t' \\ 0, & t \neq t' \end{cases}$$

and $H(z)$ and $G(z)$ are polynomials such that $H(z)$ has all its roots *outside* the unit circle. The assumption of zero mean can always be satisfied by taking all observed values as deviations from the sample mean. The type of nonstationarity permitted by the theory described in Nerlove (1972b) and allowed by Box and Jenkins (1970) in the form of what they call an autoregressive integrated moving-average process arises when some of the roots of $H(z)$ lie *on*, rather than strictly outside, the unit circle. In this case, the corresponding moving-average form contains weights that do not damp out for long lags. Such moving averages are called *integrated* moving averages (IMA).

The model proposed by Box and Jenkins (1970) for the analysis, forecasting and control of time series is just the model described above. However, in the case of economic and other time series involving seasonal fluctuations, very high-order autoregressive structures are required for representation of the time series; therefore very large numbers of parameters are required, unless some further restrictions can be placed on the process. In their chapter on seasonal models Box and Jenkins (1970, Chapter 9, especially p. 322) suggest that the data be transformed to

$$y_t = (1 - \varphi U^{12})x_t, \qquad |\varphi| < 1,$$

in the case of monthly series, or more generally to

$$y_t = (1 - \varphi U^L)x_t, \qquad |\varphi| < 1, \qquad (2)$$

where L is the number of periods over which the seasonal fluctuation is assumed to occur (e.g., $L = 4$ in the case of quarterly data, $L = 52$ for weekly data, and so forth).

The operator $(1 - \varphi U^L)$ in Eq. (2) is the most general form suggested by Box and Jenkins for handling seasonality, and at several points they appear to recommend the simple form $(1 - U^L)$. Indeed, some computer programs for analyzing time series by Box–Jenkins techniques do assume the possibility of removing seasonality by repeated application of the operator $(1 - U^L)$. Unfortunately, however, since this operator has zeros on the unit circle, it cannot be inverted in a region containing the unit circle. It can be shown that a series characterized by (1), where $H(U)$ has a factor $1 - U^L$, will have jumps in its spectral distribution function at the seasonal frequencies. Real economic time series do not appear to be characterized by distribution functions with such jumps or, equivalently, by spectral density functions having infinite lines at the seasonal frequencies (see Nerlove, 1972b). Moreover, even the use of the more general operator $(1 - \varphi U^L)$, $|\varphi| < 1$ to remove seasonality implies that the spectral density of the time series should have peaks at seasonal frequencies of nearly equal height (apart from any effects of the moving average applied to the innovations); whereas we observe that many economic time series have spectra that show peaks at the seasonal frequencies falling off, sometimes irregularly, with frequency (see Chapters VIII and IX). Thus, more complicated characterizations of seasonality in economic time series may be required; such characterizations may, in principle, involve rather high-order polynomials in the lag operator.

Use of a *few* parameters, or *parsimony* as Box and Jenkins (1970, pp. 17–18) call the principle, is especially important in the characterization of economic time series. Thus the formulation suggested by Box and Jenkins, in terms of a general mixed autoregressive integrated moving-average process may not be adequate for the characterization of many economic time series. It is for this reason that a closely related type of model, the so-called unobserved-components model (Nerlove, 1967), is suggested as a possible extension of the models discussed by Box and Jenkins. It does appear to satisfy both the criterion of parsimony and the criterion of realism with such models based upon the notion of unobserved components, more or less as envisaged in traditional economic statistics. The novelty of this approach lies in the specification of each of the components as a mixed moving-average autoregressive process after a simple transformation of the observed series (e.g., logarithmic first differences) designed to render it stationary. Models of the sort proposed are capable of reproducing the spectral shapes of a variety of economic time series and are thus capable of characterizing at least their second-moment properties.

The idea that one may divide an economic time series into several unobserved but separately meaningful components has been discussed at length in Chapter I.[1] The class of models embodying this idea was once fashionable in economics and includes the well-known errors-in-variables models. In the simplest case of such a model, we suppose that the two observed variables x_t and y_t are divided into two unobserved components—the "true" values ξ_t and η_t, respectively, and the "errors" u_t and v_t, respectively:

$$x_t = \xi_t + u_t, \qquad y_t = \eta_t + v_t. \tag{3}$$

It is also generally supposed that the "true" values of x_t and y_t are connected by an exact relation, e.g.,

$$\eta_t = \alpha \xi_t + \beta, \tag{4}$$

while u_t and v_t are independent. The problems of estimating α and β have been the subject of extensive investigation (see, for example, Malinvaud, 1970, pp. 374–411). The essential point, however, for our purpose is that *the observed variables x_t and y_t are divided into two unobserved components, and corresponding components in each series are related differently*; i.e., u_t is related to v_t in quite a different manner than ξ_t is related to η_t.

Although interest in models of errors-in-variables waned considerably following the sweep of the field by the "shock" model in the forties, the errors-in-variables approach is not entirely without recent application. Indeed, as is well known, the "permanent income" hypothesis of consumption behavior developed by Friedman (1957) can be viewed in exactly this way. Without attempting to do justice to Friedman's ingenious and complex theory, it may be described in brief as follows: Both income and consumption as observed may be divided into two unobserved components called, respectively, the permanent and the transitory component. Friedman supposes that there exists an exactly proportional relationship between the two permanent components, but no relationship between the two transitory components or between the latter and the permanent component of either income or consumption. Friedman argues that "if a consumer unit knows that its receipts in any one year are unusually high and expects lower receipts subsequently, it will surely tend to adjust its consumption to its 'normal' receipts rather than to its current receipts" (1957, p. 10). The permanent component of income, according to Friedman, "is to be interpreted as reflecting the effect of those factors that determine the con-

---

[1] The discussion here follows Nerlove (1967).

sumer unit's capital value or wealth ... ," while the transitory component "is to be interpreted as reflecting all 'other' factors, factors that are likely to be treated by the unit affected as 'accidental' or 'chance' occurrences, though they may, from another point of view, be the predictable effect of specifiable forces, for example, cyclical fluctuations in economic activity" (1957, pp. 21–22). When Friedman comes to the analysis of aggregate consumption and income over time, he specifies a relation between past income and what people consider to be the permanent component of income, which amounts to taking consumption as a function of income with an exponential distribution of lag. Indeed, Friedman's justification for this form is the continuous analog of the adaptive expectations hypothesis, which leads to distributions of lag based on geometrically declining weights (see Chapter XIII). In the next chapter we derive such an exponentially weighted moving-average of past values of a time series as an optimal extraction and prediction of an unobserved component of a two-component model.

This two-component model also serves to illustrate the general relationship that exists between any given unobserved-components model and a corresponding simple mixed moving-average autoregressive model. We call the latter the *canonical form* of the former, by analogy with the use of the term canonical factorization in the relation between a spectral density function for, and a one-sided moving-average representation of, a nondeterministic time series.

Consider the following model:

$$x_t = y_t + u_t, \qquad y_t = \alpha y_{t-1} + v_t, \qquad |\alpha| < 1, \tag{5}$$

where $\{u_t\}$ and $\{v_t\}$ are independent zero-mean white noise inputs with variance ratio

$$\mu = Ev_t^2/Eu_t^2 = \sigma_v^2/\sigma_u^2. \tag{6}$$

In order to derive a simple mixed moving-average autoregressive representation for the time series $\{x_t\}$ defined by (5) and (6) in which the single white noise input is serially independent rather than merely serially uncorrelated, we make the rather strong assumption that $\{u_t\}$ and $\{v_t\}$ are not only independent white noise inputs but also Gaussian.[2] Then the input to the canonical form of the model will also be Gaussian, as required by the estimation techniques proposed in Chapter VII.

---

[2] The estimation procedures for unobserved-components models described in Chapter VII rest on the assumption that the white noise input in the canonical form of the model is Gaussian; thus, they require that the underlying inputs to the unobserved components also be Gaussian. The prediction and extraction theory developed in Chapter V require only that the input of the canonical form be serially uncorrelated white noise; this is assured if the inputs to the unobserved components are independent white noise series, but may not be if they are simply uncorrelated white noise series. Moreover, even if the inputs to the unobserved components are independent, if they are not also Gaussian, the input to the canonical form will be a serially uncorrelated series, but the values of the series at different points in time may not be independent.

To derive the canonical form of (5) and (6) we must determine G, H, and σ^2 in

$$H(U)x_t = G(U)\epsilon_t, \tag{7}$$

where $\{\epsilon_t\}$ is white noise with zero mean and variance σ^2, so that the process satisfying (7) will have the same autocovariance generating function as the process described by (5) and (6). From (5)

$$x_t - \alpha x_{t-1} = y_t - \alpha y_{t-1} + u_t - \alpha u_{t-1}$$

or

$$(1 - \alpha U)x_t = v_t + (1 - \alpha U)u_t. \tag{8}$$

Because of the assumed independence of v_t and u_t and their assumed lack of serial dependence, it follows straightforwardly that

$$(1 - \alpha z)(1 - \alpha z^{-1})g_{xx}(z) = \sigma_v^2 + (1 - \alpha z)(1 - \alpha z^{-1})\sigma_u^2, \tag{9}$$

so that

$$g_{xx}(z) = \sigma_u^2\left[\frac{\mu + (1 - \alpha z)(1 - \alpha z^{-1})}{(1 - \alpha z)(1 - \alpha z^{-1})}\right]. \tag{10}$$

In order to express this in the form $\sigma^2 G(z)G(z^{-1})/H(z)H(z^{-1})$, it is necessary to factor the polynomial $\mu + (1 - \alpha z)(1 - \alpha z^{-1})$, which appears in the numerator on the right.

The two roots of this polynomial are

$$|\beta| = \left|\frac{(1 + \mu + \alpha^2) - [(1 + \mu + \alpha^2)^2 - 4\alpha^2]^{1/2}}{2\alpha}\right| < 1,$$

$$\left|\frac{1}{\beta}\right| = \left|\frac{(1 + \mu + \alpha^2) + [(1 + \mu + \alpha^2)^2 - 4\alpha^2]^{1/2}}{2\alpha}\right| > 1. \tag{11}$$

There is no loss in generality in taking $\alpha > 0$. In this case, we may remove the absolute value operators. Thus β in (11) is the root lying *inside* the unit circle. Thus we take

$$G(z) = 1 - \beta z, \qquad H(z) = 1 - \alpha z. \tag{12}$$

To determine the constant σ^2, observe that

$$\sigma_u^2[\mu + (1 - \alpha z)(1 - \alpha z^{-1})] = \sigma^2(1 - \beta z)(1 - \beta z^{-1}), \tag{13}$$

so that

$$\sigma^2 = \sigma_u^2\left[\frac{\mu + (1 + \alpha^2)}{1 + \beta^2}\right] = (\alpha/\beta)\sigma_u^2. \tag{14}$$

The general principles involved in obtaining the canonical form of an unobserved-components model may be further illustrated by generalizing the model of (5) and (6) to

$$x_t = y_t + u_t, \qquad Q(U)y_t = v_t, \tag{15}$$

where $Q(U)$ is a polynomial of degree n in the backward shift operator U with generating transform

$$Q(z) = \prod_{j=1}^{n} (1 - \alpha_j z) \tag{16}$$

such that $|\alpha_j| < 1$ for all j. Note that $Q(z)$ is normalized so that the coefficient of the current value of y in $Q(U)y_t$ is one. The restriction $|\alpha_j| < 1$ for all j ensures that the roots of $Q(z)$ all lie *outside* the unit circle. Hence, if we take, as before, $\{u_t\}$ and $\{v_t\}$ as independent Gaussian zero-mean white noise inputs with variance ratio

$$\mu = Ev_t^2/Eu_t^2 = \sigma_v^2/\sigma_u^2,$$

the series $\{y_t\}$ will have a one-sided moving-average representation and $\{x_t\}$ will be a stationary process with a one-sided moving-average representation in terms of independent white noise inputs $\{\epsilon_t\}$. Should some roots of $Q(z)$ lie *on* the unit circle, the process $\{x_t\}$ will be nonstationary, but our results will hold if we let some of the α_j's tend to values for which $|\alpha_j| = 1$.

$$Q(U)x_t = Q(U)y_t + Q(U)u_t = v_t + Q(U)u_t \tag{17}$$

so that by methods used above we deduce

$$g_{xx}(z) = \sigma_u^2 \left[\frac{\mu + Q(z)Q(z^{-1})}{Q(z)Q(z^{-1})} \right]. \tag{18}$$

Consider the polynomial

$$cG(z)G(z^{-1}) = \mu + Q(z)Q(z^{-1}) = \mu + \prod_{j=1}^{n} (1 - \alpha_j z)(1 - \alpha_j z^{-1}). \tag{19}$$

Clearly, if z_0 is a root, so is $1/z_0$. There are thus $2n$ roots that come in reciprocal pairs: One member of each pair lies *inside* the unit circle, the other *outside*. Let the roots be β_j and $1/\beta_j$, $j = 1, \ldots, n$, and let β_j be the member of each pair lying *inside* the unit circle. Thus factor $G(z)$ as

$$cG(z)G(z^{-1}) = c \prod_{j=1}^{n} (1 - \beta_j z)(1 - \beta_j z^{-1}), \tag{20}$$

where c is a constant of proportionality so chosen as to make the coefficients for corresponding powers of z in (19) and (20) equal. Since β_k, $k = 1, \ldots, n$ is a root of $G(z)$, we have

$$\mu = - \prod_{j=1}^{n} (1 - \alpha_j \beta_k)(1 - \alpha_j/\beta_k), \qquad k = 1, \ldots, n. \tag{21}$$

It may thus be readily verified that c should be chosen so that

$$c = \frac{\mu + \prod_{j=1}^{n}(1 + \alpha_j^2)}{\prod_{j=1}^{n}(1 + \beta_j^2)} = \frac{\prod_{j=1}^{n}(1 + \alpha_j^2) - \prod_{j=1}^{n}(1 - \alpha_j\beta_k)(1 - \alpha_j/\beta_k)}{\prod_{j=1}^{n}(1 + \beta_j^2)}, \qquad (22)$$

where k may take on any value from 1 to n.[3] Following the convention, described above, that we take both numerators and denominators in the canonical factorization of a rational spectral density to have roots *outside* the unit circle, we choose

$$\frac{G(z)}{H(z)} = \prod_{j=1}^{n}\left(\frac{1 - \beta_j z}{1 - \alpha_j z}\right), \qquad |\beta_j| < 1, \quad |\alpha_j| < 1, \qquad (23)$$

and

$$\sigma^2 = \sigma_u^2 c = \sigma_u^2\left[\frac{\prod_{j=1}^{n}(1 + \alpha_j^2) - \prod_{j=1}^{n}(1 - \alpha_j\beta)(1 - \alpha_j/\beta)}{\prod_{j=1}^{n}(1 + \beta_j^2)}\right], \qquad (24)$$

where β is any root of $G(z)G(z^{-1})$.

A still more general model, which is basic to our discussion of seasonal adjustment in Chapter VIII yet sufficiently general to permit a complete discussion of the problem of relating an unobserved-components model to its canonical form, may be illustrated by the following decomposition of the time series $\{x_t\}$, which is analogous to the classical trend-cycle–seasonal–irregular decomposition when certain properties are assumed for each component. Let the series $\{x_t\}$ be decomposed as

$$x_t = T_t + S_t + I_t. \qquad (25)$$

To give the decomposition content, we suppose that the three unobserved components $\{T_t\}$, $\{S_t\}$, and $\{I_t\}$ satisfy the following relations:

$$Q(U)T_t = P(U)v_t, \qquad S(U)S_t = R(U)w_t, \qquad I_t = u_t, \qquad (26)$$

where $Q(\ )$, $P(\ )$, $S(\ )$, and $R(\ )$ are polynomials in the lag operator U of relatively low order except for $S(\ )$, which, however, is assumed to be of low order in U^L, where L is the number of times per year the series $\{x_t\}$ is observed. The series $\{u_t\}$, $\{v_t\}$, and $\{w_t\}$ are assumed to be stationary independent white noise time series with variances σ_u^2, σ_v^2, and σ_w^2, respectively. For later purposes of estimation and to ensure the serial independence of the white noise input to the canonical form of the model, the series may also be assumed to be Gaussian. In practical situations, it may sometimes be necessary to assume that u_t is not white noise but follows a low-order moving average, e.g., that the entire process has in effect been transformed by, say, $1 - \theta U$.

How complicated one may wish to make the polynomials Q, P, S, and R depends in part on how many data points are available and how closely one

---

[3] All values so obtained must obviously be equal. This result is obtained most simply by equating the coefficients of $\zeta = z + z^{-1}$ in the two representations of $G(z)G(z^{-1})$.

wishes to approximate the observed characteristics of the series $\{x_t\}$. For most series of economic relevance rather simple, i.e., low-order, polynomials are desirable. The effect of choosing relatively low-order polynomials is to reduce greatly the number of parameters required for a mixed moving-average auto-regressive scheme of comparable order in the simplest form. By the results of Chapter III, the series $\{x_t\}$ described by the above model has a spectral density function proportional to

$$\frac{P(z)P(z^{-1})}{Q(z)Q(z^{-1})}\sigma_v^2 + \frac{R(z)R(z^{-1})}{S(z)S(z^{-1})}\sigma_w^2 + \sigma_u^2 = g_{xx}(z), \tag{27}$$

where $z = e^{i\lambda}$ lies on the unit circle. Note that if the variance of the observed series is given, the variances σ_v^2, σ_w^2, and σ_u^2 and other parameters cannot all be given independently. The variance of $\{x_t\}$ is the coefficient of z^0 in $g_{xx}(z)$ and may be obtained very simply by a method described in the next section of this chapter.

Equation (27) may be rewritten as

$$g_{xx}(z) = \sigma^2[G(z)G(z^{-1})/H(z)H(z^{-1})], \tag{28}$$

where $G(z)G(z^{-1})$ is proportional to

$$P(z)P(z^{-1})S(z)S(z^{-1})\sigma_v^2 + R(z)R(z^{-1})Q(z)Q(z^{-1})\sigma_w^2 + Q(z)Q(z^{-1})S(z)S(z^{-1})\sigma_u^2$$

and where $H(z)H(z^{-1}) = Q(z)Q(z^{-1})S(z)S(z^{-1})$.

Because the variance of $\{x_t\}$ must be the same for the representation (27) as for the representation (28), the method of the next section for the determination of the autocovariance of an arbitrary mixed moving-average autoregressive time series may be employed to determine σ^2, the variance of the white noise input in the canonical form of (28), as a function of the variances and parameters of the original unobserved-components model. The first step in this procedure is the determination of $G(\ )$ in terms of the parameters of the original model. Let $P(\ )$ be a polynomial of degree p, $Q(\ )$ of degree q, $R(\ )$ of degree r, and $S(\ )$ of degree s. Let

$$\mu_1 = \sigma_v^2/\sigma_u^2, \qquad \mu_2 = \sigma_w^2/\sigma_u^2; \tag{29}$$

then (27) may be written

$$g_{xx}(z) = \sigma_u^2 \left\{ \frac{\begin{bmatrix}[Q(z)Q(z^{-1})S(z)S(z^{-1}) + \mu_1 P(z)P(z^{-1})S(z)S(z^{-1}) \\ + \mu_2 R(z)R(z^{-1})Q(z)Q(z^{-1})]\end{bmatrix}}{Q(z)Q(z^{-1})S(z)S(z^{-1})} \right\}$$

$$= \sigma^2 \frac{G(z)G(z^{-1})}{H(z)H(z^{-1})}. \tag{30}$$

The first term in the numerator is a symmetric polynomial in z (if ζ is a root so is $1/\zeta$) of degree $2(q + s)$, the second term is a symmetric polynomial of degree $2(p + s)$, and the third term is a symmetric polynomial of degree $2(r + q)$. Thus, in general, the numerator will be a symmetric polynomial of degree $2m$, where $m = \max\{q + s, p + s, r + q\}$, and the denominator will be a symmetric polynomial of degree $2n$, where $n = q + s$.

If, for example, P is of degree 2, Q is of degree 2, R is of degree 2, and S is of degree 12 but of the form $1 - \theta U^{12}$, then G will be of degree 14 and H of degree 14, but there are not a total of 28 independent coefficients. Indeed, given the restriction on the parameters σ_v^2, σ_w^2, and σ_u^2 imposed by the given value of the variance of $\{x_t\}$, there are only $2 + 2 + 2 + 1 + 3 - 1 = 9$ independent parameters—a major reduction by any standard as compared with an unrestricted mixed moving-average autoregressive model of equivalent degree. Transformations, such as differencing, designed to render the series stationary, although they may be considered as allowing $H(\ )$ to have roots on the unit circle, do not add to the parameters it is necessary to estimate since these roots are given.

Since the numerator of (30) is a symmetric polynomial of degree $2m$, it has, in general, $2m$ roots, not all of which may be distinct. As usual, if a root is complex, its complex conjugate is also a root; moreover, since the polynomial is symmetric, for every root lying inside the unit circle, say ζ, there is a corresponding root lying outside the unit circle $1/\zeta$. Details of how these roots may be determined numerically are given in our discussion of estimation in Chapter VII. In practical applications, it is unlikely that any of the roots will lie exactly on the unit circle (in which case a real root would be of at least multiplicity two), or indeed that the roots will not be distinct, although of course two or more roots may be quite close. In any case, the assumption that the roots are distinct makes the calculation of σ^2, described below, and other results somewhat simpler and is made here for convenience. Let β_j and $1/\beta_j$, $j = 1, \dots, m$, be the $2m$ roots of the polynomial appearing in the numerator of (30) such that $|\beta_j| < 1$. Partitioning the roots so that $G(z)$ contains only those lying *outside* the unit circle, we find that the polynomial $G(z)$ is $\prod_{j=1}^{m}(1 - \beta_j z)$. The constant of proportionality c is determined, as described below, so as to make the variance of $\{x_t\}$, calculated either from (28) or from (30), the same. To see how this may be accomplished, it is useful to digress briefly and treat the general problem of finding the autocovariances of a mixed moving-average autoregressive process from the autocovariance generating transform. Our result for σ^2 in (28) is given in (3.12).

3. Digression on a General Method
   for the Determination of the Autocovariances
   of a Mixed Moving-Average Autoregressive Process

In Chapter III, we showed that the autovariance generating function of a zero-mean stationary nondeterministic time series is an analytic function in an annulus containing the unit circle and proportional to the spectral density of the time series on the unit circle itself. Moreover, if the process is invertible, i.e., if the process has a purely autoregressive representation, the autocovariance generating function has no zeros on the unit circle. If the generating function of a sequence is an analytic function in some region, then the infinite series form represents the Laurent expansion of that function in the region. Thus, the autocovariances of a zero-mean stationary purely linearly nondeterministic time series are the coefficients in a Laurent series expansion of the autocovariance generating function in the annulus about the unit circle in which the series converges. Consequently, Cauchy's integral formula (Appendix B, p. 372) and the residue theorem (Appendix B, p. 376) may be used to evaluate these autocovariances in a particularly simple fashion for time series having a rational spectral density, i.e., a mixed moving-average autoregressive process.

The covariance generating function of such a series $\{x_t\}$ is, as has been noted,

$$g_{xx}(z) = \frac{\sigma^2 \prod_{j=1}^{m}(1 - \beta_j z)(1 - \beta_j z^{-1})}{\prod_{k=1}^{n}(1 - \alpha_k z)(1 - \alpha_k z^{-1})} = \frac{\sigma^2 z^{n-m} \prod_{j=1}^{m}(1 - \beta_j z)(z - \beta_j)}{\prod_{k=1}^{n}(1 - \alpha_k z)(z - \alpha_k)}, \quad (1)$$

where $|\alpha_k| < 1$, $k = 1, \ldots, n$, and $|\beta_j| \leq 1$, $j = 1, \ldots, m$. If $|\beta_j| < 1$, for all j, the process is invertible. Clearly, $g_{xx}(z)$ is analytic in some annulus containing the unit circle but has poles, which may not be distinct, at $z = \alpha_k$ inside a circle within the unit circle and at $z = 1/\alpha_k$ outside a circle containing the unit circle. Moreover, if $m > n$, $g_{xx}(z)$ has a pole of multiplicity $m - n$ at zero. These facts permit use of the residue theorem in evaluating integrals around the unit circle of functions based on the generating function of the autocovariances.

Let $\gamma(\tau) = Ex_t x_{t-\tau}$. Then, suppressing the subscripts x for convenience,

$$g(z) = \sum_{\tau=-\infty}^{\infty} \gamma(\tau) z^{\tau}. \quad (2)$$

By the result in Appendix B (p. 375), the coefficients in a Laurent series expansion about the origin of a function analytic in an annulus containing the unit circle are

$$\gamma(\tau) = \frac{1}{2\pi i} \oint_{|z|=1} \frac{g(z)}{z^{\tau+1}} \, dz, \quad \tau = 0, \pm 1, \ldots. \quad (3)$$

Because $\{x_t\}$ is stationary, $\gamma(\tau) = \gamma(-\tau)$ so that substituting from (1) for $g(z)$,

$$\gamma(\tau) = \gamma(-\tau) = \frac{\sigma^2}{2\pi i} \oint_{|z|=1} z^{|\tau|-1} \left\{ \frac{\prod_{j=1}^{m}(1 - \beta_j z)(1 - \beta_j z^{-1})}{\prod_{k=1}^{n}(1 - \alpha_k z)(1 - \alpha_k z^{-1})} \right\} dz$$

$$= \frac{\sigma^2}{2\pi i} \oint_{|z|=1} z^{n+|\tau|-m-1} \left\{ \frac{\prod_{j=1}^{m}(1 - \beta_j z)(z - \beta_j)}{\prod_{k=1}^{n}(1 - \alpha_k z)(z - \alpha_k)} \right\} dz, \quad (4)$$

for $\tau = 0, \pm 1, \pm 2, \ldots$. Only when $n + |\tau| - m - 1 < 0$ does the expression inside the integral sign have poles at zero; thus, if $\{x_t\}$ is generated by a pure moving-average process, $n = 0$ and the integrand has poles of multiplicity $m + 1 - |\tau|$ at zero, $\tau = 0, \pm 1, \ldots, \pm m$. By the residue theorem, the integral on the right-hand side of (4) is $2\pi i$ times the sum of the residues enclosed by the unit circle, $|z| = 1$. What these are depends on whether there are poles at zero and whether the roots $1/\alpha_k$ of the generating function of the autoregressive coefficients are distinct. If the latter are not distinct, some of the poles not at zero inside the unit circle of the function appearing as the integrand in (4) will be of multiplicity greater than one.

Let α be a pole of order p, corresponding to a root of $H(\ )$ in (2.28) above of multiplicity p; then the residue at α is

$$\mathrm{res}(\alpha) = \lim_{z \to \alpha} \frac{1}{(p-1)!} \frac{d^{p-1}}{dz^{p-1}} \frac{z^{n+|\tau|-m-1} \prod_{j=1}^{m} (1 - \beta_j z)(z - \beta_j)(z - \alpha)^p}{\prod_{k=1}^{n} (1 - \alpha_k z)(z - \alpha_k)}.$$

In practical situations, however, it is unlikely that multiple roots will actually occur, although roots that are close to one another may be obtained. In the case of distinct roots, $\alpha_1, \ldots, \alpha_n$, the residue at α_q reduces to

$$\mathrm{res}(\alpha_q) = \frac{\alpha_q^{n+|\tau|-m-1} \prod_{j=1}^{m} (1 - \beta_j \alpha_q)(\alpha_q - \beta_j)}{\prod_{k=1}^{n} (1 - \alpha_k \alpha_q) \cdot \prod_{k=1, k \neq q}^{n} (\alpha_q - \alpha_k)}. \tag{5}$$

When $n + |\tau| - m - 1 < 0$ (as would be the case for a pure moving average $|\tau| < m + 1$), then, as noted, there are poles at zero of multiplicities $m + 1 - n - |\tau|$, $|\tau| < m + 1 - n$. The residues are

$$\mathrm{res}(0) = \lim_{z \to 0} \frac{1}{(m-n-|\tau|)!} \frac{d^{m-n-|\tau|}}{dz^{m-n-|\tau|}} \left\{ \frac{\prod_{j=1}^{m} (1 - \beta_j z)(z - \beta_j)}{\prod_{k=1}^{n} (1 - \alpha_k z)(z - \alpha_k)} \right\},$$

for $\tau = 0, \pm 1, \ldots, \pm(m + 1 - n)$. Unless $m - n$ is relatively small, this expression is difficult to evaluate. Hence, we show how to transform the problem so that $n \geq m + 1$. But $n \geq m + 1$ implies $n + |\tau| - m - 1 \geq 0$ for all τ so that the covariances for this series are given by

$$\gamma(\tau) = \sigma^2 \sum_{q=1}^{n} \mathrm{res}(\alpha_q) \qquad \text{for} \quad \tau = 0, \pm 1, \pm 2, \ldots, \tag{6}$$

where $\mathrm{res}(\alpha_q)$ is given by (5). The result holds as long as $n \geq m + 1$. Note that if we simply take $n \geq m$, we might have a pole at $z = 0$ for $\tau = 0$.

Let $\{y_t\}$ be a series such that $n + |\tau| - m - 1 \geq 0$; note that for $|\tau|$ sufficiently large this condition will automatically be satisfied for typical values of n and m so that the following procedure need be employed, in general, only for small values of $|\tau|$ when $n < m + 1$. The series $\{x_t\}$ whose autocovariances we wish to obtain may always be expressed as a moving average of a series $\{y_t\}$ satisfying the condition $n + |\tau| - m - 1 \geq 0$ if $\{x_t\}$ has a rational spectral density. Let p be the order of the moving average required. Then

$$x_t = \left\{ \prod_{j=1}^{p} (1 - \beta_j U) \right\} y_t, \qquad \text{where} \qquad y_t = \left\{ \frac{\prod_{j'=p+1}^{m} (1 - \beta_j U)}{\prod_{k=1}^{n} (1 - \alpha_k U)} \right\} \epsilon_t, \tag{7}$$

and

$$g_{xx}(z) = g_{yy}(z) \prod_{j=1}^{p} (1 - \beta_j z)(1 - \beta_j z^{-1}).$$ (8)

Let

$$b_0 = 1,$$

$$b_1 = -\sum_{j=1}^{p} \beta_j,$$

$$b_2 = \sum_{j<k} \beta_j \beta_k,$$

$$\vdots$$

$$b_p = (-1)^p \beta_1 \cdots \beta_p.$$

This converts the moving average in (7) from root form to coefficient form; thus

$$g_{xx}(z) = g_{yy}(z)[b_0 + b_1 z + \cdots + b_p z^p][b_0 + b_1 z^{-1} + \cdots + b_p z^{-p}]$$
$$= g_{yy}(z)[(b_0^2 + \cdots + b_p^2) + (b_1 b_0 + b_2 b_1 + \cdots + b_p b_{p-1})z$$
$$+ (b_0 b_1 + b_1 b_2 + \cdots + b_{p-1} b_p)z^{-1} + \cdots + (b_p b_0)z^p + (b_0 b_p)z^{-p}].$$ (9)

It follows that

$$\gamma_x(\tau) = \gamma_y(\tau)[b_0^2 + \cdots + b_p^2]$$
$$+ [\gamma_y(\tau+1) + \gamma_y(\tau-1)][b_0 b_1 + b_1 b_2 + \cdots + b_{p-1} b_p]$$
$$+ \cdots + [\gamma_y(\tau+p) + \gamma_y(\tau-p)][b_0 b_p].$$ (10)

For example, when $p = 1$, a first-order moving average converts the series $\{y_t\}$ into the series $\{x_t\}$. Equation (10) then yields

$$\gamma_x(\tau) = \gamma_y(\tau)[1 + \beta_1^2] + [\gamma_y(\tau+1) + \gamma_y(\tau-1)][-\beta_1].$$

When $\{y_t\}$ is white noise $\gamma_y(\tau) = \sigma^2$ for $\tau = 0$ and 0 otherwise; thus

$$\gamma_x(0) = \sigma^2[1 + \beta_1^2], \qquad \gamma_x(1) = -\beta_1 \sigma^2 = \gamma_x(-1), \qquad \gamma_x(\tau) = 0 \qquad \text{for} \quad |\tau| > 1,$$

which are the standard results.

To avoid the clumsy differentiation involved in computing the residues at zero, the result (10) may be used for all τ whenever $n < m + 1$ by removing $p = m - n + 1$ moving-average factors. Together Eqs. (6) and (10) enable us to calculate the variance and covariances of the series $\{x_t\}$ from the original or the canonical form of an unobserved-components model. Consider first the canonical form (2.28) above. From (6), assuming distinct roots of $H(z)$ and $n \geq m + 1$,

$$\sigma_x^2 = \sigma^2 \sum_{q=1}^{n} \left\{ \frac{\alpha_q^{n-m-1} \prod_{j=1}^{m} (1 - \beta_j \alpha_q)(\alpha_q - \beta_j)}{\prod_{k=1}^{n} (1 - \alpha_k \alpha_q) \prod_{k=1, k \neq q}^{n} (\alpha_q - \alpha_k)} \right\}.$$ (11)

Now consider the unobserved-components form of the model with auto-covariance generating function given by (2.27). It is simplest to consider this expression term by term: σ_u^2 has no moving-average or autoregressive part; the seasonal term will generally have a much higher-order autoregressive component than moving-average component; that is, the degree of $S(\ )$ will generally be much greater than the degree of $R(\ )$, so that (6) may be applied directly to obtain the variance of the seasonal component; the only difficulty that may arise is in connection with the trend-cycle component, in which case it is entirely possible that the degree of $P(\ )$ may exceed the degree of $Q(\ )$. In the event that the degree of the numerator exceeds that of the denominator less one, Eq. (10) must be used together with (6). For example, let the trend-cycle be a second-order autoregression with input equal to a second-order moving average of white noise $\{v_t\}$:

$$(1 - \alpha_1 U)(1 - \alpha_2 U)T_t = (1 - \beta_1 U)(1 - \beta_2 U)v_t.$$

Clearly, for $|\tau| \geq 1$, (6) may be used to calculate the result since $2 + |\tau| - 2 - 1 \geq 0$; thus

$$\gamma_{TT}(\tau) = \frac{\sigma_v^2 \alpha_1^{|\tau|-1}(1 - \beta_1\alpha_1)(\alpha_1 - \beta_1)(1 - \beta_2\alpha_1)(\alpha_1 - \beta_2)}{(1 - \alpha_1^2)(1 - \alpha_1\alpha_2)(\alpha_1 - \alpha_2)}$$

$$+ \frac{\sigma_v^2 \alpha_2^{|\tau|-1}(1 - \beta_1\alpha_2)(\alpha_2 - \beta_1)(1 - \beta_2\alpha_2)(\alpha_2 - \beta_2)}{(1 - \alpha_1\alpha_2)(1 - \alpha_2^2)(\alpha_2 - \alpha_1)},$$

for $|\tau| \geq 1$. But, for $\tau = 0$,

$$\sigma_{TT} = \sigma_{yy}[1 + \beta_1^2] + [\gamma_y(1) + \gamma_y(-1)][-\beta_1],$$

where

$$y_t = [(1 - \beta_2 U)/(1 - \alpha_1 U)(1 - \alpha_2 U)]v_t$$

so that

$$\sigma_{yy} = \sigma_v^2 \left\{ \frac{(1 - \alpha_1\beta_2)(\alpha_1 - \beta_2)}{(1 - \alpha_1^2)(1 - \alpha_1\alpha_2)(\alpha_1 - \alpha_2)} + \frac{(1 - \alpha_2\beta_2)(\alpha_2 - \beta_2)}{(1 - \alpha_1\alpha_2)(1 - \alpha_2^2)(\alpha_2 - \alpha_1)} \right\}$$

and

$$\gamma_y(1) = \gamma_y(-1) = \sigma_v^2 \left\{ \frac{\alpha_1(1 - \alpha_1\beta_2)(\alpha_1 - \beta_2)}{(1 - \alpha_1^2)(1 - \alpha_1\alpha_2)(\alpha_1 - \alpha_2)} + \frac{\alpha_2(1 - \alpha_2\beta_2)(\alpha_2 - \beta_2)}{(1 - \alpha_1\alpha_2)(1 - \alpha_2^2)(\alpha_2 - \alpha_1)} \right\}.$$

Assume we have calculated the variance of each component σ_{TT}, σ_{SS}, and σ_{II}; then given the variance of the observed series $\{x_t\}$, the variance of the innovations of the process in canonical form σ^2 is determined by the condition

$$\sigma^2 = \frac{\sigma_{TT} + \sigma_{SS} + \sigma_{II}}{(1/2\pi i)\oint_{|z|=1} [z^{-1}G(z)G(z^{-1})/H(z)H(z^{-1})]\,dz}, \tag{12}$$

where $H(U)x_t = G(U)\epsilon_t$ is the canonical form of (2.27). The expression in the denominator may be evaluated in the manner described above. For example, when P and Q are both of degree 2, R is of degree 2, and S is of degree 12, $G(z)G(z^{-1})$ will be of degree 28, in general, while $H(z)H(z^{-1})$ will be of degree 28 as well; thus, only one moving-average factor need be removed from $G(z)G(z^{-1})$ in order to evaluate the denominator without finding the residue at zero.

Of course, in estimating models, we shall seldom wish to evaluate σ^2 explicitly.[4] Rather, in maximum-likelihood estimation, we shall generally concentrate the likelihood function with respect to the variance of one component and estimate the variances of the remaining components as functions of it. See Chapter VII.

In concluding this section, it is useful to employ these results in the calculation of a number of special cases so that the concordance of the results obtained by these and more laborious methods may be observed. The cases considered are (a) a finite moving average, (b) a simple first-order autoregression, (c) second-order and higher-order autoregressions, and (d) a mixed moving-average autoregressive process in which both moving average and autoregression are first order.

(a) *A finite moving average.* As noted above, a finite moving average is a special case of (10), where $\{y_t\}$ is white noise. Thus, for the qth-order moving-average model for a zero-mean stationary series $\{x_t\}$,

$$x_t = \sum_{j=0}^{q} b_j \epsilon_{t-j}, \qquad b_0 = 1,$$

where $\{\epsilon_t\}$ is zero-mean white noise with variance σ^2, the autocorrelation function for this process is given very simply in terms of the b's:

$$\rho(\tau) = \begin{cases} \dfrac{b_\tau + b_1 b_{\tau+1} + \cdots + b_{q-\tau} b_q}{b_0^2 + b_1^2 + \cdots + b_q^2}, & \tau = 1, \ldots, q, \\ 0, & \tau > q. \end{cases} \tag{13}$$

Of course, $\rho(0) = 1$. An important point to note is that the autocorrelation function for the moving-average process has a *cutoff* at lag q, i.e., is zero after a certain point that depends on the order of the process. The existence of such a cutoff is suggested by Box and Jenkins (1970) as a means of identifying the order of a moving-average process.

(b) *A first-order autoregression.* Let

$$x_t - \rho x_{t-1} = \epsilon_t, \qquad \sigma^2 = 1.$$

---

[4] If we are considering alternative approaches to forecasting the series, the variance of the innovations will, of course, be of interest.

Then $\beta_j = 0, j = 1, \ldots, m$, and $\alpha_1 = \rho, n = 1$. Hence, applying (6)

$$\gamma(\tau) = \rho^{|\tau|}/(1 - \rho^2), \tag{14}$$

which is a standard result.

(c)   *Second-order and higher-order autoregressions.*   Let

$$(1 - \alpha_1 U)(1 - \alpha_2 U)x_t = x_t - (\alpha_1 + \alpha_2)x_{t-1} + \alpha_1\alpha_2 x_{t-2} = \epsilon_t, \qquad \sigma^2 = 1.$$

Then $\beta_j = 0, j = 1, \ldots, m$, and $n = 2$. We assume $\alpha_1 \neq \alpha_2$. Applying (6)

$$\begin{aligned}
\gamma(\tau) &= \frac{\alpha_1^{\tau+1}}{(1 - \alpha_1\alpha_2)(1 - \alpha_1^2)(\alpha_1 - \alpha_2)} + \frac{\alpha_2^{\tau+1}}{(1 - \alpha_1\alpha_2)(1 - \alpha_2^2)(\alpha_2 - \alpha_1)} \\
&= \frac{\alpha_1^{\tau+1}(1 - \alpha_2^2) - \alpha_2^{\tau+1}(1 - \alpha_1^2)}{(\alpha_1 - \alpha_2)(1 - \alpha_1\alpha_2)(1 - \alpha_1^2)(1 - \alpha_2^2)}, \qquad \tau \geq 0.
\end{aligned} \tag{15}$$

The result given by Jenkins and Watts (1968, pp. 166, 169) and Box and Jenkins (1970, p. 59) for the autocorrelation function for the second-order autoregressive process may be obtained from (15) by dividing by the variance $\gamma(0)$:

$$\frac{\gamma(\tau)}{\gamma(0)} = \frac{\alpha_1^{\tau+1}(1 - \alpha_2^2) - \alpha_2^{\tau+1}(1 - \alpha_1^2)}{(\alpha_1 - \alpha_2)(1 + \alpha_1\alpha_2)}, \qquad \tau \geq 0.$$

The general result for an autoregression of order n,

$$\prod_{k=1}^{n} (1 - \alpha_k U)x_t = \epsilon_t,$$

is

$$\gamma(\tau) = \sum_{q=1}^{n} \left\{ \frac{\alpha_q^{n+|\tau|-1}}{\prod_{k=1}^{n} (1 - \alpha_k\alpha_q) \cdot \prod_{k=1, k \neq q}^{n} (\alpha_q - \alpha_k)} \right\}. \tag{16}$$

(d)   *A mixed first-order moving-average first-order autoregressive process.*
The process is

$$(1 - \alpha U)x_t = (1 - \beta U)\epsilon_t$$

or

$$x_t = \alpha x_{t-1} + \epsilon_t - \beta\epsilon_{t-1},$$

where

$$\sigma^2 = E\epsilon_t^2 = 1.$$

In this case (6) yields

$$\gamma(\tau) = \frac{\alpha^{|\tau|}(1 - \alpha\beta)(1 - \beta/\alpha)}{1 - \alpha^2}, \qquad \tau = \pm 1, \pm 2, \ldots. \tag{17}$$

For $\tau = 1$, (17) yields

$$\gamma(1) = (\alpha - \beta)(1 - \alpha\beta)/(1 - \alpha^2),$$

and for $\tau \geq 2$,

$$\gamma(\tau) = \alpha \left\{ \frac{\alpha^{\tau-1}(1 - \alpha\beta)(1 - \beta/\alpha)}{1 - \alpha^2} \right\} = \alpha\gamma(\tau - 1),$$

which are the results obtained by Box and Jenkins (1970, p. 76) by a more laborious method. To obtain the variance, we must use both (6) and (10). By (10)

$$\sigma_{xx} = \sigma_{yy}[1 + \beta^2] - \beta[\gamma_y(1) + \gamma_y(-1)],$$

where

$$y_t = \epsilon_t/(1 - \alpha U),$$

so that

$$\sigma_{yy} = 1/(1 - \alpha^2) \qquad \text{and} \qquad \gamma_y(1) = \alpha/(1 - \alpha^2) = \gamma_y(-1).$$

Hence, $\sigma_{xx} = (1 + \beta^2 - 2\alpha\beta)/(1 - \alpha^2).$[5]

[5] The result of Box and Jenkins (1970, p. 76) corresponding to our parameterization is $\gamma(0) = (1 + \beta^2 - 2\alpha\beta)/(1 - \alpha^2)$ which is identical with ours.

Chapter V
ELEMENTS OF THE THEORY
OF PREDICTION AND EXTRACTION

1. Introduction

This chapter develops the elements of minimum-mean-square-error prediction and extraction when the true model generating a time series or several such series is known.[1] In the course of our development, we prove the important result that the white noise inputs in a moving average representation of a purely nondeterministic covariance stationary process are in fact the one-step prediction errors, on the assumption the true model is known. The problem of signal extraction, especially important in the use to which unobserved components models may be put, is also discussed. Appendix D provides a proof of an important theorem by Whittle (1963) used extensively in this chapter.

2. Prediction

In this section we develop the theory of least-squares forecasting for nondeterministic covariance stationary processes. A number of examples are given to illustrate the basic theory and to show convenient methods for calculating and updating the forecasts.

Let x_t be a process with a one-sided moving average representation

$$x_t = B(U)\epsilon_t = \sum_{j=0}^{\infty} b_j \epsilon_{t-j},$$

---

[1] Other expositions of this material are contained in Whittle (1963), Yaglom (1962), and Hannan (1960). The treatment given here is similar to that given by Whittle (1963).

where $b_0 \equiv 1$ and $\{\epsilon_t\}$ is a white noise sequence with variance σ^2. The least-squares forecast of x_{t+v} computed at time t is given by

$$\hat{x}_{t+v,t} = \varphi(U)\epsilon_t = \sum_{j=0}^{\infty} \varphi_j \epsilon_{t-j},$$

where the φ_j's are chosen in order to minimize

$$\sigma_v^2 = E\{(x_{t+v} - \hat{x}_{t+v,t})^2\}.$$

Now

$$\sigma_v^2 = E\left\{\left(\sum_{j=0}^{\infty} b_j \epsilon_{t+v-j} - \sum_{j=0}^{\infty} \varphi_j \epsilon_{t-j}\right)^2\right\}$$

$$= E\left\{\left(\sum_{j=0}^{v-1} b_j \epsilon_{t+v-j} + \sum_{j=0}^{\infty} (b_{j+v} - \varphi_j)\epsilon_{t-j}\right)^2\right\}$$

$$= \sigma^2 \sum_{j=0}^{v-1} b_j^2 + \sigma^2 \sum_{j=0}^{\infty} (b_{j+v} - \varphi_j)^2.$$

This expectation is minimized by taking

$$\varphi_j = b_{j+v}, \tag{1}$$

which yields a mean-square forecast error equal to[2]

$$\sigma_v^2 = \sigma^2 \sum_{j=0}^{v-1} b_j^2. \tag{2}$$

The forecasting rule (1) may be simply expressed in terms of generating functions, namely,

$$\hat{x}_{t+v,t} = \varphi(U)\epsilon_t,$$

$$\varphi(z) = \sum_{j=0}^{\infty} \varphi_j z^j = \left[\frac{B(z)}{z^v}\right]_+, \tag{3}$$

where $B(z) = \sum_{j=0}^{\infty} b_j z^j$. The operator $[\ ]_+$ is defined, for a sum containing both positive and negative powers of z, as the sum containing only nonnegative powers of z, namely,

$$[H(z)]_+ = [\cdots + h_{-1}z^{-1} + h_0 z^0 + h_1 z^1 + h_2 z^2 + \cdots]_+ \equiv h_0 z^0 + h_1 z^1 + \cdots.$$

Similarly, we define

$$[H(z)]_- \equiv \cdots + h_{-2}z^{-2} + h_{-1}z^{-1},$$

---

[2] In deriving the forecasting rule (1) only linear forecasts were considered; thus the predictions are minimum-mean-square error in the class of linear forecasting rules. If the random variables $\{\epsilon_t\}$ are jointly normal, then the restriction to linear rules is not binding and the forecasts are minimum-mean-square-error forecasts. In all of the following, we shall simply refer to the forecasts as least-squares forecasts.

as the sum of all terms containing *negative* powers of z (omitting the zero power term).

To understand the nature of the forecasting rule consider first the case in which the process being forecast is itself white noise; that is, $B(z) = 1$. Since $[B(z)/z^v]_+$ vanishes for all positive v, we have

$$\hat{\epsilon}_{t+v,t} = 0, \qquad v > 0.$$

In this case, the variable being forecast is uncorrelated with all the observed values of the sequence. In other words, the current and past values of the sequence provide no information about future levels of the series (at least as far as second moments are concerned). In this case, the forecasting rule simply takes the overall mean of the series as the forecast value. Even when the time series under consideration has a more complicated structure than pure noise, the least-squares forecasts simply amount to multiple applications of this quite sensible rule. For if

$$x_{t+v} = \epsilon_{t+v} + b_1\epsilon_{t+v-1} + \cdots + b_{v-1}\epsilon_{t+1} + b_v\epsilon_t + b_{v+1}\epsilon_{t-1} + \cdots,$$

the rule (1) says to take

$$\hat{x}_{t+v,t} = b_v\epsilon_t + b_{v+1}\epsilon_{t-1} + \cdots.$$

Thus, the forecast is obtained by setting each of the future ϵ's equal to their least-squares forecast value, which is zero. Note that the v-step forecast error is a moving-average process of order $v - 1$; as the forecast period increases, the forecast error process approaches the process being forecast. It may also be shown that σ_v^2 approaches the variance of x as v approaches infinity. This follows immediately from Eq. (2).

The actual forecast error is

$$x_{t+v} - \hat{x}_{t+v,t} = \epsilon_{t+v} + b_1\epsilon_{t+v-1} + \cdots + b_{v-1}\epsilon_{t+1},$$

which, for one-step predictions, gives

$$x_{t+1} - \hat{x}_{t+1,t} = \epsilon_{t+1}. \qquad (4)$$

From Eq. (4) we see that the sequence $\{\epsilon_t\}$ is simply the sequence of one-step prediction errors so that all least-squares forecasts are in a sense adaptive forecasts, i.e., are averages of past forecasting errors. The elements of the sequence $\{\epsilon_t\}$ are often called the "innovations" in the process or the sequence itself called the "innovation sequence." This seems to be reasonable terminology since each ϵ_t contains the new information in the observation x_t (the rest being predicted from past observations). As one moves through time, forecasts for a fixed future period are revised only as new information becomes available, in each period the change being proportional to the most recent innovation[3]:

$$\hat{x}_{t+v,t} - \hat{x}_{t+v,t-1} = b_v\epsilon_t = b_v(x_t - \hat{x}_{t,t-1}). \qquad (5)$$

---

[3] Equations similar to (5) have been used frequently in the literature on the term structure of interest rates. See Meiselman (1962) and Kessel (1965).

Often it may be more convenient to express the forecasts in terms of observed values of the x series itself, rather than in terms of past forecast errors. This can be done whenever the process being forecast has an autoregressive representation; that is, if $A(U)x_t = \epsilon_t$, where $A(z) = 1/B(z)$, is analytic in a circle with radius greater than unity so that the representation is what we have called "invertible." In this case the forecast may be expressed as

$$\hat{x}_{t+v, t} = \varphi(U)\epsilon_t = \varphi(U)A(U)x_t = \frac{\varphi(U)}{B(U)} x_t = \gamma(U)x_t,$$

where[4]

$$\gamma(z) = \sum_{j=0}^{\infty} \gamma_j z^j = \frac{1}{B(z)} \left[\frac{B(z)}{z^v} \right]_+. \tag{6}$$

A number of examples may be used to illustrate these results.

3. Examples of the Application of Minimum-Mean-Square-Error Forecasts

Example A

$$x_t = \rho x_{t-1} + \epsilon_t, \qquad |\rho| < 1. \tag{1}$$

This is the case of a first-order autoregressive process with $B(z) = 1/(1 - \rho z)$. Clearly,

$$\left[\frac{B(z)}{z^v} \right]_+ = \left[\frac{1}{(1 - \rho z)z^v} \right]_+ = \frac{\rho^v}{1 - \rho z}, \tag{2}$$

so the forecast is given by

$$\hat{x}_{t+v, t} = \rho^v \sum_{j=0}^{\infty} \rho^j \epsilon_{t-j} = \rho^v x_t. \tag{3}$$

Clearly, $\hat{x}_{t+v, t} \to 0$ as $v \to \infty$ and thus $\sigma_v^2 \to \sigma_x^2$, as already remarked in general.

Example B

$$x_t = (\alpha + \beta)x_{t-1} - \alpha\beta x_{t-2} + \epsilon_t, \qquad |\alpha| < 1, \ |\beta| < 1. \tag{4}$$

This example is a second-order autoregression with $B(z)$ equal to

$$1/(1 - \alpha z)(1 - \beta z).$$

To calculate the v-step predictor, we must find $[1/(1 - \alpha z)(1 - \beta z)z^v]_+$. Expanding $B(z)$ by partial fractions gives

$$B(z) = \frac{1}{\alpha - \beta} \left(\frac{\alpha}{1 - \alpha z} - \frac{\beta}{1 - \beta z} \right).$$

[4] The result in (6) may be obtained directly by minimizing $\sigma_v^2 = E\{(x_{t+v} - \gamma(U)x_t)^2\}$ with respect to the γ_j's.

For $|b| < 1$, in general,

$$\left[\frac{az^{-v}}{1-bz}\right]_{+} = [az^{-v} + abz^{-v+1} + \cdots + ab^{v} + ab^{v+1}z + \cdots]_{+}$$

$$= ab^{v} + ab^{v+1}z + ab^{v+2}z^2 + \cdots = \frac{ab^{v}}{1-bz}. \tag{5}$$

Thus, the result for the second-order autoregression is

$$\left[\frac{B(z)}{z^v}\right]_{+} = \frac{1}{\alpha - \beta}\left(\frac{\alpha^{v+1}}{1-\alpha z} - \frac{\beta^{v+1}}{1-\beta z}\right), \tag{6}$$

which for $v = 1$ simplifies to

$$\left[\frac{B(z)}{z}\right]_{+} = \frac{\alpha + \beta - \alpha\beta z}{(1-\alpha z)(1-\beta z)}. \tag{7}$$

Using (2.6), the forecast is

$$\hat{x}_{t+1,t} = \gamma(U)x_t, \tag{8}$$

where

$$\gamma(z) = (\alpha + \beta) - \alpha\beta z,$$

or

$$\hat{x}_{t+1,t} = (\alpha + \beta)x_t - \alpha\beta x_{t-1}. \tag{9}$$

For $v = 2$, we have

$$\left[\frac{B(z)}{z^2}\right]_{+} = \frac{1}{\alpha - \beta}\left(\frac{\alpha^3}{1-\alpha z} - \frac{\beta^3}{1-\beta z}\right) = \frac{\alpha^2 + \alpha\beta + \beta^2 - \alpha\beta(\alpha + \beta)z}{(1-\alpha z)(1-\beta z)}. \tag{10}$$

Since $\gamma(z)$ is simply the numerator of the above expression, we have

$$\begin{aligned} \hat{x}_{t+2,t} &= (\alpha^2 + \alpha\beta + \beta^2)x_t - \alpha\beta(\alpha + \beta)x_{t-1} \\ &= ((\alpha + \beta)^2 - \alpha\beta)x_t - \alpha\beta(\alpha + \beta)x_{t-1} \\ &= (\alpha + \beta)((\alpha + \beta)x_t - \alpha\beta x_{t-1}) - \alpha\beta x_t \\ &= (\alpha + \beta)\hat{x}_{t+1,t} - \alpha\beta x_t. \end{aligned} \tag{11}$$

Thus, once the one-step forecast is known, the two-step forecast can be easily calculated.

At time $t + 2$ we know that

$$x_{t+2} = (\alpha + \beta)x_{t+1} - \alpha\beta x_t + \epsilon_{t+2}. \tag{12}$$

From (11) we see that computing the forecast value of x_{t+2} simply involves replacing the unknown quantities in the preceding equation $(x_{t+1}, \epsilon_{t+2})$ by their least-squares forecasts $(\hat{x}_{t+1,t}, 0)$. Similarly, we can view (9) as coming from

$$x_{t+1} = (\alpha + \beta)x_t - \alpha\beta x_{t-1} + \epsilon_{t+1}, \tag{13}$$

with ϵ_{t+1} replaced by its least-squares forecast. These procedures may be followed for any finite autoregressive process and for arbitrary prediction v. That is, if

$$A(U)x_t = \sum_{j=0}^{p} a_j x_{t-j} = \epsilon_t, \tag{14}$$

with all the zeros of $A(z)$ outside the unit circle, then

$$\hat{x}_{t+v,t} + a_1\hat{x}_{t+v-1,t} + \cdots + a_p\hat{x}_{t+v-p,t} = 0, \tag{15}$$

where we have adopted the convention

$$\hat{x}_{s,t} = x_s \qquad \text{if} \quad s \le t. \tag{16}$$

To establish (15) we must show that

$$\sum_{j=0}^{p} a_j \varphi_{v-j}(z) = 0, \tag{17}$$

where $\varphi_k(z) = [1/A(z)z^k]_+$ and k may be either positive or negative. But this is immediate since

$$\sum_{j=0}^{p} a_j \varphi_{v-j}(z) = \sum_{j=0}^{p} a_j \left[\frac{1}{A(z)z^{v-j}} \right]_+ = \sum_{j=0}^{p} a_j \left[\frac{z^j}{A(z)z^v} \right]_+$$

$$= \sum_{j=0}^{p} \left[\frac{a_j z^j}{A(z)z^v} \right]_+ = \left[\frac{A(z)}{A(z)z^v} \right]_+ = 0, \qquad v > 0. \tag{18}$$

In summary, for finite autoregressive processes there is a simple recursive procedure for calculating forecasts for any period in the future. In addition to the coefficients of the autoregression, the only data that are required to forecast a pth-order autoregression are the p most recently observed values of the time series.

Example C

$$x_t = \epsilon_t - \alpha\epsilon_{t-1}, \qquad B(z) = 1 - \alpha z. \tag{19}$$

For this process

$$\left[\frac{B(z)}{z^v} \right]_+ = \begin{cases} -\alpha, & v = 1, \\ 0, & v > 1, \end{cases} \tag{20}$$

so

$$\hat{x}_{t+1,t} = -\alpha\epsilon_t$$
$$= -\alpha(x_t - \hat{x}_{t,t-1}), \tag{21}$$

and

$$\hat{x}_{t+v,\,t} = 0, \qquad v > 1. \tag{22}$$

In this example, unless α is less than one in absolute value, the process does not have an autoregressive representation and the forecasts cannot be expressed in terms of observed values of the series. When $|\alpha|$ is less than one,

$$\gamma(z) = \frac{1}{1 - \alpha z}\left[\frac{1 - \alpha z}{z^v}\right]_+, \tag{23}$$

so

$$\hat{x}_{t+v,\,t} = \begin{cases} -\alpha \displaystyle\sum_{j=0}^{\infty} \alpha^j x_{t-j}, & v = 1, \\[2mm] 0, & v > 1. \end{cases} \tag{24}$$

It should be pointed out that for moving-average processes in general, the forecasts cannot be expressed in terms of a finite number of observed values of the process. They may, of course, be given in terms of a finite number of innovations.

Example D.   Now consider the case of a mixed autoregressive moving-average process:

$$x_t - \alpha x_{t-1} = \epsilon_t - \beta \epsilon_{t-1}, \qquad |\alpha| < 1. \tag{25}$$

Here $B(z) = (1 - \beta z)/(1 - \alpha z)$ and in order for the process to possess an autoregressive representation we would have to require that $|\beta|$ also be less than one. Now

$$\left[\frac{B(z)}{z^v}\right]_+ = \left[\frac{1 - \beta z}{(1 - \alpha z)z^v}\right]_+ = \left[\frac{1}{(1 - \alpha z)z^v}\right]_+ - \left[\frac{\beta}{(1 - \alpha z)z^{v-1}}\right]_+$$

$$= \frac{\alpha^v}{1 - \alpha z} - \frac{\beta \alpha^{v-1}}{1 - \alpha z} = \frac{\alpha^{v-1}(\alpha - \beta)}{1 - \alpha z}. \tag{26}$$

Thus, to obtain the forecasts in autoregressive form we use

$$\gamma(z) = \frac{1}{B(z)}\left[\frac{B(z)}{z^v}\right]_+ = \frac{1 - \alpha z}{1 - \beta z}\frac{\alpha^{v-1}(\alpha - \beta)}{1 - \alpha z} = \frac{\alpha^{v-1}(\alpha - \beta)}{1 - \beta z}; \tag{27}$$

so

$$\hat{x}_{t+v,\,t} = \alpha^{v-1}(\alpha - \beta)\sum_{j=0}^{\infty}\beta^j x_{t-j} = \frac{\alpha^{v-1}(\alpha - \beta)}{1 - \beta U}x_t. \tag{28}$$

As α tends to one from below, the model becomes

$$\Delta x_t = \epsilon_t - \beta \epsilon_{t-1}, \tag{29}$$

and

$$\hat{x}_{t+v,t} = (1 - \beta) \sum_{j=0}^{\infty} \beta^j x_{t-j}. \tag{30}$$

Note that the forecasts are the same for all future periods. For one-period forecasts we have

$$\hat{x}_{t+1,t} - \beta\hat{x}_{t,t-1} = (1 - \beta)\left(\sum_{j=0}^{\infty} \beta^j x_{t-j} - \sum_{j=1}^{\infty} \beta^j x_{t-j} \right) = (1 - \beta)x_t \tag{31}$$

so that

$$\hat{x}_{t+1,t} = \beta\hat{x}_{t,t-1} + (1 - \beta)x_t, \tag{32}$$

which is the familiar adaptive-expectations formula.

Let

$$w_t = (1 - \alpha U)x_t = \epsilon_t - \beta\epsilon_{t-1}; \tag{33}$$

from Example C we know that

$$\hat{w}_{t+1,t} = -\beta\epsilon_t, \qquad \hat{w}_{t+v,t} = 0, \qquad v > 1. \tag{34}$$

It follows from (28) that

$$\hat{x}_{t+1,t} - \alpha x_t = \frac{(\alpha - \beta)}{1 - \beta U} x_t - \alpha x_t = \frac{(\alpha - \beta)x_t - \alpha(1 - \beta U)x_t}{1 - \beta U}$$

$$= -\frac{\beta(1 - \alpha U)x_t}{1 - \beta U} = -\beta\epsilon_t = \hat{w}_{t+1,t}. \tag{35}$$

For v greater than one

$$\hat{x}_{t+v,t} = \alpha\hat{x}_{t+v-1,t}, \tag{36}$$

so we have that, in general,

$$\hat{x}_{t+v,t} - \alpha\hat{x}_{t+v-1,t} = \hat{w}_{t+v,t}, \qquad v \geq 0, \tag{37}$$

where, as before, we take $\hat{x}_{t,t}$ equal to x_t. Thus, for this autoregressive moving-average process there is a relatively simple way of computing forecasts for any period in the future. Though the forecasts in (28) depend upon all the past values of x_t, we see that in fact the forecasts can be calculated using only the most recently observed value of the x series and the current one-step prediction error.

As was the case for autoregressive processes, the above procedure generalizes to mixed autoregressive moving-average processes of any order and to arbitrary prediction periods.

If

$$x_t = (N(U)/D(U))\epsilon_t, \tag{38}$$

where

$$N(z) = \sum_{j=0}^{n} n_j z^j,$$ (39)

$$D(z) = \sum_{j=0}^{d} d_j z^j,$$ (40)

and all the roots of $D(\ )$ lie outside the unit circle,

$$\hat{x}_{t+v,t} - d_1 \hat{x}_{t+v-1,t} - \cdots - d_d \hat{x}_{t+v-d,t} = \hat{w}_{t+v,t},$$ (41)

where

$$w_t = D(U)x_t = N(U)\epsilon_t.$$ (42)

The calculation of forecasts using (41) has been called "unscrambling" (Nerlove and Wage, 1964) and provides a general scheme for computing least-squares forecasts with relatively modest data storage. As before the forecasts are computed starting with $v = 1$.

From the definition of w_t the generating function for the weights in computing $\hat{w}_{t+v,t}$ is $[N(z)/z^v]_+$. Therefore to prove (41) we need to show that

$$\sum_{j=0}^{d} d_j \varphi_{v-j}(z) = \left[\frac{N(z)}{z^v}\right]_+,$$ (43)

where

$$\varphi_k(z) = \left[\frac{N(z)}{D(z)z^k}\right]_+$$ (44)

and k may be either positive or negative. The proof is almost exactly the same as that given for the autoregressive case and will not be repeated.

Once a v-step predictor has been calculated it is also a simple matter to update the forecasts, i.e., to calculate v-step predictors at later points in time. For instance, from Eq. (28) we have

$$\hat{x}_{t+v+1,t+1} = \alpha^{v-1}(\alpha - \beta) \sum_{j=0}^{\infty} \beta^j x_{t+1-j}$$

$$\beta \hat{x}_{t+v,t} = \alpha^{v-1}(\alpha - \beta) \sum_{j=0}^{\infty} \beta^{j+1} x_{t-j}.$$ (45)

Subtracting the second expression from the first gives

$$\hat{x}_{t+v+1,t+1} - \beta \hat{x}_{t+v,t} = \alpha^{v-1}(\alpha - \beta)x_{t+1}.$$ (46)

In the general case, updating forecasts can be done similarly. If

$$x_t = (N(U)/D(U))\epsilon_t,$$

then

$$\hat{x}_{t+v,t} + n_1\hat{x}_{t+v-1,t-1} + \cdots + n_n\hat{x}_{t+v-n,t-n} = \sum_{j=0}^{\infty} h_j x_{t-j}, \tag{47}$$

where

$$H(z) = D(z)[N(z)/D(z)z^v]_+ \tag{48}$$

is the numerator of $\gamma(z)$.[5]

In all the examples treated above it is relatively easy in each case to work out the forecasting equations directly. Our experience has been that for more complicated models or for more complex problems, such as the signal-extraction problems discussed in Section 4, it is often easier to proceed differently. The procedure that we have adopted and that is based upon the following theorem due to Whittle (1963, p. 93) has proved especially useful for numerical calculations of predictions and signal extractions. An alternative proof of this theorem is provided in Appendix D.

Whittle's Theorem.   Let $Q(z)$ be a function of z analytic in $\rho < |z| < \rho^{-1}$, and let θ be a number such that $|\theta| < 1$. Then

$$R(z) = (1 - \theta z)^p \left[\frac{Q(z)}{(1 - \theta z)^p} \right]_+ = \Pi_p(z) + [Q(z)]_+,$$

where $\Pi_p(z)$ is a polynomial in z of degree $p - 1$ so chosen that the differential coefficients of order $0, 1, 2, \ldots, p - 1$ of $R(z)$ are, respectively, equal to those of $Q(z)$ at $z = \theta^{-1}$.

$$\Pi_p(z) = \sum_{j=0}^{p-1} \frac{Q^{(j)}(\theta^{-1})}{j!} (z - \theta^{-1})^j$$

where $Q^{(j)}(\theta^{-1})$ is the jth derivative of $[Q(z)]_-$ evaluated at $z = \theta^{-1}$.

To illustrate the use of this theorem we consider one final example.

Example E

$$x_t = \frac{(1 - \alpha U)(1 - \beta U)}{(1 - \delta U)(1 - \lambda U)} \epsilon_t, \tag{49}$$

where

$$|\alpha| < 1, \quad |\beta| < 1, \quad |\delta| < 1, \quad |\lambda| < 1.$$

The generating function for the v-step predictor is given by

$$\gamma(z) = \frac{(1 - \delta z)(1 - \lambda z)}{(1 - \alpha z)(1 - \beta z)} \left[\frac{(1 - \alpha z)(1 - \beta z)}{(1 - \delta z)(1 - \lambda z)z^v} \right]_+. \tag{50}$$

---

[5] This result is given in Whittle (1963, exercise 3.3.12).

The first step in obtaining the predictor is to calculate the value of the expression under the $[\ ]_+$ operator. Expanding by partial fractions gives

$$\left[\frac{(1-\alpha z)(1-\beta z)}{(1-\delta z)(1-\lambda z)z^\nu}\right]_+ = \frac{\delta}{\delta-\lambda}\left[\frac{(1-\alpha z)(1-\beta z)z^{-\nu}}{1-\delta z}\right]_+$$
$$-\frac{\lambda}{\delta-\lambda}\left[\frac{(1-\alpha z)(1-\beta z)z^{-\nu}}{1-\lambda z}\right]_+. \tag{51}$$

Now,

$$\left[(1-\alpha z)(1-\beta z)z^{-\nu}\right]_+ = \begin{cases} -(\alpha+\beta)+\alpha\beta z, & \nu=1, \\ \alpha\beta, & \nu=2, \\ 0, & \nu>2. \end{cases} \tag{52}$$

Thus, from Whittle's theorem,

$$\left[\frac{(1-\alpha z)(1-\beta z)z^{-\nu}}{1-\pi z}\right]_+ = \begin{cases} \dfrac{-(\alpha+\beta)+\alpha\beta z}{1-\pi z}+\dfrac{\pi}{1-\pi z}, & \nu=1, \\[2mm] \dfrac{\alpha\beta}{1-\pi z}+\dfrac{\pi^2-(\alpha+\beta)\pi}{1-\pi z}, & \nu=2, \\[2mm] \dfrac{(\pi^2-(\alpha+\beta)\pi+\alpha\beta)\pi^{\nu-2}}{1-\pi z}, & \nu>2, \end{cases} \tag{53}$$

where π stands for either θ or λ and $|\pi|<1$. Here $(1-\alpha z)(1-\beta z)z^{-\nu}$ plays the role of $Q(z)$ in the statement of the theorem. Combining terms gives

$$\left[\frac{(1-\alpha z)(1-\beta z)z^{-\nu}}{(1-\delta z)(1-\lambda z)}\right]_+ = \begin{cases} \dfrac{(\delta+\lambda)-(\alpha+\beta)+(\alpha\beta-\lambda\delta)z}{(1-\delta z)(1-\lambda z)}, & \nu=1, \\[4mm] \dfrac{\left(\begin{array}{c}(\lambda+\delta)(\lambda+\delta-(\alpha+\beta))+(\alpha\beta-\lambda\delta)\\ -\lambda\delta(\lambda+\delta-(\alpha+\beta))z\end{array}\right)}{(1-\delta z)(1-\lambda z)}, & \nu=2, \\[4mm] \dfrac{\left(\begin{array}{c}C-(\alpha+\beta)C_{\nu-1}+\alpha\beta C_{\nu-2}\\ -\lambda\delta(C_{\nu-1}-(\alpha+\beta)C_{\nu-2}+\alpha\beta C_{\nu-3})z\end{array}\right)}{(1-\delta z)(1-\lambda z)}, & \nu>2, \end{cases} \tag{54}$$

where the sequence $\{C_j\}$ is defined by

$$\sum C_j z^j = \sum_{j=0}^{\infty}\delta^j z^j \sum_{k=0}^{\infty}\lambda^k z^k.$$

4. Signal Extraction

In this section we discuss the following problem:

$$\underset{\gamma}{\text{minimize}}\, E\left\{\left(y_t - \sum_{j=0}^{\infty} \gamma_j x_{t-j}\right)^2\right\}, \tag{1}$$

where (y_t, x_t) are jointly covariance stationary nondeterministic processes. If y_t is equal to x_{t+v}, then the problem is prediction, which was discussed in the previous section. In the case of signal extraction, x_t is the sum of several covariance stationary nondeterministic processes, one of which is y_t. For example, we observe $x_t = y_t + \eta_t$ and wish to estimate y_t based upon observations on x up to time t. Then the problem would be minimize $E\{(\hat{y}_t - y_t)^2\}$, where $\hat{y}_t = \sum_{j=0}^{\infty} \gamma_j x_{t-j}$.

The solution can be obtained by an argument similar to that used in Section 2. Let

$$\hat{y}_t = \varphi(U)\epsilon_t = \sum_{j=0}^{\infty} \varphi_j \epsilon_{t-j}, \tag{2}$$

where $x_t = B(U)\epsilon_t$, $E(\epsilon_t^2) = \sigma^2$. Then

$$E\{(y_t - \hat{y}_t)^2\} = E\left\{\left(y_t - \sum_{j=0}^{\infty} \varphi_j \epsilon_{t-j}\right)^2\right\}$$

$$= \sigma_y^2 + \sigma^2 \sum_{j=0}^{\infty} \varphi_j^2 - 2 \sum_{j=0}^{\infty} \varphi_j \,\text{cov}(y_t, \epsilon_{t-j})$$

$$= \sigma_y^2 - (1/\sigma^2) \sum_{j=0}^{\infty} \text{cov}(y_t, \epsilon_{t-j})^2 + \sum_{j=0}^{\infty}\left(\sigma \varphi_j - \frac{\text{cov}(y_t, \epsilon_{t-j})}{\sigma}\right)^2 \tag{3}$$

so we must choose

$$\varphi_j = \text{cov}(y_t, \epsilon_{t-j})/\sigma^2, \tag{4}$$

or

$$\varphi(z) = (1/\sigma^2)[g_{y\epsilon}(z)]_+. \tag{5}$$

Since $x_t = B(U)\epsilon_t$, it follows that

$$g_{yx}(z) = B(z^{-1})g_{y\epsilon}(z) \tag{6}$$

so

$$\varphi(z) = (1/\sigma^2)[g_{yx}(z)/B(z^{-1})]_+$$

and[6]

$$\gamma(z) = [1/\sigma^2 B(z)][g_{yx}(z)/B(z^{-1})]_+. \tag{7}$$

[6] See footnote 4.

If the problem is one of prediction, i.e., $y_t = x_{t+v}$, then

$$g_{yx}(z) = z^{-v}g_{xx}(z) = \sigma^2 z^{-v}B(z)B(z^{-1}) \tag{8}$$

and (7) reduces to

$$\gamma(z) = [1/B(z)][B(z)/z^v]_+, \tag{9}$$

which agrees with the forecasting rule in the preceding section. Consider now the problem of signal extraction in which

$$x_t = y_t + \eta_t, \qquad E(y_t\eta_{t-j}) = 0, \qquad j = 0, \pm 1, \pm 2, \ldots . \tag{10}$$

In this case

$$g_{xx}(z) = g_{yy}(z) + g_{\eta\eta}(z), \qquad g_{yx}(z) = g_{yy}(z) = g_{xy}(z). \tag{11}$$

Suppose we wish to estimate y_{t+v} using data on x up to time t. Then from (7) and (11) we get

$$\hat{y}_{t+v,t} = \gamma(U)x_t, \qquad \gamma(z) = [1/\sigma^2 B(z)][g_{yy}(z)/B(z^{-1})z^v]_+. \tag{12}$$

Note that in this problem v may be any integer—positive, negative, or zero.

5.   Examples of Minimum-Mean-Square-Error Signal Extraction

Example A

$$x_t = y_t + u_t, \qquad y_t = \alpha y_{t-1} + v_t, \tag{1}$$

where $\{u_t\}$ and $\{v_t\}$ are mutually uncorrelated white noise sequences with

$$E(v_t^2)/E(u_t^2) = \sigma_v^2/\sigma_u^2 = \mu.$$

Now $g_{yx}(z) = g_{yy}(z) = \sigma_v^2/[(1 - \alpha z)(1 - \alpha z^{-1})]$ so we first need to determine $g_{xx}(z)$ and its canonical factorization. It follows from (1) that

$$w_t = x_t - \alpha x_{t-1} = y_t - \alpha y_{t-1} + u_t - \alpha u_{t-1} = v_t + u_t - \alpha u_{t-1} \tag{2}$$

and

$$\begin{aligned} E(w_t^2) &= \sigma_v^2 + \sigma_u^2(1 + \alpha^2) = \sigma_u^2[\mu + (1 + \alpha^2)], \\ E(w_t w_{t-1}) &= -\alpha\sigma_u^2, \\ E(w_t w_{t-j}) &= 0, \qquad j \geq 2. \end{aligned} \tag{3}$$

Thus, considering second moments, w_t behaves like a first-order moving-average process

$$w_t = \epsilon_t - \beta\epsilon_{t-1},$$

where

$$E(\epsilon_t \epsilon_s) = \begin{cases} \sigma^2, & t = s, \\ 0, & t \neq s, \end{cases}$$

$$E(w_t^2) = \sigma^2(1 + \beta^2), \, .$$

$$E(w_t w_{t-1}) = -\beta\sigma^2, \tag{4}$$

$$E(w_t w_{t-j}) = 0, \quad j \geq 2.$$

Solving equations (3) and (4) for β and σ^2 yields[7]

$$\beta = \frac{(1 + \mu + \alpha^2) - \sqrt{(1 + \mu + \alpha^2)^2 - 4\alpha^2}}{2\alpha}, \qquad \sigma^2 = \frac{\alpha}{\beta}\sigma_u^2. \tag{5}$$

It follows that

$$g_{xx}(z) = \sigma^2 \frac{(1 - \beta z)(1 - \beta z^{-1})}{(1 - \alpha z)(1 - \alpha z^{-1})}. \tag{6}$$

In order to estimate y_t using current and past data on x, we must evaluate

$$\gamma(z) = \frac{1}{\sigma^2 B(z)} \left[\frac{g_{yx}(z)}{B(z^{-1})} \right]_+ = \frac{\beta\mu(1 - \alpha z)}{\alpha(1 - \beta z)} \left[\frac{1}{(1 - \alpha z)(1 - \beta z^{-1})} \right]_+. \tag{7}$$

It follows immediately from Whittle's theorem that

$$(1 - \alpha z) \left[\frac{1/(1 - \beta z^{-1})}{1 - \alpha z} \right]_+ = 1 + \frac{\beta\alpha}{1 - \alpha\beta} = \frac{1}{1 - \alpha\beta}; \tag{8}$$

thus[8]

$$\gamma(z) = \frac{\beta\mu}{\alpha(1 - \alpha\beta)} \frac{1}{1 - \beta z} = \frac{\alpha - \beta}{\alpha} \frac{1}{1 - \beta z}. \tag{9}$$

The estimate of y_t is given by

$$\hat{y}_{t,t} = \frac{\alpha - \beta}{\alpha} \sum_{j=0}^{\infty} \beta^j x_{t-j}, \tag{10}$$

and satisfies

$$\hat{y}_{t,t} - \beta\hat{y}_{t-1,t-1} = \frac{\alpha - \beta}{\alpha} x_t. \tag{11}$$

For values of μ near zero, β is approximately equal to α so that in updating the estimates almost no weight is given to the most recent observation. On the other hand, large values of μ are associated with values of β near zero, in which case the estimates of y_t are very nearly equal to the most recently observed

[7] β is a root of $\mu + (1 - \alpha z)(1 - \alpha z^{-1})$ and we have chosen the smallest root in absolute value of this equation.
[8] In simplifying the expression we have used the fact that $\mu + (1 - \alpha\beta)(1 - \alpha/\beta) = 0$.

value of the x series. This type of behavior of the estimates is quite reasonable since when μ is small most of the period-to-period variation in the observed series is, on average, due to the variation in the noise or "transitory" component, and vice versa for large values of μ.

Example B.   Suppose one wishes to predict

$$y_t = \frac{\epsilon_t}{(1 - \theta U)(1 - \rho U)}, \tag{12}$$

where y_t is observed with an error; i.e., one observes

$$x_t = y_t + \eta_t = \frac{\epsilon_t}{(1 - \theta U)(1 - \rho U)} + \eta_t, \tag{13}$$

where $\{\epsilon_t\}$, $\{\eta_t\}$ are white noise inputs uncorrelated with each other and where $E(\epsilon_t^2) = \sigma^2$, $E(\eta_t^2) = \mu\sigma^2$. Then

$$x_t = \frac{\epsilon_t + (1 - \theta U)(1 - \rho U)\eta_t}{(1 - \theta U)(1 - \rho U)} \tag{14}$$

so that

$$
\begin{aligned}
g_{xx}(z) &= \frac{\sigma^2[1 + \mu(1 - \theta z)(1 - \rho z)(1 - \theta z^{-1})(1 - \rho z^{-1})]}{(1 - \theta z)(1 - \rho z)(1 - \theta z^{-1})(1 - \rho z^{-1})} \\
&= \frac{\sigma_1^2[(1 - \alpha z)(1 - \beta z)(1 - \alpha z^{-1})(1 - \beta z^{-1})]}{(1 - \theta z)(1 - \rho z)(1 - \theta z^{-1})(1 - \rho z^{-1})},
\end{aligned} \tag{15}
$$

where α, β are the roots of $1 + \mu(1 - \theta z)(1 - \theta z^{-1})(1 - \rho z)(1 - \rho z^{-1})$ that lie inside the unit circle. To obtain $\hat{y}_{t+v,t}$, we obtain $\gamma(z)$ as

$$
\begin{aligned}
\gamma(z) &= \frac{(1 - \theta z)(1 - \rho z)}{\sigma_1^2(1 - \alpha z)(1 - \beta z)} \\
&\quad \times \left[\frac{\sigma^2(1 - \theta z^{-1})(1 - \rho z^{-1})}{(1 - \theta z)(1 - \theta z^{-1})(1 - \rho z)(1 - \rho z^{-1})(1 - \alpha z^{-1})(1 - \beta z^{-1})z^v} \right]_+ \\
&= \frac{\sigma^2}{\sigma_1^2}\frac{(1 - \theta z)(1 - \rho z)}{(1 - \alpha z)(1 - \beta z)}\left[\frac{1}{(1 - \theta z)(1 - \rho z)(1 - \alpha z^{-1})(1 - \beta z^{-1})z^v} \right]_+ \\
&= \frac{\sigma^2}{\sigma_1^2}\frac{(1 - \theta z)(1 - \rho z)}{(1 - \alpha z)(1 - \beta z)(\theta - \rho)}\left[\frac{\theta}{(1 - \theta z)(1 - \alpha z^{-1})(1 - \beta z^{-1})z^v} \right. \\
&\qquad \left. - \frac{\rho}{(1 - \rho z)(1 - \alpha z^{-1})(1 - \beta z^{-1})z^v} \right]_+ \\
&= \frac{\sigma^2}{\sigma_1^2}\frac{(1 - \theta z)(1 - \rho z)}{(1 - \alpha z)(1 - \beta z)(\theta - \rho)}\left\{ \left[\frac{\theta}{(1 - \theta z)(1 - \alpha z^{-1})(1 - \beta z^{-1})z^v} \right]_+ \right. \\
&\qquad \left. - \left[\frac{\rho}{(1 - \rho z)(1 - \alpha z^{-1})(1 - \beta z^{-1})z^v} \right]_+ \right\}.
\end{aligned} \tag{16}
$$

Letting $z^{-v}/(1 - \alpha z^{-1})(1 - \beta z^{-1})$ play the role of $Q(z)$ in Whittle's theorem and noting that for v positive $[Q(z)]_+$ vanishes,

$$
\gamma(z) = \frac{\sigma^2}{\sigma_1^2} \frac{(1 - \rho z)\theta^{v+1}}{(1 - \alpha z)(1 - \beta z)(\theta - \rho)(1 - \alpha\theta)(1 - \beta\theta)}
$$

$$
- \frac{\sigma^2}{\sigma_1^2} \frac{(1 - \theta z)\rho^{v+1}}{(1 - \alpha z)(1 - \beta z)(\theta - \rho)(1 - \alpha\rho)(1 - \beta\rho)}. \tag{17}
$$

This expression is clearly of the form

$$
\gamma(z) = (\delta + kz)/(1 - \alpha z)(1 - \beta z), \tag{18}
$$

where δ and k can be calculated by combining terms as in the earlier examples.

Example C. We noted above that the optimization problem (4.1) applies to other problems in addition to prediction and signal extraction. We conclude this section with an example of a somewhat different type of problem, namely, interpolation.
Let

$$
x_t = \rho x_{t-1} + \epsilon_t, \tag{19}
$$

where $|\rho| < 1$ and $\{\epsilon_t\}$ is white noise with variance σ^2. Suppose that for one reason or another we do not have a complete history on x_t but only have observations on every mth x; that is, suppose we have observed $\{x_{m(t-j)}, j = 0, \pm 1, \pm 2, \ldots\}$, where m is an integer greater than one. Consider the problem of estimating the unobserved x's. Specifically, we wish to find the least-squares estimate of x_{mt-k},

$$
\hat{x}_{mt-k} = \sum_{j=-\infty}^{\infty} \gamma_j x_{m(t-j)}, \qquad 0 < k < m. \tag{20}
$$

Since

$$
E(x_{mt} x_{m(t-j)}) = [\sigma^2/(1 - \rho^2)]\rho^{|mj|} = \sigma_x^2 \rho^{|mj|}, \tag{21}
$$

the covariance generating function for the observed sequence is given by

$$
g_{x_m x_m}(z) = \sigma_x^2 \sum_{j=-\infty}^{\infty} \rho^{|mj|} z^j = \frac{\sigma_x^2(1 - \rho^{2m})}{(1 - \rho^m z)(1 - \rho^m z^{-1})}
$$

$$
= \frac{\sigma^2(1 - \rho^{2m})}{1 - \rho^2} \frac{1}{(1 - \rho^m z)(1 - \rho^m z^{-1})}. \tag{22}
$$

Now

$$
\begin{aligned}
E(x_{mt-k} x_{mt-mj}) &= \sigma_x^2 \rho^{-k+mj}, & j > 0, \\
E(x_{mt-k} x_{mt+mj}) &= \sigma_x^2 \rho^{k+mj}, & j \geq 0,
\end{aligned} \tag{23}
$$

so that

$$
\begin{aligned}
g_{yx_m}(z) &= \sum_{j=-\infty}^{\infty} E(x_{mt-k}x_{mt-mj})z^j \\
&= \sigma_x^2 \left\{ \frac{(\rho^k - \rho^{2m-k}) + (\rho^{m-k} - \rho^{m+k})z}{(1-\rho^m z)(1-\rho^m z^{-1})} \right\} \\
&= \frac{(\rho^k - \rho^{2m-k}) + (\rho^{m-k} - \rho^{m+k})z}{(1-\rho^{2m})} g_{x_m x_m}(z),
\end{aligned}
\tag{24}
$$

where $y_t = x_{mt-k}$.
Thus,

$$
\gamma(z) = \frac{\rho^k - \rho^{2m-k} + (\rho^{m-k} - \rho^{m+k})z}{1-\rho^{2m}}
\tag{25}
$$

and

$$
\hat{x}_{mt-k,\,mt} = \frac{\rho^k - \rho^{2m-k}}{1-\rho^{2m}} x_{mt} + \frac{(\rho^{m-k} - \rho^{m+k})}{1-\rho^{2m}} x_{m(t-1)}.
\tag{26}
$$

Let ρ tend to one from below; using L'Hospital's rule, we find

$$
\hat{x}_{mt-k,\,mt} = \left(\frac{m-k}{m}\right) x_{mt} + \left(\frac{k}{m}\right) x_{mt-m}.
$$

That is, optimal interpolation is simply linear interpolation.

It is interesting to note that the interpolation rule (26) can be obtained by a more direct argument. Since x is a first-order autoregression,

$$
x_{mt-k} = \rho^{m-k}x_{mt-m} + \epsilon_{mt-k} + \rho\epsilon_{mt-k-1} + \cdots + \rho^{m-k-1}\epsilon_{mt-m+1}
$$
$$
x_{mt} = \rho^k x_{mt-k} + \epsilon_{mt} + \rho\epsilon_{mt-1} + \rho^2\epsilon_{mt-2} + \cdots + \rho^{k-1}\epsilon_{mt-k+1}.
$$

Thus we have two possible estimates of x_{mt-k}, namely, $\rho^{m-k}x_{mt-m}$ and $\rho^{-k}x_{mt}$ with mean-square errors $\sigma_x^2[1 - \rho^{2(m-k)}]$ and $\sigma_x^2 \rho^{-2k}(1-\rho^{2k})$, respectively. Both estimates are clearly unbiased and, given the nature of the process, uncorrelated. If we form a weighted average of these estimates with weights inversely proportional to the mean-square errors, the resulting estimate is that given above.

Chapter VI
FORMULATION OF UNOBSERVED-COMPONENTS MODELS AND CANONICAL FORMS[1]

1. Introduction

In this chapter we are concerned with the formulation of unobserved-components models, their canonical forms, and ordinary mixed moving-average autoregressive (ARMA) models for both single and multiple time series. The next chapter deals with estimation of such models by maximum-likelihood methods. The first step in the estimation of either an ARMA model or an unobserved-components (UC) model is the determination of the orders of the moving averages and autoregressions, as well as the number of components in a UC model, which is itself made up of superimposed ARMA models. This process is called "model identification" by Box and Jenkins (1970, Chapter 6, pp. 173–204); to avoid confusion with standard econometric usage we use the term model formulation rather than Box and Jenkins' term. Identification problems in the ordinary econometric sense may arise in the estimation of both ARMA and UC models and are discussed at the appropriate points in the next chapter, which deals with estimation.

An outline of this chapter is as follows: Section 2 deals with the determination of the form of ARMA models using the estimated autocorrelation and partial autocorrelation functions, as suggested by Box and Jenkins, and a method suggested by Carvalho (1971). Section 3 discusses the formulation of UC models

[1] The material presented in this chapter is based on research supported in part by the Board of Governors of the Federal Reserve System as well as by a grant from the National Science Foundation. We are indebted to Michael Ward for his able assistance.

by estimated spectral densities. Section 4 deals with the formulation of time-series models relating two or more interdependent time series. Examples of formulating and estimating univariate ARMA models are given in Chapter X, univariate unobserved-components models in Chapter XII, and multivariate ARMA models in Chapter XI.

2.   Determining the Form of a Univariate Time-Series ARMA Model

By *formulation* of a time-series model we mean here the determination of the appropriate degrees of the polynomials in the lag operators that appear in both the autoregressive part and the moving-average part of an ARMA model. What is traditionally meant in the literature of econometrics by identification and identifiability of parameters is a problem that may also occur in attempting to infer the parameters of the unobserved-components form from the canonical form of a model. This is briefly discussed in connection with estimation.

In Chapter IV, Section 3, we derived general formulas for the autocovariances, and a fortiori the autocorrelations of mixed moving-average autoregressive processes. Our result for a pure finite moving-average process $x_t = \sum_{j=0}^{q} b_j \epsilon_{t-j}, b_0 = 1$, $\{\epsilon_t\}$ zero-mean white noise with variance σ^2, is given in (IV.3.13):

$$\rho(\tau) = \begin{cases} \dfrac{b_\tau + b_1 b_{\tau+1} + \cdots + b_{q-\tau} b_q}{b_0^2 + b_1^2 + \cdots + b_q^2}, & \tau = 1, \ldots, q, \\ 0, & \tau > q, \end{cases}$$

so that $\rho(\tau)$ has a cutoff point of zero at the maximum lag of the moving average. Box and Jenkins (1970, p. 175) suggest using the existence of such a cutoff point as a means of determining the order of a purely moving-average process.

Our result for a purely autoregressive process of order n,

$$\prod_{k=1}^{n} (1 - \alpha_k U) x_t = \epsilon_t,$$

$\{\epsilon_t\}$ zero-mean white noise with variance σ^2, and $|\alpha_k| < 1$, $k = 1, \ldots, n$, from (IV. 3.16), is

$$\rho(\tau) = \frac{\gamma(\tau)}{\gamma(0)} = \frac{\sum_{q=1}^{n} \left\{ \dfrac{\alpha_q^{n+|\tau|-1}}{\prod_{k=1}^{n}(1 - \alpha_k \alpha_q) \cdot \prod_{k=1, k \neq q}^{n}(\alpha_q - \alpha_k)} \right\}}{\sum_{q=1}^{n} \left\{ \dfrac{\alpha_q^{n-1}}{\prod_{k=1}^{n}(1 - \alpha_k \alpha_q) \cdot \prod_{k=1, k \neq q}^{n}(\alpha_q - \alpha_k)} \right\}},$$

which has the general form

$$\rho(\tau) = \sum_{q=1}^{n} A_q \alpha_q^{|\tau|}, \tag{1}$$

where

$$A_q = \frac{\alpha_q^{n-1}}{\prod_{k=1}^{n}(1 - \alpha_k\alpha_q)\cdot\prod_{k=1, k\neq q}^{n}(\alpha_q - \alpha_k)}$$
$$\cdot \sum_{j=1}^{n}\alpha_j^{n-1}/\{\prod_{k=1}^{n}(1 - \alpha_k\alpha_j)\cdot\prod_{k=1, k\neq j}^{n}(\alpha_j - \alpha_k)\}$$

does not depend on τ. Thus the autocorrelation function for a pure auto-regression is the sum of damped exponentials; the rate at which these damp depends on how close the roots of $A(z)$ are to the unit circle. If any root is close, $\rho(\tau)$ will damp very slowly; the greater the number of roots close to the unit circle, the more irregularly will $\rho(\tau)$ damp.

Clearly, the structure of an autoregressive process is more simply described in terms of the original autoregressive coefficients than in terms of the rather complicated expressions for the autocorrelation coefficients. Consider now a set of p equations, called the *Yule–Walker equations*, connecting the first p autocorrelations:

$$\rho(1) = a_1 + a_2\rho(1) + \cdots + a_p\rho(p-1)$$
$$\rho(2) = a_1\rho(1) + a_2 + \cdots + a_p\rho(p-2) \tag{2}$$
$$\vdots$$
$$\rho(p) = a_1\rho(p-1) + a_2\rho(p-2) + \cdots + a_p.$$

Solving equations (2) for $a_1, \ldots, a_p$ yields the pth-*order partial autocorrelation* a_p. If we solve (2) repeatedly for $p = 1, 2, \ldots, n$, we obtain the partial auto-correlations as a function of p, the maximum-lag autocorrelation used in the formulation of the Yule–Walker equations. Note that, in general, we would *estimate* the autoregressive coefficients of the nth-order autoregression by substituting the estimated autocorrelations $\hat{\rho}(1), \hat{\rho}(2), \ldots, \hat{\rho}(n)$ in the Yule–Walker equations for $p = n$. Since the sample autocorrelations are consistent estimates of the population values, the estimates $\hat{a}_1, \hat{a}_2, \ldots, \hat{a}_n$ will be consistent estimates of the autoregressive coefficients in

$$x_t = a_1 x_{t-1} + a_2 x_{t-2} + \cdots + a_n x_{t-n} + \epsilon_t. \tag{3}$$

If we had the true autocorrelations, all $\hat{a}_j$ for $j > n$ would be zero, if we were, in fact, dealing with an nth-order autoregression. The fact that the partial auto-correlation function is zero for $p > n$ for the nth-order autoregressive process is suggested by Box and Jenkins (1970, p. 175) as a means of determining the order of such a process.

When a process is of a mixed moving-average autoregressive type, the nature of the autocorrelation and partial autocorrelation functions becomes con-siderably more complicated. In the general case of a mixed moving-average autoregressive process with autoregressive component of order n and moving-average component of order m the autocorrelation and partial autocorrelation function are both infinite in extent, but the former is dominated by damped exponentials or damped sinusoidal fluctuations after m lags, whereas the latter follows a similar pattern after n lags (Box and Jenkins, 1970, p. 79). Presumably, this result could be used to determine the orders of the relevant polynomials in the canonical form of a general mixed process, but it is difficult to attach much practical significance to a method that requires one to distinguish damped sinusoidal or exponential shapes at long lags for which the statistical reliability of the estimates is low.

Indeed, it is difficult to rationalize use of ordinary estimates of either the autocorrelation or partial autocorrelation functions in identifying the orders even of simple moving-average or autoregressive processes in view of the poor statistical properties of the estimates of both at long lags. In particular, it may be shown that the coefficient of variation of the sample autocorrelation will increase as the length of lag increases so that "the later [estimates] provide practically no information" (Hannan, 1960, p. 41). (See also Chapter III, Section 5.) This leads to a failure of the sample estimate of the correlogram to damp down. Therefore determination of a maximal order of a moving average by this method is exceedingly unreliable and biased toward finding far *too high* a value. If one knows that a process is purely autoregressive, however, the situation is much better. Here it may be shown that the estimates are consistent, asymptotically normal, and asymptotically unbiased, provided one has specified an autoregression of at least as high an order as the true autoregression. If too low an order is specified initially, however, or if the disturbance of the autoregression is itself autocorrelated either because of misspecification or because it follows a moving-average scheme (which, under certain circumstances, would be equivalent to an infinite-order autoregression), then serious estimation problems arise: The estimated partial autocorrelation coefficients will be biased and inconsistent; so will be any tests on these coefficients. In many circumstances, but not all, we are likely to estimate too low a value of the maximal lag in the autoregression. The situation is, a fortiori, much worse for mixed processes. Estimates of the orders of autoregressive and moving-average components are of extreme unreliability if the orders involved are even moderate-sized in relation to the total size of the sample. "Overfitting," or using more lags than necessary, may be helpful in the case of a pure autoregression, but is unavailing for moving-average processes and possibly positively harmful in the case of mixed processes.[2]

An alternative to using the estimated autocorrelation and partial autocorrelation functions in the determination of the form and lengths of lag in mixed models is to use the estimated spectral density. There seem to be alternative procedures for simple mixed moving-average autoregressive models, as is

---

[2] We should mention here Akaike's method for determining the order of a purely autoregressive representation by minimizing the final prediction error (see Akaike, 1970, 1974). This method was devised primarily within the context of optimal control and prediction of univariate and multivariate processes, and not for the purposes of structural identification and estimation with which we are concerned here.

discussed in this section; however, as we suggest below, there appear to be no good substitutes for spectral estimates in the formulation of unobserved-components models.

If the process for which a model is to be formulated is a moving average only, with no autoregressive component, then, as noted, the true autocorrelation function should become zero at a lag equal to the order of the process. Of course, the estimated autocorrelation function will not satisfy this property exactly and indeed may tend to behave erratically at long lags.[3] In an earlier paper (Carvalho, 1971), one of us suggested a technique for formulating a mixed moving-average autoregressive model with a possible nonstationary component of the sort arising from an integrated moving average. The first step is to attempt to reduce the series to one generated by a simple stationary moving average and to determine this model from the autocorrelation function alone. In order to avoid specifying a moving average of too high an order, only estimated autocorrelations larger than some specified value in absolute value are considered to be significant.[4] What makes this procedure different from any procedures explicitly recommended by Box and Jenkins, although it is perhaps implicit in their discussion, is first its reliance on the autocorrelation function for the initial step of the procedure and second its assumption of a rather simple form for the moving-average process to be determined. Our procedure may be described in broad outline as follows: first, compute the autocorrelation function for the original data; if it fails to damp, take ordinary differences until it does, except possibly at discrete lags that are multiples of L (ordinarily, one difference is enough). Second, if the autocorrelations are large in absolute value (relative to some cutoff level) at lags that are multiples of L, take an Lth link or repeated Lth links (ordinarily, one is enough).[5] Third, assume that the transformed series w_t is, apart from a possible low-order autoregression, a moving average of the form

$$w_t = \theta(U)\Theta(U^L)\epsilon_t, \tag{4}$$

where θ and Θ are polynomials in the lag operator U of degrees q and LQ, respectively. The orders q and Q are both assumed to be relatively small. We return in a moment to the question of how to decide if a low-order autoregressive component is present; for now, assume there is none.

---

[3] The approximate variance of the sample autocorrelation $\hat{\rho}(k)$ for long lags, i.e., large k, is

$$\text{var}\{\hat{\rho}(k)\} \cong (1/n)\{1 + 2[\hat{\rho}(1)^2 + \hat{\rho}(2)^2 + \cdots + \hat{\rho}(q)^2]\},$$

for $k > q$, where n is the number of observations, and q is a lag larger than the one at which true autocorrelation is zero. Thus, if q is fairly large and k is not much larger, the estimates $\hat{\rho}(k)$ will have large variance (see Box and Jenkins, 1970, p. 177.)

[4] This value may be arbitrary or determined, for example, in accordance with the standard errors given by the approximation reported in the previous footnote.

[5] If L is the number of observations on the series per year, so that the seasonal frequencies are given by the Lth roots of unity, then seasonal fluctuations may be removed by possibly repeated "linking," i.e., differencing by means of the operator $1 - U^L$.

A process following a moving average of the form (4), will have autocovariance generating function

$$g_{ww}(z) = \sigma^2 \theta(z)\Theta(z^L)\theta(z^{-1})\Theta(z^{-L}). \tag{5}$$

Thus, the largest autocorrelation different from zero should be that for lag $q + LQ$. Suppose $q = 1$ and $Q = 1$; then nonzero values may be expected at lags $1, L - 1, L$, and $L + 1$. Suppose $q = 2$ and $Q = 1$; then nonzero values may be expected at lags $2, L - 2$, and $L + 2$ in addition to those mentioned. Provided we place severe restrictions on the sizes of q and Q, it is apparent that only a small number of combinations of lags exist at which the autocorrelation function should differ from zero. Of course, some autocorrelations may be close to zero before the maximal lag $q + LQ$ is reached, simply because the coefficients in the polynomials take on certain values; this is why major reliance is placed on observing the maximum lag at which the autocorrelation is significantly larger in absolute value than some cutoff level.

It is possible that even after the transformation of the original series to w_t the autocorrelation function observed cannot be interpreted in terms of (5) for q and Q both small. Then the existence of an autoregressive component in w_t should be considered. The problem, of course, is that an autoregression has an autocorrelation function that is not zero even at very long lags, although it does damp down (assuming the series is stationary and has no linearly deterministic component). If it is assumed that whatever autoregression left in w_t is of low order, then the first few values of the autocorrelation function will be most affected, so that these in turn may be used to arrive at some judgment regarding the existence and order of the autoregression. We suggest using the estimated values of the first few partial autoregressive coefficients for the series w_t to transform it; then the previous analysis is applied. A problem with this approach, however, is that the estimated autoregressive coefficients will be "contaminated" by the moving-average effects on the autocorrelation function; but since the procedure is used only for model formulation, and not for final estimation, this problem may not be too serious.

In order to avoid introducing too many nonstationary elements in the original series, it is useful to fit a model that allows the operators initially applied in the formulation process to render the series stationary to have roots off the unit circle. For example, suppose the series x_t was transformed to w_t by

$$w_t = (1 - U)(1 - U^L)x_t,$$

w_t was transformed to y_t by using the first two autoregressive coefficients

$$(1 - a_1 U - a_2 U^2)w_t = y_t,$$

and y_t was represented as

$$y_t = \theta(U)\Theta(U^L)\epsilon_t;$$

then we might fit the model

$$(1 - \delta_1 U)(1 - \delta_L U^L)A(U)x_t = \theta(U)\Theta(U^L)\epsilon_t, \tag{6}$$

where $A(U)$ is of degree 2.

We present illustrations of this method of model formulation in Chapter X. This approach to the problem of model formulation is essentially a way of introducing a number of strong a priori assumptions. These are not imposed in the estimation process, although they could easily be introduced along the same lines as the restrictions resulting from an unobserved-components model, as are imposed in the modified estimation procedure described below. In fact, such restrictions could be more easily imposed since the model (6) is already in what we call canonical form. An unobserved-components model is itself nothing more than a way of introducing strong a priori assumptions in a less arbitrary manner than in our modification of Box and Jenkins' use of the autocorrelation and partial autocorrelation functions. Such models, however, require somewhat different techniques for their formulation.

3. Determining the Form of a Univariate Time-Series Unobserved-Components Model

We suggest use of the estimated spectral density function, which if properly estimated is known to have good statistical properties, for the formulation of unobserved-components models. When large or potentially large numbers of parameters are involved this method is difficult to implement; but when a good deal of structure is imposed on the problem, as, for example, in a typical unobserved-components model, the method does appear to be feasible, as we should now like to demonstrate.

Figure 1 shows estimated spectral densities for automotive sales and inventories. The estimates exhibit two features commonly found in economic time series. First, there are peaks at each of the so-called seasonal frequencies (with monthly data these frequencies correspond to 1, 2, 3, 4, 5, and 6 cycles per year). Second, apart from the seasonal peaks, the spectral densities are generally decreasing with frequency, having substantially more power at the frequencies near zero than anywhere else.

A three-component model, with components corresponding to the traditional "trend cycle," "seasonal," and "irregular," each of which is represented by a relatively simple mixed moving-average autoregressive scheme, is capable of reproducing these typical characteristics of an economic time series. In choosing such a model we seek one that is simple, i.e., has only a few parameters, and one that has a spectral density with characteristics that can be associated with particular unobserved components of the traditional kind.

Thus the "trend cycle" should be a series, the time pattern of which is dominated by gradual cumulative movements and does not have any prominent

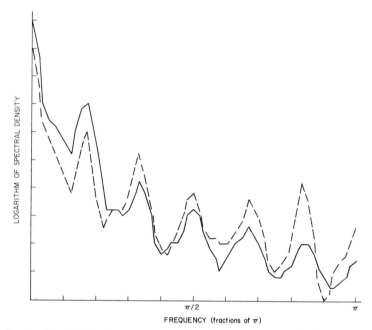

Fig. 1.   Spectral densities: ----, automotive sales; ———, automotive inventories.

short-term regularities. In terms of its spectral density, it should have maximum power at the origin and decreasing power throughout its range. Many low-order autoregressive processes have spectra of the type described. There are two points worth mentioning, however, in connection with economic time series. First, in undifferenced form very little of the variance appears to be contributed by what we have called the trend-cycle component at high frequencies. A much greater contribution is made at those frequencies by the seasonal and irregular. Purely autoregressive processes of low order, however, with real roots have spectral densities that decline less slowly with frequency than is desirable if we wish our model to allow greater contribution of seasonal and irregular components at high frequencies. In order to produce this effect, it is necessary to formulate the trend-cycle component as a mixed process with a low-order moving-average as numerator and a low-order autoregression as denominator; for example,

$$T_t = \frac{(1 + \beta_1 U + \beta_2 U^2)}{(1 - \alpha_1 U)(1 - \alpha_2 U)} \epsilon_{1t}. \tag{1}$$

Of course, the low-order moving-average numerator may, if all the roots of its generating polynomial lie outside the unit circle, be equivalent to an infinite-order autoregression, which suggests that similar spectral effects could be achieved with high-order autoregressions. High-order terms, however, require large numbers of parameters; thus parsimony dictates a mixed formulation.

Second, in differenced form many of our time series have a spectral shape that suggests stationarity in this form (absence of a sharp dip at the origin), but nonetheless have a spectral density with a moderate fall and then rise. Such shapes can be achieved by allowing complex roots. The graphs of the spectral densities of three possible models for the trend-cycle component are plotted in Fig. 2. They are

$$T_t = \frac{1}{(1 - 0.95U)(1 - 0.75U)} \epsilon_{1t}$$

$$T_t = \frac{(1 + 0.8U)}{(1 - 0.95U)(1 - 0.75U)} \epsilon_{1t} \qquad (2)$$

$$T_t = \frac{1}{1 - 1.7U + 0.9025U^2} \epsilon_{1t},$$

where $\{\epsilon_{1t}\}$ is white noise. Note that the last possibility has complex roots, $0.9418 \pm i(0.2210)^{1/2}$, that lie outside the unit circle.

The simplest process with peaks at each of the seasonal frequencies is

$$S_t = (1/1 - \gamma U^L)\epsilon_{2t}, \qquad (3)$$

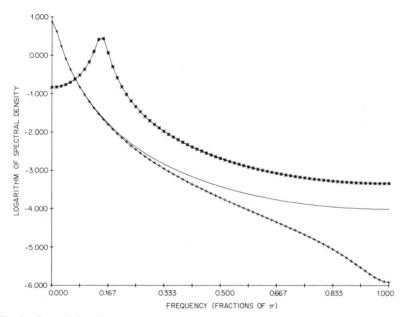

Fig. 2. Spectral densities:

$$\text{————}, \; T_t = \frac{\epsilon_{1t}}{(1 - 0.95U)(1 - 0.75U)}, \qquad + + + +, \; T_t = \frac{(1 + 0.8U)\epsilon_{1t}}{(1 - 0.95U)(1 - 0.75U)},$$

$$\text{****}, \; T_t = \frac{\epsilon_{1t}}{(1 - 1.7U + 0.9025U^2)}$$

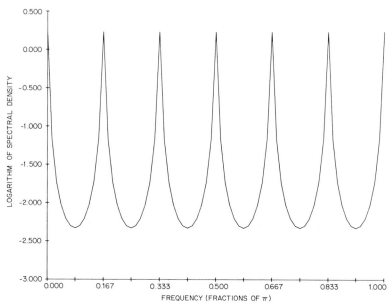

Fig. 3.   Spectral density: ——— , $S_t = \epsilon_{2t}/(1 - 0.9U^{12})$.

where $\{\epsilon_{2t}\}$ is white noise and L is the number of observations per year.[6] A process of this type amounts to specifying L independent processes each of which appears as a first-order autoregression when observed at annual intervals. Depending on whether γ is close to one or close to zero, the seasonal peaks produced will be either extremely sharp or very diffuse, respectively. Figure 3 shows the spectral density of S_t ($\gamma = 0.9$, $L = 12$); note that the peaks at each seasonal frequency are the same height, which is not characteristic of real economic time series. In undifferenced form most economic time series exhibit spectral densities with markedly higher peaks at the lower seasonal frequencies than at the higher. Merely superimposing a seasonal component with peaks of equal height on the component T_t as defined in (2) will not produce the effect characteristic of many economic time series; it is necessary, as before, to introduce a moving-average numerator in order to achieve this effect. Thus

$$S_t = \frac{1 + \beta_3 U + \beta_4 U^2}{1 - \gamma U^{12}} \epsilon_{2t} \qquad (4)$$

should be used. A second-order moving-average in the numerator can impart a wavelike motion to the height of the seasonal peaks, which is desirable since spectra of many economic time series show higher peaks at the intermediate seasonal frequencies, when account is taken of their superposition on the trend-cycle component, than at either very low or very high frequencies. A graph of

---

[6] This model also has a peak in its spectral density at the origin. This means, in effect, that part of the process may be confused empirically with a polynomial trend or even a simple autoregression.

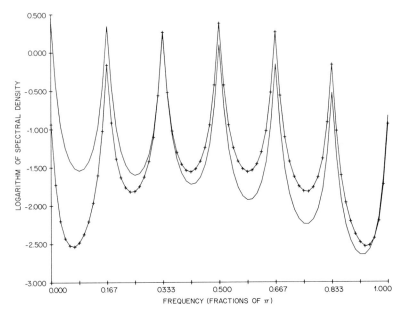

Fig. 4. Spectral densities:

$$\underline{\hspace{2cm}}, S_t = \frac{(1 + 0.6U)\epsilon_{2t}}{(1 - 0.8U^{12})}, \qquad + + + +, S_t = \frac{(1 + 0.8U)(1 - 0.8U)\epsilon_{2t}}{(1 - 0.8U^{12})}$$

the theoretical spectral densities series with seasonal component

$$S_t = \frac{1 + 0.6U}{1 - 0.8U^{12}} \epsilon_{2t} \qquad \text{and} \qquad S_t = \frac{(1 + 0.8U)(1 - 0.8U)}{1 - 0.8U^{12}} \epsilon_{2t}, \qquad (5)$$

is presented in Fig. 4.

These considerations lead to the view that a model such as

$$x_t = \frac{1 + \beta_1 U + \beta_2 U^2}{(1 - \alpha_1 U)(1 - \alpha_2 U)} \epsilon_{1t} + \frac{1 + \beta_3 U + \beta_4 U^2}{1 - \gamma U^{12}} \epsilon_{2t} + \epsilon_{3t} \qquad (6)$$

may be suitable for the representation of many economic time series.[7] The

---

[7] In private correspondence, K. F. Wallis has remarked that although this model produces a time series that closely resembles many economic time series in the frequency domain, its properties in the time domain seem less desirable: In particular, the model produces a time series whose seasonal patterns change too rapidly. A time path of a series generated by a model such as given in equation (6) is presented in Fig. 8 of Chapter VIII. Even with $\gamma = 0.9$, the seasonal pattern is very ragged. Wallis remarks that seasonality is usually smoother: "if August is high, then September isn't low." This would seem to call for a more complicated autoregressive formulation than our simple model; yet estimates of unobserved-components models typically do not support anything of greater complexity. The model leads to sets of more or less independently evolving seasonals, but neighboring seasonals need not differ by much. Thus the problem Wallis raises may be more of a difficulty for simulation than for estimation, which is precisely why we may not have been able to find empirical evidence in our estimates for the smoother character he finds more plausible.

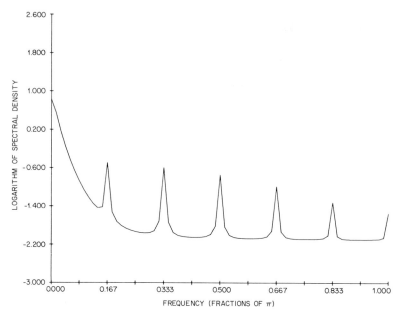

Fig. 5. Spectral density:

$$x_t = \frac{(1 + 0.8U)\epsilon_{1t}}{(1 - 0.95U)(1 - 0.75U)} + \frac{(1 + 0.6U)\epsilon_{2t}}{(1 - 0.9U^{12})} + \qquad \epsilon_{3t}$$

(weight 0.85)　　　　　(weight 0.10)　　(weight 0.05)

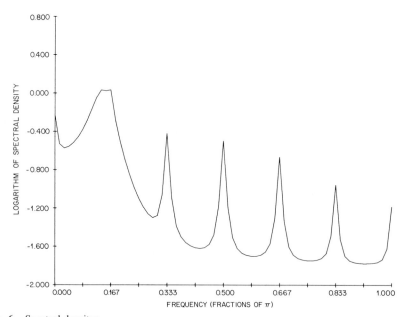

Fig. 6. Spectral density:

$$x_t = \frac{(1 + 0.6U)\epsilon_{1t}}{(1 - 1.6U + 0.8U^2)} + \frac{(1 + 0.6U)(1 - 0.2U)\epsilon_{2t}}{(1 - 0.8U^{12})} + \qquad \epsilon_{3t}$$

(weight 0.70)　　　　　(weight 0.20)　　　　　(weight 0.10)

graph of the theoretical spectral densities for two such models are presented in Figs. 5 and 6. The models are

$$x_t = \frac{1 + 0.8U}{(1 - 0.95U)(1 - 0.75U)} \epsilon_{1t} + \frac{1 + 0.6U}{1 - 0.9U^{12}} \epsilon_{2t} + \epsilon_{3t} , \qquad \text{(Fig. 5)}$$

weight $=$ $\qquad$ (0.85) $\qquad\qquad\qquad$ (0.10) $\qquad$ (0.05),

and $\hspace{11cm}$ (7)

$$x_t = \frac{1 + 0.6U}{1 - 1.6U + 0.8U^2} \epsilon_{1t} + \frac{(1 + 0.6U)(1 - 0.2U)}{1 - 0.8U^{12}} \epsilon_{2t} + \epsilon_{3t} , \qquad \text{(Fig. 6)}$$

weight $=$ $\qquad$ (0.70) $\qquad\qquad\qquad$ (0.20) $\qquad$ (0.10).

The spectral densities of each component are individually computed using $\sigma_1^2 = \sigma_2^2 = \sigma_3^2 = 1$ and then summed using the weights immediately below. This is done to avoid the problem of having to compute the variance of each component as a function of the coefficients appearing in its lag operator. Thus the weights express the contributions of each component to the overall variance of $\{x_t\}$. Note that the second of these has complex roots, $1 \pm 0.5i$, and shows a hump at frequencies slightly below $\pi/6$.

By comparing the form of the spectral density for a theoretical model such as (6) with estimated spectral density of an actual time series, it is often possible to decide whether the actual series might be characterized in terms of such an unobserved-components model.[8] The model introduces, as is shown in the next chapter, a number of strong a priori assumptions that may also be taken into account in the estimation procedure.

4. The Analysis of Time Series by More Than Its Own Past[9]

In Chapter V and in Sections 2 and 3 of this chapter, we have discussed the problem of predicting a time series from its own past and suggested the formulation of parametric ARMA and unobserved-components models as an aid in this connection. In this section we explore a slight but significant generalization

---

[8] It should be borne in mind throughout that the spectral density is nothing more than the Fourier transform of the autocorrelation function. Of course, the *estimated* spectral density is based on weighted averages of autocorrelations and has better statistical properties than the raw estimates of those autocorrelations themselves. Nonetheless, it is basically a matter of which is more easily interpretable; we often find it easier and more convenient to compare the properties of models in the frequency domain—others may find it less so under the same or other circumstances.

[9] Several recent important contributions deal with the topic of this section (discussion of which is continued in Chapters VII, XI, and XIV), namely, multiple time-series analysis and modeling. These are Granger and Newbold (1977, Chapter 7, "Multiple time series modeling and forecasting," pp. 215–267), Wallis (1977a,b), and Wallis and Chan (1976). Unfortunately, these contributions came to our attention too late to be taken properly into account in our own work or to be described fully in this book.

of this problem: We suppose that there are additional series that contain information about the future values of the series in which we are interested, not also contained in that series' own past. Let the series $\{y_t\}$ be the one in which we are primarily interested, and let $\{x_t\}$ be a related series; suppose that

$$\varphi(U)y_t + \psi(U)x_t = \theta(U)\epsilon_t, \qquad (1)$$

where $\{\epsilon_t\}$ is zero-mean white noise with variance σ^2 and $\varphi(\ )$, $\psi(\ )$, and $\theta(\ )$ are polynomials in the backward-shift operator. For the moment we say nothing about the roots of $\psi(z)$, but as usual the roots of $\varphi(z)$ and $\theta(z)$ are assumed to lie outside the unit circle. The polynomials $\varphi(\ )$, $\psi(\ )$, and $\theta(\ )$ are assumed to have no common factors.

Whether we assume that future values of the related x series are known or not makes a good deal of difference as to how we should treat the problem as a whole: If future values of the series $\{x_t\}$ relevant to the prediction of $\{y_t\}$ are known, then we may legitimately consider the estimation of (1) by itself. If these values will not be known, however, it is necessary to augment the model. Some supposition must be made concerning the manner in which the series $\{x_t\}$ is in fact generated.

Consider first the situation when future values of $\{x_t\}$ are assumed to be known, so that equation (1) may be treated in isolation. The first step in the analysis is to determine the order of each polynomial appearing in (1): An approach similar to the one suggested in Section 2 of this chapter may be employed. We first determine a model for the series $\{y_t\}$, then using this model determine an appropriate polynomial $\psi(\ )$ relating the series $\{x_t\}$ to the series $\{y_t\}$. Finally, having determined initial values for the φ's and the ψ's, we may obtain a preliminary result for the θ's.

Step 1.   We may formulate a mixed moving-average autoregressive model for which possible nonstationarities removable by differencing are allowed (ARIMA model), along exactly the lines described in Section 2. Let this model be

$$\varphi^{(1)}(U)y_t = \theta^{(1)}(U)\epsilon_t^{(1)}, \qquad (2)$$

where the superscript $^{(1)}$ denotes that this is merely the first stage in a procedure designed to determine the full model (1).

Step 2.   Initial values for the parameters of the polynomial $\varphi^{(1)}(\ )$ may be determined using the partial autocorrelation function or by applying the Box–Jenkins procedure described in Section 1 to the model (2). Let the estimated polynomial $\varphi^{(1)}(\ )$ be $\hat{\varphi}^{(1)}(\ )$; then we may calculate the "residuals"

$$w_t = \hat{\varphi}^{(1)}(U)y_t. \qquad (3)$$

Step 3.   To determine an initial estimate of the polynomial $-\psi(\ )$, we do a stepwise regression of w_t on past x's, $x_t, x_{t-1}, \ldots, x_{t-r}$.[10] The value of r, the

---

[10] Alternatively, the cross-lag correlation function between $\{w_t\}$ and $\{x_t\}$ might be used to determine the order of $\psi(\ )$. Unfortunately, as Jenkins and Watts (1968, pp. 321–340) point out, many different lag structures can yield the same cross-lag correlation function. To use this method, therefore, additional restrictions on the admissibility of the structure would have to be imposed.

longest lag considered, should depend in large part on how strongly seasonal the series $\{x_t\}$ is; generally, a good rule of thumb is to choose $r \geq 3L$, where L is the number of observations per year and therefore the period of seasonality. Should all coefficients of lagged x's be significant for $r = 3L$, the value of r should be increased by at least L. We have found, however, that $r = 3L$ is satisfactory in all our empirical work to date. The stepwise regression of w_t on past x's provides us with initial estimates of $-\psi(\ )$; thus

$$w_t = \hat{\varphi}^{(1)}(U)y_t = -\hat{\psi}^{(1)}(U)x_t + \epsilon_t^{(2)}, \tag{4}$$

where the $\epsilon_t^{(2)}$ are the residuals from the final step of the stepwise regression of w_t on past x's.

Step 4. The correlogram of the residuals $\epsilon_t^{(2)}$ may now be used to obtain a revised estimate of the order of the polynomial $\theta(\ )$.[11]

It is not really plausible to assume that future values of the x series will be known at the time the y series is to be predicted. If they are not, we must assume something about the nature of the mechanism generating the series $\{x_t\}$ so that predictions of $\{y_t\}$ will, in general, be based on past values of $\{x_t\}$ as well as those of $\{y_t\}$. (There are however, circumstances, as we show later in this section, in which it is still only necessary to use the past values of the series to be predicted despite the presence of a related series.)

Consider the model

$$\varphi_1(U)y_t + \psi_1(U)x_t = \theta_1(U)\epsilon_{1t}, \qquad \varphi_2(U)y_t + \psi_2(U)x_t = \theta_2(U)\epsilon_{2t}, \tag{5}$$

where $\{\epsilon_{1t}\}$ and $\{\epsilon_{2t}\}$ are jointly stationary zero-mean white noise series with variances σ_{11} and σ_{22}, respectively. $\{\epsilon_{1t}\}$ and $\{\epsilon_{2t}\}$ may be independent, but in general we would expect them to be correlated at least contemporaneously, and possibly to be correlated with some lags as well.

As before, the first step in the analysis of the series $\{x_t\}$ and $\{y_t\}$ is to specify the orders of the polynomials $\varphi_1(\ ), \varphi_2(\ ), \psi_1(\ ), \psi_2(\ ), \theta_1(\ )$, and $\theta_2(\ )$; we must now also be concerned with the problem of identification in the usual econometric sense. [On this problem, see Hannan (1969a, 1971).] In general, the conditions for identifiability are somewhat weaker in the case of dynamic systems of the type (5) than in usual simultaneous systems because the supposed serial correlation of the disturbances may place additional restrictions on the form of each equation.

If $\{\epsilon_{1t}\}$ and $\{\epsilon_{2t}\}$ are independent and if $\varphi_2(\ ) \equiv 0$, we have a recursive system; both equations are identified. We may use the methods of Section 2 to determine the orders of $\psi_2(\ )$ and $\theta_2(\ )$ and a modification of the method described earlier in this section to determine the orders of $\varphi_1(\ ), \psi_1(\ )$, and $\theta_1(\ )$. While

---

[11] More than one auxiliary series presents no further problem in this procedure. Steps 1 and 2 are essentially the same. Step 3 now involves a stepwise regression on past values of both series. Only if the two series are highly correlated will there be any serious problem. But in this case, one of the two series is essentially redundant, and we might as well disregard it.

recursivity in this form may often be a plausible assumption, there are circumstances when joint dependence between $\{x_t\}$ and $\{y_t\}$ will be a more plausible assumption, either because $\{\epsilon_{1t}\}$ and $\{\epsilon_{2t}\}$ cannot be assumed to be independent or because $\varphi_1(\ )$ or $\varphi_2(\ )$ cannot be assumed identically zero. In this case, unfortunately, we know of no perfectly general method for determining the orders of the polynomials in the lag operator in (5). Without further a priori information, the parameters are simply underidentified and any procedure we might develop would be completely ad hoc. In our general discussion of estimation in subsequent chapters, we therefore simply assume that enough a priori information is available to identify (5) and that this information also specifies a fortiori the orders of the relevant polynomials.

If equations (5) are a recursive system, essentially the series $\{y_t\}$ is partially "explained" by the series $\{x_t\}$ but not vice versa. In this case, we modify the procedure previously found useful in the analyses described in Chapter XI in order to allow nonstationarities in the series $\{x_t\}$ to explain, insofar as is possible, the nonstationarities in the series $\{y_t\}$. A detailed description of our procedure is given in Chapter XI; a brief outline is as follows:

Step 1. Do a single time-series analysis on the two series separately, as described in Section 2, so as to obtain

$$\varphi_1^{(1)}(U)T_y(U)y_t = \theta_1^{(1)}(U)\epsilon_{1t}^{(1)}, \qquad \psi_2^{(1)}(U)T_x(U)x_t = \theta_2^{(1)}(U)\epsilon_{2t}^{(1)}, \tag{6}$$

where the superscript $^{(1)}$ denotes that these are the first-step estimates and where

$$T_y(U) = (1 - U)^{j_1}(1 - U^L)^{k_1}, \qquad T_x(U) = (1 - U)^{j_2}(1 - U^L)^{k_2}$$

are the differencing and "linking" transformations necessary to make $\{x_t\}$ and $\{y_t\}$ stationary in the usual Box–Jenkins approach.

Step 2. To determine the appropriate lags of the series $\{x_t\}$ in explaining $\{y_t\}$, we next do a stepwise regression of the series $\varphi_1^{(1)}(U)T_y(U)y_t$ on various lagged values of $T_x(U)x_t$. It is important to include a constant term in this regression and to limit the highest order of lag permitted (otherwise very long and unreasonable lags may be obtained in practice).

Step 3. Cancel whatever common factors there are in $T_y(U)$ and $T_x(U)$, leaving those not in common either in the series to be "explained" or in the "explanatory" series. This is the essence of "allowing nonstationarity in $\{x_t\}$ to explain nonstationarity in $\{y_t\}$." Usually, $T_y(U)$ and $T_x(U)$ will be identical, in which case the implication is that the remaining steps are carried out with the raw data. If not, consider the series $\{x_t\}$ and $\{y_t\}$ as transformed by the remaining factors, not in common, in an appropriate manner.

Step 4. Calculate an ordinary least-squares regression of y_t on the lags of y_t given by $\varphi_1^{(1)}(U) - 1$ and the lags of x_t given in Step 3, to obtain

$$\varphi_1^{(2)}(U)y_t = -\psi_1^{(2)}(U)x_t + \epsilon_{1t}^{(2)}, \tag{7}$$

where the superscript $^{(2)}$ denotes the second set of estimates of φ_1 and ψ_1, $\varphi_1^{(1)}$ and 0 being the first.

Step 5. Examine the autocorrelation and partial autocorrelation functions of the residuals $\epsilon_{1t}^{(2)}$ to determine a moving average (or in some cases an auto-regression) appropriate to it, say $\theta_1^{(2)}(U)$.

Step 6. Fit the model

$$\varphi_1(U)y_t + \psi_1(U)x_t = \theta_1(U)\epsilon_{1t}, \tag{8}$$

where the orders of φ_1, ψ_1, and θ_1 are given by $\varphi_1^{(2)}$, $\psi_1^{(2)}$, and $\theta_1^{(2)}$ respectively. The result of Step 1 for the series $\{x_t\}$ is the model for that series since we assume $\varphi_2(U) \equiv 0$ and $\{\epsilon_{1t}\}$ and $\{\epsilon_{2t}\}$ uncorrelated.

Methods of estimating both multivariate and univariate time-series models of the simple ARMA type, or of the UC type, are discussed in the next chapter.

Chapter VII
ESTIMATION OF UNOBSERVED-COMPONENTS AND CANONICAL MODELS

1. Introduction

This chapter deals with maximum-likelihood estimation of univariate ARMA and unobserved-components models in both the time and frequency domain and with multivariate time-series models in the frequency domain. The method for ARMA models in the time domain is basically that of Box and Jenkins (1970, Chapters 7 and 9, pp. 208–284, 300–333), although their suggestions have a number of important antecedents in the work of Durbin (1959) and Walker (1962).[1] [See Hannan (1970, Chapter 6, pp. 325–414) for a thorough discussion of inference and hypothesis testing for models with rational spectral densities.]

Our method for the estimation of unobserved-components models in the time domain was first introduced in an earlier paper by one of us (Nerlove, 1971) and involves reducing an unobserved-components model to its canonical form, to which the maximum-likelihood procedures of Box and Jenkins may be

---

[1] Important recent contributions include Chatfield and Prothero (1973) and Nelson (1974). In a short paper Newbold (1974) derives an *exact* likelihood function for a mixed autoregressive moving-average process. Newbold's result circumvents much of the complexity of Box–Jenkins' procedure, which relies on various approximations to the likelihood function. Most available computer programs continue to use the original Box–Jenkins procedures and recent comparisons (not only ours) of time and frequency domain estimation procedures such as Pukkila (1977) are between the original procedures suggested by Box and Jenkins and various alternatives. Hence, we present a rather complete account of the Box–Jenkins methods here, although in future work we would undoubtedly make extensive use of Newbold's formulation in time domain estimation. Curiously, Granger and Newbold (1977, pp. 83–89) themselves rely on a conditional likelihood or on the approximation to the likelihood suggested by Box and Jenkins.

applied, given suitable restrictions on the parameters of the canonical ARMA model. Some recent suggestions for estimation in the frequency domain (Hannan, 1969; Hannan and Nicholls, 1972; Nicholls, 1973; Nicholls *et al.*, 1975, pp. 123–125; and Pukkila, 1977), however, lead to much simpler procedures for estimation of unobserved-components models. Indeed, frequency domain methods turn out to be a great deal more efficient computationally, even for ARMA models, and to lead to very nearly the same results as do time domain estimates.[2]

Results of fitting ARMA models to eight time series by both time and frequency domain methods are presented in Chapter X. Unobserved-components models are estimated for the same eight series in Chapter XII. Chapter XI deals with the formulation and estimation of a recursive multiple time-series model for the prices of steers, heifers, and cows, which are three of the eight time series analyzed in Chapters X and XII. The multiple time-series model of Chapter XI is estimated only in the time domain, although frequency domain methods for estimation of multiple time-series models are discussed in this chapter.

2. ARMA Model Estimation in the Time Domain

This section deals with the estimation of ARMA models by maximum-likelihood methods. We first discuss the case of a single-component model, i.e., the standard case of a mixed moving-average autoregressive model, and then, in the next section, show how the method can be adapted to handle ARMA models that have arisen from, and are therefore the canonical forms of, unobserved-components models. In the section following, some suggestions of Hannan (1969), Hannan and Nicholls (1972), Nicholls (1973), Nicholls, *et al.* (1975, pp. 123–125), and Pukkila (1977) for estimation of ARMA models in the frequency domain are discussed, and we show how to extend these methods when the models arise from unobserved components.

In Chapter VI, we termed the basic mixed moving-average autoregressive model the canonical form, or canonical model, and saw how an unobserved-components model of a high degree of complexity could be expressed in terms of a much smaller number of parameters than the derived canonical form or any canonical model of equal complexity. The procedure developed by Box and Jenkins (1970) for estimation of mixed moving-average autoregressive models in canonical form involves searching the parameter space or the use of gradient maximization procedures. It is therefore imperative that the number of parameters be kept as small as possible.

Consider the canonical model

$$P(U)x_t = Q(U)\epsilon_t, \qquad \{\epsilon_t\} \text{ white noise,} \tag{1}$$

---

[2] This result has been verified by Monte Carlo experiments by Pukkila (1977) for relatively short time series ($T = 50$).

where $P(z)$ and $Q(z)$ are polynomials of orders m and n, respectively, such that $P(z)$ has roots all lying outside the unit circle, and $Q(z)$ has roots that all lie on or outside the unit circle. The series $\{x_t\}$ may, of course, be a transformation of the observed series whose structure we wish to describe. In Chapter V (V.2.4), we showed that the values of the white noise series $\{\epsilon_t\}$ are simply the one-step prediction errors of forecasts of x_t at time $t - 1$ using all the past information on $\{x_t\}$ up to and including x_{t-1} and given knowledge of the parameters of P and Q. In similar fashion, it can be shown that if we "backcast" the past values of $\{x_t\}$ at time t, given all *future* values of the series up to and including x_{t+1}, we can express $\{x_t\}$ in terms of the forward-shift operator U^{-1} and the one-step "backcast" errors η_t:

$$P(U^{-1})x_t = Q(U^{-1})\eta_t, \qquad \{\eta_t\} \text{ white noise}, \qquad (2)$$

where P and Q are polynomials identical to those appearing in the more usual formulation (1). The series $\{\eta_t\}$ will be different, however, from the series $\{\epsilon_t\}$. These two representations of the process $\{x_t\}$ are used in the computation of the value of the likelihood function for a given set of parameter values corresponding to the coefficients of P and Q.

REMARK. (See Box and Jenkins, 1970, pp. 195–199, 205–207.) It is clear from the canonical factorization of the spectral density function that (1) and (2) represent processes with exactly the same covariance structure; (2), however, has both moving-average and autoregressive structure in terms of the *forward-shift* operator U^{-1}. Exactly the same analysis applied in Chapter V to the *past* of the x series at time t may be applied to the *future* of the x series to show that the m.s.e. predictor of x_{t-v} in terms of $\eta_t, \eta_{t+1}, \ldots$ is $\hat{x}_{t-v,t} = b_v\eta_t + b_{v+1}\eta_{t+1} + \cdots$. Then this result is used to show, as in (V.2.4), that η_t is the one-step back minimum m.s.e. "backcast" error.

Although the series $\{\eta_t\}$ is white noise and has the same variance as $\{\epsilon_t\}$, the actual values of the series $\{\eta_t\}$ will clearly not be the same as the actual values of the $\{\epsilon_t\}$ for any given realization of $\{x_t\}$. The relation is easy to see for a process that is invertible, i.e., for which $B(z)$ has no zeros on the unit circle. Then $x_t = B(U)\epsilon_t = B(U^{-1})\eta_t$, so that

$$\eta_t = A(U^{-1})B(U)\epsilon_t, \qquad \text{where} \quad A(z) = 1/B(z).$$

If the $\{\epsilon_t\}$ are normally distributed with mean zero and variance σ^2, and if we observe a sample of T x's, $x_1, \ldots, x_T$, we may express the approximate likelihood function for the parameters $p_1, \ldots, p_m$, and $q_1, \ldots, q_n$ as

$$L(p_1, \ldots, p_m, q_1, \ldots, q_n | x_1, \ldots, x_T) = (2\pi\sigma^2)^{-T/2} \exp\left\{ -\frac{1}{2\sigma^2} \sum_{t=1}^{T} \epsilon_t^2 \right\}$$

$$= (2\pi\sigma^2)^{-T/2} \exp\left\{ -\frac{1}{2\sigma^2} S(p, q | x_1, \ldots, x_T) \right\}, \qquad (3)$$

where

$$S(p, q | x_1, \ldots, x_T) = \sum_{t=1}^{T} [x_t + p_1 x_{t-1} + \cdots - q_1 \epsilon_{t-1} - \cdots]^2. \qquad (4)$$

REMARK. Strictly speaking, L in (3) is not the likelihood for $p_1, \ldots, p_m$ and $q_1, \ldots, q_n$ since the conditions on the presample values of the series $\{x_t\}$ are ignored. If the series is stationary, the likelihood can be written down and is more complicated (see Newbold, 1974). If the series is not stationary, then $x_0, x_{-1}, \ldots, x_{1-m}$ and $\epsilon_0, \epsilon_{-1}, \ldots, \epsilon_{1-n}$ may be treated as a number of initiating constants. As E. J. Hannan has noted in private correspondence (1977), "The distinction is not irrelevant. For example, the full (stationary form) likelihood could *not* be maximized at a point where the autoregressive [generating function] had a zero on the unit circle, while it is very difficult also to maximize it for such a zero in the moving average [generating function]." On the other hand, treating presample values of $\{x_t\}$ and $\{\epsilon_t\}$ as fixed unknown constants to be estimated along with $p_1, \ldots, p_m$ and $q_1, \ldots, q_n$ raises some additional problems with the asymptotic theory. As an approximation, we and Box and Jenkins therefore adopt L in (3) with presample values as "known" constants as an approximate form. The word "known" is in quotation marks because, of course, there the presample values are not really known and must be estimated from the sample data.

Newbold's approach (1974) avoids this difficulty but at the expense of a considerably more complicated likelihood function. For an application of Newbold's result, see Osborn (1977).

For another approximate likelihood function based on the asymptotic distribution of the sample observations, see Anderson (1971, pp. 238–241).

A numerical procedure for obtaining the maximum-likelihood estimates of $p_1, \ldots, p_m$ and $q_1, \ldots, q_n$ is to minimize S with respect to the p's and q's if only we observed or had estimates of $x_0, x_{-1}, \ldots, x_{1-m}$ and $\epsilon_0, \epsilon_{-1}, \ldots, \epsilon_{1-n}$ *before* the sample period. Note that $\epsilon_1, \ldots, \epsilon_T$, which enter into successive values of the squared expression in (3), could then be calculated directly. Box and Jenkins (1970, pp. 215–220) suggest *estimating* these unknown values from the observed x's for the sample period by making use of the relations (1) and (2) and replacing unknown ϵ's and η's by their expectations conditional on the observed values $x_1, \ldots, x_T$. Their suggestion is implemented by noting that the values of ϵ_t, $\epsilon_{t+1}, \ldots$ are independent of $x_{t-1}, x_{t-2}, \ldots$ and the values of $\eta_t, \eta_{t-1}, \ldots$ are independent of $x_{t+1}, x_{t+2}, \ldots$. Thus,

$$\begin{aligned} E(\epsilon_t | x_1, \ldots, x_T) &= 0 \qquad \text{for} \quad t > T, \\ E(\eta_t | x_1, \ldots, x_T) &= 0 \qquad \text{for} \quad t < 1. \end{aligned} \tag{5}$$

If we had a pure moving-average process

$$x_t = \epsilon_t + q_1 \epsilon_{t-1} + \cdots + q_n \epsilon_{t-n}, \tag{6}$$

the calculation would be further simplified by the fact that

$$E(\epsilon_t | x_1, \ldots, x_T) = 0 \qquad \text{for} \quad t \leq -n. \tag{7}$$

Box and Jenkins make use of the further approximation that

$$E(\epsilon_t | x_1, \ldots, x_T) \approx 0 \qquad \text{for} \quad t \leq -N \ll -n \tag{8}$$

when $\{x_t\}$ is stationary even if it follows an autoregressive or a mixed process. We first illustrate their method for a finite pure moving-average process and then discuss the general procedure.

In order to calculate $\hat{\epsilon}_1$ from (6), we need estimates of $\epsilon_0, \epsilon_{-1}, \ldots, \epsilon_{-n+1}$. Since $\epsilon_{-n}, \epsilon_{-n-1}, \epsilon_{-n-2}$ are independent of the sample, their values can be estimated as zero. Consequently, it suffices to have estimates of $x_0, x_{-1}, \ldots,$ x_{-n+1}. These estimates are obtained by "backcasting" using the dual relation to (6):

$$x_t = \eta_t + q_1 \eta_{t+1} + \cdots + q_n \eta_{t+n}. \tag{9}$$

Here, Box and Jenkins (1970, p. 216) make the further approximation that $\eta_{T+1} = \eta_{T+2} = \cdots = \eta_{T+n} = 0$, arguing that the transient thus introduced will have little effect by the time we come to the beginning of the sample period and the computation of $x_0, x_{-1}, \ldots$. Thus, we estimate recursively

$$\hat{\eta}_T = x_T$$
$$\hat{\eta}_{T-1} = x_{T-1} - q_1 \hat{\eta}_T$$
$$\hat{\eta}_{T-2} = x_{T-2} - q_1 \hat{\eta}_{T-1} - q_2 \hat{\eta}_T \tag{10}$$
$$\vdots$$
$$\hat{\eta}_1 = x_1 - q_1 \hat{\eta}_2 - \cdots - q_n \hat{\eta}_{n+1}.$$

Now we "backcast" to estimate $x_0, x_{-1}, \ldots, x_{-n+1}$

$$\hat{x}_0 = 0 + q_1 \hat{\eta}_1 + \cdots + q_n \hat{\eta}_n$$
$$\hat{x}_{-1} = 0 + q_1 0 + \cdots + q_n \hat{\eta}_{n-1} \tag{11}$$
$$\vdots$$
$$\hat{x}_{-n+1} = 0 + q_1 0 + \cdots + q_n \hat{\eta}_1$$

since $E(\eta_t | x_1, \ldots, x_T) = 0$ for $t < 1$. Now we calculate

$$\hat{\epsilon}_{-n+1} = \hat{x}_{-n+1} - q_1 0 - \cdots - q_n 0$$
$$\hat{\epsilon}_{-n+2} = \hat{x}_{-n+2} - q_1 \hat{\epsilon}_{-n+1} - \cdots - q_n 0 \tag{12}$$
$$\vdots$$
$$\hat{\epsilon}_0 = \hat{x}_0 - q_1 \hat{\epsilon}_{-1} - \cdots - q_{n-1} \hat{\epsilon}_{-n+1} - q_n 0$$

since $\hat{\epsilon}_{-n} = 0$ by (7). These values may now be used with the observed series $x_1, \ldots, x_T$ to calculate estimates of $\epsilon_1, \ldots, \epsilon_T$ and so to estimate $S(q|x_1, \ldots, x_T)$ for given q. The sequence of calculations must be repeated for every different value of q in order to define S as a function of q. Of course, from a practical point of view, we write the sequence of computations as a subroutine and do the calculations only for certain values of q determined by a search or gradient maximization procedure.

Now let us consider what modification of this method is necessary when the process is a mixed moving-average autoregressive process. In this case we have

$$x_t + p_1 x_{t-1} + \cdots + p_m x_{t-m} = \epsilon_t + q_1 \epsilon_{t-1} + \cdots + q_n \epsilon_{t-n}. \tag{13}$$

Thus to calculate $S(p, q|x_1, \ldots, x_T)$ we need estimates of $x_0, x_{-1}, \ldots, x_{-m+1}$ and $\epsilon_0, \epsilon_{-1}, \ldots, \epsilon_{-n+1}$. Starting our "backcast" computation therefore with

η_{T-m}, where $T > m$,

$$\hat{\eta}_{T-m} = x_{T-m} + p_1 x_{T-m+1} + \cdots + p_m x_T$$
$$\hat{\eta}_{T-m-1} = x_{T-m-1} + p_1 x_{T-m} + \cdots + p_m x_{T-1} - q_1 \hat{\eta}_{T-m}$$
$$\hat{\eta}_{T-m-2} = x_{T-m-2} + p_1 x_{T-m-1} + \cdots + p_m x_{T-2} - q_1 \hat{\eta}_{T-m-1} - q_2 \hat{\eta}_{T-m} \quad (14)$$
$$\vdots$$
$$\hat{\eta}_1 = x_1 + \cdots + p_m x_{m+1} - q_1 \hat{\eta}_2 - q_2 \hat{\eta}_3 - \cdots - q_n \hat{\eta}_{n+1},$$

where, as before, we have set the values $\eta_{T-m+1}, \eta_{T-m+2}, \ldots$ equal to zero, introducing a transient that will hopefully wash out by the time we reach the beginning of the series. Next we calculate

$$\hat{x}_0 = 0 + q_1 \hat{\eta}_1 + \cdots + q_n \hat{\eta}_n - p_1 x_1 - \cdots - p_m x_m$$
$$\hat{x}_{-1} = 0 + q_1 0 + \cdots + q_n \hat{\eta}_{n-1} - p_1 \hat{x}_0 - \cdots - p_m x_{m-1}$$
$$\vdots \qquad\qquad\qquad\qquad\qquad\qquad (15)$$
$$\hat{x}_{-n+1} = 0 + q_1 0 + \cdots + q_n \hat{\eta}_1 - p_1 \hat{x}_{-n+2} - \cdots - p_m \hat{x}_{m-n+1},$$

where, as before, we make use of (5), and where $\hat{x}_{m-n+1}$ is an actual sample value or a previously estimated value according as $m \geq n$ or $n > m$. Now, however, instead of stopping at $\hat{x}_{-n+1}$ we continue to process until we obtain $\hat{x}_{-N}$ approximately zero. At this distant point, the approximation (8) is valid and we can compute

$$\hat{\epsilon}_{-N+1} = \hat{x}_{-N+1} + p_1 0 + \cdots + p_m 0 - q_1 0 - \cdots - q_n 0$$
$$\hat{\epsilon}_{-N+2} = \hat{x}_{-N+2} + p_1 \hat{x}_{-N+1} + \cdots + p_m 0 - q_1 \hat{\epsilon}_{-N+1} - \cdots - q_n 0$$
$$\vdots \qquad\qquad\qquad\qquad\qquad\qquad (16)$$
$$\hat{\epsilon}_0 = \hat{x}_0 + p_1 \hat{x}_{-1} + \cdots + p_m \hat{x}_{-m} - q_1 \hat{\epsilon}_{-1} - \cdots - q_n \hat{\epsilon}_{-n}.$$

We now have all the values necessary to calculate $S(p, q | x_1, \ldots, x_T)$ for any specified values of $p_1, p_2, \ldots, p_m$, and $q_1, q_2, \ldots, q_n$. As before, these calculations are arranged in a function subroutine that may be called repeatedly by a search or gradient maximization procedure.

3. UC Model Estimation in the Time Domain

The method for estimating an ordinary ARMA model described above may be adapted for the estimation of an unobserved-components model by expressing the parameters of the canonical form of the latter $(p_1, \ldots, p_m, q_1, \ldots, q_n)$ in terms of the original parameters of the unobserved-components form, in the manner described in Section 2 of Chapter IV. Alternatively, we may use a method suggested by Hannan (1969) to estimate these parameters in the frequency domain without the necessity of calculating the canonical form of the model. This method is discussed in the next section. Here we show how the analysis may be carried out entirely in the time domain by factoring the auto-covariance generating transform of the unobserved-components model numerically in order to express the model in canonical form. Both methods are used in the applications presented in Chapters X and XII and the results compared.

In what follows we use $p_1, \ldots, p_m$ and $q_1, \ldots, q_n$ to represent the parameters of the canonical model rather than $a_1, \ldots, a_m$ and $b_1, \ldots, b_n$. Let the unobserved-components model to be estimated be

$$x_t = (R_1(U)/S_1(U))\epsilon_{1t} + (R_2(U)/S_2(U))\epsilon_{2t} + \epsilon_{3t}, \tag{1}$$

where $\{\epsilon_{1t}\}$, $\{\epsilon_{2t}\}$, and $\{\epsilon_{3t}\}$ are independent Gaussian white noise inputs and R_1, R_2, S_1, and S_2 are polynomials whose roots are appropriately located.

$$g_{xx}(z) = \frac{\left(\begin{array}{c} R_1(z)R_1(z^{-1})S_2(z)S_2(z^{-1})\sigma_1^2 + R_2(z)R_2(z^{-1})S_1(z)S_1(z^{-1})\sigma_2^2 \\ + S_1(z)S_1(z^{-1})S_2(z)S_2(z^{-1})\sigma_3^2 \end{array} \right)}{S_1(z)S_1(z^{-1})S_2(z)S_2(z^{-1})}. \tag{2}$$

If we have expressed S_1 and S_2 in terms of their roots or in any other parametric form, we can easily calculate the coefficients of the autoregressive part of (2.1). For example, suppose

$$S_1(U) = (1 - \alpha_1 U)(1 - \alpha_2 U), \qquad S_2(U) = 1 - \gamma U^{12};$$

then

$$P(U) = (1 - \alpha_1 U)(1 - \alpha_2 U)(1 - \gamma U^{12})$$
$$= 1 - (\alpha_1 + \alpha_2)U + \alpha_1\alpha_2 U^2 - \gamma U^{12} + \gamma(\alpha_1 + \alpha_2)U^{13} - \gamma\alpha_1\alpha_2 U^{14},$$

so

$$p_1 = -(\alpha_1 + \alpha_2)$$
$$p_2 = \alpha_1\alpha_2$$
$$p_3 = 0$$
$$\vdots$$
$$p_{11} = 0$$
$$p_{12} = -\gamma$$
$$p_{13} = \gamma(\alpha_1 + \alpha_2)$$
$$p_{14} = -\gamma\alpha_1\alpha_2.$$

The moving-average coefficients in (2.1) are determined by the numerator of the expression for $g_{xx}(z)$ in (2). This is a symmetric polynomial of degree $2\max\{m_1 + n_2, m_2 + n_1, n_1 + n_2\} = 2n$, where m_1 is the degree of R_1, m_2 the degree of R_2, n_1 the degree of S_1, and n_2 the degree of S_2. This polynomial has $2n$ roots, n of which lie on or outside the unit circle. If we can factor this polynomial and separate the roots, choosing those lying on or outside the unit circle, we can express the numerator of (2) as

$$cQ(z)Q(z^{-1}) = c \prod_{j=1}^{n} (1 - \lambda_j z)(1 - \lambda_j z^{-1}),\tag{3}$$

where $|\lambda_j| \leq 1$ for $j = 1, \ldots, n$. The coefficient c is determined as described in Section 2 of Chapter IV; c may be disregarded, however, in calculations that follow, provided the estimates of the variances, σ_1^2, σ_2^2, and σ_3^2, are scaled appropriately at the end of the process to yield a sum of squares equivalent to the process described in the previous section. We then identify Q as

$$Q(U) = 1 + q_1 U + \cdots + q_n U^n = \prod_{j=1}^{n} (1 - \lambda_j U),\tag{4}$$

so that

$$q_1 = -\sum_{j=1}^{n} \lambda_j$$

$$q_2 = \sum_{j=1}^{n-1} \sum_{k>j}^{n} \lambda_j \lambda_k\tag{5}$$

$$\vdots$$

$$q_n = (-1)^n \lambda_1 \lambda_2 \cdot \ldots \cdot \lambda_n.$$

Thus equations (5), the relation $P(U) = S_1(U)S_2(U)$, and the relation between the parameters of R_1, R_2, S_1, S_2, σ_1^2, σ_2^2, and σ_3^2 permit us to establish an exact relation between each of the parameters $p_1, \ldots, p_m, q_1, \ldots, q_n$ and the parameters of the unobserved-components model. In the form of a subroutine, this allows us to minimize $S(p, q | x_1, \ldots, x_T)$ with respect to the parameters of the unobserved-components model rather than the canonical form.

A number of computational problems arise in the implementation of this method, which we now discuss: First, the parameters of the unobserved-components model may not be identified; that is, a given set of values of the p's and q's may be consistent with multiple sets of values of the set of the coefficients and variances in the unobserved-components model. If this is the case, the latter are not identified, in the usual sense that we cannot obtain unique estimates of these parameters. If we are satisfied, however, with *some* estimate, then no harm is done. We must only be careful to use a *local* minimization procedure for minimizing $S(p, q | x_1, \ldots, x_T)$ as a function of the parameters of the unobserved-components model. A global minimization procedure will not converge in the unidentified case. Starting the local procedure at different points in the parameter space should reveal both lack of identification and/or the presence of several local minima. If these occur at different levels, the lowest should be selected; lack of identification is revealed by minima occurring at approximately the same level for different values of the parameters.

A second computational problem that must be solved is the factorization of the numerator of (2). This is a high-order polynomial, the roots of which come in reciprocal pairs. In principle, there is no difficulty in obtaining numerically the roots of a polynomial regardless of order, and a variety of methods are available to do this. Difficulties do arise, however, if the roots lie close together, and in the type of problem considered here this may well be the case. (See Couts et al., 1966.) There is, also, the question of how to take advantage of the special characteristics of the polynomial to be factored. One possibility is simply to ignore the fact that the roots come in reciprocal pairs. If the polynomial is $R(z) = \sum_{-n}^{n} a_i z^i$, one may simply multiply by z^n and then use any standard factoring procedure. If n is fairly large (14 in this case), the execution time may be quite long. More important, there is no guarantee that as many roots will be found inside the unit circle as outside it. If n is large, and many roots are close to the unit circle, this latter possibility may be a real problem.

One procedure used in our calculations reported in Chapter XII is a modification of Muller (1956). The Muller method was modified in two ways. If a root was found, both the root and its reciprocal were accepted (for a complex root four roots were taken at once: $r, 1/r, \bar{r}, 1/\bar{r}$). Another change made was to guard against clusters. If a predetermined number of iterations did not give $|R(z)|$ sufficiently small, then the search was restarted in the neighborhood of the reciprocal of the last iteration. The idea was that clusters were more likely to be inside the unit circle, and by jumping outside, the search could continue in an area where the roots were farther apart. All calculations on IBM machines were performed in double precision, those on CDC machines in single precision; in several trials no trouble was encountered. While this method adopted is probably not the most efficient way to handle this kind of polynomial, it is sufficiently fast in most cases. In all cases on which we have used the routine, the absolute value of the function was less than 10^{-14} at the roots. As a further check, the roots were convolved to reproduce the original polynomial. The least accurate term agreed to four digits (single precision was used for this check).

REMARK.   A second procedure may be necessary if a large number of calculations are to be performed. A different polynomial factorization routine may be based upon the Newton–Raphson iterative technique and designed to take advantage of the special characteristics of the polynomial to be factored that result from its properties as an autocovariance generating transform. These are, as noted, that the roots occur in double pairs so that if a number is a root, so is its reciprocal, its complex conjugate, and the reciprocal of its complex conjugate. These properties enable us to transform the problem of evaluating the roots of a polynomial of degree $2n$ to the problem of evaluating the roots of a polynomial of degree n. Let the polynomial be of the form

$$P(x) = a_0 + a_1(x + x^{-1}) + \cdots + a_n(x^n + x^{-n}). \tag{i}$$

Define

$$V_p = x^p + x^{-p}, \qquad y = x + x^{-1} = V_1. \tag{ii}$$

Then

$$V_{p+1} = V_p y - V_{p-1}, \qquad p \geq 1, \tag{iii}$$

where $V_0 = 2$. Thus, $p(x)$ may be rewritten as

$$P(x) = a_0 + a_1 V_1 + \cdots + a_n V_n = Q(y),\qquad\text{(iv)}$$

which is, in fact, a polynomial of order n in y, where the actual expressions in y follow recursively from (iii). Alternatively, let η_1 and η_2 be the two roots of the characteristic polynomial of the difference equation (iii), where the roots are assumed to be distinct,

$$z^2 - yz + 1 = 0.\qquad\text{(v)}$$

It may be verified that

$$V_p = \eta_1^p + \eta_2^p,\qquad\text{(vi)}$$

where

$$\eta_1 = \frac{y + \sqrt{y^2 - 4}}{2},\qquad \eta_2 = \frac{y - \sqrt{y^2 - 4}}{2},\qquad\text{(vii)}$$

since (iii) is a second-order difference equation subject to the initial conditions $V_0 = 2$, $V_1 = y$. Note that η_2 is the reciprocal of η_1. Substituting for V_p in (iv) yields a polynomial of degree n in y.

The coefficients of the new polynomial are rather complicated expressions in the coefficients $a_0, a_1, \ldots, a_n$ of the original polynomial obtained by collecting terms of common powers of y in

$$Q(y) = a_0 + a_1(\eta_1 + \eta_2) + \cdots + a_p(\eta_1^p + \eta_2^p) + \cdots + a_n(\eta_1^n + \eta_2^n)$$

$$= a_0 + a_1 y + \cdots + \frac{a_p}{2^p} \sum_{k=0}^{p} \binom{p}{k} y^{p-k}[(\sqrt{y^2 - 4})^k + (-1)^k(\sqrt{y^2 - 4})^k]$$

$$+ \cdots + \frac{a_n}{2^n} \sum_{k=0}^{n} \binom{n}{k} y^{n-k}[(\sqrt{y^2 - 4})^k + (-1)^k(\sqrt{y^2 - 4})^k].\qquad\text{(viii)}$$

Since the terms in square brackets vanish for odd k, $Q(y)$ "simplifies" to

$$Q(y) = a_0 + \sum_{p=1}^{n} \frac{a_p}{2^{p-1}} \sum_{j=0}^{[p/2]} \binom{p}{2j} y^{p-2j}(y^2 - 4)^j,\qquad\text{(ix)}$$

where $[p/2]$ is the greatest integer less than or equal to $p/2$. The two reciprocal roots satisfying (i) are then obtained from (ii) for each of the n roots of the polynomial in y. The latter are obtained by the Newton–Raphson iteration technique commonly employed for such purposes. A good polynomial factorization routine is given in Robinson (1967, pp. 28–38).

In the method of estimation in the time domain, the polynomial factorization routine is called each time the sum of squares of one-step prediction errors appearing in the likelihood function is computed by the minimization procedure employed since the model in unobserved-components form must be expressed in canonical form for any set of parameter values in order to carry out the calculation of the function to be minimized. For this reason it is clear that, in general, the gradient and the matrix of second-order partial derivatives of the log likelihood function or the sum of squared one-step prediction errors cannot be expressed analytically. The procedure we use in our calculations reported in Chapter XII is the functional minimization algorithm of Davidon (1959) as modified by Fletcher and Powell (1963) and further modified by Stewart (1967) in order to avoid analytical evaluation of either the gradient or the matrix of second-order partial derivatives for the function minimized. This algorithm makes use of a variable step size at each iteration determined by a local quadratic approximation to the function being minimized. Convergence of Davidon's method is guaranteed only if the gradient can be calculated analytically; since it cannot and is not in this case, convergence may not be obtained if the function minimized is not smooth or has asymptotes in a region of the point at which a local quadratic approximation is being obtained by numerical perturbation of the function itself. Lack of smoothness makes the direction of descent quite unreliable; the presence of nearby asymptotes causes the step length to become extremely large. This last effect is perhaps the most serious, since large step lengths may send the routine off into distant regions of the parameter space or, worse, into regions where the function being minimized is not well defined (e.g., regions where the process described by the unobserved-components model would be nonstationary).[3] Consequently, our version of the Davidon–Fletcher–Powell–Stewart algorithm incorporates an upper bound on the step size. We also considered, but ultimately did not employ, a transformation of the parameter space and introduction of a penalty function designed to force convergence in the region of the parameter space where the function being minimized is well defined.

REMARK.   It is worthwhile to illustrate the manner in which such constraints may be imposed, although such imposition may be seen to add greatly to the computational burden. Consider the simple three-component model set forth previously: The observed series $\{x_t\}$, which may be the first differences of the original series, is assumed to be decomposed as

$$x_t = \frac{1 + \beta_1 U + \beta_2 U^2}{(1 - \alpha_1 U)(1 - \alpha_2 U)} \epsilon_{1t} + \frac{1 + \beta_3 U + \beta_4 U^2}{1 - \gamma U^{12}} \epsilon_{2t} + \epsilon_{3t},$$

where $\{\epsilon_{1t}\}$, $\{\epsilon_{2t}\}$, and $\{\epsilon_{3t}\}$ are independent Gaussian white noise inputs with zero means and variances σ_1^2, σ_2^2, and σ_3^2, respectively. In order to ensure stationarity, $|\alpha_1|, |\alpha_2|, |\gamma| < 1$, although α_1 and α_2 may be complex, in which case α_1 and α_2 are conjugates. We further restrict the moving averages in the numerators of the first and second components to being "invertible" so that these components will have the autoregressive representations essential for the method of estimation employed; this implies the additional constraints $-(\beta_1 + \beta_2) < 1$, $\beta_1 - \beta_2 < 1$, $|\beta_2| < 1$, $-(\beta_3 + \beta_4) < 1$, $\beta_3 - \beta_4 < 1$, and $|\beta_4| < 1$, where β_1, β_2, β_3, and β_4 are assumed to be real [see Box and Jenkins (1970, p. 70)]. Let (ξ_1, ξ_2) be defined as

$$\begin{pmatrix} \xi_1 \\ \xi_2 \end{pmatrix} = \begin{pmatrix} 1 & 1 \\ -1 & 1 \end{pmatrix} \begin{pmatrix} \beta_1 \\ \beta_2 + 1 \end{pmatrix} \quad \text{or} \quad \begin{pmatrix} 1 & 1 \\ -1 & 1 \end{pmatrix} \begin{pmatrix} \beta_3 \\ \beta_4 + 1 \end{pmatrix};$$

if these values are now transformed to polar coordinates $(\xi_1, \xi_2) \to (\rho, \theta)$,

$$\rho = \sqrt{\xi_1^2 + \xi_2^2}, \qquad \theta = \arctan(-\xi_2/\xi_1),$$

where the restrictions are

$$0 < \theta < \pi/2, \qquad 0 < \rho < R = 4/(\cos \theta + \sin \theta).$$

---

[3] Since the direction and magnitude of the step is determined by updating an approximation of the inverse of the matrix of second-order partial derivatives, large jumps in the parameter values may move the point in the parameter space outside of a locally concave region, rendering the matrix useless in determining the length of the next step. Decreasing the scale of the step size uniformly mitigates such difficulties, but only at a cost of increasing computational time significantly.

A further transformation to

$$\eta_1 = \text{arc sin}\{2\theta/\pi\}, \qquad \eta_2 = \text{arc sin}\{\rho/R\}$$

ensures that the restrictions in polar coordinate form will be satisfied for *any* pair (η_1, η_2). Locally, the transformations $(\xi_1, \xi_2) \to (\eta_1, \eta_2)$ are one-to-one; hence, these transformations cannot introduce any other distinct local maxima or minima, and provided estimation is terminated once any one local maximum or minimum has been found, a unique estimate of (ξ_1, ξ_2) is obtained that satisfies the conditions for invertibility, except possibly at the boundary.

In order to prevent a boundary solution, a feasible region strictly inside the boundary may be employed to force the parameter point away from the boundary. If a boundary solution for this "inside" feasible region is obtained, the region may then be expanded so that a new feasible region still closer to the boundary is used. The rationale for this rather elaborate procedure is that near the boundaries defining stationarity and invertibility, the sum of squares function becomes extremely sensitive to small perturbations in the parameter values and the numerically calculated first and second derivatives highly unstable; thus the step size and direction of descent are ill-determined in the vicinity of a boundary. By forcing a solution away from a boundary we can ensure convergence; at the same time, solutions on "inside" boundaries ever closer to the true boundaries signal the possibility of a true boundary solution—and trouble! To enforce the restrictions on the auto-regressive part of the trend-cycle component, it suffices to take ξ_1 and ξ_2 as above with $\beta_1 = -(\alpha_1 + \alpha_2)$ and $\beta_2 = \alpha_1\alpha_2$. To force $0 \leq \gamma < 1$, take $\gamma = \sin^2\eta$.

The variances σ_1^2, σ_2^2, and σ_3^2 may be constrained to be positive by estimating their square roots. Unfortunately, in actual application, it is frequently true that a boundary solution $\sigma_3^2 = 0$ emerges as the maximum of the likelihood function, suggesting the absence of a third component.

In fact, in the calculations reported in Chapter XII, we did not impose any such constraints. The only constraint that we ever found to be violated, however, was $\sigma_3^2 \geq 0$. In such cases we simply set $\sigma_3^2 = 0$ and estimated a two-component model. In general, the computational procedures in the time domain discussed here proved to be relatively unsatisfactory, compared to those in the frequency domain, in terms of converging within a reasonable amount of time. The estimates obtained, however, were typically close to those obtained in the frequency domain; hence, although it is nice to know that unobserved-components models can be estimated in the time domain, we would recommend that if such models are to be formulated and estimated, frequency domain methods be used. Indeed, even ordinary ARMA models appear to be estimated much more efficiently in the frequency domain, with results almost always very close to estimates obtained by the procedures used in the time domain.[4]

[4] This conclusion is supported as well by recent Monte Carlo studies of Pukkila (1977). Pukkila examines a variety of time series generated by mixed moving-average autoregressive processes, pure moving-average processes, and pure autoregressive processes (altogether 77 parameter combinations). For time series of lengths 50 and 100, Pukkila computes maximum-likelihood estimates by the procedures suggested by Box and Jenkins and by two alternative procedures in the frequency domain, maximum likelihood and a least-squares approximation thereto. Although, for very short time series that have not been modified by "tapering," Pukkila finds that the Box–Jenkins procedures produce better estimates than frequency domain methods when the time parameter values lie close to the boundary of the stationarity-invertibility region, this is no longer true when the parameter values are more centrally located, when a longer time series is used without "tapering," or when shorter time series are used in modified form.

Of course, these comparisons do not make use of modified procedures in the time domain suggested by Newbold's (1974) derivation of the exact likelihood function. Conceivably, a time domain procedure for either unobserved-components or ordinary ARMA models might outperform frequency domain methods both in statistical accuracy and speed of computation.

4.   ARMA Model Estimation in the Frequency Domain

Computations in the time domain, even for ARMA models, are rather complex. For unobserved-components models, the canonical form of the unobserved-components model must be calculated at each evaluation of the sum of squares in the likelihood function for given values of the model's parameters. Fortunately, an asymptotically efficient method, which avoids the tedious canonical calculation, has been described by Hannan (1969). Hannan actually deals with straightforward ARMA models, but a simple modification of his method makes it applicable to models of the unobserved-components type. In this section, we deal with application of frequency domain methods to ARMA models; the next section discusses its extension to UC models.

It is well known that the variance–covariance matrix for a vector of T components, each of which is an observation on a member of a sequence generated by a stationary nondeterministic process, has characteristic roots that are asymptotically values of the spectral density of the process at equally spaced frequencies, $\lambda_j = 2\pi j/T, j = 0, \ldots, T - 1$, in the interval $(0, 2\pi)$ or, alternatively, $(-\pi, \pi)$. [See Grenander and Rosenblatt (1957, Chapter 7, pp. 226–240), Hannan (1960, p. 27), Watson (1967, pp. 1696–1698), and Hannan (1969); the result appears first in Whittle (1951).] Hannan's method is to consider the Fourier transform of the observed series $\{x_t\}$:

$$w_j = \frac{1}{\sqrt{2\pi T}} \sum_{t=1}^{T} x_t e^{it\lambda_j}, \tag{1}$$

where $j = 0, \ldots, T - 1$. Thus, the values $w_0, \ldots, w_{T-1}$ represent a transformation of the vector $x = (x_1, \ldots, x_T)'$ by the matrix

$$P = \frac{1}{\sqrt{2\pi T}} \begin{bmatrix} e^{i1\lambda_0} & e^{i2\lambda_0} & \cdots & e^{iT\lambda_0} \\ e^{i1\lambda_1} & e^{i2\lambda_1} & \cdots & e^{iT\lambda_1} \\ \vdots & \vdots & & \vdots \\ e^{i1\lambda_{T-1}} & e^{i2\lambda_{T-1}} & \cdots & e^{iT\lambda_{T-1}} \end{bmatrix}, \tag{2}$$

which is proportional to a unitary matrix, the factor of proportionality being $1/\sqrt{2\pi}$. The modulus of the Jacobian of this transformation is $(2\pi)^{-T/2}$.

If $\{x_t\}$ is generated by a mixed moving-average autoregressive process or unobserved-components model with Gaussian innovations, the vector x will itself be multivariate normal with some variance–covariance matrix Γ, which may be determined by the methods outlined in Chapter IV. The transformed variables

$$w = Px \tag{3}$$

will also be multivariate normal with variance–covariance matrix

$$\Omega = P\Gamma P^*, \tag{4}$$

where P^* is the complex conjugate transpose of P. Asymptotically, the matrix

Ω tends to

$$\begin{bmatrix} f(\lambda_0) & 0 & \cdots & 0 \\ 0 & f(\lambda_1) & \cdots & 0 \\ \vdots & \vdots & & \vdots \\ 0 & 0 & \cdots & f(\lambda_{T-1}) \end{bmatrix}$$

by the result stated previously.

Now consider the joint density of the innovations of the canonical form of the process generating $\{x_t\}$, which underlies the approximate likelihood function (2.3). As indicated in our earlier discussion, $\epsilon_1, \ldots, \epsilon_T$, are not directly observable, and estimation of the parameters p and q from (2.3) or the more basic parameters of an underlying unobserved-components model depends upon how we treat their values, given only the sample $(x_1, \ldots, x_T)'$ of observed values. The approximation discussed in Section 2 conditions on values prior to and subsequent to the sample period itself. The frequency domain method suggested by Hannan avoids these complexities. If the series $\{\epsilon_t\}$ is Gaussian, then so must $\{x_t\}$ be. Hence the joint density function of $(x_1, \ldots, x_T)'$ is

$$(2\pi)^{-T/2} |\Gamma^{-1}|^{1/2} \exp\{-\tfrac{1}{2} x' \Gamma^{-1} x\},$$

where Γ is determined by the variance σ^2 and the parameters of the process generating $\{x_t\}$ from $\{\epsilon_t\}$. [Newbold (1974) gives an exact representation.] Consequently, the vector w in (3) has the joint density function

$$(2\pi)^{-T/2} |\Omega^{-1}|^{1/2} \exp\{-\tfrac{1}{2} w^* \Omega^{-1} w\}.$$

Asymptotically, the logarithmic likelihood function for the parameters of the process is

$$L(p_1, \ldots, p_m; q_1, \ldots, q_n | x_1, \ldots, x_T)$$

$$= -\frac{T}{2} \log 2\pi - \frac{1}{2} \sum_{j=0}^{T-1} \log f(\lambda_j) - \frac{1}{2} \sum_{j=0}^{T-1} \frac{I(\lambda_j)}{f(\lambda_j)}, \tag{5}$$

where

$$I(\lambda_j) = |w_j|^2 = \frac{1}{2\pi T} \left| \sum_{t=1}^{T} x_t e^{it\lambda_j} \right|^2$$

is proportional to the periodogram of the series $\{x_t\}$. This result is only asymptotic since $\Omega \to \operatorname{diag} f(\lambda_j)$ only as $T \to \infty$. [See also Fishman (1969, pp. 152–154).] When this is the case, it is clear we can also neglect the second term on the right-hand side of (5) since the third term, which depends on the observations, will come to dominate the value of the likelihood function; nonetheless, for small samples, it may be useful to include the second term in the expression to be maximized since the term may then make an important difference in the estimates obtained.

Alternatively, the same result can be derived by making use of the distributional properties of the periodogram ordinates $I(\lambda_j), j = 0, 1, \ldots, T - 1$. (See Pukkila, 1977, p. 50.) The periodogram ordinates are asymptotically independently distributed (Brillinger, 1975, p. 95), and the random variables $2I(\lambda_j)/f(\lambda_j)$ have an asymptotic chi-square distribution with two degrees of freedom (L. H. Koopmans, 1974, pp. 260–265). This means that the asymptotic density of the random variable $I(\lambda_j)$ is

$$h(I(\lambda_j)) = [1/f(\lambda_j)]e^{-I(\lambda_j)/f(\lambda_j)}, \qquad I(\lambda_j) \geq 0.$$

Making use of the asymptotic independence of the $I(\lambda_j)$ then yields the approximate likelihood function in (5).

Note that the "true" spectral density of the time series $\{x_t\}$, $f(\lambda_j)$, depends on the parameters of the process assumed to generate the series, whether this be a simple ARMA model or a more complex unobserved-components model. In general, these parameters enter the likelihood function in a highly nonlinear way, so that numerical procedures must be used as in the methods described earlier. Much of Hannan (1969), for example, is devoted to the development of an iterative procedure for the solution of the equations obtained by setting the derivatives of

$$w^*\Omega^{-1}w = \sum_{j=0}^{T-1} \frac{I(\lambda_j)}{f(\lambda_j)}$$

to zero. But there is no reason why a gradient procedure cannot be used to maximize the likelihood function directly, or to minimize $w^*\Omega^{-1}w$ directly. In contrast with our earlier procedure, based on Box and Jenkins' method for maximizing the likelihood function in the time domain, the estimation of unobserved-components models does not require us to obtain the canonical form of the model at each iteration. Since determination of the canonical form for a given set of parameter values requires the factorization of a high order polynomial, it is clear that frequency domain methods may offer a considerable advantage.

Before illustrating the likelihood function, it is useful to derive some general results that are used in the applications described in Chapter XII.

First, if we are dealing with an ARMA model it is useful to "concentrate" the likelihood function by maximizing out σ^2, the parameter reflecting the variance of the innovations of the process. For convenience, define the covariance generating function of the process as $\sigma^2 g(z)$, rather than incorporating the factor σ^2 in g as before. Since $f(\lambda) = (\sigma^2/2\pi)g(e^{i\lambda})$, the likelihood function (5) becomes

$$\begin{aligned}
L &= -\frac{T}{2}\log 2\pi - \frac{T}{2}\log\frac{\sigma^2}{2\pi} - \frac{1}{2}\sum_{j=0}^{T-1}\log g(e^{i\lambda_j}) - \frac{2\pi}{2\sigma^2}\sum_{j=0}^{T-1}\frac{I(\lambda_j)}{g(e^{i\lambda_j})} \\
&= -\frac{T}{2}\log\sigma^2 - \frac{1}{2}\sum_{j=0}^{T-1}\left[\log g + \frac{2\pi}{\sigma^2}\frac{I}{g}\right],
\end{aligned} \qquad (6)$$

suppressing the explicit dependence of I and g on λ_j for convenience. Thus

$$\hat{\sigma}^2 = \frac{2\pi}{T} \sum_{j=0}^{T-1} \frac{I}{g}. \tag{7}$$

Of course, g depends on the other parameters of the autocovariance generating function. Let these for convenience be denoted as α and β, where α and β are considered as typical elements of vectors of parameters in the calculations that follow.

The likelihood function concentrated with respect to σ^2 is therefore

$$L^* = -\frac{T}{2}\left[\log\frac{2\pi}{T} + 1\right] - \frac{T}{2}\log\sum_{j=0}^{T-1}\frac{I}{g} - \frac{1}{2}\sum_{j=0}^{T-1}\log g. \tag{8}$$

The gradient of the concentrated likelihood function with respect to an arbitrary parameter α of g is

$$\frac{\partial L^*}{\partial \alpha} = \sum_{j=0}^{T-1}\left[\frac{2\pi}{\hat{\sigma}^2}\frac{I}{g} - 1\right]\left(\frac{1}{2g}\frac{\partial g}{\partial \alpha}\right). \tag{9}$$

Note that $\hat{\sigma}^2$ depends on α through its dependence on g. The gradient is used in the numerical calculations described in Chapter XII.

To obtain an asymptotic variance–covariance matrix of the maximum-likelihood estimates we may use the matrix of second-order partial derivatives of the unconcentrated or concentrated logarithmic likelihood function, even though the second-order partials of L with respect to a parameter α of g *and* with respect to σ^2 do not vanish at the maximum.

Remark. From (6)

$$\frac{\partial L}{\partial \sigma^2} = -\frac{T}{2}\frac{1}{\sigma^2} + \frac{1}{2}\frac{2\pi}{(\sigma^2)^2}\sum\frac{I}{g}. \tag{i}$$

Differentiating a second time with respect to an arbitrary parameter α of g, we have

$$\frac{\partial^2 L}{\partial \sigma^2 \partial \alpha} = \frac{1}{2}\frac{2\pi}{(\sigma^2)^2}\sum\left[\frac{-I}{g^2}\frac{\partial g}{\partial \alpha}\right]. \tag{ii}$$

At the maximum, we have

$$\frac{\partial L}{\partial \alpha} = -\frac{1}{2}\sum\frac{1}{g}\frac{\partial g}{\partial \alpha} + \frac{1}{2}\frac{2\pi}{\sigma^2}\sum\frac{I}{g^2}\frac{\partial g}{\partial \alpha} = 0, \tag{iii}$$

so that the cross-partial in (ii) becomes

$$\frac{\partial^2 L}{\partial \sigma^2 \partial \alpha} = \frac{-1}{2\hat{\sigma}^2}\sum\frac{1}{g}\frac{\partial g}{\partial \alpha} \neq 0, \tag{iv}$$

in general. $\hat{\sigma}^2$ is the value given in (7).

Despite this fact, the *asymptotic* variance–covariance matrix may still be obtained from the concentrated likelihood function, as pointed out by *T.* Amemiya (in private correspondence, 1977) or even from the sum of products of the gradients as suggested by Bernt et al. (1974).

To obtain the typical element of the matrix of second-order derivations of the logarithmic likelihood function, we may proceed as follows. Differentiate L in (6) with respect to a typical parameter α of g:

$$\frac{\partial L}{\partial \alpha} = -\frac{1}{2}\sum \frac{1}{g}\frac{\partial g}{\partial \alpha} + \frac{1}{2}\frac{2\pi}{\sigma^2}\sum \frac{I}{g^2}\frac{\partial g}{\partial \alpha}. \tag{10}$$

Now differentiate (10) with respect to a second typical parameter β and also with respect to σ^2:

$$\frac{\partial^2 L}{\partial \alpha\,\partial \beta} = \sum\left\{\left(\frac{2\pi}{\sigma^2}\frac{I}{g} - 1\right)\left(\frac{1}{2g}\right)\frac{\partial^2 g}{\partial \alpha\,\partial \beta} - 2\left(\frac{4\pi}{\sigma^2}\frac{I}{g} - 1\right)\left(\frac{1}{2g}\right)\frac{\partial g}{\partial \alpha}\left(\frac{1}{2g}\right)\frac{\partial g}{\partial \beta}\right\} \tag{11}$$

$$\frac{\partial^2 L}{\partial \alpha\,\partial \sigma^2} = -\frac{1}{2}\frac{2\pi}{(\sigma^2)^2}\sum \frac{I}{g^2}\frac{\partial g}{\partial \alpha} = -\frac{1}{\sigma^2}\sum\left(\frac{1}{2g}\right)\frac{\partial g}{\partial \alpha}, \tag{12}$$

making use of the first-order condition $\partial L/\partial \alpha = 0$. Unfortunately, it does not appear to be possible to simplify (11) by using the first-order conditions. The typical elements are combined in a single matrix, the negative of which is inverted to obtain the asymptotic variance–covariance matrix.

The likelihood function in the frequency domain may be illustrated by the simple first-order moving-average, first-order autoregression

$$(1 - \alpha U)x_t = (1 - \beta U)\epsilon_t, \qquad E\epsilon_t = 0, \qquad E\epsilon_t^2 = \sigma^2.$$

In this case,

$$f(\lambda_j) = \frac{\sigma^2}{2\pi}\frac{(1 - \beta e^{i\lambda_j})(1 - \beta e^{-i\lambda_j})}{(1 - \alpha e^{i\lambda_j})(1 - \alpha e^{-i\lambda_j})} = \frac{\sigma^2}{2\pi}\left[\frac{1 + \beta^2 - 2\beta\cos\lambda_j}{1 + \alpha^2 - 2\alpha\cos\lambda_j}\right]$$

so that, from (5),

$$L(\alpha, \beta, \sigma^2|x_1, \dots, x_T) = -\frac{T}{2}\log 2\pi - \frac{1}{2}\sum_{j=0}^{T-1}\log\left[\frac{\sigma^2}{2\pi}\left\{\frac{1 + \beta^2 - 2\beta\cos\lambda_j}{1 + \alpha^2 - 2\alpha\cos\lambda_j}\right\}\right]$$
$$-\frac{1}{2}\sum_{j=0}^{T-1}\frac{2\pi I(\lambda_j)(1 + \alpha^2 - 2\alpha\cos\lambda_j)}{\sigma^2(1 + \beta^2 - 2\beta\cos\lambda_j)} \tag{13}$$

is to be maximized subject to $\sigma^2 > 0$, $|\alpha| < 1$, and $|\beta| \le 1$. The observations $x_1, \dots, x_T$ enter through the periodogram ordinates $I(\lambda_j)$, $j = 0, \dots, T - 1$. In this case, $\partial g/\partial \alpha$ and $\partial g/\partial \beta$ take on fairly simple forms:

$$\frac{\partial g}{\partial \alpha} = -\frac{2(\alpha - \cos\lambda_j)}{1 + \alpha^2 - 2\alpha\cos\lambda_j}g, \qquad \frac{\partial g}{\partial \beta} = \frac{2(\beta - \cos\lambda_j)}{1 + \alpha^2 - 2\alpha\cos\lambda_j}, \tag{14}$$

which may be used in the expressions for the concentrated likelihood function and to calculate the matrix of second-order partial derivations of the logarithmic likelihood function.

5. Unobserved-Components Model Estimation in the Frequency Domain

As the preceding discussion makes clear, the extension of frequency domain methods to unobserved-components models presents no essential difficulties. If we neglect the normalization of the covariance generating function that reduces it to canonical form premultiplied by the variance of the innovations of the observed series, we have

$$f(\lambda_j) = (1/2\pi)g_{xx}(e^{i\lambda_j}), \tag{1}$$

where $g_{xx}(z)$ is given by (3.2) above and $f(\lambda_j)$ is the theoretical spectral density of the observed time series $\{x_t\}$ at the frequency λ_j. The logarithmic likelihood function is exactly as before, equation (4.6), except the parameter σ^2 no longer explicitly appears but is implicit in the function $g_{xx}(\cdot)$. We now retain the subscripts xx to differentiate this formulation from the preceding one.

$$L = -\frac{T}{2}\log 2\pi + \frac{T}{2}\log 2\pi - \frac{1}{2}\sum_{j=0}^{T-1} \log g_{xx} - \frac{2\pi}{2}\sum_{j=0}^{T-1}\frac{I}{g_{xx}}, \tag{2}$$

where again we suppress the arguments of both $I(\cdot)$ and $g_{xx}(\cdot)$ for convenience. Because of the disappearance of the parameter σ^2, the logarithmic likelihood function in (2) has a deceptively simple appearance. In fact, g_{xx} is more complicated than before since it represents the superposition of simpler ARMA models with unknown variance weights. To continue, $g_{xx}(\cdot)$ must be specified explicitly.

To simplify matters, write

$$G(U) = R_1(U)/S_1(U), \qquad H(U) = R_2(U)/S_2(U). \tag{3}$$

Then from (3.2) above

$$g_{xx}(z) = G(z)G(z^{-1})\sigma_1^2 + H(z)H(z^{-1})\sigma_2^2 + \sigma_3^2. \tag{4}$$

In general, $G(U)$ is the ratio of a relatively low-order moving average to a relatively low-order autoregression, and $H(U)$ is the ratio of a low-order moving average to a very low-order autoregression in U^L, where L is the number of periods per year at which the series is observed—not to be confused with the logarithmic likelihood function.

It happens frequently in empirical work that the variance of the third component is so small relative to the first two that the estimate of σ_3^2 is very close to zero, close enough in fact that it may be preferable to set it equal to zero. More rarely, the second component may also be small, thus making the estimated unobserved-components model very nearly a simple ARMA model. In order to allow for these possibilities, it is useful to concentrate the likelihood function not with respect to σ^2 in the canonical form of $g_{xx}(\cdot)$, which can be determined only from all the parameters by the methods described in Chapter

IV, nor with respect to σ_2^2 or σ_3^2, which we may wish to set equal to zero, but rather with respect to σ_1^2.

Substituting (4) into (2) for $z = e^{i\lambda_j}$ yields

$$L = -\frac{1}{2}\left\{\sum_{j=0}^{T-1} \log[G(e^{i\lambda_j})G(e^{-i\lambda_j})\sigma_1^2 + H(e^{i\lambda_j})H(e^{-i\lambda_j})\sigma_2^2 + \sigma_3^2]\right.$$

$$\left. + 2\pi \sum_{j=0}^{T-1} \frac{I(\lambda_j)}{G(e^{i\lambda_j})G(e^{-i\lambda_j})\sigma_1^2 + H(e^{i\lambda_j})H(e^{-i\lambda_j})\sigma_2^2 + \sigma_3^2}\right\}. \tag{5}$$

For notational simplicity, let

$$G(e^{-i\lambda_j}) = \bar{G}, \qquad H(e^{-i\lambda_j}) = \bar{H}$$

and suppress the arguments $e^{i\lambda_j}$ of G and H. It is also convenient to reparameterize the problem so that σ_2^2 and σ_3^2 do not appear explicitly, but only as ratios to σ_1^2:

$$\mu_2 = \sigma_2^2/\sigma_1^2, \qquad \mu_3 = \sigma_3^2/\sigma_1^2. \tag{6}$$

Estimates of σ_1^2, μ_2, and μ_3 then permit us to recover estimates of σ_2^2 and σ_3^2. These may be used directly in the matrix of second derivatives of the logarithmic likelihood function to obtain the matrix to be inverted for the matrix of asymptotic variances and covariances of the estimates. Thus

$$L = -\frac{T}{2}\log\sigma_1^2 - \frac{1}{2}\left\{\sum \log[G\bar{G} + \mu_2 H\bar{H} + \mu_3] + \frac{2\pi}{\sigma_1^2}\sum \frac{I}{G\bar{G} + \mu_2 H\bar{H} + \mu_3}\right\}. \tag{7}$$

We are clearly back in the situation described in the previous section, with σ_1^2 playing the role of σ^2 and $G\bar{G} + \mu_2 H\bar{H} + \mu_3$ playing the role of g, only now involving more parameters than before. Essentially the same maximization procedure and procedure for obtaining asymptotic standard errors may be employed.

To illustrate the method, consider the unobserved-components model (IV. 2.5) and (IV. 2.6). The spectral density of the observed series $\{x_t\}$ generated by this model is

$$f(\lambda_j) = \frac{\sigma_u^2}{2\pi}\left[\frac{\mu + (1 + \alpha^2 - 2\alpha\cos\lambda_j)}{1 + \alpha^2 - 2\alpha\cos\lambda_j}\right],$$

where $\mu = \sigma_v^2/\sigma_u^2$. The parameters σ_u^2 and σ_v^2, or alternatively σ_u^2 and μ, may be estimated, and σ_u^2 may be used to concentrate the likelihood function.

Thus the logarithmic likelihood function is

$$L = -\frac{T}{2}\log 2\pi - \frac{1}{2}\sum_{j=0}^{T-1} \log \frac{\sigma_u^2}{2\pi}\left[\frac{\mu + (1 + \alpha^2 - 2\alpha\cos\lambda_j)}{1 + \alpha^2 - 2\alpha\cos\lambda_j}\right]$$

$$-\frac{2\pi}{2\sigma_u^2}\sum_{j=0}^{T-1} \frac{I(\lambda_j)(1 + \alpha^2 - 2\alpha\cos\lambda_j)}{\mu + (1 + \alpha^2 - 2\alpha\cos\lambda_j)}. \tag{8}$$

Given α and μ the maximum-likelihood estimate of σ_u^2 is

$$\hat{\sigma}_u^2 = \frac{2\pi}{T} \sum_{j=0}^{T-1} \frac{I(\lambda_j)(1 + \alpha^2 - 2\alpha \cos \lambda_j)}{\mu + (1 + \alpha^2 - 2\alpha \cos \lambda_j)}, \tag{9}$$

so that the concentrated likelihood function is

$$L^* = -\frac{T}{2} - \frac{1}{2} \sum_{j=0}^{T-1} \log\left[\frac{\mu + (1 + \alpha^2 - 2\alpha \cos \lambda_j)}{1 + \alpha^2 - 2\alpha \cos \lambda_j}\right]$$

$$-\frac{T}{2} \log \frac{2\pi}{T} \sum_{j=0}^{T-1} \frac{I(\lambda_j)(1 + \alpha^2 - 2\alpha \cos \lambda_j)}{\mu + (1 + \alpha^2 - 2\alpha \cos \lambda_j)}. \tag{10}$$

This expression is to be maximized with respect to α and μ such that $|\alpha| < 1$ and $\mu > 0$.

6. Hypothesis Testing

Since the methods described in this chapter are all maximum-likelihood methods, the usual results concerning hypothesis testing and asymptotic standard errors apply. In particular, complicated hypotheses involving several restrictions may be tested by means of a likelihood-ratio test, and the asymptotic variances and covariances of the estimates may be found, as we have indicated, by inverting the negative of the matrix of second derivatives of the logarithmic likelihood function at the maximum (it must be positive-definite there). In the case of the time domain method, the value of the likelihood function at the maximum is at hand, but the matrix of second derivatives must generally be calculated numerically. In contrast, in the frequency domain method, the value of the likelihood function under any set of restrictions we care to impose will also generally be at hand (if a gradient procedure is used), and in addition the matrix of second derivatives of the logarithmic likelihood function may be readily calculated analytically.[5]

7. Estimation of Multiple Time-Series Models

Consider the multiple time-series model of Chapter VI (VI.4.1), under the assumption that the orders of $\varphi(\ )$, $\psi(\ )$, and $\theta(\ )$ have been determined. Both time domain and frequency domain methods are feasible and essentially similar to those developed in the previous sections for ARMA models. In the time domain, when we dealt with only a single series, it will be recalled, we were able to reconstruct the necessary presample values of the observed series by a "backcasting" procedure. Unless we are willing to assume something about how the x series is generated, however, the possibility of doing such a reconstruction in this case is ruled out. An approximate solution, useful when very long time

---

[5] See the Remark on page 135.

series are available, is to discard enough of the initial values of both the y series and the x series to yield sufficient presample values of both in the estimation of (VI.4.1) by the methods described in the previous section (see Box and Jenkins, 1970, pp. 209–212). Indeed, the multiple time-series models estimated in Chapter XI are estimated in just this way.

If we assume that $\{\epsilon_t\}$ is not only zero-mean white noise but Gaussian as well, it follows that $\{y_t\}$ *conditional* on $\{x_t\}$ is also Gaussian with mean

$$\mu_{yt} = -(\psi(U)/\varphi(U))x_t \tag{1}$$

and a variance–covariance matrix depending in the usual way on σ^2, the variance of $\{\epsilon_t\}$, and the parameters of $\theta(\ )$ and $\varphi(\ )$. Unless we say something further about $\{x_t\}$, however, we cannot say that $\{y_t\}$ is stationary, and in general μ_{yt} depends on t. Moreover, it is clear from (1) that the conditional density of the sample $(y_1, \ldots, y_T)$ depends on values of $\{x_t\}$ *prior to* the sample period. If nothing is assumed about these values and no part of the sample is to be discarded, it would appear impossible to formulate the likelihood function even in the frequency domain. Fortunately, however, this is not the case when joint stationarity of both series is assumed since the periodogram of the x series and the cross periodogram between the x and the y series appear in the likelihood function, together with the parameters of $\psi(\ )$ and $\varphi(\ )$.

Premultiply

$$y_t = \frac{-\psi(U)}{\varphi(U)} x_t + v_t = H(U)x_t + v_t, \quad \text{where} \quad v_t = \frac{\theta(U)}{\varphi(U)} \epsilon_t, \tag{2}$$

by the matrix P introduced in equation (4.2) and denote the Fourier transforms of y_t by

$$y(\lambda_j) = \frac{1}{\sqrt{2\pi T}} \sum_{t=1}^{T} y_t e^{it\lambda_j},$$

of x_t by

$$x(\lambda_j) = \frac{1}{\sqrt{2\pi T}} \sum_{t=1}^{T} x_t e^{it\lambda_j},$$

of $h_k x_{t-k}$ by

$$h_k x_{-k}(\lambda_j) = \frac{h_k}{\sqrt{2\pi T}} \sum_{t=1}^{T} x_{t-k} e^{it\lambda_j}$$

$$= \frac{h_k e^{ik\lambda_j}}{\sqrt{2\pi T}} \sum_{t=1}^{T} x_{t-k} e^{i(t-k)\lambda_j},$$

and of v_t by

$$v(\lambda_j) = \frac{1}{\sqrt{2\pi T}} \sum_{t=1}^{T} v_t e^{it\lambda_j}.$$

If we make the not too heroic assumption that, at least approximately,

$$\frac{1}{\sqrt{2\pi T}}\sum_{t=1}^{T}x_{t-k}e^{i(t-k)\lambda_j} = \frac{1}{\sqrt{2\pi T}}\sum_{t=1}^{T}x_t e^{it\lambda_j},$$

as would be true asymptotically, for example, on the assumption that $\{x_t\}$ is stationary and purely nondeterministic, then (2) reduces approximately to

$$y(\lambda_j) = H(e^{i\lambda_j})x(\lambda_j) + v(\lambda_j), \tag{3}$$

where $v = (v_1, \ldots, v_T)'$. Conditional on the x series

$$y(\lambda_j) - H(e^{i\lambda_j})x(\lambda_j) = v(\lambda_j)$$

is normal with a variance–covariance matrix asymptotically equal to

$$\Omega = \begin{bmatrix} f_{vv}(\lambda_0) & 0 & \cdots & 0 \\ 0 & f_{vv}(\lambda_1) & \cdots & 0 \\ \vdots & \vdots & & \vdots \\ 0 & 0 & \cdots & f_{vv}(\lambda_{T-1}) \end{bmatrix}.$$

In this equation $f_{vv}(\ )$ is the spectral density of

$$v_t = [\theta(u)/\varphi(u)]\epsilon_t$$

evaluated at T equally spaced frequencies in the interval $[0, 2\pi)$, i.e.,

$$\lambda_j = 2\pi j/T, \qquad j = 0, \ldots, T-1.$$

Clearly

$$f_{vv}(\lambda_j) = (\sigma^2/2\pi)|\theta(e^{i\lambda_j})/\varphi(e^{i\lambda_j})|^2 \tag{4}$$

depends on the parametric form of $\theta(\ )$ and $\varphi(\ )$. The logarithmic likelihood function is thus asymptotically

$$L(\varphi_1, \ldots, \psi_1, \ldots, \theta_1, \ldots, \sigma^2 | y_1, \ldots, y_T; x_1, \ldots, x_T)$$

$$= -\frac{T}{2}\log 2\pi - \frac{1}{2}\sum_{j=0}^{T-1}\log f_{vv}(\lambda_j) - \frac{1}{2}[y(\lambda)$$

$$- H(e^{i\lambda})x(\lambda)]'\Omega^{-1}[y(\lambda) - H(e^{i\lambda})x(\lambda)], \tag{5}$$

where $y(\lambda)$ denotes the vector $(y(\lambda_0), \ldots, y(\lambda_{T-1}))'$ and $H(e^{i\lambda})x(\lambda)$ denotes the vector

$$(H(e^{i\lambda_0})x(\lambda_0), \ldots, H(e^{i\lambda_{T-1}})x(\lambda_{T-1}))'.$$

The last term may be explicitly written out in terms of the sample periodograms of y and x and their cross periodogram:

$$[y(\lambda) - H(e^{i\lambda})x(\lambda)]'\Omega^{-1}[y(\lambda) - H(e^{i\lambda})x(\lambda)]$$

$$= \sum_{j=0}^{T-1}\left\{\frac{I_{yy}(\lambda_j) - H(e^{i\lambda_j})I_{xy}(\lambda_j) - H(e^{-i\lambda_j})I_{yx}(\lambda_j) + |H(e^{i\lambda_j})|^2 I_{xx}(\lambda_j)}{f_{vv}(\lambda_j)}\right\}. \tag{6}$$

The cross periodogram $I_{xy}(\lambda_j)$ is defined in an analogous manner to the ordinary periodogram defined in Chapter III, Section 5, i.e., as $x(\lambda_j)\overline{y(\lambda_j)}$. Now $\overline{I_{yx}(\lambda_j)} = I_{xy}(\lambda_j)$ and the sum of a complex number and its conjugate is twice the real part; hence, the likelihood function becomes

$$L = -\frac{T}{2}\log 2\pi - \frac{1}{2}\sum_{j=0}^{T-1}\left\{\log f_{vv}(\lambda_j)\right.$$

$$\left. + \frac{I_{yy}(\lambda_j) - 2\operatorname{Re}[H(e^{i\lambda_j})I_{xy}(\lambda_j)] + |H(e^{i\lambda_j})|^2 I_{xx}(\lambda_j)}{f_{vv}(\lambda_j)}\right\}. \tag{7}$$

Both $f_{vv}(\lambda_j)$ and $H(e^{i\lambda_j}) = -\psi(e^{i\lambda_j})/\varphi(e^{i\lambda_j})$ depend on the parameters of the model (VI.4.1), whereas $I_{yy}(\lambda_j)$, $I_{xy}(\lambda_j)$, and $I_{xx}(\lambda_j)$ depend on the sample data $y_1, \ldots, y_T$ and $x_1, \ldots, x_T$.

Generalization to unobserved-components models for the y series and/or the inclusion of additional observed explanatory series is immediate, along the lines described in Section 5.

Tests of hypotheses and asymptotic variances and covariances of the parameters may be obtained exactly as described in the previous section.

Now consider the more general two-equation model (VI.4.5)

$$\varphi_1(U)y_t + \psi_1(U)x_t = \theta_1(U)\epsilon_{1t}, \qquad \varphi_2(U)y_t + \psi_2(U)x_t = \theta_2(U)\epsilon_{2t}.$$

Suppose that the orders of $\varphi_1(\ )$, $\varphi_2(\ )$, $\psi_1(\ )$, $\psi_2(\ )$, $\theta_1(\ )$, and $\theta_2(\ )$ have been determined a priori so that we do not assume recursivity.[6] We discuss the problem of estimation in two simple cases and indicate the more general approach in more complex cases. First, assume that $\{\epsilon_{1t}\}$ and $\{\epsilon_{2t}\}$ are Gaussian white noise and are contemporaneously correlated but not cross-serially correlated; moreover, assume that $\theta_1(\ ) \equiv \theta_2(\ ) \equiv 1$. Array the samples thus: $\epsilon = (\epsilon_1, \epsilon_2)' = (\epsilon_{11}, \ldots, \epsilon_{1T}, \epsilon_{21}, \ldots, \epsilon_{2T})'$. Then the joint density of ϵ is

$$(2\pi)^{-T}|\Omega^{-1}|^{1/2}\exp\{-\tfrac{1}{2}\epsilon'\Omega^{-1}\epsilon\},$$

where

$$\begin{bmatrix} \sigma_{11} & 0 & \sigma_{12} & 0 \\ 0 & \sigma_{11} & 0 & \sigma_{12} \\ \sigma_{21} & 0 & \sigma_{22} & 0 \\ 0 & \sigma_{21} & 0 & \sigma_{22} \end{bmatrix} = \begin{bmatrix} \Omega_{11} & \Omega_{12} \\ \Omega_{21} & \Omega_{22} \end{bmatrix}.$$

---

[6] As we saw in Chapter VI, there is no general good method, or even plausible method, for determining these orders in the nonrecursive case without a priori information. Here, we simply assume that the theory leading to the model formulation supplies the orders of the lag polynomials.

By a standard result on the inverse of partitioned matrices (Theil, 1971, p. 18)

$$\Omega^{-1} = \frac{1}{\sigma_{11}\sigma_{22} - \sigma_{12}^2} \begin{bmatrix} \sigma_{22}I & -\sigma_{21}I \\ -\sigma_{12}I & \sigma_{11}I \end{bmatrix}.$$

We also have

$$|\Omega^{-1}| = \left(\frac{1}{\sigma_{11}\sigma_{22} - \sigma_{12}^2}\right)^T.$$

The approximate logarithmic likelihood function in terms of the parameters of (VI.4.5), which we denote by $\varphi_1, \varphi_2, \psi_1,$ and ψ_2 and the scalars $\sigma_{11}, \sigma_{22},$ and $\sigma_{12},$ is thus[7]

$$L(\varphi_1, \varphi_2, \psi_1, \psi_2, \sigma_{11}, \sigma_{22}, \sigma_{12}|x_1, \ldots, x_T, y_1, \ldots, y_T)$$

$$= -T\log 2\pi - \frac{T}{2}\log(\sigma_{11}\sigma_{22} - \sigma_{12}^2) - \frac{1}{2(\sigma_{11}\sigma_{22} - \sigma_{12}^2)}\sum_{t=1}^T \{\sigma_{22}(\varphi_1(U)y_t$$

$$+ \psi_1(U)x_t)^2 - 2\sigma_{12}(\varphi_1(U)y_t + \psi_1(U)x_t)(\varphi_2(U)y_t + \psi_2(U)x_t)$$

$$+ \sigma_{11}(\varphi_2(U)x_t + \psi_2(U)x_t)^2\} + \log|J|, \tag{8}$$

where $|J|$ is the Jacobian of the transformation from $\{\epsilon_{1t}, \epsilon_{2t}\}$ to $\{x_t, y_t\}$. In this case there are no moving-average components in the model so that pre-sample values of $\{\epsilon_{1t}\}$ and $\{\epsilon_{2t}\}$ are not required; presample values of $\{y_t\}$ and $\{x_t\}$ are, however, required for maximization of L in the time domain; these may be obtained by truncating the sample or by "backcasting" as described in Section 2.[8]

Frequency domain methods are also possible in this case as well (Hannan and Nicholls, 1972). Let the Fourier transforms of the observed series $(x_1, \ldots, x_T)$ and $(y_1, \ldots, y_T)$ be

$$x(\lambda_j) = \frac{1}{\sqrt{2\pi T}}\sum_{t=1}^T x_t e^{it\lambda_j}, \qquad y(\lambda_j) = \frac{1}{\sqrt{2\pi T}}\sum_{t=1}^T y_t e^{it\lambda_j}, \tag{9}$$

where $\lambda_j = 2\pi j/T, j = 0, 1, \ldots, T - 1$. Now, if ϵ follows a multivariate normal distribution with zero mean and variance–covariance matrix Ω, then the vector $(x, y)' = (x_1, \ldots, x_T, y_1, \ldots, y_T)'$ must also be zero-mean multivariate normal with some variance–covariance matrix Γ that, moreover, may be partitioned conformably with the vector $(x, y)'$. The Fourier transform of the observed variables (9) amounts to premultiplying each of the equations of the model (VI.4.5), by the matrix P defined in (4.2). Asymptotically, this transformation

---

[7] $|J|$ is a rather complicated expression depending on the parameters of $\varphi_1, \varphi_2, \psi_1, \psi_2, \theta_1,$ and θ_2.

[8] When $\sigma_{12} = 0,$ it is easily seen that this reduces to the single-equation case previously considered, since L becomes the sum of two independent parts involving no common parameters.

diagonalizes Γ so that the logarithmic likelihood function becomes

$$L(\varphi_1, \varphi_2, \psi_1, \psi_2, \sigma_{11}, \sigma_{22}, \sigma_{12} | x_1, \ldots, x_T, y_1, \ldots, y_T)$$

$$= -T \log 2\pi - \frac{1}{2} \sum_{j=0}^{T-1} \log[f_{yy}(\lambda_j) f_{xx}(\lambda_j) - |f_{yx}(\lambda_j)|^2]$$

$$- \frac{1}{2} \sum_{j=0}^{T-1} \left\{ \frac{f_{xx}(\lambda_j) I_{yy}(\lambda_j) - f_{xy}(\lambda_j) I_{xy}(\lambda_j) - f_{yx}(\lambda_j) I_{yx}(\lambda_j) + f_{yy}(\lambda_j) I_{xx}(\lambda_j)}{f_{xx}(\lambda_j) f_{yy}(\lambda_j) - |f_{yx}(\lambda_j)|^2} \right\},$$

$$(10)$$

where $f_{xx}(\lambda_j), f_{yy}(\lambda_j), f_{yx}(\lambda_j), f_{xy}(\lambda_j)$ are the spectral and cross-spectral densities of the two series, and where $I_{xx}(\lambda_j)$, $I_{yy}(\lambda_j)$, $I_{yx}(\lambda_j)$, and $I_{xy}(\lambda_j)$ are the sample periodograms and cross periodograms. The latter depend on the sample data, and the former depend on the parameters of the polynomials of the model and the variances and covariance of $\{\epsilon_{1t}\}$ and $\{\epsilon_{2t}\}$ as follows:

Multiply the first equation (VI.4.5) by the operator $\varphi_2(U)$ and the second by $\varphi_1(U)$; then we may eliminate $\{y_t\}$ and obtain an expression in $\{x_t\}$ alone:

$$[\varphi_2(U)\psi_1(U) - \varphi_1(U)\psi_2(U)]x_t = \varphi_2(U)\theta_1(U)\epsilon_{1t} - \varphi_1(U)\theta_2(U)\epsilon_{2t} \quad (11)$$

or

$$\Phi(U)x_t = G_1(U)\epsilon_{1t} - G_2(U)\epsilon_{2t}.$$

A similar manipulation yields an expression in $\{y_t\}$ alone

$$[\psi_2(U)\varphi_1(U) - \psi_1(U)\varphi_2(U)]y_t = \psi_2(U)\theta_1(U)\epsilon_{1t} - \psi_1(U)\theta_2(U)\epsilon_{2t} \quad (12)$$

or

$$-\Phi(U)y_t = H_1(U)\epsilon_{1t} - H_2(U)\epsilon_{2t}.$$

Thus

$$f_{yy}(\lambda_j) = \frac{1}{2\pi} \frac{\sigma_{11}|H_1(e^{i\lambda_j})|^2 - 2\sigma_{12}\text{Re}[H_1(e^{i\lambda_j})H_2(e^{-i\lambda_j})] + \sigma_{22}|H_2(e^{i\lambda_j})|^2}{|\Phi(e^{i\lambda_j})|^2}$$

$$f_{xx}(\lambda_j) = \frac{1}{2\pi} \frac{\sigma_{11}|G_1(e^{i\lambda_j})|^2 - 2\sigma_{12}\text{Re}[G_1(e^{i\lambda_j})G_2(e^{-i\lambda_j})] + \sigma_{22}|G_2(e^{i\lambda_j})|^2}{|\Phi(e^{i\lambda_j})|^2} \quad (13)$$

$$f_{xy}(\lambda_j) = -\frac{1}{2\pi} \frac{\left(\begin{array}{c} \sigma_{11}G_1(e^{i\lambda_j})H_1(e^{i\lambda_j}) - \sigma_{12}[G_1(e^{i\lambda_j})H_2(e^{-i\lambda_j}) + G_2(e^{i\lambda_j})H_1(e^{-i\lambda_j})] \\ + \sigma_{22}G_2(e^{i\lambda_j})H_2(e^{-i\lambda_j}) \end{array} \right)}{|\Phi(e^{i\lambda_j})|^2}.$$

Note that this formulation allows for moving-average error terms, although we retain the simplifying assumption that $\{\epsilon_{1t}\}$ and $\{\epsilon_{2t}\}$ are only contemporaneously correlated.[9]

---

[9] It is not necessary to make the simplification; see Quenouille (1957, pp. 19–20).

Substitution of (13) in the likelihood function L in (10) yields a function of the parameters that may be maximized by a gradient procedure to yield maximum-likelihood estimates. Hypotheses may be tested by means of likelihood ratio test statistics, and asymptotic variances and covariances may be obtained from the inverse of the negative of the matrix of analytical second derivatives of the logarithmic likelihood function evaluated at the maximum-likelihood estimates.

When $\{\epsilon_{1t}\}$ and $\{\epsilon_{2t}\}$ are more than contemporaneously correlated, the situation becomes considerably more complicated. We consider only the case where there is first-order crosslag correlation, but indicate how the analysis may be generalized. Let $\{\epsilon_{1t}\}$ and $\{\epsilon_{2t}\}$ be Gaussian white noise series with contemporaneous variances σ_{11} and σ_{22} and contemporaneous covariance σ_{12}; let

$$
\begin{aligned}
E\epsilon_{1t}\epsilon_{2t-1} &= \rho_1\sigma_{12} \\
E\epsilon_{1t-1}\epsilon_{2t} &= \rho_{-1}\sigma_{12} \\
E\epsilon_{1t}\epsilon_{2t+j} &= 0, \qquad j \neq 0, \pm 1.
\end{aligned}
\tag{14}
$$

For simplicity, we assume that $\theta_1(\ ) \equiv 1 \equiv \theta_2(\ )$, although it is easy enough to assume first-order moving-average disturbances in the time domain, and any structure in the frequency domain.

Under these assumptions, the vector ϵ has a multivariate normal distribution with zero mean and variance–covariance matrix

$$
\Omega = \begin{bmatrix} \Omega_{11} & \Omega_{12} \\ \Omega_{21} & \Omega_{22} \end{bmatrix},
$$

where

$$
\Omega_{11} = \sigma_{11}I, \qquad \Omega_{22} = \sigma_{22}I,
$$

$$
\Omega_{12} = \sigma_{12} \begin{bmatrix}
1 & \rho_{-1} & 0 & \cdots & 0 \\
\rho_1 & 1 & \rho_{-1} & \cdots & 0 \\
0 & \rho_1 & 1 & \cdots & 0 \\
\vdots & \vdots & \vdots & & \vdots \\
0 & 0 & 0 & \cdots & 1
\end{bmatrix} = \Omega'_{21}.
$$

The result on the inverse of partitioned matrices cited earlier allows us to calculate Ω^{-1} from the inverses of Ω_{11}, Ω_{22}, and Ω_{12}. Clearly, the only difficulty is the calculation of Ω_{12}^{-1}. Ω_{12} is a simple case of a finite Toeplitz matrix. The inversion of such matrices is discussed in Appendix E.

The matrix Ω_{12} may be expressed in terms of the parameters θ and η of the two-band matrix discussed in Appendix E by setting

$$
\sigma_{12} = \alpha(1 + \theta\eta), \qquad \sigma_{12}\rho_1 = -\alpha\theta, \qquad \sigma_{12}\rho_{-1} = -\alpha\eta.
$$

α is a coefficient of proportionality obtained by solving the equation

$$
\alpha^2 - \sigma_{12}\alpha + \sigma_{12}^2\rho_1\rho_{-1} = 0.
$$

With this change of variable, the inverse of Ω_{12} is proportional to V as determined in (16) and (17) of Appendix E; the constant of proportionality is clearly α since

$$
\frac{1}{\alpha}\Omega_{12} = \begin{bmatrix} 1 + \theta\eta & -\eta & 0 & \cdots & 0 \\ -\theta & 1 + \theta\eta & -\eta & \cdots & 0 \\ \vdots & \vdots & \vdots & & \vdots \\ 0 & 0 & 0 & \cdots & 1 + \theta\eta \end{bmatrix}
$$

Given the inverse of the Ω_{12} and, therefore, also of Ω'_{12}, the likelihood function may be constructed from the density function for the vector ϵ in the same manner as before. The calculations are rather complex, however, since Ω_{12}^{-1} is no longer of simple form.

Frequency domain methods may also be employed in this case, but it is simplest to begin with (11) and (12) and to find f_{yy}, f_{xx}, and f_{xy} directly, taking into account the lag correlation between $\{\epsilon_{1t}\}$ and $\{\epsilon_{2t}\}$. This will not be done here since it is straightforward. Moreover, the simpler case of no-lag correlation will generally suffice for most practical applications.

Chapter VIII
APPRAISAL OF SEASONAL ADJUSTMENT TECHNIQUES

In this chapter we consider the problem of seasonal adjustment of economic time series. We formulate several criteria for optimal seasonal adjustment that at least seem to be consistent with published statements concerning desirable features of seasonally adjusted series.[1] We show that use of these criteria leads to relationships between the spectral densities of adjusted and unadjusted series similar to those found between estimated spectra using time series adjusted by official census and BLS methods. In this chapter we also discuss the implications for parameter estimates of using seasonally adjusted data when fitting econometric models.

1. Criteria for "Optimal" Seasonal Adjustment

The problem of seasonal adjustment arises in at least three very different contexts: in historical studies of business cycles, in appraising current economic conditions, and in estimating structural parameters in relationships among economic time series. For the study of past business cycles, seasonal adjustment is essentially an estimation problem. That is, one assumes that the observed series is a function of trend-cycle, seasonal, and irregular components and attempts to estimate that part of the series due to the trend-cycle or to the trend-cycle and irregular. Closely related problems are the study of secular trends and long swings; in the earlier literature, it was often assumed that the trend and cyclical factors were separate components. In recent works, the latter

---

[1] This chapter draws heavily on the joint paper of two of the present authors (Grether and Nerlove, 1970).

147

two components are frequently treated as one, and for many applications the model is reduced to only two components, namely seasonal and nonseasonal.

In appraising current economic conditions, seasonal adjustment may be thought of as either an estimation or a prediction. For example, in the passage quoted in Chapter I, Shiskin states "A principal purpose of studying business statistics is to determine the stage of the business cycle at which the economy stands" (1958, p. 1539). While this sounds much like estimating the current value of the cyclical or trend-cycle component, there is also an element of prediction here. Typically, the business cycle is thought of as being a fluctuation lasting at least one and possibly several years. So if one knows the current stage of the business cycle, one should be able to predict at least the general direction of movement for the near future. As Shiskin says, this "helps in forecasting subsequent cyclical movements" (1958, p. 1539). Elsewhere he writes, "seasonally adjusted data not only avoid some of the biases to which same-month-year-ago comparisons are subject, but also often reveal cyclical changes several months earlier" (OECD, 1961, p. 530). Similarly, Daly states:

> No government, economic group or individual, who is interested in the current economic situation can afford to be without seasonal adjustment for those series that are of general interest. It is correct and usually persuasive to say that with seasonal adjustment one can know what is going on in the economy six months earlier than those using unadjusted data.   (OECD, 1961, p. 176)

Daly also compares seasonally adjusted data with use of same-month-a-year-ago type comparisons and notes that turning points can be detected much earlier using adjusted series. To illustrate, he quotes as follows from an internal memo of the Economics Branch of the Canadian Department of Trade and Commerce:

> These series (seasonally adjusted) have proven extremely helpful .... The current material is of considerable help in economic forecasting as the seasonally adjusted data show changes in directions of economic activity much earlier than a comparison with the same period of the year before .... The seasonally adjusted data (of industrial production) show a decline after July, 1953, fully *six months* earlier than the year-to-year changes suggest .... Similarly, the number of persons without jobs and seeking work dropped from the previous year in May, 1955, but when allowance is made for seasonal factors some declines had begun to occur by July, 1954, fully ten months earlier.   (OECD, 1961, p. 167)

The emphasis on the advantages of seasonally adjusted data for the early detection of turning points provides another indication that prediction may be the goal of seasonal adjustment. It should be noted that what is being predicted is a mean path or possibly some kind of average over several periods, rather than the value of any real economic time series.

The decision to use adjusted or unadjusted data in the estimation of economic models can have substantial effects upon the estimates of the structural parameters. There has been some discussion in the literature of such consequences of seasonal adjustment, and even some suggestions on adjusting time series prior to using them as variables in econometric models (Lovell, 1963, 1966; Jorgenson, 1964, 1967a; Sims, 1974; Wallis, 1974; and Thomas and Wallis, 1971). These suggestions have been directed to practicing econometricians and were not intended as advice to the Census Bureau concerning how series "ought" to be adjusted. In fact, while official adjustment procedures clearly have implications for the properties of parameter estimates obtained using adjusted data, it seems that these implications are best characterized as (possibly undesirable) side effects. In other words, these considerations have been of little importance in the design of methods actually in use. This should not be taken as a criticism of the standard methods since, as will be shown below, the impact of a given seasonal adjustment procedure depends crucially upon the form of the economic model being estimated. Thus these sorts of considerations cannot possibly lead to a single most desirable method, though they do make clear the need to publish the unadjusted data.

One of the difficulties in appraising methods for eliminating seasonal variation from economic times series is the lack of precise criteria by which to rank various alternative procedures. Shiskin gives four criteria for good seasonal adjustment:

> 1. Any repetitive intra-year pattern in a series should be eliminated.
> 2. Systematic fluctuations lasting a year or longer must be measured by the seasonal and cyclical-trend factors, and the changes (generally over a period of a year or more) in the residual fluctuations, designated here as the irregular, must behave like the similar changes of a random series.
> 3. The underlying cyclical movements should not be distorted; that is, seasonally adjusted series, which in unadjusted form had a large seasonal factor, must resemble, in terms of amplitude, pattern, and timing, other related economic series that either had no seasonal at all . . . or had a small seasonal factor compared to the cyclical factor . . . .
> 4. The results must be reasonable.   (OECD, 1961, pp. 84–85)

These criteria are certainly plausible, but they clearly are not sufficient to determine a "best" method of seasonal adjustment.

In two previous papers Nerlove (1964, 1965) attempted to analyze the effects of various procedures for seasonal adjustment of economic time series on the characteristics of the series to which these procedures were applied. The analysis consisted of a comparison of the estimated spectra of the two series, original and seasonally adjusted, and an examination of the cross spectrum of the two series, particularly of the coherence and phase shift at various frequencies. In the course of these investigations several informal criteria for judging the adequacy of seasonal adjustment were developed. These criteria were: First, the coherence of the original and the seasonally adjusted series should be high at all frequencies except, possibly, seasonal ones.

Second, although phase shifts are generally impossible to avoid altogether in any method of seasonal adjustment that uses past data to adjust current observations, such shifts should be minimized especially at low frequencies at which most of the power in economic time series is typically concentrated.

Finally, seasonal adjustment should remove the peaks in the original series that typically appear at the so-called seasonal frequencies, but should affect the remainder of the spectral density as little as possible; in particular, the process of seasonal adjustment should not remove excessive power at other than seasonal frequencies.

A subsidiary consideration involved the possibility that seasonal adjustment might remove more than enough power at the seasonal frequencies, thus producing dips at those frequencies. While this was not regarded as especially serious in and of itself, corresponding to the dips there must exist intermediate peaks at frequencies between the seasonal ones. Such peaks, if large enough, might induce spurious fluctuations in the adjusted series—a disturbing possibility. Nettheim (1965), however, showed how the seasonally adjusted series could be corrected for "over-adjustment" at the seasonal frequencies. When such corrections were made in a number of seasonally adjusted series (male unemployment 20+, total imports, and total civilian labor force), the overall movement and general appearance of the resulting series differed very little from the uncorrected seasonally adjusted series; however, in all three series the locations of turning points were frequently altered, in some cases by as much as two to three months. It is not possible to assess the economic significance of such effects outside a particular substantive context, but it is unlikely that most consumers of seasonally adjusted series would fail to be concerned about the possibility that seasonal adjustment methods may affect the location of turning points by as much as two to three months.

In the first of the two studies referred to above (Nerlove, 1964), it was found that, for the BLS method of adjusting unemployment, a considerable loss of power occurred at nearly all nonseasonal frequencies higher than those corresponding to a sinusoidal fluctuation of 12-months duration, and that this loss was most severe for the age–sex groups unemployed males 14–19 and unemployed females 14–19, for which the seasonal pattern is most pronounced and regular. Little difference in this respect was found between the BLS method then in use and the proposed "residual" method, which involved first adjusting employment and labor force for seasonal influences and then deriving the seasonally adjusted unemployment series as the difference between the two. However, in the second study (Nerlove, 1965), a method closely related to a proposal made by Hannan (1963) proved to be markedly superior in this respect. The two studies showed that all three methods of seasonal adjustment produced series that had low coherence with their original series at most frequencies above that corresponding to a sinusoidal fluctuation of 12-months duration. Rather violent phase shifts were found at many frequencies, including some of the lower frequencies; however, the significance of such shifts in frequency bands where coherence is low is quite limited.[2]

One purpose of this chapter is a reassessment of the earlier findings reported above and of recent work along similar lines by Rosenblatt (1965, 1966, 1967,

---

[2] For true coherence equal to zero, the phase angle is approximately uniformly distributed in the interval $[-\pi/2, \pi/2]$.

1968). It has never been denied, and indeed is repeatedly emphasized by Rosenblatt in his own work, that the effects noted in the frequency domain are significant only to the degree to which these same effects, translated into the behavior of the adjusted series over time, affect the interpretation of the movements of that series. It has been found, however, extraordinarily difficult to obtain general agreement on what constitutes "good" seasonal adjustment in the time domain, and hence there has been continued reliance on the examination of the behavior of the adjusted series in the frequency domain.[3]

The chief problem in the interpretation of the effects observed in the frequency domain is the formulation of a definite theory of what constitutes "good" seasonal adjustment. Without a clear and rigorous notion of the purpose of seasonal adjustment, optimal procedures cannot be formulated nor shortcomings assessed.

Suppose, for example, that the observed series X_t is the sum of two components, a nonseasonal component N_t, and a seasonal component S_t,

$$X_t = N_t + S_t, \tag{1}$$

and we assume, by definition, that they are uncorrelated at any lag:

$$\text{cov}(N_t, S_{t-k}) = 0, \qquad k = 0, \pm 1, \pm 2, \ldots. \tag{2}$$

Thus, the spectral density of the observed series is simply the sum of the spectral densities of each of the two components:

$$f_{XX}(\lambda) = f_{NN}(\lambda) + f_{SS}(\lambda), \tag{3}$$

where $-\pi \leq \lambda \leq \pi$. Since $f_{SS}(\lambda) \geq 0$, the spectral density of N_t is less than or equal to the spectral density of the observed series X_t. Unless S_t has a line spectrum, e.g.,

$$S_t = \sum_j c_j e^{i\lambda_j t}, \tag{4}$$

where $\lambda_j = 2\pi j/12, j = 1, \ldots, 12$, for monthly observations, so that it is positive only at the so-called seasonal frequencies (see Nerlove, 1964, pp. 259–260), the

---

[3] Rosenblatt (1967, pp. 4–5) puts the matter felicitously as follows: "Like the physician's stethoscope and electrocardiograph, the spectrum is a highly sensitive instrument. Not only will these instruments display the readily recognizable characteristics of a patient (time series) which are not too difficult to interpret, but they will also point to much finer effects which at first may not be readily understood, but whose meaning may become clearer through research, experimentation, and experience. Often, difficulty in the interpretation of the spectrum will be a reflection of the degree of deviation from the spectral criteria. This process of examination is analogous to the procedure followed by a physician in examining a patient. He compares his findings with his standards for good health; he may classify one individual as being in better health than another, yet, unless deviations from norm are extreme, it is difficult for him to say that his patient will not live a full and fruitful life."

nonseasonal component will have a spectral density lying below that of the observed series at frequencies other than these. For example, if

$$S_t = \alpha S_{t-12} + \epsilon_t, \tag{5}$$

where ϵ_t is a serially uncorrelated random variable with variance σ^2 and mean zero independent of t, again assuming monthly observations, $f_{SS}(\lambda)$ will be non-zero at every frequency. Thus, a comparison of the spectral densities of N_t and X_t would show "loss of power at nonseasonal frequencies" as well as seasonal ones. Conceivably, our objective in seasonal adjustment might be to isolate N_t, in which case we should not object to some loss of power at nonseasonal frequencies, particularly if the seasonal peaks were not expected to be exceptionally sharp.

Continuing the above example, note that the coherence $R_{XN}^2(\lambda)$ between N_t and X_t is

$$0 \leq R_{XN}^2(\lambda) = \frac{1}{1 + f_{SS}(\lambda)/f_{NN}(\lambda)} \leq 1, \tag{6}$$

with the upper inequality strict when $f_{SS}(\lambda) \neq 0$. If $f_{SS}(\lambda)$ is large at any frequency, the coherence between N_t and X_t will be low at that frequency. Some plausible models for the seasonal component and the nonseasonal component lead to contribution by the seasonal component of much of the power at high frequencies, seasonal or otherwise. This is the case for the example discussed in detail in Chapter IV. Hence, low estimated coherence of seasonally adjusted and seasonally unadjusted series at other than seasonal frequencies requires careful interpretation. Furthermore, any method of seasonal adjustment that consists of linear combinations of past and, possibly, future values of the series in question, with constant weights, will produce a series always having coherence with the unadjusted series equal to one. By itself, then, the coherence can tell us little about the adequacy of a seasonal adjustment procedure.

Essentially the same conclusion comes from consideration of phase shifts. While it is possible to transform a series without inducing a nonzero phase angle, to make this a requirement of an adjustment procedure would severely restrict the class of admissible methods. For instance, the only linear time-invariant filters with zero phase angle at every frequency are symmetric. These are filters giving adjustments of the form:

$$x_t^a = \sum_{-n}^{n} a_j x_{t-j}, \qquad a_j = a_{-j}.$$

Of course, the trouble is that using symmetric filters requires that the adjustment either uses a small number of observations or has a long lag between the observation and the adjustment. Certainly the latter alternative would be in conflict with the use of the adjusted series for appraising current economic conditions.

Suppose that the observed values of a time series $\{x_t\}$ may be represented as the sum of, say, three unobserved components: $\{y_t\}$, trend-cycle; $\{s_t\}$, seasonal; and $\{u_t\}$, irregular. Thus

$$x_t = y_t + s_t + u_t. \tag{7}$$

Further, let us suppose that the stochastic structure of each of these unobserved components can be specified in such a way that the stochastic structure of the observed time series $\{x_t\}$ is thereby determined. Along the lines of the above discussion, the problem of seasonal adjustment may be specified in the following three ways as the problem of obtaining, at a given moment of time t,

(a) an estimate or extraction of y_t based on the observed x_t either up to that time or beyond it as well;
(b) an estimate or extraction of s_t, and subtraction of this from x_t, based on observations either up to that time or beyond it as well; or
(c) a series of predictions of $x_t, x_{t+1}, \ldots, x_{t+v}$, up to v periods ahead (e.g., 12 if we are dealing with monthly data), based on past observations alone, that may or may not be summarized in the form of an average or mean value, weighted or unweighted.

All of these problems are closely related and may be solved by essentially the same method. However, in order to apply the method a number of further simplifications are necessary with regard to the criterion of optimality we shall adopt, as well as to the nature of our specification of the stochastic structure of the unobserved components.

In some fundamental sense, optimal estimation of something should depend upon what it costs to make an error. Such cost or loss functions can only be specified within the context of a specific decision problem; that is, we have to know precisely how and by whom an estimate or prediction is going to be used before we can determine an appropriate criterion of optimality and derive an estimate or prediction that satisfies that criterion. Such a specification is obviously impossible in the present context since whatever seasonal adjustment may or may not be, it is surely designed to serve a great variety of users in many different situations. The classic solution to this problem is to minimize the expected value of the squared error between whatever it is we are trying to estimate or predict and the true value. Thus the criterion of optimality we adopt is that of *minimum mean-square error*.

With each of these criteria for good seasonal adjustment it is assumed that the prediction or extraction is made at some fixed point of time and not subsequently changed. Thus, even though in principle subsequent data would allow for a better estimate of y_t [if formulations (a) or (b) were operative], it is assumed that the continued revision of past adjustments is not made. In effect, we are assuming that the only revisions in seasonally adjusted time series are the result of correcting errors in the data. While this assumption is clearly not strictly correct, it does not seem unreasonable, as frequent or large revisions in published time series are sometimes thought of as undesirable per se, presumably because the reason for revision is not well understood. We also note that the adjustment methods suggested here will be illustrated below using a linear filter. The methods actually in use are distinctly nonlinear, although Wallis (1974) and Hext (1964) have both developed linear filters that approximate the official adjustment methods. Wallis reports the results of several simulation studies that suggest that conclusions concerning some effects of seasonal adjustment derived under the assumption of a linear filter are applicable to data adjusted by official methods.

We defer until later in this chapter any discussion of the consequences of estimating econometric models using data adjusted according to any of the adopted criteria. It does turn out, however, that in some special cases use of data adjusted according to (a) yields improved parameter estimates in distributed-lag models. In general, these methods do not have such desirable side effects and, as is brought out in the discussion of the Jorgenson and Lovell proposals, procedures designed to yield "efficient" estimates of seasonal or non-seasonal components will not generally be the same as those designed to yield desirable statistical properties for estimates of structural parameters.

Throughout this chapter we assume that the stochastic structure of the series $\{x_t\}$ is known a priori. This means, in effect, that our "optimal" seasonal adjustment procedures are more optimal than realizable procedures could ever be. That they, in fact, possess many of the same spectral properties as the Census and Bureau of Labor Statistics Methods do is rather strong evidence, therefore, in support of our conclusion that the spectral criteria developed earlier do not provide an adequate basis for the evaluation of such methods.

2.   Choice of Models

In order to illustrate the effects of applying any of the above definitions of "optimal" seasonal adjustment, we adopt an explicit unobserved-components model for the observed series $\{x_t\}$. In Chapter VI we presented some parametric three-component models that have spectral densities similar to those of many real economic time series. In this section we present the derivations necessary to apply the theory of least-squares prediction or extraction to one of those models. The model with which we work is

$$X_t = T_t + S_t + I_t, \qquad T_t = \frac{\epsilon_t + 0.8\epsilon_{t-1}}{(1 - 0.95U)(1 - 0.75U)}$$

$$S_t = \frac{v_t + 0.6v_{t-1}}{1 - 0.9U^{12}}, \qquad I_t = \eta_t, \tag{1}$$

and $\{\epsilon_t\}$, $\{v_t\}$, $\{\eta_t\}$ mutually uncorrelated white noise sequences. The variances of the noise sequences were chosen so that 85 percent of the variance of X_t is accounted for by the trend-cycle, 10 percent by the seasonal component, and 5 percent by the irregular. The spectral density functions for the similar components and for the series as a whole are shown in Figs. 2–5 of Chapter VI.

To obtain the least-squares forecasts and extractions, we need the canonical factorization of the covariance generating function of X_t. Since the individual components are orthogonal,

$$g_{XX}(z) = g_{TT}(z) + g_{SS}(z) + g_{II}(z)$$

$$= \frac{\sigma_\epsilon^2(1 + 0.8z)(1 + 0.8z^{-1})}{(1 - 0.95z)(1 - 0.75z)(1 - 0.95z^{-1})(1 - 0.75z^{-1})}$$

$$+ \frac{\sigma_v^2(1 + 0.6z)(1 + 0.6z^{-1})}{(1 - 0.9z^{12})(1 - 0.9z^{-12})} + \sigma_\eta^2$$

$$= \sigma^2 \frac{P(z)P(z^{-1})}{(1 - 0.95z)(1 - 0.75z)(1 - 0.9z^{12})}, \\
\times (1 - 0.95z^{-1})(1 - 0.75z^{-1})(1 - 0.9z^{-12})$$

$$\tag{2}$$

where

$$\sigma^2 P(z)P(z^{-1}) = \sigma_\epsilon^2(1 + 0.8z)(1 + 0.8z^{-1})(1 - 0.9z^{12})(1 - 0.9z^{-12})$$
$$+ \sigma_v^2(1 + 0.6z)(1 + 0.6z^{-1})(1 - 0.95z)$$
$$\times (1 - 0.75z)(1 - 0.95z^{-1})(1 - 0.75z^{-1})$$
$$+ \sigma_\eta^2(1 - 0.95z)(1 - 0.75z)(1 - 0.9z^{12})$$
$$\times (1 - 0.95z^{-1})(1 - 0.75z^{-1})(1 - 0.9z^{-12}).$$

σ^2 is chosen so that the constant in $P(z)$ is one.[4]

Once the polynomial $P(z)$ is obtained, the predictions and extractions can be calculated, as discussed in Chapter V. As an example, consider the problem of finding the least-squares estimate of T_{t+v} at time t (v may be any integer). Since the components are uncorrelated with one another,

$$g_{TX}(z) = g_{TT}(z); \tag{3}$$

---

[4] For calculating the spectral densities shown below, the method used to obtain the roots of $P(z)P(z^{-1})$ was a variant of Muller's method (1956). See Chapter VII.3.

hence, the generating function of the sequence of weights is given by

$$\gamma(z) = 0.85 \frac{(1 - 0.95z)(1 - 0.75z)(1 - 0.9z^{12})}{P(z)}$$

$$\times \left[\frac{(1 + 0.8z)(1 + 0.8z^{-1})(1 - 0.95z^{-1})(1 - 0.75z^{-1})(1 - 0.9z^{-12})}{(1 - 0.95z)(1 - 0.95z^{-1})(1 - 0.75z)(1 - 0.75z^{-1})P(z^{-1})z^{v}} \right]_{+}$$

$$= 0.85 \frac{(1 - 0.95z)(1 - 0.75z)(1 - 0.9z^{12})}{P(z)}$$

$$\times \left[\frac{(1 + 0.8z)(1 + 0.8z^{-1})(1 - 0.9z^{-12})}{(1 - 0.95z)(1 - 0.75z)P(z^{-1})z^{v}} \right]_{+}. \tag{4}$$

Generating functions for estimates of the other components and for predictions can be obtained by evaluating similar expressions. Since

$$\hat{X}_{t+v,t} = \hat{T}_{t+v,t} + \hat{S}_{t+v,t} + \hat{I}_{t+v,t}, \tag{5}$$

it is not necessary to evaluate generating functions for each of the four cases explicitly. This is especially helpful if v is negative since in that case the best predictor of X_{t+v} as of time t is clearly X_{t+v} itself.[5]

3.   Some Results

In this section, the results of applying the various methods of "optimal" seasonal adjustment to the hypothetical series are reported.

Consider the special case of extracting the trend-cycle component when the entire history of X_t is known. The generating transform of the optimal weights is easily shown to be

$$\gamma(z) = g_{XT}(z)/g_{XX}(z) = g_{TT}(z)/g_{XX}(z). \tag{1}$$

The spectral density of the estimate is

$$f_{\hat{T}\hat{T}}(\lambda) = \gamma(e^{i\lambda})\gamma(e^{-i\lambda})f_{XX}(\lambda) = \frac{f_{TT}(\lambda)}{f_{XX}(\lambda)/f_{TT}(\lambda)}$$

$$= \frac{f_{TT}(\lambda)}{1 + f_{SS}(\lambda)/f_{TT}(\lambda) + f_{II}(\lambda)/f_{TT}(\lambda)}. \tag{2}$$

The ratios $f_{SS}(\lambda)/f_{TT}(\lambda)$ will generally be large near the seasonal frequencies. Thus "optimal" adjustment will produce dips in the spectral density of the adjusted series at those frequencies. (See, for example, Fig. 1.) Such dips do not

[5] The calculations needed to evaluate (4) can be easily handled by using the theorem by Whittle (1963) discussed in Appendix D. Identifying $(1 + 0.8z)(1 + 0.8z^{-1})(1 - 0.9z^{-12})/P(z^{-1})z^{v}$ in (4) with $Q(z)$ and expanding $(1 - 0.95z)^{-1}(1 - 0.75z)^{-1}$ by partial fractions, we may apply Whittle's theorem to each term in the sum and obtain $\gamma(z)$ as a rational function of z.

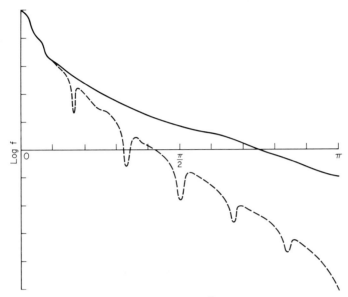

Fig. 1. Spectral densities: _ _ _ _, $\hat{T}_{t-x,t}$; ———, T_t.

represent "overadjustment," as Nerlove (1964) thought, but rather are characteristic of this sort of "optimal" adjustment.

Since the filter used is linear and symmetric, the coherence will be one at every frequency and the phase shift zero; however, the spectral density of the adjusted series will show a loss of power at every frequency. Note that not only will there be a loss of power relative to the spectrum of the observed series X_t, but from (2) it is clear that there will be a loss of power relative to the spectrum of the trend cycle itself. Figures 2 and 3 show that the same phenomena can be produced with filters which are only moderately two-sided. Clearly, these dips are in no way an indication of "overadjustment."

Using one-sided filters only does not lead to dips at the seasonal frequencies (one-sided filters occur when forecasting or estimating the current value of a component). As Figs. 4–7 show, however, the other effects noted in Nerlove (1964) are still present. Relative to the observed series, all methods produce "distortions" at all frequencies and may lead to a loss of power throughout the entire range.

In the case of one-sided filters, the filters are not symmetric, and the phase angle is thus generally different from zero, although this does not imply that the method of adjustment used is improper. The coherence between the adjusted and the unadjusted series is unity at every frequency because the filters used are linear.

To complete this example (and to see how well the prediction and extraction really works) the series analyzed are simulated by generating normal random variables, with the appropriate variances, to be used as inputs to the several

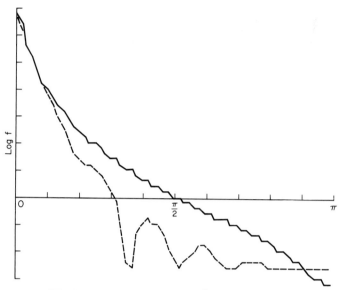

Fig. 2.   Spectral densities: _____, $\hat{T}_{t-12,t}$; _____, T_t.

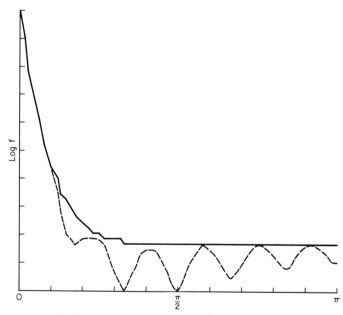

Fig. 3.   Spectral densities: _____, $\hat{T}_{t-18,t}$; _____, T_t.

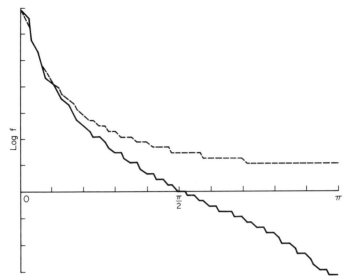

Fig. 4. Spectral densities: _ _ _ _ , $\hat{T}_{t,t}$; —————, T_t.

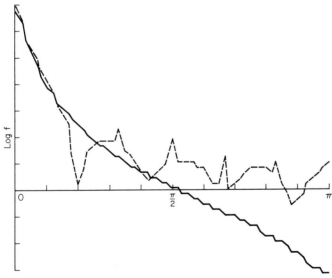

Fig. 5. Spectral densities: _ _ _ _ , $\frac{1}{12}\sum_{i=-8}^{3} \hat{x}_{t+i,t}$; —————, T_t.

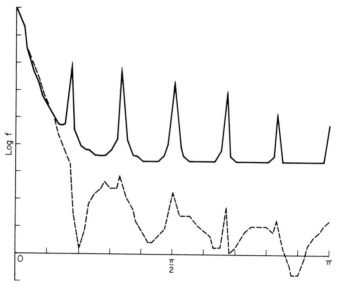

Fig. 6.   Spectral densities: $\_\_\_\_\_$, $\frac{1}{12} \sum_{i=-8}^{3} \hat{x}_{t+i,t}$; $_____$, X_t.

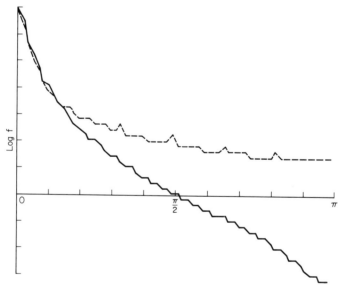

Fig. 7.   Spectral densities: $\_\_\_\_\_$, $\frac{1}{12} \sum_{i=1}^{12} \hat{x}_{t+i,t}$; $_____$, T_t.

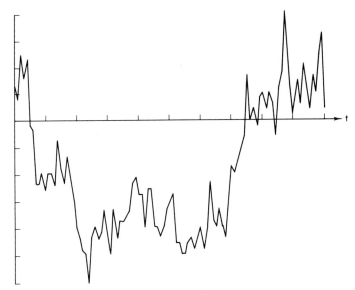

Fig. 8. The series X_t.

components of the model. Each component is initialized by picking a zero-mean random variable from a population with variance equal to the variance of the component; 480 observations are then generated, of which the first 120 are discarded. Figure 8 shows the last 100 observations of the simulated time series, and Fig. 9 shows the estimates of the trend-cycle component obtained

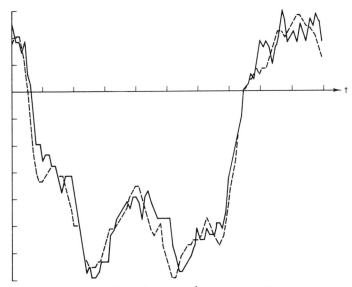

Fig. 9. The series: $----$, $\hat{T}_{t-3,t}$; $\underline{\quad\quad}$, T_{t-3}.

with a filter that uses three subsequent observations.[6] As pointed out above, using a fixed linear filter results in the coherence between the adjusted and unadjusted series which is everywhere one. However, if one were to estimate the coherence between the series using the simulated forecasts and the series X_t, the estimates might be substantially below one. When such coherences are estimated this result is indeed obtained. It should be pointed out that low coherence in this case derives only from sampling errors and truncation of the forecasting or extraction operator.

Our results clearly suggest that all of the undesirable features noted in the spectral comparisons of the unadjusted and BLS seasonally adjusted unemployment series in Nerlove (1964) are reproduced by the three sorts of "optimal" adjustments considered here. Since the criteria of optimality are rather plausible, it can only be concluded that the spectral criteria suggested in Nerlove (1964) leave much to be desired. Furthermore, the results obtained do not depend on sampling problems or the difficulties of too-short series; they are logical consequences of the alternative assumptions we have made concerning the objectives of seasonal adjustment.

Recently Cleveland and Tiao (1976, p. 581) have concluded that "the linear filter version of the Census X-11 program for time-series decomposition can be approximately justified in terms of an additive model with stochastic trend, seasonal and noise components. Optimal estimates of the trend and seasonal components are obtained from the model and found to be in close agreement with the corresponding estimates for the Census Procedure." They find that the Census X-11 approximately corresponds to signal extraction filters for the following model:

$$y_t = p_t + s_t + \epsilon_t$$
$$(1 - U)^2 p_t = (1 + 0.49U - 0.49U^2)\eta_t \tag{3}$$
$$(1 - U^{12})s_t = (1 + 0.64U^{12} + 0.83U^{24})\zeta_t$$

with $\dfrac{\sigma_\zeta^2}{\sigma_\eta^2} = 1.3$, $\dfrac{\sigma_\epsilon^2}{\sigma_\eta^2} = 14.4$, and where $\{\epsilon_t\}$, $\{\eta_t\}$, $\{\zeta_t\}$ are mutually uncorrelated noise processes.

4.   Seasonal Adjustment and the Estimation of Structural Models

As mentioned earlier in this chapter, the use of seasonally adjusted data affects parameter estimates obtained from fitting econometric models. In general, whether or not a particular adjustment procedure improves the properties of parameter estimates depends upon the nature of the models being estimated

---

[6] The generating functions derived above apply only if the entire past of the series X_t is known. In calculating the estimates shown in Fig. 9, the filters are simply truncated at the earliest observation. Thus one estimate uses 360 observations, one uses 359, and so on.

and upon the method of estimation. It may well be that there are tradeoffs between the "efficiency" of a seasonal adjustment procedure and the usefulness of the adjusted data for econometric purposes. Each of these points is well illustrated by the work of Lovell (1963, 1966) and Jorgenson (1964, 1967a).

Lovell approached the problem of seasonal adjustment axiomatically. He considered five properties for seasonal adjustment methods: sum-preserving, product-preserving, idempotency, orthogonality, and symmetry.

An adjustment procedure is called sum-preserving if summing two adjusted series gives the same result as adjusting their total. More formally, if x_t and y_t are time series and x_t^a, y_t^a are the adjusted series, then a method is sum-preserving if and only if

$$x_t^a + y_t^a = (x_t + y_t)^a.$$

Thus data adjusted by a sum-preserving method will satisfy the same linear accounting relations as the original data. It seems clear that for many purposes (e.g., when analyzing Gross National Product and its components) this would be a convenient property. Of course, in some cases one might wish for other types of consistency, e.g., when analyzing factor intensities, unemployment rates, etc. As Lovell showed, it is easy to demand too much of an adjustment method; in fact, he proved that all adjustment methods that are both sum-preserving and product-preserving $\left[x_t^a y_t^a = (x_t y_t)^a \right]$ must be trivial. That is, either x_t^a is equal to x_t or it is identically zero.

An adjustment procedure is called idempotent if $(x_t^a)^a = x_t^a$ for all t. The rationale behind requiring this property is that a method ought to remove all seasonality in a series and not alter series with no seasonal fluctuations. While idempotency seems intuitively attractive, it is important to be aware that its appeal depends upon how concretely one defines the operation of seasonal adjustment. As a property of the full process, including the selection of series to adjust and the determination of computational procedures appropriate for different individual time series, it appears inoffensive. However, as a property of the final adjustment formula itself, it is hard to justify. To be sure, the least-squares seasonal dummy variables approach does possess this property, but other perfectly reasonable procedures need not. For example, suppose one posits a model such as the one used in the examples in Section 3, and in some fashion filters or transforms, not necessarily linearly, the observed series to obtain an estimate of the trend cycle plus the irregular. Now refiltering the series or applying the filter to the actual trend-cycle component amounts to a major specification error, and it is not clear why in this situation the filter should act as the identity operator.

The property of orthogonality is that $\sum_{u \leq t} (x_u - x_u^a) x_u^a = 0$. The rationale for this requirement is similar; i.e., if it does not hold, then "some seasonality remains in the data." Notice that this requirement essentially assumes a time-series model with additive seasonal and nonseasonal components; i.e., the *difference* between the two series is somehow important (rather than their ratio or some other function). Also, if this property is satisfied at time t, then in order for it to be satisfied at time $t + 1$, either the adjusted series must be revised or the adjustment is trivial. Since both of these properties are undesirable for official adjustment methods, Lovell's orthogonality axiom is not appropriate for them. However, for adjusting data to be used in linear regression analysis, this property is desirable (see below), so this provides a nice illustration of the futility of defining a unique "best" method of adjustment independently of the intended use of the adjusted series.

The final property Lovell considers is symmetry, i.e., $\partial x_t^a/\partial x_s = \partial x_s^a/\partial x_t$ for all t and s. Lovell states that this property may be reasonable in some applications, but not in others since it may be "embarrassing to find that seasonally adjusted figures for earlier periods are subject to marked revision as a result of updating preliminary figures for recent months" (1966, p. 995).

Idempotency, orthogonality, and symmetry are not independent, and Lovell shows that any sum-preserving (i.e., linear) method that has two of these properties has the third. Lovell's main result is to show that all sum-preserving adjustment procedures that possess these latter properties are equivalent to a regression with the unadjusted series as the dependent variable. The residuals from the regression being the adjusted series, for example, subtracting out the mean for each season would correspond to regressing a series on a set of seasonal dummies.

Jorgenson (1964, 1967a) considered observed time series of the form

$$X = D\delta_x + S\sigma_x + \epsilon_x, \tag{1}$$

where X is a vector of T observations, D is a T-by-k matrix of powers of time etc. that represents the trend-cycle component, S is a matrix of seasonal dummies, and ϵ_x is the irregular component. The vectors δ_x and σ_x contain the unknown coefficients. It is assumed that the elements of ϵ_x are uncorrelated and have equal variances. Jorgenson observed that application of ordinary least-squares regression to (1) will give the unique, minimum variance, linear, unbiased estimates of σ_x and suggested using these estimates to obtain an estimate of the seasonal component and, by subtraction, the seasonally adjusted series. Lovell's procedure in this case would be to regress X on S only and take the residuals as the adjusted series. Jorgenson's method provides more efficient estimates of the seasonal component than Lovell's but, as Lovell pointed out, could cause problems in the estimation of econometric models.

Suppose that

$$\bar{Y} = \bar{X}\beta + u, \tag{2}$$

where

$$Y = \bar{Y} + S\sigma_y = D\delta_y + S\sigma_y + \epsilon_y,$$
$$X = \bar{X} + S\sigma_x = D\delta_x + S\sigma_x + \epsilon_x, \tag{3}$$
$$E(u) = E(\epsilon_x) = E(\epsilon_y) = 0.$$

Combining (2) and (3) yields the following estimating equation:

$$Y = X\beta + S(\sigma_y - \sigma_x\beta) + u. \tag{4}$$

Applying least squares to this equation will yield unbiased estimates of β. But by well-known properties of linear regressions (Goldberger, 1968, Chapter 4), this is equivalent to applying Lovell's method to each series and then calculating the regression using the adjusted data. This is not true of Jorgenson's method, however, as the orthogonality property is not satisfied. Both procedures depend upon a particular specification of the seasonal components and, Jorgenson noted (1967a), applying least squares to (4) need not provide unbiased estimates of β since some of the x's may be endogenous. The purpose of this discussion is not to choose between these two approaches, but rather to note the sort of tradeoffs involved and to emphasize that the effects of seasonal adjustment on parameter estimates are highly model dependent.

Also, as noted at the beginning of this chapter, one of the main practical conclusions to emerge from this sort of analysis is that it is extremely important to make unadjusted data available for use. Although in the example considered, using data adjusted by Lovell's method will give estimates of the structural parameters identical to those obtained by estimating (4) directly, it still seems preferable to work with the unadjusted data; the reason being that use of the unadjusted data at least ensures that the degrees of freedom will be calculated correctly.

Granger (1976) has also given some a priori desirable properties of seasonal adjustment [see also Granger and Newbold (1977, pp. 65–69)]. The one that he asserts to be the most important is that the coherence between an adjusted series and a true nonseasonal portion of a time series be unity and the phase angle zero at all frequencies. The purpose is to ensure that the adjusted series and the true nonseasonal series be identical, except possibly for scale effects. Note that the condition while necessary, is not sufficient since it is satisfied for any pair of series related by a symmetric linear filter. Further, the condition is never satisfied for extraction based upon unobserved-components models. In this case, however, the coherence may be near unity away from the seasonal frequencies, though the phase angle will in general be different from zero.

Thomas and Wallis (1971) also considered the problem of seasonal adjustment in the context of regression analysis. They considered two specifications of the seasonality, viz., seasonal dummy variables and a high order autoregressive process in the residuals. They noted, as Jorgenson had earlier, that if the first specification is correct, then efficient estimates of all the parameters can be obtained by ordinary least squares, with the dummy variables included among the set of explanatory variables (making the usual adjustment if an intercept would normally be calculated). They observed that estimating the model without the seasonal dummies amounts to a specification error and in general will yield biased estimates of the parameters. Essentially, one is combining several regressions with the same slope coefficients and different intercepts and requiring the pooled regression to have a single intercept. Thus, unless the intercepts really were all the same or the means of the other explanatory variables were equal across the regressions, there will be some bias. If the seasonal dummies are included when they need not be, then one has unnecessarily burned a few degrees of freedom, so that while no biases are introduced, there is some loss of efficiency.

If the seasonal fluctuations are treated as part of the disturbance term in the regression, then of course the efficient procedure is generalized least squares using appropriate specifications for the errors. Ignoring seasonality in this model is simply using ordinary least squares instead of generalized least squares. Notice that in this case mistakenly ignoring the seasonal does not lead to biased estimates of the regression coefficients, though there are the usual effects of autocorrelated disturbances.

Since including seasonal dummies in a regression equation is hardly a structural explanation of seasonal fluctuations, one might prefer to think of the seasonal as being part of the disturbance, i.e., that unexplained by the model. One possibility would be to adopt a variance components model. This would amount to thinking of the data as a time series of cross sections where the unit of time was a year and the "cross section" the seasons.

That is, take the disturbance to be

$$\epsilon_{kt} = S_k + \eta_{kt}, \qquad k = 1, 2, \ldots, 12, \quad t = 1, 2, \ldots, T,$$

where

$$E(S_k) = E(\eta_{kt}) = 0,$$

$$E(S_k S_j) = \begin{cases} \sigma_S^2, & j = k \\ 0, & j \neq k \end{cases}$$

$$E(\eta_{kt}\eta_{js}) = \begin{cases} \sigma^2, & k = j \quad \text{and} \quad t = s \\ 0, & \text{otherwise} \end{cases}$$

$$E(S_k \eta_{jt}) = 0, \qquad \text{for all } j, k, \text{ and } t.$$

Let W_{xx} and W_{xy} be the matrices of within-group sums of squares and cross products and B_{xx} and B_{xy} be the corresponding between-group quantities. Then for this model the generalized least-squares estimates of the regression coefficients are given by

$$\hat{\beta} = [W_{xx} + \theta B_{xx}]^{-1}[W_{xy} + \theta B_{xy}] \qquad (5)$$

where $\theta = \sigma_S^2/(\sigma_S^2 + T\sigma^2).$[7] As T becomes large, θ goes to zero, and the generalized least-squares estimates become the estimates obtained by ordinary least squares with seasonal dummies included.

---

[7] For a detailed discussion of this model, see Maddala (1971) and Nerlove (1971).

Thomas and Wallis (1971) treat the case in which the seasonal error term is given by

$$\epsilon_t = \rho\epsilon_{t-L} + \eta_t, \qquad |\rho| < 1,$$

where $\{\eta_t\}$ is a white noise process and L is the number of observations per year. They suggest estimating the parameters by a two-step feasible generalized least-squares estimate in which ρ is estimated from the residuals of an ordinary least-squares regression.

The implications of seasonal adjustment for the estimation of distributed-lag models have been studied by Wallis (1974) and Sims (1974). Both authors treat the case in which the adjustment can be represented by a time-invariant linear filter, and Wallis develops a linear approximation to the Census method X-11, as do Cleveland and Tiao (1976) in a different way. Suppose that y_t and x_t are two observed time series and that there is a distributed-lag relation between their nonseasonal components and, possibly, a different relation between the seasonal components. Let

$$\begin{aligned} y_t &= y_t^{NS} + y_t^{S}, & x_t &= x_t^{NS} + x_t^{S}, \\ y_t^{NS} &= C(U)x_t^{NS} + \epsilon_t, & y_t^{S} &= D(U)x_t^{S} + \eta_t, \end{aligned} \qquad (6)$$

where all sequences are jointly covariance stationary. To complete the specification, it is assumed that the seasonal and nonseasonal components of a series are orthogonal to each other and that the disturbances ϵ_t and η_t are uncorrelated with each other and with the x's:

$$\left. \begin{aligned} E(y_t^{S} y_{t'}^{NS}) &= E(x_t^{S} x_{t'}^{NS}) = 0 \\ E(\epsilon_t x_{t'}^{NS}) &= E(\eta_t x_{t'}^{S}) = 0 \end{aligned} \right\} \quad \text{for all } t \text{ and } t'$$

$$\text{and} \quad \left. \begin{aligned} E(\epsilon_t \eta_{t'}) &= 0 \\ E(\epsilon_t x_{t'}^{S}) &= 0 \\ E(\eta_t x_{t'}^{NS}) &= 0 \end{aligned} \right\} \quad \text{for all } t \text{ and } t'. \qquad (7)$$

Notice that if D is identical to zero, then the seasonal components are unrelated and the seasonal component of x_t acts as a measurement error. Estimation of C is further complicated since the seasonal component of y_t is a serially correlated disturbance.

It follows from the specification of the model that

$$g_{xx}(z) = g_{NS}(z) + g_{S}(z), \qquad g_{yx}(z) = C(z)g_{NS}(z) + D(z)g_{S}(z), \qquad (8)$$

where $g_{NS}(z)$ and $g_{S}(z)$ are defined for the series x. If we define the empirical lag distribution between y and x as γ, where

$$y_t = \gamma(U)x_t + w_t, \qquad E(w_t x_{t'}) = 0 \qquad \text{for all } t \text{ and } t', \qquad (9)$$

we have

$$\gamma(z) = \frac{g_{yx}(z)}{g_{xx}(z)} = C(z)\frac{g_{NS}(z)}{g_{xx}(z)} + D(z)\frac{g_S(z)}{g_{xx}(z)}$$

$$= C(z)(1 - h(z)) + D(z)h(z) = C(z) + [D(z) - C(z)]h(z), \qquad (10)$$

where $h(z) = g_S(z)/g_{xx}(z)$.

In the frequency domain it is clear what is happening. The Fourier transform of γ is simply a weighted average of the transforms of C and D. It seems reasonable to assume that $h(e^{i\lambda})$ is close to one near the seasonal frequencies and close to zero (though positive) away from them. Thus $\gamma(e^{i\lambda})$ tends to be close to $D(e^{i\lambda})$ near seasonal frequencies and closer to C elsewhere. The effects of this in the time domain are quite different. Sims reports that lag distributions fitted between unadjusted seasonal series often show spurious seasonal fluctuations in the coefficients. Even if it were considered possible for the coefficients in C to exhibit a seasonal pattern, there would be no difficulty distinguishing between C and γ. For one thing, γ will surely be a two-sided distribution, while C will be known to be one-sided. It is clear from (10) that, in general, the only case in which γ is one-sided is when the spectral densities of x^{NS} and x^S are proportional at every frequency, i.e., have the same autocorrelation functions. While mathematically this is possible, it is completely contrary to any reasonable distinction between seasonal and nonseasonal series. Thus, in principle, bias due to seasonal noise should be relatively easy to detect.

It should be clear that (10) holds whenever different lag distributions link different unobserved components of economic time series. The only way in which the seasonal–nonseasonal distinction enters at all in this discussion is that in this case we have a priori information about $h(e^{i\lambda})$ that aids in identifying the source of the trouble. In the general case of different relations between components γ will be two-sided, thus signaling that something is wrong. Unfortunately, two-sided lag distributions can result from a variety of causes, e.g., simultaneity or time aggregation (Sims, 1972a,b), so that the precise nature of the difficulty may not be so easily determined.

As a practical matter, econometricians do not generally estimate unconstrained two-sided lag distributions. Generally, estimates are constrained to be one-sided, and often parametric forms are adopted that force the estimated pattern of lag coefficients to be smooth. This procedure not only suppresses the symptoms, but in fact, as Sims (1972a) shows, can make the disease (at least the bias) worse. Since

$$y_t = \gamma(U)x_t + w_t,$$

we have

$$E(y_t - b(U)x_t)^2 = \sigma_w^2 + E(\gamma(U)x_t - b(U)x_t)^2$$

$$= \sigma_w^2 + \int_{-\pi}^{\pi} |\gamma(e^{i\lambda}) - b(e^{i\lambda})|^2 f_{xx}(\lambda)\, d\lambda. \qquad (11)$$

As Sims (1972a) points out, the usual constraints adopted in estimation amount to smoothness constraints on $b(e^{i\lambda})$, so that while the bias due to seasonal noise is still present, common practice suppresses the symptoms. If both series are adjusted using the same linear filter, then γ is unchanged, but constrained estimates may well be improved. If both series are adjusted but by different filters, the results are completely unpredictable. Let

$$y_t^a = A_y(U)y_t \qquad x_t^a = A_x(U)x_t \tag{12}$$

be the adjusted series. Then the empirical relation between the adjusted series is

$$y_t^a = [\gamma(U)A_y(U)/A_x(U)]x_t^a + w_t'. \tag{13}$$

As noted, if $A_x \equiv A \equiv A_y$, then γ is unaffected. However, in fitting by least-squares the lag distribution between the adjusted series, one is now minimizing

$$\int_{-\pi}^{\pi} |\gamma(e^{i\lambda}) - b(e^{i\lambda})|^2 |A_x(e^{i\lambda})|^2 f_{xx}(\lambda)\, d\lambda.$$

Presumably $|A(e^{i\lambda})|$ is near zero in the neighborhood of the seasonal frequencies and closer to one away from them, which should, to some extent at least, undo some of the effects of the seasonal noise. That is, relatively greater weight is now being given to those frequencies where a priori we expect $|\gamma(e^{i\lambda}) - b(e^{i\lambda})|$ to be small.

Consider now the situation in which the seasonal component x_t^S is purely an errors-in-variables problem, i.e., there is no relation between the two seasonal components. In this case $\gamma(z)$ has an especially simple form:

$$\gamma(z) = C(z)(1 - h(z)) = C(z)g_{NS}(z)/g_{xx}(z). \tag{14}$$

Thus if one used data on the unadjusted y series and the adjusted x series, the transform of the empirical lag distribution would be

$$\gamma(z) = C(z)\frac{g_{NS}(z)}{g_{xx}(z)}\frac{1}{A_x(z)}. \tag{15}$$

Notice that use of the seasonally adjusted data on x_t will yield the correct lag distribution when

$$A_x(z) = 1 - h(z). \tag{16}$$

But comparing (15) with (3.1), we see that this is precisely the adjustment filter that arises when the seasonally adjusted series is an estimate of the trend-cycle component based upon the entire history of x series. Thus, in this situation at least, the "optimal" method of seasonal adjustment, that is, optimal from the point of view of estimating the parameters of the lag distribution, is also optimal in the sense discussed in the previous sections. As mentioned earlier, this method leads to dips in the spectrum of the adjusted series at frequencies near the seasonals.

When both series are seasonally adjusted, using different filters, essentially anything can happen. The difficulty is that both $|A_y(e^{i\lambda})|$ and $|A_x(e^{i\lambda})|$ are likely to be close to zero at the seasonal frequencies, so their ratio can behave quite wildly.

All of this discussion presumes that the adjustment is performed with a linear filter, which as we know is not the case with the official adjustment methods. As noted above, Wallis (1974) has developed a linear filter designed to approximate the census method X-11. More importantly, he has conducted several Monte Carlo experiments in which the effects of using the official adjustment methods are compared with the predicted effects based upon his linear approximations, and the two sets of results are in reasonable agreement.

If estimated coefficients obtained with unadjusted data show evidence of seasonal bias, (or if this is likely a priori), then adjusting the series may be necessary. Sims (1974, pp. 621–624) suggests several methods of adjustment that he has found reasonable and gives the appropriate degrees of freedom corrections. Whether either, both, or neither series should be adjusted depends upon the model of the relationship between the series. Similarly, the choice of method of adjustment—official, using a linear filter, seasonal dummies, frequency-based regressions with certain frequencies omitted (Engle, 1974), etc.—depends upon the observed characteristics of the series. Also, the sample size is a consideration because, as Sims notes, simple fixed-seasonal-effects type models may seem adequate for short series but generally perform poorly in long series since the adjusted series will still show evidence of seasonality.

5.   Conclusion

The effects, desirable or undesirable, of a particular method of seasonal adjustment can be assessed properly only in the time domain and only in relation to the objectives of such adjustment. In making an assessment, we are greatly handicapped by the inadequate attention that practitioners of seasonal adjustment have paid to the purposes of such adjustment and by the lack of a clearly formulated conception of the nature of seasonality. In Nerlove (1964) seasonality was defined as the characteristic of an economic time series that gives rise to peaks at seasonal frequencies, and an attempt was made to develop informal but generally applicable criteria for "good" seasonal adjustment in spectral terms. Any criteria should reflect time domain effects, even if couched in frequency terms. Lack of clear objectives precludes formulation of appropriate criteria, and spectral criteria were developed in the hope that they might serve as second best.

In terms of the traditional simple three-component model, modified by the addition of appropriate stochastic assumptions, we formulate three plausible objectives of "seasonal adjustment." We show how the minimum-mean-square-error criterion may be used to obtain "optimal" methods of seasonal adjustment, neglecting sampling problems. We show both empirically and theoretically that such "optimal" methods of adjustment reproduce many of the features of the relation between seasonally adjusted and unadjusted series noted in Nerlove (1964). We cannot say that the spectral comparisons are useless; certainly such comparisons should be interpreted with great care. Clearly the criteria suggested in Nerlove (1964) were naive.

Quite apart from whatever the objectives of seasonal adjustment are assumed to be in relation to the analysis of business cycles, it is important to keep in mind that the methods of adjustment actually used can have major effects upon econometric model fitting. From the discussion in the previous section it is clear that (a) no single method of adjustment will be best for all potential users of the data and (b) it is essential to provide economic time series data in unadjusted form.

Within the last few years, the analysis of the effects of various seasonal adjustment procedures in different situations has greatly increased in sophistication and rigor and, correspondingly, suggested adjustment methods are more precisely formulated and better tailored to specific modeling circumstances. Yet in terms of modeling explicitly what is going on, there seems to have been remarkably little progress. For example, in the work of both Sims and Wallis the various components are simply there and are assumed to be interrelated in various ways. The individual components are not explicitly modeled either in terms of underlying causal forces or in terms of providing stochastic specifications.

In this book we provide several examples of explicit stochastic specifications for unobserved components for economic time series. Also, in Chapter XIV we give some models in which these components are introduced directly as explanatory variables in economic models. Ultimately, no doubt, the proper objective is explanation of economic time series in terms of basic causal variables (for seasonal fluctuations, e.g., the timing of holidays and meteorological factors). While we can hardly claim to have accomplished this objective, we do feel that we have at least moved away from the development of complicated adjustment strategies for ad hoc setups toward more basic understanding.

Chapter IX
ON THE COMPARATIVE STRUCTURE
OF SERIAL DEPENDENCE IN
SOME U.S. PRICE SERIES[1]

1. Introduction

In Chapters II–VII we have developed the theory of stationary time series in both the frequency and the time domains and shown how equivalent *descriptions* of a time series may be given in both forms. Chapter VIII discussed the particular problem of seasonality in economic time series on the basis of a simple unobserved-components model, which, we asserted, had properties typical of many economic time series. The purpose of this chapter is twofold: First, we seek to bolster the "stylized" description upon which our simulation model of Chapter VIII is based. Second, we hope to demonstrate that description in the frequency domain can be a useful adjunct in descriptive studies of time series, purely as a practical matter. The material we have chosen for both of these aims consists of selected price statistics for the United States. Many of the series produced by the Bureau of Labor Statistics were analyzed in Nerlove (1972b). Here we concentrate on the industrial price series for which Stigler and Kindahl (1970) have published a detailed analysis in the time domain, with only brief mention of some of the other types of price series and their characteristics.

[1] This chapter builds on Nerlove (1972b) and additional unpublished research that was supported in part by the Board of Governors of the Federal Reserve System as well as by the National Science Foundation.

We are indebted to Claire Friedland and George Stigler for making available some of the data from the study of Stigler and Kindahl (1970) in punchcard form, and to Uri Ben–Zion for his skillful programming assistance.

The price statistics of the United States are produced by a complicated economic, statistical, and bureaucratic mechanism. Transactions occur; these have economic significance. Some are recorded, many are not. Various devices have been adopted for making statistical inferences about the prices at which some of the millions of transactions occurring in any period take place. These bits of evidence are combined, in turn, into aggregates that, it is hoped, are useful for a variety of analytical and prescriptive purposes. Over time, the manner of making statistical inferences, the universe of discourse about which such inferences are made, and the manner of combining all these pieces are constantly changing. The methods by which the Bureau of Labor Statistics collects and infers price information and the sorts of aggregates that it constructs have been extensively criticized; see, for example, the report of the Price Statistics Review Committee of the National Bureau of Economic Research (1961) and Stigler and Kindahl (1970). A good brief description of the various price indices and the manner of their construction and collection is contained in Backman and Gainsburgh (1966).

It is not our purpose to continue this discussion. The question of the *economic* mechanism that generates price movements in the United States and of what inferences can be drawn about the mechanism on the basis of existing price statistics is exceedingly important. The fact that a great many statistical and conceptual difficulties obscure the connection between the price data we observe and the underlying economic mechanism is not a question with which we are concerned here, despite its importance. For better or for worse, the price statistics of the United States have been and will continue to be used in many forms of econometric analyses and policy discussions. Furthermore, these series have much in common with other important economic time series, including common statistical and conceptual difficulties in their collection, collation, and use. Our concern here is to seek a useful characterization, preferably a parametric characterization, of U.S. price series *as they exist*, that is, taking the processes by which these statistics are produced, with all their concomitant difficulties and all of the changes which have taken place, as given. Because our characterization is analogous to *reduced-form estimation* in econometrics as compared to *structural estimation*, it will be less useful for analysis and prediction than might otherwise be the case were we able to study separately the several parts of the mechanism that generate our observations. Such reduced-form analysis, however, is characteristic to a greater or lesser degree of all econometric analysis and, as we hope to show, can still be quite useful in a variety of ways.

In 1948, Guy Orcutt published a study of the autoregressive nature of the annual time series used for Tinbergen's econometric model of the United States. Orcutt simply fit autoregressive schemes of low order to Tinbergen's data. At that time, little was known about how to fit moving-average schemes or mixed moving-average autoregressive schemes, or about the difficulties that may arise in fitting an autoregression whose order is unknown. Despite the relatively primitive state of its technique, Orcutt's study had a major impact on econometrics. He found highly significant first- or second-order autoregressive coefficients in almost every case and finally concluded that the first differences of Tinbergen's series followed a first-order autoregressive process. Suddenly economists became aware of the problem: If economic time series were so highly dependent serially, then it seemed surely likely that the disturbances in econometric equations, supposed to represent left-out variables in part, were as well. One of the general questions to which the present investigation is addressed is whether monthly or quarterly time series, now extensively available, are characterized by serial dependencies of a more complicated nature than the simple autoregressive forms that Orcutt found adequate for the annual series used in Tinbergen's model of the U.S. economy. Our results, using spectral analytic techniques that have been obtained for U.S. price series and a variety of other monthly economic time series, suggest that, in contrast to Orcutt's findings for annual time series, relatively low-order autoregressive structures are inadequate to account for the serial dependencies that characterize monthly economic time series.

What do we mean when we say we seek to "characterize" a time series or, more specifically, to characterize the structure of serial dependence in a particular time series, say the Consumer Price Index? The approach presented in Chapters II–VII above regards observations on a time series as collections of random variables. More generally, the outcomes of stochastic processes may be thought of as collections of random variables. By "characterization," strictly speaking, we mean specification of the probability law or distribution from which these random variables arise. Such specifications may range from very simple to extremely complex and may be of varying degrees of completeness. For example, an estimated econometric model is a very complex characterization of the multiple time series consisting of the observations on all the endogenous variables over the time period covered; the current set of seasonal factors for unemployment of males aged 14–19 in the United States is a very simple and exceedingly incomplete characterization of that series.

Consider the collection of random variables consisting of observations on a single time series, e.g., the Consumer Price Index. Provided the probability law governing the generation of the series has finite moments, the series can be characterized in terms of these moments. Generally, one would seek a characterization only in terms of first and second moments, or equivalently (in the case of a time series) in terms of the *serial correlation*, or *correlogram* as the collection of these correlations is called. If the series is not stationary, it can often be transformed in such a way that the transformed series is; the nature of the transformation required is then part of the characterization.

From a purely theoretical point of view, looking at the serial correlations of a stationary time series and looking at its spectral density are equivalent modes of analysis, but as a practical matter the two characterizations may yield different, sometimes complementary, insights into the nature of the structure of serial dependence in the time series. Fitting an unobserved-components model to the series is also a way, albeit at a somewhat different level of discourse, of describing a time series. Here we consider only how descriptions in the frequency domain by estimated spectral density functions may be a useful adjunct to more traditional forms of description and analysis.

2.   Brief Characterization of Selected Nonindustrial Price Series of the Bureau of Labor Statistics[2]

What can spectral estimates reveal of the nature of serial dependence of U.S. price series as collected and published by the Bureau of Labor Statistics? In this section we examine the spectral densities for the Consumer Price Index and a number of its components; in the next section we examine some industrial prices, such as those that enter the Wholesale Price Index.

Figures 1–7 plot graphs for the normalized spectral densities of the time series of the raw data for the logarithmic first differences or logarithms of selected individual price series entering the Consumer Price Index, the CPI itself, and the food component. All are monthly series for the period January 1947–March 1970. Both the spectral density (solid line) and points one standard deviation up and one down are plotted (asterisks without connecting lines).

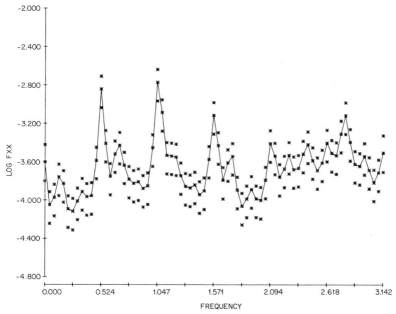

Fig. 1.   Spectral density of the logarithmic first differences of pork chop prices, Bureau of Labor Statistics, January 1947–March 1970, monthly data.

[2] This section is drawn from Nerlove (1972b, pp. 71–76, 78–112).

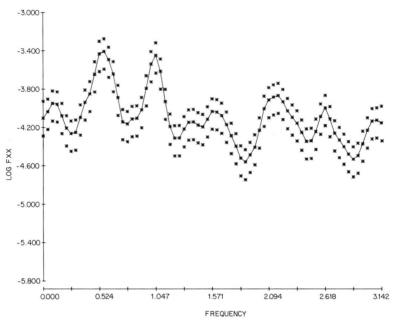

Fig. 2.   Spectral density of the logarithmic first differences of round steak prices, Bureau of Labor Statistics, January 1947–March 1970, monthly data.

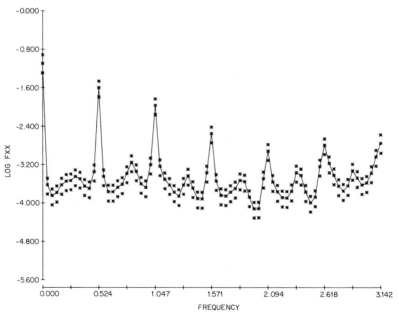

Fig. 3.   Spectral density of the logarithmic first differences of apple prices, Bureau of Labor Statistics, January 1947–March 1970, monthly data.

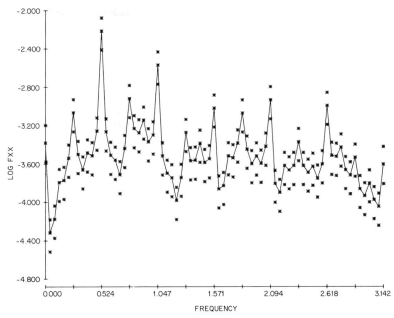

Fig. 4. Spectral density of the logarithmic first differences of orange prices, Bureau of Labor Statistics, January 1947–March 1970, monthly data.

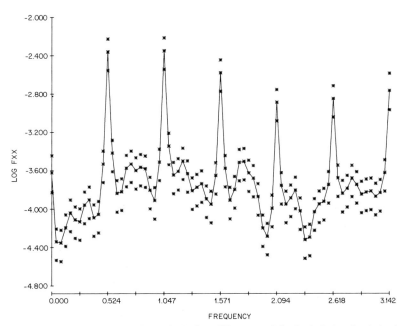

Fig. 5. Spectral density of the logarithmic first differences of the fresh fruit price index in the Consumer Price Index, Bureau of Labor Statistics, January 1947–March 1970, monthly data.

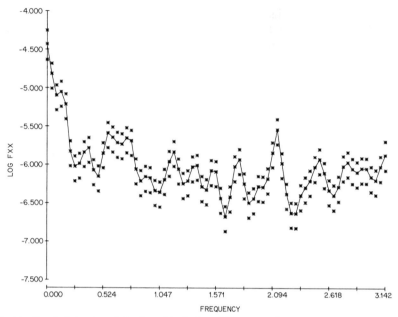

Fig. 6.   Spectral density of the logarithmic first differences of the consumer Price Index, all items, Bureau of Labor Statistics, January 1947–March 1970, monthly data.

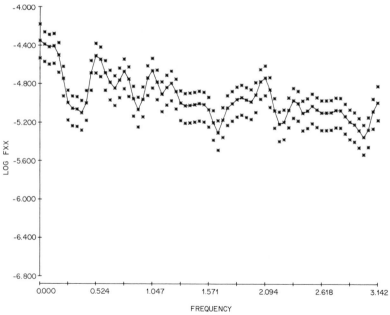

Fig. 7.   Spectral density of the logarithms of the food component of the consumer Price Index, Bureau of Labor Statistics, January 1947–March 1970, monthly data.

Examine first the graphs of the spectral densities for price series for individual items: Fig. 1, pork chops; Fig. 2, round steak; Fig. 3, apples; and Fig. 4, oranges. These graphs reveal a number of distinctive features commonly found in economic time series and noted in the previous chapter: First, there are marked peaks, but not extremely sharp spikes, at each of the so-called seasonal frequencies. (Recall that, for monthly data, these frequencies correspond to periods of 12, 6, 4, 3, 2.4, and 2 months or cycles of 1, 2, 3, 4, 5, and 6 per year; if the positive frequency axis above which the spectral estimates are plotted is represented by the interval $[0, \pi]$, the monthly seasonal frequencies divide the interval into six equal segments with endpoints $0, \pi/6, \pi/3, \pi/2, 2\pi/3, 5\pi/6, \pi$.) Second, apart from these seasonal peaks, the spectral densities generally decrease with frequency. Since the spectral density function essentially "decomposes" the variance of the times series into parts contributed by "sinusoidal components" of different frequencies, we could say that the variance contributed by the low frequency components was many times greater than that contributed by the high frequency components, apart from the contribution of components near seasonal frequencies. However, note that, in contrast to the automotive sales and inventory series examined above in Chapter VI, the difference in the contributions of low and high frequencies to the variance is much less marked. This is entirely due to the fact that we are not graphing the spectral densities of the series themselves, but of their first differences.

The logarithmic first-difference transformation allows for a form of nonstationarity, of which a particular case would be the presence of an exponential trend, but which is in fact somewhat more general. Since the estimation procedure smooths or averages the spectral density functions, the actual presence of such nonstationarity would be revealed merely by an extremely sharp peak at the origin. Similarly, since the first-difference transformation removes all the variance contributed by a sinusoidal component of zero frequency, such a transformation should result in a sharp dip near the origin if the series is not in fact nonstationary in this particular way, or indeed in any way that can be removed by differencing. As noted in Nerlove (1972b), except for the food component of the Consumer Price Index, the crude-materials-for-further-processing component of the Wholesale Price Index, and certain of the individual components of the WPI, the sharp dips at the origin that would occur if the transformation were unnecessary are absent or very insignificant. On the other hand, further differencing does introduce dips of the sort that suggest that the nonstationarity does not take the form requiring multiple differencing for removal.[3]

For the series, the spectral densities of which are graphed in Figs. 1–4, considerable evidence of seasonality exists, revealed by very sharp and relatively

---

[3] This is all quite analogous, of course, to the difficulties involved in prewhitening that led to the device of recoloring discussed in Chapter III; however, since the difference filter has a transfer function with a zero at the origin, the estimates cannot be recolored here.

high peaks at the seasonal frequencies noted above. Although the price of round steak is clearly less seasonal than pork chops, fresh apples, or fresh oranges, prices for many such individual commodities are so highly seasonal in part because some are, in fact, only intermittently available, and for these commodities prices are interpolated using averages of previous prices or group prices of commodities "in season."[4] The prices of the four specific commodities for which spectral densities are graphed in Figs. 1–4 are, however, continuously available through the period January 1947–March 1970.

In Nerlove (1972b), highly implausible behavior was exhibited by the spectral density for the logarithmic first differences of the composite *index* of all fresh fruit prices. The graph of the spectral density of the logarithmic first differences of this series showed there an extremely sharp dip at the origin, rose rapidly to a frequency of $\pi/6$ (corresponding to a period of 12 months), then more gradually to a frequency of $\pi/2$ (corresponding to a period of 4 months), and finally very slowly for the remainder of the frequency range. This behavior was entirely accounted for by a misplaced decimal point in the original series and is not repeated in the results presented here based on the corrected raw data (Fig. 5). We conclude that the raw data must *always* be examined in conjunction with any spectral analytic results if such anomalies are to be discovered and in order to guard against such possibly highly misleading conclusions.

Figures 6 and 7 show the graphs of the spectral densities of the logarithmic first differences of the Consumer Price Index and logarithms of the food component of the CPI, respectively; the data cover the same period as that for the individual items discussed above, January 1947–March 1970. The CPI as a whole shows little evidence of seasonality in contrast to the individual food items previously considered, whereas the composite index for food does show seasonality, although the seasonality is hardly as marked or regular as that observed above. The spectral density of the logarithmic first differences of the Food Price Index exhibits a marked dip near the origin, which suggests the possibility that differencing this series may have been inappropriate, in the sense that the series may be approximately stationary *without* a first-difference transformation. Nonetheless, a spectral analysis of the undifferenced logarithms shows such a peak near the origin that the matter must be regarded as moot.

Perhaps the main conclusion one can draw from Figs. 1–7 is that the structure of serial dependence in aggregates is more irregular than in subaggregates. The aggregate indices have "smoother" spectral densities and show much less evidence of seasonality than any of the corresponding subcomponents (Nerlove, 1972b, p. 73). This conclusion also holds for the Stigler–Kindahl data, which we discuss in the next section.

---

[4] See Victor Zarnowitz's excellent discussion in his Staff Paper 5, "Index Numbers and the Seasonality of Quantities and Prices," in National Bureau of Economic Research (1961, pp. 233–304, especially pp. 258–262).

3. Buyer's Prices and Seller's Prices: The National Bureau of Economic Research Series and the Stigler–Kindahl Study

In this section we report analyses of data collected by the National Bureau of Economic Research over a 10-year period and reported in Stigler and Kindahl (1970).[5] Our results show that prices collected from buyers of and sellers of industrial commodities of all types have very different structures of serial dependence as reflected in their estimated spectral densities. It is interesting to note, however, that spectral densities of the price indices constructed by Stigler and Kindahl on the basis of their data more nearly correspond to the spectral densities of comparable indices based on BLS data, and the greater the level of aggregation, the greater the degree of correspondence. This fact has been noted by other investigators who examined the series themselves directly.

In the fall of 1965, continuing through 1966 and the first half of 1967, the National Bureau of Economic Research undertook to collect a unique body of price information for the 10-year period 1957–1966. Price data were obtained from both buyers and sellers; however, the data from sellers were not used since selling prices other than list prices were almost never reported. Instead, comparisons were made between the price data collected from buyers and closely corresponding price data collected by the Bureau of Labor Statistics, which obtains its data from sellers rather than from the actual purchasers. Although the BLS does seek to obtain actual transactions prices together with discounts and allowances, it is not always successful. The data obtained by the BLS are thus reasonably representative of what would have been reported by sellers had the NBER attempted a more extensive survey of this group.

The data sources for the survey of buyers' prices for some 64 commodities, corresponding to commodities for which the BLS also collects price data, were 33 governments and governmental agencies (federal, state, and local), 137 industrial utility and transportation companies, and nine hospitals. The number of price series reported varied from a low of 601 in 1957 to a high of 1240 in 1965, falling off to 957 in 1966, the final year of the study. Price reports for a given product were combined for three or more reporters into a price index for that product; where fewer reports were available, indices are not published in the Stigler–Kindahl study. Price data were supplied by reporters from their records or, in a number of instances, the NBER was allowed direct access to the records for purposes of transcription or photocopying. The BLS bases its prices frequently on the reports of one to three respondents; the NBER series, on the other hand, are never based on fewer than three responses.

---

[5] Reference to these calculations was made in Nerlove (1972b). More recently, Bohi and Scully (1975) have reported an extensive series of similar spectral analyses of the BLS and NBER data reported in Stigler and Kindahl (1970) but with conclusions opposite to those arrived at here. Their work has been sharply criticized by Stigler (1975).

Stigler and Kindahl analyze the timing and size of price changes, overall direction of movement (trend), variation with respect to the business cycle, and price movements by type of buyer. More importantly, they compare their series with the corresponding BLS series with respect to trend and cyclical behavior, frequency of price change, and size of short-run movements. Both the NBER and BLS series are combined into 20 commodity groups, e.g., "Fuel and Related Products," "Paper, Pulp, and Allied Products," etc., and an overall Index of Industrial Prices. Our purpose in this section is to supplement the detailed and comprehensive Stigler–Kindahl analyses and comparisons with certain spectral analyses and comparisons for both individual products and the overall index of industrial prices. At one level, our comparisons must be considered vastly simplified in relation to those undertaken by Stigler and Kindahl; at a different level, they show how revealing, in some instances, consideration of second-moment serial properties as characterized by the spectral density function may be.

In all cases, we analyzed the logarithmic first differences of the prices or indices reported in Stigler and Kindahl (1970, pp. 108–192). Frequently, in the case of the BLS (sellers') prices reported, there were very few changes in price reported over the period, with long stretches of constancy in between; when differenced, such series gave rise to varied and often curious estimated spectral density functions. Indeed, one of the purposes of the material presented in this chapter is to serve as a vivid caution to the reader that no spectral estimates should ever be taken seriously unless one also has at hand the series or graph of the series itself. (See our previous comment with respect to the earlier results on fresh fruit prices.) For example, the BLS series for neoprene (SK #27)[6] changes once in January 1962, and is constant before and after that date (see Fig. 8). Thus all logarithmic first differences are zero except one. For a finite series, but one which is fairly long, the autocovariances will be nearly zero (they are inversely proportional to n^2, where n is the number of observations), but the variance is much larger (being inversely proportional to n). It follows that such a series will, from a spectral point of view, be very much like white noise with all power at the origin removed. Indeed, this is exactly the appearance of the spectral density for neoprene presented in Fig. 9. Although the NBER series of (buyers') prices for neoprene is better behaved than the BLS series, it too shows constancy for stretches up to 12 months; later in the 10-year period, however, it varies much more frequently and in an apparent pattern of negatively serially correlated differences. This pattern is confirmed by the estimated spectral density for this series presented in Fig. 9. Figure 9 shows the characteristically rising spectral density of a negatively serially correlated series with lowest power at the lowest frequencies. There is a curious peak at a frequency midway between 6 months/cycle and 4 months/cycle. As

[6] SK numbers refer to the numbers of the tables in Appendix C of Stigler and Kindahl (1970, pp. 105–192), where the series in question is presented.

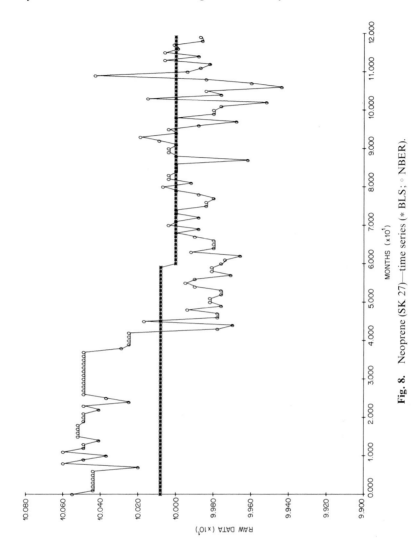

Fig. 8. Neoprene (SK 27)—time series (∗ BLS; ○ NBER).

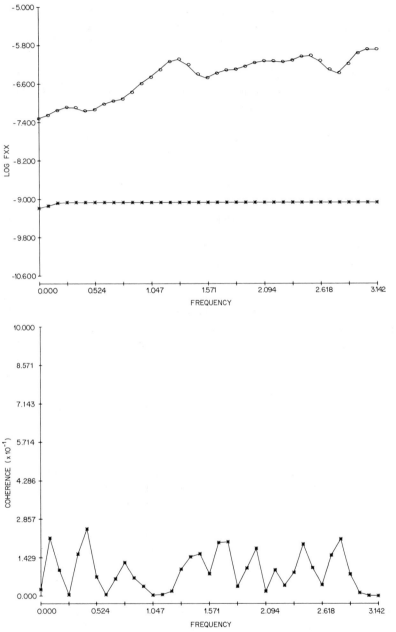

Fig. 9. Neoprene (SK 27)—spectral densities (∗ BLS; ∘ NBER) and coherence (∗ BLS and NBER series).

we shall observe below, such curiosities are often due to the location of abrupt changes within the year, even when these occur only for a few years.

A similar example, Fig. 10, is the BLS series for bulk chlorine (SK #38); this series also changes precisely once during the 10-year period in April 1960. The corresponding NBER series, however, exhibits more varied behavior than the NBER series for neoprene; indeed, it is clearly downward-trending and seasonal. These characteristics are shown clearly by the estimated spectral density of the logarithmic first-differences presented in Fig. 11: There is considerable power near the origin, but the density drops off rapidly, showing marked peaks at 12, 6, 4, and 3 months/cycle. There is a curious peak between 2.4 and 2 months/cycle.

Even for commodities in which both BLS and NBER series vary much more from month to month, the behavior of these series, particularly with respect to seasonality, can be quite different. For example, the time series for the logarithmic first differences of the BLS and NBER price series for bituminous coal (SK #23) are exhibited in Fig. 12 and the corresponding spectral densities in Fig. 13. The spectral density of the former shows sharp and clearly defined peaks at the six seasonal frequencies. On the contrary, the NBER series not only shows no seasonality whatsoever but exhibits evidence of positive serial correlation in the first differences, as shown by the considerable power of frequencies up to 6 month/cycle. Conversely, in the case of coarse paper and bags and kraft papers (SK #31; Fig. 14), the logarithmic first differences of the BLS price series show little evidence of seasonality, although there are a number of distinctive spectral peaks at intermediate frequencies, whereas the logarithmic first differences of the NBER series have a spectral density with reasonably well-defined peaks at four of the six seasonal frequencies (see Fig. 15).

On the other hand, it is clear that the appearance of strong seasonality in the spectral density of a time series may result simply from a pattern of infrequent changes, which, however, exhibit a certain timing within the year. An example of this phenomenon occurs in the BLS series for ammonia (SK #40). This series changes once or twice every year but one (see Fig. 16). The spectral density of the logarithmic first differences of the series shows very sharp and well-defined peaks at each of the seasonal frequencies (see Fig. 17). The corresponding NBER series is also quite sticky, although not nearly so sticky as the BLS series, but it changes much more irregularly within the year. The result, as may be seen in Fig. 17, is a series of rather broad peaks, three of which are more or less centered on the seasonal frequencies 6, 4, and 2.4 months/cycle.

When both the BLS and NBER series exhibit relatively infrequent and/or small changes and the timing of these changes is roughly coincident, the spectral densities of the logarithmic first differences are quite similar, as indeed they should be. This is illustrated by Figs. 18 and 19 for carbon steel bars and rods (SK #5).

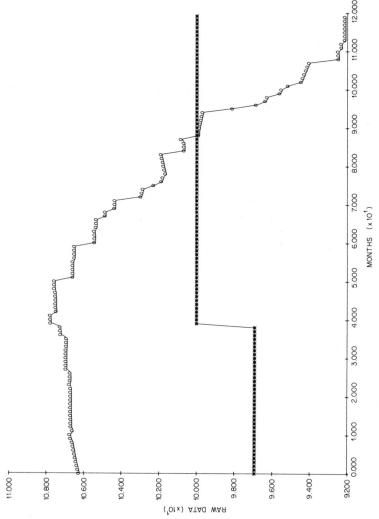

Fig. 10.   Chlorine in bulk (SK 38)—time series (∗ BLS; ○ NBER).

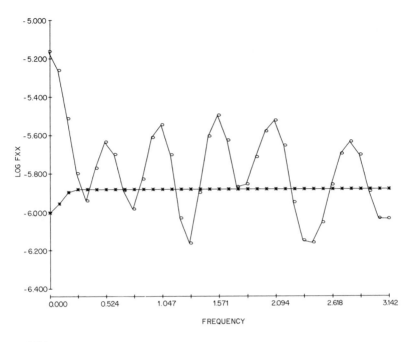

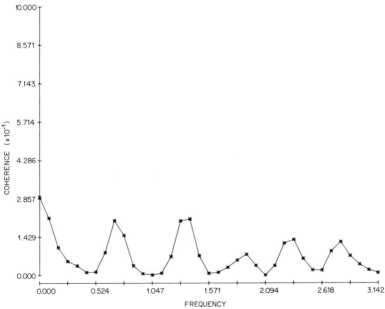

Fig. 11.   Chlorine in bulk (SK 38)—spectral densities (∗ BLS; ○ NBER) and coherence (∗ BLS and NBER series).

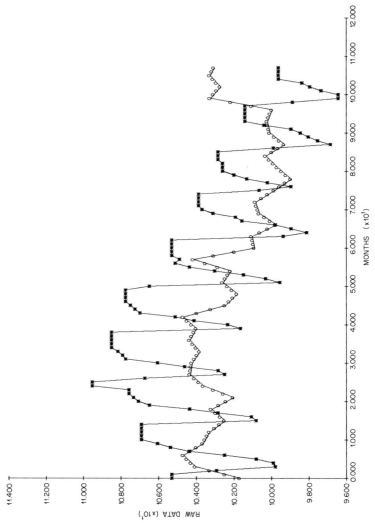

Fig. 12.   Bituminous coal (SK 23)—time series (∗ BLS; ∘ NBER).

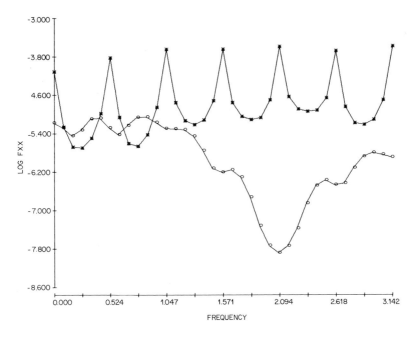

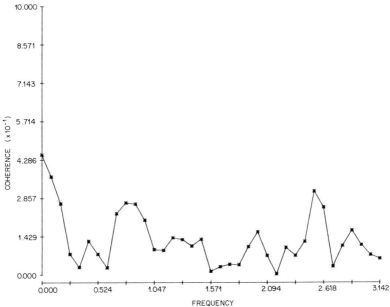

Fig. 13. Bituminous coal (SK 23)—spectral densities (∗ BLS; ◦ NBER) and coherence (∗ BLS and NBER series).

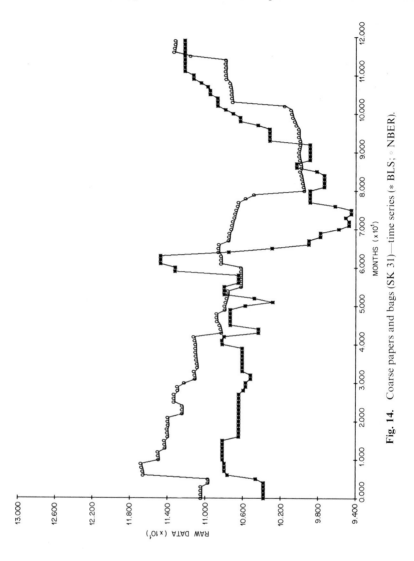

Fig. 14. Coarse papers and bags (SK 31)—time series (∗ BLS; ○ NBER).

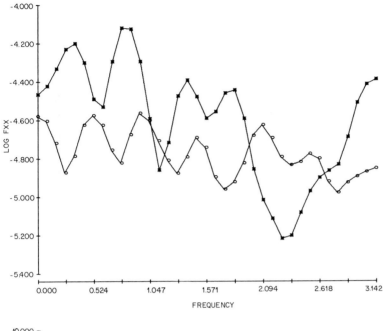

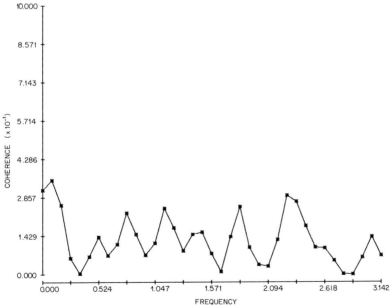

Fig. 15. Coarse papers and bags (SK 31)—spectral densities (∗ BLS; ○ NBER) and coherence (∗ BLS and NBER series).

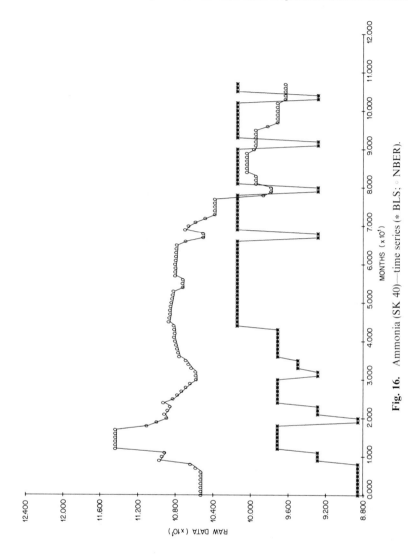

Fig. 16. Ammonia (SK 40)—time series (∗ BLS; ◦ NBER).

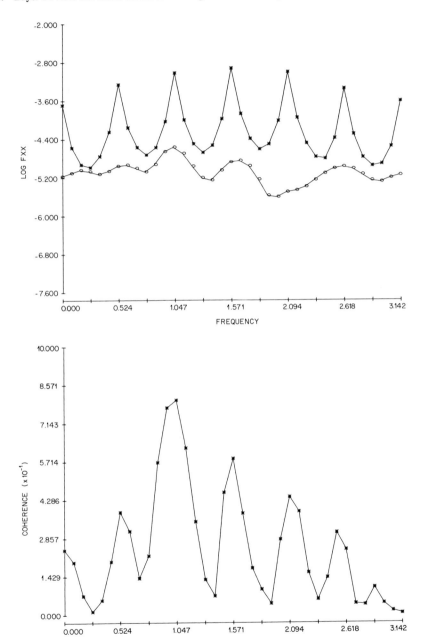

Fig. 17. Ammonia (SK 40)—spectral densities (∗ BLS; ○ NBER) and coherence (∗ BLS and NBER series).

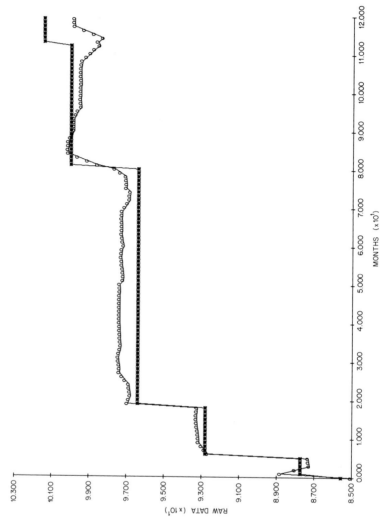

Fig. 18.   Carbon steel bars and rods (SK 5)—time series (∗ BLS; ○ NBER).

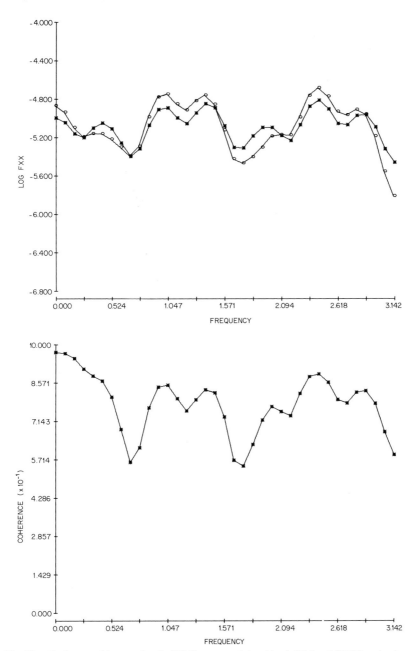

Fig. 19. Carbon steel bars and rods (SK 5)—spectral densities (* BLS; ○ NBER) and coherence (* BLS and NBER series).

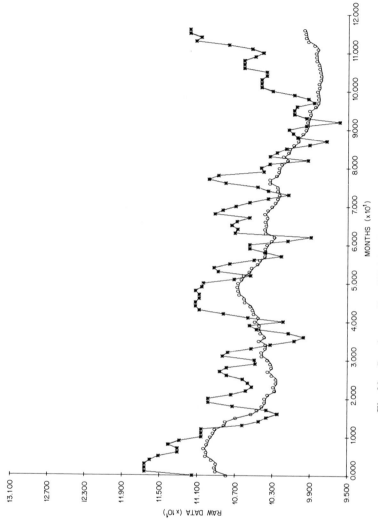

Fig. 20.   Regular gasoline (SK 20)—time series (✳ BLS; ○ NBER).

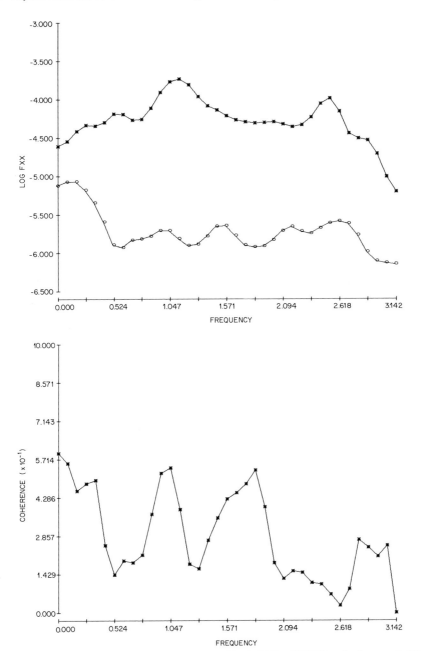

Fig. 21. Regular gasoline (SK 20)—spectral densities (∗ BLS; ○ NBER) and coherence (∗ BLS and NBER series).

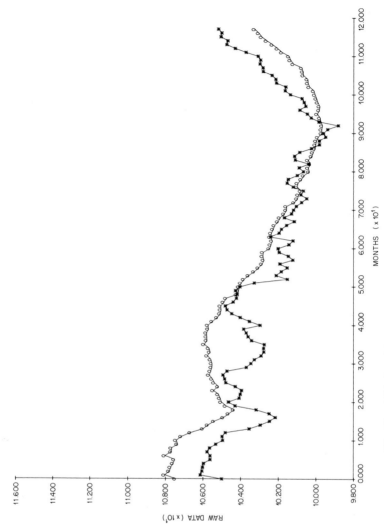

Fig. 22. All industrial commodity prices (SK 85)—time series (∗ BLS; ○ NBER).

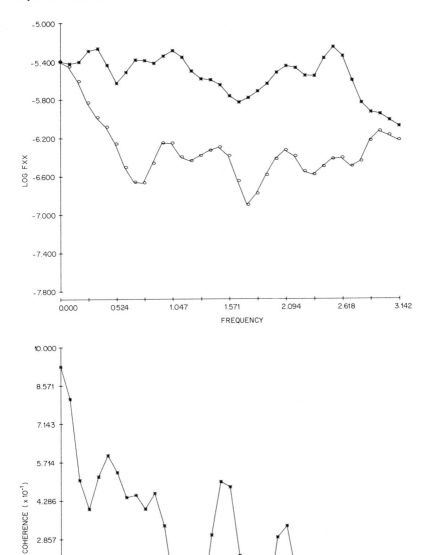

Fig. 23. All industrial commodity prices (SK 85)—spectral densities (∗ BLS; ○ NBER) and coherence (∗ BLS and NBER series).

In the case of regular gasoline (SK #20), the BLS and NBER price series both show considerable variation (see Fig. 20). The spectral densities of the two series are nonetheless quite different (see Fig. 21). The spectral density of the BLS series is relatively smooth and double-humped with broad peaks at 6 and near 2.4 months/cycle. There is a loss of power near the origin, presumably due to differencing a series that would otherwise be approximately stationary and that might conceivably account for the first peak. The NBER series has a markedly different spectral density with relatively high power near the origin, falling off relatively sharply to an irregular "plateau" at frequencies above 12 months/cycle.

Many other interesting comparisons might be made between the BLS and NBER price series having the spectral densities of their logarithmic first differences, but the above will serve to illustrate the variety of results obtainable by the method. One further comparison in closing, however, seems especially useful since it confirms what other investigators have noted: Namely, when the BLS and NBER price series are aggregated, the more highly aggregate the index, the greater the similarity of behavior. This phenomenon is illustrated for the aggregate index of all industrial commodity prices (SK #85) in Figs. 22 and 23.

4.   Conclusions

What may be concluded from our examination of the spectral densities of the BLS Consumer Price Index and several of its components in Section 2 and from our examination of selected industrial prices in Section 3?

Certainly our analysis shows how the estimated spectral density of the two series, e.g., the buyers' prices versus the sellers' (or BLS) series, may conform to and/or complement other visual evidence obtained by looking at the series themselves. For example, in Section 2 the smoother behavior of aggregates as contrasted with components is well brought out. On the other hand, the spectral results are extremely sensitive to the exact timing and spacing of price changes when few such changes occur. Spectral techniques that have proved a sensitive and suitable device for detecting and measuring the extent of seasonality for many types of series tend to break down rather badly for ill-behaved series such as are encountered in Section 3, showing all kinds of essentially spurious cyclical and seasonal behavior.

Chapter X
FORMULATION AND ESTIMATION OF MIXED MOVING-AVERAGE AUTOREGRESSIVE MODELS FOR SINGLE TIME SERIES: EXAMPLES

1. Introduction

In most analyses of economic time series, it is generally thought to be necessary to remove a polynomial trend or difference the series in order to render them stationary. Series which, when differenced, follow a mixed moving-average autoregressive model are said to follow an autoregressive *integrated* moving-average model (ARIMA model). The rationale is that ordinary differencing is representable by an autoregressive component with a root on the unit circle; when inverted, this results in an infinite moving-average representation with weights that do not die out but rather sum up (integrate) all past values with equal weight.

The purpose of this chapter is to implement the method proposed in Chapter VI for formulating ARIMA models. The emphasis is on seasonal models, but it is clear that the proposed procedure also can be used for nonseasonal models.

The proposed method is a variation of Box and Jenkins' procedure (1970). In Section 2 we summarize in an informal way the procedure for formulating ARIMA models, both with and without seasonality, as suggested by Box and Jenkins. In Section 3 we explain an alternative method when there is seasonality. In Section 4 two examples are given using data from the U.S. Department of Agriculture on slaughter prices of steers and on milk prices from January 1910 to December 1974.

After model formulation, the parameters may be estimated by methods discussed in Chapter VII, and tests performed in order to check validity of the estimated model. Two tests are suggested here in addition to those presented by Box and Jenkins (1970). One test compares serial correlation values, and the other compares spectral densities.

In addition to these tests, a prediction test is also performed for each model estimated. As we suggested in Chapter VII, the parameters in a time-series model can be estimated either in the time or in the frequency domain. In Section 5 we formulate ARIMA models for six additional time series and estimate the parameters of the corresponding models in both domains for all eight series. The parameters thus estimated are compared numerically and by their predictive ability. Note that the formulated model is the same however the estimated values are obtained. The predictive comparisons are based on standard measures such as correlation between actual and predicted values for forecasts 1, 6, 12 and 18 months ahead, the regression slope of predicted on actual values, and other measures suggested by Theil (1964).

2. The Formulation Procedure of Box and Jenkins

For the sake of completeness, we comment briefly on the procedure developed and used by Box and Jenkins in formulating ARIMA models. We discuss their formulation procedure for nonseasonal and for seasonal series, paying more attention to the latter since their discussion of the method used is not very clear (Box and Jenkins, 1970, Chapter 9). We make partial use of their notation in what follows, but keep the essentials of our own notation intact.

Nonseasonal Models

Suppose that a variable, z_t, can be represented by an ARIMA model. Assume that, for $t = 1, 2, \ldots, T$, $\{z_t\}$ is not stationary but can be transformed into a stationary series by successive differencing.[1] It is assumed that the transformed z_t contains no linearly deterministic component.

Consider the possibility of representing z_t by the following ARIMA model:

$$\varphi(U)\, \mathbf{V}^d z_t = c_0 + \theta(U)a_t, \tag{1}$$

where U is backward shift operator introduced in Chapter II; $\varphi(U)$ is a polynomial in U of order p, $\varphi(U) = \sum_{j=0}^{p} \varphi_j U^j$ and $\varphi_0 = 1$; $\mathbf{V}^d$ is a differencing operator of order d and can be expressed in terms of U as $(1 - U)^d$; d must be sufficiently large such that after d differences $\mathbf{V}^d z_t$ is a stationary series; c_0 is

---

[1] The reasons for taking differences may be justified in terms of the roots of the difference equation satisfied by the autocorrelation function. (Box and Jenkins, 1970, Chapter 3, Section 3.4.2, p. 74.) It may also be noted that repeated differencing removes a polynomial time trend of degree equal to the number of differences taken.

a constant that will be left out in future considerations; $\theta(U)$ is a polynomial in U of order q, $\theta(U) = \sum_{j=0}^{q} \theta_j U^j$, and $\theta_0 = 1$; a_t is white noise with variance σ_a^2. $\varphi(U)$ and $\theta(U)$ are assumed to satisfy conditions for stationary and invertibility. Formulation of the above model consists in finding the appropriate values for p, d, and q, making use of the autocorrelation and partial autocorrelation functions. Box and Jenkins suggest:

> Briefly, whereas the autocorrelation function of an autoregressive process of order p tails off, its partial autocorrelation function has a cut-off after lag p. Conversely, the autocorrelation function of a moving-average process of order q has a cut off after lag q, while its partial autocorrelation tails off. If both the autocorrelations and partial autocorrelations tail off, a mixed process is suggested. Furthermore, the autocorrelation function for a mixed process, containing a pth-order autoregressive component and a qth-order moving average component, is a mixture of exponentials and damped sine waves after the first $q - p$ lags. Conversely, the partial autocorrelation function for a mixed process is dominated by a mixture of exponentials and damped sine waves after the first $p - q$ lags. (Box and Jenkins, 1970, Chapter 6, Section 6.2, p. 175.)

Experience shows how difficult it is to use such an apparently easy procedure. The difficulty is due to the fact that sample autocorrelation functions in general do not follow the expected pattern, especially if a mixed process is involved. (See Hannan, 1960, pp. 34–45; Jenkins and Watts, 1968, pp. 171–188.) The method outlined in Chapter VI, Section 2, is developed in more detail in Section 3 and applied in two examples in Section 4.

Seasonal Models

Seasonal models as suggested by Box and Jenkins can be represented in a multiplicative form:

$$\varphi(U)\Phi(U^s)\nabla^d\nabla_s^D z_t = \theta(U)\Theta(U^s)a_t. \tag{2}$$

The rationale for this construction is explained in Box and Jenkins (1970, pp. 303–305) and is summarized below.

Let $z_t, t = 1, 2, \ldots, T$, be monthly observations on a seasonal variable observed for n years ($T = 12n$). We expect some relationship between successive values of z_t, i.e., month to month, as well as between values for a particular month in successive years, due to seasonality. An ARIMA model relating all Januaries, all Februaries, etc., is of a form similar to (1) except in U^s ($s = 12$) rather than in U:

$$\Phi(U^s)\nabla_s^D z_t = \Theta(U^s)b_t, \tag{3}$$

where ∇_s^D is the Dth difference for values s periods apart; thus $\nabla_s^D = (1 - U^s)^D$; s is the seasonal period; $\Phi(U^s)$ is a polynomial in U^s of order P, $\Phi(U^s) = \sum_{j=0}^{P} \Phi_j U^{js}$ and $\Phi_0 = 1$; $\Theta(U^s)$ is a polynomial in U^s of order Q, $\Theta(U^s) = \sum_{j=0}^{Q} \Theta_j U^{js}$ and $\Theta_0 = 1$; and b_t is a random variable. $\Phi(U^s)$ and $\Theta(U^s)$ are assumed to satisfy the stationarity and invertibility conditions.

It is implausible to assume that the b_t are uncorrelated; in general, we suppose that b_t itself follows an ARIMA model:

$$\varphi(U)\nabla^d b_t = \theta(U)a_t, \tag{4}$$

where $\varphi(U)$ and $\theta(U)$ are polynomials in U of order p and q, respectively, $\nabla^d = (1 - U)^d$, and a_t is a white noise input with variance σ_a^2. Substituting (4) in (3) yields

$$\varphi(U)\Phi(U^s)\nabla^d\nabla_s^D z_t = \theta(U)\Theta(U^s)a_t, \tag{5}$$

which is the general form for a multiplicative Box–Jenkins model of what they call order $(p, d, q) \times (P, D, Q)_s$.

The formulation problem is now concerned with the determination of p, d, q, P, D, and Q, given that s is known.

The way in which Box and Jenkins proceed is essentially through the auto-covariance generating function for z_t or for the transformation of z_t. We can rewrite (5) as

$$\varphi(U)\Phi(U^s)(1 - U)^d(1 - U^s)^D z_t = \theta(U)\Theta(U^s)a_t. \tag{6}$$

If stationary conditions are assumed to be satisfied by the polynomials $\varphi(\ )$ and $\Phi(\ )$, we may write

$$w_t = [\theta(U)\Theta(U^s)/\varphi(U)\Phi(U^s)]a_t, \tag{7}$$

where $w_t = (1 - U)^d(1 - U^s)^D z_t$ is the transformed series. If we call the above ratio $\psi(U)$, we have

$$w_t = \psi(U)a_t, \tag{8}$$

and the autocovariance generating function for w_t is given by

$$g_w(z) = \psi(z)\psi(z^{-1})\sigma_a^2 \tag{9}$$

(see Chapter III). It is clear that $\psi(U)$ is a complicated expression.

As indicated in Chapter VI, Box and Jenkins (1970, pp. 173–187) suggest using the sample autocorrelation and partial autocorrelation functions to deter-mine a model whose theoretical autocorrelation and partial autocorrelation functions have values that are different from zero at the same lags as the sample functions. However, as we noted in Chapter VI, the statistical properties of the sample autocorrelation, particularly at long lags, are far from optimal.[2] More-over, "over-fitting," or using a model with more lags than necessary, which may be helpful in the case of a pure autoregression, may be of positive harm in the case of mixed processes. Nor do Box and Jenkins (1970, pp. 178–179) give us any guide as to how small an autocorrelation or partial autocorrelation

---

[2] In addition to Hannan (1960, p. 41), see also Jenkins and Watts (1968, Chapter 5) for a good discussion of the poor statistical properties of sample autocorrelation functions.

ought to be, and at what length of lag, before it may properly be considered to be zero. The procedure, due to Carvalho (1971), described briefly in Chapter VI makes some attempt to resolve these difficulties by providing additional a priori constraints. We return to our elaboration of this procedure in the next section.

3. An Alternative Method for the Formulation of an ARIMA Model

By imposing somewhat stronger a priori constraints on the class of model considered, it is possible to formulate ARIMA models from the evidence of the estimated correlogram alone. We explain the method for a seasonal series, but clearly a nonseasonal model is a special case where $P = D = Q = 0$.

To avoid difficulties that arise for a mixed process, we attempt to separate the autoregressive and moving-average parts of the process by transforming the original series z_t in such a way that it can be approximated by a moving-average process alone. Thus we try to find a transformation w_t of z_t of the form

$$w_t = \varphi(U)\Phi(U^s)\mathbf{V}^d\mathbf{V}_s^D z_t, \tag{1}$$

such that w_t may be represented by a pure moving-average process

$$w_t = \theta(U)\Theta(U^s)a_t. \tag{2}$$

The details of the suggested procedure are as follows:

(1) *Compute the sample autocorrelation function for z_t.* In general, the economic time series considered will not be stationary; therefore the estimated correlogram will not damp out with increasing lag. Thus take repeated differences until the sample correlogram damps at long lags, except possibly at multiples of s (Chapter VI, p. 108). In general, a first difference is enough. For simplicity, assume that first difference does transform the series so that it may be considered stationary.

(2) *Compute the sample autocorrelation function for $(1 - U)z_t$.* If seasonality is in fact present, as assumed, the autocorrelation function will now damp, except possibly at lags that are a multiple of s and frequently also at multiples of $\frac{1}{2}s$. If seasonality is assumed to be nonstationary or perfectly regular, it may be removed by taking links of order s, i.e., the transform $(1 - U^s)$ is applied to $(1 - U)z_t$. (See Box and Jenkins, 1970, pp. 303–304.)

(3) *Compute the sample autocorrelation function for $(1 - U)(1 - U^s)z_t$.* If the transformed data follow a model with a weak or nonexistant autoregressive component, the autocorrelation function of the transformed variable at this stage gives us information about the moving-average component of the process. According to (2.2)

$$w_t = \theta(U)\Theta(U^s)a_t.$$

By observing the values of the correlogram that can be considered to be different from zero, we can determine a value for the q and Q through the identity

$$H \equiv q + sQ, \tag{3}$$

where H is the degree of the product $\psi(U) = \theta(U)\Theta(U^s)$ and thus the order of the correlation of highest order among those that can be considered to be different from zero. Provided we are willing to assume q and Q are relatively small, say at most 1 or 2, we can determine H and, therefore, a pair of values, q and Q, that satisfies (3). For example, if z_t has a seasonal period equal to 12 (as would usually be the case with series observed monthly) and the sample autocorrelation function for w_t is such that only r_1, r_{11}, r_{12}, and r_{13} are significantly different from zero, where r_j is the value of the correlation function at lag j, we have $H = 13$. There exists just one pair q and Q such that $13 = q + 12Q$, namely $q = Q = 1$; hence, w_t may be approximated by[3]

$$w_t = (1 - \theta_1 U)(1 - \Theta_1 U^{12})a_t. \tag{4}$$

The main problem after transforming z_t into w_t is to determine for which values of j the autocorrelations can be considered different from zero. One way is to use Bartlett's approximation to the standard error for each autocorrelation and use the two-standard-error rule as a test.[4] Another way is to use an arbitrary value as the cutoff point, and assume that all autocorrelations smaller than that value are zero. This arbitrary value must be such that the autocorrelations that are larger in absolute value are compatible with a simple model for w_t, i.e., a model for which q and Q may be assumed to be quite small.

It may happen that the resulting autocorrelation function for w_t has a shape from which a simple model cannot be deduced. In this case, the existence of an autoregressive component in w_t must be considered. A more detailed analysis of the correlogram may give us some clues. If w_t follows an autoregressive scheme, this fact should be reflected in the sample autocorrelation function for w_t by exponentials, damped sine waves, or a mixture of both.

(4)   *Compute the partial autocorrelation function for w_t:*   Information about the partial autocorrelation function may be used to confirm the evidence given by the correlogram: If, in fact, w_t follows an autoregressive scheme, its order will be given by the sample partial autocorrelation values of w_t that can be considered different from zero.[5] Hence, w_t will be transformed to another variable, say x_t, such that x_t can be represented by

$$x_t = \theta(U)\Theta(U^s)a_t. \tag{5}$$

---

[3] The procedure to this point is virtually identical to that suggested by Box and Jenkins for (integrated) moving-average models with no autoregressive component.

[4] For more detail concerning Bartlett's approximation to the standard error and the test procedure, see Box and Jenkins (1970, p. 177).

[5] On partial autocorrelation functions and their use in identifying AR models, see Box and Jenkins (1970, pp. 53–66). See also our discussion in Section 2 of Chapter VI.

(5) *Transform the* w_t. The values of the partial autocorrelation function of w_t considered to be different from zero are used to determine the order of the autoregressive model for w_t. Accordingly x_t is the transformation of w_t given by

$$x_t = R'_w(U)w_t. \tag{6}$$

Since w_t is z_t transformed, in turn, we have

$$x_t = (1 - U)(1 - U^s)R'_w(U)z_t, \tag{7}$$

where $R'_w(U)$ is a polynomial in U of order p with coefficients given by the autoregression. Now we compute the autocorrelation function for x_t and use the above procedure for identifying H, q, and Q.

After formulating a process that may have generated z_t, the parameters involved may be estimated using the methods discussed in Chapter VII. Once the estimated values for the parameters are obtained, various checks may be made in order to assess the plausibility of the formulation adopted. Several are suggested by Box and Jenkins (1970, especially Chapter VIII and Section IX.2.5). The correlogram of the residuals a_t provides a "quick and dirty" check: There should be no evident serial correlation since a_t is supposed to be a white noise series. Two additional checking procedures are applied in Section 4: (1) matching correlation values, and (2) comparing spectral densities.

Suppose the fitted model is:

$$x_t = (1 - U)(1 - U^{12})\Phi(U^{12})\varphi(U)z_t = \theta(U)\Theta(U^{12})a_t. \tag{8}$$

The autocovariance generating function for x_t is thus

$$g(z) = [\theta(z)\Theta(z^{12})\theta(z^{-1})\Theta(z^{-12})]\sigma_a^2. \tag{9}$$

The values for the covariances at different lags j are given by the coefficients of $(z^j + z^{-j})$ for $j = 1, 2, \ldots, H$, and the corresponding correlation values can be easily computed from (III.1.2) or (IV.3.13). Thus one obvious way to check the fitted model is to compare the values of the sample correlation with their corresponding values implied by the estimated coefficients.[6]

An alternative method for checking the model is to compute the normalized spectral density for the observed time series $\{x_t\}$ and compare it with the spectral density of a variable with variance 1 generated by the estimated model for $\{x_t\}$; i.e., compare the sample normalized spectral density with the theoretical spectral density for the estimated model.[7]

---

[6] If the estimated model is assumed to be correct, then, if $\{a_t\}$ is white noise, the autocorrelations have a known asymptotic distribution (Anderson, 1971, pp. 351–353). In a more formal treatment we would presumably make use of this distribution to decide whether the estimated autocovariances differed significantly from those predicted by the model.

[7] The relevant distribution theory for spectral estimates is discussed in Fuller (1976, pp. 287–308), Brillinger (1975, pp. 94–98), and Anderson (1971, pp. 519–546). Our graphs of spectral estimates all plot a one-standard-error deviation above and below the estimated value.

Moreover, since we are interested in constructing time-series models largely for forecasting purposes, a further desirable check may be made by using the model to forecast the time series beyond the period of fit, assuming we have saved some data at the end of the period for this purpose. All of these checking procedures are applied in the examples discussed in the next section. The forecasting performance is the only criterion in Section 5 for which we compare the performance of the estimated models in time domain versus the corresponding estimates of the same models in frequency domain.

4. The Detailed Examples

In this section, the model formulation procedure proposed above is applied to two price series: average price for slaughter steers, all grades, per 100 lb at Chicago from January 1910 to December 1964,[8] and average milk wholesale price per 100 lb from January 1910 through December 1964.[9] Data for January 1965–December 1974, are used for the predictive tests described in the next section.

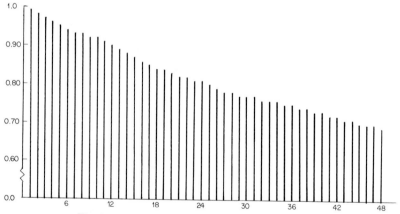

Fig. 1. Autocorrelation function for price of steers z_t.

Consider first the problem of formulating an ARIMA model for the average price of slaughter steers $\{z_t\}$, which allows for seasonality since this series may contain a seasonal component, but one not as obvious as in the case of milk prices to be considered below. If we look at the correlogram for $\{z_t\}$ in Fig. 1, we can see that the correlation values do not die out, suggesting that $\{z_t\}$ is not stationary.[10] Table 1, column 2, gives the corresponding numerical values.

[8] Source: U.S. Department of Agriculture, *Livestock and Meat Situation*, various issues.
[9] Source: U.S. Department of Agriculture, *Dairy Situation*, various issues.
[10] Though this pattern is common even for stationary series, the large values of the autocorrelations at long lags suggest the nonstationarity of the series.

TABLE 1   *Autocorrelation Function, Price of Steers, $\{z_t\}$, January 1910–December 1964 and Various Transformations*

(1) Lag	(2) z_t	(3) $(1 - U)z_t$	(4) $(1 - U)(1 - U^{12})z_t$	(1) Lag	(2) z_t	(3) $(1 - U)z_t$	(4) $(1 - U)(1 - U^{12})z_t$
1	0.99	0.35	0.29	25	0.80	−0.04	−0.08
2	0.98	0.10	0.02	26	0.79	−0.11	−0.18
3	0.97	0.00	−0.00	27	0.78	−0.13	−0.12
4	0.96	−0.16	−0.11	28	0.78	−0.09	0.00
5	0.95	−0.24	−0.13	29	0.77	−0.04	0.06
6	0.94	−0.22	−0.08	30	0.77	−0.03	0.02
7	0.93	−0.12	0.05	31	0.77	−0.01	0.07
8	0.93	0.01	0.10	32	0.76	0.02	0.05
9	0.92	0.07	0.07	33	0.76	−0.04	−0.05
10	0.92	0.17	0.11	34	0.76	0.04	0.00
11	0.91	0.20	−0.02	35	0.75	0.08	−0.00
12	0.90	0.16	−0.46	36	0.75	0.07	−0.06
13	0.89	0.02	−0.17	37	0.74	−0.04	0.04
14	0.88	0.00	0.01	38	0.74	−0.11	0.16
15	0.87	−0.06	−0.00	39	0.73	−0.13	0.10
16	0.86	−0.15	−0.02	40	0.73	−0.09	−0.02
17	0.85	−0.13	0.01	41	0.72	−0.04	−0.04
18	0.84	−0.09	0.04	42	0.72	−0.03	0.02
19	0.84	−0.08	−0.02	43	0.71	−0.01	−0.03
20	0.83	0.01	−0.00	44	0.71	0.02	−0.00
21	0.82	0.00	−0.00	45	0.70	−0.04	0.09
22	0.82	0.04	−0.07	46	0.70	0.04	0.04
23	0.81	0.08	−0.07	47	0.70	0.08	0.05
24	0.81	0.11	−0.02	48	0.69	0.07	0.09

Figure 2 plots the correlogram for $\{(1 - U)z_t\}$. Table 1, column 3, gives the corresponding numerical values. The correlation values decrease as the lag increases, but we can see that at lags that are multiples of 6, the correlation values are high, although decreasing as the multiple increases. This is an indication of seasonality.

In Fig. 3, the correlogram for $\{(1 - U)(1 - U^{12})z_t\}$ is plotted. Table 1, column 4, gives the corresponding numerical values. The autocorrelation values that stand out in Fig. 3 are those at lags 1 and 12. The values at lags 13 and 26 are relatively large, although not much larger than those at lags 4, 5, 8, and 10. This suggests two possible alternative models, one with 26 as the highest order for the autocorrelation different from zero and the other with 13. If, in fact, 13 is the highest order of autocorrelation with value different from zero, the order of the polynomial $\psi(\ )$ is 13; hence, from (3.3), $13 = q + 12Q$, which implies that $q = Q = 1$. If we were to assume 26 as the order of the polynomial $\psi(\ )$, a consistent pair of values for q and Q would be $q = Q = 2$. This model was estimated, but the value of the coefficient for U^{26} was not significantly

Fig. 2. Autocorrelation function for price of steers transformed to $\{(1 - U)z_t\}$.

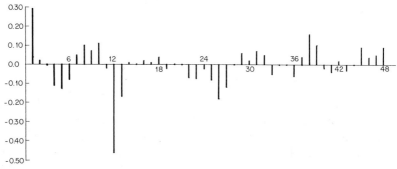

Fig. 3. Autocorrelation function for price of steers transformed to $\{(1 - U)(1 - U^{12})z_t\}$. Bartlett's standard errors (lag, S.E.): 1, 0.041; 12, 0.044; 24, 0.045; 36, 0.050.

different from zero, which suggests the simpler model with $q = Q = 1$:

$$(1 - U)(1 - U^{12})z_t = (1 - \theta_1 U)(1 - \Theta_1 U^{12})a_t. \qquad (1)$$

To make the model somewhat more general, we initially allowed the coefficient for U^{12} to be different from one, say a parameter γ_1, and estimated γ_1 together with θ_1 and Θ_1. The introduction of the additional parameter γ_1 was not helpful since its estimated value was greater than one, although not significantly different. θ_1 and Θ_1 were estimated assuming $\gamma_1 = 1$ as in (1). The values for these coefficients were not greatly different than those estimated allowing

γ_1 to differ from one. The estimated model was thus

$$(1 - U)(1 - U^{12})z_t = (1 + 0.333U)(1 - 0.958U^{12})a_t, \qquad (2)$$

$$\underset{(8.96)}{} \qquad \underset{(166.4)}{\phantom{(1-0.958U^{12})}}$$

where the numbers in parentheses are t-statistics computed from the asymptotic standard errors from the matrix of second derivatives of the logarithmic likelihood function since the Box–Jenkins procedure is an approximate maximum-likelihood method.[11] The estimate of the residual variance is $\hat{\sigma}_a = 0.565$.[12]

If we denote $(1 - U)(1 - U^{12})z_t$ as w_t, our formulation implies

$$w_t = (1 - \theta_1 U)(1 - \Theta_1 U^{12})a_t$$

or

$$w_t = (1 - \theta_1 U - \Theta_1 U^{12} + \theta_1 \Theta_1 U^{13})a_t.$$

The autocovariance generating function for $\{w_t\}$ is given by

$$g_w(z) = \{[1 + \theta_1^2 + \Theta_1^2 + (\theta_1 \Theta_1)^2] - (\theta_1 + \theta_1 \Theta_1^2)(z + z^{-1}) + \theta_1 \Theta_1(z^{11} + z^{-11})$$
$$- (\Theta_1 + \Theta_1 \theta_1^2)(z^{12} + z^{-12}) + \theta_1 \Theta_1(z^{13} + z^{-13})\}\sigma_a^2. \qquad (3)$$

The variance and autocovariances at different lags are

$$\begin{aligned}
\gamma_w(0) &= [1 + \theta_1^2 + \Theta_1^2 + (\theta_1 \Theta_1)^2]\sigma_a^2, \\
\gamma_w(1) &= -(\theta_1 + \theta_1 \Theta_1^2)\sigma_a^2, \\
\gamma_w(11) &= \theta_1 \Theta_1 \sigma_a^2, \qquad\qquad\qquad\qquad\qquad (4) \\
\gamma_w(12) &= -(\Theta_1 + \Theta_1 \theta_1^2)\sigma_a^2, \\
\gamma_w(13) &= \theta_1 \Theta_1 \sigma_a^2.
\end{aligned}$$

The estimated values of θ_1, Θ_1, and σ_a^2 determine all the above autocovariances and corresponding autocorrelations. Table 2 gives the values of the autocovariances and the variance of w_t computed from the sample and implied by the estimated parameters. Except for lag 11, the estimated autocovariances are reasonably close to their theoretical values, which suggests that our model is not a bad approximation.

A spectral comparison may also be made. Figure 4 is the theoretical spectrum for $\{w_t\}$ and Fig. 5 is the estimated spectral density for the observed w_t's. On this graph we have also plotted the points for one standard deviation above and below the estimated spectral density. The theoretical spectrum is characterized by very low values at frequencies $\pi/6$, $\pi/3$, $\pi/2$, $2\pi/3$, $5\pi/6$, and π, and these values decrease as we move from $\pi/6$ to π. The same decreasing pattern can be

[11] Box and Jenkins (1970, pp. 226–231) suggest basing this matrix on a quadratic approximation to the likelihood function.

[12] In model (2) the nonseasonal moving-average operator contains a term that virtually cancels the operator $1 - U$. This may be an indication of a fixed additional seasonal pattern that might be treated by removing seasonal means. See Prothero and Wallis (1976).

TABLE 2   *Autocovariances for w_t*

	Autocovariances	
Lag	From the sample	From the model
1	0.34	0.36
11	−0.02	−0.18
12	−0.54	−0.60
13	−0.20	−0.18
Variance	1.166	0.966

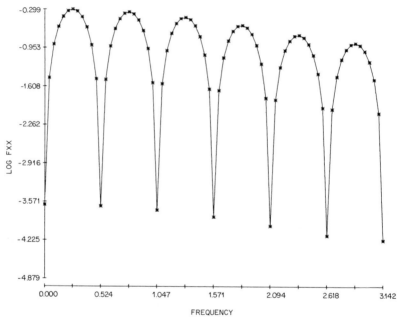

Fig. 4.   Spectral density for $(1 + 0.333U)(1 - 0.958U^{12})a_{st}$.

observed for the high values at other frequencies, i.e., they decrease as we move from low to high frequencies. The estimated spectral density exhibits the same general characteristics. Note, however, that the depth of the dips in the theoretical spectrum is greater than that for the estimated spectral density, and the peaks of the estimated density are far more irregular and fall off somewhat more rapidly. Despite these differences, it seems fair to say that the theoretical and estimated densities provide a reasonably close correspondence. This result confirms the conclusion that the fitted model used to represent slaughter steer prices is a good approximation.

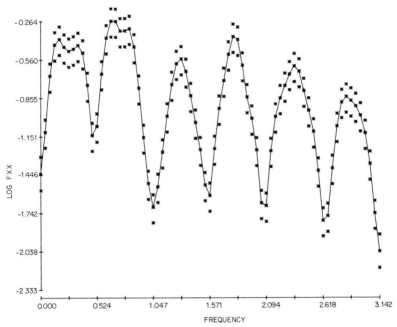

Fig. 5. Estimated spectral density for $(1 - U)(1 - U^{12})s_t$, where s_t is the price of steers January 1910–December 1964 (SK 10). (Solid line is the estimate; upper and lower points plotted are one standard deviation.)

Predictive tests for the fitted model for slaughter steer prices are given in the next section.

The same procedure was applied in our second example, using the wholesale price of milk series. In Figs. 6, 7, and 8, respectively, the autocorrelation functions

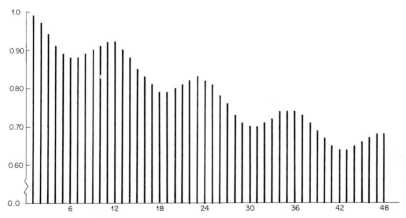

Fig. 6. Autocorrelation function for price of milk $\{z_t\}$.

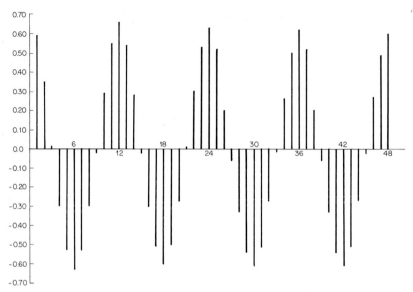

Fig. 7.   Autocorrelation function for price of milk transformed to $\{(1 - U)z_t\}$.

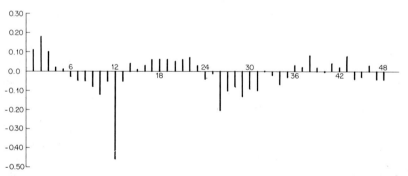

Fig. 8.   Autocorrelation function for price of milk transformed to $\{(1 - U)(1 - U^{12})z_t\}$. Bartlett's standard errors (lag, S.E.): 1, 0.037; 2, 0.038; 12, 0.038; 24, 0.041; 36, 0.049.

for z_t, i.e., the original series, $(1 - U)z_t$, and $(1 - U)(1 - U^{12})z_t$ are plotted. In Fig. 8, the values of the autocorrelation function at lags 1, 2, 3, 10, 12, 26, 27, and and 29 stand out. If we assume 27 is the highest order for the autocorrelation different from zero, we have $27 = q + 12Q$. A pair q and Q satisfying this restriction is $q = 3$ and $Q = 2$. Thus the model

$$(1 - U)(1 - U^{12})z_t = (1 - \theta_1 U - \theta_2 U^2 - \theta_3 U^3)(1 - \Theta_1 U^{12} - \Theta_2 U^{24})a_t \quad (5)$$

may be used as a first approximation to that characterizing the milk price series. The model (5) implies that the autocorrelation values at lags 1, 2, 3, 9, 10, 11, 12, 13, 14, 15, 21, 22, 23, 24, 25, 26, and 27 are different from zero.

It can be seen that the autocorrelation function for $w_t = (1 - U)(1 - U^{12})z_t$, in Fig. 8, follows approximately a sine wave pattern. This suggests that w_t may follow an autoregressive scheme. If we assume that the values for the partial autocorrelation at lags 1 and 2, i.e., $r'_w(1)$ and $r'_w(2)$, are different from zero, then w_t follows a second-order AR scheme. According to our suggested procedure, we thus transform w_t to

$$x_t = (1 - a_1 U - a_2 U^2)w_t, \tag{6}$$

where a_1 and a_2 are the autoregressive coefficients. Substituting the values for a_1 and a_2

$$x_t = (1 - 0.11U - 0.17U^2)w_t. \tag{7}$$

The sample autocorrelation function for x_t is given in Table 3 and plotted in Fig. 9. Now we use the correlogram of x_t to determine q and Q in the MA part of the model. It is clear that the correlation value at lag 12 is different from zero. The possibility that the values at lags 14 and 26 are different from zero also exists. This suggests that $26 = q + 12Q$, and a pair $q = 2$ and $Q = 2$ satisfies this relation. The correlation value at lag 1 is very small, so that we can approximate x_t by the model

$$x_t = (1 - \theta_2 U^2)(1 - \Theta_1 U^{12} - \Theta_2 U^{24})a_t \tag{8}$$

as a second alternative.

When both models (5) and (8) were estimated, a striking result emerged: Although the correlation value at lag 26 was considerably different from zero, the computed value of this correlation based on the estimated coefficients was zero. This was due to the fact that the estimated Θ_2 was very small and not significantly different from zero. Since the correlation value at lag 26 is proportional to Θ_2, it is not surprising that the implied autocorrelation is zero. Because Θ_2 was not significantly different from zero, and the estimated θ_2 was also very small, we assumed that there is only one autocorrelation value different from zero—that at lag 12—and therefore $x_t = (1 - \Theta_1 U^{12})a_t$. Note that though the autocorrelation at lag 14 is higher than most of the others, it is relatively small compared to the one at lag 12. The foregoing suggests the following model:

$$(1 - U)(1 - \gamma_1 U^{12})(1 - \varphi_1 U - \varphi_2 U^2)z_t = (1 - \Theta_1 U^{12})a_t. \tag{9}$$

Again a coefficient for U^{12} in the AR different from one was estimated initially, but, as we can see from the results below, the difference from one is not significant since the standard error of the coefficient is 0.0035:

$$(1 - U)(1 - 0.998U^{12})(1 - 0.160U - 0.194U^2)z_t = (1 - 0.879U^{12})a_t \tag{10}$$
$$\quad\;\;(281.7) \qquad\qquad (4.3) \qquad\quad (5.2) \qquad\qquad\qquad (45.9)$$

Setting $\gamma_1 = 1.0$, we obtain the following model for milk prices January 1910–December 1964:

$$(1 - U)(1 - U^{12})(1 - 0.1516U - 0.1971U^2)z_t = (1 - 0.8834U^{12})a_t,$$
$$\qquad\qquad\qquad\qquad (3.92) \qquad\quad (5.10) \qquad\qquad\qquad (48.80)$$

with $\hat{\sigma}_a^2 = 0.008227$.

TABLE 3 *Autocorrelation Function, Price of Milk, $\{z_t\}$, January 1910–December 1964 and Various Transformations*

(1) Lag	(2) z_t	(3) $(1-U)z_t$	(4) $(1-U)(1-U^{12})z_t$	(5) $(1-U)(1-U^{12})(1-0.11U-0.17U^2)z_t$
1	0.99	0.59	0.11	−0.02
2	0.97	0.35	0.17	−0.01
3	0.94	0.01	0.10	0.07
4	0.91	−0.30	0.02	−0.01
5	0.89	−0.53	0.01	0.00
6	0.88	−0.63	−0.03	−0.02
7	0.88	−0.53	−0.05	−0.03
8	0.89	−0.30	−0.05	−0.01
9	0.90	−0.02	−0.08	−0.06
10	0.91	0.29	−0.12	−0.02
11	0.92	0.55	−0.05	0.02
12	0.92	0.66	−0.46	−0.48
13	0.90	0.54	−0.05	−0.01
14	0.88	0.28	0.04	0.12
15	0.85	−0.02	0.01	0.00
16	0.83	−0.30	0.03	0.01
17	0.81	−0.51	0.06	0.04
18	0.79	−0.60	0.06	0.04
19	0.79	−0.50	0.06	0.04
20	0.80	−0.27	0.05	0.01
21	0.81	0.01	0.06	0.04
22	0.82	0.30	0.07	0.07
23	0.83	0.53	0.03	0.02
24	0.82	0.63	−0.04	−0.03
25	0.81	0.52	−0.01	0.03
26	0.78	0.20	−0.20	−0.19
27	0.76	−0.06	−0.10	−0.06
28	0.73	−0.33	−0.08	−0.01
29	0.71	−0.54	−0.13	−0.08
30	0.70	−0.61	−0.09	−0.06
31	0.70	−0.51	−0.10	−0.08
32	0.71	−0.27	0.00	0.05
33	0.72	−0.01	−0.02	0.01
34	0.74	0.26	−0.07	−0.07
35	0.74	0.50	−0.03	−0.03
36	0.74	0.62	0.03	0.03
37	0.73	0.52	0.02	0.02
38	0.71	0.20	0.08	0.08
39	0.69	−0.06	0.02	0.00
40	0.67	−0.33	0.00	−0.02
41	0.65	−0.54	0.04	0.02
42	0.64	−0.61	0.01	0.00
43	0.64	−0.51	0.08	0.10
44	0.65	−0.27	−0.04	−0.05
45	0.66	−0.02	−0.03	−0.04
46	0.67	0.27	0.03	0.04
47	0.68	0.49	−0.04	−0.02
48	0.68	0.60	−0.04	−0.04

Fig. 9. Autocorrelation function for price of milk transformed to $(1 - U)(1 - U^{12})(1 - 0.11U - 0.17U^2)z_t$.

The theoretical variance and autocovariances may be calculated from the model using the methods described in Chapter IV, Section 3. Unfortunately the order of the moving average in the model for

$$w_t = (1 - U)(1 - U^{12})z_t,$$

$m = 12$, is much larger than the order of the autoregression, $n = 2$. As indicated there this makes calculation tedious. As a quick check we may compute the implied variance and autocovariance at lag 12 (Table 4) for the series

$$(1 - U)(1 - U^{12})(1 - 0.1516U - 0.1971U^2)z_t.$$

The theoretical spectral density for the model

$$(1 - 0.1516U - 0.1971U^2)w_t = (1 - 0.8834U^{12})a_t$$

TABLE 4 *Autocovariances for* $(1 - U)(1 - U^{12}) \times$
$(1 - 0.1516U - 0.1971U^2)z_t$

	Autocovariances	
Lag	From the sample	From the model
12	-0.00685	-0.007268
Variance	0.01426	0.01465

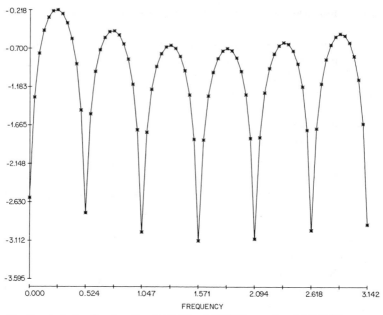

Fig. 10. Spectral density for $(1 - 0.1516U - 0.1971U^2)w_t = (1 - 0.8834U^{12})a_{mt}$, $w_t = (1 - U)(1 - U^{12})m_t$.

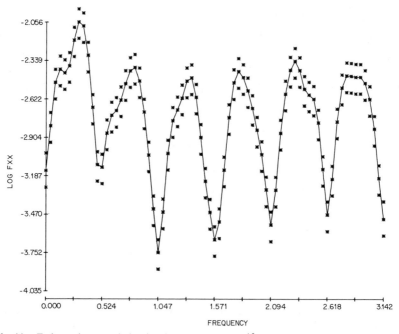

Fig. 11. Estimated spectral density for $(1 - U)(1 - U^{12})m_t$, where m_t is the price of milk January 1910–December 1964 (SK 40). (Solid line is the estimate; upper and lower points plotted are one standard deviation.)

is presented in Fig. 10. The estimated spectral density for $(1 - U)(1 - U^{12})z_t$, where z_t are milk prices January 1910–December 1964, is given in Fig. 11. The agreement is good and somewhat closer than in the case of steers.

Predictive tests are presented in the next section.

5. Comparison between Estimation Methods in the Frequency and Time Domains

Having formulated a time-series model for a series, we can estimate the parameters of the model in the time domain or in the frequency domain, as described in Chapter VII. It is clear from our discussion there that the frequency domain estimates for the parameters are much simpler to obtain. Here we formulate and estimate time-series models for an additional six series using data for various periods up to 1964. The formulation of the models follows the procedure presented above in Section 3. The parameters of each model are estimated in both the time and frequency domains. The comparison of the two estimation procedures is made by means of comparing the forecast ability of the models under the two sets of parameters obtained by the different estimation. For this forecast comparison we use the postsample period January 1965–December 1974. We thus have a total of eight series for which to make predictive comparisons. Since the estimated models tend to be very similar, no striking differences emerge. Spectral comparisons for all eight models estimated in the frequency domain are included in Appendix F.

Using the procedure described above on Section 3, we formulate and estimate the following models for the six additional series. The results for all eight series are presented in Tables 5–12. Parameters have been estimated in both the time domain and the frequency domain. The figure in parentheses beneath each estimate is its asymptotic t-ratio.[13]

TABLE 5 *Price of Steers*[a]

$$(1 - U)(1 - U^{12})s_t = (1 - \theta_1 U)(1 - \Theta U^{12})a_{st}$$

Parameters	Estimated values	
	Time domain	Frequency domain
θ_1	−0.3327	−0.3480
	(8.96)	(8.45)
Θ	0.9577	0.8363
	(166.4)	(30.56)

[a] $T = 660$.

[13] Both the t-ratio, together with the coefficient and the standard error, convey the same information, but some find the standard error more useful since it may be used as a diagnostic. Its use in this connection arises from the fact that it should be approximately the same for every coefficient in the autoregressive part; see Galbraith and Galbraith (1974). This is clearly the case for the models presented, as can be seen by dividing each t-ratio by the corresponding coefficient.

TABLE 6 *Price of Cows*[a]

$$(1 - U)(1 - U^{12})(1 - \varphi_1 U - \varphi_2 U^2 - \varphi_3 U^7)c_t$$
$$= (1 - \Theta U^{12})a_{ct}$$

	Estimated values	
Parameters	Time domain	Frequency domain
φ_1	0.1540	0.1357
	(3.35)	(2.96)
φ_2	0.1686	0.1521
	(3.71)	(3.35)
φ_3	0.1233	0.1372
	(2.72)	(3.03)
Θ	0.9222	0.8135
	(52.50)	(30.49)

[a] $T = 480$.

TABLE 7 *Price of Heifers*[a]

$$(1 - U)(1 - U^{12})(1 - \varphi_1 U - \varphi_2 U^2 - \varphi_3 U^4 - \varphi_4 U^5)h_t$$
$$= (1 - \theta_1 U^4)(1 - \Theta U^{12})a_{ht}$$

	Estimated values	
Parameters	Time domain	Frequency domain
φ_1	0.4086	0.3861
	(7.67)	(7.22)
φ_2	−0.1205	−0.1233
	(2.29)	(2.26)
φ_3	−0.1630	−0.1648
	(0.74)	(0.67)
φ_4	−0.06867	−0.06143
	(0.69)	(0.62)
θ_1	−0.05300	−0.03952
	(0.23)	(0.15)
Θ	0.9466	0.8194
	(91.30)	(24.33)

[a] $T = 360$.

REMARK.   The remaining six series were obtained from the following sources:
Average price for slaughter cows, utility grade, per 100 lb at Chicago, January 1925–December 1974. Source: U.S. Department of Agriculture, *Livestock and Meat Situation*, various issues.

Average price for slaughter heifers per 100 lb at Chicago, January 1935–December 1949 for different grades and for April 1958–1969 for all grades and for each grade separately. Source: 1935–1949, *Livestock Market News, Statistics and Related Data*, 1949, USDA, Statistical Bulletin No. 91 (August 1950). Because no information was available for all grades, the price for the choice grade was chosen because it is close in level to the all grades average;

TABLE 8   *Price of Milk[a]*

$$(1 - U)(1 - U^{12})(1 - \varphi_1 U - \varphi_2 U^2)m_t = (1 - \Theta U^{12})a_{mt}$$

	Estimated values	
Parameters	Time domain	Frequency domain
φ_1	0.1516	0.1389
	(3.92)	(3.56)
φ_2	0.1971	0.1974
	(5.10)	(5.12)
Θ	0.8834	0.8547
	(48.80)	(33.53)

[a] $T = 660$.

TABLE 9   *Cattle Slaughter[a]*

$$(1 - U)(1 - U^{12})(1 - \varphi_1 U - \varphi_2 U^2 - \varphi_3 U^9)cs_t$$
$$= (1 - \theta_1 U - \theta_2 U^2)(1 - \Theta U^{12})a_{cst}$$

	Estimated values	
Parameters	Time domain	Frequency domain
φ_1	−0.9728	−0.9227
	(14.48)	(9.88)
φ_2	−0.6314	−0.6276
	(8.20)	(6.19)
φ_3	0.2209	0.2168
	(4.64)	(4.16)
θ_1	−0.5295	−0.4189
	(5.23)	(3.55)
θ_2	−0.2705	−0.2210
	(2.47)	(2.33)
Θ	0.8615	0.6259
	(27.06)	(0.68)

[a] $T = 216$.

April 1958–1969, USDA, *Livestock and Meat Statistics*, average for all grades, various issues; 1950–March 1958, estimated accordingly to the following procedure: regress price of heifers on price of steers, PRICEH$(t) = a_0 + a_1$ PRICES(t), using the data for 1935–1949 and 1959–1969, as described above. Given estimates of a_0 and a_1, estimate the price of heifers, PRICEH, using the above relationship applied to prices of steers for 1950–March 1958 in order to complete the series.

For a quick test of the validity of this procedure, the correlogram for this series was computed for 1935–1949 and compared to the one computed for the estimated price (1950–1957). The correlograms are alike enough to remove doubts about the validity of the estimation procedure. The correlogram for the entire series PRICEH for 1935–1969 was also computed and compared to

TABLE 10   *Hog Slaughter[a]*

$$(1 - U)(1 - U^{12})(1 - \varphi_1 U - \varphi_2 U^2 - \varphi_3 U^4)hs_t$$
$$= (1 - \Theta U^{12})a_{hst}$$

	Estimated values	
Parameters	Time domain	Frequency domain
φ_1	−0.2192	−0.2340
	(5.63)	(7.93)
φ_2	−0.1706	−0.1692
	(4.40)	(4.36)
φ_3	−0.1970	−0.1907
	(5.21)	(4.97)
Θ	0.7885	0.7488
	(32.09)	(19.67)

[a] $T = 660$.

TABLE 11   *Industrial Production* (Base 1967)[a]

$$(1 - U)(1 - U^{12})(1 - \varphi_1 U - \varphi_2 U^2)i_t = (1 - \Theta U^{12})a_{it}$$

	Estimated values	
Parameters	Time domain	Frequency domain
φ_1	0.3863	0.3805
	(8.91)	(8.62)
φ_2	0.01483	0.01786
	(0.34)	(0.41)
Θ	0.6823	0.6324
	(21.10)	(19.76)

[a] $T = 552$.

the correlograms for the periods 1935–1949 and 1950–1957, and the comparison gave no cause to doubt the estimation procedure.

Cattle slaughter, federally inspected:
January 1947–December 1957, from U.S. Department of Agriculture, *Livestock and Meat Statistics* (1957);
January 1958–December 1960, from *Supplement for 1960 to Livestock and Meat Statistics*;
January 1961–December 1974, from U.S. Department of Agriculture, *Livestock and Meat Situation*, monthly issues.

Hog slaughter, federally inspected:
January 1910–December 1974, from U.S. Dept. of Agriculture, *Livestock and Meat Situation*, monthly issues.

TABLE 12 *Male Unemployment*[a]

$$(1 - U)(1 - U^{12})(1 - \varphi_1 U - \varphi_2 U^2)u_t$$
$$= (1 - \theta_1 U - \theta_2 U^3 - \theta_3 U^4)(1 - \Theta U^{12})a_{ut}$$

Parameters	Estimated values	
	Time domain	Frequency domain
φ_1	0.4636	0.4232
	(0.43)	(1.16)
φ_2	0.1405	0.1626
	(0.85)	(1.80)
θ_1	0.3353	0.3244
	(0.31)	(0.91)
θ_2	0.04031	0.02356
	(0.13)	(0.22)
θ_3	0.01534	−0.02196
	(0.16)	(0.31)
Θ	0.8978	0.7293
	(37.35)	(21.65)

[a] $T = 216$.

Male unemployment, 20 years and over:
January 1947–December 1974, from U.S. Department of Labor, Bureau of Labor statistics, *Handbook of Labor Statistics*, annual issues.

Industrial Production, 1967 = 100 base, seasonally unadjusted:
January 1919–December 1971, from private communication dated October 17, 1974, from Bernice A. Bowman, *Survey of Current Business*, Bureau of Economic Analysis, Social and Economic Statistics Administration, U.S. Department of Commerce.
January 1972–December 1974, from U.S. Department of Commerce, *Survey of Current Business*, monthly issues.

In general, the models estimated in the time and frequency domains are extremely close to one another, as they should be, given the large number of observations with which we are working. Occasionally, however, there are large discrepancies in the *t*-statistics reported. The difficulty here probably stems from the fact that these statistics are very sensitive to the local curvature of the likelihood function, which may differ substantially in the time and frequency domains. Moreover, as remarked earlier, estimation of the standard errors in the time domain relies on a quadratic approximation to the likelihood surface, and this may also prove to be a source of inaccuracy even for the sample sizes with which we deal, especially if the likelihood function is very uneven or "rough" in the space of parameters to be estimated. There are no instances of large discrepancies in the estimated parameters, although the seasonal coefficient Θ does occasionally differ by as much as 30 percent (e.g., cattle slaughter).

TABLE 13 *Comparison of Actual and Predicted Time Series for Models Estimated in the Time Domain: Summary Statistics*

Series (1)	Steps ahead forecast (2)	R^2 of regression of actual on predicted (3)	Root of mean-squared error (4)	Mean-absolute error (5)	Mean error (6)	Regression coefficient of actual on predicted (7)	Theil's inequality coefficient and decomposition of error			
							Theil's coefficient (8)	Due to bias (9)	Due to different variation (10)	Due to different covariation (11)
Price of steers	1	0.9324	1.797	1.028	0.0556	0.9475	0.0272	0.0009	0.0052	0.9939
	6	0.7548	3.508	2.513	0.5737	0.8558	0.0531	0.0267	0.0008	0.9724
	12	0.6706	4.169	3.031	1.264	0.8591	0.0632	0.0919	0.0057	0.9023
	18	0.5431	5.101	3.815	2.134	0.8860	0.0777	0.1751	0.0501	0.7749
Price of cows	1	0.9711	1.020	0.672	−0.0782	0.9653	0.0224	0.0001	0.0144	0.9856
	6	0.7496	3.181	2.105	−0.0729	0.7847	0.0688	0.0000	0.0348	0.9651
	12	0.4164	5.159	3.370	4.858	0.5634	0.1108	0.0089	0.0251	0.9660
	18	0.2809	5.490	3.840	14.300	0.5653	0.1196	0.0678	0.0041	0.9280
Price of heifers	1	0.9248	1.680	0.9965	0.0625	0.9390	0.0272	0.0014	0.0074	0.9913
	6	0.7487	3.097	2.256	0.5108	0.8846	0.0512	0.0272	0.0018	0.9710
	12	0.6582	3.710	2.724	0.9960	0.8843	0.0601	0.0721	0.0179	0.9100
	18	0.5547	4.409	3.310	1.765	0.9733	0.0718	0.1603	0.1039	0.7359
Price of milk	1	0.9926	0.1035	0.0585	0.0125	0.9961	0.0087	0.0146	0.0001	0.9853
	6	0.8513	0.4729	0.2764	0.1050	0.9157	0.0399	0.0493	0.0003	0.9503
	12	0.7375	0.6517	0.3784	0.2939	0.9901	0.0552	0.2033	0.0534	0.7433
	18	0.6822	0.7997	0.5057	0.4745	1.192	0.0680	0.3520	0.1824	0.4656

Cattle slaughter	1	0.7773	110.1	80.91	0.0718	0.9645	0.0219	0.0000	0.0329	0.9670
	6	0.5768	146.5	111.5	0.6973	0.8245	0.0290	0.0000	0.0138	0.9861
	12	0.4870	166.1	119.6	−10.30	0.7378	0.0326	0.0038	0.0051	0.9911
	18	0.4767	161.5	122.4	−35.59	0.7614	0.0314	0.0485	0.0145	0.9370
Hog slaughter	1	0.7483	422.2	335.7	−7.196	0.8594	0.0338	0.0003	0.0002	0.9996
	6	0.5764	609.7	500.9	4.699	0.6674	0.0487	0.0001	0.0334	0.9666
	12	0.3491	763.4	623.1	23.65	0.5141	0.0605	0.0009	0.0231	0.9760
	18	0.2700	909.6	726.4	35.26	0.3686	0.0713	0.0015	0.1102	0.8883
Industrial production	1	0.9881	12.40	9.855	−0.6433	0.9848	0.0057	0.0027	0.0073	0.9900
	6	0.9009	35.15	27.22	−2.880	0.9025	0.0160	0.0067	0.0242	0.9690
	12	0.7194	57.58	47.35	−4.550	0.7806	0.0260	0.0062	0.0220	0.9717
	18	0.4167	79.80	64.73	−4.354	0.6418	0.0357	0.0030	0.0000	0.9970
Male unemployment	1	0.9154	146.3	76.01	16.55	1.016	0.0471	0.0128	0.0398	0.9474
	6	0.6596	324.6	239.2	46.77	0.7563	0.1056	0.0208	0.0131	0.9662
	12	0.4312	424.4	287.1	77.11	0.6757	0.1386	0.0330	0.0011	0.9658
	18	0.2547	578.1	460.3	119.4	0.4333	0.1871	0.0427	0.0220	0.9353

TABLE 14   *Comparison of Actual and Predicted Time Series for Models Estimated in the Frequency Domain: Summary Statistics*

Series (1)	Steps ahead forecast (2)	R^2 of regression of actual on predicted (3)	Root of mean-squared error (4)	Mean-absolute error (5)	Mean error (6)	Regression coefficient of actual on predicted (7)	Theil's inequality coefficient and decomposition of error			
							Theil's coefficient (8)	Due to bias (9)	Due to different variation (10)	Due to different covariation (11)
Price of steers	1	0.9348	1.766	1.024	0.0454	0.9465	0.0268	0.0007	0.0068	0.9926
	6	0.8786	3.420	2.470	0.4723	0.8416	0.0516	0.0191	0.0074	0.9735
	12	0.6649	4.293	3.127	0.9926	0.7870	0.0647	0.0535	0.0032	0.9433
	18	0.5703	4.943	3.811	1.898	0.8344	0.0750	0.1474	0.0170	0.8356
Price of cows	1	0.9714	1.019	0.662	−0.0223	0.9618	0.0224	0.0005	0.0204	0.9791
	6	0.7467	3.287	2.094	−1.398	0.7607	0.0708	0.0018	0.0564	0.9418
	12	0.4044	5.397	3.451	1.975	0.5278	0.1150	0.0013	0.0456	0.9531
	18	0.2753	5.624	3.877	10.790	0.5195	0.1214	0.0368	0.0001	0.9631
Price of heifers	1	0.9286	1.637	0.9899	0.0604	0.9407	0.0265	0.0014	0.0079	0.9907
	6	0.7685	3.028	2.179	0.4571	0.8550	0.0489	0.0228	0.0025	0.9747
	12	0.6594	3.807	2.842	0.8757	0.8048	0.0614	0.0529	0.0002	0.9469
	18	0.5924	0.274	3.295	1.766	0.9083	0.0695	0.1706	0.0467	0.7827
Price of milk	1	0.9926	0.1035	0.0583	0.0118	0.9954	0.0087	0.0129	0.0001	0.9870
	6	0.8504	0.4739	0.2745	0.0988	0.9118	0.0399	0.0435	0.0008	0.9557
	12	0.7349	0.6487	0.3744	0.2807	0.9789	0.0549	0.1873	0.0472	0.7655
	18	0.6792	0.9707	0.4948	0.4576	1.181	0.0672	0.3349	0.1803	0.4849

Cattle slaughter	1	0.7577	115.1	84.49	−1.590	0.9462	0.0229	0.0002	0.0262	0.9736
	6	0.5109	160.2	122.6	−2.595	0.7658	0.0317	0.0003	0.0083	0.9915
	12	0.3776	187.5	137.5	−16.90	0.6533	0.0368	0.0081	0.0048	0.9871
	18	0.3447	189.3	149.6	−54.83	0.6521	0.0366	0.0839	0.0121	0.9040
Hog slaughter	1	0.7492	421.3	337.5	−7.118	0.8602	0.0338	0.0003	0.0001	0.9996
	6	0.5769	607.1	498.8	6.170	0.6709	0.0485	0.0001	0.0311	0.9688
	12	0.3441	777.5	634.6	25.50	0.5006	0.0616	0.0011	0.0296	0.9693
	18	0.2591	927.9	741.8	33.46	0.3565	0.0727	0.0013	0.1152	0.8835
Industrial production	1	0.9882	12.38	9.763	−0.6643	0.9845	0.0057	0.0029	0.0077	0.9894
	6	0.8993	35.55	27.38	−3.226	0.8994	0.0162	0.0082	0.0262	0.9656
	12	0.7114	58.73	48.14	−5.190	0.7723	0.0265	0.0078	0.0240	0.9682
	18	0.3928	82.26	67.01	−5.014	0.6180	0.0368	0.0037	0.0003	0.9960
Male unemployment	1	0.9144	147.4	74.82	18.48	1.017	0.0475	0.0157	0.0414	0.9429
	6	0.6651	327.6	246.8	54.52	0.7441	0.1067	0.0277	0.0217	0.9506
	12	0.4690	440.8	316.2	92.25	0.6164	0.1434	0.0438	0.0165	0.9397
	18	0.2791	632.6	502.3	142.4	0.3902	0.2034	0.0507	0.0847	0.8646

Tables 13 and 14 present summary statistics for the eight forecasted series in the time and frequency domains respectively.[14] Column (2) shows how far ahead the series are forecast; in column (3) the R^2 for the regression of the actual series on its predicted value is given and in column (7) the corresponding regression coefficient is presented; columns (4)–(6) give the root mean-square error, mean absolute error, and mean error, respectively; finally, columns (8)–(11) give Theil's inequality coefficient and its decomposition into components due to bias, different variation, and different covariation (Theil, 1964, pp. 24–32).

All forecasts are for the period January 1965–December 1974.

Comparing the results, we conclude that the models estimated in the time domain and frequency domain perform equally well. For some series, the frequency domain estimates perform marginally better, while for others the time domain estimates lead to marginally better forecasts. In some cases, one set of estimates performs slightly better for some period-ahead forecasts, but not for others. Although in six of the series the results are very close for the two sets of estimates, it is clear that the time domain estimates produced better forecast for two series: cattle slaughter and industrial production. The very slight differences in forecasting ability are clearly the result of the fact that the time domain and frequency domain estimates are typically very close to one another.

---

[14] It is also useful to examine the actual pattern of forecasts in relation to the series being forecast. In general, the one-step and six-step ahead forecasts are quite good, but after that the forecasts tend to deteriorate quite rapidly (except for series with an exceptionally strong seasonal component) and even, in some cases, would be negatively correlated with the observed series in the absence of common trend. There is, unfortunately, too little space to present such comparisons here. In any case, they would shed little light on the desirability of estimating models in the time domain or in the frequency domain since, once the model has been formulated, the estimated parameters are usually extremely close to one another. We present the Theil inequality coefficient and its decomposition as well. Some authors, e.g., Granger and Newbold (1977, pp. 287–289) consider this decomposition, however, to be useless if not positively misleading. We think the coefficient and its decomposition can provide some insights into the behavior of a forecast series to supplement other measures. As always, however, it is important to examine the actual data and forecasts directly. Space limitations prevent graphing the results here.

Chapter XI
FORMULATION AND ESTIMATION OF MULTIVARIATE MIXED MOVING-AVERAGE AUTOREGRESSIVE TIME-SERIES MODELS

1. Introduction

This chapter outlines a method for formulating and estimating multiple time-series models for time series that are known from other considerations to be related to one another. Indeed, such outside information about the possible connections among the various time series will generally be essential if we are to achieve identification in the traditional econometric sense.[1]

We first develop in Section 2 a single-equation approach to multiple time-series model formulation and estimation, in which the past and current values of other series are supposed to affect the behavior of the series to be forecast. In Section 3 we show how the single-equation approach may be extended to two (actually several) jointly dependent series. Our discussion parallels the suggestions of Granger (1974) and Granger and Newbold (1975; 1977, Chapter 7), although we did not see their work until much of ours was completed. The reader should also refer to several recent papers by Wallis and his co-workers (Wallis, 1977a,b; Wallis and Chan, 1976; Osborn and Wallis, 1976) for a different approach and a general discussion of the most important aspects of the multiple time-series problem.

Under certain circumstances, the general formulation may be reduced to equation-by-equation application of the single-equation approach developed

---

[1] Hannan (1971) and Hatanaka (1975) have dealt with this problem. Osborn and Wallis (1976) extend Hatanaka's analysis and consider the problem of the determination of the orders of lags appearing in each structural equation.

in Section 2.[2] Finally, in Section 4, we apply these methods to a three-equation recursive model of the prices of steers, heifers, and cows based on considerations developed in Chapter XIV and test the assumption of recursivity, which requires the residuals of each process to be uncorrelated one with the other although not necessarily serially uncorrelated. Unfortunately, although the models fit the data extremely well, their forecasting ability proves marginally inferior to simple ARIMA models.[3]

One must conclude, we believe, that, at least on the basis of our limited experience, multiple time-series modeling may not be worth the far greater effort and expense involved. Needless to say, however, one would want to examine a great many more cases before accepting such a conclusion as a general principle of time-series modeling and estimation.

2.   A Single-Equation Approach

Suppose we want to predict the series $\{y_t\}$. Let $\{x_t\}$ be a series containing useful information for the generation of the predicted values for y_t; hence, the predicted values of y_t depend not only on the past values of y_t, but also on the past values of x_t plus a disturbance component, which will generally also be serially correlated. Let us assume that this relationship can be represented as:

$$\varphi(U)y_t = \psi(U)x_t + \theta(U)a_t, \tag{1}$$

where $\varphi(U)$, $\psi(U)$, and $\theta(U)$ are polynomials in U; $\varphi(U)$ and $\psi(U)$ satisfy the stationary conditions, while $\theta(U)$ satisfies the invertibility conditions; U is a backward shift operator, such that $U^j y_t = y_{t-j}$; y_t is a stationary time series to be predicted; x_t is an auxiliary time series to be used for predicting y_t; a_t are innovations of the y_t series, after taking account of the past of $\{x_t\}$, such that

$$E(a_t) = 0, \qquad E(a_t a_{t'}) = \begin{cases} 0, & t \neq t', \\ \sigma_a^2, & t = t', \end{cases}$$

$$E(a_t x_{t'}) = 0 \qquad \text{for all } t \text{ and } t'.$$

In order to use a model such as (1), we must determine the orders of the polynomials in U and devise a way to estimate the corresponding parameters of these polynomials. We discuss first how to determine the order of each poly-

---

[2] Granger and Newbold (1977) adopt a multiple time-series representation that is such that single-equation estimation can be employed. Granger and Newbold (1977, p. 216) and Wallis and Chan (1976) note that for a general vector ARMA model that is identifiable there is only one such representation; however, certain restrictions are imposed on each univariate model by the derivation. Such restrictions are not taken into account by Granger and Newbold.

[3] Clearly, if the multiple time-series models actually fit the data worse than the single time-series models, we would suspect errors of specification. However, such models do fit better, often much better, in the period for which they are estimated; it is *outside* that period that their performance deteriorates relative to single time-series models.

nomial, then how to estimate the model and checking procedures, and finally how to use (1) to forecast future values of the series $\{y_t\}$.

We assume that the related series $\{x_t\}$ has known future values at time t or that these are forecast in some way unrelated to the series $\{y_t\}$. Thus we may consider the problem of forecasting from a single equation such as (1).

Model Formulation

The procedure we propose here for determining the order of each component (two for observed series and one for an unobserved series of "innovation") is similar to that discussed in Chapter X for the analysis of a single time series. The idea of both methods is to determine the order of one component and then use this information to determine the order of another component. The only difference is that for a multiple time-series model, even where only one equation may be considered, there are more than two components, so that the procedure must be continued. We have not been able to discover a single satisfactory systematic procedure for model formulation in the multiple time-series case, although in reality the situation is hardly significantly different for the single-series problem. Hence, our solution is offered as only one of several possible, equally plausible methods. At appropriate points in our discussion, we append suggestions for modifications or alternatives. Perhaps a crucial test of the method is found in Section 4, where we apply the technique to a model relating three time series—the prices, respectively, of steers, heifers, and cows.

Let there be two series: $\{y_t\}$, the series to be "explained," and $\{x_t\}$, the "explanatory" series. In general, of course, in a fully developed multiple time-series model the "explanatory" series will itself be explained, perhaps in part by the series $\{y_t\}$.

Step 1. The first step in the procedure is to do a single time-series analysis for each time series $\{y_t\}$ and $\{x_t\}$ in order to determine:

(a) The transformations required to make each series stationary. These will generally be of the form

$$T(U) = (1 - U)^j(1 - U^s)^k,$$

that is, with possibly repeated first differences and seasonal differences, where s is the number of times per year the series is observed.

(b) The order of the autoregressive structure for the series to be explained and, typically, since it may be necessary to restrict the number of parameters to be estimated, also what lags less than the maximal lag included should be assumed absent.

Incidentally, we shall also obtain an autoregressive structure for the "explanatory" series and a moving-average structure for both series. Let $T_1(U)$ and $T_2(U)$ be, respectively, the transformations required to render $\{y_t\}$ and $\{x_t\}$

stationary; then the result of this step is

$$T_1(U)A_1(U)y_t = B_1(U)b_{1t}, \qquad T_2(U)A_2(U)x_t = B_2(U)b_{2t}, \qquad (2)$$

where $A_1(\ )$ and $A_2(\ )$ are the autoregressive parts and $B_1(\ )$ and $B_2(\ )$ the moving-average parts, respectively. b_{1t} and b_{2t} are the innovations of the two processes.

Step 2. Having determined the necessary transformations for both series and an appropriate autoregressive structure for the "dependent" series, we may now determine the number of lagged values of the "explanatory" series in several possible ways. Practical experience suggests that it is difficult to do better than a simple ARIMA model and, therefore, that an appropriate model identification procedure ought essentially to "add" extra explanation to the single-series model rather than to change the structure of the model drastically. Hence, in determining the number of lags to be included in the "explanatory" variables, we fix the transformations in both variables and the autoregressive structure of the dependent series as determined in Step 1.[4] Thus, transform the series $\{y_t\}$ to $\{w_t\}$ by

$$w_t = T_1(U)A_1(U)y_t$$

and the series $\{x_t\}$ to $\{z_t\}$ by

$$z_t = T_2(U)x_t.$$

We discard, of course, the autoregressive structure for $\{x_t\}$ as determined in Step 1 since that is presumably of no relevance per se in the explanation of the series $\{y_t\}$. To obtain the explanatory lag structure, run a stepwise regression of w_t on z_t and its lagged values to obtain

$$w_t = C(U)z_t + \text{const} + u_t. \qquad (3)$$

In general, it is advisable to avoid very long lags or very many lagged values in the "explanatory" series, so that a fairly high cutoff F-value should be used in the stepwise procedure. Moreover, retention of the transformations $T_1(\ )$ and $T_2(\ )$ at this step will also help prevent long lags in $\{x_t\}$ from entering explicitly, although another plausible principle of model formulation is that nonstationarities in the "explanatory" variable ought, if possible, to explain nonstationarities in the dependent variable.

Step 3. In accordance with this last mentioned principle, we do now cancel whatever common factors occur in $T_1(\ )$ and $T_2(\ )$ and continue to transform $\{y_t\}$ and $\{x_t\}$ only by first or seasonal differences that are necessary to render one series stationary but not the other. Thus, for example, if

$$T_1(U) = (1 - U)^2(1 - U^s)^3 \qquad \text{and} \qquad T_2(U) = (1 - U)(1 - U^s),$$

---

[4] Of course, having fixed on a particular single time-series form, which is part of a "reduced form" of the multiple time-series model, may prevent us from finding the "correct" multiple time-series form.

we would continued to transform only the series $\{y_t\}$, and this only by the operator $(1 - U)(1 - U^s)^2$ rather than the original operator. In most cases $T_1(\ ) = T_2(\ )$, so that the result is to work with untransformed series from this step onward. Let us assume that $T_1(\ ) = T_2(\ )$ is the case, keeping in mind, however, the necessary modification should $T_1(\ ) \neq T_2(U)$.

Step 4.   We must now determine the order of the appropriate moving-average or autoregressive scheme for the unobserved part of the model (1), that is, the order of $\theta(\ )$. A number of possibilities exist at this point:

(a)   Since we already have numerical estimates of the polynomials $A_1(\ )$ and $C(\ )$, we could simply calculate the residuals

$$u_t^* = A_1(U)y_t - C(U)x_t.$$

Because, however, we have cancelled the transformation factors $T_1(\ )$ and $T_2(\ )$, equal by assumption, the residuals so calculated will not generally have mean zero. Moreover, the serial properties of the u_t^* may be quite complicated if we do not allow the parameters of $A_1(\ )$ and $C(\ )$ to vary. Hence, it is useful to obtain the residuals by means of another regression at this step.

(b)   In view of our position that one ought to keep as close as possible to the single-series ARIMA model for $\{y_t\}$, it would seem most natural to regress $A_1(U)y_t$ on those values, current and lagged, of $\{x_t\}$ given by $C(\ )$ to obtain an appropriate constant, new values of the coefficients for the lagged x's, and calculated residuals. In fact, at one point in our work on multiple time-series analysis we did exactly this but found that the calculated residuals still had a serial structure too complex to model easily. These early results are reported for comparative purposes in Section 4.

(c)   The alternative finally adopted was to regress y_t on those *lagged* values of $\{y_t\}$ given by $A_1(\ )$, clearly excluding the current value, and those values, current and lagged, of $\{x_t\}$ given by $C(\ )$ to obtain residuals

$$u_t^* = A_1^*(U)y_t - C^*(U)x_t - \text{const}^*,$$

which are then used to determine the character (MA, AR, or mixed) and order of $\theta(\ )$.

Since a new AR scheme with different parameters, albeit the same lags, is obtained at this step using alternative (c), it is wise to check whether the new scheme represents a stationary residual series, i.e., whether all of the roots of $A_1^*(z) = 0$ lie *outside* the unit circle. Such a check is particularly important in view of the fact that any stationarity-rendering transformations required in the original ARIMA models for the series $\{y_t\}$ and $\{x_t\}$ have been used to cancel one another out, to the extent possible, in Step 3. We have not encountered cases in our work in which $A_1^*(z) = 0$ had any roots inside the unit circle. Should this occur, however, the original AR determined in Step 1, $A_1(\ )$, could be imposed by choosing alternative (b) since the ARIMA model chosen in

Step 1 would not have been an acceptable one in the first place if $A_1(z) = 0$ had had a root inside the unit circle.

Step 5. The residual series $\{u_t^*\}$ may be used exactly in the manner described in Chapter X, Section 3, to determine the character and order of $\theta(\ )$ in (1) by computing autocorrelations and partial autocorrelations. It should not be necessary to make any stationarity-rendering transformations at this stage. If so, it would be a clear indication of difficulty with the model as formulated.

Another point is worthy of special mention in this connection: Whereas, in the case of a single time series, the formulation procedure described in Chapter X inevitably led us to a moving-average scheme in the innovations at this stage (otherwise the AR process could not have been correctly specified), there is no reason why it should in the multiple time-series case described here. The explanation is simply that the AR process appropriate for the original single time-series ARIMA model determined for $\{y_t\}$ in Step 1, may not be appropriate when dependence on the observed series $\{x_t\}$ is permitted.[5] We cannot say a priori, therefore, whether we expect to find a pure MA process, an AR process, or a mixed process in the unobserved part of the model $\theta(U)a_t$. If a pure MA process is found at this stage, we may proceed with estimation as described below. If, however, an AR or a mixed process is obtained, some additional further calculations are needed. Indeed, in the case of both of the multiple time-series models estimated in Section 4 below, $\theta(\ )$ was found to be of an autoregressive form.

Step 6.   If $\theta(\ )$ is of an autoregressive or mixed form, the term $\theta(U)a_t$ will be of the form $(\theta_1(U)/\theta_2(U))a_t$, where $\theta_1(\ )$ and $\theta_2(\ )$ are polynomials in U. In this situation, the model (1), in which the order and zero coefficients of the polynomial $\varphi(\ )$ correspond to those of $A_1^*(\ )$ and the order and zero coefficients of the polynomial $\psi(\ )$ correspond to those of $C^*(\ )$ should be rewritten as

$$\theta_2(U)\varphi(U)y_t - \theta_2(U)\psi(U)x_t - \text{const} = \theta_1(U)a_t \qquad (4)$$

and estimated as described below. The result must then be checked to be sure the "innovation" process $\{a_t\}$ is approximately white noise by computing the autocorrelation and partial autocorrelation functions. Indeed, since it will seldom, if ever, be possible to determine the orders of the polynomial in U for a *mixed* process in Step 5, the most likely possibility in the event this Step 6 is used will be that $\theta_1(\ ) \equiv 1$. If this is the case, the calculations proposed here will either confirm that this is so, i.e., that $\theta(\ )$ is indeed of purely AR form, or suggest the form of $\theta_1(\ )$. In the first case, of course, the process terminates, and we have obtained an estimated multiple time-series model. In the second case, if $\theta_1(\ )$ appears to be of a pure moving-average form, we may reintroduce that form in (4) and re-estimate the model. If it should turn out that another autoregression is required, it would be evidence that this step has not been fully or

---

[5] See footnote 4.

properly carried out. It could then be repeated, and one would hope that an infinite sequence of such repeats would not result. Fortunately, this circumstance has not yet occurred in our work to date.

Estimation of the parameters

Once the model (1) is specified, we may proceed in the manner outlined in Chapter VII. Thus, let us assume, without loss of generality, that in (1) the initial coefficient of $\theta(\ )$ is one; then

$$\varphi(U)y_t = \psi(U)x_t + a_t + \theta(U)a_{t-1} + \text{const.} \tag{5}$$

From (5) we may write:

$$a_t = \varphi(U)y_t - \psi(U)x_t - \theta(U)a_{t-1} - \text{const,} \tag{6}$$

$$\eta_t = \varphi(U^{-1})y_t - \psi(U^{-1})x_t - \theta(U^{-1})\eta_{t+1} - \text{const,} \tag{7}$$

where U^{-1} is the forward shift operator such that $U^{-j}y_t = y_{t+j}$. Let $y = (y_1, \ldots, y_T)'$ and $x = (x_1, \ldots, x_T)'$ be the sample values. We assume

$$\begin{aligned} E(a_t|y, x) &= 0 \quad \text{for} \quad t > T, \\ E(\eta_t|y, x) &= 0 \quad \text{for} \quad t < 1. \end{aligned} \tag{8}$$

Recalling that

$$E(a_t) = 0, \qquad E(a_t a_{t'}) = \begin{cases} 0, & t \neq t', \\ \sigma_a^2, & t = t', \end{cases}$$

by assumption, we can use (6) to write the joint probability distribution function of the a_t's and thus an approximate likelihood function for the parameters φ's, ψ's and θ's:

$$L(\varphi, \psi, \theta|y, x) = (2\pi\sigma_a^2)^{-T/2} \exp\left\{-\frac{1}{2\sigma_a^2} \sum_{t=1}^{T} a_t^2\right\}. \tag{9}$$

Substituting (6) in (9), we have an approximation to the likelihood function:

$$L(\varphi, \psi, \theta|y, x) = (2\pi\sigma_a^2)^{-T/2} \exp\{-(1/2\sigma_a^2)S(\varphi, \psi, \theta|y, x)\}. \tag{10}$$

Concentrating L with respect to σ_a^2, we see that approximations to the maximum-likelihood estimates of φ, ψ, and θ may be obtained by minimizing S with respect to these parameters:[6]

$$S(\varphi, \psi, \theta|y, x) = \left\{\sum_{t=1}^{T} [\varphi(U)y_t - \psi(U)x_t - \theta(U)a_{t-1} - \text{const}]^2\right\}. \tag{11}$$

To define S, however, we need the presample period values for y, x, and estimates of past values of a.

---

[6] Minimizing S yields only an approximation, as indicated in Chapter VII, since the past values of the a's necessary to define S are not, in fact, known but must be estimated.

Chapter VII discusses the procedure suggested by Box and Jenkins for estimating the required presample values. This procedure involves "backcasting" error values, then generating estimates of the presample period values for the time series, and then calculating estimates of the presample and sample values of the innovations.

Proceeding in a similar fashion, we may generate from (7) a series of η_t that are the "backcasted" values for the innovations. The initial values for θ's, φ's, and ψ's are used in order to get these η_t's. In so doing, we obtain a set of equations, defining η_t's, similar to the one presented in Chapter VII except that each η_t now depends, as well, on values of the auxiliary series. The next step is to generate the presample values of $\{y_t\}$. To do so, however, we need not only the η_t's, generated as explained above, but also the unknown presample values of $\{x_t\}$. There are two ways to solve this problem: One possibility is to do a time-series analysis for $\{x_t\}$, use its ARIMA model to generate the necessary presample values for $\{x_t\}$, and then proceed to get the presample values of $\{y_t\}$ in the way described in Chapter VII.[7] This would be of particular interest for short time series. The other possibility is simply to truncate the sample so that the necessary values of $\{y_t\}$ and $\{x_t\}$, say $\{y_*\}$ and $\{x_*\}$, for the generation of the a_t's are available. Then the $S(\ )$ function, conditional on these values, may be minimized. This procedure is feasible when the length of the series to be studied is relatively great compared to the number of lagged values of $\{y_*\}$ or $\{x_*\}$. In this case, to estimate the parameters we minimize

$$S(\varphi, \psi, \theta \mid y, x, y_*, x_*, a_*), \tag{12}$$

with respect to φ, ψ, and θ.[8]

Assume we generate the presample values or truncate the sample so as to have sufficient presample values y_* and x_*. We may then proceed to minimize $S(\ )$ numerically. We may use as initial values for the parameters those obtained from Steps 4 and 5 of the formulation procedure described above.[9] Exactly as in the procedure discussed in Chapter VII, we change these initial guesses and compute another value for $S(\ )$. We proceed in this fashion until $S(\ )$ is minimized. Approximations to the standard errors of parameters estimates may be obtained by computing the second-order derivatives of the likelihood function.

---

[7] In this case we would develop a set of equations similar to equations (VII.2.10)-(VII.2.16), where the presample values for y_t would be obtained, given the initial guess values for the parameters, from η_t and the presample x_t's generated by its ARIMA model.

[8] Taking y_* and x_* as given, this is equivalent to maximizing the conditional likelihood function. The importance of y_* and x_* will be nil for long series. The equivalent procedure for an ARIMA model is described in Box and Jenkins (1970, pp. 209–212).

[9] If it has been necessary to continue to Step 6, the values of the parameters obtained from the multiple time-series estimation required there and from the estimated autocorrelation or partial autocorrelation functions may be used as initial values.

Checking the model

In general, all tests used for ARIMA models described in Chapter X can be used to check models such as (1). Some of the ways to check the quality of the fitted model are:

(a)   the correlograms for the innovations a_t's;
(b)   a χ^2 test of the hypothesis that these correlations are jointly equal to zero;
(c)   the covariance generating function implied by the parameters compared with that implied by the sample; and
(d)   spectral density of the theoretical model compared with the actual spectral density.

Taking the model (1) as an example, we may compute the autocorrelation function for the estimated a_t's. We expect that all values in the correlogram should be zero if we have specified our model properly. A χ^2 test such as the one presented by Box and Jenkins (1970, pp. 290–293) may be used to test if these correlations are jointly equal to zero.

Another interesting test can be performed by comparing the autocovariance function implied by the sample

$$\text{cov}(y_t y_{t+s}) = \frac{1}{T-s} \sum_{j=1}^{T-s} (y_j - \bar{y})(y_{j+s} - \bar{y}), \qquad \text{for} \quad s = 0, 1, 2, \ldots \quad (13)$$

with the autocovariance implied by the parameters, i.e., the coefficient of $(z^s + z^{-s})$ for $s = 0, 1, 2, \ldots$ in the autocovariance generating function:

$$\hat{\gamma}_{yy}(z) = \hat{B}(z)\hat{B}(z^{-1})\sigma_y^2. \quad (14)$$

We can also test whether the covariance values are equal to those implied by the model by comparing the coefficients of $(z^s + z^{-s})$ for all s on the left side to those on the right side of

$$\hat{\varphi}(z)\hat{\varphi}(z^{-1})\hat{\gamma}_{yy}(z) = \hat{\psi}(z)\hat{\psi}(z^{-1})\hat{\gamma}_{xx}(z) + \hat{\theta}(z)\hat{\theta}(z^{-1})\sigma_a^2, \quad (15)$$

where $\hat{\gamma}_{xx}(z)$ is the estimated autocovariance generating function for the series $\{x_t\}$. Similar tests can be performed with the spectra of $\{y_t\}$, which must be a weighted sum of those for $\{x_t\}$ and $\{a_t\}$.

Forecasting

Given the estimated values of the parameters φ, ψ, and θ, the model (1) may be used to predict the future values of $\{y_t\}$. The optimal predictions are given by

$$E(y_{t+l}|y_t, y_{t-1}, \ldots, x_t, x_{t-1}, \ldots) \qquad \text{for all} \quad l \geq 1, \quad (16)$$

that is, the expected values of y_{t+l} for all l, conditional on the past history of $\{y_t\}$ and $\{x_t\}$.

If the autoregressive scheme of y_t is of order p, the corresponding one for x_t is of order g and the moving average has order q, the model (1) may be written

$$y_t - \varphi_1 y_{t-1} - \varphi_2 y_{t-2} - \cdots - \varphi_p y_{t-p}$$
$$= \psi_0 x_t - \psi_1 x_{t-1} - \cdots - \psi_g x_{t-g} + a_t - \theta_1 a_{t-1} - \cdots - \theta_q a_{t-q}. \quad (17)$$

Hence

$$y_t = \varphi_1 y_{t-1} + \varphi_2 y_{t-2} + \cdots + \varphi_p y_{t-p} + \psi_0 x_t$$
$$- \psi_1 x_{t-1} - \cdots - \psi_g x_{t-g} + a_t - \theta_1 a_{t-1} - \cdots - \theta_q a_{t-q}, \quad (18)$$

can be used to predict y_{t+l} for all l's. If a nonzero constant has been estimated in the minimization of S in (11), it will, of course, have to be added in (18). When $l = 1$, we have all the necessary information to predict y_{t+1} except x_{t+1} since

$$E(a_{t+1}|y_t, y_{t-1}, \ldots, x_t, x_{t-1}, \ldots) = 0$$

by assumption; see (8) above. Since we believe the x_t's are valuable information for predicting y_t—discounting the possibility of the x_t's being predicted by any specific form like (1)—we may consider obtaining predicted values of the x_t's by an ARIMA model. This implies that in the prediction of y_t using (18) we take

$$E(x_{t+j}|y_t, y_{t-1}, \ldots, x_t, x_{t-1}, \ldots) = E(x_{t+j}|x_t, x_{t-1}, \ldots), \qquad j \geq 1. \quad (19)$$

The situation here is similar to the one we face when we do a regression analysis and consider the explanatory variables as given, although some of them may really be endogenous, just as the dependent variable is. This difficulty is resolved in the regression analysis by considering a system of equations explaining the jointly dependent endogenous variables instead of considering just one equation. The same idea may be applied to the multivariate time-series analysis, as we show in the next section.[10]

The predicted values for the x_t's from (19) may be used to generate the predicted values for y_t's from (18). When $l > 1$, the predicted values for $\{y_t\}$ and $\{x_t\}$ prior to $t + l$ will be used in predicting y_{t+l}.

3.   A Simultaneous-Equations Approach

Although we can predict future values of $\{y_t\}$ from past values of the y's and the x's, let us assume that we can also predict the series $\{x_t\}$ using past values of the y's and the x's plus "innovations" for $\{x_t\}$. Thus we have a system

---

[10] The effect is to formulate a joint model for $\{y_t\}$ and $\{x_t\}$ that is identical to that presented by Granger (1974) and Granger and Newbold (1975). The form of the latter model is, however, dictated by considerations related to model formulation and identification, whereas our assumption is related to the question of estimation.

such as

$$\varphi(U)y_t = \alpha(U)x_t + \beta(U)a_t, \qquad \psi(U)x_t = \gamma(U)y_t + \delta(U)b_t, \qquad (1)$$

where φ, α, β, ψ, γ, and δ are polynomials in U; $\varphi(U)$, $\alpha(U)$, $\psi(U)$, and $\gamma(U)$ satisfy the stationarity conditions while $\beta(U)$ and $\delta(U)$ satisfy the invertibility conditions; U, $\{y_t\}$, $\{x_t\}$, and $\{a_t\}$ are as defined in the previous section; and $\{b_t\}$ is the innovation series for the x series such that

$$E(b_t) = 0, \qquad E(b_t b_{t'}) = \begin{cases} 0, & t \neq t', \\ \sigma_b^2, & t = t', \end{cases}$$

$$E(b_t y_{t'}) = 0, \qquad \text{for all } t \text{ and } t'.$$

The "innovations" $\{a_t\}$ and $\{b_t\}$ may be independent, but in general we should expect them to be correlated.

To obtain forecasts based on a simultaneous-equations model, we must first specify the nature of the relationships among the variables and the innovations involved. Thus it is necessary to discuss the problems of specifying the orders of the polynomials in (1).

Model Formulation

When we consider a model like (1), aside from the specification of the order of the polynomials, we must also be concerned with the identification of the parameters in the model in the usual econometric sense. The parameters are identified in this sense if the conditional expectations of y and x are uniquely determined by the parameters in the model. [See Koopmans et al. (1950), pp. 69–78 or Fisher, (1966).]

To specify the order of the polynomials in (1), we might proceed as described in Section 2 above, treating each equation separately. Having obtained a specific model for (1), we may then consider the parameter identification problem. If by any chance the polynomials in the first equation of (1) are specified to be of a certain degree and in formulating the second equation we obtain the same specification as that obtained for the first equation—that is, if the degrees of the polynomials $\varphi(\ )$ and $\gamma(\ )$, $\alpha(\ )$ and $\psi(\ )$, $\beta(\ )$ and $\delta(\ )$ are pairwise equal—we do not have a system of equations but just one equation.[11] In this case single-equation methods must be used and the same equation is used to predict either y_t or x_t.

When the orders of the relevant polynomials are different, we have two distinct equations, and the parameter identification problem must be considered. If the parameters are exactly identified or over-identified, the conditional

---

[11] Of course, this assumes the coefficients are completely unspecified. It is possible to have perfectly good multiple time-series models in which the polynomials are pairwise of equal degree, but it is not possible to estimate such a model unless it is known a priori that a sufficient number of coefficients, for the right lags, are, for example, equal to zero.

expectations for $\{y_t\}$ and $\{x_t\}$ are uniquely determined and predictions can be obtained. If the model is under-identified, some a priori information must be used to impose identifying constraints on the parameters of model (1).

Estimation of the Parameters and Forecasting

Let us begin with a very simple model

$$\varphi(U)y_t + \alpha(U)x_t = a_t, \qquad \gamma(U)y_t + \psi(U)x_t = b_t, \tag{2}$$

where all symbols are as defined before, $Ea_t = 0 = Eb_t$ for all t, and

$$E(a_t b_{t'}) = \begin{cases} 0, & t \neq t', \\ \sigma_{ab}^2, & t = t'. \end{cases}$$

Define $\epsilon = \begin{bmatrix} a \\ b \end{bmatrix}$, where $a' = (a_1, a_2, \ldots, a_T)$ and $b' = (b_1, b_2, \ldots, b_T)$. If the a's and b's are normally distributed, we can write their joint p.d.f.

$$f(a, b) \propto |\Omega|^{-1/2} \exp\{-\tfrac{1}{2}\epsilon'\Omega^{-1}\epsilon\}, \tag{3}$$

where Ω is the variance–covariance matrix

$$\Omega = \left[\begin{array}{cccc|cccc} \sigma_a^2 & 0 & \cdots & 0 & \sigma_{ab}^2 & 0 & \cdots & 0 \\ 0 & \sigma_a^2 & \cdots & 0 & 0 & \sigma_{ab}^2 & \cdots & 0 \\ \vdots & \vdots & & \vdots & \vdots & \vdots & & \vdots \\ 0 & 0 & \cdots & \sigma_a^2 & 0 & 0 & \cdots & \sigma_{ab}^2 \\ \hline \sigma_{ab}^2 & 0 & \cdots & 0 & \sigma_b^2 & 0 & \cdots & 0 \\ 0 & \sigma_{ab}^2 & \cdots & 0 & 0 & \sigma_b^2 & \cdots & 0 \\ \vdots & \vdots & & \vdots & \vdots & \vdots & & \vdots \\ 0 & 0 & \cdots & \sigma_{ab}^2 & 0 & 0 & \cdots & \sigma_b^2 \end{array}\right].$$

From (3) we can write an approximate likelihood function

$$L(\varphi, \alpha, \gamma, \psi, \sigma_a^2, \sigma_b^2, \sigma_{ab}^2 | y, x) \propto |\Omega|^{-1/2} \exp\{-\tfrac{1}{2}\epsilon'\Omega^{-1}\epsilon\}. \tag{4}$$

Substituting ϵ and Ω^{-1} in (4), we obtain the likelihood function corresponding to that in (VII.7.8), where

$$\epsilon'\Omega^{-1}\epsilon = S(\varphi, \alpha, \gamma, \psi, \sigma_a^2, \sigma_b^2, \sigma_{ab}^2 | y, x)$$

$$= \frac{1}{\sigma_a^2\sigma_b^2 - \sigma_{ab}^4} \sum_{t=1}^{T} \{\sigma_b^2[\varphi(U)y_t + \alpha(U)x_t]^2$$

$$- 2\sigma_{ab}^2[\varphi(U)y_t + \alpha(U)x_t][\gamma(U)y_t + \psi(U)x_t]$$

$$+ \sigma_a^2[\gamma(U)y_t + \psi(U)x_t]^2\}.$$

An approximation to the maximum-likelihood estimates of the parameters $\varphi, \alpha, \gamma, \psi$, given σ_a^2, σ_b^2, and σ_{ab}^2, may thus be obtained by minimizing this function, using estimated values of the presample values of the innovation processes $\{a_t\}$ and $\{b_t\}$.[12]

To minimize S, we follow the standard procedures: Given the initial values for the parameters, we compute $S(\cdots|y,x,y_*x_*)$; we change the values of the parameters iteratively and compute until this function is minimized, the corresponding values for $S(\cdots|y,x,y_*,x_*)$. Note that if there are no moving-average schemes in the model, it is not necessary to generate presample values for a's or b's. On the other hand, the presample values for x_t and y_t are required; these may be obtained by truncating the sample or as described in Chapter VII. Note that if $\sigma_{ab}^2 = 0$, minimization of S reduces to minimization of

$$S(\cdots|y,x) = \sum_{t=1}^{T} \frac{1}{\sigma_a^2} [\varphi(U)y_t + \alpha(U)x_t]^2 + \sum_{t=1}^{T} \frac{1}{\sigma_b^2} [\gamma(U)y_t + \psi(U)x_t]^2, \quad (5)$$

and it is clear that each equation may be estimated separately since $S(\cdots|y,x)$ is a sum of two functions, one depending only on σ_a^2, the φ's, and the α's and the other on σ_b^2, the γ's, and the ψ's. This result is general, irrespective of the MA scheme followed by $\{a_t\}$ or $\{b_t\}$. (Indeed, in our empirical work reported below, we have assumed the correlation between a_t and $b_{t'}$ to be zero for any t and t', then tested this assumption by calculating the cross correlations of the estimated values of the "innovations."[13])

In Chapter VI, Section 4, we analyzed the following model

$$\varphi_1(U)y_t + \psi_1(U)x_t = \epsilon_{1t}, \qquad \varphi_2(U)y_t + \psi_2(U)x_t = \epsilon_{2t}, \qquad (6)$$

where, for example,

$$\epsilon_{1t} = (1 - \theta_1 U)a_t \qquad \text{and} \qquad \epsilon_{2t} = (1 - \theta_2 U)b_t.$$

The processes $\{a_t\}$ and $\{b_t\}$ have the same properties as in the model previously discussed. The variance–covariance matrix of the ϵ's and its inverse are derived in Appendix E.

Let $\epsilon = (\epsilon_{11}, \ldots, \epsilon_{1T}, \epsilon_{21}, \ldots, \epsilon_{2T})'$ and let $\Omega = E\epsilon\epsilon$. Then the likelihood function to be minimized is a function of the parameters entering the polynomials $\varphi_1, \varphi_2, \psi_1, \psi_2$, and the parameters θ_1 and θ_2.

To obtain approximations to the maximum-likelihood estimator for the parameters, we may proceed in much the same way as described above. y_* and a_*, as well as x_* and b_*, may be generated in the same fashion. Alternatively, the first equation of (6) may be used to generate an initial set of past values of y, y_*^1; then these values are used to generate an initial x_*^1; the x_*^1 are used to

---

[12] This neglects the Jacobian of the transformation defined by (2). See the remark in Chapter VII below equation (VII.7.8).

[13] As K. F. Wallis points out (private correspondence, 1977), this is not a correct procedure since the estimated innovations are from estimates of the model assuming $\sigma_{ab} = 0$. Under certain circumstances, e.g., $\gamma(\ ) \equiv 0$ and degree $\alpha(\ ) =$ degree $\psi(\ )$, the estimated covariance for the equation estimated separately must be zero.

generate a second-round estimate y_*^2, and these to obtain x_*^2. This process may be repeated until the values for y_* and x_* do not change very much. Then a_* and b_* may be conveniently obtained as before.

We should note that backcasted values for $\{a_t\}$ and $\{b_t\}$ may be obtained in the same manner described in Chapter VII as well.

If in model (6) the parameters are exactly identified, we can specify the model in its reduced form, and for the reduced-form parameters there will be just one set of structural parameters. Let the reduced form be

$$y_t = M_1(U)a_t + M_2(U)b_t, \qquad x_t = N_1(U)a_t + N_2(U)b_t, \qquad (7)$$

where $M_1(U)$, $M_2(U)$, $N_1(U)$, and $N_2(U)$ are polynomials in U compatible with (6). Thus the reduced form of any model such as (6) will be a set of unobserved-components models such as those described in Chapter IV except that the $\{a_t\}$ and the $\{b_t\}$ are not assumed to be independent. If in fact $\{a_t\}$ and $\{b_t\}$ are uncorrelated for all lagged values, i.e., $E(a_tb_{t'}) = 0$ for all t and t', and the model is just identified, we can estimate the model in its reduced form as proposed in Chapter VII and then, from these reduced-form parameters, obtain just one set of structural parameters. For any model such as (6), we may initially consider $\{a_t\}$ and $\{b_t\}$ to be independent; once the model has been estimated, this hypothesis may be tested by computing the covariances between the estimated a_t's and b_t's obtained from the fitted model.

When the parameters of a system have been estimated, the accuracy of the models used for each equation should be checked. If the innovations of each equation are independent of each other, we can use the procedures indicated above in Section 2 and check each equation separately. If the innovations are correlated with each other, we may use the reduced form to check the accuracy of our models when the parameters of the system are identified. We should in this case apply the same tests we use in the single-equation approach to each of the reduced-form equations.

In order to obtain the forecast values for each variable, it is necessary to use the reduced form. Thus for the model (6) we use (7) to forecast future values of $\{y_t\}$ and $\{x_t\}$. If the parameters of the model are not identified, but we can obtain estimates for the reduced-form parameters by the methods developed in Chapters IV and VII for unobserved-components models, then predicted values can be obtained using the reduced-form equations.

4.   Estimation of Multiple Time-Series Models for Interrelated Agricultural Prices

In this section we test the multiple time-series approach suggested in this chapter by comparing its predictive power to that of a single time-series ARIMA model. The series to which these methods are applied are three of those considered in the previous chapter: the price of steers, the price of heifers, and the price of cows. The simple ARIMA models corresponding to those presented in Section 5 of Chapter X are as follows:[14]

Price of steers (s_t), from Chapter X, Table 5:

$$(1 - U)(1 - U^{12})s_t = (1 + 0.333U)(1 - 0.958U^{12})a_{st}, \qquad 1910-1964. \quad (1)$$
$$\phantom{(1 - U)(1 - U^{12})s_t = (1 + } (8.96) (166.4)$$

Price of heifers (h_t), from Chapter X, Table 7:

$$(1 - U)(1 - U^{12})(1 - 0.409U + 0.120U^2 + 0.163U^4 + 0.069U^5)h_t$$
$$\phantom{(1 - U)(1 - U^{12})(1 - } (7.67) (2.29) (0.74) (0.69)$$

$$= (1 + 0.053U^4)(1 - 0.947U^{12})a_{ht}, \qquad 1935-1964. \quad (2)$$
$$ (0.23) (91.3)$$

Price of cows (c_t), from Chapter X, Table 6:

$$(1 - U)(1 - U^{12})(1 - 0.154U - 0.169U^2 - 0.123U^7)c_t$$
$$\phantom{(1 - U)(1 - U^{12})(1 - } (3.35) (3.71) (2.72)$$

$$= (1 - 0.922U^{12})a_{ct}, \qquad 1925-1964. \quad (3)$$
$$ (52.5)$$

We argue in Chapter XIV that the predictions of the price of heifers may be improved by using information on prices of steers. We also argue that, although the price of steers may be used to predict prices of heifers, there is no reason to consider the price of heifers when predicting the price of steers. However, the price of steers may be useful information in predicting the price of heifers since heifers may produce calves that will be heifers or steers in the future, and thus heifers will be sold in the market if the actual price of steers is high compared to the expected future prices. For the same reason, the prices of steers and heifers may be used to improve the prediction of the price of cows. On the other hand, the future prices of cows and heifers should have no predictive power for those of steers since the latter will be fully taken into account in the former.

Thus we consider the following model for predicting prices of steers, heifers, and cows, respectively:

$$
\begin{aligned}
\gamma(U)s_t &= v(U)a_t, \\
-\delta(U)s_t + \varphi(U)h_t &= \theta(U)b_t, \\
-\alpha(U)s_t - \beta(U)h_t + \psi(U)c_t &= \eta(U)d_t.
\end{aligned} \quad (4)
$$

This is a triangular model, so that each equation may be treated separately, provided we assume that

$$E(a_t b_{t'}) = 0, \qquad E(a_t d_{t'}) = 0, \qquad E(b_t d_{t'}) = 0, \qquad (5)$$

for all t and t'.[15] Under the assumption, the first equation in (4) is tantamount to

---

[14] The figures in parentheses beneath the estimates are asymptotic t-ratios.

[15] These assumptions are usually made for vector moving-average processes for $t \neq t'$. To assume, in addition, that they hold for $t = t'$ is one way of normalizing the system, and a representation such as presented in (4) always exists.

a single time-series analysis and (1) gives us the appropriate ARIMA model. It remains to formulate the models for the second and the third equations of (4) in order to estimate the corresponding parameters.

Let us follow the procedure outlined in Section 2 for the two equations of (4) related to the prices of heifers and cows, respectively, since by assumption each may be treated separately. To keep the line of argument clear, we formulate and estimate a multiple time-series model, first for heifers, then for cows. Next we examine the assumption (5), which enables us to treat the equations separately, and finally compare forecasts of the prices for heifers and cows generated by the multiple time-series models with those for simple ARIMA models. We may do this because the hypothesis (5) cannot be rejected on the basis of our results, thus implying (a) that each equation may indeed be treated separately and (b) that the appropriate model for the price of steers is indeed the simple ARIMA model estimated in Chapter X.

Model Formulation and Estimation: Heifers

Step 1. The ARIMA models for the prices of heifers and steers are given above, equations (2) and (1), respectively. Note that

$$T_1(U) = T_2(U) = (1 - U)(1 - U^{12}).$$

Step 2. From (2),

$$w_t = (1 - U)(1 - U^{12})(1 - 0.409U + 0.120U^2 + 0.163U^4 + 0.069U^5)h_t. \quad (6)$$

From (1),

$$z_t = (1 - U)(1 - U^{12})s_t. \quad (7)$$

The results for a stepwise regression in which the F-value to enter a variable is 4.1 and the F-value to delete a variable is 4.0 are presented in Table 1 for a maximal lag permitted of 25. After z_{t-19} had been entered, no further lagged values of z could be found to increase the R^2 of the regression significantly.

TABLE 1   *The First Eight Lagged Values of Transformed Steers' Price z_t, Appearing in a Stepwise Regression of w_t on z_t and Lags Thereof in the Order in Which They Appear, and Corresponding R^2 Values*

Lag	0	4	1	17	22	21	24	19
R^2	0.65	0.69	0.73	0.74	0.74	0.75	0.76	0.76

REMARK.   For comparative purposes, we reproduce here the corresponding results when a full 50 lags of z_t are considered in the stepwise procedure (Table 1′). After inclusion of 11 lagged values, no further lagged values of z could be found to increase the R^2 of the regression significantly. Not only are many more lagged values included by allowing consideration of a full 50 lags, (the maximum R^2 is increased from 0.76 to 0.83), but it is disconcerting to note that some very long lags, 40 and 39, enter almost at once, producing quite significant increases in the R^2. Not only do such long lags

TABLE 1'   *The First Lagged Values of Transformed Steers' Price z_t, Appearing in a Stepwise Regression of w_t on z_t and Lags Thereof in the Order in Which They Appear, and Corresponding R^2 Values*

Lag	0	4	1	40	39	17	41	19	2	24	23
R^2	0.65	0.69	0.73	0.75	0.79	0.80	0.81	0.82	0.82	0.83	0.83

appear implausible, but previous experience with multiple time-series models suggests that their inclusion is bound to cause difficulty in forecasting: Multiple time-series models containing a second series with long lags invariably forecast much worse than simple ARIMA models. For this reason, we have restricted the stepwise regression of Step 2 to a maximum of 25 lags. At a later point, however, we find an autoregression for the unobserved part of the model that is probably partially the result of the significant effect of rather longer lags than were included in the initial model specification—at least for the particular sample period.

It is also worth noting some special characteristics of the stepwise regression at this point for future reference: The partial correlations and F-values of the variables that entered the final stepwise regression at each step are given in Table 2. It is clear that in the initial stages z_{t-19} is a good deal more significant in terms of its F-value than z_{t-21}, z_{t-22}, or z_{t-24}. Yet, at the point at which z_{t-22} enters, it is essentially a toss-up between the two variables, the difference in F-values being only 0.06. If z_{t-19} had been forced to enter after z_{t-17}, it is doubtful that it would have made any great difference to the subsequent analysis. Indeed, below we do estimate a model that includes lags only up to 19 in the price of steers and one that includes lags of 21, 22, and 24. The addition of the

TABLE 2   *Partial Correlations and F-values of Variables Entering Final Regression between w_t and Lagged z_t at Each Stage*

Variable just entered	Variables eventually entered						
	z_{t-4}	z_{t-1}	z_{t-17}	z_{t-22}	z_{t-21}	z_{t-24}	z_{t-19}
z_t	0.34	−0.31	0.15	0.086	−0.086	−0.087	−0.12
	41.74	32.91	7.71	2.40	2.36	2.43	4.97
z_{t-4}	—	−0.35	0.22	0.080	−0.095	−0.092	−0.13
		43.02	15.63	2.02	2.89	2.71	5.85
z_{t-1}	—	—	0.21	0.11	−0.11	−0.12	−0.12
			15.06	3.78	3.55	4.78	4.60
z_{t-17}	—	—	—	0.14	−0.094	−0.13	−0.14
				6.53	2.80	5.85	6.47
z_{t-22}	—	—	—	—	−0.15	−0.15	−0.15
					7.19	7.05	7.13
z_{t-21}	—	—	—	—	—	−0.15	−0.14
						6.94	6.15
z_{t-24}	—	—	—	—	—	—	−0.16
							8.74

latter three lagged values turns out to reduce the final sum of squares by a negligible amount.

Step 3. Since the ARIMA models for both heifers and steers include the stationarity-rendering transformation $(1 - U)(1 - U^{12})$, this common factor may be cancelled to allow this form of nonstationarity in the steers' price to "explain" the corresponding nonstationarity in the heifers' price.

Step 4. In order to determine the order of the appropriate moving-average, autoregressive, or mixed scheme for the unobserved part of the model, we require residuals from an ordinary least-squares regression of the current heifers' price on the lagged values of heifers' prices and the current and lagged values of steers' prices, where the appropriate lags are given by the analysis of the preceding steps. The result is

$$h_t = 0.1647 + 0.9105h_{t-1} - 0.1248h_{t-2} + 0.1085h_{t-4} - 0.0028h_{t-5}$$
$$\ (1.96)\qquad\ (20.23)\qquad\qquad\ (3.85)\qquad\qquad\ (2.37)\qquad\qquad\ (0.11)$$

$$+ 0.8440s_t - 0.6332s_{t-1} - 0.1044s_{t-4} + 0.0709s_{t-17} - 0.0981s_{t-19} \qquad (8)$$
$$\ (33.50)\qquad\ (13.09)\qquad\qquad\ (2.78)\qquad\qquad\ (4.19)\qquad\qquad\ (4.01)$$

$$- 0.0001s_{t-21} + 0.0335s_{t-22} - 0.0135s_{t-24} + u_t^*, \qquad R^2 = 0.9964.$$
$$\ (0.00)\qquad\qquad\ (0.99)\qquad\qquad\ (0.83)$$

We see that the very high-order lags of s, 21, 22, and 24, are insignificant in the stepwise regression; h_{t-5} is also, although it is by no means such a high-order lag.[16,17]

The roots of the autoregressive structure in h_t estimated in (8) are as follows:

Root	Modulus	Root	Modulus
1.096	1.096	−2.4167	2.417
$0.6724 \pm 1.7403i$	1.866	39.4547	39.455

All are well outside the unit circle.

Step 5. Autocorrelation and partial autocorrelation functions for u_t^* obtained in Step 4 may be used to determine the nature of $\theta(U)b_t$ in (4). These functions are given in Table 3 and Figs. 1 and 2 for various lags. It may be seen that large values of the autocorrelations (relative to their standard errors) occur for lags of 12, 23, 37, and 38. Indeed, the value at lag 38, -0.23, is larger than

---

[16] The figures in parentheses beneath the coefficients are their *t*-ratios.

[17] The result obtained, constraining the autoregressive structure in h_t to be what was obtained in the previous ARIMA model, is

$$w_t = 1.4073 + 0.8638s_t - 0.1924s_{t-1} + 0.2435s_{t-4} + 0.1096s_{t-17} - 0.0879s_{t-19}$$
$$\ (9.83)\qquad\ (18.76)\qquad\quad\ (3.52)\qquad\qquad\ (9.92)\qquad\qquad\ (3.35)\qquad\qquad\ (1.86)$$

$$- 0.0145s_{t-21} + 0.0503s_{t-22} - 0.1024s_{t-24} + u_t^{*\prime}, \qquad R^2 = 0.984. \qquad (8')$$
$$\ (0.22)\qquad\qquad\ (0.77)\qquad\qquad\ (3.38)$$

TABLE 3 *Autocorrelations and Partial Autocorrelations of Residuals from the OLS Regression for Heifers' Price in Step 4, Equation (8)[a]*

Lag	Autocorrelation	Partial autocorrelation	Lag	Autocorrelation
1	−0.06	−0.06	25	−0.01
2	0.02	0.02	26	−0.04
3	0.02	0.03	27	−0.08
4	−0.11	−0.11	28	−0.02
5	−0.06	−0.08	29	0.02
6	0.08	0.08	30	0.03
7	0.01	0.03	31	0.01
8	−0.01	−0.02	32	−0.06
9	0.01	−0.01	33	0.01
10	−0.07	−0.06	34	0.05
11	0.04	0.05	35	0.05
12	0.17	0.17	36	0.10
13	0.07		37	0.18
14	0.11		38	−0.23
15	−0.02		39	−0.05
16	−0.06		40	−0.08
17	−0.08		41	−0.05
18	−0.01		42	0.00
19	−0.05		43	0.06
20	−0.02		44	−0.01
21	0.07		45	0.01
22	0.02		46	−0.02
23	0.21		47	−0.01
24	0.08		48	0.05

[a] Standard errors (lags, S.E.): 1–12, 0.05; 13–48, 0.06.

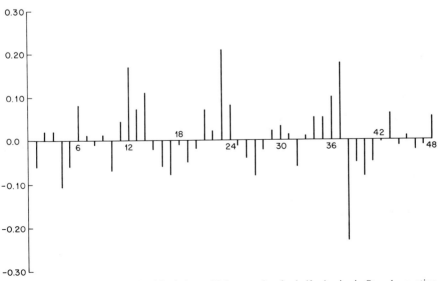

Fig. 1. Autocorrelations of residuals from OLS regression for heifers' price in Step 4, equation (8). Bartlett's standard errors (lag, S.E.): 12, 0.05; 24, 0.06; 36, 0.06; 48, 0.06.

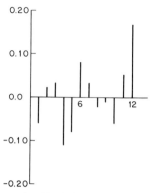

Fig. 2. Partial autocorrelations of residuals from the OLS regression for heifers' price in Step 4, equation (8). Bartlett's standard error: lag 12, S.E. 0.05.

any other value encountered. The partial autocorrelation function shows relatively high values at lags 4 and 12. The failure of the autocorrelation function to damp (at least relative to the standard error of the estimate) is somewhat disconcerting, suggesting possible failure to remove a factor $1 - U^{12}$. However, the partial autocorrelation function suggests an autoregressive component with a root of approximately $1/0.2 = 5$, rather than a root on the unit circle. A moving-average component does not appear evident. Hence, the factor $b_t/(1 - \theta U^{12})$ is introduced, with $\theta = 0.2$ as a plausible starting value, in the multiple time-series analysis described below. This implies that both h_t and s_t are premultiplied by $(1 - \theta U^{12})$ in the analysis, and b_t is treated as white noise.[18]

[18] In contrast to these results, the residuals from (8') exhibit strong autocorrelations and partial autocorrelations, suggesting a relatively complex mixed process. For example, the first 12 autocorrelations and partial autocorrelations are as follows:

Lag	Autocorrelation	Partial autocorrelation
1	0.83	0.83
2	0.80	0.36
3	0.74	0.05
4	0.73	0.14
5	0.70	0.06
6	0.68	0.07
7	0.64	−0.06
8	0.59	−0.08
9	0.55	−0.02
10	0.53	0.01
11	0.52	0.08
12	0.53	0.13
Standard error	0.05	0.05

Step 6. The foregoing implies that we begin with a multiple time-series analysis of the form

$$(1 - \theta U^{12})(1 - \varphi_1 U - \varphi_2 U^2 - \varphi_3 U^4 - \varphi_4 U^5)h_t$$
$$= (1 - \theta U^{12})(\delta_0 - \delta_1 U - \delta_2 U^4 - \delta_3 U^{17}$$
$$- \delta_4 U^{19} - \delta_5 U^{21} - \delta_6 U^{22} - \delta_7 U^{24})s_t + \text{const}, \tag{9}$$

with starting values

$\theta = 0.20$	$\delta_0 = 0.84$	$\delta_5 = 0.0001$
$\varphi_1 = 0.91$	$\delta_1 = 0.63$	$\delta_6 = -0.034$
$\varphi_2 = -0.12$	$\delta_2 = 0.10$	$\delta_7 = 0.014$
$\varphi_3 = 0.11$	$\delta_3 = -0.071$	$\text{const} = 0.165$
$\varphi_4 = -0.0028$	$\delta_4 = 0.098$	

Indeed, because of their relatively small values, we might be tempted to set φ_4, δ_5, δ_6, and δ_7 to zero, especially δ_5, δ_6, and δ_7 since these coefficients attached to exceptionally long lags in the supposed effect of past steers' prices on current heifers' price. Both analyses were performed, with the final choice being the one that omitted steers' price lagged 21, 22, and 24 months:

$$(1 - 0.1713U^{12})(1 - 0.8886U + 0.1304U^2 - 0.1185U^4 + 0.00670U^5)h_t$$
$$\quad(3.00) \qquad\qquad (20.01) \qquad\qquad (4.13) \qquad (2.68) \qquad\qquad (0.28)$$

$$= (1 - 0.1713U^{12})(0.8497 - 0.6171U - 0.1060U^4 + 0.0641U^{17} - 0.0721U^{19})s_t$$
$$\quad(3.00) \qquad\qquad (33.98) \qquad (13.04) \qquad (2.88) \qquad (4.17) \qquad (4.99)$$

$$+ 0.1750 + b_t, \tag{10}$$

where the figure in parentheses beneath each coefficient is its asymptotic t-ratio. The value of the sum of squares at the minimum is 56.1119.[19]

To check the equation, but not the entire model, it is useful to compare the autocorrelations and partial autocorrelations of the calculated series $\{b_t\}$ from (10). These are given in Table 4 and Figs. 3 and 4. The autocorrelation function

---

[19] Inclusion of lags of 21, 22, and 24 months in the steers' price yielded the following multiple time-series analysis:

$$(1 - 0.1971U^{12})(1 - 0.9028U + 0.1285U^2 - 0.1115U^4 + 0.00483U^5)h_t$$
$$\quad(12.66) \qquad\qquad (6.21) \qquad\quad (0.88) \qquad (2.01) \qquad\quad (0.19)$$

$$= (1 - 0.1971U^{12})(0.8510 - 0.6410U - 0.0857U^4$$
$$\quad(12.66) \qquad\qquad (33.85) \qquad (4.83) \qquad (2.01)$$

$$+ 0.0730U^{17} - 0.0963U^{19} - 0.0161U^{21} + 0.0570U^{22} - 0.0242U^{24})s_t + 0.1692 + b_t. \tag{10'}$$
$$\quad(2.85) \qquad\quad (3.33) \qquad\quad (0.28) \qquad\quad (1.17) \qquad\quad (0.22) \qquad\quad (14.67)$$

The sum of squares at the minimum is 54.0384. Only one of the added lagged variables has a t-ratio above one. Moreover, the sum of squares differs by less than 4 percent. Under these circumstances, and because long lags in an explanatory series are almost bound to cause difficulties in forecasting, we feel justified in omitting the lags of 21, 22, and 24 months in the further analysis of heifers' price.

TABLE 4   *Autocorrelations and Partial Autocorrelations of Residuals from a Multiple Time-Series Model for Heifers' Price, Equation (10)*[a]

Lag	Autocorrelation	Partial autocorrelation	Lag	Autocorrelation
1	0.07	0.07	25	−0.09
2	−0.02	−0.02	26	−0.11
3	0.01	0.02	27	−0.12
4	−0.09	−0.10	28	−0.03
5	−0.12	−0.11	29	0.09
6	−0.06	−0.05	30	−0.04
7	−0.01	−0.00	31	0.06
8	0.02	0.02	32	0.07
9	0.07	0.05	33	−0.04
10	−0.00	−0.03	34	0.06
11	0.07	0.07	35	0.07
12	0.07	0.05	36	0.05
13	−0.02		37	0.01
14	0.09		38	0.03
15	0.02		39	−0.14
16	−0.14		40	0.02
17	0.02		41	0.01
18	−0.03		42	−0.08
19	−0.12		43	0.07
20	0.12		44	0.04
21	0.03		45	0.05
22	0.01		46	0.02
23	0.15		47	0.03
24	−0.01		48	−0.03

[a] Standard errors (lags, S.E.): 1–12, 0.05; 13–48, 0.06.

Fig. 3.   Autocorrelations of the residuals from a multiple time-series model for heifers' price, equation (10). Bartlett's standard errors (lag, S.E.): 12, 0.05; 24, 0.06; 36, 0.06; 48, 0.06.

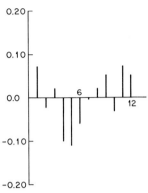

Fig. 4. Partial autocorrelations of the residuals from a multiple time-series model for heifers' price, equation (10). Bartlett's standard error: lag 12, S.E. 0.05.

is now relatively close to zero, especially at longer lags, relative to the standard error for the estimate, although significant departures occur at lags 5, 16, 23, and 39. Moreover, only at lag 5 does the partial autocorrelation rise above twice the appropriate standard error. Taken as a whole, the results suggest that the departure of $\{b_t\}$ from white noise is relatively slight and that further attempts to account for the serial properties of the residual series would be worth little.

After the model for the price of cows has been estimated, it will be possible to examine the relation among the residuals for steers', heifers', and cows' prices to see whether they are indeed uncorrelated at all lags as required by the assumption that we can estimate each equation separately.

Model Formulation and Estimation: Cows

Step 1. The ARIMA models for the prices of cows, heifers, and steers are given by equations (1), (2), and (3) above. Note that the stationarity-rendering transformations required are all the same.

$$T_1(U) = T_2(U) = T_3(U) = (1 - U)(1 - U^{12}).$$

Step 2. From (3)

$$w_t = (1 - U)(1 - U^{12})(1 - 0.154U - 0.169U^2 - 0.123U^7)c_t \qquad (11)$$

and

$$z_{1t} = (1 - U)(1 - U^{12})s_t, \qquad z_{2t} = (1 - U)(1 - U^{12})h_t. \qquad (12)$$

The results for a stepwise regression in which the F-value to enter a variable is 4.1 and the F-value to delete a variable is 4.0 are presented in Table 5 for a

TABLE 5   *The First Five Lagged Values of Transformed Steers' Price z_{1t} and Transformed Heifers' Price z_{2t}, Appearing in a Stepwise Regression of w_t on z_{1t} and z_{2t} and Lags Thereof in the Order in Which They Appear, and Corresponding R^2 Values*[a]

Variable	S	H	S	H	H
Lag	0	19	4	12	5
R^2	0.21	0.25	0.28	0.30	0.31

[a] Variable z_1 denoted by S and z_2 by H.

maximal lag permitted of 25.[20] After entering z_{2t-5}, no further lagged values of either z_1 or z_2 could be found to increase the R^2 of the regression significantly.

Step 3.   Since the ARIMA models for all three series include the same stationarity-rendering transformation $(1 - U)(1 - U^{12})$, we cancel this common factor in order to let the nonstationarity in the steers' and heifers' price series "explain" the nonstationarity in the cows' price series.

Step 4.   To determine the order of the appropriate moving-average, autoregressive, or mixed scheme for the unobserved part of the model, we require the residuals from an ordinary least-squares regression of the current price of cows on those lagged prices of cows suggested by the ARIMA model in (3) and those lagged or current prices of steers and heifers suggested by Step 3. The result is[21]

$$c_t = 0.0931 + 1.2211c_{t-1} - 0.3249c_{t-2} + 0.0318c_{t-7} + 0.0586s_t$$
$$\quad (0.91) \qquad\qquad (23.04) \qquad\qquad\quad (5.86) \qquad\qquad (1.49) \qquad\qquad (3.92)$$

$$- 0.0148s_{t-4} + 0.0576h_{t-5} - 0.0662h_{t-12} + 0.00414h_{t-19} + u_t^*, \quad (13)$$
$$\quad (0.60) \qquad\qquad (2.51) \qquad\qquad (4.56) \qquad\qquad\quad (0.41)$$

$$R^2 = 0.9873.$$

We see that the relatively high-order lagged variables c_{t-7}, s_{t-4}, and h_{t-19} have low t-ratios, but h_{t-12} appears to be highly significant.

The roots of the autoregressive structure in c_t estimated in (13) are as follows:

Root	Modulus	Root	Modulus
1.086	1.086	$-1.750 \pm 1.025i$	2.029
$1.194 \pm 0.8137i$	1.445	$0.01293 \pm 1.835i$	1.835

All are well outside the unit circle.

[20] Increasing the number of possible lags to 45 for both steers and heifers leaves the order of introduction of the variables unchanged and adds only transformed heifers lagged 27 months at the final stage before the stepwise procedure terminates. This last variable increases the R^2 of the regression only to 0.32 from 0.31 at the point at which transformed heifers' price lagged 5 months has been entered.

[21] The figures in parentheses beneath the coefficients are their t-ratios.

Step 5. Autocorrelation and partial autocorrelation functions for u_t^* obtained in Step 4 may be used to determine the nature of $\eta(U)$ in (4). These functions are given in Table 6 and Figs. 5 and 6 for various lags. While the values of the autocorrelations are not much larger than the standard errors, there is a notable failure to damp at longer lags: Values somewhat more or less than three times the standard error are obtained for lags of 2, 11, 12, 24, 36, 42, and 48 months. Examination of the partial autocorrelation function suggests that this effect may be due to an autoregressive, rather than a moving-average, structure in the residual of the form $d_t/(1 - \theta_1 U^2 - \theta_2 U^6 - \theta_3 U^{12})$ with $\theta_1 = \theta_3 = 0.2$ and $\theta_2 = -0.15$, approximately. This implies that all three series are premultiplied by the factor $(1 - \theta_1 U^2 - \theta_2 U^6 - \theta_3 U^{12})$ in the analysis and d_t is treated as white noise.[22]

Step 6. The foregoing implies that we begin with a multiple time-series analysis of the form

$$
\begin{aligned}
(1 - \theta_1 U^2 &- \theta_2 U^6 - \theta_3 U^{12})(1 - \psi_1 U - \psi_2 U^2 - \psi_3 U^7)c_t \\
&= (1 - \theta_1 U^2 - \theta_2 U^6 - \theta_3 U^{12})(\alpha_0 + \alpha_1 U^4)s_t \\
&+ (1 - \theta_1 U^2 - \theta_2 U^6 - \theta_3 U^{12})(\beta_1 U^5 + \beta_2 U^{12} + \beta_3 U^{19})h_t + \text{const} \quad (14)
\end{aligned}
$$

---

[22] In contrast, the residuals obtained by constraining the autoregressive component to be what it was in the previous ARIMA model, i.e., from the regression

$$
w_t = -0.1405 + 0.3397 s_t - 0.0798 s_{t-4} + 0.2527 h_{t-5} - 0.1524 h_{t-2} - 0.0183 h_{t-19} + u_t^{*'}, \quad (13')
$$
$$
\quad (0.68) \qquad (13.61) \qquad (1.63) \qquad (5.54) \qquad (5.73) \qquad (0.90)
$$

$$R^2 = 0.8343,$$

exhibit strong autocorrelations and partial autocorrelations, suggesting a relatively mixed process. For example, the first 12 autocorrelations and partial correlations are as follows:

Lag	Autocorrelation	Partial autocorrelation
1	0.86	0.86
2	0.68	−0.23
3	0.49	−0.12
4	0.30	−0.14
5	0.15	0.04
6	0.06	0.05
7	0.04	0.18
8	0.12	0.24
9	0.20	0.00
10	0.29	0.04
11	0.38	0.06
12	0.39	−0.09
Standard error	0.05	0.05

TABLE 6 *Autocorrelations and Partial Autocorrelations of the Residuals from the OLS Regression for Cows' Price in Step 4 Equation (13)[a]*

Lag	Autocorrelation	Partial autocorrelation	Lag	Autocorrelation
1	−0.03	−0.03	25	0.03
2	0.18	0.18	26	0.01
3	0.07	0.09	27	−0.03
4	0.07	0.04	28	−0.09
5	−0.05	−0.08	29	−0.07
6	−0.09	−0.13	30	−0.12
7	−0.06	−0.06	31	−0.12
8	−0.04	0.00	32	−0.01
9	−0.04	0.01	33	0.01
10	−0.03	−0.01	34	0.04
11	0.15	0.16	35	0.07
12	0.14	0.16	36	0.24
13	0.04		37	0.05
14	0.07		38	0.01
15	0.02		39	0.01
16	−0.12		40	−0.08
17	−0.02		41	−0.09
18	−0.14		42	−0.23
19	−0.11		43	−0.14
20	−0.04		44	−0.05
21	−0.05		45	−0.02
22	0.05		46	−0.03
23	−0.03		47	0.03
24	0.20		48	0.20

[a] Standard errors (lags, S.E.): 1–12, 0.05; 13–36, 0.06; 37–48, 0.07.

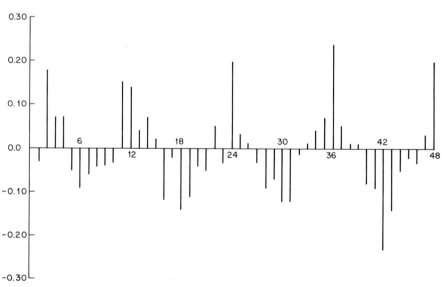

Fig. 5. Autocorrelations of the residuals from the OLS regression for cows' price in Step 4, equation (13). Bartlett's standard errors (lag, S.E.): 12, 0.05; 24, 0.06; 36, 0.06; 48, 0.07.

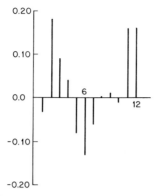

Fig. 6. Partial autocorrelations of the residuals from the OLS regression for cows' price in Step 4, equation (13). Bartlett's standard error: lag 12, S.E. 0.05.

with starting values

$$
\begin{array}{lll}
\theta_1 = 0.20 & \psi_2 = -0.32 & \beta_1 = 0.058 \\
\theta_2 = -0.15 & \psi_3 = 0.032 & \beta_2 = -0.066 \\
\theta_3 = 0.20 & \alpha_0 = 0.059 & \beta_3 = 0.0041 \\
\psi_1 = 1.22 & \alpha_1 = -0.015 & \text{const} = 0.093
\end{array}
$$

Despite the relatively low value of β_3, we did not set it to zero in the multiple time-series analysis. The result of the multiple time-series analysis is

$$(1 - 0.2204U^2 + 0.1651U^6 - 0.2692U^{12})(1 - 1.016U + 0.1309U^2 - 0.003088U^7)c_t$$
$$\quad {\scriptstyle (3.26) \qquad\qquad (2.63) \qquad\qquad (4.03) \qquad\qquad (16.50) \qquad\qquad (1.88) \qquad\qquad (0.10)}$$

$$= (1 - 0.2204U^2 + 0.1651U^6 - 0.2692U^{12})(0.1016 - 0.02827U^4)s_t$$
$$\quad {\scriptstyle (3.26) \qquad\qquad (2.63) \qquad\qquad (4.03) \qquad (5.87) \qquad\qquad (0.95)}$$

$$+ (1 - 0.2204U^2 + 0.1651U^6 - 0.2692U^{12})$$
$$\quad {\scriptstyle (3.26) \qquad\qquad (2.63) \qquad\qquad (4.03)}$$

$$\times (0.04124U^5 - 0.04919U^{12} - 0.004542U^{19})h_t + 0.1006 + d_t, \tag{15}$$
$$\quad {\scriptstyle (1.41) \qquad\qquad (2.60) \qquad\qquad (0.39) \qquad\qquad (0.98)}$$

where the figure in parentheses beneath each coefficient is its asymptotic t-ratio. The value of the sum of squares at the minimum is 94.9672.

To check whether the calculated residuals d_t from equation (15) are approximately white noise, we compute their autocorrelation and partial autocorrelations. These are given in Table 7 and in Figs. 7 and 8. Only for lags of 11, 16, 30, and 42 months does the autocorrelation exceed twice its standard error, and then by very little. For the partial autocorrelations this occurs only for 11 months. Taken as a whole, the results suggest, as before, that the departure of $\{d_t\}$ from white noise is relatively slight and that further attempts to account for the serial properties of the residual series would be worth little.

TABLE 7   *Autocorrelations and Partial Autocorrelations of the Residuals from a Multiple Time-Series Model for Cow's Price, Equation (15)[a]*

Lag	Autocorrelation	Partial autocorrelation	Lag	Autocorrelation
1	0.05	0.05	25	0.03
2	0.01	0.00	26	−0.01
3	0.09	0.09	27	0.01
4	0.08	0.07	28	−0.04
5	−0.04	−0.04	29	−0.08
6	0.06	0.05	30	−0.16
7	0.02	−0.00	31	−0.10
8	−0.01	−0.01	32	−0.02
9	−0.05	−0.05	33	0.01
10	−0.01	−0.02	34	−0.08
11	0.18	0.19	35	0.01
12	−0.10	−0.12	36	0.06
13	0.01		37	0.03
14	0.06		38	−0.01
15	0.00		39	0.01
16	−0.14		40	−0.04
17	0.02		41	−0.08
18	−0.04		42	−0.16
19	−0.01		43	−0.10
20	−0.04		44	−0.02
21	−0.02		45	0.01
22	0.01		46	−0.08
23	−0.04		47	0.01
24	0.12		48	0.06

[a] Standard errors (lags, S.E.): 1–48, 0.06.

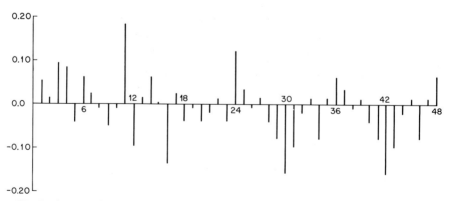

Fig. 7. Autocorrelation of the residuals from a multiple time-series model for cows' price, equation (15). Bartlett's standard errors (lag, S.E.): 12, 0.06; 24, 0.06; 36, 0.06; 48, 0.06.

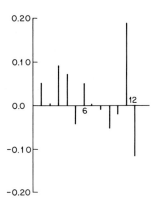

Fig. 8. Partial autocorrelations of the residuals from a multiple time-series model for cows' price, equation (15). Bartlett's standard error: log 12, S.E. 0.06.

5. Testing and Checking the Multiple Time-Series Models for Interrelated Agricultural Prices

In this section we check whether the disturbances a_{st} or a_t, a_{ht} or b_t, and a_{ct} or d_t are in fact uncorrelated at all lags as required by the assumption that we can estimate the equations independently and, finding this to be approximately the case, we compare the forecasting ability of the multiple time-series models for heifers' price and cows' price with the corresponding ARIMA models. There is, of course, no need to do this for the steers' price model since it is identical with the corresponding ARIMA model.

Tables 8–10 present the lag correlations of the calculated residuals from the three time series models making up our multiple time-series model explaining

TABLE 8 *Lag Correlations of Steers' and Heifers' Residual Series*

Lag	Correlation	Lag	Correlation
0	0.0882		
1	0.0374	−1	0.0722
2	0.0123	−2	0.0283
3	0.0009	−3	0.0227
4	−0.0932	−4	−0.0315
5	−0.0783	−5	−0.1124
6	−0.0826	−6	−0.1030
7	−0.0767	−7	−0.0356
8	0.0329	−8	−0.0036
9	0.0452	−9	0.0224
10	0.0600	−10	0.0191
11	0.0700	−11	0.0845
12	0.0743	−12	0.0753
13	−0.0443	−13	0.0057
14	0.0362	−14	0.0032
15	−0.0090	−15	0.0021

the three interrelated price series. We estimated each of the equations separately on the assumption that the residuals were uncorrelated. As Tables 8–10 show, this assumption is very nearly satisfied, the largest lag correlation being about 0.1. Note that the second series is lagged or led, according to whether the lag is plus or minus.

TABLE 9   *Lag Correlations of Cows' and Heifers' Residual Series*

Lag	Correlation	Lag	Correlation
0	0.0365		
1	0.0123	−1	−0.0370
2	0.0181	−2	−0.0166
3	0.0204	−3	−0.0245
4	0.0418	−4	0.0190
5	0.0203	−5	−0.0193
6	0.0336	−6	0.0031
7	0.0420	−7	0.0293
8	−0.0276	−8	−0.0189
9	−0.0431	−9	−0.0049
10	−0.0005	−10	−0.0207
11	−0.0150	−11	−0.0105
12	0.0048	−12	−0.0820
13	−0.0206	−13	−0.0252
14	−0.0043	−14	0.0348
15	0.0464	−15	0.0320

TABLE 10   *Lag Correlations of Steers' and Cows' Residual Series*

Lag	Correlation	Lag	Correlation
0	0.0387		
1	0.0064	−1	−0.0306
2	0.0249	−2	0.0072
3	0.0413	−3	−0.0401
4	0.0562	−4	0.0325
5	0.0230	−5	−0.0145
6	0.0426	−6	−0.0015
7	0.0419	−7	0.0370
8	−0.0280	−8	−0.0097
9	−0.0363	−9	−0.0184
10	0.0189	−10	−0.0019
11	−0.0065	−11	0.0124
12	0.0106	−12	−0.0759
13	−0.0136	−13	−0.0195
14	0.0164	−14	0.0092
15	0.0373	−15	0.0269

TABLE 11 Comparison of Actual and Predicted Time Series for ARIMA and Multiple Time-Series Models Estimated in the Time Domain, 1965–1974

Series and model (1)	Steps ahead forecast (2)	R^2 of regression of actual on predicted (3)	Root of mean-squared error (4)	Mean-absolute error (5)	Mean error (6)	Regression coefficient of actual on predicted (7)	Theil's inequality coefficient and decomposition of error			
							Theil's coefficient (8)	Due to bias (9)	Due to different variation (10)	Due to different covariation (11)
Price of Heifers										
ARIMA model	1	0.9248	1.680	0.9965	0.0625	0.9390	0.0272	0.0014	0.0074	0.9913
	6	0.7487	3.097	2.256	0.5108	0.8846	0.0512	0.0272	0.0018	0.9710
	12	0.6582	3.710	2.724	0.9960	0.8843	0.0601	0.0721	0.0179	0.9100
	18	0.5547	4.409	3.310	1.765	0.9733	0.0718	0.1603	0.1039	0.7359
MTS model	1	0.9226	1.725	1.011	−0.0842	0.9252	0.0279	0.0024	0.0174	0.9802
	6	0.7320	3.307	2.405	0.0073	0.8078	0.0530	0.0000	0.0113	0.9887
	12	0.6549	3.733	2.620	0.4067	0.8111	0.0598	0.0119	0.0001	0.9881
	18	0.5090	4.511	3.374	1.093	0.7994	0.0725	0.0587	0.0208	0.9205
Price of cows										
ARIMA model	1	0.9711	1.020	0.6720	−0.007822	0.9653	0.0224	0.0001	0.0144	0.9856
	6	0.7496	3.181	2.105	−0.007290	0.7847	0.0688	0.0000	0.0348	0.9651
	12	0.4164	5.159	3.370	0.4858	0.5634	0.1108	0.0089	0.0251	0.9660
	18	0.2809	5.490	3.840	1.430	0.5653	0.1196	0.0678	0.0041	0.9280
MTS model	1	0.9680	1.066	0.7099	0.1746	0.9923	0.0235	0.0269	0.0022	0.9709
	6	0.6743	3.583	2.527	1.336	0.8942	0.0802	0.1391	0.0171	0.8437
	12	0.4494	4.949	3.599	2.387	0.7627	0.1116	0.2326	0.0189	0.7484
	18	0.2505	6.247	4.958	3.815	0.7720	0.1445	0.3729	0.1006	0.5265

Unfortunately, the results of the predictive tests are not so favorable. By every measure reported in Table 11,[23] except in the case of the regression co-efficient of actual on predicted for the price of cows, the multiple time-series models perform marginally *worse* than the ordinary single time-series ARIMA model. Indeed, as a general observation, this is not an entirely surprising result.[24] For example, Nelson (1972) found that the large scale structural FRB–MIT–PENN model does not outperform and, in fact, gives worse one-quarter ahead predictions than simple ARIMA models for the major series. This does not mean, of course, that we should give up structural equation models and concentrate on forecasting using simple ARIMA models. Structural models tell us a great deal more, both about behavior and about the possible effects of policy changes, than do ARIMA models. In the case at hand, the multiple time-series models are based to a greater extent, although far from fully, on structural considerations. For that reason, they may be preferred in a context in which the forecast values are used to represent expectations governing be-havior. This is especially so inasmuch as their forecasting ability is only mar-ginally worse (by construction it could hardly be much worse) than that of simple ARIMA models. However, as we shall show in Chapter XIV, replacing the forecasts of the price of cows and heifers generated by simple ARIMA models with forecasts generated from the above models, refit to data through 1969, does not improve the estimates of the parameters of the structural model of cattle producer behavior there developed. Our conclusion must be that the case for multiple time-series modeling is far from good, especially in view of the substantially greater effort and cost involved in formulating and estimating such models.

[23] See footnote 14, p. 228, Chapter X.
[24] For the period for which the models are estimated, the joint model must, and does, outperform the univariate models. But, of course, this need not be true outside the period of forecast.

Chapter XII
FORMULATION AND ESTIMATION OF UNOBSERVED-COMPONENTS MODELS: EXAMPLES

1. Introduction

The purpose of this chapter is to implement and compare the methods proposed in Chapters VI and VII for formulating and estimating unobserved-components models. We have removed a polynomial trend from each series, and calculated the estimated spectral densities for these deviations from trend. In every case, the estimated spectral densities have the same general shape as that suggested in Chapter VI. Thus it seems reasonable to simplify the formulation procedure by fitting the same basic unobserved-components model to all series after removal of polynomial trend.[1] Since few parameters are involved, variations in the extent of seasonality or in the magnitude of the trend-cycle component relative to the other components, for example, may be most simply handled as a problem in estimation.

All models are estimated in both time and frequency domains; however, as reported below, we often had convergence problems in the time domain and frequently were able to estimate only a two-component model lacking an irregular component ($\sigma_3^2 = 0$). Both sets of estimates are presented, the fit of models in the frequency domain assessed by comparison of the theoretical

---

[1] Fitting the *same* model to all series, even after removal of a polynomial trend, probably gives some advantage to the simple ARIMA models in forecast comparisons presented at the end of this chapter, although, as noted below, the differencing employed in fitting an ARIMA model is equivalent to removal of a polynomial of appropriate degree.

spectral density of the estimated model with that of the actual trend-reduced series and by comparison of the forecasts generated, with those produced in Chapter X for ARIMA models fit to the same eight series.

2.   Formulation of the Models; Trend Reduction

Because the eight series examined in this chapter are fairly clearly nonstationary, we removed a polynomial trend from each series before fitting a standard unobserved-components model of the form

$$x_t = \frac{1 + \beta_1 U + \beta_2 U^2}{(1 - \alpha_1 U)(1 - \alpha_2 U)} \epsilon_{1t} + \frac{1 + \beta_3 U + \beta_4 U^2}{1 - \gamma U^{12}} \epsilon_{2t} + \epsilon_{3t}. \tag{1}$$

Graphs of the original series, together with the fitted polynomial trends, are presented in Figs. 1–8. Figures 1–4 and 6 and 7 are found at the back of this volume. Table 1 exhibits the trend coefficients and selected information for the trend regressions for each series. It should be noted that the differencing employed in fitting an ARIMA model to the data is equivalent to removing a polynomial of appropriate degree corresponding to the order of the difference (Anderson, 1971, p. 63), so that removal of a polynomial trend in fitting an unobserved-components model does not result in an unfair comparison with the former.

TABLE 1   *Trend Regressions for Eight Series*

Series	Period	Constant	T	T^2	T^3	R^2
Price of steers	1910–1974	3.596 (9.66)[a]	0.0378 (45.81)	—	—	0.730
Price of cows	1925–1974	387.1 (8.06)	2.092 (5.67)	0.00234 (3.94)	—	0.710
Price of heifers	1935–1974	9.772 (13.80)	0.0786 (11.55)	−0.000071 (5.18)	—	0.599
Price of milk	1910–1974	2.095 (26.45)	−0.00191 (4.08)	0.000010 (16.88)	—	0.777
Cattle slaughter	1947–1974	1043.5 (33.37)	2.983 (6.96)	0.00762 (6.19)	—	0.892
Hog slaughter	1910–1974	2529.0 (35.49)	4.738 (29.97)	—	—	0.536
Industrial production	1919–1974	164.5 (27.82)	−0.3805 (9.38)	0.00300 (51.36)	—	0.977
Male unemployment, 20 +	1947–1974	1116.7 (8.92)	14.33 (4.46)	−0.0906 (4.09)	0.000161 (3.74)	0.059

[a] Figures in parentheses are *t*-ratios of corresponding coefficients. Omitted coefficients were less than twice their estimated standard errors.

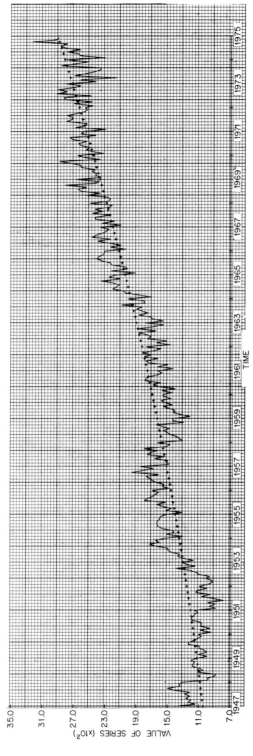

Fig. 5. Cattle slaughter, 1947–1974, and polynomial trend ($+++$).

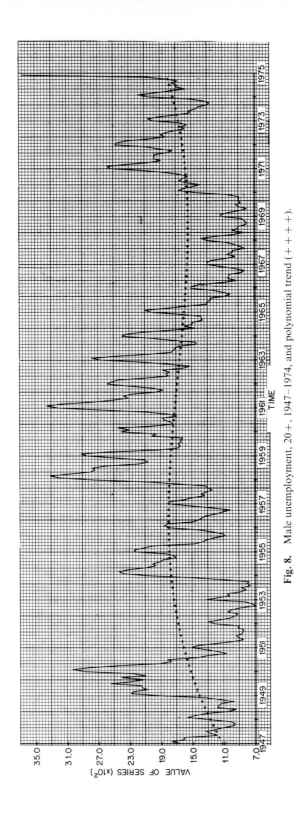

Fig. 8. Male unemployment, 20+, 1947–1974, and polynomial trend $(+++)$.

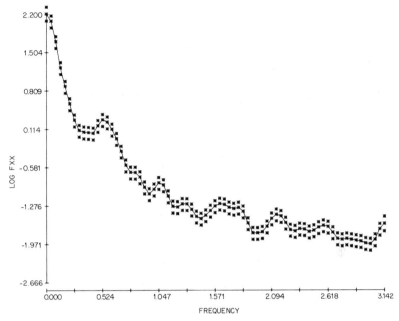

Fig. 9.   Estimated spectral density, detrended price of steers, 1910–1974.

In the case of hog slaughter and steer prices, a simple linear trend sufficed to remove apparent nonstationarity. In the other cases, except male unemployment, 20+, a quadratic trend appeared to be necessary. For male unemployment, 20+, a cubic was used, but it should be noted that in contrast to the other series, very little of the variation was explained by trend. In the case of hog slaughter, the variance of the series about trend appears to be *decreasing* with time. We experimented with exponentiating the series (the opposite of taking logarithms to offset the effect of *increasing* variance over time), but found no improvement in our results.

Figures 9–16 present the estimated spectral densities for the detrended series, estimated at 72 points in addition to the origin using a Parzen window [see Chapter III, Section 5, especially equation (III.5.32)]. The estimates of the densities, represented by asterisks at each frequency, are connected by a solid line. The asterisks above and below each estimated density represent points one standard error of estimate away.[2] The numerically marked points along the abscissa are the seasonal frequencies as fractions of π. It may be noted that all of the spectral densities have the same general shape and form as the typical shape described in Chapter VI. All series show some evidence of

---

[2] Due to a problem in the plotting routine, the top set of asterisks is actually a little closer to the estimates than the bottom set.

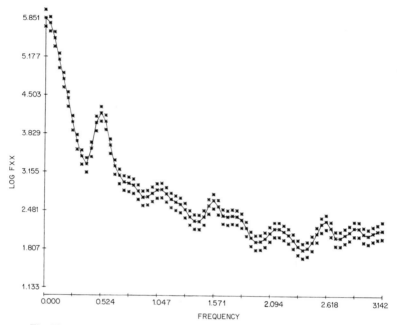

Fig. 10.   Estimated spectral density, detrended price of cows, 1925–1974.

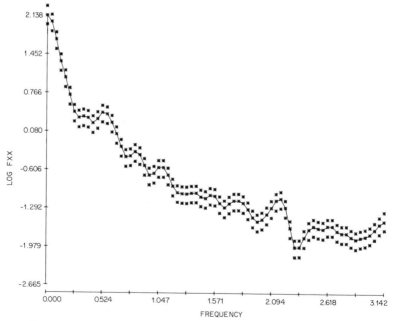

Fig. 11.   Estimated spectral density, detrended price of heifers, 1935–1974.

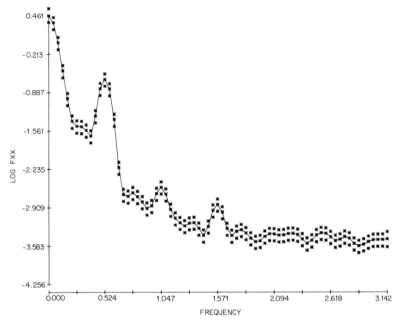

Fig. 12. Estimated spectral density, detrended price of milk, 1910–1974.

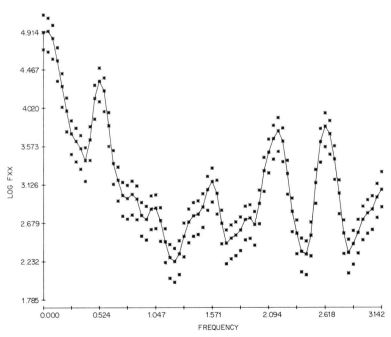

Fig. 13. Estimated spectral density, detrended federally inspected cattle slaughter, 1947–1974.

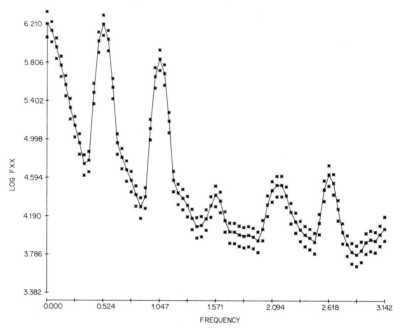

Fig. 14.   Estimated spectral density, detrended federally inspected hog slaughter, 1910–1974.

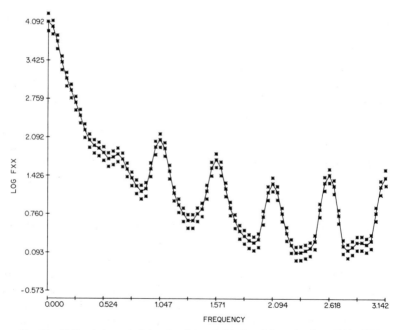

Fig. 15.   Estimated spectral density, detrended industrial production, 1919–1974.

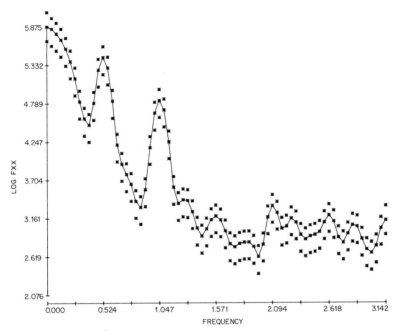

Fig. 16. Estimated spectral density, detrended male unemployment, 20+, 1947–1974.

seasonality, although this is most marked for cattle and hog slaughter, industrial production, and male unemployment, 20+. Curiously, the price series show much less evidence of seasonality except for the rather marked peak at $0.524 = \pi/6$, which corresponds to a sinusoidal fluctuation period of 12 months, in the milk price and cows' price series. The absence of much evidence of seasonality in the price of a storable commodity would not be at all surprising, but meat and milk were not easily storable throughout much of the period under consideration. Moreover, the peak at 12 months cannot be explained in this manner. Apart from this somewhat irregular evidence of seasonality, each series exhibits a spectral density that falls off rapidly with frequency, suggesting a trend-cycle component with a first- or second-order autoregression tempered by a moving average. There is little or no suggestion in any of the spectral densities that an autoregressive component in the trend-cycle with complex roots may be found, but we nonetheless allow for such a possibility in estimation and, indeed, find such complex roots in a number of cases.

In view of the above, the common model (1) was estimated for all eight series by the methods described in detail in Chapter VII, Sections 3 and 5. Certain details of the computations are described in Section 3, in which the results are presented, together with an account of the difficulties encountered with time domain estimation. The theoretical spectral densities of the estimated models are compared with the spectral densities estimated for the actual detrended series. Finally, in Section 4, we present the results of forecasting 1, 6, 12, and 18 months ahead for the eight models estimated in the frequency domain for the 10-year period 1965–1974, not used in the estimation of the models. These results suggest that unobserved-components models do about as well as simple ARIMA models, although, of course, they lend themselves to more appealing interpretations and a variety of applications, such as seasonal adjustment, which ARIMA models do not.

3. Estimation of the Models in Time and Frequency Domains

As indicated in Chapter VII, Section 3, our method for estimating unobserved-components models in the time domain was to impose the restrictions implied by the unobserved-components model on the parameters of the canonical form, i.e., the corresponding ARIMA model, by converting the former to the latter at each iteration in the numerical maximization of the likelihood function. Given numerical values of the parameters, $\alpha_1, \alpha_2, \beta_1, \beta_2, \beta_3, \beta_4, \gamma$, and of the variances of the innovations of each unobserved process, σ_1^2, σ_2^2, and σ_3^2, the corresponding canonical form is calculated as described in Chapter VII. From the canonical form parameters, a value of the sum of squares appearing in the likelihood function (VII.2.3) may be calculated by the methods described in Chapter VII, Section 2. It is this sum of squares we wish to minimize with respect to the parameters of the UC model. The function to be minimized is defined in terms of the underlying parameters only numerically. Moreover, as indicated in Chapter VII, the component variances are determined only up to a scale factor, which must be chosen at the end of the process. This is most simply done by choosing that value of the scale factor such that the variance of the unobserved series implied by the model is equal to the actual variance of the observed series.[3]

Numerical minimization of the sum of squares of the canonical model associated with the underlying parameters of the unobserved-components model was carried out using the algorithm of Davidon (1959), as modified by

---

[3] In the procedure described below for estimation in the frequency domain, the likelihood function is concentrated with respect to one of the original variances, σ_1^2, σ_2^2, or σ_3^2—usually σ_1^2 since the trend-cycle component will rarely, if ever, be found to be absent. The problem of scaling the variances appropriately therefore does not arise. In the case of an ordinary ARIMA model, the concentrated likelihood involves only the sum of squares of the innovations of the process, as may be seen from the form of the unconcentrated likelihood function in (VII.2.3); moreover, the ML estimate of the variance σ^2 in this case is simply min S/T. The difficulty here encountered with respect to the scaling of the estimated variances in the unobserved-components model is that the canonical form does not determine the scale factor without reference to the observed data. Since the estimated sample variance of the observed data is the maximum-likelihood estimate of the population variance of $\{x_t\}$, our scaling does yield ML estimates. Of course, any other sample moment could have been used; all are implicitly used in the estimation of σ^2 in an ordinary ARIMA model or in the frequency-domain estimation of the component variances in an unobserved-components model.

Fletcher and Powell (1963) and further modified by Stewart (1967), in order to avoid analytical evaluation of either the gradient or the matrix of the second-order partial derivatives of the function minimized.[4]

The results for the eight time series considered are presented in Table 2. For each series, the coefficients of all moving-average and autoregressive parts are presented, together with estimates of variances, and the percent contribution of each component to the variance of the observed series is given immediately above the estimated variance of the innovations of that component (*not* equal to the variance of the component). Since complex roots were allowed in the autoregressive part of the trend-cycle component, this was estimated in the form $1 + a_1 U + a_2 U^2$ rather than in the form $(1 - \alpha_1 U)(1 - \alpha_2 U)$. The roots, whether real or complex, are presented in the next to last line of the block for each series, and the modulus of the root follows in the next line. In the line below the estimated coefficients, estimates of the corresponding standard errors are given. These estimates are based on a numerically calculated matrix of second derivatives. Since this matrix is repeatedly updated starting from an arbitrary positive-definite matrix, it does not give reliable estimates. Moreover, the accuracy depends on the number of iterations so the problem is further exacerbated by the fact that the procedure had to be restarted frequently because of failure to converge or because of the occurrence of a boundary condition. These figures, therefore, cannot be compared directly with the standard errors given for the frequency domain estimates since the latter are calculated from an analytically derived matrix of second derivatives of the logarithmic likelihood function. Following the estimated standard errors, the final values of the gradients are given. In many cases, these are rather large, although not in comparison with the final estimate of the sum of squares presented in column (12). (If the reader finds such large gradients troubling, he is invited to rescale the data mentally!) This is because convergence was presumed to have occurred *either* when the largest gradient value became very small *or* when the step size fell below a preassigned limit.[5] Since the step size depends in part on how much the value of the function being minimized changes between iterations, and since the likelihood function was frequently flat,

---

[4] Actually these programs were modified in a number of important respects, the key modification being one to ensure that the approximate numerically calculated second derivatives used in the Fletcher–Powell algorithm always formed a positive-definite matrix. Other modifications concerned the procedure for searching along the gradient whenever the step size indicated by the Fletcher–Powell algorithm became large. See also Wells (1965).

[5] It is, of course, possible that the gradients may be quite large in the vicinity of a true maximum if the likelihood function is very sharply peaked there. The presence of a very well-defined maximum would then be signalled by very small standard errors. As indicated, however, our estimates of the standard errors are unreliable in the case of the time domain estimates, so that they are of little help in deciding the question of whether convergence to a maximum has in fact occurred but with large gradients.

TABLE 2 Time Domain Estimates of Unobserved-Components Models for Eight Detrended Series

Series, period of fit, item (1)	Trend-cycle component — Moving-average β_1 (2)	β_2 (3)	Autoregression $a_1\ \alpha_1$ (4)	$a_2\ \alpha_2$ (5)	Variance σ_1^2 (6)	Seasonal component — Moving-average β_3 (7)	β_4 (8)	Autoregression γ (9)	Variance σ_2^2 (10)	Irregular component variance σ_3^2 (11)	Sum of squares at the minimum (12)	Number of iterations to minimum (13)
1. Price of Steers, 1910–1964[a]												
Coefficients	0.9240	0.8350	-1.2429	0.2668	99.5% 147.098	-0.1455	-0.4169	0.1156	0.5% 113.865	0% Suppressed	387.8557	72[b]
Standard error[a]	0.0273	0.1282	0.000547	0.00249	0.0884	0.0643	0.00284	0.0541	0.0882			
Gradient	-8.0×10^{-2}	-2.6×10^{-2}	1.3×10^{0}	-2.8×10^{-1}	1.3×10^{-4}	2.1×10^{-2}	4.0×10^{-1}	3.0×10^{-3}	-1.7×10^{-4}			
Roots	-0.5533	$\pm\,0.9442i$	1.0341	3.6251		1.3840	-1.7329	—				
Modulus	1.0944			Same		Same	1.7329					
2. Price of Cows,[c] 1925–1964												
Coefficients	0.1547	0.0000	-1.9099	0.9140	97.2% 737.912	1.1141	0.9986	0.9849	2.5% 46.553	0.2% 628.022	1039921.	22
Standard error[a]	0.0000	0.0000	0.0000	0.0000	0.0000	0.0000	0.0000	0.0000	0.0000	0.0002		
Gradient	-8.3×10^{3}	3.3×10^{3}	3.6×10^{4}	1.3×10^{6}	-3.5×10^{3}	-1.5×10^{6}	2.9×10^{5}	3.9×10^{5}	8.6×10^{2}	-1.5×10^{1}		
Roots	-1.0665	1.2772	1.0448	$\pm\,0.0500i$		-0.5578	$\pm\,0.8308i$	—				
Modulus	1.0665	Same		1.0460			1.00068					
3. Price of Heifers, 1935–1964												
Coefficients	1.1984	0.4020	-1.2057	0.2367	99.0% 0.1836	0.4341	-0.00534	0.1974	1.0% 0.2163	0% Suppressed	295.517	31[b]
Standard error[a]	0.6542	1.1205	0.1613	0.1562	0.000367	0.3604	0.1716	0.0775	0.3218			
Gradient	-2.5×10^{-2}	-1.1×10^{-1}	-1.3×10^{-1}	-1.6×10^{-1}	-7.3×10^{-2}	1.2×10^{-2}	-1.2×10^{-1}	-9.1×10^{-3}	4.1×10^{-2}			
Roots	-1.4906	$\pm\,0.5155i$	1.0430	4.0500		-2.2420	83.554	—				
Modulus		1.5772		Same		2.2420	Same					
4. Price of Milk, 1910–1964												
Coefficients	-0.2655	0.2146	-1.4523	0.4605	89.7% 56.732	1.0199	0.9189	0.9936	10.2% 2.8959	0.1% 6.9831	5.3413	51
Standard error[a]	0.4066	0.3823	0.0379	0.0458	0.3906	0.8376	0.7392	0.0544	1.2916	0.4121		
Gradient	-2.9×10^{-2}	3.2×10^{-2}	-3.9×10^{-1}	-4.5×10^{-1}	-2.0×10^{-3}	5.8×10^{-3}	3.2×10^{-2}	8.1×10^{-1}	5.1×10^{-2}	4.5×10^{-3}		
Roots	0.6185	$\pm\,2.0680i$	1.0157	2.1380		-0.5549	$\pm\,0.8833i$	—				
Modulus	2.1586		Same	Same			1.0432					

5. Cattle Slaughter, 1947–1964												
Coefficients	0.6990	−0.3070	−0.3732	−0.5762	61.3%	−0.5609	0.9873	0.9216	38.7%	0%	1487158.	11[b]
Standard error[a]	0.0000	0.0000	0.0000	0.0000	3005.7	0.0000	0.0000	0.0000	1565.0	Suppressed		
Gradient	1.1×10^4	6.5×10^4	-1.0×10^4	-1.1×10^4	0.0000	8.5×10^4	3.2×10^4	4.0×10^4	0.0000			
Roots	−0.9954	3.2725	1.0327	1.6804	-3.4×10^1	$0.2841 \pm 0.9655i$		—	6.6×10^1			
Modulus	0.9954	Same	Same	1.6804		1.0064						
6. Hog Slaughter, 1910–1964												
Coefficients	0.2666	−0.2835	−0.3702	−0.5451	40.3%	1.4131	1.1276	0.9879	59.7%	0%	11471240.	54[b]
Standard error[a]	0.0002	0.0001	0.0002	0.0002	135808.	0.0006	0.0008	0.0000	4715.	Suppressed		
Gradient	-3.8×10^5	-4.7×10^5	1.5×10^6	-2.3×10^6	0.0002	9.7×10^5	-5.2×10^5	-3.3×10^6	0.0047			
Roots	−1.4660	2.4065	1.0568	−1.7360	-1.1×10^3	$-0.6266 \pm 0.7030i$		—	3.1×10^4			
Modulus	1.4660	Same	Same	1.7360		0.9417						
7. Industrial Production, 1919–1964												
Coefficients	−0.2216	−0.1446	−1.6754	0.6873	78.9%	0.5539	0.2901	0.9955	21.1%	0%	36476.95	31[b]
Standard error[a]	0.0006	0.0008	0.0000	0.0000	53.876	0.0017	0.0006	0.0006	5.1408	Suppressed		
Gradient	3.1×10^0	-5.8×10^0	-1.8×10^2	5.2×10^1	0.0068	1.4×10^0	1.1×10^0	1.6×10^1	0.0343			
Roots	1.973	−3.5057	1.0438	1.3940	3.5×10^{-3}	$-0.9548 \pm 1.5925i$		—	-4.5×10^{-2}			
Modulus	Same	3.5057	Same	Same		1.8568						
8. Male Unemployment, 1947–1964												
Coefficients	−0.6022	0.1830	−1.6584	0.6826	78.8%	0.9149	0.7213	0.9834	21.2%	0%	4164697.	46[b]
Standard error[a]	0.0004	0.0003	0.0000	0.0000	1466.2	0.0012	0.0010	0.0001	121.346	Suppressed		
Gradient	2.6×10^4	3.6×10^4	-5.4×10^5	-5.2×10^5	0.0048	-5.9×10^4	-1.5×10^4	1.0×10^6	0.0304			
Roots	$1.6454 \pm 1.6605i$		1.1114	1.3181	-1.7×10^2	$-0.6342 \pm 0.9921i$		—	2.1×10^3			
Modulus		2.3376	Same	Same		1.1774						

[a] Derived numerically from H matrix used in the calculation of the direction of descent and step length. Unreliable.

[b] After restart from last values for which $\hat{\sigma}_3^2 > 0$.

[c] Transformed to $(1 - 0.1\,U^{12})x_t$. Estimation did not converge for untransformed detrended series x_t.

[d] Converged in 35 iterations but with a noninvertible moving-average in the seasonal component. Root was inverted and calculations restarted. Convergence was obtained in 16 more iterations with nearly the same sum of squares at the minimum.

calculations were terminated by the step-size condition for all cases except heifers and milk. The number of iterations is given in column (13) from start to convergence or from restart, with σ_3^2 set equal to zero, to convergence. In all but two cases, cows and milk, only a two-component model with $\sigma_3^2 = 0$ could be estimated.

The actual results are in most cases not very different from the frequency domain estimates, which were obtained much more reliably, with fewer iterations, and using substantially less computer time. Even where differences in the coefficients are appreciable, however, the forecasting ability of a particular model estimated in the two ways does not appear to be affected much. Since the results presented in Table 2 are largely of academic interest in view of the greater ease of computation in the frequency domain, we discuss the latter in more detail.

Estimation of ARIMA models in the frequency domain is discussed in Chapter VII, Section 4, and for unobserved-components models in Section 5. The latter contains a full discussion of the concentration of the likelihood function with respect to σ_1^2, the variance of the innovations of the trend-cycle component. Essentially, the same numerical procedures were used to maximize the likelihood function in the frequency domain, except that an analytically derived gradient was supplied to the function minimization routine rather than a numerically calculated one. Moreover, at the end of the maximization of the concentrated likelihood function, the matrix of second derivatives of the full likelihood function was evaluated at the ML estimates of all parameters and used to derive an asymptotic variance–covariance matrix for the estimates. In general, estimation in the frequency domain is considerably more reliable and more rapid than in the time domain. This is true despite the time-consuming need to calculate the periodogram ordinates at equispaced frequencies in the interval $[0, \pi]$ equal in number to half the number of observations. Once this is accomplished, however, convergence to the maximum-likelihood estimates is generally rapid, although subject to some minor difficulties as noted. Moreover, each iteration generally takes far less time in the frequency than in the time domain because of the analytically supplied gradient and because the likelihood function appears to be smoother and better behaved. If one were doing large numbers of calculations with a given set of series, it would pay to compute the Fourier transforms of the data and work with these series rather than the original observations. Such a device would cut down subsequent computational costs considerably even if different periods were explored so that periodogram ordinates would have to be recomputed.[6]

---

[6] The suggestions of Pukkila (1977, pp. 32–39) are relevant here. Very considerable savings in computer time may be achieved, even without fast Fourier transform methods, by recursive calculation as compared with use of the standard trigonometric function routines. Table lookup, as suggested here, might be still faster but it uses up a considerable amount of storage space.

Results for the eight series are presented in Table 3 in the same format as those for the time domain estimates in Table 2. In only one case, cattle slaughter, were we unable to estimate a three-component model. Moreover, in general the gradients are very small, both relative to the value of the logarithmic likelihood function at the maximum and relative to the size of the coefficients themselves. Unfortunately, with few exceptions, the estimated standard errors of the coefficients tend to be rather large, suggesting that the likelihood function is quite flat in the vicinity of the maximum. Such a conclusion may also be drawn from the fact that, even where different to a notable degree, models estimated in the time domain forecast about as well as models estimated in the frequently domain. Apparently, considerable variation in the parameters is required before either forecasting ability or the value of the likelihood of the sample can be much affected.[7]

The price of steers, 1910–1964, shows a strong and reliably estimated first-order autoregression in its trend-cycle component, which, partly as a consequence, contributes 99.5% of the variance of the observed series. The time domain estimates presented in Table 2 reveal a similar result (disregarding the order of the roots, which is immaterial). The second root in both cases is farther away from the unit circle, the consequence of a smaller coefficient attached to the second lag. The second-order moving average in the trend-cycle component is not significantly different from 1. A mild seasonal is apparent from the estimate of the autoregressive parameter in the corresponding component of about 0.10 in both frequency and time domain. This value is not large enough to produce a pronounced seasonal effect, and its effect is further reduced by the small estimated variance of this component. Here we were successful in estimating an irregular component ($\sigma_3^2 > 0$), but because of the larger variances attached to the other components, and especially because of the strong autoregression in the trend-cycle, the contribution of this component was effectively zero. A graph of the theoretical spectral density for the estimated model is presented in Fig. 17. Disregarding the scale, which is essentially arbitrary for the theoretical spectral density, the model provides only a mediocre fit: The first order autoregression is far too strong, producing a rapid falloff in the spectral density for the model, which does not occur for the series itself. The mild peak in the actual series at $\pi/6$ is also almost totally suppressed in the model. Correspondingly, the model has somewhat excessive power at frequencies between $\pi/3$ and $2\pi/3$.

The price of cows, 1925–1964, offered the greatest difficulty in estimation: Convergence simply could not be obtained with a positive variance for the seasonal component; moreover, when σ_2^2 was set to zero, σ_3^2 also went to zero,

---

[7] Examination of the computer runs also reveals little change in the value of the concentrated logarithmic likelihood function during rather more of the final iterations than one would have expected, given the fairly substantial changes taking place in the parameter values themselves.

TABLE 3   *Frequency Domain Estimates of Unobserved-Components Models for Eight Detrended Series*

Series, period of fit item (1)	Trend-cycle component					Seasonal component				Irregular component variance, σ_3^2 (11)	Value of the likelihood function at the maximum (12)	Number of iterations to maximum (13)
	Moving-average		Autoregression		Variance, σ_1^2 (6)	Moving-average		Autoregression	Variance, σ_2^2 (10)			
	β_1 (2)	β_2 (3)	α_1 (4)	α_2 (5)		β_3 (7)	β_4 (8)	γ (9)				
1. Price of Steers, 1910–1964												
Coefficients	0.8068	0.9943	−1.1841	0.2117	99.5% 0.1369	−0.02676	−0.4158	0.1039	0.5% 0.1069	0.0% 0.000934	−182.4015	29
Standard error	1.6075	2.5246	0.1832	0.1781	0.3784	2.2791	1.4254	0.1318	0.3134	0.1568		
Gradient	7.3×10^{-5}	-1.0×10^{-4}	5.6×10^{-4}	4.6×10^{-4}		1.2×10^{-4}	-2.7×10^{-4}	-6.6×10^{-5}	3.7×10^{-6}	-2.3×10^{-5}		
Roots	$-0.4057 \pm 0.9171i$		4.5579	1.0366		−1.5833	1.5189	—				
Modulus	1.0029		Same	Same		1.5833	Same					
2. Price of Cows[a], 1925–1964												
Coefficients	0.1309	−0.7583	−1.8934	0.8984	97.9% 737.912	1.1131	0.99998	0.9579	1.6% 46.553	0.5% 628.023	−2121.2394	20
Standard error	55.3166	44.6897	0.0442	0.0433	42097.	0.2390	0.2853	0.0181	23.712	1175.76		
Gradient	-5.7×10^{-4}	-5.2×10^{-4}	4.7×10^{-2}	4.7×10^{-2}		1.9×10^{-4}	-3.4×10^{-4}	-5.2×10^{-4}	-6.2×10^{-4}	2.1×10^{-4}		
Roots	−1.0653	1.2379	$1.0538 \pm 0.0516i$			$-0.5565 \pm 0.8308i$		—				
Modulus	1.0653	Same	1.0550			1.000008						
3. Price of Heifers, 1935–1964												
Coefficients	0.7981	−0.1579	−1.2271	0.2565	98.6% 0.3766	1.1978	0.7467	0.9161	1.0% 0.01245	0.4% 0.1031	−173.9255	28[b]
Standard error	98.602	16.284	0.4042	0.3900	37.806	0.5590	0.6205	0.0581	0.01231	0.6285		
Gradient	-9.3×10^{-6}	1.1×10^{-4}	7.2×10^{-4}	8.4×10^{-4}		6.2×10^{-5}	1.2×10^{-4}	-2.7×10^{-4}	-4.9×10^{-4}	1.5×10^{-4}		
Roots	−1.0392	6.0929	3.7417	1.0419		$-0.8020 \pm 0.8342i$		—				
Modulus	1.0392	Same	Same	Same		1.1572						
4. Price of Milk, 1910–1964												
Coefficients	0.6491	0.8801	−1.4851	0.4965	94.1% 0.000784	1.5163	1.0000	0.9687	5.4% 0.000355	0.5% 0.0028	1191.7266	30[c]
Standard error	19.530	41.112	0.0983	0.0972	0.0376	0.2373	0.1945	0.0106	0.000114	0.00173		
Gradient	-2.3×10^{-4}	-2.2×10^{-4}	4.8×10^{-4}	-4.4×10^{-4}		9.1×10^{-5}	1.3×10^{-3}	4.2×10^{-3}	4.2×10^{-4}	3.6×10^{-5}		
Roots	$-0.3688 \pm 1.0001i$		1.9672	1.0238		$-0.7581 \pm 0.6521i$		—				
Modulus	1.0659		Same	Same		1.00005						

Parameter												
5. Cattle Slaughter, 1947–1964												
Coefficients	0.7012	-0.2988	-0.3677	-0.5594	63.1%	-0.5077	1.0000	0.8692	36.9%	0%	-1091.6112	16[d]
Standard error	0.3147	0.1555	0.2222	0.2103	2735.9	0.1749	0.4717	0.0447	1565.0	Suppressed		
Gradient	-1.3×10^{-6}	-2.8×10^{-6}	2.8×10^{-5}	2.8×10^{-5}	1153.9	-5.2×10^{-8}	4.0×10^{-7}	9.2×10^{-7}	837.6			
Roots	-1.00005	3.3471	-1.7054	1.0481		$0.2538 \pm 0.9672i$			8.6×10^{-7}			
Modulus	1.00005	Same	1.7054	Same		1.000002						
6. Hog Slaughter, 1910–1964												
Coefficients	0.7253	-0.2699	0.2366	-0.6477	45.4%	1.0882	0.7533	0.9656	50.9%	3.7%	-4336.3101	22
Standard error	148.55	37.726	0.1904	0.1720	73506.8	0.1923	0.1885	0.01124	11915.0	34938.		
Gradient	-1.8×10^{-4}	-3.8×10^{-4}	8.1×10^{-4}	5.2×10^{-4}	1119696.	1.6×10^{-4}	-3.3×10^{-4}	1.3×10^{-3}	3492.9	384050.		
Roots	-1.00383	3.6914	-1.4385	1.0733		$-0.7223 \pm 0.8977i$			-3.2×10^{-4}	2.9×10^{-4}		
Modulus	1.00383	Same	1.4385	Same		1.1522						
7. Industrial Production, 1919–1964												
Coefficients	0.4490	-0.5166	-1.6764	0.6887	95.5%	0.5949	0.2810	0.9280	4.2%	0.3%	-1502.0965	47
Standard error	68.998	36.492	0.2537	0.2466	20.442	0.1431	0.1457	0.0215	10.0998	6.7140		
Gradient	-5.0×10^{-4}	-7.7×10^{-4}	6.1×10^{-2}	6.1×10^{-2}	1425.9	4.8×10^{-6}	3.0×10^{-5}	2.5×10^{-5}	2.3746	13.2997		
Roots	-1.0230	1.8922	1.3883	1.0459		$-1.0587 \pm 1.5616i$			9.7×10^{-5}	1.4×10^{-4}		
Modulus	1.0230	Same	Same	Same		1.8866						
8. Male Unemployment, 1947–1964												
Coefficients	0.7799	-0.1162	-1.7028	0.7308	80.8%	1.4145	1.0000	0.9138	17.8%	1.3%	-1200.7316	46
Standard error	158.142	21.5693	0.2388	0.2258	1460.3	0.4773	0.6546	0.0296	2449.4	4384.3		
Gradient	-2.9×10^{-5}	-3.1×10^{-5}	2.4×10^{-3}	2.3×10^{-3}	239854.	2.3×10^{-5}	2.2×10^{-5}	1.9×10^{-5}	1773.4	4916.9		
Roots	-1.1014	7.8149	$1.1650 \pm 0.1056i$			$-0.7074 \pm 0.7068i$			4.1×10^{-6}	5.6×10^{-6}		
Modulus	1.1014	Same	1.1697			1.00004						

[a] Transformed to $(1 - 0.1\,U^{12})x_t$. Estimation did not converge for untransformed detrended series x_t.

[b] Converged in 18 iterations with a nonnegative-definite Hessian and a noninvertible moving average in the trend-cycle. The root was inverted and calculations restarted. Convergence was obtained in 10 more iterations with a negative-definite Hessian. The value of the likelihood function was exactly the same as before.

[c] Converged in 21 iterations with a nonnegative-definite Hessian and a noninvertible moving average in the trend-cycle. The root was inverted and calculations restarted. Convergence was obtained in 9 more iterations with a negative-definite Hessian. The value of the likelihood function was exactly the same as before

[d] After restart from last values for which $\hat{\sigma}_3^2 > 0$.

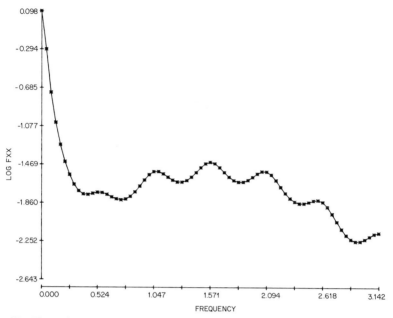

Fig. 17. Theoretical spectral density, model for detrended price of steers estimated in the frequency domain, 1910–1964.

and the resulting ARIMA model had estimated innovations containing a strong and significant seasonal component. As may be seen from Fig. 10, the series itself has relatively little seasonality except for a rather marked peak at $\pi/6$. The partial autocovariance at lag 12 in the estimated innovations of a simple ARIMA model of the form

$$x_t = [(1 + \beta_1 U + \beta_2 U^2)/(1 - \alpha_1 U)(1 - \alpha_2 U)]\epsilon_t$$

fitted to the detrended series was about 0.10. Suppose then we assume a common autoregression in all components of the form $1/(1 - 0.1U^{12})$; this suggests transforming the data to $(1 - 0.1 U^{12})x_t$. When this was done, the fitted models presented in Tables 2 and 3 were obtained. The time and frequency domain estimates differ little. There is a relatively powerful second-order autoregression with complex roots in the trend-cycle component, which has an insignificant moving-average component. The moving average of the seasonal component has complex roots very nearly on the unit circle and a surprisingly marked 12th-order autoregression. In both frequency and time domains, it was possible to estimate a three-component model, although the variances of the seasonal and irregular components are quite small, so that these components account, respectively, for only 1.6% and 0.5% of the variance in the model estimated in the frequency domain. A graph of the theoretical spectral density of the theoretical model

$$x_t = \frac{1 + 0.1309U - 0.7583U^2}{(1 - 1.8934U + 0.8984U^2)(1 - 0.1U^{12})} \epsilon_{1t}$$

$$+ \frac{1 + 1.1131U + 0.9999U^2}{(1 - 0.9579U^{12})(1 - 0.1U^{12})} \epsilon_{2t} + \frac{1}{1 - 0.1U^{12}} \epsilon_{3t}$$

is given in Fig. 18. The fit at the upper end of the spectrum of frequencies is good, but the theoretical spectral density falls off much too rapidly between 0 and $\pi/3$, so that, despite an unusually sharp peak at $\pi/6$, the theoretical density badly misses the marked peak at $\pi/6$ in the estimated density of the actual series. The problem again appears to lie with an overly powerful autoregressive part in the trend-cycle component.

The price of heifers, 1935–1964, offered a new and unexpected problem, encountered also in connection with the price of milk. The computations converged rapidly (in 18 iterations) in the frequency domain, but the matrix of second derivatives of the log–likelihood function was not negative–definite, as it should have been at a true maximum. On inspection, the trend-cycle component was found to have a noninvertible moving-average part, i.e., a moving average with roots *inside* the unit circle. Since the actual value of the likelihood function is unaffected by whether the estimated roots lie inside or

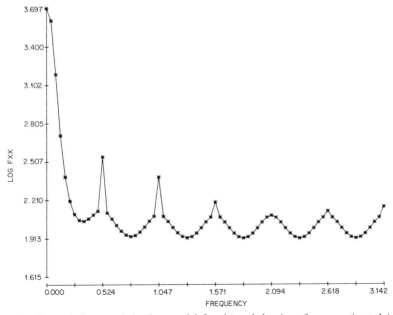

Fig. 18. Theoretical spectral density, model for detrended price of cows estimated in the frequency domain, 1925–1964.

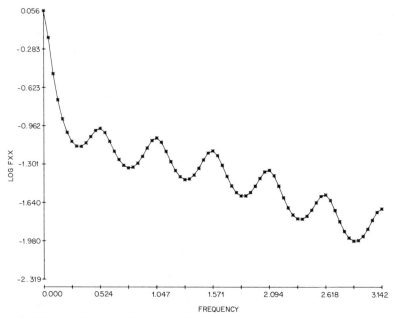

Fig. 19.   Theoretical spectral density, model for detrended price of heifers estimated in the frequency domain, 1935–1964.

outside the unit circle (a corresponding root always enters the likelihood function symmetrically), the estimation procedure was restarted using as initial values all the coefficients previously obtained except those in the trend-cycle moving average, which were replaced by the coefficients corresponding to the reciprocal of the root found to be inside the unit circle.[8] Convergence to a new model with a negative-definite matrix of second derivatives of the log–likelihood function, the same value of the function, and all roots well outside the unit circle was obtained in 10 more iterations. Figure 11 shows that the price of heifers does not have any marked trends or other important distinguishing characteristics. Figure 19 shows that the theoretical spectral density of the estimated model fits the actual tolerably well: There is a bit too much power at the high end of the frequency spectrum and a bit too little at the low end.

The price of milk, 1910–1964, presented the same problem as the price of heifers: After 21 iterations the procedure converged but with a nonnegative-definite matrix of second derivatives of the log–likelihood function and a non-invertible moving average in the trend-cycle component. Restarting with the same modification as outlined above resulted in convergence in nine more

[8] The value of the likelihood function was numerically identical to the previous value with this change—as it should have been.

iterations to the estimates presented in the table. The estimated spectral density for the actual series, shown in Fig. 12, suggests a very strong seasonal component at $\pi/6$. This is mirrored in the substantial autoregressive part, in the seasonal component of the estimated model with a highly damping moving-average part. This is not sufficient to damp successive spikes at seasonal frequencies to the extent they are damped in the estimated spectral density for the actual series (see Fig. 20), but we should remember that the smoothing, i.e., averaging of the estimated values, will have this effect. Again, the problem seems to be too strong an autoregressive part in the trend-cycle component: The theoretical density for the model falls off far too rapidly at very low frequencies.

Cattle slaughter, 1947–1964, represents another type of series in contrast to the four discussed above. Seasonality is very marked and strong in this series, as may be seen from the estimated spectral density of the actual series presented in Fig. 13. This is revealed by a substantial contribution to the overall variance of the series by the estimated seasonal component, 36.9% for the model estimated in the frequency domain and 38.7% for the model estimated in the time domain. For neither method of estimation was it possible to obtain convergence for a positive σ_3^2. Hence, the irregular component was suppressed. The trend-cycle component has a definite moving-average part, although not significantly second-order. The seasonal component is well-defined and damped by a second-order moving average in its numerator.

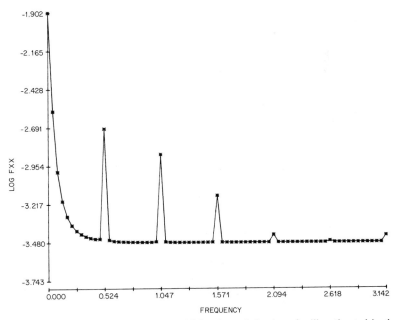

Fig. 20. Theoretical spectral density, model for detrended price of milk estimated in the frequency domain, 1910–1964.

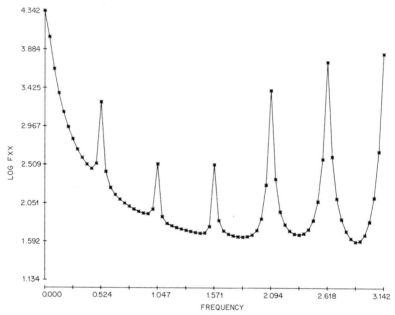

Fig. 21. Theoretical spectral density, model for detrended federally inspected cattle slaughter estimated in the frequency domain, 1947–1964.

Comparison of the estimated spectral density of the actual series, Fig. 13, with the theoretical spectral density of the fitted model, Fig. 21, reveals a moderately good match, albeit one which suggests that the seasonal effect has been dominated by the peaks at high frequencies, $\pi/2$, $2\pi/3$, $5\pi/6$, and π, rather than by the well-defined and marked peak at $\pi/6$.

Hog slaughter, 1910–1964, is similar to cattle slaughter in having very well-defined and marked peaks in the spectral density of the actual series at the seasonal frequencies (Fig. 14). Estimation of the basic model proved to be extraordinarily difficult in the time domain, but quite simple in the frequency domain. Although the seasonal component accounted for over 50% of the variance of the observed series, the estimated model fails to capture the marked peaks at $\pi/6$ and $\pi/3$ (see Fig. 22). The trend-cycle component, however, appears to fit quite well.

Industrial production, 1919–1964, shows very marked seasonality at all seasonal frequencies except $\pi/6$, where the presence of a seasonal peak may be partly obscured by a strong autoregressive part in the trend-cycle component (see Fig. 15). The fitted model reflects partly the importance of the 12th-order autoregression in the seasonal component but surprisingly, despite the marked peaks in the theoretical spectral density (see Fig. 23), relatively little is contributed by this component to the overall variance in comparison with the model for hog slaughter. A strong second-order autoregression appears in the trend-cycle component and the closeness of one of the roots to the unit circle probably

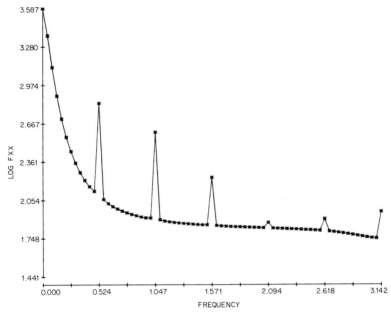

Fig. 22. Theoretical spectral density, model for detrended federally inspected hog slaughter estimated in the frequency domain, 1910–1964.

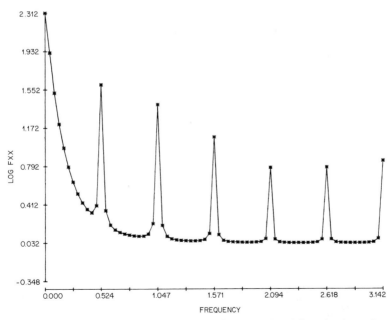

Fig. 23. Theoretical spectral density, model for detrended industrial production estimated in the frequency domain, 1919–1964.

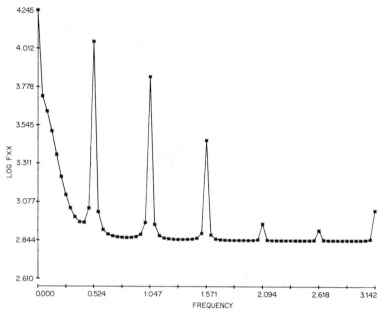

Fig. 24.   Theoretical spectral density, model for detrended male unemployment, 20+, estimated in the frequency domain, 1947–1964.

accounts for the high contribution to the overall variance. The spectral density of the fitted model follows the estimated spectral density of the actual series well at frequencies above $\pi/3$, but again drops too quickly at frequencies below this level.

Male unemployment, 1947–1964, shows marked seasonal peaks at $\pi/6$ and $\pi/3$, but little elsewhere. The estimated spectral density for the actual series, as is the case with the other series examined, does not tail off sufficiently rapidly to suggest the absence of a moving-average part in the trend-cycle component (see Fig. 16). Nonetheless, the fitted model contains a well-defined autoregression in its trend-cycle component, but the moving average is insignificantly different from 1.0. The moving average in the seasonal component is highly significant, with complex roots nearly on the unit circle, and this accounts for the heavy damping of the theoretical spectral density of the fitted model (see Fig. 24). The model thus does well in picking up the marked seasonal peaks at $\pi/6$ and $\pi/3$ and suppressing those at all higher frequencies except $\pi/2$.

4.   Predictive Properties of Unobserved-Components Models

Tables 4 and 5, respectively, present summary statistics for predictions from the models estimated in the time and frequency domains presented in the previous section for the postsample period 1965–1974.[9] Forecasts from the models were added to the fitted trend (see Table 1) to generate forecasts of the actual levels of the variables. These forecasts may thus be compared directly with those presented in Table 13 and 14 of Chapter X for ARIMA models fitted in time and frequency domains respectively. Since the unobserved-components models estimated in the time domain are almost identical with those estimated in the frequency domain, except for the irregular component, we may concentrate on a comparison of Tables 14 of Chapter X and 5 of this chapter.

In nearly every case, the one-step ahead forecasts from the ARIMA models are marginally more highly correlated with the actual series than those from the corresponding unobserved-components model. The exceptions are the price of milk and male unemployment, for which the one-step ahead forecasts are marginally better from the unobserved-components model than from the ARIMA model. The correlations between actual and forecast values tail off with increasing step length, notably less rapidly for the unobserved-components model for hog slaughter, and more rapidly for the price of cows.

A similar pattern may be observed for the root mean-squared error and the mean-absolute error. Differences between the forecasts generated by unobserved-components and ARIMA models, however, emerge in a comparison of the regression slopes: Whereas in the case of ARIMA models the slope of the regression of the actual series on the forecast level is almost always less than one (the exceptions are the price of milk, 18 steps ahead, and male unemployment, 1 step ahead), this is not true for unobserved-components models, for which quite large values of the slope are obtained in a variety of cases. One such, for example, is for the price of heifers, 18 steps ahead, for which a slope to nearly 2 is obtained. These results are in large part responsible for the shift in that part of the Theil coefficient accounted for by differences in covariation to differences in variation. Except for cattle slaughter, the portion due to bias typically remains small.

What may we conclude from these results? Unobserved-components models have considerably more structure than do ARIMA models. Corresponding to the greater structure are a greater variety of uses, which include seasonal adjustment, component extraction, and the representation of reduced forms of multiple time-series models. Unfortunately, unobserved-components models are also a good deal harder to fit. As we have seen, the forecasts generated by unobserved-components models tend to be inferior to those generated by ARIMA models, marginally so by some criteria and more significantly by others. Of course, part of the difficulty may well be that we have forced each series to fit a common unobserved-components model; to the extent this model

---

[9] See our comments in Chapters X and XI regarding Theil's inequality coefficient and its decomposition.

TABLE 4 *Comparison of Actual and Predicted Time Series, 1965–1974 for Unobserved-Components Models Estimated in the Time Domain: Summary Statistics*

Series (1)	Steps ahead forecast (2)	R^2 of regression of actual on predicted (3)	Root of mean-squared error (4)	Mean-absolute error (5)	Mean error (6)	Regression coefficient of actual on predicted (7)	Theil's coefficient (8)	Theil's inequality coefficient and decomposition of error		
								Due to bias (9)	Due to different variation (10)	Due to different covariation (11)
1. Price of steers	1	0.9287	1.831	1.032	0.07392	0.9573	0.02777	0.001631	0.000608	0.9978
	6	0.7601	3.374	2.331	0.7755	0.9875	0.05135	0.05282	0.05416	0.8930
	12	0.6782	4.182	2.787	1.472	1.178	0.06388	0.1238	0.2349	0.6413
	18	0.6024	5.086	3.492	2.118	1.496	0.07784	0.1735	0.4128	0.4137
2. Price of cows	1	0.9726	99.92	66.52	−19.67	0.9794	0.02188	0.03876	0.001670	0.9596
	6	0.3797	515.6	337.9	−105.6	0.6124	0.1094	0.04193	0.000047	0.9580
	12	0.2337	561.4	392.1	−177.2	0.5722	0.1161	0.09960	0.02416	0.8762
	18	0.2241	574.3	482.4	−287.3	0.8903	0.1155	0.2503	0.2110	0.5388
3. Price of heifers	1	0.9212	1.695	0.9819	0.05681	0.9582	0.02745	0.001124	0.000034	0.9988
	6	0.7486	3.044	2.177	0.5455	1.060	0.04942	0.03212	0.1284	0.8395
	12	0.6609	3.845	2.620	0.9677	1.347	0.06253	0.06333	0.3842	0.5525
	18	0.5683	4.701	3.420	1.411	1.832	0.07639	0.09013	0.5740	0.3358
4. Price of milk	1	0.9930	0.1010	0.05756	0.01116	1.008	0.008542	0.01222	0.01845	0.9693
	6	0.8606	0.4446	0.2446	0.08594	1.012	0.03748	0.03736	0.04750	0.9151
	12	0.7557	0.6166	0.3082	0.2167	1.160	0.05198	0.1235	0.2125	0.6640
	18	0.7128	0.7403	0.3971	0.3195	1.475	0.06225	0.1863	0.4119	0.4019

5.	Cattle slaughter	1	0.6963	129.6	100.6	0.1545	0.9136	0.02580	0.000001	0.02421	0.9758
		6	0.5834	146.7	109.3	2.492	0.8052	0.02904	0.000288	0.005848	0.9939
		12	0.5816	149.5	110.5	−6.242	0.7764	0.02940	0.001743	0.000675	0.9976
		18	0.4257	176.3	135.0	−16.60	0.6413	0.03436	0.008866	0.000423	0.9907
6.	Hog slaughter	1	0.7324	422.8	345.6	16.52	0.9262	0.03399	0.001526	0.02119	0.9773
		6	0.5976	528.2	427.6	93.28	0.8872	0.04259	0.03119	0.03891	0.9299
		12	0.4480	611.1	483.4	165.4	0.8246	0.04911	0.07325	0.05742	0.8693
		18	0.4167	638.9	516.8	264.8	0.7640	0.05120	0.1718	0.03198	0.7962
7.	Industrial production	1	0.9880	12.49	9.826	−1.014	0.9843	0.005735	0.006598	0.007950	0.9855
		6	0.9237	30.94	23.84	−5.379	0.9217	0.01407	0.03023	0.02132	0.9484
		12	0.8386	43.30	35.76	−9.161	0.8606	0.01949	0.04477	0.02144	0.9338
		18	0.7340	52.63	41.38	−12.57	0.8383	0.02348	0.05702	0.001546	0.9414
8.	Male unemployment	1	0.9168	147.5	75.11	−8.102	1.070	0.04730	0.003015	0.1270	0.8700
		6	0.6301	335.2	248.2	−137.3	1.035	0.1046	0.1678	0.1216	0.7106
		12	0.4473	465.8	386.7	−264.1	1.197	0.1394	0.3214	0.2337	0.4448
		18	0.2437	568.2	481.8	−343.4	0.9737	0.1650	0.3653	0.2039	0.4308

TABLE 5 *Comparison of Actual and Predicted Time Series, 1965–1974 for Unobserved-Components Models Estimated in the Frequency Domain: Summary Statistics*

Series (1)	Steps ahead forecast (2)	R^2 of regression of actual on predicted (3)	Root of mean-squared error (4)	Mean-absolute error (5)	Mean error (6)	Regression coefficient of actual on predicted (7)	Theil's coefficient (8)	Theil's inequality coefficient and decomposition of error		
								Due to bias (9)	Due to different variation (10)	Due to different covariation (11)
1. Price of steers	1	0.9291	1.822	1.032	0.0778	0.9602	0.02764	0.001822	0.000203	0.9980
	6	0.7643	3.349	2.313	0.7918	1.006	0.05099	0.0589	0.06857	0.8755
	12	0.6832	4.191	2.778	1.487	1.213	0.06405	0.1260	0.2625	0.6115
	18	0.6097	5.109	3.519	2.124	1.559	0.07823	0.1728	0.4397	0.3875
2. Price of cows	1	0.9516	98.74	64.76	−3.538	0.9778	0.1107	0.001284	0.000115	0.9986
	6	0.5740	297.3	199.4	−22.95	0.8379	0.3511	0.00596	0.02041	0.9736
	12	0.1529	440.8	290.9	−5.507	0.5066	0.5577	0.000156	0.05245	0.9474
	18	0.0191	466.2	327.0	30.47	0.3181	0.7158	0.004273	0.2978	0.6979
3. Price of heifers	1	0.9252	1.644	0.9703	0.07458	0.9699	0.02664	0.002058	0.000898	0.9970
	6	0.7629	2.984	2.110	0.5737	1.093	0.04848	0.03696	0.1598	0.8033
	12	0.6732	3.820	2.591	0.9951	1.371	0.06216	0.06785	0.3996	0.5326
	18	0.5878	4.698	3.452	1.454	1.905	0.07641	0.09582	0.5926	0.3116
4. Price of milk	1	0.9932	0.1334	0.1070	−0.09003	1.004	0.01119	0.4556	0.004001	0.5404
	6	0.8632	0.4339	0.2541	−0.00628	1.039	0.03631	0.000209	0.08135	0.9184
	12	0.7614	0.5910	0.3151	0.1247	1.196	0.04946	0.04450	0.2699	0.6856
	18	0.7318	0.7120	0.3896	0.2275	1.588	0.05943	0.1021	0.5185	0.3793

5.	Cattle slaughter	1	0.6786	143.0	109.3	45.28	0.8587	0.02873	0.1003	0.004385	0.8954
		6	0.4705	262.6	218.4	181.9	0.5930	0.05382	0.4798	0.01703	0.5032
		12	0.4477	427.9	370.7	350.5	0.4431	0.09020	0.6710	0.06798	0.2610
		18	0.2817	692.8	599.4	595.3	0.2652	0.1521	0.7385	0.09105	0.1705
6.	Hog slaughter	1	0.7218	429.6	353.9	18.60	0.9424	0.03454	0.001874	0.03449	0.9636
		6	0.5927	527.1	421.2	96.86	0.9467	0.04253	0.03378	0.08239	0.8838
		12	0.4532	602.5	471.9	164.9	0.8800	0.04842	0.07489	0.09198	0.8331
		18	0.4187	627.3	497.3	264.2	0.8398	0.05029	0.1774	0.07261	0.7500
7.	Industrial production	1	0.9857	13.56	10.88	0.02795	0.9843	0.00623	0.00000	0.005183	0.9948
		6	0.9210	31.25	25.96	3.777	0.9200	0.01427	0.01461	0.02139	0.9640
		12	0.8394	43.08	37.49	8.449	0.8603	0.01954	0.03846	0.02222	0.9393
		18	0.7343	52.64	45.37	12.56	0.8371	0.02375	0.05697	0.001795	0.9412
8.	Male unemployment	1	0.9189	147.6	74.33	5.201	1.090	0.04755	0.001241	0.1658	0.8330
		6	0.6734	306.2	227.3	−45.16	1.305	0.09878	0.02176	0.3712	0.6070
		12	0.4791	394.6	326.5	−85.69	1.463	0.1249	0.04717	0.4650	0.4879
		18	0.2763	462.9	378.9	−103.4	1.465	0.1449	0.04995	0.5196	0.4304

departs significantly from an appropriate one, we have "stacked the deck," so to speak, against unobserved-components models. Nonetheless, at least on the basis of the evidence presented in this chapter, it is safe to say that if one is interested only in prediction, ARIMA models offer the cheapest and most reliable means to that end. On the other hand, to the extent that structure is meaningful or important, there is no substitute for unobserved-components or for multiple time-series models, which allow an expression of that structure in a manner in which ARIMA models do not. Of course, the structure imposed must be reasonably correct and appropriate.

Chapter XIII
APPLICATION TO THE FORMULATION OF DISTRIBUTED-LAG MODELS

1. Introduction

Since the invention of the distributed lag by Irving Fisher early in this century, the concept has been used in a great variety of contexts. Fisher himself used a distributed lag in his investigation of the relations among money, prices, and interest rates (Fisher, 1925, 1930). A complete survey of the literature on distributed lags up to about 1958 is contained in Nerlove (1958a); subsequent surveys include Griliches (1967) and Nerlove (1972a). Since the publication of Koyck's book (1954), there has been a great revival of interest in distributed lags, methods of estimating relationships containing them, and their application in a considerable variety of empirical contexts.

The extent and variety of topics to which distributed-lag analysis has been applied in empirical economics is astounding, but what is more remarkable is the virtual lack of theoretical justification for the lag structures superimposed on basically static models. This extraordinary neglect of the dynamic underpinning of the models actually fitted to the data is what Griliches (1967, p. 42) has called "theoretical ad-hockery."

Perhaps the most important application of distributed-lag analysis has been to the study of investment: Koyck's pioneering work was on this topic; Eisner (1960, 1967), Diamond (1962), de Leeuw (1962), Greenberg (1964), Griliches and Wallace (1965), and Almon (1965) all made important contributions, but the most extensive, sophisticated, and elaborate studies have been those of Jorgenson and his co-workers (Jorgenson, 1963, 1965, 1967b; Jorgenson and Siebert, 1968a,b; Jorgenson and Stephenson, 1967a,b, 1969; Hall and Jorgenson, 1967, 1969).

A wide variety of economic models include as explanatory variables either expectational variables or variables representing the result of some decision-making process. The first category includes both expectations about the future values of variables, e.g., next period's sales, the level of unemployment two quarters ahead, etc., and other subjective variables such as permanent income or the "normal" level of prices and interest rates. Examples of the second type are "desired" capital stock, planned production or inventory accumulation, and so on.

Distributed-lag models based on *expectation formation* have perhaps a longer history than any. Cagan's (1956) and Nerlove's (1956, 1958b) uses of the adaptive expectations model to justify a lag distribution with geometrically declining weights are more or less ad hoc. In 1960, however, Muth (1960) attempted to put the adaptive expectations model on a sounder footing. He showed that for a certain kind of nonstationary process, the simple adaptive expectations model used by Cagan and Nerlove in fact yields the conditional expectation of *all* future values of the variable being forecast. Later Muth (1961) elaborated this idea in a more general theory of expectation formulation, the so-called *rational* expectations hypothesis. Rational expectations or forecasts are simply the conditional expectations of the variable being forecast, based on all observations on it and related variables up to the time of the forecast. They assume a knowledge of the structure generating the data observed. In very simple models, rational expectations can be generated analytically even when the variables being forecast are endogenous to the model; the analytical difficulties encountered, however, increase rapidly with increasing complexity of the model unless the variables forecast are exogenous.

In "Distributed Lags and Unobserved Components in Economic Time Series," Nerlove (1967) shows that Muth's formulation may be generalized. As long as the variables forecast are treated as exogenous in the behavior relationship studied, and if we assume that those economic agents whose behavior we are observing have knowledge of the underlying structure generating the time series to which they react, all manner of distributed-lag relations may be developed. For stationary processes, minimum mean-square-error forecasts and conditional expectations are equivalent. That part of the lag structure arising from expectation formation may be estimated independently of the behavior studied from observations on the variables that are assumed to be forecast. Additional generalization results in what are frequently very difficult and intractable estimation problems. However, the question of how seasonal time series should be handled is easily answered in this context. Generalization for certain types of nonstationarity is also possible. Of course, there is a price that is paid for such substantial benefits; it is the very strong assumption that the economic agents whose behavior we are attempting to describe are fully aware of the stochastic structure generating the time series to which they themselves respond and that, at least to a first approximation, they respond to conditional expectations of the variables rather than to higher moments.

In this chapter we show how time series analysis can be used to generate expectation models similar to those suggested by Muth (1961).[1]

The other common way of generating lag distributions is through the introduction of *adjustment costs*. Search costs and transactions costs are, in one sense, special cases of a general adjustment-cost approach, but both search- and transactions-cost models are characterized by increasing returns to scale, and therefore lead to models with "bang-bang solutions" at the micro level. [See Nerlove (1972b, p. 229), for an elaboration of this point.] Adjustment-cost models with decreasing returns to scale of transaction or increasing costs, lead generally, on the other hand, to smooth forms of behavior at the micro level. Because such models are characteristic of recent theoretical work on investment, we discuss them here in that context and bring out the potential fertility of a marriage between the expectation-formation and adjustment-cost approaches. Our discussion shows that excessive preoccupation with the static concept of long-run equilibrium has retarded the development of econometrically relevant dynamic microeconomic theory. This is not to say that comparative statics has no place in economic theory, but merely that it is not a useful approach when one is explicitly concerned with the dynamics of behavior.[2]

Without strong theoretical justification for a particular form of lag distribution, and perhaps even a strong prior belief about the quantitative properties of that distribution and the factors on which those properties depend, it is generally impossible to isolate the lag distribution in any very definitive way from the sort of data generally available. It is this lack of a well-defined implication of the data that accounts for the sensitivity of the estimates to changes in the sample period and various assumptions concerning the absence or presence of serial correlation among the disturbances of the relationships to be estimated that has been found in numerous empirical investigations. The issue is whether we can in fact obtain a better and truly dynamic theory that will determine the form and perhaps even some parameters of the lag distributions encountered in empirical contexts. It is certainly not possible to resolve this deep and difficult issue here, but we should like to indicate a few of the directions in which such theoretical approaches to the problem of lags in economic behavior might be developed.

Since data on expectations or specific decisions (desired stock of capital) are frequently unavailable, these models are often made empirically testable by specifying the way in which the expectational or choice variables are related to observable quantities. As is well known, this specification often leads to a

[1] Wallis (1977b) is highly relevant to this discussion. Unfortunately, his paper arrived too late to be taken into account here.

[2] In two papers Mundlak (1966, 1967) suggests that dynamic theory should be formulated in a manner that takes explicit account of the restrictions of static theory. Unfortunately, as Treadway has shown in several recent unpublished papers, the propositions of traditional comparative statics do not always hold in a dynamic context.

distributed-lag model such as the familiar adaptive-expectations model or the stock adjustment model. In this chapter we consider models of the form

$$y_t = a + bx_t^* + u_t, \tag{1}$$

where x_t^* is one of the types of variables mentioned above. We show that in a large variety of cases (1) reduces to a distributed-lag model in which the lag distribution is a rational distributed lag (Jorgenson, 1966).

In this case, the model may be written

$$y_t = a + b[N(U)/D(U)]x_t + u_t \tag{2}$$

where $N(\ )$ and $D(\ )$ are polynomials in the lag operator, and x_t is an exogenous variable. Specifically, it is shown that rational distributed lags arise when the exogenous variable (or its pth difference) has a mixed autoregressive moving-average representation and x_t^* is chosen to minimize the expected value of a quadratic objective function. For example, x_t^* could be the least-squares forecast of x_t made at time $t - v$, i.e., $x_t^* = \hat{x}_{t,t-v}$. It is also shown that the orders of the polynomials in the lag operator depend in a simple way upon the structure of the exogenous variable and upon the nature of the optimization problem. The results are illustrated with a number of examples, and their implications for estimation are discussed.

2.   Prediction and Expectation-Formation Models

That individuals react to current values of variables and to their anticipated future values is well established in economic theory. How anticipations are formed is still a matter of debate. It is unlikely that there is a unique explanatory mechanism. As one important application of time-series analysis, we propose that models of anticipation formation be generated as conditional expectations by time-series analysis techniques.

In this section we describe and discuss the most popular models of expectation formation used in previous economic studies.

In the first three subsections, the cobweb, the extrapolative, and the adaptive theories are analyzed, the relationships among the models discussed, and the implications of each theory compared.

In the fourth subsection, Muth's model of rational expectation formation is discussed (Muth, 1961). An alternative to Muth's theory is suggested in the fifth subsection. We call this alternative the model of "quasi-rational" expectation formation. The theory is shown to have wider applicability in empirical work than Muth's theory because of its greater simplicity. We call the theory one of "quasi-rational" expectation formation because, although it follows Muth's rational theory, in actual estimation certain restrictions implied by "fully rational" expectation formation are ignored. Estimation of quasi-rational expectations is possible by time-series-analytic techniques, such as those discussed in Chapters VI and VII.

The Cobweb Theory

The "cobweb" theory was developed to explain possible dynamic relationships in economics, although it is in fact a simple adaptation of existing static theory. Studies of farmers' response to prices gave the theory an empirical flavor, opening a new avenue in economics (e.g., Bean, 1929).

A good historical background and a summary of the cobweb theory can be found in Ezekiel's classic paper "The Cobweb Theorem" (Ezekiel, 1938). The theory, as pointed out by Ezekiel, can be applied only if three conditions are met:

(a) production is determined by producers' response to price under conditions of pure competition;

(b) the time needed for production requires at least one full period before production can be changed;

(c) price is set by the supply available (Ezekiel, 1938, p. 274).

The basic idea of the cobweb theory is that the supply of a product (generally an agricultural product) is a function of its past price, while the demand of this same good is a function of current price. Since production decisions must be made in advance (the period of production is at least one period), these decisions must be based on anticipated prices. The cobweb theorem postulates that these anticipations are simply current prices at the time of the production decisions. In the analysis of the stability of the system, there are three possible outcomes according to the elasticities of demand and supply:

(a) continuous cyclic fluctuations when elasticity of demand is equal to elasticity of supply;

(b) divergent explosive fluctuations when elasticity of demand is smaller than the elasticity of supply;

(c) convergent damped fluctuations when the elasticity of demand is greater than the elasticity of supply (Ezekiel, 1938, p. 257).

Numerous qualifications were made to adapt the cobweb theory in ways more compatible with observed price and quantity fluctuations (Cochrane, 1947). Despite such efforts, the poor theoretical and empirical support of the theory and its extraneous implications have been frequently used as arguments against it. Among the early studies, those done by Coase and Fowler (1937) and by Buchanan (1939) are the most relevant. Coase and Fowler show that the cobweb model implies a shorter price cycle than the one observed in the pig market for Great Britain. This observation is confirmed by later empirical studies (Lorie, 1947). Buchanan concludes that the cobweb theory is valid only under very special circumstances because, in general, it implies that producers suffer constant losses and that they never learn from experience (Buchanan, 1939, p. 81). Alternatives to the cobweb theory are discussed below.

It is interesting to note that when the cobweb theory was formulated, much work had been done on forecasting economic variables (Ezekiel, 1927; Moore,

1917; Smith, 1925). Although this work was relatively sophisticated, the model of expectation formation incorporated in the cobweb theory was always the naive model that the expected price in period $t - 1$ for period t, P_t^*, is given by the observed price at period $t - 1$, P_{t-1}, i.e., $P_t^* = P_{t-1}$.

Extrapolative Expectations

To assume expected prices in future periods are all equal to the observed price in period $t - 1$ is not a very plausible hypothesis unless prices are a random walk so the information contained in other past prices is nil.

In a classic paper, Metzler (1941) presented an alternative to the naive cobweb expectation model, defining what he called the "coefficient of expectation"; the model was later used by Goodwin (1947). This model of expectation generation was subsequently analyzed by Enthoven and Arrow (1956). Under the extrapolative expectation theory, the expected price is defined as

$$P_t^* = P_{t-1} + \eta(P_{t-1} - P_{t-2}), \tag{1}$$

where P_t^* is the expected price for period t at period $t - 1$, P_{t-1} the observed price in period $t - 1$, P_{t-2} the observed price in period $t - 2$, and η Metzler's coefficient of expectation.

The purpose of the extrapolative expectation model is to modify the cobweb theory to take into account the most recent trend in prices: "It is natural to object that expectations of future sales may depend not only upon the past level of sales, but also upon the direction of change of such sales" (Metzler, 1941, p. 119).

An alternative approach was given by Hicks in his *Value and Capital* (1939). Metzler compares his coefficient of expectations to Hicks' elasticity of expectations and concludes that one plus his coefficient of expectations was exactly Hicks' elasticity (Metzler, 1941, footnote 13, pp. 119–120).

As pointed out by Arrow and Nerlove (1958), the extrapolative property of this expectation formation model holds only if $\eta \geq 0$ in (1). If $\eta = 0$, the model becomes the traditional cobweb model and expectations are said to be static; if $\eta > 0$, the expected price will be a weighted average of the past two prices with weights $(1 + \eta)$ and $-\eta$ for P_{t-1} and P_{t-2}. Enthoven and Arrow (1956) show that, under certain circumstances, a stable dynamic model can incorporate the extrapolative expectation model and remain stable.

The simplicity of the extrapolative expectations model, its weak theoretical appeal in terms of its relation to Hicks' elasticity of expectations, and its compatibility with a stable dynamic model, as well as its incorporation of the cobweb theory as a special case, made the model popular for a time.

Adaptive Expectations

Based on Hicks' definition of elasticity of expectations, the adaptive expectations model first appears in Cagan (1956). However, the history of the idea is unclear: A. W. Phillips may have suggested the idea to M. Friedman about 1950.

Under the adaptive expectation hypothesis, the individuals are assumed to revise their expectations according to their most recent experience:

$$P_t^* - P_{t-1}^* = \gamma(P_{t-1} - P_{t-1}^*) \qquad \text{for } |\gamma| < 1, \tag{2}$$

where P_t^* is the expected price for period t at period $t - 1$, P_{t-1}^* the expected price for period $t - 1$ at period $t - 2$, P_{t-1} the observed price in period $t - 1$, and γ the coefficient of expectation.

If the above prices are the logarithms of the absolute levels of actual prices, γ is simply Hicks' elasticity of expectation. Note that if $\gamma = 1$, (2) reduces to $P_t^* = P_{t-1}$, so that the simple cobweb model is a special case.

Expansion of (2) yields a more useful expression for P_t^*. Collecting terms in P^* on the left-hand side,

$$P_t^* - (1 - \gamma)P_{t-1}^* = \gamma P_{t-1}. \tag{3}$$

Replacing $(1 - \gamma)$ by β and introducing the lag operator U, such that $U^j x_t = x_{t-j}$, we obtain

$$(1 - \beta U)P_t^* = (1 - \beta)P_{t-1}, \tag{4}$$

so that

$$P_t^* = [(1 - \beta)/(1 - \beta U)]P_{t-1}.$$

Provided $|\beta| < 1$, we can expand $1/(1 - \beta U)$ as $1 + \beta U + \beta^2 U^2 + \beta^3 U^3 + \cdots$ and thus write[3]

$$P_t^* = (1 - \beta) \sum_{k=0}^{\infty} \beta^k P_{t-1-k}. \tag{5}$$

Under the adaptive expectation hypothesis, the expected price may be expressed by an infinite weighted average of past realized prices with weights that decline geometrically with the lag.

Using the adaptive expectations model, Nerlove (1958b, pp. 46–59) develops the idea of an expected normal price. Since the model predicts just one price, it may be convenient for some purposes, as pointed out by Arrow and Nerlove (1958), to consider this price as an average of all future prices, i.e., an expected "normal" price. Accordingly, this notion of expected normal price may have been in Hicks' mind when he defined the elasticity of expectations. On this interpretation, Arrow and Nerlove (1958) prove that, provided the conditions for ordinary stability are met, a system of multiple markets has dynamic stability if anticipations are generated by the adaptive theory.

Adaptive expectations have been popular for their simplicity since maximum-likelihood estimates for β can be easily obtained and because such models appear to work well in a number of empirical studies.

---

[3] If $|\beta| < 1$, the roots of $(1 - \beta z) = 0$ are outside the unit circle. Since $|\gamma| < 1$, β can vary only in $[0, 1)$ for the infinite moving-average representation to be possible.

Several unsolved problems, however, make the concept of expected normal price questionable. First, there is no real theoretical justification for the model, although it is related to Hicks' definition of elasticity of expectations. From an economic viewpoint, there is no more justification than for the extrapolative model. Second, there are at least two technical problems in the use of the model. One is an identification problem. As one can see from (5), expected normal price can be represented by a distributed lag of past prices, with weights declining geometrically; hence, when the expected normal price is introduced in a supply function, the new form of this function will incorporate a distributed lag in prices. This final form can be obtained just as well by a different model that does not incorporate expected normal price but instead incorporates a distributed-lag model arising from lagged adjustment of production over time (Goodwin, 1947; Koyck, 1954). A second technical problem is that the estimated values of β or γ may be particularly sensitive to omission of relevant variables in the fitted functions, as noted by Brandow (1958) and by Nerlove (1958c). Much of the criticism of the adaptive expectations theory has to do with its implication of a geometrically decaying lag structure. There is no economic explanation for the lag structure implied by the adaptive expectations theory other than the form of the expectation model. If, in fact, there is a lag in response to price changes in the formation of expectations about future prices, this suggests a weight structure in which the weights increase at first and after some point decrease (Solow, 1960). If the weights are transformed in such way that they sum up to one, we can associate a distribution function to any system of weights in which the weights correspond to probabilities, provided that all the weights are nonnegative. In this way, Solow (1960) obtains a more general weighting system by assuming a Pascal distribution. The Pascal system can incorporate an initial lag with an increasing and then decreasing weight structure, and can be interpreted in terms of a cascaded series of adaptive lags.

The adaptive model has been widely used, despite its limitations, for the following reasons:

(a)   models including normal prices perform better when applied to empirical data than those without such distributed lags or with other substitutes;

(b)   adaptive expectations are compatible with dynamic stability under nonrestrictive assumptions;

(c)   there appears to have been no better alternative for generating expectations until Muth (1961) suggested rational expectations;

(d)   there is some empirical evidence supporting the adaptive expectation model: "the respondents tended to overestimate sales for periods in which sales actually fell and to underestimate them for periods in which sales rose" (Modigliani and Sauerlender, 1955). We should note, however, that the Modigliani–Sauerlender findings are compatible with other expectation formation models.

Muth's Rational Expectations

As indicated, the adaptive and extrapolative expectations models lack theoretical justification. In his paper "Rational Expectations and the Theory of Price Movements," Muth (1961) develops an expectations model that eliminates the theoretical weakness common to previous theories of expectation formation.

Muth's theory is based on three hypotheses about individual behavior: "(1) Information is scarce, and the economic system generally does not waste it. (2) The way expectations are formed depends specifically on the structure of the relevant system describing the economy. (3) A 'public prediction,' in the sense of Grunberg and Modigliani . . . , will have no substantial effect on the operation of the economic system (unless it is based on inside information)" (Muth, 1961, p. 316).

The theory implies that economic behavior underlies the formation of expectations. Expectations are based on information, assumed implicitly to be costless, and generated according to perceptible forces affecting the economic activity to be investigated. It is not difficult, however, to extend the rational expectations theory to incorporate the cost of generating predictions.

If a producer operating under free competition has some idea of market conditions, he will use the information available to him about demand and supply conditions in generating his expectations about the relevant variables for decision purposes. This theory agrees with the evidence presented by Heady and Kaldor (1954) in their study of farmers' price expectations:

> For their 1948 and 1949 forecasts, the majority was not using simple mechanical models such as the projection of the current price or recent price trend into next year but was attempting to analyze and predict the more complex price-making forces. A rather common procedure appeared to start the process of devising expected prices from current prices. The current price then was adjusted for the expected effects of important supply-and-demand forces. Where farmers possessed little information about these forces, there was a tendency to project either the current price or the recent price trend.   (Heady and Kaldor, 1954, p. 35)

Since future prices are stochastic variables, and an economic model can be represented in a great many possible ways, Muth introduces three simplifying assumptions: "(1) The random disturbances are normal. (2) Certainty equivalents exist for the variable to be predicted. (3) The equations of the system, including the expectation formulas are linear." Any one of the above assumptions implies the other two (Muth, 1961, p. 317).

Under these conditions, the rational expectations hypothesis implies that a new linear equation should be added to the system in order to define the process of anticipation formation. Muth suggested that the anticipated price for period $t + 1$ at period t must be equal to the expected value (in a statistical sense) of the market equilibrium price for period $t + 1$, conditional on information available up to period t:

$$P^*_{t+1} = E_t\{P_{t+1}\}.$$

That is, expectations are unbiased and the expected price is treated as endogenous to the system. Evidence presented by Heady and Kaldor (1954, p. 85) lends plausibility to this hypothesis: "The idea of a distribution of possible prices seemed to be crudely visualized by farmers. Most of them used the concept of a distribution of distributions."

Consider a simple example given by Muth (1961, p. 317):

$$
\begin{aligned}
C_t &= -bP_t & \text{(demand)}, \\
Q_t &= cP_t^* + u_t & \text{(supply)}, \\
Q_t &= C_t & \text{(market equilibrium)}, \\
P_t^* &= E_{t-1}(P_t) & \text{(expectation function)}.
\end{aligned}
\tag{6}
$$

It is also assumed that

$$
u_t = \sum_{k=0}^{\infty} w_k \epsilon_{t-k}, \qquad E(\epsilon_k \epsilon_j) = \begin{cases} \sigma^2 & \text{if} \quad k = j, \\ 0 & \text{if} \quad k \neq j. \end{cases}
\tag{7}
$$

All the variables are taken as deviations from equilibrium values:

C_t = quantity demanded in period t,

Q_t = quantity supplied in period t,

P_t = market price in period t,

P_t^* = expected price for period t in period $t - 1$.

In this model there are four endogenous variables: C_t, Q_t, P_t, and P_t^*. Considering all w_k in (7) equal to one and solving the system for P_t^*, we obtain (Muth, 1961, p. 320)

$$
P_t^* = \frac{b}{c} \sum_{j=1}^{\infty} \left(\frac{c}{b+c} \right)^j P_{t-j}.
\tag{8}
$$

The expected price can be rewritten as

$$
P_t^* = \frac{b}{c} \sum_{j=1}^{\infty} \left(\frac{1}{1 + (b/c)} \right)^j P_{t-j}.
\tag{9}
$$

Because the model (6) involves only one random variable u_t, the parameter c can be estimated by generalized least squares. When the w_k in (7) are all equal to one, this amounts to ordinary least squares on the first differences of Q_t and P_t^*. Since P_t^* is the same as the expected price generated by an adaptive expectations model, c can be estimated by an iterative maximum-likelihood method; therefore b and c can be identified. Although the same adaptive expectation formation is implied by this model, the interpretation is quite different. If we compare (5) with (9), we can see that in the second expression, the coefficient of expectations is a function of the parameters b and c. On the other hand, the adaptive expectations model arbitrarily defines a coefficient of expectations; whereas, the rational expectation approach, under the assumption of the unbiasedness of the expectations, leads to a similar formulation in which the coefficient of expectations is a function of parameters from the structural form of the model considered (6). See Nerlove (1961) for an explicit relationship between the expectation coefficient and the structural parameters in a more general case.

How much better is the rational expectations theory compared to any other theory when applied to an economic model? Is it true that rational expectations are always better?[4]

From the economic point of view, rational expectations are more consistent with the underlying structure of economic behavior considered in the model studied; whereas alternative models of expectations (cobweb, extrapolative, and adaptive) are not necessarily compatible with the economic behavior implied by the underlying economic structure. From the technical viewpoint, rational expectations are more difficult to estimate than other alternatives. To obtain rational expectations in our model, it must be solved for the expected values of the uncertain variables. Although this solution is linear in the exogenous variables, the coefficients are combinations of the structural parameters that are generally not linear. What makes rational expectations attractive is that economic behavior is directly incorporated in their definition, and it is this, of course, that makes expectations depend on the parameters of the model itself. Provided the model is complete, we can always derive the relationship between expected variables and structural parameters, although, if the model is not identified, we may not be able to obtain estimates for the structural parameters. Such identification problems thus present a difficulty in the use of rational expectations. Even in unidentified cases, rational expectations do yield the proper forms of the relationships of the expected variables to the exogenous variables. If the structural parameters of the model are assumed not to change, there is no loss of generality in using the reduced-form version of the rational expectations when the model is not identified—a standard result of econometric theory. In this case, the relation between the expected variable and other exogenous variables can be inferred. If some structural parameters change in values, however, empirical inferences cannot be made in the unidentified case.

Another source of possible difficulty is the evidence of serial correlation in the structural disturbances. Despite the fact that (6) is a very simple model, imposing the simple autocorrelation structure of the u_i's as we did in (7) was not enough to simplify estimation. Considering $w_j = 1$ for all j makes the estimation and identification of the parameters possible by a simple method. Other hypotheses about the autocorrelation function of the structural residuals may render the identification of the structural parameters impossible or complicate estimation a great deal. Moreover, any such assumption will generally be quite arbitrary.

The rational expectation formation model is theoretically satisfactory but presents some problems in use. If the model considered is linear and complete,

---

[4] If forecast efficiency is the criterion, the answer is yes; see Wallis (1977b, Section 2.1).

the explicit form of the anticipated variables as functions of the exogenous variables may be obtained. The anticipated series may then be obtained by first constructing the conditional expectations for the exogenous variables and then substituting these expected values of the exogenous variables in the expression derived from the solution of the model for the anticipated endogenous variables. Introducing these anticipated values in the model, the remaining relationships implied by the model can then be estimated.[5] The expected values of the exogenous variables must also be unbiased predictions, just as we assume to be the case for predictions of the endogenous variables.

Essentially, the rational expectation hypothesis defines a function that specifies the anticipation as an integral part of the economic model considered. This is represented in (6) by the expectation function

$$P_t^* = E_{t-1}(P_t).$$

As the Modigliani and Sauerlender study suggests, it is possible that individuals have biased expectations about future values of variables. This possibility can be incorporated in the rational expectation framework by the introduction of a specific expectation function that incorporates such a bias. Biased expectation functions can persist under the assumption of rationality, if the cost of generating expectations is explicitly considered (Pashigian, 1970).

Quasi-Rational Expectations

In this subsection we present a method for generating anticipations based on time-series analysis as developed by Box and Jenkins. These anticipations have most of the properties of the rational expectations and are easier to implement empirically. All hypotheses and assumptions made by Muth are retained. To make the procedure more easily understood, we use a specific model to explain how the expectations are generated.

It is well known that in some cases, least-squares forecasts lead to distributed-lag models. For example, consider the following time series model with which we dealt as Example D in Chapter V (V.3.25):

$$x_t - \alpha x_{t-1} = \epsilon_t - \beta \epsilon_{t-1} \qquad \text{or} \qquad x_t = [(1 - \beta U)/(1 - \alpha U)]\epsilon_t, \qquad (10)$$

where $|\alpha|, |\beta| < 1$, and

$$E(\epsilon_t) = 0, \qquad E(\epsilon_t \epsilon_{t'}) = \begin{cases} \sigma^2, & t = t', \\ 0, & \text{otherwise.} \end{cases}$$

The least-squares forecast of x_{t+1} at time t is given by

$$\hat{x}_{t+1,t} = \gamma(U)x_t, \qquad \text{where} \quad \gamma(z) = \frac{1 - \alpha z}{1 - \beta z}\left[\frac{1 - \beta z}{(1 - \alpha z)z}\right]_+. \qquad (11)$$

---

[5] Note that to substitute forecast variables for the anticipated endogenous variables requires knowledge of the structural parameters in general for the whole model (see Wallis, 1977b, Section 3). It is for this reason that we introduce the concept of "quasi-rational" expectations.

[See equation (V.2.6).] Now

$$(1 - \beta z)/(1 - \alpha z) = 1 + z(\alpha - \beta)/(1 - \alpha z);$$

hence,

$$\gamma(z) = (\alpha - \beta)/(1 - \beta z), \tag{12}$$

and

$$\hat{x}_{t+1,t} = (\alpha - \beta) \sum_{j=0}^{\infty} \beta^j x_{t-j}, \tag{13}$$

which is a special case of (V.3.28), for $v = 1$. Lagging (13) once, multiplying by β, and subtracting the result from (13) gives

$$\hat{x}_{t+1,t} - \beta\hat{x}_{t,t-1} = (\alpha - \beta)x_t. \tag{14}$$

As α goes to unity, (14) yields the familiar adaptive expectations model:

$$\hat{x}_{t+1,t} = \beta\hat{x}_{t,t-1} + (1 - \beta)x_t, \tag{15}$$

which we derived as equation (V.3.32).

If in the structural model (1.1) we take x_t^* to be $\hat{x}_{t,t-1}$, then the model can be transformed to

$$y_t = \beta y_{t-1} + a(1 - \beta) + b(1 - \beta)x_{t-1} + u_t - \beta u_{t-1}. \tag{16}$$

Though the forecast of x_t depends upon all the previous values of the series, the fact that the lag distribution γ is rational allows the structural equation to be transformed into one containing only a finite number of variables, which is thus suitable for estimation. Of course, except for a very special case, the disturbances in the equations to be estimated will be serially correlated. While the above example is well known, econometricians do not seem to be aware that it generalizes to the case of any covariance-stationary process of the autoregressive moving-average type.

Theorem. Let $x_t = [N(U)/D(U)]\epsilon_t$ be a covariance-stationary time series, where $N(\ )$ and $D(\ )$ are polynomials of degree n and d, respectively. Then the least-squares forecast of x_{t+v} made at time t is given by

$$\hat{x}_{t+v,t} = [N_v(U)/N(U)]x_t,$$

where $N_v(\ )$ is a polynomial of degree $\max(n - v, d - 1, 0)$.

Proof. The proof is a straightforward extension of Exercise 3.3.5 in Whittle (1963, p. 34).

$$B(z) = \frac{N(z)}{D(z)} = \sum_{j=0}^{v-1} b_j z^j + \frac{z^v N_v(z)}{D(z)}. \tag{17}$$

The least-squares forecast is given by

$$\hat{x}_{t+v,t} = \gamma(U)x_t, \qquad \gamma(z) = [1/B(z)][B(z)/z^v]_+ = N_v(z)/N(z).$$

From (17) we have

$$N_v(z) = z^{-v}N(z) - z^{-v}D(z)\left(\sum_{j=0}^{v-1} b_j z^j\right), \tag{18}$$

so the degree of N_v is $\max(n - v, d - 1, 0)$.   Q.E.D.

If in the structural model (1.1) x_t^* is the least-squares forecast of some covariance-stationary process, the model becomes

$$y_t = a + b\gamma(U)x_t + u_t. \tag{19}$$

Except for the case of finite-order autoregressions, these forecasts in general depend upon the entire past history of the x series. The preceding result shows that, for arbitrary autoregressive moving-average processes, the lag distribution is rational and, therefore, as in the example above, the equation may be transformed into one with a finite number of lagged x's and y's.

Knowing that the lag distribution is rational does not by itself allow one to obtain efficient or even consistent estimates of the structural parameters since the orders of the lag operators will not in general be known a priori. This could be a particularly serious problem if the disturbances in the structural equation are autocorrelated. Note that the assumptions made also provide a source of information about the lag distribution, namely, the nature of the x series. In order to avoid repetition, we defer the discussion of estimation problems to Section 5 of this chapter. Consider the following model borrowed from Pashigian (1970):

$$
\begin{aligned}
q_t^d &= a + bP_t + eI_t + v_t && \text{(demand)} \\
q_t^s &= c + dP_t^* + fC_t + u_t && \text{(supply)} \\
E_{t-1}(P_t) &= P_t^* && \text{(expectation formation)} \\
q_t^d &= q_t^s && \text{(market equilibrium)},
\end{aligned}
\tag{20}
$$

where q_t^d is the quantity demand in period t, q_t^s the quantity supplied in period t, P_t the observed price in period t, P_t^* the expected price for period t in period $t - 1$, I_t the expected income for period t in period $t - 1$, C_t the expected costs for period t in period $t - 1$, and a, b, c, d, e, and f are structural parameters such that $b < 0$, $e > 0$, $d > 0$, $f < 0$, and $a > c$.

In order to proceed as Muth suggested, the system must be solved for P_t^*. Taking conditional expectations as of time $t - 1$, replacing $E_{t-1}(P_t)$ by P_t^*, and equating demand and supply, we obtain P_t^* (see Pashigian, 1970, p. 340):

$$P_t^* = \frac{c - a}{b - d} + \frac{f}{b - d}C_t - \frac{e}{b - d}I_t + \frac{1}{b - d}E_{t-1}(u_t) - \frac{1}{b - d}E_{t-1}(v_t), \tag{21}$$

which is the rational expectation for the market price. To obtain P_t^* explicitly, it is necessary to make special assumptions about the errors u_t and v_t and the stochastic determination of the exogenous variables C_t and I_t. It is assumed that each exogenous variable can be represented by an ARIMA model.[6] Hence

$$\psi_C(U)C_t = \theta_C(U)\epsilon_{Ct}, \qquad \psi_I(U)I_t = \theta_I(U)\epsilon_{It}, \tag{22}$$

where $\psi_C(\ )$, $\psi_I(\ )$, $\theta_C(\ )$, and $\theta_I(\ )$ are polynomials in U, satisfying the stability and invertibility conditions (Box and Jenkins, 1970, pp. 49–51). C_t and I_t may be written

$$C_t = \frac{\theta_C(U)}{\psi_C(U)}\epsilon_{Ct}, \qquad I_t = \frac{\theta_I(U)}{\psi_I(U)}\epsilon_{It}. \tag{23}$$

If we further assume that

$$E(u_t v_t) = E(u_t u_{t'}) = E(v_t v_{t'}) = 0, \qquad t \neq t', \tag{24}$$

substituting (23) in (21), we obtain

$$P_t^* = \left(\frac{c-a}{b-d}\right) + \left(\frac{f}{b-d}\right)\frac{\theta_C(U)}{\psi_C(U)}\epsilon_{Ct} - \left(\frac{e}{b-d}\right)\frac{\theta_I(U)}{\psi_I(U)}\epsilon_{It}. \tag{25}$$

The expression for P_t^* in (25) can be written as

$$P_t^* = \Theta_0 + \frac{\Theta(U)}{\Phi(U)}\xi_t, \tag{26}$$

where[7] $\Theta_0 = \dfrac{c-a}{b-d}$, and

$\dfrac{\Theta(U)}{\Phi(U)}\xi_t$ has the same distribution as

$$\left(\frac{f}{b-d}\right)\frac{\theta_C(U)}{\psi_C(U)}\epsilon_{Ct} - \left(\frac{e}{b-d}\right)\frac{\theta_I(U)}{\psi_I(U)}\epsilon_{It}. \tag{27}$$

A representation for P_t^* as in (26), satisfying (27), is the rational expectation.[8] Estimation of P_t^* is possible by a time-series analysis along the lines suggested by Box and Jenkins (1970) subject, however, to the restrictive condition (27). The problem is to minimize the mean-square error subject to the stability and invertibility restrictions on the ARIMA representation of the exogenous variables and subject to (27). Some of these restrictions may be replaced by a weaker assumption that the mean and the variance–covariance matrices of the two variables should be equal.

---

[6] It is assumed that if the exogenous variables are not stationary, the model is transformed in such a way that these transformed variables are stationary. Transforming to first differences is usually sufficient in dealing with most economic series (Box and Jenkins, 1970, p. 74).

[7] Note that if the exogenous variables can be represented by ARIMA models, the observations made by Pashigian (1970, pp. 342–347) about the relationship between the distributed lag in past prices implied in P_t^* and the hypothesis about the errors in demand and supply are not valid.

[8] For an opposing view, see Nelson (1975). Wallis argues that the model (26)–(27), if used for prediction, will have a larger m.s.e. than the rational expectations model (private correspondence, 1977).

What we propose as quasi-rational expectations is the representation of P_t^* as in (26) but without imposing the constraints implied by (27). Under quasi-rational expectations, we simply replace the expectations about endogenous and exogenous variables in (20) by their corresponding minimum-mean-square-error predictions. These predictions may be generated by applying the estimation procedure suggested in Chapter VII to each one of the variables individually.

If we relax the assumption that the disturbances in the demand and supply are not serially independent, so that

$$u_t = \sum_{j=0}^{\infty} w_j \epsilon_{t-j}, \qquad \{\epsilon_t\} \text{ white noise, } E(\epsilon_t) = 0,$$

$$v_t = \sum_{j=0}^{\infty} r_j \eta_{t-j}, \qquad \{\eta_t\} \text{ white noise, } E(\eta_t) = 0, \tag{28}$$

where $E(\epsilon_t)$ and $E(\eta_t)$ are the unconditional expectations, P_t^* is now defined as[9]

$$P_t^* = \frac{c-a}{b-d} + \frac{f}{b-d} C_t - \frac{e}{b-d} I_t + \frac{1}{b-d} \sum_{j=1}^{\infty} w_j \epsilon_{t-j} - \frac{1}{b-d} \sum_{j=1}^{\infty} r_j \eta_{t-j}. \tag{29}$$

We can define the infinite sums in terms of polynomials in the lag operator:[10]

$$\frac{1}{b-d} \sum_{j=1}^{\infty} w_j \epsilon_{t-j} = \theta_\gamma(U)\gamma_{t-1}, \qquad \frac{1}{b-d} \sum_{j=1}^{\infty} r_j \eta_{t-j} = \theta_\mu(U)\mu_{t-1}. \tag{30}$$

Substituting (23) and (30) into (29), we obtain

$$P_t^* = \left(\frac{c-a}{b-d}\right) + \left(\frac{f}{b-d}\right)\frac{\theta_C(U)}{\psi_C(U)}\epsilon_{Ct} - \left(\frac{e}{b-d}\right)\frac{\theta_I(U)}{\psi_I(U)}\epsilon_{It}$$
$$+ \theta_\gamma(U)\gamma_{t-1} - \theta_\mu(U)\mu_{t-1}. \tag{31}$$

As before, provided the conditions for stationarity and invertibility are satisfied, P_t^* may be rewritten

$$P_t^* = \Theta_0 + [\Theta(U)/\Phi(U)]\xi_t, \tag{32}$$

where $\Theta_0 = \left(\dfrac{c-a}{b-d}\right)$ and

$\dfrac{\Theta(U)}{\Phi(U)}\xi_t$ has the same distribution as

$$\left(\frac{f}{b-d}\right)\frac{\theta_C(U)}{\psi_C(U)}\epsilon_{Ct} - \left(\frac{e}{b-d}\right)\frac{\theta_I(U)}{\psi_I(U)}\epsilon_{It} + \theta_\gamma(U)\gamma_{t-1} - \theta_\mu(U)\mu_{t-1}. \tag{33}$$

---

[9] We might assume that u_t and v_t have an ARIMA representation. Equations (28) are used because this is a frequent assumption and is, moreover, a special kind of ARIMA representation.

[10] Provided the conditions for stationarity are satisfied, we can represent an infinite autoregressive process by a finite moving average (Box and Jenkins, 1970, p. 72).

Retaining all assumptions, except those about the disturbances which can be of almost any kind, and assuming that all exogenous variables can be represented by ARIMA models, the quasi-rational expectation model implies that the necessary anticipated values of both endogenous and exogenous variables may be replaced by their minimum-mean-square-error predictions. The restrictions implied by (27) and (33) are neglected in this formulation.

Quasi-rational expectations cannot be obtained in any very simple way. Time-series analyses are needed for all endogenous variables, the conditional expectations of which enter the model, and therefore all difficulties common to such analyses are encountered. However, in applying quasi-rational expectations the problem of solving the system is avoided; moreover, it is not necessary to predict all exogenous variables that determine the future values of endogenous variables whose expectations enter the model. In addition, it is not necessary to specify the structure of serial dependence in the disturbances; however, quasi-rational expectations can be generated by maximum-likelihood methods for the ARIMA models assumed to apply to each expected variable in the model. As suggested by Nerlove (1972a), and in Chapter VIII, the use of quasi-rational expectations will correspond to the use of unrestricted reduced-form estimation when the model is overidentified: fully rational expectations yield expected prices as functions of the exogenous variables in the system and incorporate the whole economic structure of the model considered. They correspond, therefore, to full-information estimates of the reduced-form equations, incorporating all overidentifying restrictions. Quasi-rational expectations correspond to a reduced form of fully rational expectations that do not specify all of the appropriate restrictions and that therefore may not allow the structural parameters to be identified. If it is assumed that the structural parameters do not change, or if the model considered is underidentified in any case, the gain from using fully rational expectations over quasi-rational expectations is nil. In the first instance, there is no need for knowing the effects of changes in the structural parameters on expectation formation since the structural parameters are assumed to be constants. In the second instance, the structural parameters that enter in the expectation formation cannot be identified under any circumstance; the additional restrictions implied by fully rational expectations cannot matter.

An alternative way to generate quasi-rational expectations is by the unobserved-components theory discussed in Chapter IV above. Indeed, as we can see from (25) and (31), rational expectations imply a representation of expected price as the sum of several unobserved components. The number of components depends on the number of exogenous variables and on the way in which they can be represented. In (25) and (31), for example, they have two and four unobserved components, respectively. The number of components also depends on the assumptions about the disturbances in the model's structural equations. The unobserved-components approach can be implemented empirically as suggested in Chapters VI, VII, and XII. Nonetheless, the ordinary canonical technique is applied to the example presented in Chapter XIV since it is easier to compute the relevant estimates. (Use of the multiple time-series models and forecasts suggested in Chapter XI did not improve the results.) It is interesting to note that all expectation formation models analyzed in this chapter can be seen as particular cases of the version of quasi-rational expectations, where the time-series model is imposed on the data instead of being obtained from its analysis.

3.　Signal Extraction

Consider the case in which the expectational variable is not the forecast value of an observed series, but instead is an estimate of an unobserved component of an economic time series. In this case, it is assumed that "the causative variables are divided by economic agents into two or more unobserved components having definite stochastic properties, and that these agents react not to the observed variables but rather to estimates of the current values of the unobserved components" (Nerlove, 1967, p. 180). As with forecasts, we assume that the economic agents react to minimum-mean-square-error estimates.

Chapters IV and V presented several examples in which least-squares extractions of unobserved components led to distributed-lag models. In this section we generalize the previous results to the case of all covariance-stationary processes of the autoregressive moving-average type.

Let

$$x_t = y_t + \eta_t, \qquad y_t = \frac{N(U)}{D(U)} \epsilon_t, \qquad \eta_t = \frac{R(U)}{S(U)} \zeta_t, \tag{1}$$

where $N(\ )$, $D(\ )$, $R(\ )$, and $S(\ )$ are polynomials of degree n, d, r, and s, respectively, and $\{\epsilon_t\}$, $\{\zeta_t\}$ are mutually uncorrelated white noise sequences with variances σ_ϵ^2 and σ_ζ^2, respectively. Further, let $T(\ )$ be a polynomial of degree $\max(n+s, d+r)$, satisfying

$$\sigma^2 T(z)T(z^{-1}) = \sigma_\epsilon^2 N(z)S(z)N(z^{-1})S(z^{-1}) + \sigma_\zeta^2 R(z)R(z^{-1})D(z)D(z^{-1}), \tag{2}$$

with the roots of $T(\ )$ lying outside the unit circle and σ^2 chosen so that $t_0 = 1$.

Theorem.　Let $\hat{y}_{t+v,t}$ be the least-squares estimate of y_{t+v} made at time t. Then

$$\hat{y}_{t+v,t} = \gamma(U)x_t, \qquad \gamma(z) = [S(z)N_v(z)/T(z)],$$

where $N_v(\ )$ is a polynomial of order $\max(n-v, d-1, 0)$.

Proof.　From (1) we have

$$g_{yy}(z) = \sigma_\epsilon^2 \frac{N(z)N(z^{-1})}{D(z)D(z^{-1})}, \qquad \text{and} \qquad g_{xx}(z) = \sigma^2 \frac{T(z)T(z^{-1})}{D(z)S(z)D(z^{-1})S(z^{-1})}.$$

Thus $\gamma(z)$ is given by

$$\gamma(z) = \frac{D(z)S(z)}{\sigma^2 T(z)} \left[\frac{\sigma_\epsilon^2 N(z)N(z^{-1})S(z^{-1})D(z^{-1})}{D(z)D(z^{-1})T(z^{-1})z^v} \right]_+$$

$$= \frac{D(z)S(z)}{\sigma^2 T(z)} \left[\frac{\sigma_\epsilon^2 N(z)N(z^{-1})S(z^{-1})}{T(z^{-1})D(z)z^v} \right]_+ . \tag{3}$$

The expression under the $[\ ]_+$ operator can be evaluated using Whittle's theorem, proved in Appendix D. To see this, note that

$$\left[\frac{\sigma_\epsilon^2 N(z)N(z^{-1})S(z^{-1})}{T(z^{-1})D(z)z^v} \right]_+ = \left[\frac{\sigma_\epsilon^2 N(z)N(z^{-1})S(z^{-1})}{T(z^{-1})z^v} \right]_+ \bigg/ D(z)$$

$$+ \left[\left[\frac{\sigma_\epsilon^2 N(z)N(z^{-1})S(z^{-1})}{T(z^{-1})z^v} \right]_- \bigg/ D(z) \right]_+ .$$

The first term is of the form $A_1(z)/D(z)$, where $A_1(\ )$ is of order $\max(n - v, 0)$. To obtain the second term we may expand $1/D(z)$ by partial fractions and apply Whittle's theorem to each term in the resulting sum. On recombining terms, the second expression is of the form $A_2(z)/D(z)$, where $A_2(\ )$ is of order $d - 1$.   Q.E.D.

Two Examples

Probably the best-known example is the one we presented in Chapter IV, pp. 73–74 and as Example A in Chapter V, pp. 98–100:

$$x_t = y_t + u_t, \qquad y_t = \alpha y_{t-1} + v_t, \qquad |\alpha| < 1, \tag{4}$$

and $\{u_t\}$ and $\{v_t\}$ are mutually uncorrelated white noise sequences. The least-squares estimate of y_t based on current and past observed x_t's is

$$\hat{y}_{t,t} = \left(1 - \frac{\beta}{\alpha}\right) \sum_{j=0}^{\infty} \beta^j x_{t-j}, \tag{5}$$

where[11]

$$\beta = \frac{(1 + \lambda + \alpha^2) - \sqrt{(1 + \lambda + \alpha^2)^2 - 4\alpha^2}}{2\alpha} .$$

For α equal to one, this gives the same relation as the adaptive expectations model and leads to the same estimating equation (2.16) for the structural equation.[12]

---

[11] For details on this example see Chapter IV, pp. 73–74.

[12] Nerlove (1958b) estimated equations of the form (2.16) in which the dependent variable was the acreage that farmers allotted to a given crop and x_t^* was the expected "normal" price of that crop. Note that for those results to be interpreted as an optimal extraction requires the additional assumption that (4) adequately describe the annual agricultural price series.

For the second example, which was presented before as Example B of Chapter V, pp. 100–101, suppose one wishes to predict $x_t = \epsilon_t/(1 - \theta U)(1 - \rho U) + \eta_t$, where the observed series is $x_t = y_t + \eta_t$; $\{\epsilon_t\}$, $\{\eta_t\}$ are mutually uncorrelated white noise sequences. Since

$$x_t = \frac{\epsilon_t + (1 - \theta U)(1 - \rho U)\eta_t}{(1 - \theta U)(1 - \rho U)},$$

we have

$$
\begin{aligned}
g_{xx}(z) &= \frac{\sigma_\epsilon^2 + \sigma_\eta^2(1 - \theta z)(1 - \rho z)(1 - \theta z^{-1})(1 - \rho z^{-1})}{(1 - \theta z)(1 - \rho z)(1 - \theta z^{-1})(1 - \rho z^{-1})} \\
&= \frac{\sigma^2(1 - \alpha z)(1 - \beta z)(1 - \alpha z^{-1})(1 - \beta z^{-1})}{(1 - \theta z)(1 - \rho z)(1 - \theta z^{-1})(1 - \rho z^{-1})},
\end{aligned}
\tag{6}
$$

where α and β are both less than one in absolute value and where σ^2 is defined in such a way that the two expressions on the right-hand side of (6) are equal for all z. Thus the observed series has the second moment properties of a second-order moving-average and autoregressive process. Since the cross-covariance generating function between y_t and x_t is simply the covariance generating function of y_t, we have for v non-negative

$$
\begin{aligned}
\gamma(z) &= \frac{\sigma_\epsilon^2(1 - \theta z)(1 - \rho z)}{\sigma^2(1 - \alpha z)(1 - \beta z)}\left[\frac{1}{(1 - \theta z)(1 - \rho z)(1 - \alpha z^{-1})(1 - \beta z^{-1})z^v}\right]_+ \\
&= \frac{\sigma_\epsilon^2}{\sigma^2}\frac{(1 - \theta z)(1 - \rho z)}{(1 - \alpha z)(1 - \beta z)(\theta - \rho)}\left\{\left[\frac{\theta}{(1 - \theta z)(1 - \alpha z^{-1})(1 - \beta z^{-1})z^v}\right]_+\right. \\
&\quad \left. - \left[\frac{\rho}{(1 - \rho z)(1 - \alpha z^{-1})(1 - \beta z^{-1})z^v}\right]_+\right\} \\
&= \frac{\sigma_\epsilon^2}{\sigma^2}\frac{1}{(1 - \alpha z)(1 - \beta z)(\theta - \rho)}\left\{\frac{(1 - \rho z)\theta^{v+1}}{(1 - \alpha\theta)(1 - \beta\theta)} - \frac{(1 - \theta z)\rho^{v+1}}{(1 - \alpha\rho)(1 - \beta\rho)}\right\}.
\end{aligned}
\tag{7}
$$

From (6)

$$\frac{\sigma_\epsilon^2}{\sigma^2} = (1 - \alpha\theta)(1 - \beta\theta)(1 - \alpha\theta^{-1})(1 - \beta\theta^{-1}) = (1 - \alpha\rho)(1 - \beta\rho)(1 - \alpha\rho^{-1})(1 - \beta\rho^{-1}).$$

$$\tag{8}$$

Thus

$$\gamma(z) = \frac{(1 - \rho z)\theta^{v+1}(1 - \alpha\theta^{-1})(1 - \beta\theta^{-1}) - (1 - \theta z)\rho^{v+1}(1 - \alpha\rho^{-1})(1 - \beta\rho^{-1})}{(1 - \alpha z)(1 - \beta z)(\theta - \rho)}.$$

$$\tag{9}$$

So if x_t^* is the least-squares extraction of y_{t+v}, i.e., $x_t^* = \hat{y}_{t+v,t}$, the estimating equation is

$$y_t = a + \frac{b(c_1 + c_2 U)}{1 - (\alpha + \beta)U + \alpha\beta U^2} x_t + u_t, \tag{10}$$

c_1 and c_2 determined from (9).

4. Distributed Lags in Dynamic Models

In the previous sections we showed that least-squares forecasts or extractions of autoregressive moving-average processes generate distributed lags. Suppose that the decision problem is not forecasting or estimating a noise-corrupted signal, but instead is to optimize an objective function that depends upon the future values of a time series or upon some unobserved component of a time series. It is well known that if the objective function is suitably restricted, the unknown variables may be replaced by their conditional expectations and the solution obtained in terms of the certainty equivalents (Simon, 1956; Theil, 1957; Malinvaud, 1969). Replacing these conditional expectations by the optimum forecasts or extractions will then lead to a distributed-lag model. As before, the order of the lag operators will depend relatively simply upon the characteristics of the process being forecast and upon the nature of the objective function. An empirical example of such a model is given in Chapter XIV, where the U.S. cattle industry is analyzed. While this does provide a considerable generalization of the results of the previous sections, we emphasize at the outset that the approach has some severe limitations. First, it is restricted to problems in which the objective function is quadratic, which rules out many, perhaps most, interesting applications. Second, it requires either that only linear decision rules be allowed, or that the conditional expectations be linear functions of the observed variables. This condition, of course, will not in general be optimal for nonnormal processes.

Consider the following generalization of the prediction problem:

$$\min_{\gamma} E\{([A(U)\gamma(U) + B(U)]x_t)^2\}, \qquad \gamma(z) = \sum_{j=k}^{\infty} \gamma_j z^j, \tag{1}$$

where x_t is a covariance-stationary process.[13]

The value of the objective function is equal to

$$\frac{1}{2\pi i} \oint_{|z|=1} [A(z)\gamma(z) + B(z)][A(z^{-1})\gamma(z^{-1}) + B(z^{-1})]g_{xx}(z)\frac{dz}{z}, \tag{2}$$

---

[13] Adding a deterministic component to x_t does not create any difficulty (see Whittle, 1963, Section 10.6).

where all series expansions are assumed to converge in an annulus containing the unit circle. Differentiating with respect to the coefficients of $\gamma(z)$ gives the first-order conditions:

$$\frac{1}{2\pi i} \oint_{|z|=1} [\{z^j A(z)[A(z^{-1})\gamma\iota. \qquad B(z^{-1})]$$

$$+ z^{-j}A(z^{-1})[A(z)\gamma(z) + B(z)]\} g_{xx}(z)]\frac{dz}{z} = 0, \qquad j = k, k+1, \ldots. \quad (3)$$

From the residue theorem, each of the above integrals is equal to the constant term of the series within the outer square brackets. Thus, taken together, the first-order conditions imply that $A(z^{-1})[A(z)\gamma(z) + B(z)]g_{xx}(z)$ contains only powers of z less than k.

Let $C(z)C(z^{-1})$ be the canonical factorization of $g_{xx}(z)$. Then the first-order conditions imply that $C(z^{-1})A(z^{-1})[A(z)C(z)\gamma(z) + B(z)C(z)]$ contains only terms with negative powers of z and positive powers up to $k - 1$. Since the term outside the bracket contains only nonpositive powers of z, the solution is[14]

$$\gamma(z) = -\frac{z^k}{C(z)A(z)}\left[\frac{B(z)C(z)}{z^k}\right]_+. \quad (4)$$

Similarly, if instead of (1) we wish to minimize the sum of several such terms, e.g., $E\{\sum_{j=1}^J \lambda_j[(A_j(U)\gamma(U) - B_j(U))x_t]^2\}$, the solution is

$$\gamma(z) = -\frac{z^k}{A(z)C(z)}\left[\frac{\sum_{j=1}^J \lambda_j B_j(z)A_j(z^{-1})C(z)}{A(z^{-1})z^k}\right]_+, \quad (5)$$

where $A(z)A(z^{-1}) = \sum_{j=1}^J \lambda_j A_j(z)A_j(z^{-1})$ and $A(z)$ has its roots outside the unit circle.

As an example, consider the case of a firm that produces to stock, i.e., holds inventories.[15] Assume that the firm's costs in period t are given by

$$C_t = \lambda_1(\hat{P}_t - \hat{P}_{t-1})^2 + \lambda_2(\hat{I}_t - a - \alpha\hat{S}_t)^2 + \lambda_3\hat{P}_t + \lambda_4\hat{I}_t, \quad (6)$$

where $\hat{P}_t$ = production in period t, $\hat{S}_t$ = sales in period t, $\hat{I}_t$ = inventories at the end of period t, and $\hat{P}_t = \hat{S}_t + \hat{I}_t - \hat{I}_{t-1}$. We also assume that the firm must choose the level of production for period t before the amount of sales for that period is known. Given the accounting identity between production, sales, and the change in inventories, it suffices to determine either inventory holdings or the rate of production. While formally it makes little difference, it seems more natural to assume that it is the rate of production that is decided upon rather

---

[14] If we take $A(z) = -1$ and $B(z) = 1$, the problem reduces to predicting x_t at time $t - k$. Note that in this case (4) agrees with (V.2.6).

[15] This problem is similar to, but simpler than, those treated by Hay (1969), Childs (1967), Belsley (1969), Holt et al. (1960), and Whittle (1963). It is presented as an example for expository purposes only and is not intended to be very realistic.

than the level of inventories. Thus any discrepancy between expected and actual sales will show up as unplanned inventory accumulation rather than as unanticipated fluctuations in the rate of production.

Let

$$
\begin{aligned}
\hat{S}_t &= \bar{S} + S_t, & E(S_t) &= 0, \\
\hat{I}_t &= \bar{I} + I_t, & E(I_t) &= 0, \\
\hat{P}_t &= \bar{P} + P_t, & E(P_t) &= 0, & \bar{P} &= \bar{S},
\end{aligned} \tag{7}
$$

$$
P_t = \gamma(U)S_t = \sum_{j=k}^{\infty} \gamma_j S_{t-j}, \qquad k \geq 1,
$$

so that the expected costs for period t are given by

$$
E(C_t) = E\{\lambda_1(P_t - P_{t-1})^2 + \lambda_2(I_t - \alpha S_t)^2\} + [\lambda_3\bar{P} + \lambda_4\bar{I} + \lambda_2(\bar{I} - a - \alpha\bar{S})^2]. \tag{8}
$$

If the firm behaves so as to minimize $V = E\{\sum_{v=0}^{\infty} \rho^v C_{t+v}\}$, the problem is

$$
\min_{\{P_{t+v}\}, \bar{I}} E\left\{ \frac{\lambda_1(P_t - P_{t-1})^2 + \lambda_2(I_t - \alpha S_t)^2}{1 - \rho U^{-1}} \right\} + \left\{ \frac{\lambda_3\bar{P} + \lambda_4\bar{I} + \lambda_2(\bar{I} - a - \alpha\bar{S})^2}{1 - \rho} \right\}, \tag{9}
$$

where $P_t = \gamma(U)S_t$. The second term is easily minimized, so we consider only the first term.

Assuming that the current level of inventories is simply the sum of past differences between production and sales (i.e., initial inventories I_0 equals zero), the problem reduces to[16]

$$
\min_{\gamma} E\left\{ \frac{\lambda_1((1-U)\gamma(U)S_t)^2 + \lambda_2\left[\left(\dfrac{\gamma(U)-1}{1-\delta U} - \alpha\right)S_t\right]^2}{1 - \rho U^{-1}} \right\}, \qquad |\delta| < 1.
$$

This problem is clearly of the type just discussed with

$$
A_1(U) = 1 - U, \qquad B_1(U) = 0,
$$

$$
A_2(U) = \frac{1}{1-\delta U}, \qquad B_2(U) = -\frac{1 + \alpha(1 - \delta U)}{1 - \delta U}.
$$

The solution is given by

$$
\gamma(z) = \frac{z(1-\delta z)}{R(z)C(z)}\left[\frac{\lambda_2(1 + \alpha(1 - \delta z))C(z)}{(1 - \delta z)R(z^{-1})z} \right]_+, \tag{10}
$$

where

$$
R(z)R(z^{-1}) = \lambda_1(1-z)(1-\delta z)(1-z^{-1})(1-\delta z^{-1}) + \lambda_2.
$$

[16] For convenience, we have added the constant δ. Once the solution is obtained, we consider the limiting case when δ tends to unity from below.

If the sales series is a mixed autoregressive moving-average process, say, $S_t = (N(U)/D(U))\,\epsilon_t$, where $N(\ )$ and $D(\ )$ are polynomials of orders n and d, respectively, then it is easily seen that

$$\gamma(z) = zP(z)/N(z)R(z), \tag{11}$$

where $P(\ )$ is of order $\max(n,d)$. If in the structural equation (1.1) x_t^* is the planned level of production for time period t, then, as in the previous examples, the estimating equation is a rational lag distribution.[17]

If the firm attempts to minimize V rather than expected cost in period t (or the average cost per period), then because of the form of the objective function, the certainty equivalence principle applies. That is, one may choose future levels of production to minimize V in which all unknown future variables (in this problem the S_{t+j}'s) are replaced by their conditional expectations as of time $t - k$. Thus, assuming normality or alternatively restricting ourselves to linear forecasting rules, the future sales may be replaced by their least squares forecasts and P_{t+j} chosen to minimize

$$\hat{V} = \sum_{v=0}^{\infty} \rho^v [\lambda_1(P_{t+v} - P_{t+v-1})^2 + \lambda_2(I_{t+v} - \alpha \tilde{S}_{t+v,t-k})^2],$$

subject to

$$P_{t+v} = \tilde{S}_{t+v,t-k} + I_{t+v} - I_{t+v-1}.$$

where $\tilde{S}_{t+v,t-k}$ is the predicted value of S_{t+v} at time $t - k$. Note that the solution involves determining a production plan for all future periods, though as more information becomes available and the forecasts for future sales are revised, the production plans for future periods will also be revised. The solution (see Appendix G) will obviously be a distributed lag between production and expected future sales. If these latter variables are expressed as linear combinations of current and past sales, one ends up with a distributed lag between current (and past) production and the current and lagged values of sales. See the empirical example below in Chapter XIV.

In this example, as in the others, the derived distributed-lag model is exact (i.e., does not contain a disturbance term) and thus is not really suitable for estimation purposes. So far we have assumed that the equation to be estimated is obtained by substituting the derived lag distribution into the structural equation (1.1), which does contain an error term. It is tempting to posit a cost minimization model, derive the optimal decision rule, and fit the corresponding distributed-lag model; e.g., a rational lag distribution between production and past sales,[18]

$$P_t = [N(U)/D(U)]S_{t-1} + u_t. \tag{12}$$

---

[17] Other examples are given by Nerlove (1972b).
[18] See, for example, Hay (1969), Childs (1967), and Belsley (1969).

The question we consider now is whether such a procedure can be rationalized. That is, is it possible to introduce an error term into the estimating equation without seriously damaging either the model itself or the interpretation of the empirical results: The answer, which seems to have been first noted by Shiller (1972, pp. 65–85), is that it is possible.

Suppose that we have derived the following model:

$$Y_t = \sum_j a_j \hat{x}_{t+j,t}, \tag{13}$$

where $\hat{x}_{t+j,t}$ is the minimum-mean-square-error forecast of x_{t+j} based upon current and past observations on x. Assume, however, that the true model is of the form

$$Y_t = \sum_j a_j \hat{x}^*_{t+j,t}, \tag{14}$$

where $\hat{x}^*_{t+j,t}$ is the minimum-mean-square-error forecast of x_{t+j} based upon current and past x's *and* other variables. Thus in the previous example the firm may use other information in addition to historical sales figures to forecast future sales. Now

$$Y_t = \sum_j a_j \hat{x}_{t+j,t} + \sum_j a_j (\hat{x}^*_{t+j,t} - \hat{x}_{t+j,t}) = \sum_j a_j \hat{x}_{t+j,t} + \epsilon_t, \tag{15}$$

where ϵ_t has mean zero and is uncorrelated with the current and past values of x (and, therefore, with $\hat{x}_{t+j,t}$). It follows that the parameters of (15) can be consistently estimated by ordinary least squares. Note, however, that it will generally be the case that the distrubances will be serially correlated and will be correlated with the future values of the x's.

As we have pointed out, equation (15) may be converted into a distributed-lag relation between Y_t and current and past x's.

While there are alternative assumptions that result in an error term, they all seem to be unsatisfactory. For instance, one might argue that the model only gives planned production, while actual production differs from planned production due to random accidents—machinery breakdowns, labor disputes, etc. This clearly does not save things, because in this case the firm's problem is to minimize costs, and instead of by (7) production is given by

$$P_t = \gamma(U)S_t + \eta_t, \tag{16}$$

where P_t and S_t are production and sales rates at period t, and η_t is a covariance-stationary process.[19] This is a different problem, and it will have a different solution. The assumption that the otherwise rather sophisticated firm does not know that its production plans are not carried out is far from compelling. Omitted variables, aggregation problems, or measurement errors (except in production only) all do allow for error terms in the equation but

[19] For an example of this kind of problem, see the discussion in Whittle (1963, pp. 119–121).

unfortunately make interpretation of estimated coefficients doubtful (see Grether and Maddala, 1973).

It is apparent that the lag distributions derived using the theory of optimal forecasting or signal extraction depend upon both the nature of the optimization problem *and* the covariance structure of the time series being forecast. This point is illustrated in Fig. 1, which shows the first few terms in the distributed-lag relation between production and sales for two hypothetical firms with identical cost functions and different sales series. As the figure shows, these models do not in general result in lag distributions with nonnegative coefficients, so that mean lags may not be meaningful. One of the lag distributions is quite smooth and damps quickly to zero, while the other is jagged with large fluctuations in the coefficients. Thus estimates based on Almon techniques or prior smoothness restrictions such as discussed by Shiller (1972) and Leamer (1972) may be unreliable and certainly cannot be assumed a priori to be applicable for these kinds of models.

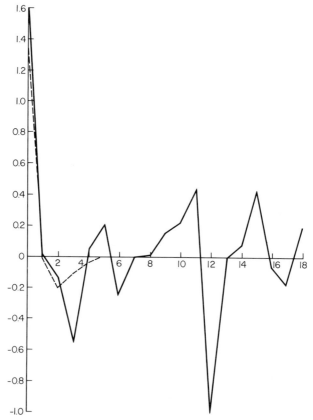

Fig. 1.   Distributed-lag relation between production and sales for two hypothetical firms with identical cost functions but different sales series ($\lambda = 0.3$, $\alpha = 0.3$, $\rho = 1.0$). $---(1 - 0.75 \ U)S_t = \epsilon_t$; $\underline{\hspace{1cm}}(1 - 0.75 \ U)(1 - 0.3 \ U^3)(1 - 0.2 \ U^6)(1 - 0.8 \ U^{12})S_t = \epsilon_t$.

Let us now consider a model of adjustment cost. Neglecting labor and assuming a fixed capital–output ratio and separable quadratic adjustment cost for gross investment, we construct the following discrete time model. Let

$X(t)$ = output at time t,

$K(t)$ = capital stock at time t,

$I(t)$ = gross investment at time t,

$p(t)$ = the price of a unit of output at time t,

$q(t)$ = the price of a unit of capital at time t, and

$\alpha(t)$ = the factor by which the firm discounts future cash flows.

We assume that $p(t)$, $q(t)$, and $\alpha(t)$ are taken as exogenous by the firm, as is its initial capital stock $K(0) = K_0$. For simplicity, we often drop the explicit representation of variables as functions of time; the following, however, is assumed constant over time:

$$\delta = \text{the depreciation rate.}$$

Define $\beta(t) = \alpha(t + 1)/\alpha(t)$ as the *rate* at which the firm discounts; then if $\beta(t)$ is assumed to be a constant, $\beta < 1$ for all t, we have $\alpha(t) = \beta^t$.

Under the assumption of a constant capital–output ratio, output and capital stock are proportional:

$$X = aK, \qquad a > 0. \tag{17}$$

If we assume that capital depreciates at the fixed rate δ, we have

$$K(t) = I(t) + (1 - \delta)K(t - 1). \tag{18}$$

Suppose that adjustment costs are both separable and quadratic, so that in addition to paying a price q per unit of new capital, a premium is also paid which depends on the square of the number of units added. It is immaterial whether these costs are made to depend on net capital formation ΔK or on gross investment I, but the latter is more reasonable. Separability is a more serious assumption, however, for it is most easily justified in terms of a rising supply price of capital to the individual firm, which is not entirely consistent with the assumption of competitive conditions. The cash flow each period of the firm is thus

$$R = pX - qI - (c/2)I^2, \qquad c > 0, \tag{19}$$

where $c/2$ is the additional premium paid for rapid investment.

Assume that the firm maximizes the *conditional expectation* at each point in time of the present value of these cash flows over an infinite horizon; at $t = 0$

$$EV = E\left\{ \sum_{j=0}^{\infty} \beta^j \left[ap(j)K(j) - q(j)I(j) - \frac{c}{2} I(j)^2 \right] \right\}. \tag{20}$$

The exogenous variables of this model enter the maximand in a very special way, namely, *linearly*; moreover I^2, which depends on these prices, does not enter in combination with them. Therefore we can pass the expectation operator inside the summation and replace the stochastic variables $p(j)$ and $q(j)$ by their conditional expectations $\hat{p}(j)$ and $\hat{q}(j)$ at $t = 0$. Provided that $\hat{p}(j)$ and $\hat{q}(j)$ do not take on values which would require the value of gross investment maximizing EV to be negative at any future time, maximizing EV is equivalent to maximizing

$$\hat{V} = \sum_{j=0}^{\infty} \beta^j \left[a\hat{p}(j)K(j) - \hat{q}(j)I(j) - \frac{c}{2}I(j)^2 \right] \tag{21}$$

as if the conditional expectations at $t = 0$ of the future values of output price $\hat{p}(j)$ and the price of capital goods $\hat{q}(j)$ were certain values.[20] Of course, some assumption must be made in order to guarantee that the sum in (21) converges. Essentially this assumption will be equivalent to the *transversality condition* that we find in the infinite-horizon continuous-time case. In this very simple problem, the assumption will be that the conditional expectations of output price do not increase at a geometric rate faster than β^{-j}, so that the distant future becomes negligible as far as the current investment decision is concerned. If $p(t)$ is the realization of a stationary stochastic process or a nonstationary process whose nonstationarity can be removed by differencing, such a transversality condition will be satisfied *a fortiori*.

The condition that the expectations of the distributions of prices be such that the problem of maximizing EV has an interior solution is an extremely important one; if it were not satisfied, it would no longer be possible always to replace the problem of maximizing EV by the problem of maximizing $\hat{V}$; that is, the conditional expectations of prices would no longer be their *certainty equivalents*.

The solution to the maximization of $\hat{V}$ with respect to $I(t)$ for $t = 0, 1, \ldots$ is obtained by replacing $K(t)$ in $\hat{V}$ by its value in terms of $I(t)$ from (18),

$$K(t) = \sum_{j=0}^{t} (1 - \delta)^j I(t - j) + (1 - \delta)^t K_0, \qquad K_0 = (1 - \delta)K(-1), \tag{22}$$

and then maximizing the resulting expression with respect to $I(t)$. This yields

$$I(t) = -\frac{\hat{q}(t)}{c} + \frac{a}{c} \sum_{\tau=t}^{\infty} \beta^{\tau-t}(1 - \delta)^{\tau-t}\hat{p}(\tau). \tag{23}$$

---

[20] That this can be done in this case depends crucially on the linearity of the production function. If K were to be replaced by a fractional power of K, say its square root, it would no longer be possible to demonstrate a first-period certainty equivalent except in some approximate sense such as that discussed by Malinvaud (1969). Asymmetries and irreversibilities introduced by boundary conditions violate even the conditions under which a first-period certainty equivalence can be established approximately.

We can make explicit the distributed lag in the relationship between current investment and past output prices by assuming a particular form for the stochastic process which generates these prices.

For illustrative purposes, suppose that prices are generated by the very simple two-component process discussed in Nerlove (1967):

$$p(t) = \bar{p} + p^*(t) + u(t), \qquad p^*(t) = \gamma p^*(t-1) + v(t), \qquad |\gamma| < 1, \qquad (24)$$

where $\{u(t)\}$ and $\{v(t)\}$ are independent, zero-mean white noise inputs with variance ratio $\lambda = \sigma_v^2/\sigma_u^2$. Of course, this is an extremely simple and unrealistic process, but the model under discussion is also simple and unrealistic; both serve to illustrate general principles of analysis in the combination of adjustment costs and expectations, but we do not maintain that either could serve as an adequate basis for a real econometric investigation. As argued in Nerlove (1967), $\bar{p} + p^*(t)$ may be interpreted as a "permanent" or "long-run normal" price. The generating transform of the weights in the minimum-mean-square-error predictor of $p(t) - \bar{p}$, the deviations of price from its mean, is

$$\theta_\tau(z) = \left(\frac{\gamma - \eta}{\gamma}\right)\gamma^\tau \sum_{j=0}^{\infty} \eta^j z^j, \qquad (25)$$

where

$$\eta = \frac{(1 + \lambda + \gamma^2) - \sqrt{(1 + \lambda + \gamma^2)^2 - 4\gamma^2}}{2\gamma}$$

can be shown to be less than one in absolute value. See Chapter IV, p. 74 and Nerlove (1967, pp. 142–144). The minimum-mean-square-error forecasts of $p(t + \tau) - \bar{p}$ are just the conditional expectations of the price deviations at times $t + \tau$ based on price data up to and including period t.

To obtain the distributed-lag relationship for investment based on the dynamic optimization model with adjustment costs and incorporating conditional price expectations for prices generated by the simple scheme (24), we simply substitute our optimal forecasts of the deviations plus the mean in (23). Note that only the current value of the price of capital goods enters, and its conditional expectation is just equal to its current observed value. The equation that exhibits investment as an explicit distributed-lag function of past prices is a complicated one, despite the great simplicity of the underlying model:

$$I(t) = -\frac{q(t)}{c} + \frac{a}{c}\left\{\left[\frac{1}{1 - \beta(1 - \delta)} - \left(\frac{\gamma - \eta}{\gamma(1 - \eta)}\right)\left(\frac{\gamma^t}{1 - \beta\gamma(1 - \delta)}\right)\right]\bar{p}\right.$$

$$\left. + \frac{\gamma - \eta}{\gamma} \sum_{\tau=t}^{\infty} \sum_{j=0}^{\infty} [\beta(1 - \delta)]^{\tau - t}\gamma^\tau \eta^j p(t - j)\right\}. \qquad (26)$$

Although β and δ are not separately identifiable in (26), one could presumably obtain an outside estimate from the way in which capital stock is constructed or from equation (22). In more complicated models, separate identification of β and δ is possible. If the parameters of that part of the lag distribution resulting from the conditional expectations occuring in the problem are estimated directly from the time series themselves, as Nerlove (1967) suggested, parameters a, c, and $\beta(1 - \delta)$ are overidentified. No stochastic disturbances have been introduced in any of the equations; where and how such disturbances are introduced and what interpretation they are given will make a great deal of difference in the final result and to the appropriate statistical procedure. To deal here with this matter in detail would unfortunately take us far beyond the limited scope of the present investigation; however, we shall turn to some of the intricate estimation problems raised by the approach suggested here in Section 5.

In this section we have considered problems that are generalizations of least-squares forecasting. Analogous generalizations of signal extraction problems are also possible, but since the derivations are quite similar to those above, we do not present them. For example, if the problem is to minimize $E\{[A(U)x_t + B(U)\gamma(U)x_t + D(U)\gamma(U)\epsilon_t]^2\}$, where x_t and ϵ_t are covariance-stationary time series with $E(x_t\epsilon_{t-k}) = 0$ for all k, then the corresponding first-order conditions imply that $\gamma(z)B(z)B(z^{-1})C_x(z)C_x(z^{-1}) + D(z)D(z^{-1})C_\epsilon(z)C_\epsilon(z^{-1}) + A(z)B(z^{-1})C_x(z)C_x(z^{-1})$ contains only powers of z less than k.

5. Estimation

Econometricians are well aware of the difficulties inherent in estimating distributed-lag relations. Insufficient degrees of freedom and the often associated problem of multicollinearity make precise estimation of arbitrary lag distributions an essentially hopeless task. A common response to these problems is to use an approximation that depends upon a relatively small number of parameters, e.g., a rational distributed-lag model. Though this type of approximation reduces the problem to one involving a finite number of parameters, several serious difficulties remain. For one thing, the parameters of the distribution typically appear in a highly nonlinear fashion. Though rational lag distributions may be transformed so that the parameters enter in a more linear way, this transformation will almost surely result in disturbances that are serially correlated. An additional problem is that the orders of the polynomials in the lag operator are often not known a priori. Quite apart from computational difficulties, this latter problem can result in identification problems if the disturbances in the equation to be estimated are themselves autocorrelated.[21]

In this chapter, we have shown that in a variety of situations one can derive lag distributions that are rational. This does not alter the computational problems due to the nonlinearities or serially correlated disturbances, but it

---

[21] For a thorough discussion of other difficulties in approximating infinite-parameter lag distributions, see Sims (1971).

does provide information about the order of the lag operators. In all cases, the order of the lag operators depends upon the covariance structure of the exogenous variables and the particular decision problem, e.g., the forecast period. Since data on the exogenous variable are available, one could determine an appropriate parametric model for this time series using the methods discussed in Chapter VI. If one is willing to assume that the economic agent correctly perceives the structure of the time series, then this allows one to make use of the parametric model in estimating the structural relation.

If the situation is one of least-squares forecasting or extraction with the forecast interval known, then there are two obvious alternatives. First, one could estimate simultaneously the parameters of the structural equation and the parameters of the autoregressive moving-average representation of the exogenous variable. Alternatively, one could adopt computationally simpler but less efficient procedures which should produce at least consistent estimates of all the parameters. The example below is intended to illustrate these approaches.

Suppose the structural equation is

$$y_t = a + bx_t^* + z_t'c + u_t, \qquad t = 1, 2, \ldots, T, \tag{1}$$

where x_t^* is a least-squares forecast or extraction based upon observations of an exogenous variable x_t, z_t is a vector of other exogenous variables, c is a vector of coefficients, and $\{u_t\}$ are independent normally distributed random variables with mean zero and variance σ_u^2. We assume that preliminary analysis has "identified" the model for the exogenous variable, and that initial estimates of the parameters of that model have been obtained. For purposes of illustration only, assume that the exogenous variable is a second-order autoregression:

$$x_t = \rho x_{t-1} + \delta x_{t-2} + \epsilon_t, \qquad \{\epsilon_t\} \text{ independent } n(0, \sigma_\epsilon^2). \tag{2}$$

We take x_t^* to be the predicted value of x_{t+k} (or the predicted average, total, etc. over some future period) based upon information up to time t. Thus in this case we have

$$x_t^* = \theta x_t + \phi x_{t-1}, \tag{3}$$

where $\theta = \theta(\rho, \delta)$ and $\phi = \phi(\rho, \delta)$ are in general nonlinear functions of ρ and δ, the exact forms depending upon the length of the forecast interval.[22] Notice that the assumption that x_t is an autoregressive process makes the length of the lag distribution in (3) independent of the prediction period, though, of course, the coefficients vary. We assume that the interval of prediction is known so that the functions $\theta(\,,\,)$ and $\phi(\,,\,)$ are known a priori.

---

[22] One could at least obtain consistent estimates of the parameters using an instrumental variable procedure with, for example, lagged values of the exogenous variable (or variables) as instruments. If the restrictions are imposed, this amounts to a two-step procedure, the first step of which determines only the order of the lag distribution. In the second step, all the identifiable parameters would be jointly estimated.

Under these assumptions, the log likelihood function is given approximately by

$$\ln L \cong \left[-\frac{T}{2} \ln \sigma_u^2 - \frac{1}{2\sigma_u^2} \sum_t (y_t - b\theta x_t - b\phi x_{t-1} - z_t'c)^2 \right]$$
$$+ \left[-\frac{T}{2} \ln \sigma_\epsilon^2 - \frac{1}{2\sigma_\epsilon^2} \sum_t (x_t - \rho x_{t-1} - \delta x_{t-2})^2 \right]$$
$$= \ln L_1 + \ln L_2. \tag{4}$$

For notational convenience we assume that the observation periods for all series are identical, and we treat the initial values x_0, x_{-1}, as constants. Also, we have suppressed the intercept term a, and take all variables as deviations from population means.

Treating the two terms in the likelihood function separately allows for consistent estimates of ρ, δ, σ_ϵ^2, $b\theta$, $b\phi$, c, and σ_u^2. The parameter b is unidentified in this approach, but from the estimates of ρ and δ and the a priori knowledge of θ and ϕ, b can also be consistently estimated. Of course, in finite samples $\widehat{b\theta}/\theta(\hat{\rho}, \hat{\delta})$ and $\widehat{b\phi}/\phi(\hat{\rho}, \hat{\delta})$ will not be equal, so that this approach leads to multiple (consistent) estimates of b. This difficulty is easily resolved by noting that

$$\ln L_1 = -\frac{T}{2} \ln \sigma_u^2 - \frac{1}{2\sigma_u^2} \sum_t (y_t - b[\theta(\rho, \delta)x_t + \phi(\rho, \delta)x_{t-1}] - z_t'c)^2$$
$$= -\frac{T}{2} \ln \sigma_u^2 - \frac{1}{2\sigma_u^2} \sum_t (y_t - bx_t^*(\rho, \delta) - z_t'c)^2. \tag{5}$$

Using the estimates of ρ and δ obtained from maximizing $\ln L_2$, the remaining parameters can be estimated by maximizing $\ln L_1$ using the estimated values of ρ and δ in computing $\hat{x}_t^*$.

The above procedure, while producing consistent estimates of all parameters, is somewhat unsatisfactory on two grounds. First, the estimates are likely to be inefficient as none of the information in $\ln L_1$ relevant to the determination of ρ and δ has been used. In general,

$$-\frac{1}{T} \frac{\partial^2 \ln L}{\partial b \, \partial \rho} \quad \text{and} \quad -\frac{1}{T} \frac{\partial^2 \ln L}{\partial b \, \partial \delta}$$

do not converge to zero, so the information matrix is not block diagonal, which implies that the estimate of b is also inefficient. The second problem is more a matter of practice than of principle; namely, in practice the standard errors used in making inferences about the parameters of the structural equations are calculated *conditional* upon the values of ρ and δ actually used. Thus they will be incorrect, even in large samples. One could avoid this by estimating the information matrix for the full set of parameters, but this is rarely done except when obtaining maximum-likelihood estimates of all the parameters.

Let

$$\begin{bmatrix} \rho_1 \\ \delta_1 \end{bmatrix} = \begin{bmatrix} \sum x_{t-1}^2 & \sum x_{t-1}x_{t-2} \\ \sum x_{t-1}x_{t-2} & \sum x_{t-2}^2 \end{bmatrix}^{-1} \begin{bmatrix} \sum x_t x_{t-1} \\ \sum x_t x_{t-2} \end{bmatrix} \tag{6}$$

be the estimates of ρ, δ obtained by maximizing $\ln L_2$. Also, let θ_0 and ϕ_0 be the estimates of θ and ϕ obtained by maximizing $\ln L_1$ *given* a value of b. The first-order conditions for maximizing $\ln L$ are as follows.

$$\frac{\partial \ln L}{\partial b} = \frac{1}{\hat{\sigma}_u^2} \sum (y_t - \hat{b}\hat{\theta}x_t - \hat{b}\hat{\phi}x_{t-1} - z_t'\hat{c})(\hat{\theta}x_t + \hat{\phi}x_{t-1}) = 0, \tag{7a}$$

$$\frac{\partial \ln L}{\partial c_i} = \frac{1}{\hat{\sigma}_u^2} \sum (y_t - \hat{b}\hat{\theta}x_t - \hat{b}\hat{\phi}x_{t-1} - z_t'\hat{c})z_{ti} = 0, \qquad i = 1, \ldots, K, \tag{7b}$$

$$\frac{\partial \ln L}{\partial \sigma_u^2} = -\frac{T}{2}\frac{1}{\hat{\sigma}_u^2} + \frac{1}{2\hat{\sigma}_u^4} \sum (y_t - \hat{b}\hat{\theta}x_t - \hat{b}\hat{\phi}x_{t-1} - z_t'\hat{c})^2 = 0, \tag{7c}$$

$$\frac{\partial \ln L}{\partial \rho} = \frac{1}{\hat{\sigma}_u^2} \sum (y_t - \hat{b}\hat{\theta}x_t - \hat{b}\hat{\phi}x_{t-1} - z_t'\hat{c})(\hat{b}\hat{\theta}_\rho x_t + \hat{b}\hat{\phi}_\rho x_{t-1})$$

$$+ \frac{1}{\hat{\sigma}_\epsilon^2} \sum (x_t - \hat{\rho}x_{t-1} - \hat{\delta}x_{t-2})x_{t-1} = 0, \tag{7d}$$

$$\frac{\partial \ln L}{\partial \delta} = \frac{1}{\hat{\sigma}_u^2} \sum (y_t - \hat{b}\hat{\theta}x_t - \hat{b}\hat{\phi}x_{t-1} - z_t'\hat{c})(\hat{b}\hat{\theta}_\delta x_t + \hat{b}\hat{\phi}_\delta x_{t-1})$$

$$+ \frac{1}{\hat{\sigma}_\epsilon^2} \sum (x_t - \hat{\rho}x_{t-1} - \hat{\delta}x_{t-2})x_{t-2} = 0, \tag{7e}$$

$$\frac{\partial \ln L}{\partial \sigma_\epsilon^2} = -\frac{T}{2}\frac{1}{\hat{\sigma}_\epsilon^2} + \frac{1}{2\hat{\sigma}_\epsilon^4} \sum (x_t - \hat{\rho}x_{t-1} - \hat{\delta}x_{t-2})^2 = 0. \tag{7f}$$

Now from the first three equations above, it is clear that b and c are simply estimated by a least-squares regression with $x^*(\hat{\rho}, \hat{\delta})$ and z_t as independent variables, and that σ_u^2 is estimated from the residual sum of squares in the usual fashion. In order to keep the algebra as simple as possible, we now assume that there are no other exogenous variables in the model.

Expand θ and ϕ about the point ρ_0, δ_0 defined by

$$\theta_0 = \theta(\rho_0, \delta_0), \qquad \phi_0 = \phi(\rho_0, \delta_0) \tag{8}$$

to obtain

$$\theta(\hat{\rho}, \hat{\delta}) = \theta_0 + \theta_{\rho_0}(\hat{\rho} - \rho_0) + \theta_{\delta_0}(\hat{\delta} - \delta_0) + R_\theta,$$
$$\phi(\hat{\rho}, \hat{\delta}) = \phi_0 + \phi_{\rho_0}(\hat{\rho} - \rho_0) + \phi_{\delta_0}(\hat{\delta} - \delta_0) + R_\phi, \tag{9}$$

with partial derivatives evaluated at the point (δ_0, ρ_0). We have

$$\frac{\partial \ln L}{\partial \rho} = \frac{1}{\hat{\sigma}_u^2} \sum ((\rho_0 - \hat{\rho})w_t + (\delta_0 - \hat{\delta})v_t)w_t$$

$$+ \frac{1}{\hat{\sigma}_\epsilon^2} \sum (x_t - \hat{\rho}x_{t-1} - \hat{\delta}x_{t-2})x_{t-1} + \text{remainder terms} = 0,$$

$$\frac{\partial \ln L}{\partial \delta} = \frac{1}{\hat{\sigma}_u^2} \sum ((\rho_0 - \hat{\rho})w_t + (\delta_0 - \hat{\delta})v_t)v_t$$
(10)

$$+ \frac{1}{\hat{\sigma}_\epsilon^2} \sum (x_t - \hat{\rho}x_{t-1} - \hat{\delta}x_{t-2})x_{t-2} + \text{remainder terms} = 0,$$

where

$$w_t = \theta_{\rho_0}\hat{b}x_t + \phi_{\rho_0}\hat{b}x_{t-1}, \qquad v_t = \theta_{\delta_0}\hat{b}x_t + \phi_{\delta_0}\hat{b}x_{t-1},$$

and we have used the fact that

$$\sum(y_t - \hat{b}\theta_0 x_t - \hat{b}\phi_0 x_{t-1})w_t = \sum(y_t - \hat{b}\theta_0 x_t - \hat{b}\phi_0 x_{t-1})v_t = 0 \qquad (11)$$

since residuals from least-squares regressions are orthogonal to the regressors. Rearranging terms and ignoring the remainder gives

$$\begin{bmatrix} \dfrac{1}{T}\dfrac{\partial \ln L}{\partial \rho} \\[2mm] \dfrac{1}{T}\dfrac{\partial \ln L}{\partial \delta} \end{bmatrix} = \frac{1}{\hat{\sigma}_u^2}\begin{bmatrix} \hat{\sigma}_w^2 & \hat{\sigma}_{wv} \\ \hat{\sigma}_{wv} & \hat{\sigma}_v^2 \end{bmatrix}\begin{bmatrix} \rho_0 - \hat{\rho} \\ \delta_0 - \hat{\delta} \end{bmatrix} + \frac{1}{\hat{\sigma}_\epsilon^2}\begin{bmatrix} \hat{\sigma}_x^2 & \hat{\sigma}_{xx}^{(1)} \\ \hat{\sigma}_{xx}^{(1)} & \hat{\sigma}_x^2 \end{bmatrix}\begin{bmatrix} \rho_1 - \hat{\rho} \\ \delta_1 - \hat{\delta} \end{bmatrix} = 0, \quad (12)$$

where

$$\hat{\sigma}_{xx}^{(1)} = \frac{1}{T}\sum_{t=1}^{T} x_{t-2}x_{t-1}.$$

Solving for $\hat{\rho}$ and $\hat{\delta}$ we obtain

$$\begin{bmatrix} \hat{\rho} \\ \hat{\delta} \end{bmatrix} = \left(\frac{1}{\hat{\sigma}_u^2}\begin{bmatrix} \hat{\sigma}_w^2 & \hat{\sigma}_{wv} \\ \hat{\sigma}_{wv} & \hat{\sigma}_v^2 \end{bmatrix} + \frac{1}{\hat{\sigma}_\epsilon^2}\begin{bmatrix} \hat{\sigma}_x^2 & \hat{\sigma}_{xx}^{(1)} \\ \hat{\sigma}_{xx}^{(1)} & \hat{\sigma}_x^2 \end{bmatrix}\right)^{-1}$$

$$\cdot \left(\frac{1}{\hat{\sigma}_u^2}\begin{bmatrix} \hat{\sigma}_w^2 & \hat{\sigma}_{wv} \\ \hat{\sigma}_{wv} & \hat{\sigma}_u^2 \end{bmatrix}\begin{bmatrix} \rho_0 \\ \delta_0 \end{bmatrix} + \frac{1}{\hat{\sigma}_\epsilon^2}\begin{bmatrix} \hat{\sigma}_x^2 & \hat{\sigma}_{xx}^{(1)} \\ \hat{\sigma}_{xx}^{(1)} & \hat{\sigma}_x^2 \end{bmatrix}\begin{bmatrix} \rho_1 \\ \delta_1 \end{bmatrix}\right). \qquad (13)$$

Thus we see that the maximum-likelihood estimates of ρ and δ are simply weighted averages of two estimates, one obtained from maximizing $\ln L_2$ with respect to ρ and δ, and the other obtained from maximizing $\ln L_1$ with respect to ρ and δ *conditional* on a value of b. In fact, equation (13) is simply an example of the standard procedure for combining two estimates to obtain a single more efficient estimator by taking a weighted average of the two estimates (the weights being proportional to the precision of the estimates).

The preceding discussion suggests the following procedure:

(1) Obtain estimates of ρ_1, δ_1, and σ_ϵ^2 from the x_t series.

(2) Regress y_t on $\theta(\rho_1,\delta_1)x_t + \phi(\rho_1,\delta_1)x_{t-1}$ to obtain initial estimates of b and σ_u^2.

(3) Regress y_t on x_t and x_{t-1} to obtain estimates of $b\theta_0$ and $b\phi_0$, which combined with the initial estimate of b provide estimates of θ_0 and ϕ_0.

(4) Use equation (13) to obtain new estimates of ρ and δ.

(5) Repeat Step 2 to obtain a new estimate of b.

(6) Using the estimates of b, ρ, and δ, calculate new estimates of σ_ϵ^2 and σ_u^2.

The assumption that x_t is a second-order autoregression has three rather different effects on the preceding discussion. First, it clearly simplifies the discussion as well as the computations in Steps 1, 3, and 4, though in substance the treatment for autoregressive moving-average processes would be the same. Second, assuming that the order of the autoregression process is *greater* than one makes the full model overidentified and thus requires iteration via equation (13). Note that if x_t is known to be a first-order autoregression, then the model is exactly identified and all the parameters are estimated from Steps 1 and 2. Finally, it was assumed that the structure of the x series was known or obtained from analyzing the data on x_t only. In fact, of course, the specifications of the structural equation can also be used to aid in "identifying" the model for x_t. In this case, for instance, including more lagged values of $\{x_t\}$ in the structural equation should not lead to a significant increase in explanatory power.

In general, if one wanted a computationally simpler procedure, one could stop with Step 2, which should provide consistent estimates of all parameters. Alternatively, one could use the model of the x_t series only to determine the order of the lag operators and then estimate the structural equation, with or without imposing whatever restrictions there are among the parameters. In this case the estimating equation is of the form

$$y_t = a + b\gamma(U)x_t + u_t = a + b[N(U)/D(U)]x_t + u_t,\tag{14}$$

so that b is not in general identified without some normalization rule such as $\gamma(1) = \sum n_j/\sum d_j = 1$. If the series being forecast or the signal being extracted is of the type

$$(1 - \theta U)^p x_t = z_t, \qquad |\theta| < 1,\tag{15}$$

where z_t is a covariance-stationary process, then, as Whittle has proved, $\gamma(\theta^{-1}) = \theta^k$.[23] So if the pth difference of x is covariance-stationary, $\gamma(1)$ will be exactly one. This condition will not necessarily be exactly satisfied for economic time series; hence, one would have to adopt the normalization rule that $\gamma(1) = 1$ in order to determine b uniquely.[24]

---

[23] This is shown in Whittle (1963, Theorems 2 and 3, pp. 93–94).

[24] Since all forecasts or extractions have been expressed in autoregressive form, we have implicitly excluded the possibility that the covariance-generating function has a zero on the unit circle.

If the forecast period is not known, then the first method suggested above is obviously not feasible. While in this case the order of the lag distribution is not exactly known, note that the order of the denominator of the rational distribution is known, and there is a known upper bound for the order of the numerator.[25] Though there is a loss of efficiency, as before it should be possible to obtain at least consistent estimates of the parameters.

If x_t^* is planned production or some similar variable, then it would appear that only the order of the lag distribution (and some nonlinear restrictions on the parameters) can be determined. The difficulty is that in these cases the co-efficients of the lag distribution are not determined solely by the autocovariance function of x_t, but also depend upon parameters of, say, the firm's cost functions. Whether or not all the parameters are identified would depend upon the structure of the entire model. If they are not, one might proceed along the lines of the latter alternative suggested.

---

[25] This is not true for extractions when v is negative.

Chapter XIV
A TIME-SERIES MODEL OF
THE U.S. CATTLE INDUSTRY

1. Introduction

In the previous chapter we explored the possibility of generating distributed-lag models through the use of quasi-rational expectations and derived some simple models of dynamic optimization incorporating explicit parametric models of the time-series structure of the exogenous series thought to be driving the behavioral model. In our final chapter we attempt to carry these ideas a step further and to illustrate how to dispense with a "static concept of a long-run equilibrium toward which adjustment occurs" (Nerlove, 1972a, p. 222) and arrive at empirically useful constructs in a true dynamic context.

The object of this chapter is to show that an econometrically relevant theory may be derived from a model that contains dynamic relationships derived from optimizing behavior of economic agents over time and not simply dictated by *ad hoc* considerations or considerations related to the convenience of estimation.

The U.S. cattle industry is chosen to provide the substance of our investigation for four reasons: (1) The volume of information is relatively large and covers a long period of time; (2) capital and product can be measured in the same units; (3) the period of production is fixed (it takes about nine months for a cow to give birth to a calf); and (4) the production technology is well defined. The study is for the United States as a whole and it aggregates over the whole sector, although the model is based on an analysis of individual behavior: The cattleman is assumed to maximize profits over time. To test the model, the solution obtained for the individual's optimal behavior is assumed to apply to the whole sector. This is a valid aggregation procedure if the solution form does not vary across individuals.

In Section 2, the particular features of cattle raising are discussed and some simplifying assumptions are imposed.

A dynamic model, based on the behavior of individuals whose objective is to maximize expected profits over an infinite horizon, is presented in Section 3. A temporal profit function is constructed in such a way that a unique maximum is guaranteed, that the conditions for certainty equivalence are satisfied, and that dynamic programming can be used to obtain the optimal solution.

A large number of future prices appear as exogenous variables in the individual optimal solutions. These values are generated as conditional expectations from past price data, in accordance with the theory of quasi-rational expectations developed in Chapter XIII. Both single-time-series methods and multiple-time-series methods have been used; the results are compared with the conclusion that multiple-time-series methods add little, if anything, to the analysis. The model developed in Section 4 is tested for both models of forecasting behavior in Section 5. The results are exceptionally encouraging, considering the large number of parameters to be estimated and the complexity of the underlying dynamic model of behavior.

We conclude that, despite considerable difficulties, it is indeed both possible and desirable to base econometric investigations on explicit models of dynamic optimizing behavior rather than to invoke *ad hoc* distributed lags and to impose them on essentially static behavioral models.

2.   The Cattle Industry

In this section, we give a brief description of the options open to the cattleman during each period in which optimizing decisions must be taken. The terms used are explained, and some assumptions made are considered. The flow diagram, presented in Fig. 1, will help us to describe the special features of beef cattle production in the U.S. To simplify matters, we shall not consider the model

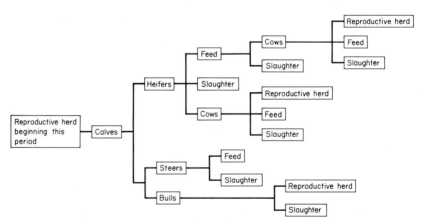

Fig. 1.   Flow diagram for cattle production decisions.

in a complete form and therefore do *not* consider either the market for feed nor the milk sector explicitly.

We start with the reproductive herd. These are animals used to produce beef cattle and consist of cows, heifers older than two years of age, and bulls. Heifers are those female animals that have not yet reproduced. A heifer can be used for reproductive purposes only after eighteen months of age. Because of data limitations, we assume that heifers can reproduce only after two years of age. Little attention will be paid to bulls. It is assumed that they are a fixed proportion of the number of cattle kept in the beef sector.[1]

The production of young animals, calves, is assumed to be proportional to the total number of animals kept in the stock of capital, i.e., the reproductive herd. Hence, if $B(t)$ is the number of calves born at period t, and $K(t)$ is the reproductive herd at the beginning of period t, we have:

$$B(t) = \lambda K(t) \qquad \text{for} \quad \lambda < 1. \tag{1}$$

Because nearly all male calves are castrated and therefore unable to reproduce, a distinction between males and females is necessary. It is assumed that $\frac{1}{2}B(t)$ are males for all t. After nine months of age, calves are considered heifers if they are female, or steers if they are castrated males. It is assumed, as indicated in the flow diagram, that the cattleman does not sell veal (young calves) or calves.[2]

Male calves which are not castrated are saved to become bulls; the castrated males will grow to steers and the female calves will grow to heifers. Each period, the initial stock of heifers and the age distribution of this stock are given from the producer's point of view. Hence, the optimal decision about heifers concerns sale of heifers for slaughter, or placement of heifers on feed, or selection of heifers for the stock of capital (reproductive herd) and breeding heifers. Breeding increases the stock of cows, since, once bred, heifers are cows by definition. Similar decisions have to be taken with respect to the stock of steers; however, the cattleman has only two alternatives in this case: a steer can be sold now for slaughter or it can be kept on feed to be sold in the future.

The variation of the actual stock of cows derives from the addition of newly bred heifers and from the sale of cows for slaughter. Cows may be kept in the reproductive herd, placed on feed, or sold for slaughter.

3. Cattleman Behavior: A Simple Example

The cattleman is assumed to maximize profits, not only for this period but over his entire productive horizon. Thus the producer will try tc maximize the expected net present value of his enterprise. Our problem is, therefore, to derive

---

[1] The stock of bulls has been about five percent of the total number of cattle for the past 50 years.

[2] Although this is not strictly true, the main source of veal and calves is the dairy sector. Because of the small fraction of calves sold by the beef sector, and since most of the veal sold is from the dairy sector, it is safe to disregard the sale of calves and veal in the model to be developed.

an expression for the producer's present value as a function of the decision variables and to maximize its expected value with respect to those decision variables. We proceed as follows.

First, a very simple profit function is constructed using the calendar year as the unit period. This profit function is quadratic in its arguments, a fact that guarantees a unique maximum and that satisfies the condition for the existence of certainty equivalents. This function is maximized to obtain the relevant behavioral functions. Second, a more complete profit function is defined in the next section using a quarter of the calendar year as the unit period. It is constructed in such a way that all properties holding for the simple example continue to hold. Difficulties in maximizing this more complete function are discussed, and two alternative ways to simplify the problem are shown to be impossible for lack of data and because of computational costs. Finally, the forms of the optimal solutions are obtained by an algebraic computer routine, and a detailed discussion of the meaning of these solutions is presented.

The Function to be Maximized

Assume that the cattleman maximizes his profits not only for this period, but for the whole period for which he is in business. Assume further that we know that the cattleman will be in business m periods and then retire. In each period, he must make decisions based on actual facts and on facts that he does not yet know for the future periods. Let the periods be numbered in ascending order backwards from his retirement, so that period n refers to a period n periods prior to the retirement. Let each period be a calendar year.

To make the problem still simpler, we assume that there are no male animals other than steers and that these are strictly proportional to the number of female animals. Steers can be sold now or kept on feed for at least one more period. The decision clearly does not affect future production of calves. The number of calves born is determined by the choice of the number of cows in the production capital stock; thus, as we have assumed that male calves constitute a fixed proportion of the calf crop, it can be assumed that decisions about male animals are independent of the other decisions. In this sense, it is possible to neglect the sex of animals in the model.

Assume that we have only three kinds of animals according to age: I_{0j}, the animals born in period j, which cannot be sold in this period; I_{1j}, the animals less than one year of age at beginning of period j which can be sold for slaughter at their market price c_j; and the animals over one year of age in period j. It is assumed that all animals are alike after one year of age.

Besides the age factor, we distinguish three kinds of animals for decision-making purposes: (1) animals in the stock of capital, (2) fed or feeder cattle to be sold this period or in future periods, and (3) calves. The capital stock K_j, consists of all the animals kept for reproductive purposes. This stock of capital depends on two decisions: gross investment δ_j, i.e., new animals added to the herd, and on depreciation V_j, i.e., animals from the stock of capital that are "retired" in period j. Gross investment comes from the actual stock of animals that are one year old, and "retired" animals are sold in the market at their slaughter price q_j. Fed or feeder cattle to be sold in the future F_j are all animals that are on feed in period j. Variation in this stock depends on actual sales of fed animals S_j at a price p_j, and actual placement on feed of one-year-old animals $I_{1j} - C_j - \delta_j$. Thus $F_{j-1} = F_j + I_{1j} - C_j - \delta_j - S_j$. C_j represents the number of calves sold for slaughter. There are three alternative uses of calves: (1) calves can be sold for slaughter C_j at their market price c_j; (2) they can be selected for breeding, i.e., added to the herd δ_j; or, finally, (3) the remainder are those kept on feed $I_{1j} - C_j - \delta_j$, i.e., the number of one-year-old animals placed on feed at the beginning of the period.

Thus calves can be a gross investment good, a final good when sold to slaughter, and a good in process when kept on feed to be sold in the future.

We know that keeping an animal one more period entails a cost and yields the benefit of being able to sell it in the future. If the cattleman acts rationally, he will decide how many cattle to keep in such a way as to equate marginal expected cost and marginal expected benefit, both discounted to the present period. Suppose the unit costs are fixed for the overall period considered by the cattleman in his decision. If we have only the animals described above, we may assume that the function to be maximized by the cattleman may be approximated by

$$
\begin{aligned}
V(&S_n, \delta_n, V_n, C_n | K_n, F_n, I_{1n}, n) \\
&= q_n V_n + p_n S_n + c_n C_n \\
&\quad - \tfrac{1}{2} a(K_n + \delta_n - V_n)^2 - \tfrac{1}{2} b(K_n - V_n)^2 - \tfrac{1}{2} d(I_{0n})^2 \\
&\quad - \tfrac{1}{2} f(F_n + I_{1n} - \delta_n - C_n - S_n)^2 - \tfrac{1}{2} g(F_n - S_n)^2 \\
&\quad + \alpha E_n [V(S_{n-1}, \delta_{n-1}, V_{n-1}, C_{n-1} | K_{n-1}, F_{n-1}, I_{1n-1}, n-1)], \quad (1)
\end{aligned}
$$

subject to the restrictions

$$
\begin{aligned}
F_n &= F_{n+1} + I_{1n+1} - \delta_{n+1} - C_{n+1} - S_{n+1}, \\
K_n &= K_{n+1} + \delta_{n+1} - V_{n+1}, \\
I_{0n} &= \lambda K_n, \qquad I_{1n} = I_{0n+1} = \lambda K_{n+1},
\end{aligned} \qquad (2)
$$

where $V(S_n, \delta_n, V_n, C_n | K_n, F_n, I_{1n}, n)$ is the expected present value of profits when there are n periods left until the cattleman's retirement; K_n the actual stock of cattle as capital; F_n the actual stock of animals on feed; I_{1n} the number of one-year-old animals; $q_n V_n + p_n S_n + c_n C_n = $ total revenue; $\tfrac{1}{2} a(K_n + \delta_n - V_n)^2 = $ maintenance cost of animals kept in stock; $\tfrac{1}{2} b(K_n - V_n)^2 = $ aging cost of animals kept in stock; $\tfrac{1}{2} d(I_{0n})^2 = $ cost of producing calves in this period; $\tfrac{1}{2} f(F_n + I_{1n} - \delta_n - C_n - S_n)^2 = $ feeding cost for animals on feed (note that $I_{1n} - \delta_n - C_n$ consists of new animals placed on feed this period); $\tfrac{1}{2} g(F_n - S_n)^2 = $ aging cost of animals on feed; $\alpha = $ one period discount factor; $E_n [V(S_{n-1}, \delta_{n-1}, V_{n-1}, C_{n-1} | K_{n-1}, F_{n-1}, I_{1n-1}, n-1)] = $ expected value of next period profits; and $E_n = $ expectation operator at period n, i.e., expectation conditional on all events up to n and including those occurring in period n. The advantages of approximating the maximizing function in this way are numerous: First, because the function is quadratic, a unique maximum or minimum is assured by the global convexity or concavity of the function; second, the simple form of the function permits us to solve the dynamic programming problem explicitly; and third, as we show below, the maximand satisfies the conditions for first-period certainty equivalence.

The Maximizing Solution

The method to be used for solving the above maximization problem is "dynamic programming." This is a recursive maximization procedure starting from the last period, i.e., the period after which the cattleman will retire; having obtained the solution for this period, the problem is to solve for the next to last period; and so on, as many times as necessary for determination of the general solution when there are n periods left, for any n (Howard, 1966, pp. 317–320).

We first solve this problem on the assumption that the cattleman knows with certainty the values of the future prices. This assumption does not invalidate the analysis, provided that the conditions for first-period certainty equivalence are satisfied. That these conditions are satisfied is verified below. For this reason we introduce the expectation operator where appropriate.

To obtain the solution to this maximization problem, we follow the standard dynamic programming procedure as described above. If the cattleman retires at the end of the last period, he must sell all his animals; there is no investment nor production. Thus,

$$S_1 = F_1, \quad V_1 = K_1, \quad C_1 = I_{11}, \quad \delta_1 = 0, \quad I_{01} = 0. \tag{3}$$

Hence, profit is

$$V(\ldots|\ldots, 1) = q_1 V_1 + p_1 S_1 + c_1 C_1, \tag{4}$$

which is in fact total revenue since there are no costs of keeping animals for future periods. Substituting (3) into (4), we obtain the maximized value of the profits in the last period:

$$V(\ldots|\ldots, 1) = q_1 K_1 + p_1 F_1 + c_1 I_{11}. \tag{5}$$

Substituting the dynamic restrictions given by (2) for $n = 1$,

$$V(\ldots|\ldots, 1) = q_1(K_2 + \delta_2 - V_2) + p_1(F_2 + I_{12} - \delta_2 - C_2 - S_2) + c_1 \lambda K_2. \tag{6}$$

The profit function when there are two periods left before the retirement is thus

$$
\begin{aligned}
V(\ldots|\ldots, 2) = {} & q_2 V_2 + p_2 S_2 + c_2 C_2 - \tfrac{1}{2}a(K_2 + \delta_2 - V_2)^2 \\
& - \tfrac{1}{2}b(K_2 - V_2)^2 - \tfrac{1}{2}d(I_{02})^2 - \tfrac{1}{2}f(F_2 + I_{12} - \delta_2 - C_2 - S_2)^2 \\
& - \tfrac{1}{2}g(F_2 - S_2)^2 + \alpha E_2[q_1(K_2 + \delta_2 - V_2) \\
& + p_1(F_2 + I_{12} - \delta_2 - C_2 - S_2) + c_1 \lambda K_2].
\end{aligned}
\tag{7}
$$

To maximize $V(\ldots|\ldots,2)$ with respect to S_2, δ_2, V_2, and C_2, take its partial derivatives:

$$\partial V(\ldots|\ldots,2)/\partial S_2 = p_2 + f(F_2 + I_{12} - \delta_2 - C_2 - S_2) + g(F_2 - S_2)$$
$$- \alpha E_2(p_1);$$
$$\partial V(\ldots|\ldots,2)/\partial \delta_2 = -a(K_2 + \delta_2 - V_2) + f(F_2 + I_{12} - \delta_2 - C_2 - S_2)$$
$$+ \alpha E_2(q_1) - \alpha E_2(p_1);$$
$$\partial V(\ldots|\ldots,2)/\partial V_2 = q_2 + a(K_2 + \delta_2 - V_2) + b(K_2 - V_2) - \alpha E_2(q_1);$$
$$\partial V(\ldots|\ldots,2)/\partial C_2 = c_2 + f(F_2 + I_{12} - \delta_2 - C_2 - S_2) - \alpha E_2(p_1).$$

Equating these to zero yields the first-order conditions for a maximum, the solution to which describes the cattleman's behavior two periods from retirement:

$$(f + g)S_2 + f\delta_2 + 0V_2 + fC_2 = p_2 - \alpha E_2(p_1) + (f + g)F_2 + fI_{12},$$
$$fS_2 + (a + f)\delta_2 - aV_2 + fC_2 = \alpha E_2(q_1) - \alpha E_2(p_1) - aK_2 + f(F_2 + I_{12}),$$
$$0S_2 - a\delta_2 + (a + b)V_2 + 0C_2 = q_2 - \alpha E_2(q_1) + (a + b)K_2, \qquad (8)$$
$$fS_2 + f\delta_2 + 0V_2 + fC_2 = c_2 - \alpha E_2(p_1) + f(F_2 + I_{12}).$$

The second-order conditions for a maximum are satisfied at this point automatically because the profit function is quadratic and because of our assumptions concerning q, p, c, a, b, d, f, g, and α.

Solving the system (8) for S_2, δ_2, V_2, and C_2, we obtain

$$S_2 = \frac{1}{g} p_2 - \frac{1}{g} c_2 + F_2,$$

$$\delta_2 = \frac{1}{b} q_2 - \left(\frac{1}{b} + \frac{1}{a}\right) c_2 + \frac{1}{a} \alpha E_2(q_1),$$

$$V_2 = \frac{1}{b} q_2 - \frac{1}{b} c_2 + K_2, \qquad (9)$$

$$C_2 = \left(\frac{1}{a} + \frac{1}{b} + \frac{1}{f} + \frac{1}{g}\right) c_2 - \frac{1}{g} p_2 - \frac{1}{b} q_2 - \frac{1}{f} \alpha E_2(p_1) - \frac{1}{a} \alpha E_2(q_1) + I_{12}.$$

max $V(\ldots|\ldots,2)$ is obtained by replacing S_2, δ_2, V_2, and C_2 by their maximizing values from (9) in $V(\ldots|\ldots,2)$. $V(\ldots|\ldots,3)$ is defined similarly and the same procedure followed in order to obtain the maximizing solution when there are three periods left. This analysis is carried out until iteration five, i.e., until five periods from retirement. At the end of iteration five, the same solution as for iteration four is obtained with all subscripts increased by one unit. It follows that after four iterations, all solutions are alike; therefore we can immediately write down the general solution when there are n periods left:

$$S_n = \frac{1}{g} p_n - \frac{1}{g} c_n - \frac{1}{g} \alpha^2 E_n(p_{n-2}) + F_n,$$

$$\delta_n = \frac{1}{b} q_n - \left(\frac{1}{a + \lambda^2 \alpha d} + \frac{1}{b} \right) c_n + \frac{1}{a + \lambda^2 \alpha d} \alpha E_n(q_{n-1})$$

$$+ \frac{1}{a + \lambda^2 \alpha d} \alpha^2 E_n(c_{n-2})$$

$$+ \left(\frac{1}{a + \lambda^2 \alpha d} + \frac{1}{d} \right) \alpha^2 E_n(p_{n-2}),$$

$$V_n = \frac{1}{b} q_n - \frac{1}{b} c_n + K_n, \tag{10}$$

$$C_n = \left(\frac{1}{a + \alpha \lambda^2 d} + \frac{1}{b} + \frac{1}{f} + \frac{1}{g} \right) c_n - \frac{1}{g} p_n - \frac{1}{b} q_n - \frac{1}{f} \alpha E_n(p_{n-1})$$

$$- \frac{1}{a + \alpha \lambda^2 d} \alpha E_n(q_{n-1}) - \frac{1}{a + \alpha \lambda^2 d} \alpha^2 E_n(c_{n-2})$$

$$- \left(\frac{1}{a + \alpha \lambda^2 d} + \frac{1}{b} + \frac{1}{f} + \frac{1}{g} \right) \alpha^2 E_n(p_{n-2}) + I_{1n}.$$

Each equation in (10), the general solution, may be estimated by OLS procedures on the assumption that the disturbances are not serially correlated. Because the decisions are not independent, however, we expect correlation among the residuals of different equations. Thus joint estimation procedures as proposed by Zellner (1962) should improve the quality of the estimated coefficients because the equations have different sets of explanatory variables. Demand functions might be added to complete the system, although we shall not undertake to introduce them here. If demand considerations are introduced, however, simultaneous-equation techniques should be used.

The estimated coefficients in (10) make it possible to identify some of the shadow costs implied in the profit function and to analyze the effects of changes in these shadow costs on each supply curve.

It can be shown, along the lines suggested by Simon (1956) and Theil (1957) that the above maximization problem satisfies all the conditions for one-period certainty equivalence; i.e., the first-period action that maximizes V is equivalent to the action that disregards uncertainty and maximizes V with the expected values of the uncertain variables in place of their actual values as if they were certain.

Certainty Equivalence

The concept of one-period certainty equivalence is discussed in detail by Theil (1964). For completeness, we reproduce here his Theorem 4.1. The problem is to maximize $W(x, y) = a'x + b'y + \frac{1}{2}(x'Ax + y'By + x'Cy + y'C'x)$ subject to $y = Rx + s$, where x is a vector of instruments and y a vector of noncontrolled variables (Theil, 1964, pp. 121–123).

Assume that x and y are real and a, b, A, B, C have fixed elements. If x and y contain stochastic values, the decision maker should maximize the expected value of $W(x, y)$. Assume further that x and y are connected by the linear constraints above, such that R is a nonstochastic lower triangular matrix; that the elements of s are stochastic variables with a joint distribution such that the distribution of a subvector of s, say s_t, is independent of $x_{t'}$ for $t \geq t'$; and that the variances of the elements of s are all finite.

Then the strategy $\tilde{x}$ which maximizes the mean value of the preference function $W(x, y)$ subject to the stochastic constraints, $y = Rx + s$, if existent and unique, has the following properties:

(i) The difference $\tilde{x}_t - x_t^0$ is independent of $\tilde{x}_{t-1}$ for $t = 1, \ldots, T$, where $\tilde{x}_t$ is the tth subvector of $\tilde{x}$, x_t^0 is the tth subvector of $x^0 = -K^{-1}k$, K and k being defined below, and t is the information available at end of tth period.

(ii) The expected value of $\tilde{x}$ is $E(x) = -K^{-1}E(k)$.

(iii) The first-period decision of $\tilde{x}$ is identical with the first-period subvector of the decisions which maximize $W(x, y)$ subject to $y = Rx + s$ after s (the additive structure of the constraints) is replaced by its expectation (first-period certainty equivalence); and this first-period decision is the subvector consisting of the first m elements of the vector $E(x)$.

If x is the solution,

$$Wx = W(x, Rx + s) = k_0 + k'x + \tfrac{1}{2}x'Kx,$$

where

$$k_0 = b's + \tfrac{1}{2}s'Bs, \qquad k = a + R'b + (C + R'B)s,$$

$$K = A + R'BR + CR + R'C'.$$

(Theil, 1964, p. 135)

In order to verify first-period certainty equivalence, our V function must be written in the form of Theil's W function, the linear constraints identified, and the assumptions of the theorem verified.

Only four periods are needed to solve the dynamic programming problem since, after four periods, the solutions are alike. Thus the case $n = 4$ involves no loss of generality.

The function to be maximized is

$$\begin{aligned}
V(S_4, &\delta_4, V_4, C_4 | K_4, F_4, I_{14}, 4) \\
&= q_4 V_4 + p_4 S_4 + c_4 C_4 - \tfrac{1}{2}a(K_4 + \delta_4 - V_4)^2 - \tfrac{1}{2}b(K_4 - V_4)^2 \\
&\quad - \tfrac{1}{2}d(I_{04})^2 - \tfrac{1}{2}f(F_4 + I_{14} - \delta_4 - C_4 - S_4)^2 - \tfrac{1}{2}g(F_4 - S_4)^2 \\
&\quad + \alpha E_4[V(S_3, \delta_3, V_3, C_3, | K_3, F_3, I_{13}, 3)],
\end{aligned} \tag{11}$$

subject to the constraints summarized by

$$F_n = F_{n+1} + I_{1n+1} - \delta_{n+1} - C_{n+1} - S_{n+1}, \quad K_n = K_{n+1} + \delta_{n+1} - V_{n+1}, \tag{12}$$
$$I_{0n} = \lambda K_n, \quad I_{1n} = I_{0n+1} = \lambda K_{n+1},$$

for $n = 1, 2, 3, 4$. To these must be added the constraint that introduces uncertainty about the prices in the future and corresponds to Theil's $y = Rx + s$.

Rewriting our problem in Theil's notation we have

$$x' = [S_4, S_3, S_2, \delta_4, \delta_3, \delta_2, V_4, V_3, V_2, C_4, C_3, C_2],$$

$$y' = [p_4, p_3, p_2, p_1, q_4, q_3, q_2, q_1, c_4, c_3, c_2, c_1],$$

$$a = \begin{bmatrix}
\alpha^2 \lambda f K_4 + (1 + \alpha + \alpha^2)(f + g)F_4 + [(1 + \alpha + \alpha^2)f + (\alpha + \alpha^2)g]I_{14} \\
\quad + [(\alpha + \alpha^2)f + \alpha^2 g]I_{04} \\[4pt]
(\alpha^2 g + \alpha f)(F_4 + I_{14} + I_{04}) + \alpha g(F_4 + I_{14}) + \alpha^2 f[F_4 + I_{14} + 2I_{04}] \\[4pt]
(\alpha^2 f + \alpha^2 g)(F_4 + I_{14} + I_{04}) + \alpha^2 f \lambda K_4 \\[4pt]
(1 + \alpha + \alpha^2)[f(F_4 + I_{14}) - aK_4] + (\alpha + \alpha^2)[g(F_4 + I_{14}) \\
\quad + fI_{04} - (b + d\lambda^2)K_4] + \alpha^2 g I_{04} \\
\quad - \alpha^2 \lambda f[F_4 + I_{14} + I_{04} - (1 - \lambda)K_4] \\[4pt]
(\alpha f + \alpha^2 f + \alpha^2 g)(F_4 + I_{14} + I_{04}) - (\alpha^2 d\lambda^2 + \alpha^2 a + \alpha^2 b \\
\quad + \alpha a)K_4 + \alpha^2 f(F_4 + I_{14} + I_{04}) + \alpha^2 f \lambda K_4 \\[4pt]
\alpha^2 f(F_4 + I_{14} + I_{04}) + (\alpha^2 f \lambda - \alpha^2 a)K_4 \\[4pt]
[(1 + \alpha + \alpha^2)(a + b) + (\alpha + \alpha^2)\,d\lambda^2 + \alpha^2 f \lambda^2]K_4 + \alpha^2 f \lambda(F_4 + I_{14} \\
\quad + I_{04}) \\[4pt]
[\alpha^2 d\lambda^2 + \alpha^2 a + \alpha^2 b + \alpha a + \alpha b]K_4 \\[4pt]
\alpha^2(a + b)K_4 \\[4pt]
f(1 + \alpha + \alpha^2)(F_4 + I_{14}) + (\alpha + \alpha^2)(gF_4 + gI_{14} + fI_{04}) + \alpha^2 g I_{04} \\
\quad + \alpha^2 f \lambda K_4 \\[4pt]
(\alpha f + \alpha^2 f + \alpha^2 g)(F_4 + I_{14} + I_{04}) + \alpha^2 f \lambda K_4 \\[4pt]
\alpha^2 f(F_4 + I_{14} + I_{04}) + \alpha^2 f \lambda K_4
\end{bmatrix},$$

$$b' = [0, 0, 0, [(F_4 + I_{14} + I_{04} + \lambda K_4)\alpha^3], 0, 0, 0, (K_4 \alpha^3), 0, 0, 0, (\alpha^3 \lambda K_4)],$$

$$B = [0], \qquad R = [0],$$

$$C = \begin{bmatrix}
1 & 0 & 0 & -\alpha^3 & 0 & 0 & 0 & 0 & 0 & 0 & 0 & 0 \\
0 & \alpha & 0 & -\alpha^3 & 0 & 0 & 0 & 0 & 0 & 0 & 0 & 0 \\
0 & 0 & \alpha^2 & -\alpha^3 & 0 & 0 & 0 & 0 & 0 & 0 & 0 & 0 \\
0 & 0 & 0 & -(1 - \lambda)\alpha^3 & 0 & 0 & 0 & \alpha^3 & 0 & 0 & 0 & \alpha^3 \lambda \\
0 & 0 & 0 & -\alpha^3 & 0 & 0 & 0 & \alpha^3 & 0 & 0 & 0 & \alpha^3 \lambda \\
0 & 0 & 0 & -\alpha^3 & 0 & 0 & 0 & \alpha^3 & 0 & 0 & 0 & 0 \\
0 & 0 & 0 & -\lambda\alpha^3 & 1 & 0 & 0 & -\alpha^3 & 0 & 0 & 0 & -\alpha^3 \lambda \\
0 & 0 & 0 & 0 & 0 & \alpha & 0 & -\alpha^3 & 0 & 0 & 0 & -\alpha^3 \lambda \\
0 & 0 & 0 & 0 & 0 & 0 & \alpha^2 & -\alpha^3 & 0 & 0 & 0 & 0 \\
0 & 0 & 0 & -\alpha^3 & 0 & 0 & 0 & 0 & 1 & 0 & 0 & 0 \\
0 & 0 & 0 & -\alpha^3 & 0 & 0 & 0 & 0 & 0 & \alpha & 0 & 0 \\
0 & 0 & 0 & -\alpha^3 & 0 & 0 & 0 & 0 & 0 & 0 & \alpha^2 & 0
\end{bmatrix}$$

(see also matrix A). Thus our problem can be expressed as

$$\max V(x, y) = a'x + b'y + \tfrac{1}{2}(x'Ax + y'By + x'Cy + y'C'x), \tag{13}$$

subject to

$$y = Rx + s. \tag{14}$$

Note that the constraints on F_n, K_n, and I_{0n} are introduced in the function $V(x, y)$; therefore we need not consider them further. Moreover, F_4, I_{14}, K_4, and consequently I_{04}, are given when there are four periods left; therefore, a, b, A, B, and C satisfy the assumptions for the validity of the theorem. Since $R = [0]$, this implies that y, the price vector, is a simple random vector; clearly, R is a special kind of triangular matrix. Thus the condition on s is satisfied and, hence Theil's theorem is immediately applicable to our problem.

The conditions for the existence and uniqueness of a maximum are trivially satisfied for our case since the function to be maximized is quadratic with appropriate coefficients and the constraints are linear. Note that the K matrix in Theil's notation reduces to our matrix A. To extend this proof when there are n periods left, it is only necessary to increase the number of elements in each vector and in each matrix accordingly. When we add one more period, we gain one more element in each subvector that corresponds to each variable and one more row in each matrix. Increasing the number of periods left therefore does not change the structure of the problem but only increases its dimensionality.

4. Cattleman Behavior: A Quarterly Model

It is clear from the simple example of the preceding section that once the profit function is given in an explicit form, we can obtain the cattleman's behavior through profit maximization over time by using dynamic programming.

Due to dependence over time, e.g., carry-over stocks, the definition of the unit period is very important. In our simple example, using the year as the unit period, the number of iterations needed to obtain the general solution is not large. When the unit period is a quarter of a year (three months), the lags involved are greater, and therefore the number of iterations needed increases.

Explicit maximization by dynamic programming is, for all practical purposes, impossible if the number of arguments is large and the number of iterations needed to get the general solution is high. If the number of arguments is large, this implies a large system of equations to be solved at each iteration. Because the expressions grow in proportion to the number of iterations, a large number of iterations will make the expressions to be handled so large that algebraic manipulation becomes impractical.

Maximization by dynamic programming is repetitive as can be seen from the simple example. With the advent of computers, solution of a great many laborious numerical problems is no longer prohibitive. As the development of a language capable of handling algebraic expressions proceeds, the same will

$$A = 2 \begin{bmatrix}
-(f+g)(1+\alpha+\alpha^2)/2 & 0 & 0 & 0 & 0 \\[4pt]
-(f+g)(1+\alpha^2) & -(f+g)(\alpha+\alpha^2)/2 & 0 & 0 & 0 \\[4pt]
-\alpha^2(f+g) & -\alpha^2(f+g) & -\alpha^2(f+g)/2 & 0 & 0 \\[4pt]
\begin{aligned}&-(1+\alpha+\alpha^2)(f+g)\\&+\alpha^2 f\lambda+g\end{aligned} & \begin{aligned}&-(f+g)(\alpha+\alpha^2)\\&+\alpha^2 f\lambda\end{aligned} & -\alpha^2(f+g) & \begin{aligned}&-\{(f+a)(1+\alpha+\alpha^2)\\&+(b+g+d\lambda^2)(\alpha+\alpha^2)\\&+f\lambda\alpha^2(\lambda-2)\}/2\end{aligned} & 0 \\[4pt]
-f(\alpha+\alpha^2)-\alpha^2 g & -f(\alpha+\alpha^2)-\alpha^2 g & -\alpha^2(f+g) & \begin{aligned}&-(a+f)(\alpha+\alpha^2)\\&-\alpha^2(\lambda f+g+\lambda^2 d+b)\end{aligned} & \begin{aligned}&-\{(a+f)(\alpha+\alpha^2)\\&+\alpha^2(g+d\lambda^2+b)\}\end{aligned} \\[4pt]
-\alpha^2 f & -\alpha^2 f & -\alpha^2 f & \begin{aligned}&-\alpha^2 f(1-\lambda)\\&-\alpha^2 a\end{aligned} & -\alpha^2 a-f\alpha^2 \\[4pt]
-\alpha^2\lambda f & -\alpha^2 f\lambda & -\alpha^2 f\lambda & \begin{aligned}&a(1+\alpha+\alpha^2)\\&+(d\lambda^2+b)(\alpha+\alpha^2)\\&-\alpha^2 f\lambda(1-\lambda)\end{aligned} & \begin{aligned}&\alpha^2(d\lambda^2+a+b)\\&+\alpha a-\lambda f\alpha^2\end{aligned} \\[4pt]
0 & 0 & 0 & \begin{aligned}&(\alpha+\alpha^2)(a+b)\\&+\alpha^2 d\lambda^2\end{aligned} & \begin{aligned}&\alpha^2(a+b+d\lambda^2)\\&+\alpha a\end{aligned} \\[4pt]
0 & 0 & 0 & \alpha^2(a+b) & \alpha^2(a+b) \\[4pt]
\begin{aligned}&-(f+g)(\alpha+\alpha^2)\\&-f\end{aligned} & -(f+g)(\alpha+\alpha^2) & -\alpha^2(f+g) & \begin{aligned}&-(f+g)(\alpha+\alpha^2)\\&+f(\alpha^2\lambda-1)\end{aligned} & \begin{aligned}&-f(\alpha+\alpha^2)\\&-\alpha^2 g\end{aligned} \\[4pt]
-f(\alpha+\alpha^2)-\alpha^2 g & -f(\alpha+\alpha^2)-\alpha^2 g & -\alpha^2(f+g) & \begin{aligned}&-(\alpha+\alpha^2)f\\&-\alpha^2(g-f\lambda)\end{aligned} & \begin{aligned}&-f(\alpha+\alpha^2)\\&-\alpha^2 g\end{aligned} \\[4pt]
-\alpha^2 f & -\alpha^2 f & -\alpha^2 f & -\alpha^2 f(1-\lambda) & -\alpha^2 f
\end{bmatrix}$$

be true for laborious and repetitive algebraic calculations such as characterize our problem. There is a language FORMAC, developed a few years ago under IBM sponsorship, that allows manipulation of algebraic expressions. Below we examine the use of such a language to perform maximizations with dynamic programming techniques (Tobey, 1971).

The Function to be Maximized

We now define explicitly a profit function, taking a quarter of a year (three months) as the unit period. All of the assumptions and simplifications introduced in the previous section are maintained; additional assumptions are introduced in the course of the discussion.

Assuming that calves are not sold, animals born this period are equal to animals with three months of age at the beginning of next period if there is no calf mortality. For the theoretical solution of the problem, it is assumed that calf mortality is zero, although an explicit allowance for mortality can be introduced in the empirical implementation of the model. The simplification does not change the final results, since the mortality rate is very small and can be neglected in the maximization of the profit function. If calves are defined as animals less than three periods old, i.e., less than nine months of age, the total stock of calves in period t, say C_t, is given by

$$C_t = B_t + B_{t-1} + B_{t-2}, \tag{1}$$

$$
\begin{bmatrix}
0 & 0 & 0 & 0 & 0 & 0 & 0 \\
0 & 0 & 0 & 0 & 0 & 0 & 0 \\
0 & 0 & 0 & 0 & 0 & 0 & 0 \\
0 & 0 & 0 & 0 & 0 & 0 & 0 \\
0 & 0 & 0 & 0 & 0 & 0 & 0 \\
-\alpha^2(f+a)/2 & 0 & 0 & 0 & 0 & 0 & 0 \\
\alpha^2(a-f\lambda) & -\{(a+b)(1+\alpha+\alpha^2) + d\lambda^2(\alpha+\alpha^2) + \alpha^2 f\lambda^2\}/2 & 0 & 0 & 0 & 0 & 0 \\
\alpha^2 a & -(a+b)(\alpha+\alpha^2) - \alpha^2 d\lambda^2 & -\{(a+b)(\alpha+\alpha^2) + \alpha^2 d\lambda^2\}/2 & 0 & 0 & 0 & 0 \\
\alpha^2 a & -\alpha^2(a+b) & -\alpha^2(a+b) & -\alpha^2(a+b)/2 & 0 & 0 & 0 \\
-\alpha^2 f & -\alpha^2 f\lambda & 0 & 0 & -\{(f+g)(\alpha+\alpha^2) + f\}/2 & 0 & 0 \\
-\alpha^2 f & -\alpha^2 f\lambda & 0 & 0 & -f(\alpha+\alpha^2) - g\alpha^2 & -\{f(\alpha+\alpha^2) + \alpha^2 g\}/2 & 0 \\
-\alpha^2 f & -\alpha^2 f\lambda & 0 & 0 & -\alpha^2 f & -\alpha^2 f & -\alpha^2 f/2
\end{bmatrix}
$$

where t refers to actual time and not to the number of periods until retirement, and the stock of calves three periods old at the beginning of period t is

$$I_t = B_{t-3}. \tag{2}$$

As before, we assume that the ratio between male and female births is fixed and equal to one. Steers are animals that, from the decision-making point of view, can either be sold now or in the future. Heifers can also be sold now or in the future or can be bred and thereby be transformed into cows in turn used to produce new calves. The reproductive capacity of heifers makes them different, and this difference is expressed in the profit function.

The profit function assumed for the cattleman is of the same quadratic form as in Section 3:

$$
\begin{aligned}
V(S_n&, H_n, \delta_n, V_n | M_n, F_n, K_n, I_n, n) \\
&= s_n S_n + h_n H_n + v_n V_n - \tfrac{1}{2}a(K_n + \delta_n - V_n)^2 - \tfrac{1}{2}b(K_n - V_n)^2 \\
&\quad - \tfrac{1}{2}c(C_n)^2 - \tfrac{1}{2}d(B_n)^2 - \tfrac{1}{2}f(M_n - S_n + \tfrac{1}{2}I_n)^2 \\
&\quad - \tfrac{1}{2}g(F_n - H_n - \delta_n + \tfrac{1}{2}I_n)^2 - \tfrac{1}{2}j(M_n - S_n)^2 - \tfrac{1}{2}k(F_n - H_n - \delta_n)^2 \\
&\quad + \alpha E_n\{V(S_{n-1}, H_{n-1}, \delta_{n-1}, V_{n-1} | M_{n-1}, F_{n-1}, K_{n-1}, I_{n-1}, n-1)\},
\end{aligned}
\tag{3}
$$

subject to the constraints

$$K_n = K_{n+1} + \delta_{n+1} - V_{n+1},$$
$$M_n = M_{n+1} - S_{n+1} + \tfrac{1}{2}I_{n+1},$$
$$F_n = F_{n+1} - H_{n+1} - \delta_{n+1} + \tfrac{1}{2}I_{n+1}, \tag{4}$$
$$B_n = \lambda K_{n+3}(n \geq 4), \qquad C_n = B_n + B_{n+1} + B_{n+2}, \qquad I_n = B_{n+3},$$

where the subscript n, as before, refers to the number of periods left before the cattleman retires, and where s_n is the slaughter price of steers, h_n the slaughter price of heifers, v_n the slaughter price of cows, K_n the reproductive herd, C_n the stock of calves, B_n the calves born, I_n the animals three periods of age (nine months), F_n the stock of heifers, H_n the heifers sold for slaughter, M_n the stock of steers, S_n the steers sold for slaughter, V_n the cows sold for slaughter, and δ_n the gross investment (new animals placed in the reproductive herd). The terms of V may be interpreted as follows:

$s_n S_n + h_n H_n + v_n V_n =$ total revenue,
$\tfrac{1}{2}a(K_n + \delta_n - V_n)^2 =$ maintenance cost of the capital stock,
$\tfrac{1}{2}b(K_n - V_n)^2 =$ cost of holding the capital stock due to aging,
$\tfrac{1}{2}c(C_n)^2 =$ maintenance cost of calves,
$\tfrac{1}{2}d(B_n)^2 =$ production cost of calves,
$\tfrac{1}{2}f(M_n - S_n + \tfrac{1}{2}I_n)^2 =$ feeding cost of steers,
$\tfrac{1}{2}g(F_n - H_n - \delta_n + \tfrac{1}{2}I_n)^2 =$ feeding cost of heifers,
$\tfrac{1}{2}j(M_n - S_n)^2 =$ cost of holding steers due to aging,
$\tfrac{1}{2}k(F_n - H_n - \delta_n)^2$ cost of holding heifers due to aging,
$\alpha =$ one-period discount rate,
$E =$ expectation operator, and
$V(S_{n-1}, H_{n-1}, \delta_{n-1}, V_{n-1} | M_{n-1}, F_{n-1}, K_{n-1}, I_{n-1}, n-1)$
   $=$ profit function for the period $n - 1$.

Feeding costs for heifers in (3) are assumed to differ from those for steers for the following reasons: First, if heifers are kept in part for possible future breeding, there is no need to feed them as much as steers. Second, the capacity of heifers for transforming feed into weight is less than the capacity of steers; hence, the producer ought to keep heifers on feed for a smaller number of periods than he keeps steers.[3] f and g are shadow costs that reflect the amount of time needed for the animals to transform feed into pounds of beef. Thus the parameters f and g should be different.

Aging costs are also assumed to be different for cows, heifers, and steers in (3). The aging cost is the cost or the additional cost involved in keeping the animal one more period, resulting from the need for more feed and the higher probability of death, etc., as the animal becomes older. The principal element of the aging cost, however, is the loss in value at sale. Animals sold for slaugh-

---

[3] This is indeed the case. See, for example, Gustafson and Van Arsdall (1970, p. 56).

ter are classified by weight, sex, and age. Older animals are generally worth less, *ceteris paribus*. Aging costs must be considered because what is important is not the net investment, i.e., $\delta_n - V_n$, but rather gross investment and depreciation since the productivities and the expected benefits and costs differ according to age. Thus the retirement of a 10-year-old cow and the addition of a two-year-old heifer does not leave the capital stock unchanged, although we have assumed the production function is $B_n = \lambda K_n$.

The Maximizing Solution

To maximize $V(\ldots|\ldots, n)$ in (3) with respect to S_n, H_n, δ_n, and V_n subject to (4) is much more difficult than for our simple example. Although there are four arguments, it is only necessary to solve a system of three equations since the solution for steers is independent of the others. This is to be expected because the profit function is constructed so that it has this property. The number of males born is given once the size of the stock of capital is determined since the male-to-female ratio is assumed to be one and the calf crop is assumed to be proportional to the stock of capital. Bulls are about five percent of the total herd and their number can be assumed to be a small fixed proportion of the number of cattle. Castrated males, steers, can only be used for beef production. Once the number of steers is determined, the only decision is to sell them this period or to keep them on feed for future sale. This decision cannot have any effect on other maximizing values, except to the extent that fixed costs change as the total number of animals changes. For simplicity, we neglect this effect and assume the marginal change in the fixed costs due to the decision to sell one more steer is negligible.

The number of iterations needed to reach the general solution depends on the time unit considered. When a shorter time unit is used, many more than five iterations are needed to reach the general solution.

Following the standard procedure, we define the solution at last period $(n = 1)$:

$$S_1 = M_1, \qquad H_1 = F_1, \qquad V_1 = K_1, \qquad \delta_1 = 0. \qquad (5)$$

Since the cattleman is to retire at the end of the period, there is no point in further investment to produce calves that cannot be sold. Thus

$$B_1 = 0, \qquad C_1 = 0, \qquad I_1 = B_4. \qquad (6)$$

The impossibility of selling calves and the production period (nine months) implies

$$\delta_j = 0 \quad \text{for } j = 1, 2, \ldots, 6,$$
$$B_j = 0 \quad \text{for } j = 1, 2, 3, 4. \qquad (7)$$

Hence the maximization problem must be solved for six periods before any investment occurs. From iteration seven on, there is a system of equations to be solved (order three) because all decisions (except those for steers) are connected through the investment decision. The problem must be solved to iteration nine before we reach the general solution; i.e., the solution nine periods from the last is identical to those obtained $10, 11, \ldots,$ and n periods from the last.

Initially we attempted to solve this problem in completely algebraic form with the help of a computer using the FORMAC language. For technical reasons, it was not possible to obtain the final solution in completely algebraic form. The problem is that the expressions grow in size rapidly using FORMAC, which does not allow for certain simplifications automatically; hence, the total amount of storage space available in the computer is not enough to solve the problem.[4] Thus a completely analytical solution, such as the one presented in the previous section, cannot be obtained directly.

There are at least two alternative ways to avoid the storage problem, not counting simplification of the profit function or the elimination of decision variables. The first is to replace the shadow costs by their estimated values and then solve the maximization problem. We can see from (3) that part of the expression is actual total costs (TC_n):

$$
\begin{aligned}
\text{TC}_n = {} & \tfrac{1}{2}a(K_n + \delta_n - V_n)^2 + \tfrac{1}{2}b(K_n - V_n)^2 + \tfrac{1}{2}c(C_n)^2 \\
& + \tfrac{1}{2}d(B_n)^2 + \tfrac{1}{2}f(M_n - S_n + \tfrac{1}{2}I_n)^2 \\
& + \tfrac{1}{2}g(F_n - H_n - \delta_n + \tfrac{1}{2}I_n)^2 + \tfrac{1}{2}j(M_n - S_n)^2 \\
& + \tfrac{1}{2}k(F_n - H_n - \delta_n)^2.
\end{aligned}
\tag{8}
$$

An OLS regression based on (8) might be used to obtain numerical estimates of the shadow costs. These estimates might then be substituted in (3) and the maximization carried out as before. The numerical character of the profit function would eliminate the difficulty and permit standard numerical techniques to be used. The form of the solution is well defined, although the dependence of each coefficient of the final form on shadow costs is not identifiable. By trying various values of the shadow costs in a sensitivity analysis, we may obtain an idea of the effect of each shadow cost on the coefficients of the solution. The problem with this approach is that there are no available data on total costs.

A second alternative would be to get information about the possible values of the shadow costs. Using such values in (3), the maximization may then be performed numerically. The form of the solution is determined by the maximization procedure; if these solutions, in parametric form, i.e., equations determining the decision variables, were in turn estimated, the estimated coefficients could be compared to the coefficients obtained from the numerical

---

[4] Superior programs for algebraic manipulation may now be available that were not in 1971–1972 when the bulk of the research reported in this chapter was done. We have not explored such a possibility.

maximization for the initially specified values of the shadow costs as determined by outside information. By the following trial-and-error procedure, we eventually could obtain reasonable estimates for the shadow costs if they were exactly identifiable. The procedure is (1) make initial guesses and find the solution numerically; (2) re-estimate the equations so obtained to modify the initial guesses; (3) obtain different numerical solutions; (4) re-estimate the equations so obtained and again modify the values of the shadow costs; (5) repeat the above sequence until the solution values based on guesses are close to the final estimated values for the corresponding coefficients in the equations of the maximizing solutions. The problem with this procedure is that the computational cost involved is prohibitive. Each numerical solution for the maximizing problem takes about 45 min in computer time using almost all core available on an IBM 360/65 or comparable machine.

It is clear, given our problem and the actual state of the art, that the best thing to do is to guess the shadow costs as accurately as possible and then maximize (3). Though the numerical solution may not have much meaning, it does yield the *form* for each of the maximizing solutions; i.e., we obtain the variables relevant to the explanation of S_n, H_n, δ_n, and V_n. Once the form of these functions is determined, we can estimate the corresponding coefficients and make inferences about the response of cattlemen to changes in prices or changes in expected prices, although, of course, nothing can be said about the effects of changes in costs.

The Solution Form

By assuming numerical values for the shadow costs, we eliminate the serious problem of storage space for the long expressions generated during the maximization process. The cost of this simplification is what we call the "computer zero effect." In an algebraic expression like $(axzy - axzy)$, it is clear that the two terms cancel out, but if numerical values are substituted for a, x, and z, it is possible that a very small number will appear as the coefficient of y as a result of the above subtraction; hence, due to the "computer zero effect" when the general solution is reached, some variables will generally have very tiny coefficients that should be interpreted as zero.

Another inconvenience of using numerical values for the shadow costs is that, due to the arbitrariness of these values, we cannot place much confidence in the signs of those coefficients that are very small in absolute value; however, economic theory may suggest the proper sign in many instances.

The maximization of (3) subject to (4) was done, replacing the values of shadow costs by numerical values.[5] The equations for optimal decisions are as follows. Supply of steers for slaughter,

$$S_n = a_1 s_n - a_2 s_{n-1} - a_3 K_{n+4} + M_n. \tag{9}$$

---

[5] The FORMAC program used is reproduced in Appendix F of Carvalho (1972).

Supply of heifers for slaughter,

$$H_n = b_1 h_n - b_2 h_{n-1} - b_3 h_{n-2} - b_4 v_n + b_5 v_{n-1} + b_6 v_{n-2} + b_7 v_{n-3} - b_8 v_{n-4}$$
$$- b_9 h_{n-5} + b_{10} h_{n-6} + b_{11} h_{n-7} - b_{12} s_{n-5} + b_{13} s_{n-6} + b_{14} s_{n-7}$$
$$+ b_{15} K_{n+4} + b_{16} K_{n+3} + b_{17} K_{n+1} - b_{18} K_n + F_n. \tag{10}$$

Gross investment (heifers added to the stock of capital),

$$\delta_n = -d_1 h_n + d_2 h_{n-1} + d_3 h_{n-2} + d_4 v_n + d_5 v_{n-1} - d_6 v_{n-2} - d_7 v_{n-3} + d_8 v_{n-4}$$
$$+ d_9 h_{n-5} - d_{10} h_{n-6} - d_{11} h_{n-7} + d_{12} s_{n-5} - d_{13} s_{n-6} - d_{14} s_{n-7}$$
$$- d_{15} K_{n+3} - d_{16} K_{n+1} + d_{17} K_n - d_{18} F_n. \tag{11}$$

Worn-out capital (supply of cows for slaughter),

$$V_n = -c_1 h_n + c_2 h_{n-2} + c_3 v_n + c_4 v_{n-1} - c_5 v_{n-2} - c_6 v_{n-3} + c_7 v_{n-4} + c_8 h_{n-5}$$
$$- c_9 h_{n-6} - c_{10} h_{n-7} + c_{11} s_{n-5} - c_{12} s_{n-6} - c_{13} s_{n-7} + c_{14} K_{n+3}$$
$$- c_{15} K_{n+1} + K_n. \tag{12}$$

The solution for slaughter of steers is simple, as we expected, since steers are used for beef production and nothing else. In fact, we can get the analytical solution for S_n because it is exactly the same in any period more than one period from the last. This solution is

$$S_n = \left(\frac{1}{f} + \frac{1}{j} \right) s_n - \alpha \left(\frac{1}{f} + \frac{1}{j} \right) s_{n-1} - \frac{1}{2} \left(\frac{f}{f+j} \right) \lambda K_{n+4} + M_n. \tag{13}$$

Recall that f is the unit feeding cost for steers and j is the unit aging cost.

The interpretation of (13) is straightforward. It is better to analyze it not in terms of the slaughter decision, but in terms of demand for stock of steers by producers. Define $\text{STOCKS}_n = M_n - S_n$; then

$$\text{STOCKS}_n = -\left(\frac{1}{f} + \frac{1}{j} \right)(s_n - \alpha s_{n-1}) + \frac{1}{2} \left(\frac{f}{f+j} \right) \lambda K_{n+4}. \tag{14}$$

Thus the stock of steers kept by the producer increases if the expected change in prices between this period and next period (quarter) decreases or if there are a large number of young steers reaching nine months of age.

The supply of heifers and cows for slaughter is more complicated. In the long run, increasing slaughter of heifers or cows today is a substitute for slaughter of heifers, steers, and cows in the future, or conversely, reducing slaughter of heifers today is complementary with slaughter of heifers, steers, and cows in the future. On the other hand, in the short run there is a substitution between actual sales of heifers and actual sales of cows: If more heifers are sold this period, fewer cows need to be sold in order to obtain the same revenue, and vice versa. Moreover, if more cows are retired today, more heifers are needed for their replacement and, consequently, fewer heifers can be sold this period. We analyze the supply of heifers, the gross investment in cows, and the supply of cows separately in order to identify all these effects.

The supply of heifers for slaughter is given by (10). The first three elements of this expression are what may be called the short-run price for heifers: $b_1 h_n - b_2 h_{n-1} - b_3 h_{n-2}$. These terms express the short-run substitution between actual sales of heifers and sales over the next two quarters. The coefficient b_3 may be interpreted as αb_2, where α is the one-period discount factor. Thus the short-run price effect for heifers can be written as $b_1 h_n - b_2(h_{n-1} + \alpha h_{n-2})$. This implies that in the short run more heifers will be sold as the actual price of heifers increases, provided this increase is larger than the discounted expected increase in the price of heifers for the next two quarters, interpreting b_2 as αb_1.

The short-run price effect for cows reflects the substitution between cows and heifers in their contribution to the total revenue. It is $-b_4 v_n$. As expected, as the price of cows increases, more cows are sold this period, and therefore fewer heifers need be sold to obtain a given total revenue.

The long-run price effects may all be considered as long-run gross revenue effects, made up of the long-run price effects for heifers, steers, and cows. The term "gross revenue effects" is used because heifers produce calves, males or females, and eventually become cows. The long-run steer and heifer price effects are similar, differing only in magnitude due to different feeding and aging costs for males and females. In (10), these effects are

$$-b_{12}s_{n-5} + b_{13}s_{n-6} + b_{14}s_{n-7} \qquad \text{for steers,}$$

and

$$-b_9 h_{n-5} + b_{10} h_{n-6} + b_{11} h_{n-7} \qquad \text{for heifers.}$$

Again, we may interpret successive coefficients in terms of the discount factor α. Thus $b_{13} = \alpha b_{12}$, $b_{14} = \alpha^2 b_{12}$, $b_{10} = \alpha b_9$, and $b_{11} = \alpha^2 b_9$. Therefore the long-run price effects are

$$-b_{12}(s_{n-5} - \alpha s_{n-6} - \alpha^2 s_{n-7}) \qquad \text{for steers,}$$

and

$$-b_9(h_{n-5} - \alpha h_{n-6} - \alpha^2 h_{n-7}) \qquad \text{for heifers.}$$

An interpretation of these effects is as follows: If expectations about future prices of steers or heifers are high compared with current prices, this implies sale of fewer heifers, *ceteris paribus*. Included in the *ceteris paribus* is the relation between the expected price five periods from now and the present value at five periods from now of the expected prices for steers and heifers seven periods from now. Alternatively, a high expected value of the calf crop (steers or heifers) implies a decrease in the sale of heifers now if the gain from not selling the heifers (h_{n-5}) can be postponed to the future with an additional gain of ($\alpha h_{n-6} - h_{n-5}$) or ($\alpha^2 h_{n-7} - h_{n-5}$). This is similar to the general problem of when an investment should be made. In that case, the optimal procedure is to make the investment when the present value of the net benefit from this investment is maximum. This is just our interpretation of the long-run steer and heifer price effects.

The five-period lead in these price effects can be explained as follows: Once the heifer is selected for the reproductive herd (δ_n), she does not contribute to actual production because production is defined as $B_n = \lambda K_n$, but she will affect the next period's production ($K_{n-1} = K_n + \delta_n - V_n$). A calf born in period $n - 1$ can be sold only in period $n - 5$ because it is assumed that animals cannot be sold unless they are at least nine months old. No great loss of generality results by altering the assumptions as follows: A decision to breed a heifer now will only increase the production of calves three periods from now. If we assume that animals can be sold after six months of age, then the same expected prices appear in the steer and heifer price effects. If a heifer is bred in period n, she will produce a calf in period $n - 3$ that will be six months of age in period $n - 5$.

The long-run price effect for cows is different. When heifers are bred, they become cows after the first calf crop. Since the potential revenue is contributed not only by a calf but also by what the cow would bring if slaughtered, the expected price for cows four periods from now must be considered as benefit from *not* selling a heifer now, while the expected price for cows for the next three periods is a cost involved in transforming heifers into cows. Another aspect of breeding heifers is that cows must be retired at some point and therefore replaced by heifers. The retirement of a cow will depend, among other things, on actual and expected slaughter price for cows: A higher actual slaughter price for cows induces more retirements now while higher expected prices for cows in the future induces postponement of retirements. From (10) the long-run price effect for cows is given by

$$b_5 v_{n-1} + b_6 v_{n-2} + b_7 v_{n-3} - b_8 v_{n-4}.$$

Interpreting successive coefficients in terms of the discount factor,

$$b_6 = \alpha b_5 \quad \text{and} \quad b_7 = \alpha^2 b_5,$$

we find the long-run cow price effect on the slaughter of heifers can be written

$$b_5(v_{n-1} + \alpha v_{n-2} + \alpha^2 v_{n-3}) - b_8 v_{n-4}.$$

Interpretation of other elements in the supply of heifers for slaughter is straightforward. Past stocks of reproductive animals represent the stocks of young heifers at different ages, which affects actual decisions. The larger the stock of reproductive animals in the past, the less need for keeping large stocks of heifers now since (1) there is a large number of calves that will increase the stock of heifers in the future, and (2) there is less need for increasing the reproductive herd. Thus it is assumed that the sign of K_{n+3} is positive, but its magnitude may be small.[6]

---

[6] The numerical solution yields a very small number for the coefficient of K_{n+3}; however, as indicated above, not much confidence can be placed on the sign of this coefficient.

The supply of heifers for slaughter may be redefined as a demand for a stock of heifers by the cattleman, where this stock is defined as

$$STOCKH_n = F_n - H_n.$$

Thus

$$
\begin{aligned}
STOCKH_n = & -b_1 h_n + b_2(h_{n-1} + \alpha h_{n-2}) + b_4 v_n \\
& - b_5(v_{n-1} + \alpha v_{n-2} + \alpha^2 v_{n-3}) + b_8 v_{n-4} \\
& + b_9(h_{n-5} - \alpha h_{n-6} - \alpha^2 h_{n-7}) \\
& + b_{12}(s_{n-5} - \alpha s_{n-6} - \alpha^2 s_{n-7}) - b_{15} K_{n+4} \\
& - b_{16} K_{n+3} - b_{17} K_{n+1} + b_{18} K_n.
\end{aligned}
\tag{15}
$$

The gross investment function is quite similar to the supply of heifers, and the price effects should be of opposite sign to those determined for heifers. Comparing δ_n in (11) with H_n in (10), it can be seen that, except for the sign of v_{n-1}, all the price effects have the expected signs, i.e., signs opposite to those obtained in the supply of heifers. A possible explanation is the numerical nature of our solution. With respect to the other elements in the gross investment decision, we expect K_{n+3} to have the opposite sign as before. The stock of females F_n appears in the solution for δ_n with a negative coefficient. On the one hand, we expect that the larger the stock of heifers with ages between one and two years, the larger the number of heifers that can be bred. On the other hand, the larger F_n, the more heifers can be slaughtered today, whereas the decision to place them in the reproductive herd can be postponed since F_n is large. The second effect should be stronger than the first since the coefficient for F_n in the equation for the slaughter of heifers is one. Gross investment can be written

$$
\begin{aligned}
\delta_n = & -d_1 h_n + d_2(h_{n-1} + \alpha h_{n-2}) + d_4 v_n \\
& + d_5(v_{n-1} - \alpha v_{n-2} - \alpha^2 v_{n-3}) + d_8 v_{n-4} \\
& + d_9(h_{n-5} - \alpha h_{n-6} - \alpha^2 h_{n-7}) \\
& + d_{12}(s_{n-5} - \alpha s_{n-6} - \alpha^2 s_{n-7}) - d_{15} K_{n+3} \\
& - d_{16} K_{n+1} + d_{17} K_n - d_{18} F_n.
\end{aligned}
\tag{16}
$$

The supply of cows for slaughter is now easy to interpret. The short-run heifer price effect is given by $-c_1 h_n + c_2 h_{n-2}$. Defining the demand for cows and heifers older than two years of age as

$$STOCKC_n = K_n - V_n,$$

we have

$$
\begin{aligned}
STOCKC_n = & \ c_1 h_n - c_2 h_{n-2} - c_3 v_n - c_4(v_{n-1} - \alpha v_{n-2} - \alpha^2 v_{n-3}) \\
& - c_7 v_{n-4} - c_8(h_{n-5} - \alpha h_{n-6} - \alpha^2 h_{n-7}) \\
& - c_{11}(s_{n-5} - \alpha s_{n-6} - \alpha^2 s_{n-7}) - c_{14} K_{n+3} + c_{15} K_{n+1}.
\end{aligned}
\tag{17}
$$

In order to use (14)–(17), to draw inferences about the cattleman's behavior, we need a theory to explain how price expectations are formed. If the futures market in the cattle industry were well developed, the futures prices could be used as approximations to the expected prices, as suggested in Johnson (1947). However, these markets are not well developed. We therefore adopt the quasi-rational expectations models discussed in the preceding chapter.

5.   Tests of the Model with Quasi-Rational Expectations

Profit maximization over time provides us with relations governing the optimal decisions that should be taken each period. Unfortunately, data on individuals are not available to test the model at a disaggregated level. Thus we assume that the optimal behavioral functions obtained in Section 4 are the same for all; then we can aggregate over all producers in the U.S. beef sector to obtain the following set of equations to be estimated:

Own-demand for stock of steers

$$\text{STOCKS}_t = -\alpha_1(s_t - \alpha s_{t+1}) + \alpha_2 K_{t-4} + u_{1t}; \tag{1}$$

Own-demand for the stock of heifers

$$\begin{aligned}
\text{STOCKH}_t = &-\beta_1 h_t + \beta_2(h_{t+1} + \alpha h_{t+2}) + \beta_3 v_t \\
&- \beta_4(v_{t+1} + \alpha v_{t+2} + \alpha^2 v_{t+3}) + \beta_5 v_{t+4} \\
&+ \beta_6(h_{t+5} - \alpha h_{t+6} - \alpha^2 h_{t+7}) + \beta_7(s_{t+5} - \alpha s_{t+6} - \alpha^2 s_{t+7}) \\
&- \beta_8 K_{t-4} - \beta_9 K_{t-3} - \beta_{10} K_{t-1} + \beta_{11} K_t + u_{2t};
\end{aligned} \tag{2}$$

Gross investment

$$\begin{aligned}
\delta_t = &-\gamma_1 h_t + \gamma_2(h_{t+1} + \alpha h_{t+2}) + \gamma_3 v_t \\
&+ \gamma_4(v_{t+1} - \alpha v_{t+2} - \alpha^2 v_{t+3}) + \gamma_5 v_{t+4} \\
&+ \gamma_6(h_{t+5} - \alpha h_{t+6} - \alpha^2 h_{t+7}) + \gamma_7(s_{t+5} - \alpha s_{t+6} - \alpha^2 s_{t+7}) \\
&- \gamma_8 K_{t-3} - \gamma_9 K_{t-1} + \gamma_{10} K_t - \gamma_{11} F_t + u_{3t};
\end{aligned} \tag{3}$$

Own-demand for the stock of cows

$$\begin{aligned}
\text{STOCKC}_t = &\,\epsilon_1 h_t - \epsilon_2 h_{t+2} - \epsilon_3 v_t - \epsilon_4(v_{t+1} - \alpha v_{t+2} - \alpha^2 v_{t+3}) \\
&- \epsilon_5 v_{t+4} - \epsilon_6(h_{t+5} - \alpha h_{t+6} - \alpha^2 h_{t+7}) \\
&- \epsilon_7(s_{t+5} - \alpha s_{t+6} - \alpha^2 s_{t+7}) - \epsilon_8 K_{t-3} + \epsilon_9 K_{t-1} + u_{4t}. \tag{4}
\end{aligned}$$

All variables have the same meaning as before, but the time subscript t refers to actual time and not to the number of periods until retirement, as in Section 4. Thus K_{t-4} is the stock of cows kept in the beef sector four periods prior to period t, and h_{t+5} is the expected price of heifers five periods ahead of period t as expected in period t. The u's added to each equation are random disturbances introduced to allow for aggregation errors, misspecification of variables, and other errors in the model such as omitted variables, including those which may be used by cattlemen in forming their price expectations other than past prices themselves. Note also that prices with subscripts $t + j$ are in fact expected prices for period $t + j$ in period t.

Attention should be called to the fact that almost all dependent variables in our model are stocks and are explained by other stocks and prices. In general, estimation of stock equations presents certain difficulties. Two particular aspects of the problem are worth commentary: First, estimation of the stock equations is based on the assumption that the observed stock is equal to the desired stock because the desired stock adjustment model is not used in the formulation of the model. Because we did not use this concept, the identification and other problems associated with it do not arise. Second, the usual difficulty with the error term in a stock function does not occur in all of our equations. If stocks are explained by flows that are, in turn, used to define stocks, it is possible that errors in the flow variables may generate autocorrelated errors in the stock equations. This cannot occur in our equation explaining the stock of steers because the stock of steers is a function of past stocks of cows and actual and expected prices, not of past flows of steers. Such difficulties might arise, however, in the equations explaining the stock of heifers and of cows for the following reasons: In the case of heifers, the stock of females F_t is computed as $F_{t+1} = F_t - H_t - \delta_t + \frac{1}{2}I_t$; hence, errors in flow variables such as H_t and δ_t are incorporated in the following stocks of females. Since we want to estimate $STOCKH_t = F_t - H_t$ as the dependent variable, the errors in the equation for this variable may well be autocorrelated. For cows, a similar situation arises. $STOCKC_t = K_t - V_t$ is the dependent variable, while K_t is defined as $K_t = K_{t-1} + \delta_{t-1} - V_{t-1}$. Fortunately, this potential autocorrelation does not appear to be an important consideration in the results reported below.

The data needed for estimating the model are described in Carvalho (1972). The expected prices were generated by the quasi-rational approach, and the time-series models used are those reported in Chapters X and XI. The data on stocks and heifers retained in the beef sector are available for 1944–1969 as described in Carvalho (1972, Appendix A). Price data are available for longer periods, as indicated in Chapter X. Using the models developed in Chapter X, we derived monthly forecasts for the prices of steers, cows, and heifers various steps ahead for the period 1944–1969 and aggregated these into quarterly forecasts.

Due to lack of other information, we can only estimate the steer and heifer relationships.[7]

Own-demand for the stock of steers

$$STOCKS_t = -\alpha_1(s_t - \alpha s_{t+1}) + \alpha_2 K_{t-4} + u_{1t}; \tag{5}$$

---

[7] For a complete discussion of this matter see Carvalho (1972, pp. 119–138). The own-demand for cows can also be estimated, but since it is not possible to predict the signs of some coefficients, the results are not reported here.

Supply of heifers for slaughter

$$H_t = \beta_1 h_t - \beta_2(h_{t+1} + \alpha h_{t+2}) - \beta_3 v_t$$
$$+ \beta_4(v_{t+1} + \alpha v_{t+2} + \alpha^2 v_{t+3}) - \beta_5 v_{t+4}$$
$$- \beta_6(h_{t+5} - \alpha h_{t+6} - \alpha^2 h_{t+7})$$
$$- \beta_7(s_{t+5} - \alpha s_{t+6} - \alpha^2 s_{t+7}) + \beta_8 K_{t-4}$$
$$+ \beta_9 K_{t-3} + \beta_{10} K_{t-1} - \beta_{11} K_t + \beta_{12} F_t + u_{5t}. \tag{6}$$

Our model is tested by fitting each of the behavioral functions by ordinary least squares for the period 1944–1969. The model can be considered a good approximation to cattlemen's behavior if the empirical results agree with the responses predicted by the theory. Joint estimation procedures might be used to improve the efficiency of the estimated coefficients as mentioned above; however, the lack of information, especially on gross investment δ_t, does not allow us to proceed in this fashion.

As noted above, the coefficient of K_{t-4} in (5) should be positive, and the coefficient for K_t in (6) should be negative, while the coefficient for F_t should be positive. This should be so in the first case due to the fact that STOCKS$_t$ as computed from the available information includes $\frac{1}{2}\lambda K_{t-4}$; in the second case, it is due to the fact that δ_t is included in the definition of K_t and F_t (Carvalho, 1972, Appendix A).

Estimation of the relationships described in (4.14) allow us to identify the one-period discount factor, which should therefore be used in the estimation of (6). From the estimates of (4.14) in Table 1, we find the one-period gross rate of return to be 25%, which seems quite large. In turn, this value implies $\alpha = 0.8$, a value that appears to be too small. Alternatively, we may impose the constraints in (4.14) and use a maximum-likelihood procedure to determine the value of α. Unfortunately, the likelihood function is very flat with respect to α, making the determination of this parameter difficult. Evidence on futures prices suggests a value of α close to 0.975, which was imposed in a second set of regressions for steers and for heifers (Carvalho, 1972, pp. 122–123). The own-demand for steers with the constraint $\alpha = 0.975$ is reported in Table 1 in the second panel. All coefficients have the predicted sign and are significantly different from zero.

The results are reported in Table 2 for the supply of heifers.

If we use a 10-percent one-tailed significance test, of the 12 coefficients only two are not significantly from zero, EXPS57 and K_{t-4}. All have the sign predicted by the theory. Note that EXPS57 is highly correlated with EXPH57, which may account for the low t-ratio.

As pointed out in Chapters VI and XI, formation of the expectations about future values of economic variables may be simultaneously determined. In Chapter XI we used price data for the beef cattle industry and constructed a simultaneous model for the formation of expectations about the prices of steers, heifers, and cows. In Chapter XI we derived multiple-time-series models and monthly forecasts for the period 1965–1974. For the purposes of this

TABLE 1 *Own-Demand for Stock of Steers*[a]

Independent variable	Predicted sign	Estimated coefficients[b]
Unconstrained estimates		
s_t	−	−626.632
		(2.79)
s_{t+1}	+	504.164
		(2.27)
K_{t-4}	+	0.504
		(13.89)

$R^2 = 0.6479$ S.E.R.[c] = 3229.03
AVER[d] = 11915.5
D.W.[e] = 2.02

$F_{(2,97)} = 89.23$

Constrained estimates $\alpha = 0.975$		
$(s_t - \alpha s_{t+1}^*)$	−	−616.804
		(2.67)
K_{t-4}	+	0.415
		(37.95)

$R^2 = 0.6241$ S.E.R.[c] = 3319.3
AVER[d] = 11915.5
D.W.[e] = 2.26

$F_{(1,98)} = 162.68$

[a] Unconstrained and constrained for $\alpha = 0.975$, 1944–1969, dependent variable: STOCKS$_t$.
[b] Figure in parentheses beneath each coefficient is its *t*-ratio.
[c] Standard Error of Regression.
[d] Sample average of the dependent variable.
[e] Durbin–Watson Statistic.

chapter we computed monthly forecasts various steps ahead for the period 1944–1969 and aggregated them to quarter forecasts.

Using the multiple-time-series model forecasts to define the expected prices needed to estimate equation (6), we obtained the results reported in Table 3. From the overall indicators of the fit, the single-time-series approach to the expectation formation models used appears to perform somewhat better. The coefficient for EXPH57 has the wrong sign, although it is not significantly different from zero. The magnitudes of the remaining coefficients are implausible in many instances and often have lower associated *t*-ratios. In short, one cannot regard the use of forecasts generated by the multiple-time-series models presented in Chapter XI as a significant improvement *in this context* over the simple single-time-series models developed in Chapter X. This does not mean, of course, that the multiple-time-series approach is not appropriate or would not significantly improve the results in another context.

TABLE 2 *Supply of Heifers[a]*

Independent variable	Predicted signs	Estimated coefficients[b]
h_t	+	47.004
		(1.68)
EXPH12[c]	−	−23.018
		(2.28)
v_t	−	−178.458
		(3.05)
EXPC13[d]	+	152.544
		(3.67)
v_{t+4}	−	−296.942
		(3.27)
EXPH57[e]	−	−10.526
		(1.60)
EXPS57[f]	−	−14.694
		(0.51)
K_t	−	−0.143
		(3.71)
K_{t-4}	+	0.039
		(1.23)
K_{t-3}	+	0.081
		(5.25)
K_{t-1}	+	0.031
		(1.82)
F_t	+	0.202
		(4.52)

$R^2 = 0.7992$ S.E.R. = 300.867
AVER = 2550.46
D.W. = 1.93
$F_{(11,88)} = 31.84$

[a] With constraint $\alpha = 0.975$, 1944–1969, dependent variable: HEIFER$_t$.

[b] Figure in parentheses beneath each coefficient is its t-ratio.

[c] EXPH12 $= (h^*_{t+1} + \alpha h^*_{t+2})$.

[d] EXPC13 $= (v^*_{t+1} + \alpha v^*_{t+2} + \alpha^2 v^*_{t+3})$.

[e] EXPH57 $= (h^*_{t+5} - \alpha h^*_{t+6} - \alpha^2 h^*_{t+7})$.

[f] EXPS57 $= (s^*_{t+5} - \alpha s^*_{t+6} - \alpha^2 s^*_{t+7})$.

The example presented in this chapter represents an alternative to the traditional stock adjustment models. In a dynamic problem, it is desirable to have an objective function maximized over time and thus to have a technique that allows us to perform the maximization analytically. It is shown here that dynamic programming can be of practical use even though the number of decision variables is greater than two. We regard the development of an analytical dynamic programming maximization procedure on an electronic com-

TABLE 3 *Supply of Heifers[a]*

Independent variable	Predicted signs	Estimated coefficients[b]
h_t	+	6.395
		(0.16)
EXPH12[c]	−	−51.601
		(1.27)
v_t	−	−81.662
		(2.42)
EXPC13[d]	+	53.402
		(2.32)
v_{t+4}	−	−111.155
		(1.81)
EXPH57[e]	−	16.494
		(0.19)
EXPS57[f]	−	−129.423
		(2.30)
K_t	−	−0.177
		(4.61)
K_{t-4}	+	0.099
		(3.27)
K_{t-3}	+	0.024
		(1.83)
K_{t-1}	+	0.085
		(6.86)
F_t	+	0.146
		(3.51)

$R^2 = 0.793$ S.E.R. = 305.768
AVER = 2550.46
D.W. = 1.95
$F_{(11,88)} = 30.54$

[a] With constraint $\alpha = 0.975$, expected prices estimated from a multiple-time-series model approach (see Chapter XI).

[b] Figure in parentheses beneath each coefficient is its *t*-ratio.

[c] $\text{EXPH12} = (h_{t+1}^* + \alpha h_{t+2}^*)$.

[d] $\text{EXPC13} = (v_{t+1}^* + \alpha v_{t+2}^* + \alpha^2 v_{t+3}^*)$.

[e] $\text{EXPH57} = (h_{t+5}^* - \alpha h_{t+6}^* - \alpha^2 h_{t+7}^*)$.

[f] $\text{EXPS57} = (s_{t+5}^* - \alpha s_{t+6}^* - \alpha^2 s_{t+7}^*)$.

puter, through the use of languages such as FORMAC that allow us to manipulate algebraic expressions, as a priority development if we are to further implement this approach. As the difficulties in FORMAC are overcome, analytical solutions may be obtained for problems as complicated or more complicated. The imposition of restrictions in the objective function allows us to obtain econometrically relevant behavioral functions to approximate individual behavior.

Appendix A
THE WORK OF BUYS BALLOT

Christoph Hendrik Didericus Buys Ballot (1817–1890) occupies a peculiar place in the literature surveyed in Chapter I. None of the nineteenth century British work considered contains any reference to him, although his work is referenced occasionally in contemporary literature. In a previous paper, one of us stated rather casually that work on unobserved components of time series has been going on at least since the publication of Buys Ballot's *Les Changements Périodiques de Témperature* in 1847, perhaps giving the impression that it originated there (Nerlove, 1967, p. 130). Guilbaud (1951) presents monthly data on the circulation of money in France using a table with 12 columns, one for each month of the year. "Cette disposition est connue sous le nom de Table de Buys Ballot," he says (1951, p. 8) and refers to Buys Ballot's 1847 book. According to Guilbaud, if one records time-series data in a rectangular table and calculates the column averages, one is using "le filtre de Buys Ballot" (1951, p. 12). Despite recent references, however, no detailed account of Buys Ballot's work appears anywhere in the econometric literature. We present one here because Buys Ballot appears to have anticipated many of the nineteenth century contributions to the analysis of economic time series by means of unobserved-components models.

Buys Ballot was a meteorologist and had a distinguished career as the Director of the Royal Netherlands Meteorological Institute, a position he held from 1854 until shortly before his death in 1890. He is remembered today primarily for Buys Ballot's law: The direction of the wind is perpendicular to the pressure gradient. Thus if one stands in the northern hemisphere with the wind at his back, one will have high pressure on one's right and low pressure on one's left (the directions are reversed in the southern hemisphere).

The empiricism characteristic of nineteenth century science, in general, is central to Buys Ballot's work; his approach was the careful analysis of meteorological data to discover the underlying laws. Buys Ballot's "law" was deduced from strictly empirical evidence in 1857, and he was apparently unaware that the same law had been derived theoretically by the American meteorologist, William Ferrel. During the 1850s, Buys Ballot studied meteorological records from several locations in the hope of finding a means for determining the weather at different places using observations taken at one point (Buys Ballot, 1861). His book, *Les Changements Périodiques de Témperature*, describes his attempts to find periodicities in meteorological phenomena and to relate the periodicities to their specific causes. Buys Ballot's purpose in the study was to find regularities that could be used in weather forecasting. In the book, Buys Ballot analyzes time-series data, and the major analytic device employed is the table that bears his name.

Presenting time-series data in a rectangular array was not uncommon in Buys Ballot's time; his innovation is not the table itself but the use made of it. The problem that Buys Ballot considers is the following: If one observes the sum of several periodic sequences what can be deduced about the patterns of the individual components of the series? Buys Ballot presents his method in the form of five theorems (the first three theorems are attributed to a Professor Nervander of Helsinki). Proofs of the theorems are not given, but the truth of each of the theorems is illustrated by means of numerical examples.

In the discussion following, all sequences $\{x_t\}$ are indexed by $t = 1, 2, 3, \ldots$. Let $r(x_t: t = 1, 2, \ldots, p) = (r_1, r_2, \ldots, r_p)$ be the p-tuple giving rank orderings of $\{x_t: t = 1, 2, \ldots, p\}$. For instance, if $r_j = 1$, then x_j is the smallest of the p numbers. A sequence $\{x_t\}$ is said to be periodic with period n if

$$x_t = x_{t+n}, \qquad t = 1, 2, 3, \ldots, \tag{1}$$

and n is the smallest integer satisfying (1). In the theorems, sequences are recorded in arrays from left to right starting with the top row.

Theorem 1. Let $\{x_t\}$ be a periodic sequence with period n. Suppose that $n \cdot m$ consecutive terms are recorded in a table with m rows and n columns, and let $(Y_1, Y_2, \ldots, Y_n)$ be the column sums; then

$$r(x_t: t = 1, 2, \ldots, n) = r(Y_1, Y_2, \ldots, Y_n).$$

This theorem is illustrated by writing the sequence $1, 3, 5, 7, 9, 7, 5, 3, 1, 3, \ldots$ in a table with eight columns. The fifth column, of course, had the largest sum, the fourth and sixth columns the second largest sums, and so on.[1]

---

[1] Theorem 1:

> Si l'on a une série de nombres qui croissent et décroissent suivant une certaine loi, et dont le $n + 1^e$ terme ait la même valeur que le premier (conséquemment une série périodique de n termes), et que l'on dispose cette serie de manière à ce que le $n + 1^e$ terme se trouve sous le premier, les sommes résultantes de l'addition des diverses colonnes formeront également une série périodique. (1847, p. 34)

Theorem 2. Let $\{x_t\}$ be a periodic sequence with period n. If $m(n + 1)$ consecutive elements are recorded in a table with $n + 1$ columns and $m \equiv 0 \bmod n$ rows, then the column sums will be identical.[2]

The truth of this theorem is demonstrated by writing the series from the previous example in a table with eight rows and nine columns. The sum of each column is equal to 40, showing that the periodic pattern has been destroyed.

Theorem 3. Let $\{x_t^i\}$, $i = 1, 2, \ldots, k$, be k periodic sequences with periods $n^i \neq n^j$ if $i \neq j$. Let $\{z_t\} = \{\sum_{i=1}^k x_t^i\}$; then $\{z_t\}$ is periodic with period n, where n is the least common multiple of the n^i. Suppose that $m \cdot n^i$ consecutive elements of z_t are recorded in a table with n^i columns and m rows, where m is chosen so that $m \cdot n^i \equiv 0 \bmod n$. If Y_j is the sum of the jth column, then $r(Y_j : j = 1, \ldots, n^i) = r(x_t^i : t = 1, \ldots, n^i)$.[3]

To illustrate this theorem Buys Ballot sums across the following three sequences:
(a) $1, 3, 5, 7, 5, 3, 1, 3, 5, \ldots$
(b) $6, 4, 2, 4, 6, 4, \ldots$
(c) $1, 2, 2, 1, 2, 2, \ldots$
By this procedure one obtains the following series with a period of 12:

$$8, 9, 9, 12, 13, 9, 4, 9, 13, 12, 9, 9, \ldots$$

To show that it is possible to recapture the pattern of the underlying periodicities, Buys Ballot presents the tables shown below:

(a)						(b)				(c)		
8	9	9	12	13	9	8	9	9	12	8	9	9
4	9	13	12	9	9	13	9	4	9	12	13	9
8	9	9	12	13	9	13	12	9	9	4	9	13
4	9	13	12	9	9	8	9	9	12	12	9	9
24	36	44	48	44	36	13	9	4	9	36	40	40
						13	12	9	9			
						68	60	44	60			

[2] Theorem 2:

Si l'on dispose les termes d'une série périodique de n termes . . . de manière à ne pas écrire sous le premier terme, le premier de la seconde période, mais le 2ᵉ, le 3ᵉ, etc., et que l'on continue ainsi un certain nombre de fois, les sommes obtenues ne formeront presque plus une série périodique. (1847, p. 34)

Buys Ballot suggests the following addition to this theorem:

On devra continuer à poser de nouvelles rangées jusqu' à ce que chaque chiffre des périodes suivantes se trouve un égal nombre de fois dans chaque colonne, et dans ce cas, il ne restera *rien* de ces périodes. (1847, p. 35)

[3] Theorem 3:

Si l'on dispose l'une sous l'autre, deux ou plusieurs séries périodiques et que l'on prenne les sommes des diverse colonnes, on obtiendra une série de nombres, qui étant disposés de diverses manières en rangées placées l'une sous l'autre, donneront par leur réunion des périodes d'un

Is it possible to find the individual components of the series? Suppose that a constant is added to one of the components and subtracted from another. Their sum is not affected by this operation, so clearly the components can at best be determined up to an additive constant. Calculating the column averages in the tables and setting the minimum to zero in each case gives

(a) $0, 3, 5, 6, 5, 3$
(b) $4, 2\frac{2}{3}, 0, 2\frac{2}{3}$
(c) $0, 1, 1$.

In each case the rank ordering of the numbers is the same as that of the original components, but only in the third case are the differences between successive terms the same. Buys Ballot states that this is because the period of the third series (3) has no common factors with the periods of the other two (6 and 4). As with his other theorems and statements, he gives no proof of this assertion; indeed, it is false! Suppose, for example, that instead of sequence (a) Buys Ballot had used the sequence 1, 2, 3, 4, 5, 6, 1, 2, 3, . . . , which when added to (b) and (c) gives 8, 8, 7, 9, 13, 12, 4, 8, 11, 9, 9, 12 with period of 12. Repeating the calculations used to estimate the sequence (c) gives

8	8	7
9	13	12
4	8	11
9	9	12
30	38	42

Averaging columns and setting the minimum average to zero yields 0, 2, 3, which does not correspond to the actual sequence. The problem is that three and six have a common factor greater than 1, so that in general it is not possible to recover the exact pattern of either sequence from their sum. A correct version of the result is

Assertion (corrected). Let Y^n be the family of all sequences $\{Y_t\}$ with period n, and let $\{X_t\}$ be a sequence with period m. Take $\{Z_t\} = \{X_t + Y_t\}$. $\{Z_t\}$ is periodic; let its period be N. Suppose that $r \cdot m$ consecutive elements of $\{Z_t\}$ are recorded in a table with m columns and r rows, where $r \cdot m \equiv 0 \bmod N$. Then the differences between average of the ith column and the $(i + 1)$th column is given by $X_{i+j} - X_{i+j+1}, j \equiv 0 \bmod m$, for all $\{Y_t\} \in Y^n$ if and only if m and n have no common factors greater than one.[4]

---

[4] *Proof*: Let A_i be the average of the ith column:

$$A_i = \frac{1}{r} \sum_{j=0}^{r-1} z_{i+jm} = \frac{1}{r} \sum_{j=0}^{r-1} x_{i+jm} + \frac{1}{r} \sum_{j=0}^{r-1} y_{i+jm} = x_i + \frac{1}{r} \sum_{j=0}^{r-1} y_{i+jm}.$$

Thus, the "filtre de Buys Ballot" can determine the location of the maximum, the minimum, and the "periodic order" in general, but it cannot determine the exact quantitative patterns of the unobserved components except in special cases.

The fourth theorem of Buys Ballot[5] is a generalization of Theorem 2. Freely interpreted,

Theorem 4. Let $\{X_t\}$ be a periodic sequence with period n. Suppose the sequence is recorded in a table with c columns and r rows, where c and r have no common factors greater than one. If $r \equiv 0 \bmod n$, then the column sums will be identical.

Buys Ballot uses his theorems to search for periodicities in meteorological data. Of course, he does not simply search through all possible periods, but only in rather narrow ranges. For example, if he sought an influence of the moon in his data, he had only to look for periods whose length was close to the lunar month, confident that each of the periodicities sought lay within a fairly narrow range. Consider a series with period $n = 5$ arranged in tables with four and six

---

Hence

$$A_i - A_{i+1} = x_i - x_{i+1} + \frac{1}{r}\left\{\sum_{j=0}^{r-1}\left[y_{i+jm} - y_{i+1+jm}\right]\right\} = x_i - x_{i+1} + B.$$

In this discussion let each member of the sequence $\{Y_i\}$ be represented by its index (modulo n). Consider any index; it occurs a certain number of times in the ith column depending on n, m, and r. Suppose that every index in the ith column appears an equal number of times in the $i + 1$st column; then B will be zero. Clearly this is the only way in which B can be zero for every sequence in Y^n. Let $I(y)^i$ be the set of indices appearing in the ith column. Then

$$I(y)^i = \{k : i + jm \equiv k \bmod n, j = 0, 1, \ldots, r - 1\}.$$

Since $a \equiv b \bmod n$ implies $a + 1 \equiv (b + 1) \bmod n$, $I(y)^i = I(y)^{i+1}$ if and only if $I(y)^i = \{0, 1, 2, \ldots, n - 1\}$. But this can only happen when m and n have no common factors greater than one. Let D be the largest common divisor of m and n. We want to show that $I(y)^i = \{0, 1, \ldots, n - 1\}$ implies $D = 1$. The number of elements in $I(y)^i$ is less than or equal to r. But $rm = 0 \bmod N$. Since $ND = m \cdot n$, $r = Qn/D$, where Q is an integer ≥ 1. Thus the number of elements in $I(y)^i$, n, is less than or equal to $r = Qn/D$ for any $Q \geq 1$. Hence, $D = 1$. On the other hand, if $I(y)^i$ does not have n elements, then there must exist distinct numbers j and k both of which are less than n such that $i + jm \equiv i + km$ mod n. Thus $(j - k)m \equiv 0 \bmod n$, which means that m and n have a common factor.

[5] Theorem 4:

> Si l'on s'est mépris sur la durée d'une période composée de nombres donnés, l'addition répétée rendra cette période moins perceptible, d'autant plus rapidement que l'on se sera plus écarté de la vraie durée de la période, et que l'on aura additionné un plus grand nombre de termes. (1847, p. 38)

columns, with each element represented by its index (modulo 5)

1	2	3	4		1	2	3	4	5	1
5	1	2	3		2	3	4	5	1	2
4	5	1	2		3	4	5	1	2	3
3	4	5	1		4	5	1	2	3	4
2	3	4	5		5	1	2	3	4	5
1	2	3	4		1	2	3	4	5	1
5	1	2	3		2	3	4	5	1	2
4	5	1	2		3	4	5	1	2	3

In the table with four columns (corresponding to a guess of too small a period) the elements in the sequence appear in successive rows of the table displaced to the right. In the case where the "guess" as to the length of the period is too large, the opposite occurs. If one takes sums of successive rows, a similar phenomenon may be expected; as more rows are added, the location of the maximum and minimum column sums should tend to shift to the right or left depending upon whether the number of columns is smaller or larger than the true period. Thus, by observing the behavior of the column sums, it is possible to determine whether the period is greater or less than the number of columns in the table. These observations are all included in Buys Ballot's Theorem 5, which we do not translate here.[6] One part of Buys Ballot's theorem that can be proved is our

Theorem 5. Let $\{X_t\}$ be a periodic sequence with period n. Suppose that $\{X_t\}$ is recorded in a table with m columns and that the column sums for rows j to $j + k$ and $j + na$ to $j + na + k$ are calculated separately; then the sums of corresponding columns will be the same.

The periodicities sought by Buys Ballot were exact periodicities. In addition to assuming strict periodicity, Buys Ballot associates each component with a specific external force, e.g., the phases of the moon or the rotation of the sun.

---

[6] Theorem 5:

Si au lieu de la vraie période, on en suppose une trop petite ou trop grande, et que l'on dispose des rangées dans cette supposition; que l'on additionne de temps en temps il en résultera.

1. Dans le premier cas, le maximum des sommes s'écartera de plus en plus vers la droite, et dans le deuxième cas le maximum ainsi que le minimum des sommes s'écartera de plus en plus vers la gauche. La même chose aura lieu si l'on réunit quelques rangées par groupes, et que l'on confronte les sommes de ces groupes.

2. On aura trouvé la vraie période, si des groupes quelconques fournissent des sommes dont le maximum se trouve dans la même colonne et pour faire cet examen, il faudra y soumettre au moins trois groupes, qui soient assez voisins l'un de l'autre, pour que dans l'intervalle on ne puisse se méprendre de deux unités à l'égard du nombre des périodes.

3. La distance des colonnes où tombe le maximum des différents groupes fournit le moyen de calculer combien on est éloigné de la vraie période . . . . (1847, p. 39–40)

Buys Ballot did not believe that all meteorological data could be exactly represented as the sum of several periodic components; he recognized that there could be some stochastic irregularities, for example, due to volcanic activity. It is clear, however, that such irregularities were of minor importance for him; he believed that his methods could lead ultimately to near-perfect weather forecasts. The model underlying Buys Ballot's model is the unobserved-components model common to astronomy: several independent periodic components with an irregular component superimposed upon them.

Appendix B
SOME REQUISITE THEORY OF FUNCTIONS OF A COMPLEX VARIABLE

1. Complex Numbers

Complex numbers were invented to fill a void in the theory of equations. For example, an equation $x^2 + 1 = 0$ has no solution if we restrict ourselves to the real number system. It was found that by introducing a "number" i to denote the solution to this equation, every polynomial equation had a solution expressible in terms of entities of the form $z = a + bi$, where a and b are real numbers and i is the "solution" to $x^2 + 1 = 0$ (sometimes called $\sqrt{-1}$). Such a number is called *complex*. a is called the *real part* of z, and b is called the *imaginary part* of z. We often write

$$a = \operatorname{Re} z, \qquad b = \operatorname{Im} z.$$

The real numbers are a subset of the set of all complex numbers such that $\operatorname{Im} z = 0$. Complex numbers can be represented as ordered pairs of real numbers (vectors of dimension 2) or as points in the plane.

The number $\bar{z} = a - bi$ is called the *complex conjugate* of the number z. Its geometric interpretation is as the reflection of the point z about the *real axis* as shown in Fig. 1. The rules of operating with complex numbers all derive from their interpretation as expressions of the form $z = a + bi$, where i is the "solution" to $x^2 + 1 = 0$. Let z_1, z_2, and z_3 be three complex numbers of the form

$$z_1 = x_1 + iy_1, \qquad z_2 = x_2 + iy_2, \qquad z_3 = x_3 + iy_3.$$

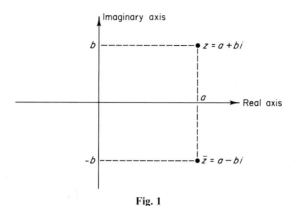

Fig. 1

We have the following definitions and rules:

Equality: $z_1 = z_2 \Leftrightarrow x_1 = x_2$ and $y_1 = y_2$.

Addition: $z_3 = z_1 + z_2 \Leftrightarrow x_3 = x_1 + x_2$ and $y_3 = y_1 + y_2$.

Multiplication: $z_3 = z_1 \cdot z_2 \Leftrightarrow x_3 = x_1 x_2 - y_1 y_2$ and $y_3 = x_1 y_2 + y_1 x_2$.

Note how this can be interpreted:

$$z_1 \cdot z_2 = (x_1 + iy_1) \cdot (x_2 + iy_2) = x_1 x_2 + iy_1 x_2 + ix_1 y_2 + i^2 y_1 y_2.$$

Division: $z_3 = \dfrac{z_1}{z_2}, z_2 \neq 0 \Leftrightarrow x_3 = \dfrac{x_1 x_2 + y_1 y_2}{x_2^2 + y_2^2}$ and $y_3 = \dfrac{x_2 y_1 - x_1 y_2}{x_2^2 + y_2^2}$.

Note how this can be interpreted:

$$\frac{z_1}{z_2} = \frac{z_1 \bar{z}_2}{z_2 \bar{z}_2} = \frac{x_1 x_2 - i^2 y_1 y_2 - x_1 y_2 i + x_2 y_1 i}{z_2 \bar{z}_2}.$$

The product of a complex number and its conjugate is called the *squared modulus* of the number:

$$|z|^2 = z \cdot \bar{z} = x^2 + y^2.$$

The modulus itself, which is a real number, can be interpreted as the *length* of the vector in E_2 representing the complex number. The geometric representation also permits us to express a complex number in *polar form* as shown in Fig. 2, where $\tan \theta = y/x$, so that $\theta = \tan^{-1} y/z \equiv \arg z$, $|z| = r$. θ is called the argument of z. It follows that $y = r \sin \theta$, and $x = r \cos \theta$, so that

$$z = r(\cos \theta + i \sin \theta).$$

r and θ are the polar coordinates of the point representing z.

Clearly, for any given $z \neq 0$, there corresponds only one value of θ in the interval $[0, 2\pi)$ or any other interval of length 2π; however, there is another

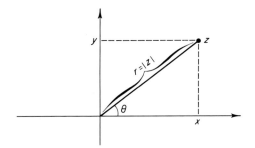

Fig. 2

value θ in the interval $[2\pi, 4\pi)$, etc., that yields exactly the same point for given r, and hence exactly the same complex number. If a particular interval, say $[-\pi, \pi)$, is chosen, it is called the *principal range*, and the *unique* value of θ for each complex number in that range is called its *principal value*.

Using the polar form of the complex numbers, the following can be proved by mathematical induction:

$$z_1 z_2 = r_1 r_2 [\cos(\theta_1 + \theta_2) + i \sin(\theta_1 + \theta_2)]$$
$$z_1 / z_2 = (r_1 / r_2)[\cos(\theta_1 - \theta_2) + i \sin(\theta_1 - \theta_2)],$$

and in general

$$\frac{z_1 \cdots z_n}{z_{n+1} \cdots z_{n+m}} = \frac{r_1 \cdots r_n}{r_{n+1} \cdots r_{n+m}}\left[\cos\left(\sum_{j=1}^{n} \theta_j - \sum_{j=n+1}^{n+m} \theta_j\right) + i \sin\left(\sum_{j=1}^{n} \theta_j - \sum_{j=n+1}^{n+m} \theta_j\right)\right].$$

Setting $m = 0$ and $z_1 = \cdots = z_n = z$, we have

DeMoivre's Theorem

$$z^n = r^n(\cos\theta + i\sin\theta)^n = r^n(\cos n\theta + i \sin n\theta).$$

We define roots of a complex number as follows: w is the nth root of z if $w^n = z$, i.e., $w = z^{1/n}$. Now write

$$w = \rho(\cos\varphi + i\sin\varphi),$$

so that

$$w^n = \rho^n(\cos n\varphi + i \sin n\varphi)$$
$$= r(\cos\theta + i\sin\theta) = z.$$

This is certainly true for $\rho = r^{1/n}$ and $\varphi = \theta/n$. But note that because of the periodicity of the trigonometric functions sine and cosine, we can satisfy the above for any number φ such that $n\varphi = \theta + 2\pi k$, where k is an integer. Hence there are n distinct points in the complex plane representing the solutions to the equation $w^n = z$, where z is a specified complex number:

$$w = r^{1/n}\left[\cos\left(\frac{\theta}{n} + k\frac{2\pi}{n}\right) + i\sin\left(\frac{\theta}{n} + k\frac{2\pi}{n}\right)\right], \qquad k = 0, 1, \ldots, n-1.$$

Note that the value for $k = n$ is the same as the value for $k = 0$ and any integral multiple of n. If $w = 0$, $\theta = \arg z$ is not well defined, but w is clearly a real number and $w^n = 0$.

An especially important cases arises when we solve the equation $z^n = 1$. Then $\rho = 1$ and $\theta = 0$, so that the solutions are

$$\cos k \frac{2\pi}{n} + i \sin k \frac{2\pi}{n}, \qquad k = 0, 1, \ldots, n - 1.$$

These numbers are called the nth *roots of unity*. All complex numbers lying on a circle of radius 1 with its center at the origin, the *unit circle*, are of the form

$$z = \cos \theta + i \sin \theta, \qquad 0 \le \theta < 2\pi \quad \text{or} \quad -\pi \le \theta < \pi, \quad \text{etc.}$$

The nth roots of unity are the vertices of an inscribed regular polygon of n sides in the unit circle.

Since we have now defined product and power, we can introduce the notion of a *polynomial*

$$P(z) = a_0 + a_1 z + a_2 z^2 + \cdots + a_n z^n$$

of degree n, where $a_n \ne 0$. $a_0, a_1, \ldots, a_n$ are given numbers that may be complex. The solutions to $P(z) = 0$ are called the *roots* or *zeros* of $P(z)$.

The *fundamental theorem of algebra* states that every polynomial of the above form has at least one root, which may be complex. From this it can be shown to follow that a polynomial of degree n has n possibly complex roots $z_1, \ldots, z_n$ and, hence, can be factored as

$$P(z) = a_n(z - z_1) \cdots (z - z_n).$$

Some or all of the n roots may be identical. If a root is complex, its complex conjugate is also a root, provided $a_0, \ldots, a_n$ are real.

2. Simple Functions of a Complex Variable

We have already encountered simple examples of functions of a complex variable in the form of positive and negative integral and rational powers and polynomials with real or complex coefficients. In general, a function of a complex variable z may be thought of as a mapping from E_2 onto or into E_2 itself. Thus f relates all numbers z of the domain of f to complex numbers w of its range: $w = f(z)$. f may be single- or multiple-valued. If f is multiple-valued, we may consider it as a collection of single-valued functions, which are called *branches* of the function f. One of these is termed the *principal branch*. For example, $w = z^2$ is a single-valued function, whereas $w = z^{1/2}$ has two branches. Inverse functions are uniquely defined for single-valued functions, but the example illustrates they may be multiple-valued.

Another simple function of z is the *rational function*: $w = P(z)/Q(z)$, where $P(z)$ and $Q(z)$ are polynomials in z. In order to derive more general functions, we need the notion of a power series since most functions encountered in complex variable theory are defined in this way. All the notions of power series in real variables carry over to the study of such series in complex variables if we replace the notion of absolute value by modulus. (It is not accidental that the same notation is used.) A power series is of the form

$$f(z) = a_0 + a_1 z + a_2 z^2 + \cdots + a_n z^n + \cdots = \sum_{j=0}^{\infty} a_j z^j,$$

where a_j and z are typically complex. If the series converges for z in some region, it defines a function $f(z)$ for that domain. For example,

$$1 + z + \cdots + z^n + \cdots,$$

the geometric series, converges to the function $f(z) = 1/(1-z)$ for $|z| < 1$ and diverges for $|z| \geq 1$.

The following important theorem is due to the nineteenth century Norwegian mathematician Abel:

Theorem. For every power series

$$a_0 + a_1 z + a_2 z^2 + \cdots,$$

there exists a real number R, $0 \leq R \leq \infty$, called the *radius of convergence*, such that

(i) $\sum a_j z^j$ converges *absolutely* for every z with $|z| < R$. For any ρ such that $0 \leq \rho < R$, $\sum a_j z^j$ converges *uniformly* for $|z| \leq \rho$.

(ii) If $|z| > R$, $\sum a_j z^j$ diverges.

When we have introduced the notion of a derivative we can also add

(iii) The derivative of $\sum a_j z^j = f(z)$ for $|z| < R$ can be obtained by termwise differentiation. $f'(z)$ has the same radius of convergence.

Note that nothing is said about the behavior of $f(z)$ *on* the *circle of convergence*, $|z| = R$. The theorem, in effect, states that we can define a function by a power series *within* its circle of convergence.

The *exponential function* may now be defined as

$$e^z = 1 + \frac{z}{1!} + \frac{z^2}{2!} + \cdots + \frac{z^n}{n!} + \cdots, \tag{1}$$

which can be shown to converge in the whole plane, i.e., $R = \infty$. When z is real, $z = x + i0$, (1) reduces to the familiar series expansion of the exponential. The function defined in (1) can be shown to have the usual properties of the real exponential function, which is a special case of the complex exponential.

The trigonometric functions $\sin z$ and $\cos z$ are also defined by power series:

$$\sin z = z - \frac{z^3}{3!} + \frac{z^5}{5!} - \cdots + \cdots$$

$$\cos z = 1 - \frac{z^2}{2!} + \frac{z^4}{4!} - \cdots + \cdots,$$

(2)

which reduce to the usual series expansions for z real. If follows from (1) and (2) that

$$e^{iz} = 1 + \frac{iz}{1!} - \frac{z^2}{2!} - \frac{iz^3}{3!} + \frac{z^4}{4!} + \frac{iz^5}{5!} - \frac{z^6}{6!} + \cdots$$

$$= \cos z + i \sin z,$$

(3)

which is known as Euler's theorem. It follows from (3) that

$$\cos z = (e^{iz} + e^{-iz})/2, \qquad \sin z = (e^{iz} - e^{-iz})/2i.$$

(4)

The radius of convergence of the series defining both $\sin z$ and $\cos z$ is infinite. Now suppose z is real; for any real number θ, (3) becomes

$$e^{i\theta} = \cos \theta + i \sin \theta$$

(5)

and (4) becomes

$$\cos \theta = (e^{i\theta} + e^{-i\theta})/2, \qquad \sin \theta = (e^{i\theta} - e^{-i\theta})/2i.$$

(6)

Equation (5) leads to an important representation of an arbitrary complex number, which may be written

$$z = r(\cos \theta + i \sin \theta) = re^{i\theta}.$$

Equations (5) and (6) are also useful in proving many trigonometric identities.

The *logarithmic function* is defined as the inverse of the exponential function. Thus

$$w = \ln z \qquad \text{if and only if} \quad z = e^{w}.$$

(7)

The exponential function is periodic, which means that the log function is multiple-valued.

We say $f(z)$ has period c if $f(z + c) = f(z)$. Thus $e^{z+c} = e^z$ if $e^c = 1$, so that e^z has period c for $c = i\theta$, where θ is an integral multiple of 2π since

$$e^{i\theta} = \cos \theta + i \sin \theta = 1 \qquad \text{for} \quad \theta = 2\pi$$

(8)

Indeed, one can show this is the smallest period of the function e^z. We also have in a similar fashion

$$e^{i\theta} = -1 \qquad \text{for} \quad \theta = (2k + 1)\pi,$$

$$e^{i\theta} = (-1)^k i \quad \text{for} \quad \theta = (2k + 1)(\pi/2), \quad k = 0, 1, \ldots.$$

It follows that $\ln(-1) = (2k + 1)\pi i$ for $k = 0, 1, \ldots$. Notice that the logarithmic function is defined for all complex numbers *except* zero (since e^z can never be 0).

By (8), $\ln z$ is a multiple-valued function: Every complex number other than zero has infinitely many logarithms that differ from each other by multiples of $2\pi i$. Another example of a multiple-valued function is

$$\sqrt{z} = \sqrt{r}e^{i\theta/2}, \qquad \text{where} \quad z = re^{i\theta},$$

since, letting θ vary from 0 to 2π (a complete circuit around 0), we have $\sqrt{r}e^{i\pi} = -\sqrt{r}$ rather than $\sqrt{r}e^{i0} = \sqrt{r}$. However, going around again (from 2π to 4π) we eventually return to $\sqrt{r}e^{i4\pi/2} = \sqrt{r}$ again. A point about which circuits such as this result in different values of a function is called *a branch point*. The number of different values is the *order* of the branch point. ln z has an infinite branch point at zero since

$$\ln z = \ln r + i\theta,$$

where $z = re^{i\theta}$ takes on an infinite number of values as θ sweeps around the circle. The principal value of ln z is usually taken to be that for the first branch, $0 \le \theta < 2\pi$.

3. Limits, Continuity, Derivatives, Singularities, and Rational Functions

A function $f(z)$ is said to have the limit α as $z \to \zeta$ if for every real $\epsilon > 0$ there exists a real $\delta > 0$ such that $|f(z) - \alpha| < \epsilon$ for all values of $z \ne \zeta$ such that $|z - \zeta| < \delta$. Thus the definition of limit is the same as that for real variables, replacing absolute values by moduli.

The derivative of a function, if it exists, is defined just as in the real case, and the usual rules for forming the derivative of a sum, product, or quotient are all valid, as is the chain rule for determining the derivative of a composite function. A function is said to be continuous at ζ if $\lim_{z \to \zeta} f(z) = f(\zeta)$.

Functions that possess a derivative wherever the functions are defined are called *analytic functions*. The terms *holomorphic function* or *regular function* are also used. One can easily show that an *analytic* function is continuous everywhere defined and that its real and imaginary parts are also continuous. But the existence of the derivative of a function of a complex variable is a stronger condition than for a real function since

$$f'(z) = \lim_{h \to 0} [f(z + h) - f(z)]/h$$

must be the same however the complex number h approaches zero. Let $h = x + iy$ and $u(z)$ and $v(z)$ be the real and imaginary parts of $f(z)$, respectively. First set $y = 0$ and let $x \to 0$; then

$$f'(z) = \frac{\partial u}{\partial x} + i\frac{\partial v}{\partial x} = \frac{\partial f}{\partial x}.$$

Now set $x = 0$ and let $y \to 0$; we have

$$f'(z) = -i\frac{\partial u}{\partial y} + \frac{\partial v}{\partial y} = \frac{\partial f}{\partial (iy)} = \lim_{y \to 0} \frac{f(z + iy) - f(z)}{iy}.$$

It follows that

$$\frac{\partial u}{\partial x} = \frac{\partial v}{\partial y} \quad \text{and} \quad \frac{\partial v}{\partial x} = -\frac{\partial u}{\partial y}. \tag{1}$$

Conditions (1), which must be satisfied by any analytic function, are called the *Cauchy–Riemann equations*.

It can be shown that the derivative of an analytic function is itself analytic in the same region, so that the existence of a derivative in a region *implies* the existence of all higher order derivatives in that region which, of course, is not the case for real-valued functions.

A point at which $f(z)$ fails to be analytic is called a *singular point* or a *singularity* of $f(z)$. Various types of singularities exist:

(1) *An isolated singularity*: z_0 such that z_0 is a singular point of $f(z)$ and there exists a $\delta > 0$ such that $|z - z_0| < \delta$ encloses no other singularity. Otherwise z_0 is a nonisolated singularity. For example, $z_0 = 0$ is an isolated singularity of $f(z) = 1/z$.

(2) *A pole*: If there exists an integer $n > 0$ such that $\lim_{z \to z_0} (z - z_0)^n f(z) = \alpha \neq 0$, then z_0 is called a *pole of order n*. For example, $1/(z - 1)^3$ has pole of order 3 at 1.

(3) *Branch points*: These have already been defined, e.g., $\ln z(z^2 + z - 2)$ has branch points at $z_0 = 1, -2$ since $(z - 1)(z + 2) = 0$.

(4) *Removable singularity*: If $\lim_{z \to z_0} f(z)$ exists but z_0 is a singular point, then z_0 is called a *removable singularity*. For example, $z_0 = 0$ is a removable singularity for $\sin z/z$ since $\lim_{z \to 0} (\sin z/z) = 1$.

(5) *Essential singularity*: These are singularities that are neither poles, branch points, nor removable, e.g., $z_0 = 2$ for $e^{1/(z-2)}$. Equivalently for single-valued functions, the singularity is essential if we cannot find any integer $n > 0$ such that $\lim_{z \to z_0} (z - z_0)^n f(z) = \alpha \neq 0$.

We are now in a position to discuss the nature of polynomials and rational functions in terms of their zeros and poles.

As we saw, a polynomial $P(z)$ of degree n has exactly n roots, not necessarily distinct. Normalizing so that $a_n = 1$, we write the factorization

$$P(z) = (z - z_1) \cdots (z - z_n),$$

which is unique except for the order of the factors. If exactly k roots are identical, their common value is called a zero of order k. The sum of the orders of all the zeros of a polynomial is equal to its degree.

A useful theorem about these zeros is

Theorem.　The smallest convex polygon that contains the zeros of $P(z)$ also contains those of $P'(z)$.

Consider the special rational function $R(z) = 1/P(z) = 1/[(z - z_1) \cdots (z - z_n)]$. Clearly every zero of order k of $P(z)$ is a pole of order k of $R(z)$. In general, for $R(z) = P(z)/Q(z)$, where $P(z)$ and $Q(z)$ are polynomials with *no common* factors, the zeros of $Q(z)$ are the poles of $R(z)$. The number of zeros and poles of $R(z)$ is called *the order of* $R(z)$, provided we also count in the zeros and poles at the point $z = \infty$ as follows:

$$R(z) \text{ has a pole of order } k \text{ at } z = \infty,$$
$$\text{if } R(1/z) \text{ has a pole of order } k \text{ at } z = 0.$$

$$R(z) \text{ has a zero of order } k \text{ at } z = \infty,$$
$$\text{if } R(1/z) \text{ has a zero of order } k \text{ at } z = 0.$$

Rational functions admit of an important representation in terms of *partial fractions.* Suppose that the denominator $Q(z)$ of $R(z)$ may be factored as

$$Q(z) = (z - z_1)^{k_1}(z - z_2)^{k_2} \cdots (z - z_m)^{k_m},$$

where k_j is the order of the jth zero and $\sum_{j=1}^{m} k_j = q$. Then it can be shown that

Theorem.　Every rational function can be represented uniquely as the sum of a polynomial $G(z)$ and a finite number m of terms that are polynomials in $1/(z - z_j)$, where z_j is a root of $Q(z)$. These polynomials are of degree equal to the order of the zero at z_j, i.e., k_j, and have no constant term. The latter is absorbed in $G(z)$. Thus

$$R(z) = G(z) + \sum_{j=1}^{m} H_j\left(\frac{1}{z - z_j}\right),$$

where

$$H_j\left(\frac{1}{z - z_j}\right) = \frac{a_1}{(z - z_j)} + \frac{a_2}{(z - z_j)^2} + \cdots + \frac{a_{k_j}}{(z - z_j)^{k_j}}.$$

(See Alfors, 1966, p. 32; Knopp, 1945, pp. 138–139.)

4.　Complex Integration: Cauchy's Theorem

The integral of a complex function along a curve in the complex plane may be defined in terms of the familiar line integral. Let C be a continuous piecewise differentiable curve in the complex plane as shown in Fig. 3. The points z along such a curve may be characterized in terms of their coordinates x and y, which may be expressed parametrically in terms of some variable t, $a \leq t \leq b$, as $x(t)$ and $y(t)$. Within any interval where the arc is differentiable, $x(t)$ and $y(t)$ will

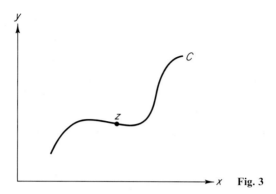

Fig. 3

also be. Now it is an elementary property of integrals that they sum. Thus if C is a segmentable curve with segments $C_1, \ldots, C_n$, then the integral over C is the sum of integrals each over the individual segments. If we write $f(z) = u(x, y) + iv(x, y)$, the integral of $f(z)$ along C may be defined as

$$\int_C f(z)\, dz = \sum_{j=1}^{n} \int_{C_j} f(z)\, dz,$$

where

$$\int_{C_j} f(z)\, dz = \int_{a_j}^{b_j} f(z(t))z'(t)\, dt$$

$$= \int_{a_j}^{b_j} \{u(x(t), y(t)) + iv(x(t), y(t))\}\{x'(t) + iy'(t)\}\, dt$$

$$= \int_{a_j}^{b_j} \{ux' - vy'\}\, dt + i \int_{a_j}^{b_j} \{vx' + uy'\}\, dt.$$

As an example, determine $\int_C z\, dz$, where C is the upper-right-hand corner of the unit circle, that is, the set of all points z in the complex plane that can be represented as $z = e^{i\theta} = \cos\theta + i\sin\theta$ for $0 \le \theta \le \pi/2$. Making use of the definition above,

$$\int_C z\, dz = \int_0^{\pi/2} (\cos\theta + i\sin\theta)(-\sin\theta + i\cos\theta)\, d\theta$$

$$= \int_0^{\pi/2} -(\cos\theta\sin\theta + \sin\theta\cos\theta)\, d\theta + i\int_0^{\pi/2}(-\sin^2\theta + \cos^2\theta)\, d\theta$$

$$= -\int_0^{\pi/2} \sin 2\theta\, d\theta + i\int_0^{\pi/2} \cos 2\theta\, d\theta$$

$$= \tfrac{1}{2}\cos 2\theta\big|_0^{\pi/2} + \tfrac{1}{2}i\sin 2\theta\big|_0^{\pi/2}$$

$$= \tfrac{1}{2}(-1 - 1) + \tfrac{1}{2}i(0 - 0) = -1.$$

Clearly it makes a difference which way the arc C is traversed. Had the direction of traversal been clockwise, the integral's sign would have been reversed.

All the usual formulas for integration by parts, change of variables, etc., hold.

In general, the integral of a function defined in a region depends on the path of integration. However, the following important theorem holds:

Theorem. The integral $\int_C f(z)\,dz$ on any continuous path C between two given points A and B in a simply connected set R and lying entirely within or on the boundary of R is independent of the exact choice of C satisfying the conditions if and only if $f(z)$ is analytic in and on the boundary of R.

A region may be *simply* or *multiply connected* or *disconnected* as shown in Fig. 4.

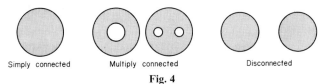

| Simply connected | Multiply connected | Disconnected |

Fig. 4

With regard to traversal of a closed path, the following convention is adopted: The positive direction is that along which the region lies to the left as, for example, in Fig. 5.

Fig. 5

Since the sign of the integral is reversed when the path is retraced, the above theorem, together with the fact that a closed curve that does not intersect itself defines a simply connected region, implies that if $f(z)$ is analytic on the curve C and inside the region R bounded by C, then $\oint_C f(z)\,dz = 0$. The little circle in the integral sign means that the integration is performed *around a closed curve*.

Morera's Theorem. If $f(z)$, continuous in a simply connected region R, has $\oint_C f(z)\,dz = 0$ for every closed curve in R, then $f(z)$ is analytic in R.

Indeed, this result, when $f(z)$ is assumed analytic, is still more generally valid for both simply and multiply connected regions and is

Cauchy's Theorem. If $f(z)$ is analytic in R and on its boundary C, then $\oint_C f(z)\,dz = 0$.

Note we have to integrate around *all* parts of the boundary. Because the boundaries of each of the subregions are segmentable curves, and because the integral along any series of segments or curves is the sum of the integrals along each, we have

$$\oint_C f(z)\,dz = \sum_{i=1}^{n} \oint_{C_i} f(z)\,dz,$$

where each individual term is *not necessarily zero*. The reason each integral is not necessaily zero is that, in the regions enclosed by the boundary segments, the function f may not be analytic. In fact, if the smallest region containing the curve C contains a nonremovable singularity of the function $f(z)$, which is thus not analytic at that point, then the integral will not be zero. For example, let C be the unit circle; then

$$\oint_C \frac{dz}{z} = \oint_0^{2\pi} \frac{-\sin\theta + i\cos\theta}{\cos\theta + i\sin\theta} \, d\theta$$

$$= \oint_0^{2\pi} i \frac{(\cos\theta + i\sin\theta)}{\cos\theta + i\sin\theta} \, d\theta = 2\pi i.$$

A simple closed curve is a continuous piecewise differentiable curve that does not intersect itself; for such curves the following remarkable theorem, known as Cauchy's integral formula, holds:

Theorem. If $f(z)$ is analytic on and inside the simple closed curve C (note *any* simple closed curve) enclosing the point α, then $f(\alpha)$ and its derivatives at α are given by

$$f^{(n)}(\alpha) = \frac{n!}{2\pi i} \oint_C \frac{f(z)}{(z-\alpha)^{n+1}} \, dz,$$

where $f^{(0)}(\alpha) = f(\alpha)$ and $0! = 1$.

This theorem shows that if an analytic function is known on a simple closed curve C lying entirely in a region where $f(z)$ is analytic, then its value and the values of all its derivatives are known anywhere inside the curve. Thus there is a powerful connection between the values of an analytic function of a complex variable that goes far beyond that for an analytic function of a real variable.

Many important results, including the fundamental theorem of algebra, can be deduced from this theorem. One rather useful result is this: If $f(z)$ is analytic on and inside a simple closed curve C except for a finite number P of poles inside C, then

$$\frac{1}{2\pi i} \oint_C \frac{f'(z)}{f(z)} \, dz = N - P,$$

where N is the number of zeros inside C.

The Cauchy integral formula is not only fundamental to complex function theory but has many direct applications. For example, suppose we want to integrate the rational function $R(z) = P(z)/Q(z)$ around a closed curve enclosing precisely one of its poles ζ that is of multiplicity k. Then

$$\oint_C R(z) \, dz = \oint_C \frac{P(z)}{(z-\zeta)^k Q_0(z)} \, dz$$

$$= \frac{2\pi i}{(k-1)!} \frac{d^{k-1}[P(z)/Q_0(z)]}{dz^{k-1}} \bigg|_{z=\zeta}$$

where $Q_0(z) = Q(z)/(z - \zeta)^k$, by the theorem. For example,

$$\oint_{|z-i|=1/2} \frac{dz}{1 + z^2} = \oint_{|z-i|=1/2} \frac{dz}{(z + i)(z - i)}.$$

Here $1/(1 + z^2)$ has poles at $z = i$ and $z = -i$; the curve $|z - i| = \frac{1}{2}$ encloses one pole at $z = i$; hence, $Q_0 = z + i$ and

$$\oint_{|z-i|=1/2} \frac{dz}{(z + i)(z - i)} = \frac{2\pi i}{(i + i)} = \pi.$$

5. Series Expansions; Taylor's Series; Laurent's Series

Infinite series in complex variables are discussed above and used to define certain elementary functions such as e^z, $\ln z$, $\cos z$, and $\sin z$. Now we are in a position to develop the theory for arbitrary analytic functions. Such a development requires the use of Cauchy's integral formula. Recall the earlier result on power series,

$$f(z) = \sum_0^\infty a_j(z - \zeta)^j$$

such that there exists a real number $R \geq 0$ such that for $|z - \zeta| < R$, the series converges absolutely; and such that there exists $\rho \geq 0$, $\rho < R$, such that, for $|z - \zeta| \leq \rho$, the series converges uniformly, and for $|z - \zeta| > R$, the series diverges. When a series converges, derivatives may be obtained by termwise differentiation of series. For example, the series

$$f(z) = \frac{1}{1 - \alpha z} = \sum_0^\infty \alpha^j z^j, \qquad |\alpha| < 1,$$

converges for all z inside the circle with radius $1/|\alpha|$. Indeed, it converges uniformly inside the same region. The reader may verify that all the derivatives of $f(z)$ may be obtained by termwise differentiation inside the circle of convergence.

There are various "tests" for convergence that should be familiar to the reader from elementary calculus.

Let $f(z)$ be a function analytic in a region formed by the circle $C: |z| \leq R$. Let z be an arbitrary point in this region. Then

$$f(z) = \frac{1}{2\pi i} \oint_C \frac{f(\zeta)}{\zeta - z} \, d\zeta \qquad \text{by the Cauchy integral formula}$$

$$= \frac{1}{2\pi i} \oint_C \frac{f(\zeta)}{\zeta \left(1 - \dfrac{z}{\zeta}\right)} \, d\zeta = \frac{1}{2\pi i} \oint_C \frac{f(\zeta)}{\zeta} \sum_0^\infty \left(\frac{z}{\zeta}\right)^j d\zeta$$

$$= \sum_0^\infty \frac{1}{2\pi i} \left(\oint_C \frac{f(\zeta)}{\zeta^{j+1}} \, d\zeta\right) z^j = \sum_0^\infty \frac{f^{(j)}(0)}{j!} z^j.$$

This expression is called the Taylor's series expansion of the function $f(z)$ about the point $z = 0$. Such a series expansion may be derived for any point in a region in which $f(z)$ is analytic. For example, let such a point be $z = \alpha$; then

$$f(z) = \sum_{0}^{\infty} \frac{f^{(j)}(\alpha)}{j!} (z - \alpha)^j.$$

In general, we take R as large as possible without including a singularity inside $|z - \alpha| \leq R$.

The Taylor's series expansion is unique and always exists in some neighborhood of a point at which $f(z)$ is analytic. Uniqueness shows that, given any power series convergent in the neighborhood of a point α, such a series uniquely represents an analytic function at that point with that series as its Taylor's series expansion.

Now consider an annulus $\mathscr{A}$ about the point $z = 0$ (or α), defined by $\mathscr{A} = \{0 \leq R_1 \leq |z| \leq R_2 < \infty\}$ (see Fig. 6).

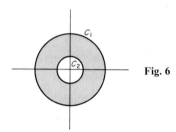

Fig. 6

Let $f(z)$ be analytic in this annulus and on its boundary (last part is stronger than need be). In much the same way as the Taylor's series result was derived, it can be shown that $f(z)$ for z an arbitrary point in the annulus $\mathscr{A}$ may be written

$$f(z) = \sum_{0}^{\infty} a_j z^j + \sum_{-1}^{-\infty} a_j z^j,$$

where

$$a_j = \frac{1}{2\pi i} \oint_{C_2} \frac{f(\zeta)}{\zeta^{j+1}} \, d\zeta, \qquad C_2 : |z| = R_2, \quad j = 0, 1, \ldots,$$

$$a_{-j} = \frac{1}{2\pi i} \oint_{C_1} \zeta^{j-1} f(\zeta) \, d\zeta, \qquad C_1 : |z| = R_1, \quad j = 1, 2, \ldots,$$

where the integration is in the counterclockwise direction in both cases. Combining terms appropriately,

$$f(z) = \sum_{-\infty}^{\infty} a_j z^j,$$

where

$$a_j = \frac{1}{2\pi i} \oint_C \frac{f(\zeta)}{\zeta^{j+1}} \, d\zeta \qquad \text{for} \quad j = 0, \pm 1, \pm 2, \ldots,$$

and where C is any circle *between* C_1 and C_2 [since the integral will be the same for any circle inside the annulus as long as $f(z)$ is analytic in the annulus]. In general, such an expansion can be made in an annulus around any point α in which the function $f(z)$ is analytic:

$$f(z) = \sum_{-\infty}^{\infty} a_j(z - \alpha)^j,$$

where

$$a_j = \frac{1}{2\pi i} \oint_C \frac{f(\zeta)}{(\zeta - \alpha)^{j+1}} \, d\zeta \qquad \text{for} \quad j = 0, \pm 1, \ldots,$$

and C is any circle *between* C_1 and C_2. Note that for $j = -1$, we obtain $2\pi i a_{-1}$ as the integral of $f(z)$:

$$a_{-1} = \frac{1}{2\pi i} \oint_C f(\zeta) \, d\zeta.$$

The expansion in terms of positive and negative powers of z is called the *Laurent series expansion* of $f(z)$. The part involving negative powers of z or $z - \alpha$ is called the *principal part* or the *singular part* of the Laurent series. Clearly, if there are only removable singularities of $f(z)$ or none at all in the doughnut hole of the annulus, the principal part of the Laurent expansion will vanish since then

$$a_{-j} = \frac{1}{2\pi i} \oint_C (\zeta - \alpha)^{j-1} f(\zeta) \, d\zeta = 0 \qquad \text{for} \quad j = 1, 2, \ldots.$$

Thus if $f(z)$ is analytic inside $|z| = R_2$, the Laurent expansion reduces to the Taylor's series expansion. That part of the Laurent expansion involving only positive powers of z is called the *analytic part* of the Laurent series.

Suppose α is an isolated singularity. Clearly, if the Laurent expansion has only a finite number, say k, of terms involving negative powers of $(z - \alpha)$, then α is a *pole of order* k according to our previous definition. Thus it is possible to discover poles by examining the Laurent expansion of a function. If α is a removable singularity, the principal part of the Laurent expansion will vanish, as in the case of analytic functions. If $f(z)$ is single-valued, and the principal part has an infinite number of terms, α must be an essential singularity. Branch points are more complicated and are not discussed here.

The value of $a_{-1} = (1/2\pi i) \oint_C f(\zeta) \, d\zeta$ is called the *residue* of $f(z)$ at $z = \alpha$. This is because if we integrate the Laurent expansion of a function term by term, all integrals vanish except for

$$a_{-1} \oint_C \frac{dz}{z - \alpha} = 2\pi i a_{-1}.$$

It is often easier to obtain the residue of a function than the entire Laurent expansion or the integral $\oint_C f(\zeta)\,d\zeta$.

Before leaving the subject area, however, note that if one looks at all the autocovariances or serial correlations of a time series and forms a series with these as the coefficients of positive and negative powers of z, the powers corresponding to the order of the lag involved, this is a Laurent expansion of a function about $z = 0$, provided the time series is what we call stationary (see Chapter II). This expansion is valid in an annulus including the unit circle and *on the unit circle*. A multiple of the function $f(z)$ on the unit circle is the spectral density of the time series. (As shown in Chapter IV, this result yields a very useful method of evaluating autocovariances for mixed-moving-average autoregressive time series using the residue theorem.)

6. The Residue Theorem and Its Applications

To obtain the residue of a function $f(z)$ at $z = \alpha$, it would appear necessary to obtain the Laurent expansion of $f(z)$ about $z = \alpha$. Fortunately this is not the case when α is a pole of order k. Then

$$a_{-1} = \lim_{z \to \alpha} \frac{1}{(k-1)!} \frac{d^{k-1}\{(z-\alpha)^k f(z)\}}{dz^{k-1}}.$$

Thus when $k = 1$ we have

$$a_{-1} = \lim_{z \to \alpha} (z - \alpha) f(z).$$

For example, $e^z/(z - 1)$ has a pole at $z = 1$ of order 1, so that

$$a_{-1} = \lim_{z \to 1} \frac{(z-1)e^z}{z-1} = e.$$

Similarly, $z/(z - i)^2$ has a pole at $z = i$ of order 2. Thus

$$a_{-1} = \lim_{z \to i} \frac{1}{1!} \frac{d[(z-i)^2 z/(z-i)^2]}{dz} = \lim_{z \to i} 1 = 1$$

These results are special cases of the following important theorem:

Residue Theorem. If $f(z)$ is analytical and single-valued on and inside a simple curve, except for a countable number of isolated singularities at the points $\zeta_1, \zeta_2, \zeta_3, \ldots$ with residues $r_1, r_2, r_3, \ldots$, then

$$\oint_C f(z)\,dz = 2\pi i \sum_1^\infty r_j.$$

Cauchy's theorem and integral formulas are also special cases of this theorem.

The primary use of the residue theorem is in the evaluation of difficult *real* integrals. For example, suppose we wish to evaluate

$$\int_0^{2\pi} R(\cos\theta, \sin\theta)\,d\theta,$$

where R is a rational function. Substitution of $z = e^{i\theta}$, so that $\cos\theta = (z + z^{-1})/2$,

$\sin\theta = (z - z^{-1})/2i$, and $d\theta = dz/iz$, transforms this integral to

$$\frac{1}{i}\oint_{|z|=1} R\left(\frac{z+z^{-1}}{2}, \frac{z-z^{-1}}{2i}\right)\frac{dz}{z}.$$

Evaluation can then proceed by means of determination of the residues of poles lying inside the unit circle. For example, let $a > 1$:

$$\int_0^\pi \frac{d\theta}{a+\cos\theta} = \frac{1}{2}\int_0^{2\pi}\frac{d\theta}{a+\cos\theta}$$

$$= \frac{1}{2i}\oint_{|z|=1}\frac{2\,dz/z}{2a+z+z^{-1}}$$

$$= \frac{1}{i}\oint_{|z|=1}\frac{dz}{z^2+2az+1}$$

$$= \frac{1}{i}\oint_{|z|=1}\frac{dz}{[z-\frac{1}{2}(-2a+\sqrt{4a^2-4})][z-\frac{1}{2}(-2a-\sqrt{4a^2-4})]}$$

$$= \frac{1}{i}\oint_{|z|=1}\frac{dz}{(z-\alpha)(z-\beta)}$$

since $[z - (-a + \sqrt{a^2-1})][z - (-a - \sqrt{a^2-1})]$ has poles

$$-a+\sqrt{a^2-1} = \alpha \quad \text{and} \quad -a-\sqrt{a^2-1} = \beta.$$

Now $|\alpha| < 1$ and $|\beta| > 1$ since $(z-\alpha)(z-\beta) = z^2 - (\alpha+\beta)z + \alpha\beta$, so $\alpha\beta = 1$ and $|\alpha|^2|\beta|^2 = 1$ because $\alpha + \beta = -2a$ and $\alpha\beta = 1$. Thus one pole lies inside the unit circle, and the other pole lies outside. Since $a > 1$, both are real and α lies inside. The residue at α is clearly $1/(\alpha - \beta) = 1/(2\sqrt{a^2-1})$; hence

$$\int_0^\pi \frac{d\theta}{a+\cos\theta} = \frac{1}{i}2\pi i\left(\frac{1}{2\sqrt{a^2-1}}\right) = \frac{\pi}{\sqrt{a^2-1}}.$$

The following theorem is useful in many instances.

   Theorem. If c is the upper semicircle of radius R and $f(z)$ is a single-valued function such that $|f(z)| \le M/R^k$ for $z = Re^{i\theta}$, $k > 0$, and M constant, then

$$\lim_{R\to\infty}\int_c f(z)\,dz = 0 \quad \text{and} \quad \lim_{R\to\infty}\int_c e^{imz}f(z)\,dz = 0, \text{ where } m \text{ is real.}$$

Use of this theorem may be helpful in situations of the following types:

   (1) $\int_{-\infty}^\infty f(x)\,dx$, $f(x)$ rational. Here we take $\oint_\Gamma f(z)\,dz$, where Γ is the upper semicircle of radius R plus segment $-R$ to R and take

$$\lim_{R\to\infty}\oint_\Gamma f(z)\,dz = \int_{-\infty}^\infty f(x)\,dx$$

since

$$\oint_\Gamma f(z)\,dz = \int_c f(z)\,dz + \int_{-R}^R f(z)\,dz,$$

where c is the upper semicircle of radius R alone.

(2) $\int_0^{2\pi} g(\sin\theta, \cos\theta)\,d\theta$, g rational function of $\sin\theta$ and $\cos\theta$. Here we take

$$\oint_\Gamma g\left(\frac{z - z^{-1}}{2i}, \frac{z + z^{-1}}{2}\right)\frac{dz}{iz}$$

where $z = e^{i\theta}$ and Γ is the unit circle.

(3) $\int_{-\infty}^\infty f(x)\cos mx\,dx$, $f(x)$ is rational or $\int_{-\infty}^\infty f(x)\sin mx\,dx$, $f(x)$ is rational. Here take $\oint_\Gamma f(z)e^{imz}\,dz$, Γ is the upper semicircle c plus the segment $-R$ to R.

Many other special cases illustrate the use of the theorem. The following are examples:

(1)
$$\int_{-\infty}^\infty \frac{dx}{1 + x^2} = \lim_{R\to\infty}\oint_\Gamma \frac{dz}{z^2 + 1} \quad \text{since} \quad \lim_{R\to\infty}\left[\oint_\Gamma = \int_c + \int_{-R}^R\right],$$

$$= \oint_\Gamma \frac{dz}{(z + i)(z - i)} = 2\pi i \text{ residue} = 2\pi i \lim_{z\to i}\frac{1}{z + i} = \pi.$$

This is the same result as that which is obtained by much more laborious real methods.

(2) The evaluation of $\int_{-\infty}^\infty (\sin x/x)\,dx$, is a somewhat more complicated example. Let Γ be the curve described in Fig. 7; c is the upper semicircle of radius R, and A is the upper semicircle of radius δ, each with the origin as center.

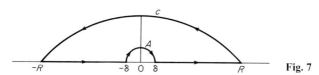

-R   -δ 0 δ   R   **Fig. 7**

Since $e^{iz} = \cos z + i\sin z$, we can look at the complex part of an integral involving e^{iz}: note e^{iz}/z is analytic inside and on the boundary Γ; thus

$$\oint_\Gamma \frac{e^{iz}}{z}\,dz = \int_{-R}^{-\delta}\frac{e^{iz}}{z}\,dz + \int_A \frac{e^{iz}}{z}\,dz + \int_\delta^R \frac{e^{iz}}{z}\,dz + \int_c \frac{e^{iz}}{z}\,dz = 0.$$

Now

$$\int_{-R}^{-\delta}\frac{e^{iz}}{z}\,dz + \int_\delta^R \frac{e^{iz}}{z}\,dz = \int_\delta^R \frac{e^{iz} - e^{-iz}}{z}\,dz$$

$$= 2i\int_\delta^R \frac{\sin x}{x}\,dx,$$

since z is real on $[\delta, R]$. Thus

$$2i\int_0^\infty \frac{\sin x}{x}\,dx = -\lim_{R\to\infty, \delta\to 0}\left\{\int_A \frac{e^{iz}}{z}\,dz + \int_c \frac{e^{iz}}{z}\,dz\right\}.$$

However, the second term tends to zero since $|e^{iz}/z|^2 = 1/R^2$ for $z = Re^{i\theta}$. Now we may apply the residue theorem: The first term is $\lim_{\delta\to 0} \int_A (e^{iz}/z)\,dz$. Consider $\oint_\Delta (e^{iz}/z)\,dz = -2\int_A (e^{iz}/z)\,dz$, where Δ is the full circle of radius δ.

The factor -2 appears because the integral around Δ in a counterclockwise direction traverses A in the reverse direction as compared to that implied by Γ. By the residue theorem

$$\oint_\Delta \frac{e^{iz}}{z}\,dz = 2\pi i \text{ residue} \left(\frac{e^{iz}}{z}\right) \qquad \text{at} \quad z = 0$$

$$= (2\pi i \cdot 1).$$

It follows that

$$-\lim_{\delta\to 0} \int_A \frac{e^{iz}}{z}\,dz = \pi i,$$

and thus

$$\int_0^\infty \frac{\sin x}{x}\,dx = \frac{\pi i}{2i} = \frac{\pi}{2}.$$

Since $(\sin x)/x$ is an even function, $\int_{-\infty}^\infty (\sin x)/x = \pi$.

Appendix C
FOURIER SERIES AND ANALYSIS[1]

1. Introduction

Certain concepts and results from the theory of Fourier series and integrals are used freely throughout the main text of this book. The purpose of this appendix is to acquaint the reader unfamiliar with this material with its rudiments in an intuitive rather than a rigorous fashion. Further insights may be obtained from Hamming (1962, Chapters 6, 17, 21–23), Lighthill (1962), Parzen (1963), Tolstov (1962, Chapters 1–7), and above all from Lanczos (1966). This appendix is divided into four sections:

Section 2 deals with the nature of periodic functions and the notion of frequency. The representation of periodic functions by trigonometric series is discussed.

Section 3 introduces the notion of orthogonal systems of functions, and discusses the representation of an arbitrary function over a finite interval in terms of linear combinations of an infinite number of the elements of an orthogonal system. This process is much like representing an arbitrary vector in terms of a system of orthogonal basis vectors; the difference, however, is that a function (even a well-behaved one) over a finite interval is a nondenumerably infinite collection of points.

In Section 4 the question of the speed of convergence of Fourier series (if it converges) is taken up and related to the problem of approximating a function over a finite interval by a finite sum of orthogonal (or trigonometric) functions. The question of the speed of convergence in the neighborhood of a discontinuity

---

[1] Appendix C is based on material prepared in November 1964 at Stanford University with the support of the National Science Foundation under Grant NSF-GS-142.

of the function is related to the notion of a "window" through which, in effect, we "view" the function when we consider its approximation by the partial sum of a Fourier series.

Section 5 introduces the Fourier integral and the Fourier transform. The results are used to illuminate some of the preceding material. "Windows" in the frequency domain are related to "windows" in the time domain.

The treatment aims throughout at intuitive appeal rather than rigor and is based in great measure upon the references cited above.

2.   Periodic Functions and Trigonometric Series of a Periodic Function

A function $f(t)$ is called *periodic* if there exists a constant $T > 0$ such that

$$f(t + T) = f(t)$$

for any t and $t + T$ for which $f(t)$ and $f(t + T)$ are defined. The sum, difference, product, and quotient of periodic functions with the same *period* T are also periodic with period T. If T is the period of a function f, then so is kT, where k is any positive integer. A periodic function (one with great importance in practical applications) is the so-called *harmonic* function

$$f(t) = A \sin(\lambda t + \varphi)$$

of *amplitude* $|A|$, (angular) *frequency* λ, and *phase* φ. The period of $f(t)$ is $T = 2\pi/\lambda$ since

$$f(t + 2\pi/\lambda) = A \sin(\lambda t + \varphi + 2\pi)$$
$$= A \sin(\lambda t + \varphi)$$

since $\sin(x + 2k\pi) = \sin x$, where k is any integer. The phase φ determines the point at which the function $f(t)$ "starts"; when $\varphi = 0$, this is the origin. If φ is not zero, replace $t + \varphi/\lambda$ by z; we see

$$f(z - \varphi/\lambda) = A \sin \lambda z$$

"starts" at the origin, so that $f(t)$ "starts" at $-\varphi/\lambda$. Setting $\varphi = 0$, $\lambda = 1$, and $t = k\pi/2$, we see that A determines the height of the sinusoidal variation. Letting $A = 1$ and $\varphi = 0$, $f(t)$ becomes the familiar sine curve, albeit uniformly compressed along the t-axis by a factor λ if $\lambda > 1$, or expanded uniformly by a factor $1/\lambda$ if $\lambda < 1$. The meaning of frequency is best understood by considering it in relation to period.

Clearly, if a harmonic function has period T, its frequency must be $\lambda = 2\pi/T$. The period T measures the distance in *time units* from peak to peak or trough to trough of the function $f(t)$ *through one cycle*. As T increases, λ falls; so we see that harmonics of low frequency are sinusoidal variations that take long periods of time to go through one full cycle. Conversely, high frequencies correspond to short periods or rapid cyclic variations.

In many analyses in economics in which harmonic functions enter, it is useful to measure frequency not in angular terms (as above, fractions of 2π) but in terms of *cycles per unit time*. Such a measure is called the *true frequency* and may be obtained from angular frequency by dividing the latter by 2π.

Just as a function with period T may be said to have periods $2T, 3T, \ldots$ as well, harmonic functions of frequencies $\lambda, 2\lambda, 3\lambda, \ldots$ all have period $T = 2\pi/\lambda$. The frequencies $2\lambda, 3\lambda, \ldots$ are called the harmonics of the frequency λ. It can be shown that well-behaved periodic functions can be well approximated by linear combinations of the harmonics of the so-called *fundamental* frequency $\lambda = 2\pi/T$, where T is the shortest period over which the function repeats itself. The circumstances and extent to which this is true are discussed below.[2]

By making use of a well-known trigonometric identity

$$\sin(\alpha + \beta) = \sin\beta\cos\alpha + \cos\beta\sin\alpha,$$

the general *harmonic* function $f(t)$ given above may be rewritten

$$f(t) = a\cos\lambda t + b\sin\lambda t,$$

where

$$a = A\sin\varphi, \qquad b = A\cos\varphi.$$

The constant function

$$f(t) = A\sin(0 \cdot t + \pi/2) = A\cos(0 \cdot t) = A$$

may be considered to be a harmonic of *zero frequency* or infinite period.

Given a period T, consider the harmonic functions

$$a_k\cos\lambda_k t + b_k\sin\lambda_k t,$$

where $\lambda_k = 2\pi k/T$, $k = 0, 1, \ldots, N$, are $N + 1$ harmonics of the fundamental frequency $2\pi/T$. The function

$$f_N(t) = \sum_{k=0}^{N} (a_k\cos\lambda_k t + b_k\sin\lambda_k t) \tag{1}$$

is clearly also a function of period T since it is the sum of functions with this same period. Such a function is called a *trigonometric polynomial of order or degree N*. Note that the term for $k = 0$ is

$$a_0\cos 0 + b_0\sin 0 = a_0 \cdot 1 = a_0,$$

---

[2] The harmonics of a given frequency are usually identified with *higher* frequencies, so that it is convenient to think of the fundamental frequency of all that are harmonics of one another as that positive frequency closest to zero.

so that the constant term of the polynomial is given by the zero frequency component. It is convenient to rescale this constant to be $a_0/2$. An infinite *trigonometric series* may be obtained from (1) by letting N increase without bound:

$$s(t) = a_0/2 + \sum_{k=1}^{\infty} (a_k \cos \lambda_k t + b_k \sin \lambda_k t). \tag{2}$$

If the series converges, it too represents a periodic function with period T.

A large part of the literature on Fourier series is concerned with the circumstances under which the series (2) will converge to a certain periodic function $f(t)$. We are concerned here with this issue only to a limited extent. In the remainder of this section, however, we simply assume that $s(t)$ does represent a convergent series and examine its properties. Subsequently, the notion of approximating an arbitrary function over a finite interval by a trigonometric polynomial such as $f_N(t)$ in (1) will be discussed; this, in fact, brings in by the back door the questions related to the convergence of $s(t)$.

By making use of the trigonometric representation of the complex exponential, trigonometric polynomials can be written in a more useful and suggestive form:

$$f_N(t) = \sum_{k=-N}^{N} C_k e^{i\lambda_k t} = \sum_{k=-N}^{N} C_k z^k, \tag{3}$$

where $C_k = \frac{1}{2}(a_k - ib_k)$, and we define $C_{-k} = \bar{C}_k = \frac{1}{2}(a_k + ib_k)$ for $k \neq 0$ and $C_0 = a_0/2$. Since $\lambda_k = 2\pi k/T$, letting $z = e^{i2\pi t/T}$ shows that (3) does in fact represent a polynomial (with complex coefficients) in the complex variable z, albeit one that is to be evaluated on the unit circle $|z| = 1$.[3]

Suppose that the series given in (2) does converge to a periodic function $s(t)$. Then by the results just obtained for the complex form of a trigonometric polynomial, we can write

$$s(t) = \sum_{k=-\infty}^{\infty} C_k z^k, \quad \text{where} \quad |z| = 1. \tag{4}$$

Thus we see that the Fourier series representation of $s(t)$ is just the Laurent expansion of a function in an annulus about the unit circle evaluated on the unit circle itself (see Appendix B, Section 5). The fact that $s(t)$ is a real rather than complex valued function is reflected by the condition $C_{-k} = \bar{C}_k$.[4] Unless the function $s(t)$ is itself a trigonometric polynomial, it has what is called an *essential*

---

[3] Any point in the unit circle can, of course, be represented by $e^{i\theta}$ for some real θ. See Section 1 of Appendix B.

[4] Note that on the unit circle $\bar{z} = z^{-1}$ and that the sum of a complex number and its conjugate is always real.

singularity at the origin.[5] This, however, need not concern us since we are interested in the representation only in the neighborhood of the unit circle.

The concept of *negative frequency* arises in connection with the complex form of trigonometric series. A negative frequency has the same meaning as a positive one in the appropriate trigonometric representation of the complex variable z in (3) or (4).

The complex form of the series or polynomial allows a particularly elegant derivation of the coefficients C_k. If the series (2) does converge, $s(t)$ is analytic in the annular region around the unit circle, and we have by the main result stated in Section 5, Appendix B

$$C_k = \frac{1}{2\pi i} \oint_\Gamma \frac{s(z)}{z^{k+1}} \, dz, \qquad k = 0, \pm 1, \dots, \tag{5}$$

where the path of integration Γ is taken to be the unit circle, $|z| = 1$, and where $s(z)$ is the function

$$s(z) = \sum_{k=-\infty}^{\infty} C_k z^k$$

not necessarily evaluated on the unit circle. Along the unit circle we have $s(z) = s(t)$ with $z = e^{i\lambda t}$, where $\lambda = 2\pi/T$ is the fundamental frequency of $s(t)$, so that (5) becomes

$$C_k = \frac{1}{2\pi i} \int_{-\pi/\lambda}^{\pi/\lambda} \frac{s(t)e^{i\lambda t}}{(e^{i\lambda t})^{k+1}} \, i\lambda \, dt = \frac{1}{T} \int_{-\pi/\lambda}^{\pi/\lambda} s(t) e^{-i\lambda_k t} \, dt \tag{6}$$

since $k\lambda = \lambda_k$. By the definition of C_k

$$C_k + C_{-k} = \frac{1}{T} \int_{-\pi/\lambda}^{\pi/\lambda} s(t) \{e^{-i\lambda_k t} + e^{i\lambda_k t}\} \, dt$$

$$= \frac{2}{T} \int_{-\pi/\lambda}^{\pi/\lambda} s(t) \cos \lambda_k t \, dt = a_k,$$

$$C_k - C_{-k} = \frac{1}{T} \int_{-\pi/\lambda}^{\pi/\lambda} s(t) \{e^{-i\lambda_k t} - e^{i\lambda_k t}\} \, dt \tag{7}$$

$$= \frac{(-2i)}{T} \int_{-\pi/\lambda}^{\pi/\lambda} s(t) \sin \lambda_k t \, dt$$

$$= -ib_k, \qquad k = 0, \pm 1, \pm 2, \dots.$$

---

[5] Recall that the singular part of a Laurent expansion is that part consisting of negative powers of z; as noted in Section 5 of Appendix B, if $f(z)$ is single-valued at 0 and the singular part of its Laurent expansion has an infinite number of terms, then the singularity at zero is essential.

For $T = 2\pi$ (i.e., a function periodic over the interval $[-\pi, \pi]$), $\lambda = 1$ and these formulas reduce to the standard textbook versions[6]

$$a_k = \frac{1}{\pi} \int_{-\pi}^{\pi} s(t) \cos kt \, dt, \qquad k = 0, 1, \dots,$$

$$b_k = \frac{1}{\pi} \int_{-\pi}^{\pi} s(t) \sin kt \, dt, \qquad k = 1, \dots. \tag{8}$$

Let $f(t)$ be a function defined either over the whole real axis or in some symmetric interval containing the origin. $f(t)$ is said to be an *even* function if $f(t) = f(-t)$ and an *odd* function if $f(t) = -f(-t)$. The cosine is an example of an even function, and the sine an example of an odd function. Clearly an odd function must pass through the origin, $f(0) = -f(-0) = 0$. We also have for any interval $[-a, a]$ over which $f(t)$ is integrable that

$$\int_{-a}^{a} f(t) \, dt = 2 \int_{0}^{a} f(t) \, dt$$

for $f(t)$ an even function and

$$\int_{-a}^{a} f(t) \, dt = 0$$

for $f(t)$ an odd function.

The fact that the product of two odd or even functions is an even function and that the product of an even and an odd function is odd follows immediately from the definitions of even and odd functions.

It follows that the function $s(t)$ defined by the (convergent) series in (4) or the trigonometric polynomial of (3) is even if and only if the right-hand sides of the defining relations contain only cosines, and odd if and only if the sums contain only sines. Sufficiency follows at once from the fact that the sum of even functions is even and the sum of odd functions is odd. To prove necessity it is simplest to evaluate the expression for a_k and b_k in (8). For even functions $s(t)$ we have

$$a_k = \frac{2}{\pi} \int_{0}^{\pi} s(t) \cos kt \, dt, \qquad k = 0, 1, 2, \dots,$$

$$b_k = 0, \qquad k = 1, 2, \dots,$$

---

[6] See, for example, Tolstov (1962, p. 13). The reader may wish to derive (8) entirely in real terms by making use of the concept of orthogonal functions:

Two functions $f(z)$ and $g(x)$ are said to be orthogonal on the interval $[a, b]$ if $\int_a^b f(x) g(x) \, dz = 0$. First show that the functions in the set

$$\cos kt, \qquad k = 0, 1, 2, \dots$$
$$\sin kt, \qquad k = 1, 2, 3, \dots$$

are orthogonal on the interval $[-\pi, \pi]$ by using the elementary trigonometric identities for $\sin(\alpha + \beta)$, $\cos(\alpha + \beta)$, $\cos \alpha \cos \beta$, etc.

Next use this result to give an alternative derivation of (8) entirely in real terms. (Hint: recall the manner in which the normal equations of least-squares regression are formed.)

since $s(t)\cos kt$ is even and $s(t)\sin kt$ is odd. For odd functions, conversely,

$$a_k = 0, \qquad b_k = \frac{2}{\pi}\int_0^\pi s(t)\sin kt\, dt, \qquad k = 0, 1, 2, \ldots,$$

since $s(t)\cos kt$ is odd and $s(t)\sin kt$ is even.

Let $s(t)$ and $\sigma(t)$ be two functions with period 2π defined in terms of the (convergent) series

$$s(t) = \sum_{k=-\infty}^{\infty} C_k z^k, \qquad \sigma(t) = \sum_{k=-\infty}^{\infty} \gamma_k z^k,$$

where $C_k = \bar{C}_{-k}$, $\gamma_k = \bar{\gamma}_{-k}$, and $|z| = 1$. The *convolution* of $s(t)$ and $\sigma(t)$ on the interval $[-\pi, \pi]$ is defined as the function

$$\rho(t) = \frac{1}{2\pi}\int_{-\pi}^\pi s(\tau)\sigma(t - \tau)\, d\tau.$$

In a straightforward manner, it can be seen that

$$s(\tau)\sigma(t - \tau) = \sum_{k=-\infty}^{\infty} s(\tau)\gamma_k e^{i\lambda_k(t - \tau)}.$$

Integrate this expression with respect to τ from $-\pi$ to π and multiply by $1/2\pi$. We obtain

$$\rho(t) = \sum_{k=-\infty}^{\infty} \left(\frac{1}{2\pi}\int_{-\pi}^\pi s(\tau)e^{-i\lambda_k \tau}\, d\tau\right)\gamma_k e^{i\lambda_k t}$$

$$= \sum_{k=-\infty}^{\infty} C_k \gamma_k z^k, \qquad |z| = 1, \qquad (9)$$

by (6). It follows that the series representation of the convolution of $s(t)$ and $\sigma(t)$ is just in terms of the products of the coefficients C_k and γ_k. *Thus convolution in the time domain corresponds to multiplication in the frequency domain.* This result, called the "convolution theorem," suggests that in problems involving convolution we would do well to view the functions in the frequency rather than the time domain.

Suppose that we are given a function $f(t)$ that is defined (or only observed) at the $2N$ discrete points

$$t_k = k\pi/N, \qquad k = 0, 1, \ldots, 2N - 1.$$

It can be shown that $f(t)$ has an *exact* representation as a trigonometric polynomial such as (3). To see this rewrite (3) as

$$f(t_k) = f\left(\frac{k\pi}{N}\right) = \sum_{j=-N+1}^{N-1} C_j e^{i\lambda_j t_k} + \left(\frac{C_N e^{iNt_k} + C_{-N} e^{-iNt_k}}{2}\right), \qquad (10)$$

where $\lambda_j = j$ and $t_k = k\pi/N$, since the period of this function can be taken as $T = 2\pi$.[7] Multiplying by $e^{-i\lambda_{j'}t_k}$ and summing over $k = 0, 1, \ldots, 2N - 1$, we obtain

$$\sum_{k=0}^{2N-1} e^{-i\lambda_{j'}t_k} f(t_k) = \sum_{j=-N+1}^{N-1} \sum_{k=0}^{2N-1} C_j e^{i(\lambda_j - \lambda_{j'})t_k} + \frac{a_N}{2} \sum_{k=0}^{2N-1} (-1)^k e^{-i\lambda_{j'}t_k}$$

$$\text{for} \quad j' = 0, \pm 1, \ldots, \pm N. \quad (11)$$

The last term on the right vanishes for all $\lambda_{j'} = j' = 0, \pm 1, \ldots, \pm(N-1)$ since it is equal to

$$\frac{a_N}{2} \left(\frac{1 - e^{-ij'2\pi}}{1 + e^{-ij'\pi/N}} \right),$$

and $e^{-i\theta} = 1$ for θ an integral multiple of 2π since $e^{i2\pi k} = \cos k2\pi + i \sin k2\pi \equiv 1$. The expression on the right may be rewritten as

$$\sum_{j=-N+1}^{N-1} C_j \left\{ \sum_{k=0}^{2N-1} \left[e^{i(\lambda_j - \lambda_{j'})\pi/N} \right]^k \right\} = \sum_{j=-N+1}^{N-1} C_j \left\{ \frac{1 - e^{i2\pi(\lambda_j - \lambda_{j'})}}{1 - e^{i(\lambda_j - \lambda_{j'})\pi/N}} \right\}.$$

However, $\lambda_j = j$; hence the expression in braces is identically zero for $j \neq j'$. Thus, returning to (11) with $j = j'$, we find

$$C_j = \frac{1}{2N} \sum_{k=0}^{2N-1} e^{-ijt_k} f(t_k), \qquad j = 0, \pm 1, \ldots, \pm(N-1). \quad (12)$$

Equating real and imaginary parts,

$$a_j = \frac{1}{N} \sum_{k=0}^{2N-1} \cos\left[k\left(\frac{j\pi}{N}\right) \right] f(t_k), \qquad j = 0, 1, \ldots, N-1,$$

$$b_j = \frac{1}{N} \sum_{k=0}^{2N-1} \sin\left[k\left(\frac{j\pi}{N}\right) \right] f(t_k), \qquad j = 1, \ldots, N-1. \quad (13)$$

Note that there are exactly $2N - 1$ coefficients determined by (13) because $b_N \equiv 0$ since $\sin k\pi = 0$ for $k = 0, 1, \ldots$. To obtain the coefficient a_N, note that it is determined from (1) by the "end condition" that $f(\pi) = f(-\pi)$ and the

---

[7] Since the value of the function is determined only at $2N$ discrete points, $k = 0, 1, \ldots, 2N - 1$, or alternatively at $2N$ of the $2N + 1$ points $k = 0, \pm 1, \ldots, \pm N$, it is necessary in (10) to limit the range of the summation in a symmetric fashion. Thus we let $f_N(t) = a_0/2 + \sum_{j=1}^{N-1} \{a_j \cos \omega_j t + b_j \sin \omega_j t\} + (a_N/2) \cos \omega_N t$. In this way the representation (1) for f_{2N-1} and (3) for f_N are made equivalent at either the $2N$ points $k = 0, 1, \ldots, 2N - 1$ or the points $k = -N, \ldots, 0, \ldots, N$. In fact, this "end-correction" is a consequence of the imposition of the so-called *Dirichlet conditions* whereby we assign the value $f(x) = \frac{1}{2}[f(x+) + f(x-)]$ to the function $f(x)$ at any point of discontinuity x such that $f(x)$ approaches $f(x+)$ from the right and $f(x-)$ from the left. See Lanczos (1966, p. 46).

remaining coefficients:

$$(-1)^N a_N = -2\left\{ f(\pi) - \sum_{j=-N+1}^{N-1} C_j e^{i\lambda_j t_N} \right\}$$

$$= -2\left\{ f(\pi) - \frac{a_0}{2} - \sum_{j=1}^{N-1} [C_j + C_{-j}] e^{ij\pi} \right\}$$

$$= a_0 + 2[a_1 - a_2 + \cdots + (-1)^{j+1} a_j + \cdots + (-1)^N a_{N-1} - f(\pi)].$$

$$(14)$$

3. Orthogonal System of Functions

An infinite system of real functions

$$\varphi_0(x), \quad \varphi_1(x), \quad \ldots, \quad \varphi_n(x), \quad \ldots$$

defined on the interval $[a, b]$ is said to be *orthogonal* on that interval if

$$(\varphi_m, \varphi_n) = \int_a^b \varphi_n(x)\varphi_m(x)\, dx = 0, \qquad m \neq n = 0, 1, 2, \ldots,$$

and

$$|\varphi_n|^2 = \int_a^b \varphi_n^2(x)\, dx = \mu_n \neq 0, \qquad n = 0, 1, 2, \ldots.$$

If $\mu_n = 1$ for all n, we say the system is *orthonormal*. Clearly, an orthogonal system can trivially be reduced to an orthonormal one by dividing each $\varphi_n(x)$ by $\sqrt{\mu_n}$. $\sqrt{\mu_n}$ is called the *norm* of the function φ_n on the interval $[a, b]$.

The system $1, \cos t, \cos 2t, \ldots, \sin t, \sin 2t, \ldots$ is orthogonal on any interval of length 2π, in particular the interval $[-\pi, \pi]$.[8]

The system $1, \cos t, \cos 2t, \ldots$ is orthogonal on the interval $[0, \pi]$ since

$$\int_0^\pi \cos nt \cos mt\, dt = \frac{1}{4} \int_{-\pi}^\pi (e^{i(m+n)t} + e^{i(m-n)t})\, dt$$

$$= \begin{cases} \dfrac{1}{4}\left[\dfrac{e^{i(m+n)t}}{i(m+n)} + \dfrac{e^{i(m-n)t}}{i(m-n)} \right]_{-\pi}^\pi = 0, & \text{for} \quad m \neq n, \\[4mm] \dfrac{1}{4}\left[\dfrac{e^{i2nt}}{2in} + t \right]_{-\pi}^\pi = \dfrac{\pi}{2}, & \text{for} \quad m = n. \end{cases}$$

In particular, the first of these formulas holds for $m \neq n$, $n = 0$, which shows $\cos nt$ is orthogonal to the function 1.

The system $\sin t, \sin 2t, \ldots$ is also orthogonal on the same interval $[0, \pi]$ since

$$\int_0^\pi \sin nt \sin mt\, dt = \begin{cases} 0, & m \neq n, \\ \pi/2, & m = n \end{cases}$$

by an argument exactly as above.

[8] See footnote 6.

The system of odd sines, $\sin t$, $\sin 3t$, $\sin 5t$, . . . , is orthogonal on the interval $[0, \pi/2]$ since

$$\int_0^{\pi/2} \sin(2n+1)t \, \sin(2m+1)t \, dt = \begin{cases} 0, & m \neq n, \\ \pi/4, & m = n. \end{cases}$$

For complex functions of a real variable, we define orthogonality over the real interval $[a, b]$ by

$$(\varphi_m, \varphi_n) = \int_a^b \varphi_m(x)\overline{\varphi_n(x)} \, dx = 0 \qquad \text{for} \quad m \neq n,$$

where, as above, the overbar denotes conjugation. The functions $1, e^{it}, e^{2it}, \ldots$ are clearly orthogonal over any interval of length 2π, e.g., $[-\pi, \pi]$, since

$$\int_{-\pi}^{\pi} e^{i(m-n)t} \, dt = \begin{cases} 0, & m \neq n, \\ 2\pi, & m = n. \end{cases}$$

A system of functions $\varphi_0(x), \varphi_1(x), \ldots, \varphi_n(x), \ldots$ is said to be *linearly independent* on the interval $[a, b]$ if, for any n, there are no constants $a_0, a_1, \ldots, a_n$ not all zero such that

$$a_0\varphi_0(x) + \cdots + a_n\varphi_n(x) \equiv 0 \tag{1}$$

on the interval. It is worth noting that the functions of an orthogonal system are always linearly independent on the interval over which they are orthogonal, since we may multiply (1) by $\varphi_m(x)$ and integrate over the interval to obtain $a_m = 0$ for all m.

From a system of functions $\psi_0(x), \psi_1(x), \ldots$ that are linearly independent but not necessarily orthogonal, an orthogonal system may be constructed by taking appropriate linear combinations of $\psi_0(x), \psi_1(x), \ldots$ in a manner entirely analogous to the well-known Gram–Schmidt procedure in the theory of ordinary vector spaces.

Let $\varphi_0 = \lambda_0\psi_0$, where $|\varphi_0|^2 = 1$, by an appropriate normalization. Next choose a_{01} so that $\psi_1 - a_{01}\varphi_0$ is orthogonal to φ_0. Note that $\psi_1 - a_{01}\varphi_0$ does not vanish identically because ψ_1 and $\psi_0 = \varphi_0$ are linearly independent. Clearly $a_{01} = (\varphi_0, \psi_1)$ will do the trick. Thus

$$\varphi_1 = \lambda_1(\psi_1 - a_{01}\varphi_0), \qquad |\varphi_1|^2 = 1,$$

is the next in the system of orthogonal functions under construction. The following function is

$$\varphi_2 = \lambda_2(\psi_2 - a_{02}\varphi_0 - a_{12}\varphi_1), \qquad |\varphi_2|^2 = 1,$$

where $a_{02} = (\varphi_0, \psi_2)$ and $a_{12} = (\varphi_1, \psi_2)$. Continuing this process indefinitely, we arrive at the desired orthogonal system.

A function defined on the interval $[a, b]$ is defined to be *square integrable* if both the function and its squares are integrable. Every bounded integrable function is square integrable, but unbounded integrable functions are not always square integrable. In the following discussion explicit mention of the interval $[a, b]$ is suppressed.

Let $\varphi_0, \varphi_1, \ldots$ be an orthonormal system (i.e., an orthogonal system for which $|\varphi_n| = 1$, $n = 0, 1, \ldots$) and $f(t)$ be square integrable. The numbers

$$C_n = (f, \bar{\varphi}_n), \qquad n = 0, 1, \ldots \tag{2}$$

are called the *Fourier coefficients* or *components* of the function $f(t)$ with respect to the system $\varphi_0, \varphi_1, \ldots$.[9]

Now consider the finite linear combination of the first N orthogonal functions $\sum_{k=0}^{N} C_k \varphi_k(t)$. Clearly

$$0 \leq \int \left[f(t) - \sum_{k=0}^{N} C_k \varphi_k(t) \right] \overline{\left[f(t) - \sum_{k=0}^{N} C_k \varphi_k(t) \right]} \, dt$$

$$= \int f(t) \overline{f(t)} \, dt - \sum_{k=0}^{N} C_k \int \overline{f(t)} \varphi_k(t) \, dt \tag{3}$$

$$- \sum_{k=0}^{N} \bar{C}_k \int f(t) \overline{\varphi_k(t)} \, dt + \sum_{k=0}^{N} \sum_{j=0}^{N} C_k \bar{C}_j \int \varphi_k(t) \overline{\varphi_j(t)} \, dt.$$

Since $C_n = (f, \bar{\varphi}_k)$, and because the functions $\varphi_0, \varphi_1, \ldots$ are orthonormal, the above reduces to

$$(f, \bar{f}) = \int f(t) \overline{f(t)} \, dt = \int |f(t)|^2 \, dt \geq \sum_{k=0}^{N} C_k \bar{C}_k. \tag{4}$$

Since the number on the left does not depend upon N, it follows that the sum of squared moduli (sum of squares if the C_k are real) of the Fourier coefficients of a square integrable function always converges and

$$\sum_{k=0}^{\infty} |C_k|^2 \leq (f, \bar{f}) = \int |f|^2 \, dt, \tag{5}$$

which is known as Bessel's inequality.

Consider the question of the approximation of the function $f(t)$ on an interval by a linear combination of orthogonal functions. One sense in which the linear combination, say $\sum_{k=0}^{N} \gamma_k \varphi_k(t)$, can be said to be a "good approximation" to the function $f(t)$ is that the mean-square error

$$M = \int \left| f(t) - \sum_{k=0}^{N} \gamma_k \varphi_k(t) \right|^2 \, dt$$

is as small as possible. Coefficients γ_k for which M is minimized give what is called the *least-squares approximation* to $f(t)$. Now by the orthonormality of

---

[9] When $\varphi_n(t) = (1/2\pi)e^{int}$ (and the interval considered is $[-\pi, \pi]$), for example, the C_n are just the Fourier coefficients defined by (2.6). Equation (2) is thus a straightforward generalization.

$\varphi_0, \varphi_1, \ldots$ we have

$$M = \int \left| f(t) - \sum_{k=0}^{N} (\gamma_k - C_k)\varphi_k(t) - \sum_{k=0}^{N} C_k\varphi_k(t) \right|^2 dt$$

$$= \int |f(t)|^2 \, dt + \sum_{k=0}^{N} |\gamma_k - C_k|^2 - \sum_{k=0}^{N} |C_k|^2,$$

from which it at once follows that M takes on its minimum value

$$M_{\min} = \int |f(t)|^2 \, dt - \sum_{k=0}^{N} |C_k|^2$$

when γ_k is chosen equal to the Fourier coefficients C_k.

Approximation in the least-squares sense is also sometimes called *approximation in the mean.*

If, for some orthonormal system of functions $\varphi_0, \varphi_1, \ldots$, the minimum mean square error $M_{\min}$ can be made as small as we please by choosing N sufficiently large, then the system $\varphi_0, \varphi_1, \ldots$ is called *complete*. For a complete system $M_{\min} \to 0$, so that (3) implies

$$\int |f|^2 \, dt = \sum_{k=0}^{\infty} |C_k|^2. \tag{6}$$

The following important theorem regarding completeness is valid:

Theorem. A necessary and sufficient condition for the system $\varphi_0, \varphi_1, \ldots$ of orthonormal functions to be complete is that the relation

$$\lim_{N \to \infty} \int \left| f(t) - \sum_{k=0}^{N} C_k\varphi_k(t) \right|^2 dt = 0$$

holds for any square integrable function $f(t)$, where the C_k are the Fourier coefficients $(f, \overline{\varphi}_k)$.

Ordinary convergence of a Fourier series to the function from which it is formed is not always guaranteed.[10] However, the theorem shows that convergence in the mean (or in the least-squares sense) always occurs if the orthogonal system considered is complete, i.e., if (6) holds. It may be shown that the systems

$$1, \cos t, \cos 2t, \ldots, \sin t, \sin 2t, \ldots; \qquad 1, e^{it}, e^{i2t}, \ldots, e^{-it}, e^{-i2t}, \ldots$$

are all complete.

---

[10] A good discussion of the conditions for convergence is given by Lanczos (1966, pp. 45–51) from an historical point of view. Essentially, all that is required is that the function to be approximated be single-valued Riemann integrable in the entire domain $[-\pi, \pi]$ and of bounded variation in the neighborhood of points where convergence is required.

In a complete system, linear combinations of functions determine each square integrable function uniquely except at a number of points. To prove this fact, we may make use of the above theorem. Suppose there exist two square integrable functions $f(t)$ and $F(t)$ for which the theorem holds, where the C_k are the same in both cases and equal to (f, φ_k). Then

$$\lim_{N \to \infty} \int \left| F(t) - \sum_{k=0}^{N} C_k \varphi_k(t) \right|^2 dt = 0,$$

$$\lim_{N \to \infty} \int \left| f(t) - \sum_{k=0}^{N} C_k \varphi_k(t) \right|^2 dt = 0. \tag{7}$$

We show (7) implies that $f(t) = F(t)$ except possibly at a number of points. Clearly,

$$0 \le \int |F(t) - f(t)|^2 \, dt$$

$$= \int \left| \left(F(t) - \sum_{k=0}^{N} C_k \varphi_k(t) \right) + \left(\sum_{k=0}^{N} C_k \varphi_k(t) - f(t) \right) \right|^2 dt$$

$$\le 2 \left\{ \int \left| F(t) - \sum_{k=0}^{N} C_k \varphi_k(t) \right|^2 dt + \int \left| f(t) - \sum_{k=0}^{N} C_k \varphi_k(t) \right|^2 dt \right\}$$

since $|a + b|^2 \le 2\{|a|^2 + |b|^2\}$. By (7) both terms following the rightmost inequality above tend to zero as N increases; hence

$$\lim_{N \to \infty} \int |F(t) - f(t)|^2 \, dt = 0,$$

which implies that $F(t) = f(t)$ except possibly at a number of points of discontinuity.

An especially important property of complete systems is the fact that any continuous function $f(t)$ that is orthogonal to all the functions of the system must be identically zero. This property follows because the assumed orthogonality implies the Fourier coefficients $C_k = (f, \overline{\varphi}_k)$ all vanish; hence, by (6)

$$\int |f(t)|^2 \, dt = 0,$$

which, since $f(t)$ is assumed to be continuous, implies that $f(t) \equiv 0$.

Other properties of complete systems may be found in Tolstov (1962, Chapter 2). The same volume contains a proof that the system of trigonometric functions

$$1, \cos t, \cos 2t, \dots ; \qquad \sin t, \sin 2t, \dots$$

is complete. This, of course, implies that the complex system $1, e^{it}, e^{2it}, \dots, e^{-it}, e^{-i2t}, \dots$ is also complete and that, as remarked above, *convergence in the mean* is guaranteed for the Fourier series of every continuous function, although ordinary convergence may not obtain.

It can be shown that the completeness of the trigonometric system implies that

$$\frac{1}{\pi} \int_{-\pi}^{\pi} [f(t)]^2 \, dt = \frac{a_0^2}{2} + \sum_{k=1}^{\infty} (a_k^2 + b_k^2),$$

where

$$a_k = \frac{1}{\pi} \int_{-\pi}^{\pi} f(t) \cos kt \, dt, \qquad k = 0, 1, \dots,$$

$$b_k = \frac{1}{\pi} \int_{-\pi}^{\pi} f(t) \sin kt \, dt, \qquad k = 1, 2, \dots,$$

$$= 0, \qquad\qquad\qquad\qquad k = 0,$$

and $f(t)$ is square integrable on the interval $[-\pi, \pi]$. This result is known as *Parseval's theorem*. The expressions on the right-hand side, $a_k^2 + b_k^2$, considered as a function of k are sometimes called the *spectrum* of $f(t)$.

4. Questions of Convergence and Goodness of Approximation

The notion of a Fourier series derives its ultimate utility from the fact that it enables us to approximate a function over a finite interval by a trigonometric polynomial of finite degree. There are three main questions of interest connected with the evaluation of just how good an approximation the finite degree polynomial will be: (1) How large should N be? (2) What happens if there are discontinuities in the function to be approximated? and (3) What is the effect of approximating the function only at a finite number of points and implicitly interpolating the remaining values according to the approximating polynomial? In this section we take up each of these questions, beginning with the last.

In Section 2 we discussed a function $f(t)$ that was defined only at $2N$ points, or only observed at such points, and showed there that such a function has *at those points* an exact representation as a trigonometric polynomial of degree N. It is now necessary to distinguish between functions that are only defined at the $2N$ points and those that are only observed at such points but are defined throughout the interval. It is the latter with which we are concerned here.

Let $f(t)$ be a continuous function defined on the interval $[-T, T]$, which we divide by $2N + 1$ points

$$t_k = k\left(\frac{2T}{2N + 1}\right), \qquad k = 0, \pm 1, \dots, \pm N.$$

From (2.10) we find that at the $2N + 1$ points

$$f(t_k) = \sum_{j=-N}^{N} C_j^{(N)} e^{i(j\pi 2/2T)k(2T/(2N+1))}$$

$$= \sum_{j=-N}^{N} C_j^{(N)} e^{i(j\pi 2/(2N+1))k}, \qquad k = 0, \pm 1, \dots, \pm N. \qquad (1)$$

The superscript (N) on the Fourier coefficients C_j is used to indicate that these coefficients are derived from an equispaced sample of points in the interval $[-T, T]$. These coefficients may be obtained from the $2N + 1$ observed points of the function $f(t)$ by means of a relation corresponding to (2.12):

$$C_j^{(N)} = \frac{1}{2N+1} \sum_{k=-N}^{N} e^{-i(j\pi 2/(2N+1))k} f(t_k), \qquad j = 0, \pm 1, \ldots, \pm N. \qquad (2)$$

The proper Fourier coefficients appropriate to the continuous form of the function are given by (2.6) with appropriate substitution:

$$C_k = \frac{1}{2T} \int_{-T}^{T} e^{-i(k\pi/T)t} f(t)\, dt. \qquad (3)$$

These coefficients appear in the expansion

$$f(t) = \sum_{j=-\infty}^{\infty} C_j e^{i(j\pi/T)t}. \qquad (4)$$

At the points $t_k = k(2T/2N + 1)$ these values are

$$f(t_k) = \sum_{j=-\infty}^{\infty} C_j e^{i(j\pi/T)k(2T/2N+1)} = \sum_{j=-\infty}^{\infty} C_j e^{i(j\pi 2/(2N+1))k}. \qquad (5)$$

The function $e^{i(j\pi 2/(2N+1))}$ is periodic of period $2N + 1$ since

$$e^{i(j\pi 2/(2N+1))} = e^{i(j\pi 2/(2N+1)\pm 2\pi)} = e^{i(j\pm(2N+1))2\pi/(2N+1)}.$$

Thus, (5) may be rewritten

$$f(t_k) = \sum_{j=-N}^{N} e^{i(j\pi 2/(2N+1))k} \{ C_j + (C_{j-2N-1} + C_{j+2N+1})$$

$$+ (C_{j-4N-2} + C_{j+4N+2}) + \cdots \}$$

$$= \sum_{j=-N}^{N} \left\{ C_j + \sum_{\tau=1}^{\infty} (C_{j-(2N+1)\tau} + C_{j+(2N+1)\tau}) \right\} e^{i(j\pi 2/(2N+1))k}. \qquad (6)$$

Equating common powers of $e^{i(j\pi 2/(2N+1))}$ in (1) and (5), we find

$$C_j^{(N)} = C_j + \sum_{\tau=1}^{\infty} (C_{j-(2N+1)\tau} + C_{j+(2N+1)\tau}), \qquad j = 0, \pm 1, \ldots, \pm N. \qquad (7)$$

In the special case of $j = 0$, for example, we have

$$C_0^{(N)} = a_0^{(N)}/2 = C_0 + \sum_{\tau=1}^{\infty} (C_{-(2N+1)\tau} + C_{(2N+1)\tau})$$

$$= a_0/2 + \sum_{\tau=1}^{\infty} (\bar{C}_{(2N+1)\tau} + C_{(2N+1)\tau}) = a_0/2 + \sum_{\tau=1}^{\infty} a_{(2N+1)\tau}$$

(see Hamming, 1962, p. 278).

These results imply that the Fourier coefficients for the sampled function will be sums of Fourier coefficients; the coefficient C_j is associated with the single frequency $\lambda_j = j\pi 2/(2N + 1)$, but the coefficient $C_j^{(N)}$ for the sampled function is the sum of coefficients associated not only with λ_j but the higher (and lower) frequencies

$$\lambda_{j \pm (2N+1)\tau} = \lambda_j \pm 2\pi\tau, \qquad \tau = 1, 2, \ldots . \tag{8}$$

The frequencies $\lambda_{j \pm (2N+1)\tau}$ are called the *aliases* of the principal frequency λ_j. The highest observable frequency (in terms of Fourier coefficients) is $\lambda_N = [2N/(2N + 1)]\pi$. Conversely, $\lambda_{-N} = -[2N/(2N + 1)]\pi$ is the lowest observable frequency. Frequencies higher than λ_N or lower than λ_{-N} are "folded" over these two frequencies into the interval between. That is, they are associated with frequencies in the interval. The frequencies λ_N and λ_{-N} are called the *folding frequencies* or *Nyquist frequencies*. Aliasing or the confounding of the Fourier coefficients associated with different frequencies cannot be undone once sampling has taken place. Note too that, at the folding frequency, sampling takes place at the rate of two sample points per full cycle since a sinusoidal wave at frequency $\lambda_N \doteq \pi$ has period $= 2\pi/\lambda_N \doteq 2$.

In our discussion of Parseval's theorem in the previous section it was noted that $|C_j|^2$ considered as a function of the associated frequencies λ_j is called the spectrum of $f(t)$. The effects of aliasing on the spectrum, i.e., the relation between the spectrum of the sampled functions $f(t_k)$, $k = 0, \pm 1, \ldots, \pm N$, to the spectrum of the underlying continuous function may be discussed with the help of (8). It may be shown that only aliases of the principal frequency λ_j affect $|C_j^{(N)}|^2$. If the true spectrum at frequencies greater than λ_N or less than λ_{-N} falls off very rapidly, the magnitude of the error due to sampling is small; e.g., consider the effect if the spectrum falls off as $1/j^2$, $j = 0, \pm 1, \pm 2, \ldots$.

Above we noted that Bessel's inequality implies that the series $\sum_{k=0}^{\infty} |C_k|^2$ always converges for any square integrable function $f(t)$ since

$$\sum_{k=0}^{N} |C_k|^2 \le (f, \bar{f}) = \int_{-\pi}^{\pi} f(t)\overline{f(t)}\, dt$$

independently of N. Thus $\sum_{k=0}^{\infty} |C_k|^2 < \infty$, which implies $\lim_{k \to \infty} C_k = 0$, which is the usual test for convergence. It is also true (not proved here) that this series diverges if $f(t)$ is not square integrable. It follows immediately that

$$\lim_{k \to \infty} C_k = \frac{1}{\sqrt{2\pi}} \lim_{k \to \infty} \int_{-\pi}^{\pi} f(t)e^{-ikt}\, dt$$

$$= \frac{1}{\sqrt{2\pi}} \lim_{k \to \infty} \left\{ \int_{-\pi}^{\pi} f(t)\cos kt\, dt - i \int_{-\pi}^{\pi} f(t)\sin kt\, dt \right\} = 0,$$

so that

$$\lim_{k \to \infty} \int_{a}^{b} f(t)\cos kt\, dt = \lim_{k \to \infty} \int_{a}^{b} f(t)\sin kt\, dt = 0$$

for any interval over which $f(t)$ is square integrable. The Fourier coefficients of a square integrable function thus tend to zero with increasing frequency; how fast they do so, as noted above, has a bearing on how well the Fourier coefficients estimated from a sampled series of points of a theoretically continuous function will approximate the true coefficients.

An issue related to this point is how well the *partial sum* of a Fourier series, i.e., the trigonometric polynomial based on the finite sample of points, approximates the true function at any point of the interval. If attention is restricted to square integrable functions, for which $f_N(t)$ as defined in (2.3) always converges to $f(t)$, we are, in effect, asking how well we can *interpolate* the values of a function over some interval by a trigonometric polynomial based on knowing the values of the function at only a finite number of points.[11]

From (1) we find that the trigonometric polynomial based on a sample of $2N + 1$ points is

$$f_N(t) = \sum_{j=-N}^{N} C_j^{(N)} e^{i(j\pi/T)t}. \tag{9}$$

Note that for $t = t_k = 2T/(2N + 1)$, $k = 0, \pm 1, \ldots, \pm N$, $f_N(t)$ as defined in (9) is numerically equal to $f(t_k)$, the exact value of the function. The coefficients $C_k^{(N)}$ are given by (2). Inserting this result in (9) yields

$$f_N(t) = \sum_{j=-N}^{N} \frac{e^{i(j\pi/T)t}}{2N + 1} \sum_{k=-N}^{N} e^{-i(j\pi 2/(2N+1))k} f(t_k)$$

$$= \frac{1}{2N + 1} \sum_{j=-N}^{N} \sum_{k=-N}^{N} e^{-i(j\pi/T)(t - t_k)} f(t_k)$$

$$= \frac{1}{2N + 1} \sum_{k=-N}^{N} f(t_k) \left\{ 1 + 2 \sum_{j=1}^{N} \cos j \left(\frac{\pi}{T} \right)(t - t_k) \right\}. \tag{10}$$

To evaluate the expression in braces we proceed as follows: Let

$$S = 1 + 2\cos\varphi + 2\cos 2\varphi + \cdots + 2\cos N\varphi, \quad \text{where} \quad \varphi = (\pi/T)(t - t_k),$$
$$S \sin \varphi/2 = \sin \varphi/2 + 2 \sin \varphi/2 \cos \varphi + \cdots + 2 \sin \varphi/2 \cos N\varphi,$$

so that, making use of an elementary trigonometric identity,

$$S \sin \varphi/2 = \sin \varphi/2 + [\sin(1 + \tfrac{1}{2})\varphi - \sin(1 - \tfrac{1}{2})\varphi]$$
$$+ [\sin(2 + \tfrac{1}{2})\varphi - \sin(2 - \tfrac{1}{2})\varphi]$$
$$+ \cdots + [\sin(N + \tfrac{1}{2})\varphi - \sin(N - \tfrac{1}{2})\varphi]$$
$$= \sin(N + \tfrac{1}{2})\varphi$$

since each of the second terms in square brackets cancels one in the square brackets before it. Inserting this result for S in (10) we obtain the value of $f_N(t)$

---

[11] In Chapter III we discuss Fourier transforms of the autocovariance function. *Interpolation* of this Fourier transform is equivalent to *extrapolation* of the autocovariance function.

at *a particular point t* as a weighted average of the values of $f(t)$ *at all the sample points*:

$$f_N(t) = \frac{1}{2N+1} \sum_{k=-N}^{N} f(t_k) \frac{\sin[\frac{1}{2}(2N+1)(\pi/T)(t-t_k)]}{\sin[\frac{1}{2}(\pi/T)(t-t_k)]}. \tag{11}$$

Let $x = (2\pi/2T)(t - t_k)$, i.e., 2π divided by the period of $f(t)$ times the distance of the point at which $f_N(t)$ is evaluated from the point t_k. The weight function

$$D_N(x) = \frac{1}{2N+1} \frac{\sin\frac{1}{2}(2N+1)x}{\sin\frac{1}{2}x} \tag{12}$$

is called Dirichlet's kernel.

The function $D_N(x)$ is an even periodic function. Since

$$\sin[\tfrac{1}{2}(2N+1)](x+2\pi) = \sin\{\tfrac{1}{2}(2N+1)x + (2N+1)\pi\} = -\sin[\tfrac{1}{2}(2N+1)]x$$

for all N including $N = 0$, we see that $D_N(x)$ is periodic with period 2π, and it thus suffices to consider it only over the interval $[-\pi, \pi]$. Over this interval $\sin x/2$ is zero only for $x = 0$. Thus the function $D_N(x)$ has zeros at the points where

$$\sin[\tfrac{1}{2}(2N+1)]x = 0,$$

i.e., at $\pm 2\pi/(2N+1)$, $\pm 4\pi/(2N+1)$, $\pm 6\pi/(2N+1)$,... in the interval $[-\pi, \pi]$. Clearly $D_N(x)$ reaches an absolute maximum within the interval at the point $x = 0$. This value may be found using L'Hopital's rule:

$$\max D_N(x) = \lim_{x \to 0} \frac{1}{2N+1} \frac{\sin[\frac{1}{2}(2N+1)]x}{\sin\frac{1}{2}x}$$

$$= \lim_{x \to 0} \frac{1}{2N+1} \frac{[\frac{1}{2}(2N+1)]\cos[\frac{1}{2}(2N+1)]x}{\frac{1}{2}\cos\frac{1}{2}x} = 1.$$

Consider the case in which $f(t) \equiv 1$. In this case (11) reduces, say over the interval $[-\pi, \pi]$, to

$$1 = \sum_{k=-N}^{N} D_N(k\pi/N),$$

so that the sum of the weights at $2N + 1$ equally spaced points in an interval corresponding to the period of the kernel function is just unity.

In the Fourier analysis of time series a weighting function such as $D_N(x)$ is called a *window*, and we may well adopt this term here. The properties of the Dirichlet window are

(a) It is even, i.e., symmetric about the origin.
(b) It reaches a maximum of 1 at the origin.
(c) The sum of the values at $2N + 1$ discrete points dividing the interval of its period is 1.

A graph of the Dirichlet window for $N = 6$ is given in Parzen (1963, p. 244). It is the graph in Fig. 3a there labeled $D_6(z)$. Since the window is symmetric about 0, only the part for positive z has been given.

Parzen's graph shows clearly what is implicit in our previous discussion: At any given point t in the interval of definition (and period) of the function $f(t)$, the partial sum $f_N(t)$ given by (11) is a weighted average of values of the function at the equispaced points for which the Fourier coefficients $C_k^{(N)}$ are calculated; it is a "view" of the function through the "window" shown in the figure. The "view" of the function $f(t)$ given by the partial sum $f_N(t)$ contains contributions from all parts of the interval, and while heaviest weight is given to values of the function at points near to the value being estimated, some weight is given to distant values. Furthermore, the weight given to distant values may be either positive or negative. It is apparent that, if the function $f(t)$ being approximated in this way is relatively flat (i.e., does not change rapidly or very much) over the interval of its definition, then it will not matter very much that relatively distant values are averaged into the estimate of the value at a particular point. On the other hand, if the function $f(t)$ changes rapidly over the interval, is not, for example, flat, and has sharp peaks and troughs, then it is clear that the view through the window, especially for small values of N, will be a relatively poor one since quite different values of the function will be averaged in (some even with negative weight!) to form the estimate of the value we seek. We might say in this case that "leakage" through the edges of the window may be a severe problem. It is even possible, for example, that the estimate of a small positive value of the function will turn out to be negative if it happens to be the right distance from a very large positive value of the function since under certain circumstances this may be averaged in with a negative weight.

For any given value of N, the ideal window would be concentrated as closely as possible about the origin and should have "side lobes" that are as small as possible and preferably nonnegative. It is clear that as N increases, the Dirichlet window does become more and more concentrated near the origin. Its first zero, for example, moves in from $\frac{2}{11}\pi$ for $N = 5$ to $\frac{2}{101}\pi$ for $N = 50$; indeed it moves toward zero approximately as $1/N$. However, it continues to have side lobes of nonnegligible height. The second largest peak, in this case a negative one, occurs between the first two zeros—for large N at approximately $x = 3\pi/(2N + 1)$. At this value the value of $D_N(x)$

$$D_N\left(\frac{3\pi}{2N + 1}\right) = \frac{1}{2N + 1} \frac{\sin 3\pi/2}{\sin[3\pi/2(2N + 1)]} \to \frac{\sin 3\pi/2}{3\pi/2}$$

as $N \to \infty$.[12] This value is $-2/3\pi = -0.2122$, and since in this discrete case the main peak has height independent of N, this is also the ratio of the height

---

[12] This follows from the fact that $\lim_{\alpha \to 0}(\sin \alpha/\alpha) = 1$ by replacing $3\pi/2(2N + 1)$ by α in the denominator of the expression for $D_N[3\pi/(2N + 1)]$.

of the first side lobe to the height of the main peak.[13] Thus, no matter how large N is, the first side lobe is certainly nonnegligible, approaching one-fifth the value at the maximum center value; and while the location of this side lobe moves toward the center with increasing N, it does not disappear. Hence, if we are trying to estimate the function in the neighborhood of a point where it is changing rapidly, we shall certainly have to take N very large in order to overcome the bad effects produced by the Dirichlet window. This matter is closely related to the question of the convergence of the partial sum $f_N(t)$ in the neighborhood of a discontinuity of $f(t)$.

The behavior of the series $f_N(t)$ in the neighborhood of a point of discontinuity entails a failure of convergence known as *Gibbs' phenomenon*.[14] This phenomenon is of interest primarily because it reveals the inadequacy of traditional Fourier analysis, based on the Dirichlet kernel, for the analysis of functions that may change very rapidly in the neighborhood of some point, although they may not actually be discontinuous at such points. In our discussion we neglect the problem of aliasing. To study the behavior of the truncated Fourier series $f_N(t)$ at a point of discontinuity of the function $f(t)$, consider the function

$$f(t) = \begin{cases} -1, & -\pi < t < 0, \\ 1, & 0 < t < \pi, \end{cases} \qquad (13)$$

which is undefined at $t = 0$. Assume $f(t)$ is periodic with period 2π.

The function $f(t)$ is certainly square integrable, and hence the Fourier series converges at every point of continuity; i.e., $f_N(t) \to f(t)$ as $N \to \infty$ for $t \neq 0$. By a standard result in the theory of Fourier series (Tolstov, 1962, p. 77), the series converges to

$$\tfrac{1}{2}[f(t + 0) + f(t - 0)] = 0$$

at $t = 0$, where $f(t + 0) = \lim_{t \to +0} f(t)$ and $f(t - 0) = \lim_{t \to -0} f(t)$.

---

[13] This is not true in the continuous case, as the following development of the theory neglecting the problem of aliasing shows: In the continuous case, we have

$$f_N(t) = \int_{-T}^{T} D_N\left(\frac{2\pi}{2T}[x - t]\right) f(x)\, dx,$$

where

$$D_N\left(\frac{2\pi}{2T}[x - t]\right) = \frac{1}{2T}\left\{1 + 2\sum_{k=1}^{N} \cos\frac{k2\pi}{2T}[x - t]\right\}.$$

Let $z = (2\pi/2T)[x - t]$. It may be shown that $D_N(z)$ is an even periodic function with period 2π; that it has zeros at the same points $\pm 2\pi/(2N + 1), \pm 4\pi/(2N + 1), \ldots$; that $D_N(0) = (2N + 1)/2T$ is its maximum value; and that

$$\int_{-\pi}^{\pi} D_N(z)\, dz = 1.$$

[14] Lanczos (1966, pp. 51–54) discusses Gibbs' phenomenon and the origin of its discovery as well as an early attempt to resolve the problem (pp. 55–61).

It may be shown that

$$f_N(t) = \int_{-\pi}^{\pi} D_N(t - x)f(x)\,dx, \tag{14}$$

where

$$D_N(z) = \frac{1}{2\pi}\frac{\sin(N + \tfrac{1}{2})z}{\sin\tfrac{1}{2}z},$$

taking account of the fact that $D_N(-z) = D_N(z)$.[15] Substituting for $f(t)$ from (13),

$$f_N(t) = \int_0^{\pi} D_N(t - x)\,dx - \int_{-\pi}^0 D_N(t - x)\,dx$$

$$= \int_{-t}^{\pi-t} D_N(z)\,dz + \int_{\pi+t}^{t} D_N(z)\,dz,$$

letting $z = -(t - x)$ in the first integral and $z = (t - x)$ in the second. Expanding the integrals in sums of integrals over shorter ranges we find, suppressing $D_N(z)\,dz$ for convenience,

$$f_N(t) = \int_{-t}^{t} + \int_{t}^{\pi-t} - \int_{t}^{\pi-t} + \int_{\pi+t}^{\pi-t} = \int_{-t}^{t} + \int_{\pi+t}^{\pi-t},$$

so that

$$f_N(t) = \int_{-t}^{t} D_N(z)\,dz - \int_{\pi-t}^{\pi+t} D_N(z)\,dz.$$

Provided t is small, the second integral will be approximately the value

$$D_N(\pi) = \frac{1}{2\pi}\frac{\sin[\tfrac{1}{2}(2N + 1)]\pi}{\sin(\tfrac{1}{2}\pi)}$$

integrated over the interval $[\pi - t, \pi + t]$, which is approximately zero. The first integral, however, does *not* vanish for small t. Thus in the neighborhood of the discontinuity at $t = 0$ we have

$$f_N(t) \cong \frac{1}{2\pi}\int_{-t}^{t}\frac{\sin(N + \tfrac{1}{2})z}{\sin\tfrac{1}{2}z}\,dz$$

$$= \frac{1}{\pi}\int_0^{t}\frac{\sin(N + \tfrac{1}{2})z}{\sin\tfrac{1}{2}z}\,dz, \qquad t > 0$$

$$\cong \frac{1}{\pi}\int_0^{t}\frac{\sin(N + \tfrac{1}{2})z}{\tfrac{1}{2}z}\,dz, \qquad t > 0$$

since $\sin z \cong z$ for small z.[16]

---

[15] See footnote 13.

[16] The integral $\mathrm{Si}(x) = \int_0^x [\sin \xi/\xi]\,d\xi$ is called the *sine integral* and has been extensively tabulated (National Bureau of Standards, 1964, pp. 238–243).

For $t > 0$ one can show $f_N(t) \to 1$ as $N \to \infty$ and $f_N(t) \to 0$ as $t \to 0$.[17] At the point $t = 0$, however, the value of $f_N(t)$ does not equal 1. For fixed N, it can be shown that the partial sum "overshoots" the value of the function near the point $t = 0$ and that the maximum overshoot occurs at $t_0 = 2\pi/(2N + 1)$. (see Carslaw, 1930, p. 297). For example, for $N = 10$, one can calculate that the maximum overshoot of 0.1789 occurs at $t_0 = 0.2992$. Moreover, the amount of the overshoot does not depend upon N; its location merely moves towards the origin, and inasmuch as the oscillations about 1 are of decreasing amplitude with increasing t, the partial sum becomes a better and better approximation to the time function at values of t away from the point of discontinuity. *No matter how large N, however, the overshoot of 0.1789 at $t_0 = 2\pi/(2N + 1)$ always occurs.*

The importance of this phenomenon lies in showing certain unsatisfactory aspects of the Dirichlet window: The overshoot, a distance $2\pi/(2N + 1)$ from the point of discontinuity of $f(t)$ is indicative of the poor approximation achieved using the Dirichlet window when the function is rapidly changing. Various devices are available for reducing the magnitude of this problem and, indeed, eliminating it all together, albeit at a price. Each of these devices may be expressed in terms of an alternative form of window; the price paid is a slowing of the rate of convergence at points distant from the point of discontinuity or excessively rapid change.

One of the first alternatives to the Dirichlet window was discovered by Fejèr (see Lanczos, 1966, pp. 55–61). He suggested using the arithmetic mean of the first N partial sums of the trigonometric approximations to the function $f(t)$:

$$\overline{f_N(t)} = (1/N + 1)[f_0(t) + f_1(t) + \cdots + f_N(t)]. \tag{15}$$

Fejèr was concerned primarily with the fact that if $f(t)$ is not square integrable, $f_N(t)$ does not necessarily converge to $f(t)$ even if $f(t)$ is continuous; he showed that $\overline{f_N(t)}$ was a trigonometric polynomial of degree N that converged uniformly to $f(t)$ provided only $f(t)$ was continuous. In the process, Fejèr also eliminated Gibbs' phenomenon at points of discontinuity of the type discussed above (Carslaw, 1930, p. 308). To derive the window implied by the approximation $\overline{f_N(t)}$, it is simplest to insert our previous result (14) in (15):

$$\overline{f_N(t)} = \sum_{n=0}^{N} \frac{1}{N + 1} \int_{-\pi}^{\pi} D_n(t - x) f(x) \, dx$$

$$= \int_{-\pi}^{\pi} F_N(t - x) f(x) \, dx,$$

---

[17] This can be shown since $\lim_{x \to \infty} \text{Si}(x) = \pi/2$ (see the derivation at the end of Section 6 of Appendix B), and $\lim_{x \to 0} \text{Si}(x) = \lim_{x \to 0} \int_0^x 1 \, dx = 0$. Setting $\xi = \frac{1}{2}(2N + 1)z$, we have

$$f_N(t) = (2/\pi) \text{Si}[(N + \tfrac{1}{2})t], \qquad t > 0,$$

which yields the desired result.

where

$$F_N(z) = \frac{1}{N+1} \sum_{n=0}^{N} D_n(z)$$

is the Fejer window. To evaluate $F_N(z)$ we write

$$2\pi F_N(z) = \frac{1}{(N+1)\sin(z/2)} \sum_{n=0}^{N} \sin(n + \tfrac{1}{2})z$$

$$= \frac{1}{(N+1)\sin(z/2)} \sum_{n=0}^{N} \{\cos(z/2)\sin nz + \sin(z/2)\cos nz\}$$

$$= \frac{1}{(N+1)\sin(z/2)} \left\{ \frac{\cos^2(z/2) - \cos(z/2)\cos(N + \tfrac{1}{2})z}{2\sin(z/2)} \right.$$

$$\left. + \frac{\sin(z/2)}{2} + \frac{\sin(z/2)\sin(N + \tfrac{1}{2})z}{2\sin(z/2)} \right\}$$

$$= \frac{1 - \cos(z/2)\cos(N + \tfrac{1}{2})z + \sin(z/2)\sin(N + \tfrac{1}{2})z}{2(N+1)\sin^2(z/2)}$$

$$= \frac{1 - \cos 2(N+1)(z/2)}{2(N+1)\sin^2(z/2)}$$

$$= \frac{1}{N+1} \left[\frac{\sin(N+1)(z/2)}{\sin(z/2)} \right]^2$$

since

$$1 + 2\cos\varphi + 2\cos 2\varphi + \cdots + 2\cos N\varphi = \frac{\sin(N + \tfrac{1}{2})\varphi}{\sin(\varphi/2)},$$

as was proved earlier, and

$$\sin\varphi + \sin 2\varphi + \cdots + \sin N\varphi = \frac{\cos\varphi/2 - \cos(N + \tfrac{1}{2})\varphi}{2\sin(\varphi/2)},$$

which may be proved by similar methods.

The Fejèr window has zeros at the points $\pm 2\pi/(N+1)$, $\pm 4\pi/(N+1)$, ..., but in contrast to the Dirichlet window, the Fejèr window never becomes negative and the first zero is nearly twice the distance from the origin. For large N the peak of the first side lobe occurs approximately at $3\pi/(N+1)$. The main peak has a height

$$\lim_{z\to 0} F_N(z) = \frac{1}{N+1} \left[\lim_{z\to 0} \frac{\sin(N+1)z/2}{\sin(z/2)} \right]^2 = N + 1,$$

which depends upon N. The ratio of the first side peak to the main peak is thus

$$\frac{F_N[3\pi/(N+1)]}{N+1} = \frac{1}{(N+1)^2} \left(\frac{\sin(3\pi/2)}{\sin[3\pi/2(N+1)]} \right)^2 \to \left(\frac{2}{3\pi} \right)^2$$

as $N \to \infty$. Thus this ratio is approximately 0.04 for the Fejèr window as compared with -0.21 for the Dirichlet window. Thus the Fejèr window is always positive and has side lobes of much smaller height than the Dirichlet window. However, the width of the main lobe of the Fejèr window, as indicated by the location of the first zero, is nearly twice that of the main lobe of the Dirichlet window. Consequently, one might expect that the Gibbs' phenomenon would be sharply reduced or eliminated for the Fejèr window but that the overall speed of convergence at points distant from the point of discontinuity would be slowed. Both expectations are justified (Carslaw, 1930, pp. 308–309).

A number of additional windows are available with properties intermediate to the Dirichlet and Fejèr windows or superior to them both in certain respects. These have been called "modified truncated Fourier series," "Tukey means," and "Lanczos means" by Parzen (1963, pp. 214–217). We also deal with an analogous result due to Parzen in the next section.

Because the window to which it leads has slightly better properties than the Dirichlet window, the following modification of the truncated Fourier series has been considered:

$$f_N^*(t) = f_N(t) - \tfrac{1}{2}(A_N \cos Nt + B_N \sin Nt),$$

where we suppose for simplicity that $f(t)$ has period 2π. Then

$$f_N^*(t) = \int_{-\pi}^{\pi} D_{N-1}(t-x)f(x)\,dx + \frac{1}{2\pi}\int_{-\pi}^{\pi} \cos N(t-x)f(x)\,dx$$

$$= \int_{-\pi}^{\pi} \frac{1}{2\pi} \left\{ \frac{\sin(N-\tfrac{1}{2})(t-x)}{\sin(t-x)/2} + \cos N(t-x) \right\} f(x)\,dx.$$

The window

$$D_N^*(z) = \frac{1}{2\pi} \left\{ \frac{\sin(N-\tfrac{1}{2})z}{\sin(z/2)} + \cos Nz \right\}$$

$$= \frac{1}{2\pi} \left\{ \frac{\sin Nz \cos(z/2) + \cos Nz \sin(z/2) - \sin(z/2)\cos Nz}{\sin(z/2)} \right\}$$

$$= \frac{1}{2\pi} \frac{\sin Nz}{\tan(z/2)}$$

has somewhat smaller side lobes than an ordinary Dirichlet window and may be termed a "modified Dirichlet window."

An alternative is the so-called Tukey window (Blackman and Tukey, 1958, p. 14), which corresponds to considering

$$f_N^{(t)}(t) = \tfrac{1}{2}f_N^*(t) + \tfrac{1}{4}f_N^*(t + \pi/N) + \tfrac{1}{4}f_N^*(t - \pi/N),$$

where $f_N^*(t)$ is the modified truncated Fourier series defined above for a function $f(t)$ on the interval $[-\pi, \pi]$. The window corresponding to this form of the series is clearly

$$T_N(z) = \tfrac{1}{2}D_N^*(z) + \tfrac{1}{4}D_N^*(z + \pi/N) + \tfrac{1}{4}D_N^*(z - \pi/N).$$

One is led most naturally to this window by considering the defects of the modified Dirichlet window. This window has zeros at the points $z = \pm \pi/N$, $\pm 2\pi/N, \ldots$ and the largest side lobe (which is a trough in this case) occurs at approximately $3\pi/2N$ for large N. The main peak occurs at the origin and has height N/π. The ratio of the first side lobe height to the main peak as N becomes large is

$$\frac{\sin 3\pi/2}{2N \tan(3\pi/4N)} = \frac{-\cos(3\pi/4N)}{2N \sin(3\pi/4N)} = \frac{-\cos(3\pi/4N)}{(3\pi/2)\sin(3\pi/4N)/(3\pi/4N)} \to \frac{-2}{3\pi} = -0.2122.$$

The idea behind the Tukey window is to reduce the size of the negative trough at $3\pi/2N$ by combining it with a shifted version of itself that is sufficiently positive. The values chosen for combination with the negative value at $3\pi/2N$ are the values at $\pm \pi/N$. These values are simply averaged in with equal weights so that

$$T_N(z) = \tfrac{1}{2}D_N^*(z) + \tfrac{1}{2}\{\tfrac{1}{2}[D_N^*(z - \pi/N) + D_N^*(z + \pi/N)]\}$$

is the overall formula for which the preceding remark is true.

If instead of averaging the modified truncated Fourier series for three discrete points as in $T_N(z)$ the unmodified values are averaged over the interval $[-\pi/2N, \pi/2N]$, we obtain

$$f_N^{(L)}(t) = \frac{N}{2\pi} \int_{t-\pi/N}^{t+\pi/N} f_N(u)\, du,$$

corresponding to the window

$$L_N(z) = \frac{N}{2\pi} \int_{-\pi/N}^{\pi/N} D_N(z + u)\, du.$$

This window is due to Lanczos (1956, p. 227) and is similar to the Tukey window in that it reduces the size of negative side lobes (very markedly) by averaging.

In order to study the important work of Parzen in this area, it is necessary to introduce the concept of a Fourier transform. This is done in the next section.

5. Fourier Transforms and "Windows"[18]

In previous sections we saw that it was possible to represent a square integrable function over a finite interval, say $[-l, l]$, by an infinite trigonometric series:

$$f(t) = \sum_{k=-\infty}^{\infty} C_k e^{ik\lambda t}, \tag{1}$$

[18] The subject of this section is beautifully treated by Lanczos (1966, pp. 158–216) on whose work our discussion is based.

where $\lambda = 2\pi/2l$ is the fundamental frequency of the representation. Since the system of complex exponentials is complete, the representation (1) holds in the sense of *convergence in the mean*. The coefficients C_k, the Fourier coefficients, are given by

$$C_k = \frac{1}{2l} \int_{-l}^{l} f(t)e^{-ik\lambda t}\, dt. \tag{2}$$

If the function $f(t)$ is extended beyond the range $[-l, l]$, we are either assuming it is periodic with period $2l$ or we are, in effect, constructing a periodic function from one defined only over the finite interval as a purely mathematical device. The question now arises as to whether we can develop the tools of harmonic analysis in such a way as to apply equally to functions defined over the entire real axis, i.e., to those whose fundamental period may become arbitrarily large. The answer to this question is yes, and to carry out the analysis the concept of a Fourier series must be extended to the notion of a *Fourier integral*.

To begin, consider a function $f(t)$, square integrable over the interval $[-l, l]$, for which (1) and (2) hold. Suppose that this function is now extended to the range $[-L, L]$ by defining $f(t)$ to be zero on the intervals $[-L, -l)$ and $(l, L]$. The relations corresponding to (1) and (2) are obtained by replacing l everywhere by L. The new frequencies are now $k\lambda = k\pi/L$, $k = 0, \pm 1, \ldots$, and it is at these frequencies, which are denser on the real line than before, that the function $f(t)$ is analyzed. If L, for example, is twice l, the fundamental frequency will be half of what it was in the former case, and there will be twice as many ordinates per unit distance on the abscissa in the graphs of the real and imaginary parts of C_k as before. If we write

$$\gamma_k = \int_{-l}^{l} f(t)e^{-i\lambda_k t}\, dt, \qquad C_k = \gamma_k/2L, \qquad \lambda_k = 2\pi k/2L, \tag{3}$$

we will find that for a given value of λ_k, the value γ_k does not change; i.e., no matter how small or how large L is, the γ_k are ordinates of a common function,

$$F(\omega) = \int_{-l}^{l} f(t)e^{-i\omega t}\, dt, \tag{4}$$

where $\gamma_k = F(\lambda_k)$. The function $F(\omega)$ is always continuous and indeed differentiable any number of times no matter how unpleasant $f(t)$ is, provided only that it is absolutely integrable on the interval $[-l, l]$.[19] $F(\omega)$ is called the *Fourier transform* of $f(t)$.

As we increase L, the fundamental frequency $\lambda = 2\pi/2L$ will grow smaller and smaller and the values $\lambda_k = k(2\pi/2L)$, $k = 0, \pm 1, \ldots$ will grow closer and

---

[19] Tolstov (1962, p. 183, 191). When l is allowed to increase, however, it is no longer true in general that $F(\omega)$ has derivatives of any order. For $F(\omega)$ to have an nth derivative it is sufficient that $t^n f(t)$ be absolutely integrable on the whole real line. This means, of course, that $f(t)$ must tend to zero fairly fast. If $f(t)$ is everywhere differentiable and both it and all its derivatives satisfy the above condition, it is called a "good function" by Lighthill (1962).

closer. Eventually, as $L \to \infty$, we shall no longer discriminate among discrete frequencies but shall regard ω as varying continuously. Let $G(\omega) = F(\omega)e^{i\omega t}$ and $\epsilon = 2\pi/2L$. Then (1) may be rewritten as

$$f(t) = \frac{1}{2L} \sum_{k=-\infty}^{\infty} F(\lambda_k)e^{i\lambda_k t} = \frac{\epsilon}{2\pi} \sum_{k=-\infty}^{\infty} G(k\epsilon) \to \frac{1}{2\pi} \int_{-\infty}^{\infty} G(\omega)\,d\omega \qquad (5)$$

as $L \to \infty$ and therefore $\epsilon \to 0$, by the definition of the integral. Thus in the limit we have the reciprocal relations between the function $f(t)$ and its Fourier transform $F(\omega)$:

$$f(t) = \frac{1}{2\pi} \int_{-\infty}^{\infty} F(\omega)e^{i\omega t}\,d\omega, \qquad F(\omega) = \int_{-l}^{l} f(t)e^{-i\omega t}\,dt. \qquad (6)$$

Provided that $f(t)$ is of bounded variation and absolutely integrable in any interval, no matter how large, we can allow l to increase without bound. Equations (6) still hold; however, while $F(\omega)$ remains continuous it may not have derivatives of every order. The final result of all of this is often summed up in a single formula called the *Fourier integral theorem*:

$$f(t) = \frac{1}{2\pi} \int_{-\infty}^{\infty} e^{i\omega t} \int_{-\infty}^{\infty} f(\tau)e^{-i\omega\tau}\,d\tau\,d\omega. \qquad (7)$$

If $f(t)$ is not continuous at a particular point t_0, at $t = t_0$ we must replace the left-hand side of (7) as well as of (1) by $(f(t_0 + 0) + f(t_0 - 0))/2$ (Tolstov, 1962, pp. 188–190).

If $F(\omega)$ and $G(\omega)$ are the Fourier transforms of $f(t)$ and $g(t)$, respectively, then

$$\int_{-\infty}^{\infty} f(t)\overline{g(t)}\,dt = \int_{-\infty}^{\infty} \overline{g(t)} \int_{-\infty}^{\infty} e^{i\omega t} \frac{1}{2\pi} F(\omega)\,d\omega\,dt$$

$$= \frac{1}{2\pi} \int_{-\infty}^{\infty} F(\omega)\overline{G(\omega)}\,d\omega \qquad (8)$$

from (6). Equation (8) is sometimes known as *Parseval's identity* and has, as a special case, the implication that

$$\int_{-\infty}^{\infty} |f(t)|^2\,dt = \frac{1}{2\pi} \int_{-\infty}^{\infty} |F(\omega)|^2\,d\omega.$$

A great deal of the importance of Fourier techniques stems from their use in the analysis of electrical networks. But as the operation of such networks represents merely a transformation of one function of time, e.g., voltage, into another function, of *input* to *output*, the principles involved are considerably more general and, as we shall see, provide an exceptionally useful tool in the analysis of "windows" in Fourier approximation theory.

Let $f(t)$ be an input function and $h(t)$ be an output function resulting from some transformation of $f(t)$. This transformation may result from an actual physical transformation of the quantity represented by $f(t)$ for each value of the argument t (at each point in time, for example, if t represents time), or it may merely represent a series of arithmetic manipulations. In either case the transformation is called a *filter*. The operation of a filter is illustrated by the following diagram:

$$\text{Input } f(t) \longrightarrow \boxed{\text{Filter}} \longrightarrow \text{Output } h(t).$$

If the filter is of a certain special type the relation between the input and output functions may be characterized by

$$h(t) = \int_{-\infty}^{\infty} K(\tau) f(t - \tau) \, d\tau. \qquad (9)$$

Such a filter is called a *linear time-invariant filter* since if $f_1(t)$ and $f_2(t)$ are two input functions and α and β are constants, then the output resulting from an input $\alpha f_1(t) + \beta f_2(t)$ will be just $\alpha h_1(t) + \beta h_2(t)$, where $h_1(t)$ and $h_2(t)$ are the outputs resulting from inputs of $f_1(t)$ and $f_2(t)$, respectively. For such filters, the output function $h(t)$ is simply the *convolution* of two functions, the input $f(t)$ and a function $K(\tau)$ called the *kernel* of the filter. The Fourier transform of the output function, say $H(\omega)$, is simply the product at each frequency ω of the Fourier transform of the input function $F(\omega)$ and the Fourier transform of the filter kernel, say $l(\omega)$.[20] Thus for linear time-invariant filters,

$$H(\omega) = l(\omega) F(\omega), \qquad -\infty < \omega < \infty. \qquad (10)$$

The function $l(\omega)$ is called the *frequency response function* of the filter. [It is sometimes also called the transfer function, but here we shall reserve this term for the squared modulus of $l(\omega)$.]

The properties of the frequency response function may be best understood by considering a particular form of input:

$$f(t) = e^{i\lambda t} = \cos \lambda t + i \sin \lambda t.$$

Thus

$$h(t) = \int_{-\infty}^{\infty} K(\tau) e^{i\lambda(t - \tau)} \, d\tau$$
$$= l(\lambda) e^{i\lambda t} = G(\lambda) e^{i[\lambda t + \varphi(\lambda)]},$$

---

[20] Let $f(t)$ and $g(t)$ be absolutely integrable on the whole real line, and let $h(t)$ be the *convolution* of $f(t)$ and $g(t)$, i.e., $h(t) = \int_{-\infty}^{\infty} f(t - \tau) g(\tau) \, d\tau$. Then one can easily show

(a) $\int_{-\infty}^{\infty} |h(t)| \, dt \le \left(\int_{-\infty}^{\infty} |f(t)| \, dt \right) \left(\int_{-\infty}^{\infty} |g(t)| \, dt \right)$.

(b) $H(\omega) = F(\omega) \cdot G(\omega)$,

where $H(\omega)$, $F(\omega)$, and $G(\omega)$ are the Fourier transforms of $h(t)$, $f(t)$, and $g(t)$, respectively. Also,

(c) $\int_{-\infty}^{\infty} f(t - \tau) g(\tau) \, d\tau = \int_{-\infty}^{\infty} f(\tau) g(t - \tau) \, d\tau$.

where the generally complex-valued frequency response function $l(\lambda)$ has been written in polar form

$$l(\lambda) = u(\lambda) + iv(\lambda)$$
$$= G(\lambda)[\cos \varphi(\lambda) + i \sin \varphi(\lambda)]$$
$$= G(\lambda)e^{i\varphi(\lambda)}. \tag{11}$$

$G(\lambda) = [u^2(\lambda) + v^2(\lambda)]^{1/2}$ is called the *gain* of the filter and $\varphi(\lambda) = \arctan[v(\lambda)/u(\lambda)]$ is called the *phase angle* of the filter. The expression for $l(\lambda)$ shows that if the input function is a sinusoidal variation of unit amplitude and (in this case) a phase angle of $\pi/4$, the output function will also be sinusoidal but of amplitude $G(\lambda)$ and phase angle $\pi/4 + \varphi(\lambda)$.

From Parseval's identity, equation (8), we deduced that the *spectrum* of $f(t)$, namely the squared modulus of the Fourier transform $|F(\omega)|^2$, was essentially a decomposition of the "sum of squares" of $f(t)$. We may also deduce that the spectrum of the output series of the filter (9) is

$$|G(\omega)|^2 = |l(\omega)|^2 |F(\omega)|^2. \tag{12}$$

The factor of proportionality $|l(\omega)|^2$ at each frequency ω is sometimes called the *transfer function* of the filter.

In Section 4 we showed that under rather general circumstances functions may be well approximated over finite intervals by trigonometric polynomials of finite degree. The importance of the present discussion in this connection is that, since certain kinds of transformations, linear time-invariant filters, can be described by their effects on trigonometric functions, i.e., the frequency response functions of the corresponding filters, the effects of such transformations on arbitrary functions may be approximately described in terms of their effects on the approximating trigonometric polynomial. Of course, in such applications of Fourier analysis, the filters considered will be discrete in the sense that they operate only on the observed points of the input function; hence, the frequency response functions will typically be for filters characterized by a summation of the form

$$h(t) = \sum_{\tau=-\infty}^{\infty} K(\tau) f(t - \tau)$$

rather than the integral expression in (9). Correspondingly, the frequency response functions considered will normally also be discrete of the form

$$l(\omega) = \sum_{\tau=-\infty}^{\infty} K(\tau) e^{-i\omega\tau}.$$

The most frequent use of filtering operations of the type discussed here is in the transformations of functions of time; and, in general, it is not physically possible to transform future observations but only current and past. Thus "physically realizable filters" will be "one-sided," i.e., of the form

$$h(t) = \int_{-\infty}^{0} K(\tau)f(t + \tau)\,dt \quad \text{or} \quad h(t) = \sum_{\tau=-\infty}^{0} K(\tau)f(t + \tau).$$

Indeed, it will not usually be possible, in general, to include the infinite past either. It may be shown that the frequency response functions of one-sided filters will invariably be complex. Such filters must also affect the phase. (Consider the input function to be approximated by a trigonometric series.) Moreover, the frequency response function will generally have infinite domain even if the kernel of the filter is of bounded domain.

In Section 4 we saw that to approximate a function by a finite trigonometric polynomial based on a sample of points was equivalent to regarding the function at a particular point as a weighted average of the values at all the sample points. We called the system of weights a "window." Neglecting the problem of aliasing, we showed that the value of the approximating polynomial was just the convolution of the actual (continuous) function over the interval of definition with the window function. As we have found here, however, when Fourier transforms are taken convolution corresponds to multiplication. Since, by the Fourier integral theorem, there is a one-to-one correspondence for the class of square integrable functions between the Fourier transform and the function, it would appear that examination of the transforms of various functions and various windows might be simpler than the analysis of their convolutions. In other words, in the study of types of trigonometric polynomial approximations it is useful to examine the relation between the Fourier transform of the approximating polynomial and the Fourier transform of the function itself rather than to compare the two directly.

The important work of Parzen (1961) on harmonic approximation derives largely from the simple notions expressed above, i.e., his analysis amounts to describing the effects of the particular approximation in terms of its effects on the Fourier coefficients of the function being approximated rather than the window through which the approximation "views" the function.

The polynomial approximation to a function $f(t)$ defined on the interval $[-\pi, \pi]$ based on a sample of $2N + 1$ points is given by (4.9). Neglecting the problem of aliasing simply means we compute the Fourier coefficients on the basis of (4.3). Thus $f(t)$ is approximated by

$$f_N(t) = \sum_{j=-N}^{N} k_N(j)C_j e^{i\lambda_j t}, \tag{13}$$

where for the moment we take $k_N(j) = 1$ for all j, and where $\lambda_j = j$ and

$$C_j = \frac{1}{2\pi} \int_{-\pi}^{\pi} e^{-i\lambda_j t} f(t)\,dt.$$

As deduced earlier, such an approximation amounts to viewing $f(t)$ through the Dirichlet window

$$D_N\left(\frac{2\pi}{2T}[x-t]\right) = \frac{1}{2\pi}\left\{1 + 2\sum_{k=1}^{N}\cos\lambda_k[x-t]\right\}$$

$$= \frac{1}{2\pi}\frac{\sin\{\frac{1}{2}(\lambda_{2N+1}[x-t])\}}{\sin\{\frac{1}{2}(\lambda_1[x-t])\}},$$

where we now write

$$f_N(t) = \int_{-\pi}^{\pi} D_N(\lambda_1[x-t])f(x)\,dx. \tag{14}$$

The window is an even function of $z = (2\pi/2T)(x-t)$, with

$$\int_{-\pi}^{\pi} D_N(z)\,dz = 1$$

and zeros at $k(2\pi/(2N+1))$, $k = \pm 1, \pm 2, \dots$, and period 2π. The maximum of $2N + 1$ occurs at $z = 0$. If we take the Fourier transform of the Dirichlet window, we find

$$\int_{-\pi}^{\pi} D_N(z)e^{-i\lambda z}\,dz = \frac{1}{2\pi}\int_{-\pi}^{\pi}\sum_{j=-N}^{N}e^{ijz}e^{-i\lambda z}\,dz$$

$$= \begin{cases} 2\pi/2\pi = 1, & \lambda = 0, \pm 1, \dots, \pm N, \\ 0, & \lambda = \pm(N+1), \pm(N+2), \dots. \end{cases}$$

Thus $k_N(j)$ of (13) is just the Fourier transform of $D_N(z)$, the Dirichlet window. Hence, straightforward approximation by truncated Fourier series amounts to weighting the Fourier coefficients equally over a finite range.

The general properties of a window were listed in conjunction with our discussion of the Dirichlet window (p. 397). Consider a window $K_N(z)$ and let $k_N(\lambda)$ be the corresponding coefficient window. Property (a), that $K_N(z)$ is even, clearly requires

(a') $k_N(\lambda)$ is an even function of λ.

Property (b), that $K_N(z)$ reaches a maximum of 1 at $z = 0$, translates into

(b') $1 = \dfrac{1}{2\pi}\displaystyle\int_{-\infty}^{\infty} k_N(\lambda)e^{i\lambda\times 0}\,d\lambda = \dfrac{1}{2\pi}\displaystyle\int_{-\infty}^{\infty} k_N(\lambda)\,d\lambda.$

Similarly, property (c), that the integral of the window over the period of the function is one, requires that

(c') $k_N(0) = 1 = \displaystyle\int_{-\pi}^{\pi} K_N(z)e^{-i\cdot 0\cdot z}\,dz.$

We now call a function $k(\lambda)$ a *coefficient window generator* if it has properties (a′)–(c′). Its Fourier transform

$$K(z) = \frac{1}{2\pi} \int_{-\pi}^{\pi} k(\lambda)e^{i\lambda z}\, d\lambda, \qquad -\infty < z < \infty,$$

will be called (following Parzen) an *amplitude window generator*. $K(z)$ may not be absolutely integrable over $[-\infty, \infty]$; in this case we require it to be a "good function" in the sense of Lighthill (1962, p. 15). We should also require $k(\lambda) = 0$ for $|\lambda| > \pi$ in order that $K(z)$ be the most general expression for the Fourier transform of $k(\lambda)$.

The importance of the notion of coefficient window, as opposed to amplitude window, is this: When we represent a function by a weighted trigonometric polynomial such as (13), it is necessary to determine the weights $k_N(j)$; but these are not intuitively obvious. Indeed, the nature of the behavior of the truncated Fourier series in the neighborhood of rapid changes in the function $f(t)$ may be best understood in terms of the amplitude window: If this is broad but with small side lobes, overshoot or other erratic behavior is not likely to occur; on the other hand convergence will tend to be slow. Conversely, if the amplitude window is concentrated near the origin but with large and possibly negative slide lobes, erratic behavior near the point of very rapid change is very likely to occur, but the rate of convergence away from such points may be quite rapid. Parzen's work makes clear how one may relate the intuitive situation to the one of practical importance. In order to complete the link, however, we must establish a correspondence between $k_N(j)$ and the more abstract $k(\lambda)$. This is done by observing that the interval $[-\pi, \pi]$, over which we are supposing $f(t)$ to be defined, is divided into the $2N + 1$ points, at which $f_N(t)$ fits exactly, by the points

$$t_j = j(\pi/N), \qquad j = 0, \pm 1, \ldots, \pm N.$$

If we take λ over the same interval $[-\pi, \pi]$ at the same points, our correspondence will be

$$k(j\pi/N) = k_N(j), \qquad j = 0, \pm 1, \pm 2, \ldots, \pm N,$$
$$= 0, \qquad |j| \geq N + 1.$$

In order to circumvent some of the undesirable features of the Dirichlet amplitude window for functions containing discontinuities (or points of exceptionally rapid change), Fejèr and Tukey constructed the windows discussed in the previous section. As these are simply superpositions of several Dirichlet windows they present no insurmountable difficulties of interpretation in terms of coefficient windows.

In his work on statistical spectral analysis, Parzen (1961) suggested the coefficient window

$$k(\lambda) \begin{cases} = 1 - 6|\lambda|^2 + 6|\lambda|^3, & |\lambda| \le \pi/2, \\ = 2(1 - |\lambda|)^3, & \pi/2 < |\lambda| \le \pi, \\ = 0, & \pi < |\lambda|. \end{cases}$$

This has the Fourier transform

$$K(z) = \frac{1}{2\pi} \int_{-\pi}^{\pi} k(\lambda) e^{-i\lambda z} \, dz, \qquad -\infty < z < \infty,$$

$$= \frac{3}{8\pi} \left[\frac{\sin(z/4)}{z/4} \right]^4,$$

which has exceptionally desirable characteristics from the standpoint of adequate treatment in the neighborhood of points of rapid change.

Appendix D
WHITTLE'S THEOREM[1]

Theorem. Let $Q(\ )$ be a function of z analytic in the annulus $\rho < |z| < \rho^{-1}$, $|\rho| < 1$, and let θ be a number such that $|\theta| < 1$. Then

$$R(z) = (1 - \theta z)^p [Q(z)/(1 - \theta z)^p]_+ = [Q(z)]_+ + \pi_p(z), \tag{1}$$

where

$$\pi_p(z) = \sum_{j=0}^{p-1} d^j \left. \frac{[Q(z)]_-}{dz^j} \right|_{z = \theta^{-1}} \frac{(z - \theta^{-1})^j}{j!}. \tag{2}$$

Proof:

$$R(z) = (1 - \theta z)^p \left[\frac{[Q(z)]_+ + [Q(z)]_-}{(1 - \theta z)^p} \right]_+$$

$$= (1 - \theta z)^p \left\{ \left[\frac{[Q(z)]_+}{(1 - \theta z)^p} \right]_+ + \left[\frac{[Q(z)]_-}{(1 - \theta z)^p} \right]_+ \right\} \tag{3}$$

$$= [Q(z)]_+ + (1 - \theta z)^p [[Q(z)]_-/(1 - \theta z)^p]_+$$

since $[Q(z)]_+/(1 - \theta z)^p$ already contains only nonnegative powers of z. To prove the theorem it must be shown that

$$(1 - \theta z)^p [[Q(z)]_-/(1 - \theta z)^p]_+ = \pi_p(z). \tag{4}$$

[1] Whittle (1963, p. 93).

The proof is by induction on p. For $p = 1$

$$(1 - \theta z)\left[\frac{[Q(z)]_-}{(1 - \theta z)}\right]_+ = (1 - \theta z)\left[\frac{q_{-1}z^{-1}}{1 - \theta z} + \frac{q_{-2}z^{-2}}{1 - \theta z} + \cdots + \frac{q_{-n}z^{-n}}{1 - \theta z} + \cdots\right]_+$$

$$= (1 - \theta z)\left[\sum_{j \geq 1} \frac{q_{-j}z^{-j}}{1 - \theta z}\right]_+ = (1 - \theta z)\sum_{j \geq 1}\left[\frac{q_{-j}z^{-j}}{1 - \theta z}\right]_+$$

$$= (1 - \theta z)\sum_{j \geq 1}\frac{q_{-j}\theta^j}{1 - \theta z} = [Q(z)]_-|_{z = \theta^{-1}} = \pi_1(z) \qquad (5)$$

since

$$\left[\frac{q_{-j}z^{-j}}{1 - \theta z}\right]_+ = \left[q_{-j}z^{-j}\sum_{k=0}^{j-1}\theta^k z^k + q_{-j}z^{-j}\sum_{k \geq j}^{\infty}\theta^k z^k\right]_+$$

$$= q_{-j}\theta^j\sum_{k=0}^{\infty}\theta^k z^k = \frac{q_{-j}\theta^j}{1 - \theta z}. \qquad (6)$$

Since

$$\pi_{n+1}(z) = \pi_n(z) + \frac{d^n[Q(z)]_-}{dz^n}\bigg|_{z=\theta^{-1}}\frac{(z - \theta^{-1})^n}{n!}, \qquad (7)$$

to complete the proof, it suffices to show that

$$A(z, \theta) = (1 - \theta z)^{n+1}\left[\frac{[Q(z)]_-}{(1 - \theta z)^{n+1}}\right]_+ - (1 - \theta z)^n\left[\frac{[Q(z)]_-}{(1 - \theta z)^n}\right]_+$$

$$= \frac{d^n[Q(z)]_-}{dz^n}\bigg|_{z=\theta^{-1}}\frac{(z - \theta^{-1})^n}{n!}. \qquad (8)$$

Using the identity

$$\frac{1}{(1 - \theta z)^n} = \sum_{j=0}^{\infty}\binom{j + n - 1}{n - 1}(\theta z)^j, \qquad (9)$$

$A(z, \theta)$ may be written

$$A(z, \theta) = (1 - \theta z)^n\left\{(1 - \theta z)\left[\frac{[Q(z)]_-}{(1 - \theta z)^{n+1}}\right]_+ - \left[\frac{[Q(z)]_-}{(1 - \theta z)^n}\right]_+\right\}$$

$$= (1 - \theta z)^n\left\{(1 - \theta z)\left[\sum_{k \geq 1}q_{-k}z^{-k}\sum_{j=0}^{\infty}\binom{j + n}{n}\theta^j z^j\right]_+\right.$$

$$\left. - \left[\sum_{k \geq 1}q_{-k}z^{-k}\sum_{j=0}^{\infty}\binom{j + n - 1}{n - 1}\theta^j z^j\right]_+\right\}. \qquad (10)$$

Applying the $[\ ]_+$ operator term by term gives

$$A(z, \theta) = (1 - \theta z)^n \left\{ (1 - \theta z) \sum_{k \geq 1} q_{-k}\theta^k \sum_{j=k}^{\infty} \binom{j+n}{n} (\theta z)^{j-k} \right.$$

$$\left. - \sum_{k \geq 1} q_{-k}\theta^k \sum_{j=k}^{\infty} \binom{j+n-1}{n-1} (\theta z)^{j-k} \right\}$$

$$= (1 - \theta z)^n \left\{ \sum_{k \geq 1} q_{-k}\theta^k \sum_{j=k}^{\infty} \left[\binom{j+n}{n} - \binom{j+n-1}{n-1} \right] (\theta z)^{j-k} \right.$$

$$\left. - \sum_{k \geq 1} q_{-k}\theta^k \sum_{j=k}^{\infty} \binom{j+n}{n} (\theta z)^{j-k+1} \right\}$$

$$= (1 - \theta z)^n \left\{ \sum_{k \geq 1} q_{-k}\theta^k \sum_{j=k}^{\infty} \binom{j+n-1}{n} (\theta z)^{j-k} \right.$$

$$\left. - \sum_{k \geq 1} q_{-k}\theta^k \sum_{j=k}^{\infty} \binom{j+n}{n} (\theta z)^{j+1-k} \right\}. \tag{11}$$

This follows from the combinatorial identity

$$\binom{j+n}{n} - \binom{j+n-1}{n-1} = \frac{(j+n)!}{n!j!} - \frac{(j+n-1)!}{(n-1)!j!}$$

$$= \frac{(j+n-1)!}{(n-1)!j!} \left[\frac{j+n}{n} - 1 \right]$$

$$= \frac{(j+n-1)!}{n!(j-1)!} = \binom{j+n-1}{n}.$$

In the next to last term in (11) let $m = j - k$, and in the last term let $m = j - k + 1$. Then

$$A(z, \theta) = (1 - \theta z)^n \left\{ \sum_{k \geq 1} q_{-k}\theta^k \sum_{m=0}^{\infty} \binom{m+k+n-1}{n} (\theta z)^m \right.$$

$$\left. - \sum_{k \geq 1} q_{-k}\theta^k \sum_{m=1}^{\infty} \binom{m+k+n-1}{n} (\theta z)^m \right\}$$

$$= (1 - \theta z)^n \sum_{k \geq 1} q_{-k}\theta^k \binom{n+k-1}{n}$$

$$= \theta^n(\theta^{-1} - z)^n \sum_{k \geq 1} q_{-k}\theta^k \binom{k+n-1}{n}$$

$$= (-1)^n(z - \theta^{-1})^n \sum_{k \geq 1} q_{-k}\theta^{k+n} \binom{k+n-1}{n}$$

$$= \frac{(z - \theta^{-1})^n}{n!} \left. \frac{d^n[Q(z)]_-}{dz^n} \right|_{z = \theta^{-1}}. \tag{12}$$

This completes the proof.

Appendix E

INVERSION OF TRIDIAGONAL MATRICES
AND A METHOD FOR INVERTING
TOEPLITZ MATRICES

A Toeplitz matrix is one for which each element depends only on the difference of two indices (see Grenander and Szegö, 1958). The general element of a Toeplitz matrix is c_{t-j}, which may be complex; in this case it is usual to assume $c_{-n} = \bar{c}_n$. The general finite Toeplitz matrix is

$$C = \begin{bmatrix} c_0 & c_1 & c_2 & \cdots & c_{T-1} & c_T \\ c_{-1} & c_0 & c_1 & \cdots & c_{T-2} & c_{T-1} \\ \vdots & \vdots & \vdots & & \vdots & \vdots \\ c_{-T+1} & c_{-T+2} & c_{-T+3} & \cdots & c_0 & c_1 \\ c_{-T} & c_{-T+1} & c_{-T+2} & \cdots & c_{-1} & c_0 \end{bmatrix}. \tag{1}$$

In econometric problems, we frequently encounter special cases of C in (1) in which many of the higher-order elements are zero; such matrices are called *band* matrices because, besides the diagonal consisting of equal elements, there are one or more bands of equal elements on either side of the diagonal. A special important case is the symmetric two-band matrix, which has the form

$$\begin{bmatrix} a & b & 0 & \cdots & 0 \\ b & a & b & \cdots & 0 \\ 0 & b & a & \cdots & 0 \\ \vdots & \vdots & \vdots & & \vdots \\ 0 & 0 & 0 & \cdots & a \end{bmatrix}.$$

Such matrices are called tridiagonal (Press, 1972, p. 16). In this appendix we show first how to obtain an exact inverse for a tridiagonal matrix, then show how to generalize the method for the asymmetric two-band matrix, and finally suggest a general procedure for the general Toeplitz matrix.

Let us reparameterize the problem so that

$$a = 1 + \theta^2, \qquad b = -\theta,$$

which we may do without loss of generality since we need only to determine the inverse up to a scalar factor. Now let

$$W = \begin{bmatrix} w_{11} & w_{12} & \cdots & w_{1T} \\ w_{21} & w_{22} & \cdots & w_{2T} \\ \vdots & \vdots & & \vdots \\ w_{T1} & w_{T2} & \cdots & w_{TT} \end{bmatrix}$$

be the inverse of

$$\Theta = \begin{bmatrix} 1 + \theta^2 & -\theta & \cdots & 0 \\ -\theta & 1 + \theta^2 & \cdots & 0 \\ \vdots & \vdots & & \vdots \\ 0 & 0 & \cdots & 1 + \theta^2 \end{bmatrix}.$$

Since Θ is symmetric, W must be as well; thus we need only to obtain w_{tj}, $t \geq j$, for $t = 1, \ldots, T$ in order to find W. From

$$\Theta W = I, \tag{2}$$

we deduce

$$(1 + \theta^2)w_{11} - \theta w_{21} = 1$$
$$-\theta w_{T-1,1} + (1 + \theta^2)w_{T1} = 0 \tag{3}$$
$$-\theta w_{t-1,1} + (1 + \theta^2)w_{t1} - \theta w_{t+1,1} = 0 \qquad \text{for} \quad t = 2, \ldots, T - 1.$$

The last equations of (3) are a system of homogeneous second-order difference equations with characteristic polynomial

$$-\theta + (1 + \theta^2)z - \theta z^2 = 0 \tag{4}$$

having roots $z_1 = \theta$ and $z_2 = 1/\theta$. The general solution to the difference equation in (3) is thus

$$w_{tj} = c_1(j)\theta^t + c_2(j)\theta^{-t} \qquad \text{for} \quad t \geq j, \tag{5}$$

where $c_1(j)$ and $c_2(j)$ are constants to be determined so that certain initial conditions are satisfied. To see how this works, consider the case $j = 1$; then

$$w_{t1} = c_1(1)\theta^t + c_2(1)\theta^{-t} \qquad \text{for} \quad t = 1, 2, \ldots, T. \tag{6}$$

Substituting (6) in the first two equations of (3), we find

$$(1 + \theta^2)[\theta c_1(1) + \theta^{-1}c_2(1)] - \theta[\theta^2 c_1(1) + \theta^{-2}c_2(1)] = 1$$
$$-\theta[\theta^{T-1}c_1(1) + \theta^{-T+1}c_2(1)] + (1 + \theta^2)[\theta^T c_1(1) + \theta^{-T}c_2(1)] = 0.$$

Collecting terms and solving for $c_1(1)$ and $c_2(1)$:

$$c_1(1) = \frac{1}{\theta}\left[\frac{1}{1 - (\theta^2)^{T+1}}\right], \qquad c_2(1) = \frac{1}{\theta}\left[1 - \frac{1}{1 - (\theta^2)^{T+1}}\right]. \tag{7}$$

Hence,

$$w_{t1} = \frac{1}{\theta}\left[\frac{1}{1 - (\theta^2)^{T+1}}\right]\theta^t + \frac{1}{\theta}\left[1 - \frac{1}{1 - (\theta^2)^{T+1}}\right]\theta^{-t}, \tag{8}$$

$t = 1, 2, \ldots, T$. This gives the first row and column of the inverse.

The second row and column may be obtained in the same manner: The equations corresponding to (3) are

$$(1 + \theta^2)w_{12} - \theta w_{22} = 0$$
$$-\theta w_{12} + (1 + \theta^2)w_{22} - \theta w_{32} = 1 \tag{9}$$
$$-\theta w_{T-1,2} + (1 + \theta^2)w_{T2} = 0$$
$$-\theta w_{t-1,2} + (1 + \theta^2)w_{t2} - \theta w_{t+1,2} = 0 \qquad \text{for} \quad t = 3, \ldots, T - 1.$$

The last series of equations may be considered as a second-order difference equation and has the same characteristic equation as before, (4). Thus

$$w_{t2} = c_1(2)\theta^t + c_2(2)\theta^{-t} \qquad \text{for} \quad t = 2, 3, \ldots, T. \tag{10}$$

The constants $c_1(2)$ and $c_2(2)$ may be determined, as before, by substituting (10) in (9), but note carefully that w_{12} *cannot* be written in the form (10) since $t = 1$. Thus in (9) we obtain w_{12} in terms of w_{22} from the first equation of (9) and replace its value in the second. The second and third equations of (9) are then used to determine the constants $c_1(2)$ and $c_2(2)$ exactly as before: From (9) $w_{12} = [\theta/(1 + \theta^2)]w_{22}$ so that the second and third equations become

$$\left[(1 + \theta^2) - \frac{\theta^2}{1 + \theta^2}\right]w_{22} - \theta w_{32} = 1 \qquad \text{and} \qquad -\theta w_{T-1,2} + (1 + \theta^2)w_{T2} = 0.$$

Hence

$$c_1(2) = \frac{1 + \theta^2}{\theta^2}\frac{1}{1 - (\theta^2)^{T+1}}, \qquad c_2(2) = \frac{1 + \theta^2}{\theta^2}\left[1 - \frac{1}{1 - (\theta^2)^{T+1}}\right].$$

Consequently,

$$w_{t2} = \frac{1 + \theta^2}{\theta^2}\frac{1}{1 - (\theta^2)^{T+1}}\theta^t + \frac{1 + \theta^2}{\theta^2}\left[1 - \frac{1}{1 - (\theta^2)^{T+1}}\right]\theta^{-t} \tag{11}$$

for $t = 2, 3, \ldots, T$, which yields the second row and column of W.

In exactly the same way, we find

$$w_{t3} = \frac{1 + \theta^2 + \theta^4}{\theta^3} \frac{1}{1 - (\theta^2)^{T+1}} \theta^t + \frac{1 + \theta^2 + \theta^4}{\theta^3} \left[1 - \frac{1}{1 - (\theta^2)^{T+1}} \right] \theta^{-t}$$

(12)

for $t = 3, 4, \ldots, T$, which yields the third row and column of W. In general we obtain

$$w_{tj} = \frac{\sum_{k=1}^{j} (\theta^2)^{k-1}}{\theta^j} \left\{ \frac{\theta^t}{1 - (\theta^2)^{T+1}} + \left[1 - \frac{1}{1 - (\theta^2)^{T+1}} \right] \theta^{-t} \right\}$$

(13)

for $t \geq j = 1, \ldots, T$. In fact, (13) is valid for all t and j since W is symmetric. Thus we have obtained an exact inverse for the tridiagonal matrix. [Theil (1964, pp. 211–223) gives only an asymptotic result for an infinite band matrix, although he allows an extra band. Our method, as indicated below, may be generalized to obtain an exact result in this case as well. Taking the limit of w_{tj} as $T \to \infty$ in (13) yields Theil's result for the tridiagonal case as a special case of ours.[1]]

Now consider the asymmetric band matrix

$$\begin{bmatrix} a & b & 0 & \cdots & 0 \\ c & a & b & \cdots & 0 \\ 0 & c & a & \cdots & 0 \\ \vdots & \vdots & \vdots & & \vdots \\ 0 & 0 & 0 & \cdots & a \end{bmatrix},$$

which we may reparameterize, without loss of generality, as

$$a = 1 + \theta\eta, \qquad b = -\eta, \qquad c = -\theta,$$

since we need only determine the inverse up to a scalar multiplier. Denote the inverse of this matrix by

$$V = \begin{bmatrix} v_{11} & v_{12} & \cdots & v_{1T} \\ v_{21} & v_{22} & \cdots & v_{2T} \\ \vdots & \vdots & & \vdots \\ v_{T1} & v_{T2} & \cdots & v_{TT} \end{bmatrix}.$$

From the first column of V we obtain

$$(1 + \theta\eta)v_{11} - \eta v_{21} = 1$$
$$-\theta v_{T-1,1} + (1 + \theta\eta)v_{T1} = 0$$
$$-\theta v_{t-1,1} + (1 + \theta\eta)v_{t1} - \eta v_{t+1,1} = 0 \qquad \text{for} \quad t = 2, \ldots, T - 1.$$

(14)

[1] Balestra (1972) gives a recursive formula for the inverse of a tridiagonal matrix similar to ours. In a subsequent unpublished paper (1978), he derives the same result in a different and more elegant way.

The last is a homogeneous difference equation with characteristic polynomial

$$-\theta + (1 + \theta\eta)z - \eta z^2$$

having roots $z_1 = 0$ and $z_2 = \eta^{-1}$. Proceeding exactly as before, we find

$$v_{t1} = \frac{1}{\theta}\left[\frac{1}{1 - (\theta\eta)^{T+1}}\right]\theta^t + \frac{1}{\theta}\left[1 - \frac{1}{1 - (\theta\eta)^{T+1}}\right]\eta^{-t} \tag{15}$$

for $t \geq 1$. In general,

$$v_{tj} = \frac{\sum_{k=1}^{j}(\theta\eta)^{k-1}}{\theta^j}\left\{\frac{\theta^t}{1 - (\theta\eta)^{T+1}} + \left[1 - \frac{1}{1 - (\theta\eta)^{T+1}}\right]\eta^{-t}\right\} \tag{16}$$

for $t \geq j$. Note, however, that V is not symmetric. To obtain the remaining elements of V, we simply reverse the role of θ and η to obtain

$$v_{jt} = \frac{\sum_{k=1}^{t}(\theta\eta)^{k-1}}{\eta^t}\left\{\frac{\eta^j}{1 - (\theta\eta)^{T+1}} + \left[1 - \frac{1}{1 - (\theta\eta)^{T+1}}\right]\theta^{-j}\right\} \tag{17}$$

for $j \geq t$. Thus the matrix V is fully determined.

The procedures described above for inverting symmetric two-band (tridiagonal) and asymmetric two-band matrices may easily be generalized. For example, suppose the matrix to be inverted is of the form

$$\begin{bmatrix} g & f & c & 0 & \cdots & 0 & 0 & 0 \\ h & g & f & c & \cdots & 0 & 0 & 0 \\ b & h & g & f & \cdots & 0 & 0 & 0 \\ \vdots & \vdots & \vdots & \vdots & & \vdots & \vdots & \vdots \\ 0 & 0 & 0 & 0 & \cdots & g & f & c \\ 0 & 0 & 0 & 0 & \cdots & h & g & f \\ 0 & 0 & 0 & 0 & \cdots & b & h & g \end{bmatrix}$$

$$\begin{aligned} gw_{11} + fw_{21} + cw_{31} &= 1 \\ hw_{11} + gw_{21} + fw_{31} + cw_{41} &= 0 \\ bw_{11} + hw_{21} + gw_{31} + fw_{41} + cw_{51} &= 0 \\ bw_{T-4,1} + hw_{T-3,1} + gw_{T-2,1} + fw_{T-1,1} + cw_{T,1} &= 0 \qquad (18) \\ bw_{T-3,1} + hw_{T-2,1} + gw_{T-1,1} + fw_{T,1} &= 0 \\ bw_{T-2,1} + hw_{T-1,1} + gw_{T,1} &= 0 \\ bw_{t-4,1} + hw_{t-3,1} + gw_{t-2,1} + fw_{t-1,1} + cw_{t,1} &= 0 \end{aligned}$$

for $t = 5, \ldots, T$. The last of these is a fifth-order difference equation that has a characteristic polynomial with four roots, say $\zeta_1, \zeta_2, \zeta_3, \zeta_4$, expressible in terms of the elements $b, h, g, f,$ and c. The solution for w_{t1} is

$$w_{t1} = c_1(1)\zeta_1^t + c_2(1)\zeta_2^t + c_3(1)\zeta_3^t + c_4(1)\zeta_4^t.$$

The constants $c_1(1), \ldots, c_4(1)$ are determined by using the first, second, fifth, and sixth equations of (18). Thus the first column of W is determined. In the same fashion as before we may determine all the columns for $t \geq j = 1, \ldots, T$. Reversing the procedure and *pre*multipling by W, we determine its rows for $j \geq t = 1, \ldots, T$.

Clearly, the method outlined will work for any Toeplitz matrix, although the orders of the difference equations to be solved become very large as the number of bands in the Toeplitz matrix increase.

Appendix F

SPECTRAL DENSITIES, ACTUAL AND THEORETICAL, EIGHT SERIES

This appendix contains graphs of the estimated spectral densities for a transformation of all eight of the series discussed in Chapter X. The series are

price of steers,	cattle slaughter,
price of cows,	hog slaughter,
price of heifers,	industrial production,
price of milk,	male unemployment.

The transformation is $(1 - U)(1 - U^{12})z_t$, where z_t is the observed series.

The appendix also contains graphs of the spectral densities implied by the theoretical models presented in Section 5 of Chapter X and estimated in the frequency domain. The points plotted on either side of the estimated spectral densities are one standard deviation. The models for the price of steers and the price of milk should be compared with the estimated spectral densities presented in Section 4 of Chapter X in connection with the time domain estimates of the models. For convenience these graphs are reproduced here as Figs. 1a and 4a, respectively.

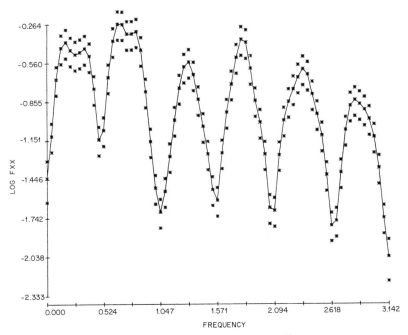

Fig. 1a. Price of steers $(1 - U)(1 - U^{12})z_t$.

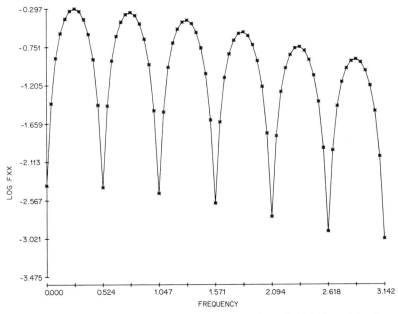

Fig. 1b. Theoretical spectral density, price of steers transformed. ARMA model estimated in the frequency domain.

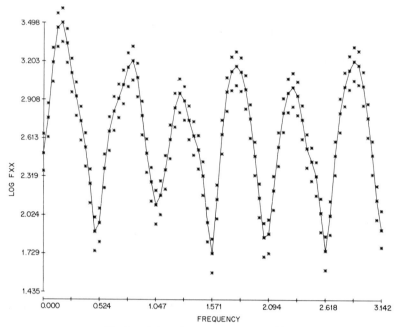

Fig. 2a.   Price of cows $(1 - U)(1 - U^{12})z_t$.

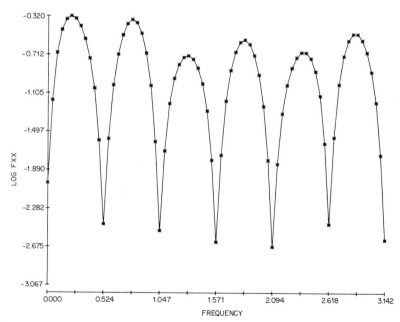

Fig. 2b.   Theoretical spectral density, price of cows transformed. ARMA model estimated in the frequency domain.

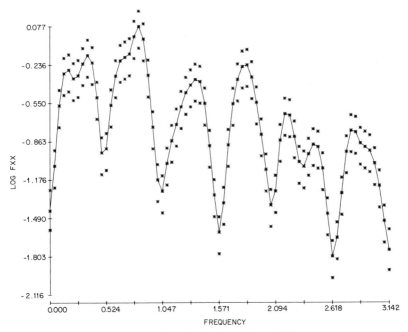

Fig. 3a. Price of heifers $(1 - U)(1 - U^{12})z_t$.

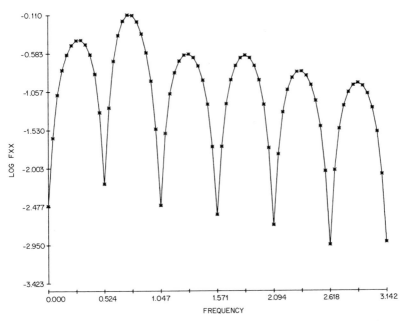

Fig. 3b. Theoretical spectral density, price of heifers transformed. ARMA model estimated in the frequency domain.

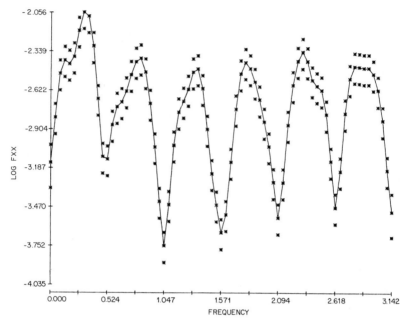

Fig. 4a. Price of milk $(1 - U)(1 - U^{12})z_t$.

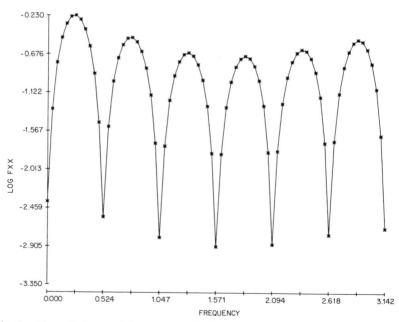

Fig. 4b. Theoretical spectral density, price of milk transformed. ARMA model estimated in the frequency domain.

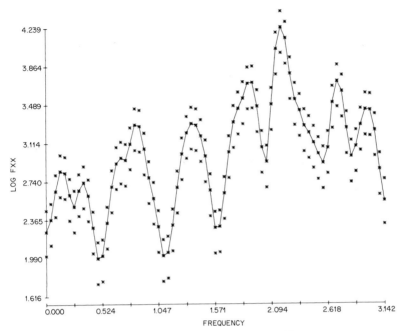

Fig. 5a.   Cattle slaughter $(1 - U)(1 - U^{12})z_t$.

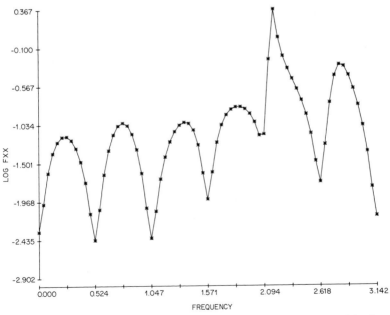

Fig. 5b.   Theoretical spectral density, cattle slaughter transformed. ARMA model estimated in the frequency domain.

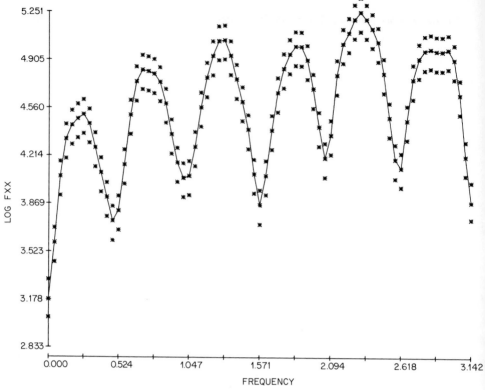

Fig. 6a. Hog slaughter $(1 - U)(1 - U^{12})z_t$.

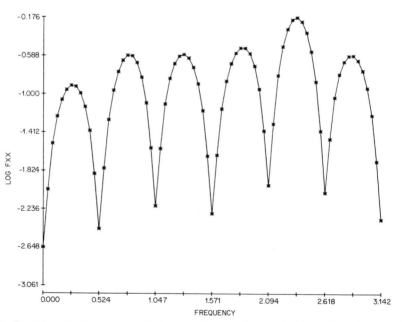

Fig. 6b. Theoretical spectral density, hog slaughter transformed. ARMA model estimated in the frequency domain.

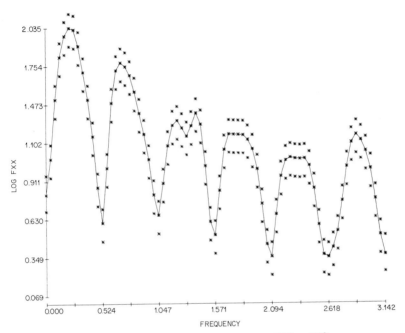

Fig. 7a. Index of industrial production $(1 - U)(1 - U^{12})z_t$.

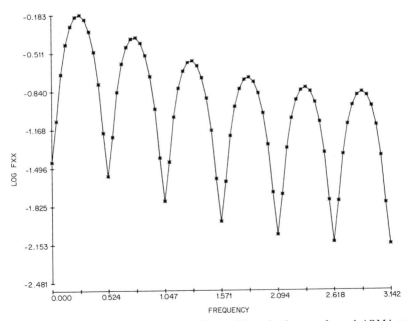

Fig. 7b. Theoretical spectral density, index of industrial production transformed. ARMA model estimated in the frequency domain.

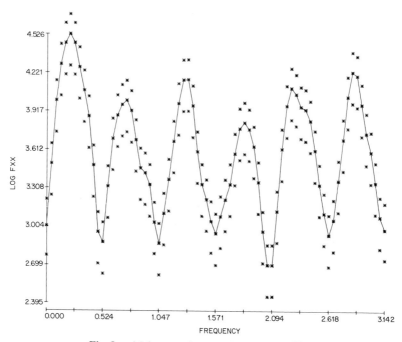

Fig. 8a. Male unemployment $(1 - U)(1 - U^{12})z_t$.

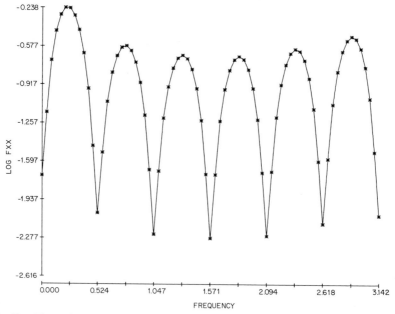

Fig. 8b. Theoretical spectral density, male unemployment $20+$ transformed. ARMA model estimated in the frequency domain.

Appendix G
DERIVATION OF A DISTRIBUTED-LAG RELATION BETWEEN SALES AND PRODUCTION: A SIMPLE EXAMPLE

Assume that a firm's costs in period t are given by

$$C_t = \lambda_1(\hat{P}_t - \hat{P}_{t-1})^2 + \lambda_2(\hat{I}_t - a - \alpha\hat{S}_t)^2 + \lambda_3\hat{P}_t + \lambda_4\hat{I}_t \qquad (1)$$

where $\hat{P}_t$ = production in period t, $\hat{S}_t$ = sales in period t, $\hat{I}_t$ = inventories at the end of the tth period, and $\hat{P}_t = \hat{S}_t + \hat{I}_t - \hat{I}_{t-1}$. At time $t - 1$, the firm is assumed to choose the level of production for period t in order to minimize

$$V = E\left\{\sum_{v=0}^{\infty} \rho^v C_{t+v}\right\}, \qquad 0 \leq \rho \leq 1. \qquad (2)$$

Let

$$\hat{S}_t = \bar{S} + S_t, \qquad E(S_t) = 0, \qquad \bar{S} = \text{const.},$$

$$\hat{I}_t = \bar{I} + I_t, \qquad E(I_t) = 0, \qquad \hat{P}_t = \bar{P} + P_t, \qquad E(P_t) = 0, \qquad \bar{P} = \bar{S}. \qquad (3)$$

Then (2) may be written as

$$V = E\left\{\sum_{v=0}^{\infty} \rho^v(\lambda_1(P_{t+v} - P_{t-1+v})^2 + \lambda_2(I_{t+v} - \alpha S_{t+v})^2)\right\}$$

$$+ \sum_{v=0}^{\infty} \rho^v(\lambda_3\bar{P} + \lambda_4\bar{I} + \lambda_2(\bar{I} - a - \alpha\bar{S})^2). \qquad (4)$$

Let $\lambda_1 = \lambda$ and $\lambda_2 = (1 - \lambda)$. The second term is easily minimized, so the problem reduces to

$$\min E\left\{\sum_{v=0}^{\infty} \rho^v(\lambda(P_{t+v} - P_{t+v-1})^2 + (1 - \lambda)(I_{t+v} - \alpha S_{t+v})^2)\right\},$$

where $P_t = S_t + I_t - I_{t-1}$ and all series have mean zero. Substituting,

$$I_t = (P_t - S_t)/(1 - U) \tag{5}$$

the problem becomes

$$\min_{\{P_{t+v}\}} E\left\{\sum_{v=0}^{\infty} \rho^v\left(\lambda(P_{t+v} - P_{t+v-1})^2 + (1 - \lambda)\left(\frac{P_{t+v} - S_{t+v}}{1 - U} - \alpha S_{t+v}\right)^2\right)\right\},$$

$$0 \le \lambda \le 1.$$

Differentiating the objective function with respect to P_{t+v} gives the following first-order conditions:

$$\frac{(\lambda(1 - U)^2(1 - \rho U^{-1})^2 + (1 - \lambda))P_{t+v} - (1 - \lambda)(1 + \alpha(1 - U))\hat{S}_{t+v,t-1}}{(1 - U)(1 - \rho U^{-1})} = 0,$$

$$v = 0, 1, 2, \ldots . \tag{6}$$

In (6) S_{t+v} has been replaced by its least-squares forecast $\hat{S}_{t+v,t-1}$. Now

$$\lambda(1 - z)^2(1 - \rho z^{-1})^2 + (1 - \lambda) = \eta z^{-2}(z - \beta)(z - \bar{\beta})\left(z - \frac{\rho}{\beta}\right)\left(z - \frac{\rho}{\bar{\beta}}\right)$$

$$= \eta|\beta|^2\left(1 - \frac{1}{\beta}z\right)\left(1 - \frac{1}{\bar{\beta}}z\right)$$

$$\times\left(1 - \frac{\rho}{\beta}z^{-1}\right)\left(1 - \frac{\rho}{\bar{\beta}}z^{-1}\right)$$

$$= R(z)Q(z^{-1}), \tag{7}$$

where η is a normalizing constant that is positive, and where

$$R(z) = \sqrt{\eta}|\beta|\left(1 - \frac{1}{\beta}z\right)\left(1 - \frac{1}{\bar{\beta}}z\right),$$

$$Q(z^{-1}) = \sqrt{\eta}|\beta|\left(1 - \frac{\rho}{\beta}z^{-1}\right)\left(1 - \frac{\rho}{\bar{\beta}}z^{-1}\right).$$

By inspection it is seen that if β is a root of (7), then ρ/β is also a root. Next it will be shown that there is always a root β with $|\beta| > 1$.

If z_0 is a root of (7), then ($\lambda \neq 0$).

$$(1 - z_0)(1 - \rho z_0^{-1}) = \pm i \sqrt{\frac{1 - \lambda}{\lambda}} \tag{8}$$

or

$$z_0 = \tfrac{1}{2}\left(1 + \rho \pm i \sqrt{\frac{1 - \lambda}{\lambda}} \pm \sqrt{\left(1 + \rho \pm i \sqrt{\frac{1 - \lambda}{\lambda}}\right)^2 - 4\rho}\right).$$

From (7) it is easily seen that for any λ in $(0, 1)$ there must be at least one root outside the unit circle if $\rho = 0$ or if $\rho = 1$. Further, it is clear that for any value of ρ in $(0, 1)$ there can be no roots on the unit circle. But for any fixed λ the roots are bounded continuous functions of ρ, so there must be at least one root outside the unit circle, i.e., $|\beta| > 1$.

The preceding argument implies that (6) may be written as

$$\frac{R(U)Q(U^{-1})P_{t+v} - (1 - \lambda)(1 + \alpha(1 - U))\hat{S}_{t+v,t-1}}{(1 - U)(1 - \rho U^{-1})} = 0, \tag{9}$$

$$v = 0, 1, 2, \ldots,$$

where the roots of $R(z)$ lie outside the unit circle, and the roots of $Q(z^{-1})$ lie inside the unit circle. Now

$$\frac{R(U)Q(U^{-1})P_{t+v} - (1 - \lambda)(1 + \alpha(1 - U))\hat{S}_{t+v,t-1}}{(1 - U)(1 - \rho U^{-1})}$$

$$= \frac{R(U)Q(U^{-1})P_{t+v} - (1 - \lambda)(1 + \alpha(1 - U))\hat{S}_{t+v,t-1}}{1 - U}$$

$$+ \rho \left[\frac{R(U)Q(U^{-1})P_{t+v+1} - (1 - \lambda)(1 + \alpha(1 - U))\hat{S}_{t+v+1,t-1}}{(1 - U)(1 - \rho U^{-1})}\right]. \tag{10}$$

But the second term is zero, so one may write

$$\frac{R(U)P_{t+v}}{1 - U} - \frac{(1 - \lambda)(1 + \alpha(1 - U))\tilde{S}_{t+v,t-1}}{1 - U} = 0, \tag{11}$$

where $\tilde{S}_{t+v,t-1} = \hat{S}_{t+v,t-1}/Q(U^{-1})$ is a weighted average of all sales expected in future periods. Now

$$\frac{(1 + \alpha(1 - U))\tilde{S}_{t+v,t-1}}{1 - U} = \text{const} + (1 + \alpha)\tilde{S}_{t+v,t-1}$$

$$+ \tilde{S}_{t+v-1,t-1} + \tilde{S}_{t+v-2,t-1} + \cdots \tag{12}$$

and

$$\frac{(1 + \alpha(1 + U))\tilde{S}_{t+v-1,t-2}}{1 - U} = \text{const} + (1 + \alpha)\tilde{S}_{t+v-1,t-2}$$

$$+ \tilde{S}_{t+v-2,t-2} + \tilde{S}_{t+v-3,t-2} + \cdots,$$

so that

$$R(U)P_{t+v} = (1 - \lambda)\left[(1 + \alpha)\tilde{S}_{t+v,t-1} - \alpha\tilde{S}_{t+v-1,t-2}\right.$$

$$\left. + \sum_{j=0}^{\infty} (\tilde{S}_{t+v-1-j,t-1} - \tilde{S}_{t+v-1-j,t-2})\right]. \tag{13}$$

The last steps in the derivation of (13) assumed that the firm has been behaving optimally in previous periods. If one were to estimate the parameters of such a model, one would typically have to use data on firms (or more likely industries) over a relatively short period of time. In general, there will be no reason to assume that the optimization began with the first observation the investigator has; rather it seems more natural to assume a long (but unobserved) history of optimal behavior and to expect that the initial conditions are sufficiently far in the past so that their influence on the observed behavior is negligible.

To gain some understanding of the preceding equation, consider the case in which changing the level of production is costless. If $\lambda = 0$, $R(U)Q(U^{-1}) = 1$, so $\tilde{S}_{t+v,t-1} = \hat{S}_{t+v,t-1}$ and the solution is

$$P_t = \alpha(\hat{S}_{t,t-1} - \hat{S}_{t-1,t-2}) + \hat{S}_{t,t-1} + (S_{t-1} - \hat{S}_{t-1,t-2}). \tag{14}$$

In this case, production is simply set equal to expected sales plus the expected change in the desired level of inventories plus a correction factor for the error in forecasting the sales of the current period.

If one assumes that $S_t = C(U)\epsilon_t$, that is, S_t is a nondeterministic covariance stationary time series,

$$R(U)P_t = \gamma(U)S_{t-1},$$

where

$$\gamma(z) = \lim_{\delta \to 1} \frac{1 - \delta z}{C(z)}\left[\frac{C(z)(1 - \lambda)(1 + \alpha(1 - \delta z))}{(1 - \delta z)Q(z^{-1})z}\right]_+. \tag{15}$$

Proof:

$$\frac{1 - \delta z}{C(z)}\left[\frac{C(z)(1 - \lambda)(1 + \alpha(1 - \delta z))}{(1 - \delta z)Q(z^{-1})z}\right]_+$$

$$= \frac{(1 - \lambda)\alpha(1 - \delta z)}{C(z)}\left[\frac{C(z)}{Q(z^{-1})z}\right]_+ + \frac{(1 - \lambda)(1 - \delta z)}{C(z)}\left[\frac{C(z)}{(1 - \delta z)Q(z^{-1})z}\right]_+. \tag{16}$$

Now $[1/C(z)][C(z)/Q(z^{-1})z]_+$ is the generating function of the operator that estimates $S_t/Q(U^{-1})$. Thus as δ goes to one, the first term will give $(1-\lambda)\alpha(\tilde{S}_{t,t-1} - \tilde{S}_{t-1,t-2})$. Applying Whittle's theorem to the second term gives

$$\frac{(1-\lambda)(1-\delta z)}{C(z)}\left[\frac{C(z)}{(1-\delta z)Q(z^{-1})z}\right]_+ = \frac{(1-\lambda)}{C(z)}\left[\frac{C(z)}{Q(z^{-1})z}\right]_+$$

$$+ (1-\lambda)\frac{([C(z)/Q(z^{-1})z]_-)|_{z=1/\delta}}{C(z)}. \quad (17)$$

The first term clearly gives $(1-\lambda)\tilde{S}_{t,t-1}$, so all that remains to be shown is that the second term leads to $\sum_j (\tilde{S}_{t-j-1,t-1} - \tilde{S}_{t-j-1,t-2})$. Now

$$\tilde{S}_{t-j-1,t-1} = \sum_{k=0}^{\infty} q_k \hat{S}_{t-j-1+k,t-1}, \quad \text{where} \quad \frac{1}{Q(z^{-1})} = \sum_{k=0}^{\infty} q_k z^{-k} \quad (18)$$

and

$$\frac{1}{C(z)}\left[\frac{C(z)}{z^{k-j}}\right]_+ - \frac{z}{C(z)}\left[\frac{C(z)}{z^{k-j+1}}\right]_+ = \begin{cases} 0, & k < j, \\ c_{k-j}/C(z), & k \geq j. \end{cases} \quad (19)$$

So the generating function for

$$\sum_{j=0}^{\infty} (\tilde{S}_{t-j-1,t-1} - \tilde{S}_{t-j-1,t-2}) = \sum_{j=0}^{\infty} \sum_{k=0}^{\infty} q_k(\hat{S}_{t-j+k-1,t-1} - \hat{S}_{t-j+k-1,t-2})$$

$$(20)$$

is given by

$$\frac{1}{C(z)} \sum_{j=0}^{\infty} \sum_{k=0}^{\infty} q_{k+j} c_k = \frac{([C(z)/Q(z^{-1})z]_-)|_{z=1}}{C(z)}. \quad (21)$$

Q.E.D.

Now suppose that S_t is a moving-average autoregressive process; e.g., let

$$C(z) = B(z)/D(z), \quad (22)$$

where $B(\ )$ and $D(\ )$ are polynomials of order b and d, respectively. Then

$$\frac{\gamma(z)}{1-\lambda} = \lim_{\delta \to 1} \frac{(1-\delta z)D(z)}{B(z)}\left[\frac{B(z)(1+\alpha(1-\delta z))}{D(z)Q(z^{-1})z(1-\delta z)}\right]_+. \quad (23)$$

Letting

$$S(z) = B(z)(1+\alpha(1-\delta z))/Q(z^{-1})z, \quad (24)$$

it is not hard to show that

$$\frac{\gamma(z)}{1-\lambda} = \frac{[S(z)]_+}{B(z)} + \frac{T(z)}{B(z)}, \quad (25)$$

where $T(z)$ is of order d. $[S(z)]_+$ is obviously of order b, so

$$\gamma(z) = (1 - \lambda) \frac{V(z)}{B(z)} \tag{26}$$

where $V(z)$ is of order $\max[b, d]$. This gives

$$R(U)B(U)P_t = (1 - \lambda)V(U)S_{t-1}, \tag{27}$$

a rational lag distribution.

REFERENCES

Abramovitz, M. (1964). *Evidences of long swings in construction since the Civil War.* Occasional Paper No. 90, National Bureau of Economic Research.

Adelman, I. (1965). "Long cycles—fact or artifact." *American Economic Review* **60**:443–463.

Ahlfors, Lars V. (1966). *Complex analysis*, 2nd ed. New York: McGraw-Hill.

Akaike, H. (1970). "Statistical predictor identification." *Annals of the Institute of Statistical Mathematics* **22**:203–217.

Akaike, H. (1974). "Markovian representation of stochastic processes and its application to the analysis of autoregressive moving-average processes." *Annals of the Institute of Statistical Mathematics* **26**:363–387.

Almon, Shirley (1965). "The distributed lag between capital appropriations and expenditures." *Econometrica* **33**:178–196.

Amemiya, T., and Fuller, W. A. (1967). "A comparative study of alternative estimators in a distributed lag model." *Econometrica* **35**:509–529.

Ames, Edward (1948). "A theoretical and statistical dilemma—the contributions of Burns, Mitchell and Frickey to business cycle theory." *Econometrica* **16**:347–369.

Anderson, T. W. (1971). *The statistical analysis of time series.* New York: Wiley.

Anonymous (1838). "On the mathematical law of the cycle." *Herapath's Railway Magazine* **5** (November).

Arrow, K. J., and Nerlove, M. (1958). "A note on expectations and stability." *Econometrica* **26**:297–305.

Babbage, Charles (1856). "Analysis of the statistics of the clearing house during the year 1839." *Statistical Journal* **19**.

Backman, Jules, and Gainsburgh, Martin R. (1966). *Inflation and the price indexes.* Subcommittee on Economic Statistics of the Joint Economic Committee, Congress of the United States. Washington, D.C.: U.S. Govt. Printing Office.

Balestra, P. (1972). *Calcul matriciel pour économistes.* Albeuve, Suisse: Éditions castella.

Balestra, P. (1978). "Determinant and inverse of a sum of matrices with applications in economics and statistics." Unpublished working paper, Universities of Fribourg and Dijon.

Bartlett, M. S. (1946). "On the theoretical specification and sampling properties of auto-correlated time series." *Journal of the Royal Statistical Society (Supp.)* **8**:27–41; Correction **10** (1948).

Bartlett, M. S. (1950). "Periodogram analysis and continuous spectra." *Biometrika* **37**:1–16.

Bartlett, M. S. (1955). *An introduction to stochastic processes*, 1st ed. London and New York: Cambridge Univ. Press.

Bean, L. A. (1929). "The farmers' response to price." *Journal of Farm Economics* 11:368–385.

Bell, G. M. (1842). *The country banks and the currency—an examination of the evidence on banks of issue, given before a select committee of the House of Commons in 1841.* London: Longman Brown, Green and Longman.

Belsley, D. A. (1969). *Industry production behavior: the order–stock distinction.* Amsterdam: North-Holland Publ.

Bernt, E. K., Hall, R. E., Hall, B. H., and Hausman, J. (1974). "Estimation and inference in non-linear structural models." *Annals of Economic and Social Measurement* 3:653–666.

Beveridge, W. H. (1921). "Weather and harvest cycles." *Economic Journal* 31:429–452.

Beveridge, W. H. (1922). "Wheat prices and rainfall in Western Europe." *Journal of the Royal Statistical Society* 85:412–459.

Billingsley, P. (1968). *Convergence of probability measures.* New York: Wiley.

Blackman, R. B., and Tukey, J. W. (1958). *The measurement of power spectra from the point of view of communications engineering.* New York: Dover.

Bloomfield, P. (1976). *Fourier analysis of time series: an introduction.* New York: Wiley.

Bohi, D. R., and Scully, G. W. (1975). "Buyer's prices, seller's prices and price flexibility: comment." *American Economic Review* 65:517–525.

Bowley, Arthur L. (1901). *Elements of statistics.* London: P. S. King and Sons, Ltd.

Bowley, Arthur L. (1926). *Elements of statistics*, 5th ed. London: P. S. King and Sons, Ltd.

Box, G. E. P., and Jenkins, G. M. (1970). *Time series analysis, forecasting and control.* San Francisco, California: Holden-Day.

Bradley, P. D., and Crum, W. L. (1939). "Periodicity as an explanation of variation in hog production." *Econometrica* 7:221–234.

Brainard, William C., and Tobin, J. (1968). "Pitfalls in financial model building." *American Economic Review Papers and Proceedings* 58:99–122.

Brandow, G. E. (1958). "A note on the Nerlove estimate of supply elasticity." *Journal of Farm Economics* 40:719–722.

Brillinger, D. R. (1975). *Time series: data analysis and theory.* New York: Holt.

Buchanan, N. S. (1939). "A reconsideration of the cobweb theorem." *Journal of Political Economy* 47:67–81.

Burns, Arthur F. (1934). *Production trends in the United States since 1870.* New York: National Bureau of Economic Research.

Burns, Arthur F., and Mitchell, W. C. (1947). *Measuring business cycles.* New York: National Bureau of Economic Research.

Buys Ballot, C. H. D. (1847). *Les changements périodiques de température.* Utrecht: Kemink et Fils.

Buys Ballot, C. H. D. (1861). Sur la marche annuelle du thermomètre et du baromètre en Neêrlande. Academie Royale des Sciences à Amsterdam.

Cagan, P. (1956). "The monetary dynamics of hyper-inflation." In *Studies in the Quantity of Money* (M. Friedman, ed.). pp. 25–117. Chicago: Univ. of Chicago Press.

Cannon, W. H., and Jensen, O. G. (1975). "Terrestrial timekeeping and general relativity—a discovery." *Science* 188 (4186):317–327.

Carslaw, H. S. (1930). *Introduction to the Theory of Fourier's Series and Integrals*, reprint 3rd Ed. New York: Dover.

Carvalho, J. L. (1971). "An alternative method for identifying ARIMA models." Center for Mathematical Studies in Business and Economics. Report 7152, Univ. of Chicago.

Carvalho, J. L. (1972). *Production, investment and expectations: a study of the United States cattle industry.* Unpublished Ph.D. dissertation, Dept. of Economics, Univ. of Chicago.

Chatfield, C., and Prothero D. L. (1973). "Box–Jenkins seasonal forecasting: problems in a case study." *Journal of the Royal Statistical Society Ser. A* 136:295–315.

Childs, Gerald L. (1967). *Unfilled orders and inventories.* Amsterdam: North-Holland Publ.

Clarke, Hyde (1838). "On the political economy and capital of joint-stock banks." *Herapath's Railway Magazine* **5**.

Cleveland, W. S. (1972). "The inverse autocorrelations of a time series and their application." *Technometrics* **14**:277–293.

Cleverland, W. S., and Tiao, G. C. (1976). "Decomposition of seasonal time series: a model for the Census X-11 program." *Journal of the American Statistical Association* **71**: 581–587.

Coase, R. M., and Fowler, R. F. (1937). "The pig-cycle in Great Britain: an explanation." *Economica* **4**:55–82.

Cochrane, Willard W. (1947). "Farm price gyration—an aggregative hypothesis." *Journal of Farm Economics* **29**:383–408.

Cooley, J. W., Lewis, P. A. W., and Welch, P. D. (1967). "Historical notes on the fast Fourier transform." *IEEE Transactions Audio Electroacoustics* **AU-15**:76–79.

Cooley, J. W., and Tukey, J. W. (1965). "An algorithm for the machine calculation of complex Fourier series." *Mathematics of Computation* **19**:297–301.

Cournot, Augustin (1927). *Researches into the mathematical principle of the theory of wealth* (Nathaniel T. Bacon, transl.). New York: Macmillan.

Couts, D., Grether, D. M., and Nerlove, M. (1966). "Forecasting non-stationary economic time series." *Management Science* **13**:1–21.

Cox, D. R., and Miller, H. D. (1965). *The theory of stochastic processes*. New York: Wiley.

Cramér, H. (1942). "On harmonic analysis of certain function spaces." *Arkiv. Mat. Astron. Fysik.* **28B** (12):1–7.

Cramér, H. (1946). *Mathematical methods of statistics*. Princeton: Princeton Univ. Press.

Crum, W. L. (1918). "The perturbations caused by a close approach of two asteroids." *The Astronomical Journal* **31**:173–180.

Crum, W. L. (1923). "Cycles of rates of return on commercial paper." *Review of Economic Statistics* **5**:17–27.

Davidon, W. C. (1959). "Variable metric method for minimization." Atomic Energy Commission Research and Development Report ANL-5900 (Rev.).

de Leeuw, Frank (1962). "The demand for capital goods by manufacturers: a study of quarterly time series." *Econometrica* **30**:407–423.

de Leeuw, Frank (1967). "The demand for money: speed of adjustment, interest rates, and wealth." In *Monetary Process and Policy* (G. Horwich, ed.). Homewood, Illinois: Richard D. Irwin.

Dhrymes, P. J. (1970). *Econometrics*. New York: Harper.

Diamond, J. J. (1962). "Further development of a distributed lag investment function." *Econometrica* **30**:788–800.

Doob, J. (1953). *Stochastic processes*. New York: Wiley.

Durbin, J. (1959). "Efficient estimators of parameters in moving average models." *Biometrika* **46**:306–316.

Eisner, R. (1960). "A distributed lag investment function." *Econometrica*. **28**: 1–29.

Eisner, R. (1967). "A permanent income theory for investment: some empirical explorations." *American Economic Review* **57**:363–390.

Eisner, R., and Strotz, R. H. (1963). "Determinants of business investment." In *Impacts of Monetary Policy*. A series of research studies prepared for the Commission on Money and Credit. Englewood Cliffs, New Jersey: Prentice-Hall.

Engle, Robert F. (1974). "Band spectrum regression." *International Economic Review* **55**:1–11.

Enthoven, Alain C., and Arrow, K. J. (1956). "A theorem on expectations and the stability of equilibrium." *Econometrica* **24**:288–293.

Everest, Robert (1843). "On the famines that have devastated India and on the probability of their being periodical." *Statistical Journal* **6**.

Ezekiel, M. (1927). "Two methods of forecasting hog prices." *Journal of the American Statistical Association* **22**:22–30.

Ezekiel, M. (1938). "The cobweb theorem." *Quarterly Journal of Economics* **52**:255–280.

Fabricant, Solomon (1961). "Basic research and the analysis of current business conditions." In *Business cycle indicators* (Geoffrey H. Moore, ed.). New York: National Bureau of Economic Research.

Feller, W. (1966). *An introduction to probability theory and its applications*, Vol. 2. New York: Wiley.

Fellner, William (1956). *Trends and cycles in economic activity.* New York: Holt.

Fisher, F. (1966). *The identification problem in econometrics.* New York: McGraw-Hill.

Fisher, I. (1925). "Our unstable dollars and the so-called business cycle." *Journal of the American Statistical Association* **20**:179–202.

Fisher, I. (1930). *The theory of interest as determined by impatience to spend income and the opportunity to invest it.* New York: Macmillan.

Fishman, G. S. (1969). *Spectral methods in econometrics.* Cambridge, Massachusetts: Harvard Univ. Press.

Fletcher, R., and Powell, M. (1963). "A rapidly convergent descent method for minimization." *Computer Journal* **6**:163–168.

Forbes, James D. (1832). "On the horary oscillations of the barometer near Edinburg, deduced from 4410 observations; with an inquiry into the law of the geographical distribution of the phenomenon." *Edinburgh Journal of Science* **12**.

Frickey, Edwin (1942). *Economic fluctuations in the United States.* Cambridge, Massachusetts: Harvard Univ. Press.

Friedman, Milton (1957). *A theory of the consumption function.* New York: National Bureau of Economic Research.

Fuller, Wayne A. (1976). *Introduction to statistical time series.* New York: Wiley.

Galbraith, R. F., and Galbraith, J. I. (1974). "On the inverses of some patterned matrices arising in the theory of stationary time series." *Journal of Applied Probability* **11**:63–71.

Gilbart, James W. (1854). "The laws of the currency, as exemplified in the circulation of country bank notes in England since the passing of the Act of 1844." *Statistical Journal* **17**.

Gilbart, James W. (1856). "The laws of the currency in Scotland." *Statistical Journal* **19**.

Gilbart, James W. (1865). *Logic for the million, a familiar exposition of the art of reasoning.* London: Bell and Daldy.

Godfrey, M. D., and Karreman, H. (1967). "A spectrum analysis of seasonal adjustment." In *Essays, Mathematical Economics* (M. Shubik, ed.). Princeton, New Jersey: Princeton University Press.

Goldberger, Arthur S. (1968). *Topics in regression analysis.* New York: Macmillan.

Goodwin, R. M. (1947). "Dynamical coupling with especial reference to markets having production lags." *Econometrica* **25**:181–204.

Gordon, Robert A. (1949). "Business cycles in the interwar period: the 'quantitative historical' approach." *American Economic Review Papers and Proceedings* **39**:47–63.

Granger, C. W. J. (in association with M. Hatanaka) (1964). *Spectral analysis of economic time series.* Princeton, New Jersey: Princeton University Press.

Granger, C. W. J. (1966). "The typical spectral shape of an economic variable." *Econometrica* **34**:150–161.

Granger, C. W. J. (1974). *Approaches to multivariate model building.* Department of Economics, University of California, San Diego, Discussion Paper No. 74-12.

Granger, C. W. J. (1976). "Seasonality: causation, interpretation and implications." Paper presented to NBER/Census Conference on Seasonal Analysis of Economic Time Series, Washington, D.C.

Granger, C. W. J., and Newbold, P. (1975). *Identification of two-way causal systems.* Dept. of Economics, Univ. of California, San Diego, Discussion Paper No. 75-13.

Granger, C. W. J., and Newbold, P. (1977). *Forecasting economic time series.* New York: Academic Press.

Greenberg, E. (1964). "A stock-adjustment investment model." *Econometrica* **32**:339–357.

Grenander, U., and Rosenblatt, M. (1957). *Statistical analysis of stationary time series.* New York: Wiley.

Grenander, U., and Szegö, G. (1958). *Toeplitz forms and their applications.* Berkeley, California: Univ. of California Press.

Grether, D. M. (1968). "Studies in the analysis of economic time series." Unpublished Ph.D. dissertation, Stanford University.

Grether, D. M. (1977). "A note on distributed lags, prediction, and signal extraction." *Econometrica* 45:1729–1734.

Grether, D. M., and Maddala, G. S. (1973). "Errors in variables and serially correlated disturbances in distributed lag models." *Econometrica* 41:255–262.

Grether, D. M., and Nerlove, M. (1970). "Some properties of 'optimal' seasonal adjustment." *Econometrica* 38:682–703.

Griliches, Z. (1967). "Distributed lags: a survey." *Econometrica* 35:16–49.

Griliches, Z., and Wallace, N. (1965). "The determinants of investment revisited." *International Economic Review* 6:311–329.

Guilbaud, G. (1951). "L'étude statistique des oscillations économiques." *Cahiers du Séminaire d'économétrie.*

Gustafson, R. A., and Van Arsdall, R. N. (1970). "Cattle feeding in the United States." *Agricultural Economic Report* No. 186. Economic Research Service, U.S. Dept. of Agriculture.

Guy, William, A. (1843). "An attempt to determine the influence of the seasons and weather on sickness and mortality." *Statistical Journal* 6.

Hall, R. E., and Jorgenson, D. W. (1967). "Tax policy and investment behavior." *American Economic Review* 57:391–414.

Hall, R. E., and Jorgenson, D. W. (1969). "Tax policy and investment behavior: reply and further results." *American Economic Review* 59:388–401.

Hamming, R. W. (1962). *Numerical Methods for Scientists and Engineers.* New York: McGraw-Hill.

Hannan, E. J. (1960). *Time series analysis.* London: Methuen.

Hannan, E. J. (1963). "The estimation of seasonal variation in economic time series." *Journal of the American Statistical Association* 58:31–44.

Hannan, E. J. (1969a). "The identification of vector mixed autoregressive-moving average systems." *Biometrika* 56:223–225.

Hannan, E. J. (1969b). "The estimation of mixed moving average autoregressive systems." *Biometrika* 56:579–593.

Hannan, E. J. (1970). *Multiple time series.* New York: Wiley.

Hannan, E. J. (1971). "The identification problem for multiple equation systems with moving average errors." *Econometrica* 39:751–765.

Hannan, E. J., and Nicholls, D. F. (1972). "The estimation of mixed regression, autoregression, moving average, and distributed lag models." Econometrica 40:529–547.

Hatanaka, M. (1975). "On the global identification of the dynamic simultaneous equations model with stationary disturbances." *International Economic Review* 16:545–554.

Hatanaka, M., and Howery, E. Philip (1965). "Another view of the long swing hypothesis: comment on Adelman's study of long cycles." Research Memorandum No. 77. Econometric Research Program, Princeton Univ.

Hay, George (1969). "Production, price and inventory theory: an integrated model of firm behavior." Unpublished Ph.D. dissertation, Dept. of Economics, Northwestern Univ.

Heady, Earl D., and Kaldor, Donald R. (1954). "Expectations and error in forecasting agricultural prices." *Journal of Political Economy* 62:34–47.

Herschel, William (1801). "Observations tending to investigate the nature of the sun in order to find the causes or symptoms of its variable emission of light and heat; with remarks on the use that may possibly be drawn from solar observation." *Philosophical Transactions* 91, Part 2.

Hext, G. R. (1964). "Transfer functions for two seasonal adjustment filters." Technical Report No. 3, Institute for Mathematical Studies in the Social Sciences, Stanford Univ.

Hext, George R. (1966). "A new approach to time series with mixed spectra." Unpublished Ph.D. dissertation, Stanford Univ.

Hicks, J. R. (1939). *Value and Capital*, 1st ed. London and New York: Oxford Univ. Press.

Holt, C. C., Modigliani, F., Muth, J. F., and Simon, H. (1960). *Planning production, inventories, and work force*. Englewood Cliffs, New Jersey: Prentice-Hall.

Horwich, George (1967). *Monetary process and policy: a symposium*. Homewood, Illinois: Richard D. Irwin.

Hotelling, Harold (1927). "Differential equations subject to error and population estimates." *Journal of the American Statistical Association* 22:283–314.

Howard, R. A. (1966). "Dynamic programming." *Management Science* 12:317–348.

Howery, E. Philip (1965). "A spectral analysis of the long-swing hypothesis." Research Memorandum No. 78, Econometric Research Program, Princeton Univ.

Jenkins, G. M., and Watts, D. G. (1968). *Spectral analysis and its applications*. San Francisco, California: Holden-Day.

Jevons, W. Stanley (1862). "On the study of periodic commercial fluctuations." In Jevons (1884, pp. 1–12).

Jevons, W. Stanley (1863). "A serious fall in the value of gold ascertained and its social effects set forth." In Jevons (1884, pp. 13–118).

Jevons, W. Stanley (1866). "On the frequent autumnal pressure in the money market, and the action of the Bank of England." In Jevons (1884, pp. 160–193).

Jevons, W. Stanley (1878). "The periodicity of commercial crises and its physical explanation." In Jevons (1884, pp. 206–220).

Jevons, W. Stanley (1884). *Investigations in currency and finance*. London: Macmillan.

Johnson, D. G. (1947). *Forward prices for agriculture*. Chicago, Illinois: Univ. of Chicago Press.

Jorgenson, D. W. (1963). "Capital theory and investment behavior." *American Economic Review* 53:247–259.

Jorgenson, D. W. (1964). "Minimum variance, linear, unbiased seasonal adjustment of economic time series." *Journal of the American Statistical Association* 59:681–724.

Jorgenson, D. W. (1965). "Anticipations and investment behavior." In *The Brookings Quarterly Econometric Model of the United States* (J. S. Duesenberry, G. Fromm, L. R. Klein and E. Kuh, eds.), pp. 35–94. Chicago, Illinois: Rand-McNally.

Jorgenson, D. W. (1966). "Rational distributed lag functions." *Econometrica* 34:135–149.

Jorgenson, D. W. (1967a). "Seasonal adjustment of data for econometric analysis." *Journal of the American Statistical Association* 62:137–140.

Jorgenson, D. W. (1967b). "The theory of investment behavior." In *Determinants of Investment Behavior*, pp. 129–155. New York: National Bureau of Economic Research.

Jorgenson, D. W., and Siebert, C. D. (1968a). "A comparison of alternative theories of corporate investment behavior." *American Economic Review* 58:681–712.

Jorgenson, D. W., and Siebert, C. D. (1968b). "Optimal capital accumulation and corporate investment behavior." *Journal of Political Economy* 76:1123–1151.

Jorgenson, D. W., and Stephenson, J. A. (1967a). "Investment behavior in U.S. manufacturing, 1947–60." *Econometrica* 35:169–220.

Jorgenson, D. W., and Stephenson, J. A. (1967b). "The time structure of investment behavior in U.S. manufacturing, 1947–60." *Review of Economics and Statistics* 49:16–27.

Jorgenson, D. W., and Stephenson, J. A. (1969). "Issues in the development of the neoclassical theory of investment behavior." *Review of Economics and Statistics* 51:346–353.

Kessel, Reuben A. (1965). *The cyclical behavior of the term structure of interest rates*. New York: National Bureau of Economic Research.

Keynes, J. M. (1951). *Essays in biography*. London: Rupert Hart-Davis.

Khinchin, A. Y. (1934). "Korrelationstheorie der stationären stochastischen Prozesse." *Mathematische Annalen* 109:604–615.

Kingman, J. F. C., and Taylor, S. J. (1966). *Introduction to measure and probability*. London and New York: Cambridge Univ. Press.

Knopp, Konrad (1945). *Theory of functions*, Vol. 1. New York: Dover.

Kolmogorov, A. N. (1940). "Kurven in Hilbertschen Raum die gegenüber eine einparametrigen Gruppe von Bewegungen invariant sind." *C. R. (Doklady) de l'Academie des Sciences de l'URSS, New Series* **26**:6–9.

Kondratieff, N. D. (1935). "The long waves of economic life." *Review of Economic Statistics* **17**:105–115.

Koopmans, L. H. (1974). *The spectral analysis of time series*. New York: Academic Press.

Koopmans, T. C. (1965a). "Measurement without theory." In *Readings in business cycle theory* (R. A. Gordon and L. R. Klein, eds.). Homewood, Illinois: Richard D. Irwin.

Koopmans, T. C. (1965b). "A reply." In *Readings in business cycle theory* (R. A. Gordon and L. R. Klein, eds.). Homewood, Illinois: Richard D. Irwin.

Koopmans, T. C., Rubin, H., and Leipnik, R. B. (1950). "Measuring the equation systems of dynamic economics," In *Statistical Inference in Dynamic Economic Models* (T. C. Koopmans, ed.), pp. 53–237. New York: Wiley.

Koyck, L. M. (1954). *Distributed lags and investment analysis*. Amsterdam: North-Holland Publ.

Kuznets, Simon (1926). *Cyclical fluctuations*. New York: Adelphi.

Kuznets, Simon (1930). *Secular movements in production and prices*. New York: Houghton-Mifflin.

Kuznets, Simon (1933). *Seasonal variations in industry and trade*. New York: National Bureau of Economic Research.

Lanczos, C. (1956). *Applied Analysis*. Englewood Cliffs, New Jersey: Prentice-Hall.

Lanczos, C. (1966). *Discourse on Fourier Series*. London: Oliver and Boyd.

Leamer, Edward E. (1972). "A class of informative priors and distributed lag analysis." *Econometrica* **40**:1059–1081.

Lighthill, M. J. (1962). *Introduction to Fourier Analysis and Generalized Functions*. London and New York: Cambridge Univ. Press.

Lorie, James H. (1947). "Causes of annual fluctuations in the production of livestock and livestock products." In *Studies in business administration:* **17**. Chicago, Illinois: Univ. of Chicago Press.

Lovell, Michael C. (1961). "Manufacturers' inventories, sales expectations, and the acceleration principle." *Econometrica* **29**:293–314.

Lovell, Michael C. (1963). "Seasonal adjustment of economic time series and multiple regression analysis." *Journal of the American Statistical Association* **58**:993–1010.

Lovell, Michael C. (1966). "Alternative axiomatizations of seasonal adjustment." *Journal of the American Statistical Association* **61**:800–802.

Lukacs, E. (1970). *Characteristic functions*, 2nd ed. New York: Hafner.

Maddala, G. S. (1971). "The use of variance components models in pooling cross-section and time-series data." *Econometrica* **39**:341–358.

Malinvaud, E. (1969). "First-order certainty equivalence." *Econometrica* **37**:706–718.

Malinvaud, E. (1970). *Statistical methods of econometrics*, 2nd rev. ed. Amsterdam: North-Holland Publ.

Meiselman, David (1962). *The term structure of interest rates*. Englewood Cliffs, New Jersey: Prentice-Hall.

Metzler, Lloyd A. (1941). "The nature and stability of inventory cycles." *The Review of Economic Statistics* **23**:113–129.

Mitchell W. C. (1928). *Business cycles—the problem in its setting*. New York: National Bureau of Economic Research.

Modigliani, F., and Sauerlender, O. H. (1955). "Economic expectations and plans of firms in relation to short-term forecasting." In *Short-term economic forecasting studies in income and wealth* **16**, pp. 261–362. Princeton, New Jersey: National Bureau of Economic Research.

Moore, Geoffrey H. (ed.) (1961). *Business cycle indicators*. New York: National Bureau of Economic Research.

Moore, Henry L. (1914). *Economic cycles: their law and cause*. New York: Macmillan.

Moore, Henry L. (1917). *Forecasting the yield and price of cotton*. New York: Macmillan.

Moore, Henry L. (1923). *Generating economic cycles*. New York: Macmillan.

Morrison, Philip, and Morrison, Emily (1961). *Charles Babbage and his calculating engines: selected writings of Charles Babbage and others.* New York: Dover.

Mosely, Mabeth (1964). *Irascible genius—a life of Charles Babbage, inventor.* London: Hutchinson.

Muller, David E. (1956). "A method for solving algebraic equations using an automatic computer." *Mathematical Tables and Other Aids to Computation* **10**:208–215.

Mundlak, Y. (1966). "On the microeconomic theory of distributed lags." *Review of Economic Statistics* **48**:51–60.

Mundlak, Y. (1967). "Long-run coefficients and distributed lag analysis: a reformulation." *Econometrica* **35**:278–293.

Muth, J. F. (1960). "Optimal properties of exponentially weighted forecasts." *Journal of the American Statistical Association* **55**:299–305.

Muth, J. F. (1961). "Rational expectations and the theory of price movements." *Econometrica* **29**:315–335.

National Bureau of Economic Research, Price Statistics Review Committee (1961). *Price statistics of the federal government.* General Series No. 73. New York: National Bureau of Economic Research.

National Bureau of Standards (1964). *Handbook of Mathematical Functions*, Applied Mathematics Series No. 55. Washington, D.C.: U.S. Govt. Printing Office.

Nelson, C. R. (1972). "The prediction performance of the FRB–MIT–PENN model of the U.S. Economy." *The American Economic Review* **62**:902–917.

Nelson, C. R. (1974). "The first-order moving average process: identification, estimation, and prediction." *Journal of Econometrics* **2**:121–141.

Nelson, Charles (1975). "Rational expectations and the predictive efficiency of econometric models." *Journal of Business* **48**:331–343.

Nerlove, M. (1956). "Estimates of the elasticies of supply of selected agricultural commodities." *Journal of Farm Economics* **38**:496–509.

Nerlove, Marc (1958a). *Distributed lags and demand analysis.* Agricultural Marketing Service, U.S. Department of Agriculture. Washington, D.C.: U.S. Govt. Printing Office.

Nerlove, Marc (1958b). *The dynamics of supply: estimation of farmers' response to price.* Baltimore, Maryland: Johns Hopkins Press.

Nerlove, Marc (1958c). "The implications of Friedman's permanent income hypothesis for demand analysis." *Agricultural Economic Research* **10**:1–14.

Nerlove, Marc (1958d). "On the Nerlove estimate of supply elasticity: a reply." *Journal of Farm Economics* **40**:723–728.

Nerlove, Marc (1961). "Time series analysis of the supply of agricultural products." In *Agricultural supply functions estimating techniques and interpretation* (Earl O. Heady *et al.*, eds.), pp. 31–59 Ames, Iowa: Iowa State Univ. Press.

Nerlove, Marc (1964). "Spectral analysis of seasonal adjustment procedures." *Econometrica* **32**:241–286.

Nerlove, Marc (1965). "A comparison of a modified Hannan and the BLS seasonal adjustment filters." *Journal of the American Statistical Association* **60**:442–491.

Nerlove, Marc (1967). "Distributed lags and unobserved components of economic time series." In *Ten economic essays in the tradition of Irving Fisher* (W. Fellner, *et al.* eds.). pp. 126–169. New York: Wiley.

Nerlove, Marc (1971). "Further evidence on the estimation of dynamic economic relations from a time series of cross sections." *Econometrica* **39**:359–382.

Nerlove, Marc (1972a). "Lags in economic behavior." *Econometrica* **40**:221–251.

Nerlove, Marc (1972b). "On the structure of serial dependence in some U.S. price series." In *The econometrics of price determination* (O. Eckstein, ed.), pp. 60–112. Washington, D.C.: Board of Governors of the Federal Reserve System.

Nerlove, Marc and Wage, S. (1964). "On the optimality of adaptive forecasting." *Management Science* **10**:207–224.

Nerlove, Marc and Wallis, Kenneth F. (1966). "Use of the Durbin–Watson statistic in inappropriate situations." *Econometrica* **34**:235–238.

Nettheim, Nigel F. (1965). "A spectral study of 'overadjustment' for seasonality." Working Paper No. 21, U.S. Bureau of the Census.

Newbold, P. (1974). "The exact likelihood function for a mixed autoregressive–moving average process." *Biometrika* **61**:423–426.

Nicholls, D. F. (1973). "Frequency domain estimation procedures for linear models." *Biometrika* **60**:202–205.

Nicholls, D. F., Pagan, A. R., and Terrell, R. D. (1975). "The estimation and use of models with moving average disturbance terms: a survey." *International Economic Review* **16**:113–134.

Olshen, R. (1967). "Asymptotic properties of the periodogram of a discrete stationary process." Unpublished Ph.D. dissertation, Yale Univ. (summarized in *Journal of Applied Probability* **4**:508–528).

Orcutt, G. H. (1948). "A study of the autoregressive nature of the time series used for Tinbergen's model of the economic system of the United States, 1919–1932." *Journal of the Royal Statistical Society Ser. B* **10**:1–53.

Organization for Economic Co-operation and Development (1961). *Seasonal adjustment on electronic computers*. Paris: OECD.

Osborn, D. R. (1977). "Exact and approximate maximum likelihood estimators for vector moving average processes." *Journal of the Royal Statistical Society Ser. B* **39**:114–118.

Osborn, D. R., and Wallis, K. F. (1976). "On the practical implications of identification conditions for dynamic simultaneous equation models." Unpublished, London School of Economics.

Otnes, R. K., and Enochson, L. (1972). *Digital time series analysis*. New York: Wiley.

Pannekoek, A. (1961). *A history of astronomy*. New York: Wiley (Interscience).

Parzen, Emanuel (1960). *Modern probability theory and its applications*. New York: Wiley.

Parzen, Emanuel (1961). "An approach to time series analysis." *Annals of Mathematical Statistics* **32**:951–989.

Parzen, E. (1962). "Notes on Fourier Analysis and Spectral Windows," unpublished multilithed memorandum.

Parzen, E. (1963). "Notes on Fourier analysis and spectral windows." Technical Report No. 48, Dept. of Statistics, Stanford Univ. Reprinted in Parzen (1967), pp. 190–250.

Parzen, Emanuel (1967). *Time series analysis papers*. San Francisco, California: Holden-Day.

Pashigian, B. Peter (1970). "Rational expectations and the cobweb theory." *Journal of Political Economy* **78**:338–352.

Persons W. M. (1919). "Indices of business conditions." *Review of Economic Statistics* **1**:5–107.

Persons, W. M. (1925). "Statistics and economic theory." *Review of Economic Statistics* **7**:179–197.

Petty, William (1899). *The economic writings of Sir William Petty* (H. C. Hull, ed.). London and New York: Cambridge Univ. Press.

Press, S. J. (1972). *Applied multivariate analysis*. New York: Holt.

Prothero, D. L., and Wallis, K. F. (1976). "Modelling macroeconomic time series." *Journal of the Royal Statistical Society Ser. A* **139**:468–500.

Pukkila, T. (1977). *Fitting of autoregressive moving average models in the frequency domain*. Report A-6. Dept. of Mathematical Sciences, Univ. of Tampere, Finland.

Quenouille, M. H. (1957). *The analysis of multiple time series*. London: Charles Griffen.

Robinson, E. A. (1967). *Multichannel time series analysis with digital computer programs*. San Francisco, California: Holden-Day.

Rosenblatt, Harry M. (1965). "Spectral analysis and parametric methods for seasonal adjustment of economic time series." Working Paper No. 23, U.S. Bureau of the Census.

Rosenblatt, Harry M. (1966). "Spectral evaluation of BLS and Census revised seasonal adjustment procedures." Paper presented to the American Statistical Association meeting in Los Angeles, California.

Rosenblatt, Harry M. (1967). "Some research on the evaluation of time series methods." Memorandum presented to the Census Advisory Committee of the American Statistical Association, Washington, D.C.

Rosenblatt, Harry M. (1968). "Spectral evaluation of BLS and Census revised seasonal adjustment procedures." *Journal of the American Statistical Association* **63**:472–501.

Rozanov, Y. A. (1967). *Stationary random processes*. San Francisco, California: Holden-Day.

Schaerf, M. C. (1964). "Estimation of the covariance and autoregressive structure of a stationary time series." Tech. Report No. 12. Dept. of Statistics, Stanford Univ.

Schumpeter, J. A. (1939). *Business cycles*. New York: McGraw-Hill.

Schuster, A. (1898). "On the investigation of hidden periodicities with application to the supposed 26-day period of meteorological phenomena." *Terrestrial Magnetism and Atmospheric Electricity* (now *Journal of Geophysical Research*) **3**.

Shiller, Robert J. (1972). "Rational expectations and the structure of interest rates." Unpublished Ph.D. dissertation, MIT.

Shiskin, Julius (1958). "Decomposition of economic time series." *Science* **128**:1539–1546.

Simon, H. (1956). "Dynamic programming under uncertainty with a quadratic criterion function." *Econometrica* **24**:74–81.

Sims, Christopher A. (1968). "Estimating distributed lags by approximation." Harvard University. Mimeographed.

Sims, Christopher A. (1971). "Discrete approximations to continuous time distributed lags in econometrics." *Econometrica* **39**:545–564.

Sims, Christopher A. (1972a). "The role of approximate prior restrictions in distributed lag estimations." *Journal of the American Statistical Association* **67**:169–175.

Sims, Christopher A. (1972b). "Money, income and causality." *American Economic Review* **62**: 57–72.

Sims, Christopher A. (1974). "Seasonality in regression." *Journal of the American Statistical Association* **69**:618–626.

Slutzky, E. (1927). "The summation of random causes as the source of cyclic processes." *Econometrica* **5**:105–146 (1937). Translated from the earlier paper of the same title in *Problems of economic conditions* (Conjuncture Institute, Moscow, eds.).

Smith, B. B. (1925). "Forecasting the acreage of cotton." *Journal of the American Statistical Association* **20**:31–47.

Solow, R. M. (1960). "On a family of lag distributions." *Econometrica* **28**:393–406.

Stanley, Lord (1856). "Presidential address to the British Association for the Advancement of Science." *Statistical Journal* **19**.

Stewart, G. W. (1967). "A modification of Davidon's minimization method to accept difference approximations of derivatives." *Journal of the Association of Computing Machinery* **14**:72–83.

Stigler, George J. (1962). "Henry L. Moore and statistical economics." *Econometrica* **30**:1–21.

Stigler, George J. (1975). "Buyer's prices, seller's prices, and price flexibility: reply." *American Economic Review* **65**:526.

Stigler, George J., and Kindahl, James K. (1970). *The behavior of industrial prices*. New York: National Bureau of Economic Research.

Stokes, G. C. (1879). "Note on searching for periodicities." *Proceedings of the Royal Society* **29**:122–125.

Taylor L. D., and Wilson, T. A. (1964). "Three-pass least squares: a method of estimating models with a lagged dependent variable." *Review of Economics and Statistics* **46**:329–346.

Theil, H. (1957). "A note on certainty equivalence in dynamic planning." *Econometrica* **25**:346–349.

Theil, H. (1964). *Optimal decision rules for government and industry*. Amsterdam: North-Holland Publ.

Theil, H., and Wage, S. (1964). "Some observations on adaptive forecasting." *Management Science* **10**:198–206.

Thomas, J. J., and Wallis, K. F. (1971). "Seasonal variations in regression analysis." *Journal of the Royal Statistical Society, Ser. A* **134**:57–72.

Tobey, R. (1971). PL/1-FORMAC: *Symbolic mathematics interpreter*. (IBM Manual). New York: International Business Machines Corp.

Tolstov, G. P. (1962). *Fourier Series*, Chapters 1–7. Englewood Cliffs, New Jersey: Prentice-Hall.

U.S. Department of Commerce Bureau of Economic Analysis (1961–). *Business cycle developments*. (Now published monthly under the title *Business conditions digest*.)

Vining, Rutledge (1965a). "Koopmans on the choice of variables to be studied and methods of measurement." In *Readings in business cycle theory* (R. A. Gordon and L. R. Klein, eds.), pp. 204–217. Homewood, Illinois: Richard D. Irwin.

Vining, Rutledge (1965b). "A rejoinder." In *Readings in business cycle theory* (R. A. Gordon and L. R. Klein, eds.). Homewood, Illinois: Richard D. Irwin.

Walker, A. M. (1962). "Large sample estimation of parameters for autoregressive processes with moving-average residuals." *Biometrika* **49**:117–132.

Wallis, Kenneth F. (1966). "Some econometric problems in the analysis of inventory cycles." Cowles Foundation Discussion Paper No. 209.

Wallis, Kenneth F. (1967). "Lagged dependent variables and serially correlated errors: a reappraisal of three-pass least squares." *Review of Economics and Statistics* **49**:555–567.

Wallis, Kenneth F. (1974). "Seasonal adjustment and relations between variables." *Journal of the American Statistical Association* **69**:18–32.

Wallis, K. F. (1977a). "Multiple time series analysis and the final form of econometric models." *Econometrica* **45**:1481–1497.

Wallis, K. F. (1977b). "Econometric implications of the rational expectations hypothesis." Discussion Paper No. 77-3. Dept. of Economics, Univ. of California, San Diego.

Wallis, K. F., and Chan, W.-Y. T. (1976). "Multiple time series modelling: another look at the mink–muskrat interaction." Working Papers in Economics and Econometrics No. 37, Australian National Univ.

Watson, G. S. (1967). "Linear least-squares regression." *Annals of Mathematical Statistics* **38**:1679–1699.

Wells, M. (1965). "Function minimization-algorithm 251." *Collected Algorithms from the Communications of the Association for Computing Machinery* **8**:169.

Whewell, William (1847). *History of the inductive sciences*. London: John W. Parker.

Whittle, P. (1951). *Hypothesis testing in time series*. Uppsala: Almqvist and Wiksell.

Whittle, P. (1963). *Prediction and regulation by linear least-squares methods*. London: English Universities Press.

Wold, H. (1938). *A study in the analysis of stationary time series*. Stockholm: Almqvist and Wiksell.

Yaglom. A. M. (1962). *An introduction to the theory of stationary random functions*. Englewood Cliffs, New Jersey: Prentice-Hall.

Yule, G. U. (1921). "On the time-correlation problem, with especial reference to the variate-difference correlation method." *Journal of the Royal Statistical Society* **84**:497–526.

Yule, G. U. (1926). "Why do we sometimes get nonsense correlations between time series? A study in sampling and the nature of time series." *Journal of the Royal Statistical Society* **89**:1–64.

Yule, G. U. (1927). "On a method of investigating periodicities in disturbed series, with special reference to Wolfer's sunspot numbers." *Philosophical Transactions* **226A**.

Zellner, A. (1962). "An efficient method of estimating seemingly unrelated regressions and a test for aggregation bias." *Journal of the American Statistical Association* **58**:348–368.

Zellner, A., and Palm, F. (1974). "Time series analysis and simultaneous equation econometric models." *Journal of Econometrics* **2**:17–54.

AUTHOR INDEX

SUBJECT INDEX

A

Abel's theorem, 365

Adaptive expectations, *see* Expectations, adaptive

Adaptive-expectations model, *see* Distributed-lag models, based on expectation formation

Algorithm, *see* Minimization; Polynomial factorization

Aliasing, *see* Fourier coefficients; Spectrum, effects of aliasing

Amplitude, 56

Amplitude window generator, 411

Analytic engine, 8

Analytic function, *see* Functions of a complex variable, analytic

Annulus, defined, 374

Approximation in the mean of a function, 391

Approximation of a smooth periodic function, by window, *see* Window

AR, *see* Autoregressive

ARIMA, *see* Autoregressive integrated moving-average (ARIMA) model

ARMA, *see* Autoregressive moving-average (ARMA) model

Astronomy
 Babbage's interest in, 8

celestial mechanics, 3
Jevons' interest in, 9
moon, 358, 359
planetary orbits, 2
planets
 Jupiter, 3
 Saturn, 3
solar radiation, 19
sun, 359
sunspots, 4, 9, 22

Autocorrelation
 estimation
  approximate variance, 107, 206
  asymptotic distribution of estimates, 207
  standard error, Bartlett's approximation, 206
  statistical properties, 106
 infinite sample, defined, 26
 relation to spectral distribution function, 47
 use in formulation, *see* specific models

Autocorrelation function
 estimate, failure to damp, 106
 use in model formulation, Box and Jenkins procedure, 203–204; *see also* specific models, formulation

Autocovariance
 defined, 25
 infinite sample, 26

453

ECONOMIC THEORY, ECONOMETRICS, AND MATHEMATICAL ECONOMICS

Consulting Editor: Karl Shell

UNIVERSITY OF PENNSYLVANIA
PHILADELPHIA, PENNSYLVANIA

Edmund S. Phelps. Studies in Macroeconomic Theory, Volume 1: *Employment and Inflation.*

Marc Nerlove, David M. Grether, and José L. Carvalho. Analysis of Economic Time Series: *A Synthesis*

Thomas J. Sargent. Macroeconomic Theory

In preparation

Michael J. Boskin (Ed.). Economics and Human Welfare: *Essays in Honor of Tibor Scitovsky*

Jerry Green and Jose Alexander Scheinkman (Eds.). General Equilibrium, Growth, and Trade: *Essays in honor of Lionel McKenzie*